bottome of Hudso
but two foote, and in the bottome of Fretum Dauis was found by M
Baffin to be but one foote, wheras by the nearenes of the South Sea i
orte Nelson, it was cons tantly 15 foote or more.

AMERICA SEPTENTRION

Uirginia

REAL DE NVEVA
MEXICO

GRANADA   Florida

ASTABLAN

Breua Costa
R. de Picmadores
R. del Spirto Santo

R. de Flores
Cabo de Canaueral
Marta
R. de Niños
P.º de Maria
B. Luca
B. de S.t
Joseph
B. de Baxas

NEWE
R. Segundo
Villa Magdalena
R. de Palmas
R. de Barba
de y mude

Nauito
ILLA DE S
SEBASTIAN

Chiametlen   CVCHILLO
Paternan

Tertug

P.º de xalisco

Negros

SPAINE
Tomalo
tipan
anico

Alacrane
C. S.t Antonio

Tringo

Front endpaper.
Henry Briggs's 1625 map *The North part of America* depicted California as a massive island, a concept that arose from the observation that no major rivers entered the Pacific along the southern part of the West Coast. The notion was finally proven wrong by exploration of the head of the Gulf of California, but so persistent was the myth that it took a royal decree by the king of Spain in 1747 to stop at least Spanish mapmakers from showing the island of California on their maps.

Historical Atlas of the American West

Historical Atlas
of the
American West

With Original Maps

Derek Hayes

☐ **University of California Press** · **Berkeley** · **London** · **Los Angeles**

University of California Press, one of the most distinguished university presses in the United States, enriches lives around the world by advancing scholarship in the humanities, social sciences, and natural sciences. Its activities are supported by the UC Press Foundation and by philanthropic contributions from individuals and institutions. For more information, visit www.ucpress.edu.

University of California Press
Berkeley and Los Angeles, California

University of California Press, Ltd.
London, England

Originated by Douglas & McIntyre, a division of D&M Publishers Inc., 2323 Quebec Street, Suite 201, Vancouver, B.C., Canada V5T 4S7
www.dmpibooks.com

© 2009 by Derek Hayes

Cataloging-in-Publication Data for this title is on file with the Library of Congress.

ISBN 978-0-520-25652-1 (cloth : alk. paper)

Manufactured in China by C&C Offset Printing Co., Ltd.

17 16 15 14 13 12 11 10 09
10 9 8 7 6 5 4 3 2 1

Printed on acid-free paper

Design and layout: Derek Hayes
Editing and copyediting: Iva Cheung
Jacket design: Lia Tjandra

To contact the author: www.derekhayes.ca / derek@derekhayes.ca

Acknowledgments

Many people helped with the research, image sourcing, and preparation of this book. As always, map collector David Rumsey, creator of arguably the finest private online collections of maps, has been most generous in permitting his maps to be reproduced in the present volume.

The author would also like to thank Kenton Forrest, Chuck Yungkurth, and Robert L. Brown, Colorado Railroad Museum Library, Golden, Colorado; Peggy Ford, Greeley History Museum, Greeley, Colorado; Lee Osmonson, Central Energy Resources Team, United States Geological Survey, Denver; Roger Rowland, Sheridan Historical Society, Sheridan, Colorado; Tomas Jaehn, New Mexico History Museum, Santa Fe; Katie Lage, Map Library, University of Colorado, Boulder; the staff at the Colorado Historical Society, Denver, and the Western History Department at the Denver Public Library; the staff at the Map Library at the Arizona State University Library, Tempe, Arizona; Karen Leong, Arizona State University; Debbie Newman, Arizona Historical Society, Tucson; Bill Frank, Huntington Library; John R. Lovett, University of Oklahoma; Bill Warren; Warren Heckrotte; Brian Croft; Steve Boulay, Salt Lake City; Sarah Jensen, Storey County (Nevada) Recorder; James Willinger, Wide World of Maps, Inc., Phoenix; and Katherine Kalsbeek, University of British Columbia.

Thanks are due to David Wrobel of the University of Nevada, Las Vegas, for the suggestion that this book be expanded to include all aspects of the history of the American West rather than just exploration, as was initially planned. Thanks are also due to my publisher at Douglas & McIntyre, Scott McIntyre, and to the publisher at the University of California Press, Sheila Levine, for her continued enthusiasm for my books. Finally, an especial big thank-you to my editor and copyeditor, Iva Cheung, whose attention to detail and untiring checking of the facts has expunged many an error and produced a much more readable text.

MAP 1 (*half-title page*).
An early train puffs west on an 1879 Union Pacific map of the West, a composite illustration.

Title-page illustration.
Modified to suit this book's title page is this artistic illustration taken from the front cover of a 1930 tourist map and information booklet from the state of Idaho. Tourist literature and road map covers from the 1920s and 1930s were often illustrated with excellent specially commissioned period art such as this.

MAP 2 (*left, top*) and MAP 3 (*left, bottom*).
In 1889 the Arbuckle Coffee Company began giving away cards such as these two examples, each with a map of a U.S. state and an illustration pertinent to that state. They were a delightful collectible in an age when color images were few and far between. Here we have Arizona (MAP 2), with an Indian village scene, and Wyoming (MAP 3), with a range scene. Others are illustrated on page 276.

Contents

A NEW PERSPECTIVE ON THE HISTORY OF THE WEST

No region has entered the public psyche more than the American West. Writers of fiction and fact, Hollywood, and, later, television glorified the outlaw West, the Indian West, the cowboy West—the stuff of Wild Bill Hickok, Calamity Jane, Wyatt Earp, or the gunfight at OK Corral—mixing in myth but at least grounding it in truth. What is more famous than the Alamo or the Pony Express or the Union Pacific? The romance of the West, part fact, part fiction, is strong, and it has remained so long after the western frontier—if there ever was one—closed for good.

The West was developed by the railroad—"opened," in popular parlance—settled by the homesteader, then converted to a tourist playground, an Eden of irrigated and fertile lands, if still with many miles of barren aridity between its watered oases. Today the West has been integrated into the rest of the nation by the freeway and the airlines and boasts some of the largest urban metropolises in the country. The West is at once a state of mind and a place millions call home.

Making it so took monumental effort and countless lives. It has been calculated that so many died trekking west in the middle nineteenth century that it is as if there were a grave every eighty yards on the trails between the Lower Missouri and the Willamette and Central valleys. "Go West, Young Man," exhorted New York newspaperman Horace Greeley, and millions did.

The motivation for the EuroAmerican drive west ultimately comes down to one thing: a search for new wealth. At first it was for quick riches—a passage to the Orient, then a quest for gold. Later it was a search for land—wealth in the form of a new beginning, wealth gained by settlement, hard work, and the diversion of water. Then it was a search for the sun, a beautiful and healthful place to live, and a place to visit spectacular natural beauty. The West of today is still young and vibrant but is massively urbanized, though still with vast, open spaces.

This book is a collection of historical maps illustrating and documenting the history and development of the West. It also has an accompanying text and a caption for each map to explain what it shows. The book should be viewed as essentially a supplement to conventional histories, for here the map is king. Many excellent histories offer greater textual explanation, and a bibliography (page 278) suggests some of them.

Almost every map in this book is a contemporary one; that is, it was drawn or published at the time of the event it depicts. As such, the maps offer a unique view—the West the explorer understood, perhaps indistinctly or inaccurately; a planned route for a railroad that might differ from what was actually built; or explanations of projects, often shown in imaginative ways.

These maps, in addition to a myriad of others, give us a different, spatial perspective on the history of the West. Included is the account of the long American westward march toward Manifest Destiny; the ousting of Spain and then Britain, Mexico, and, to the north, Russia; the stories of the explorers and the pioneers, the wagon and the stagecoach men,

MAP 4.
Why the West is a unique region. This is a Landsat satellite view of land cover in the contiguous United States, photographed in 1992 and produced by the United States Geological Survey in conjunction with the Environmental Protection Agency. Land cover is divided into a number of categories, as shown in the key. The West is immediately and obviously apparent. The major categories of land use in the West, apart from the mountainous islands of deciduous and evergreen forest (two shades of dark green), are shrubland (light brown) and grassland (yellow brown), with a cultivated area of "small grains" (such as wheat) pushing west onto the Plains generally reflecting areas able to be irrigated from the rivers. One of the principal distinguishing features of much of the West is its uncompromising aridity.

the trails and the railroads that "opened" the West at first. There are tales of instant towns and ghost towns, miners and homesteaders, those who eked out a living and those who became rich overnight, the gold rushes—and there were many—and the building of commercial empires. Later we have the rise of cities, the building of aqueducts, the irrigation of the desert, the building of great dams and water diversions, the planning of roads, and the construction of freeways that opened a wider West.

The maps themselves are of many types; some of them may not even be considered maps by all. The promotional bird's-eye maps of cities and towns seeking to advertise their prowess and encourage their growth is a good example, yet these maps are invaluable historical records of what was or what might have been. Some are accurate surveys; many more are field sketches; some are advertisements or otherwise promotional in nature; some are geological, scientific, or political, defining boundaries actual or hoped for. All have been chosen for their historical significance, cartographic interest, or artistic merit—and a host of other reasons. They are of course but a selection, and a personal one at that, but hopefully a selection that will help to illuminate the history of the West in new ways.

In this book Native Americans are referred to as Indians because that is what they were called throughout history and still call themselves, despite the term's erroneous origin. Settlers of European–American origin are referred to as EuroAmericans, purely as a convenient term but one that seems to describe them simply yet accurately.

The West has been defined in many ways, but for the purposes of the present book, we define it geographically as North and South Dakota, Nebraska, Kansas, Oklahoma, Texas, and all states west of them, including Alaska but excluding Hawaii.

MAP 5 (*right*).
The railroads opened the West not only to settlement but also to visitors, and all the major railroads expended a great deal of effort marketing the wonders of the West to potential customers back east. This is a 1939 pictorial map of Glacier National Park and the adjacent Canadian Waterton Lakes National Park across the border, published by the Great Northern Railway. The railroad was responsible for much of the early success of this national park, as it was the only practical way visitors could get there. See page 214.

Above.
John Gast's well-known *American Progress*, painted in 1872, an allegory of the American seizure of the West. In the nineteenth century many Americans viewed the West in this way, as a land rightfully theirs. A glowing Progress floats westward, driving Indian, buffalo, and bear alike before her, stringing telegraph wire in her wake as a symbol of civilization. She is followed by settlers and miners, railroads, a stagecoach, and wagons while homesteaders with house and fence plow their newly acquired land.

THE NATIVE WEST

Often dismissed as savages requiring civilization or, worse, elimination, the Indians of the West were often treated with extreme brutality as Euro-Americans sought to take over their lands for themselves. Yet, far from being savages, many of the Indians possessed considerable civilizations of their own, manifested all over the West.

The date archaeologists think humans first entered North America has been receding as new evidence comes to light. Humans were long thought to have crossed a land bridge created across the Bering Strait by a lowering of sea levels around 13,000 years ago, but recent finds of chipped bones in the Yukon now suggest the migration may have been as early as 28,000 years ago. Alternatively, humans could have migrated by sea in small boats along the coastline as early as 30,000 years ago. And in 2003 scientists found what appear to be human footprints dating to 40,000 years ago in volcanic ash at Puebla, near Mexico City. The only thing that is clear is that we do not know exactly when humans appeared in America.

Adding to the confusion was the discovery of human remains along the banks of the Columbia River at Kennewick, Washington, in

MAP 6 (*right*).
The western part of a map showing the distribution of Indians, distinguished by linguistics, published in 1890 by the then new U.S. Bureau of Ethnology, directed by John Wesley Powell. The Pacific Coast has much smaller linguistic areas than the rest of the continent owing to the relative natural richness of the region, based on the salmon as a food source; this abundance permitted a multiplicity of cultures to develop. About six hundred autonomous Native groups have been identified as living in North America by 1500, and they spoke more than 170 languages; estimates of population totals vary from fourteen to fifty million.

Below.
Reconstructed walls of the pueblo of Kuau'a, on the Rio Grande a few miles north of Albuquerque, now part of the Coronado State Monument. The pueblo was created around 1300 by Native groups looking for a location with a reliable water source. Kuau'a means "evergreen" in the Tiwa language. Its inhabitants were accomplished farmers who cultivated small fields watered by the river. The pueblo was abandoned around 1600.

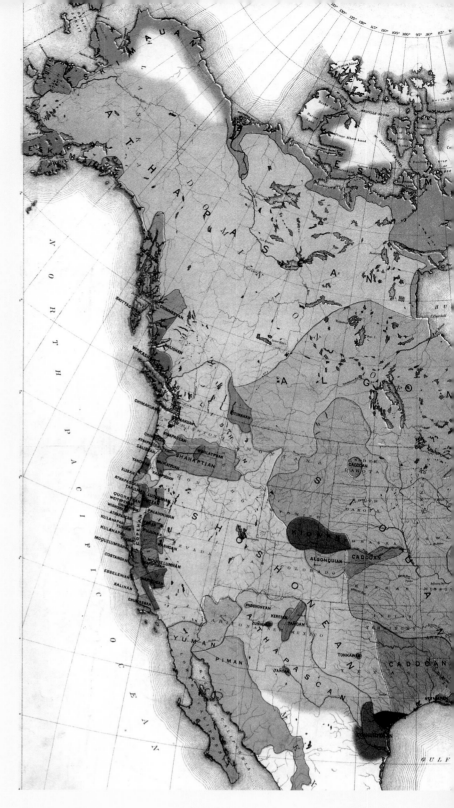

Above.

Ancient Puebloan ruins called Antelope House in the Canyon del Muerto in northeast Arizona, in part of the Canyon de Chelly National Monument. The ruins date from between AD 750 and 1300. They were abandoned about 1300 with the arrival of the Hopi, who in turn were displaced by the Navajo around 1700.

1996. "Kennewick Man" has been radiocarbon-dated to about 9,300 years ago and is of an origin most closely related to the Ainu of northeast Asia. There is documentary evidence of a number of shipwrecked Asian fishermen arriving on the West Coast, propelled by the prevailing currents in the Pacific. Kennewick Man may have arrived in this way; we do not know.

Nevertheless, we can be reasonably sure that at the time of Columbus's arrival in America, at least a million and perhaps as many as five million Native Americans were already living here.

Approximately six hundred identifiable Native groups spread over areas of unequal size, based largely on the land's ability to support a population. Thus, the West Coast, with relatively easy living based on the sea, and in particular the salmon, supported the densest population. The Plains demanded mobility, for the livelihood was based on the buffalo—more correctly the bison—and tribes had to follow the herds wherever they went. And, of course, when Euro-Americans finally all but wiped out the buffalo (see Map 314, *page 153*) the Plains Indian lifestyle vanished forever.

In the Southwest the climate allowed a more sedentary lifestyle to develop, and considerable towns were constructed—the pueblos. All were based on agriculture,

Map 7 (*right*).
This 1876 map from the German geographer Augustus Petermann shows pueblos and the areas of each Native group in northeastern New Mexico. The German public was fascinated by the North American Indian.

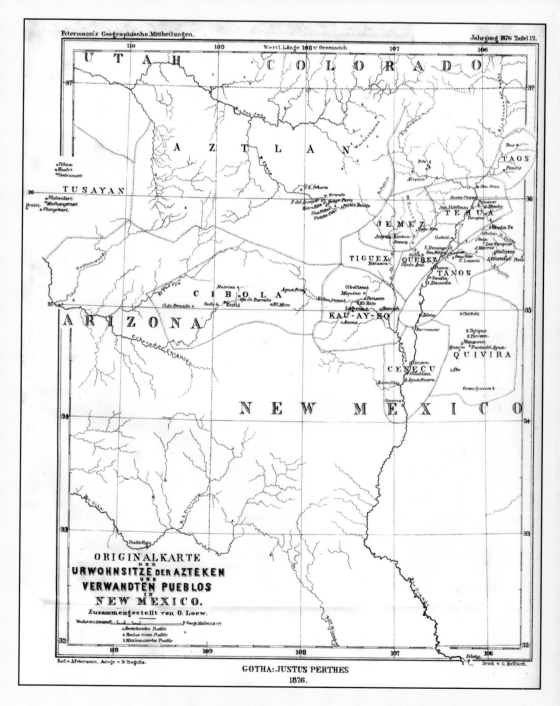

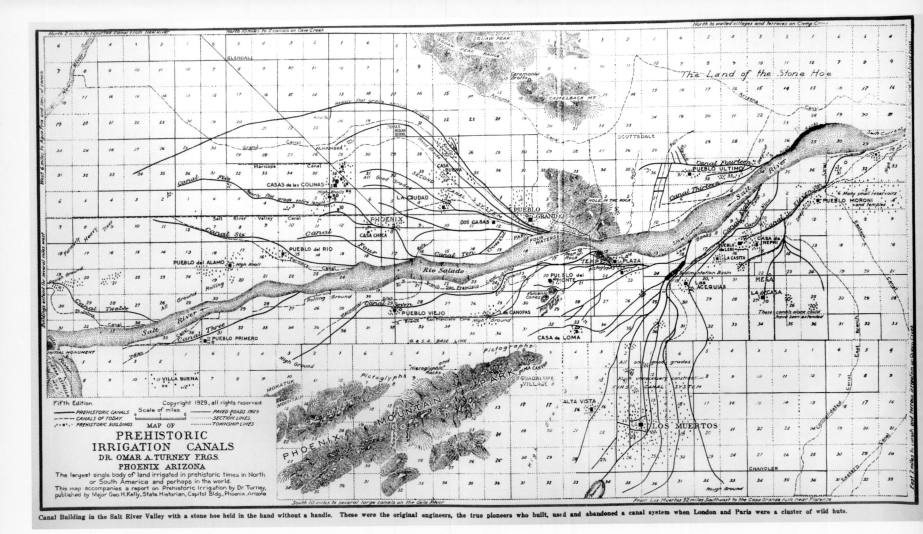

MAP OF

PREHISTORIC IRRIGATION CANALS

DR. OMAR A. TURNEY, F.R.G.S.
PHOENIX ARIZONA

The largest single body of land irrigated in prehistoric times in North or South America and perhaps in the world.
This map accompanies a report on Prehistoric Irrigation by Dr. Turney, published by Major Geo. H. Kelly, State Historian, Capitol Bldg., Phoenix, Arizona

Canal Building in the Salt River Valley with a stone hoe held in the hand without a handle. These were the original engineers, the true pioneers who built, used and abandoned a canal system when London and Paris were a cluster of wild huts.

MAP 8 (*above*).
Hohokam irrigation canals in the Salt River Valley around Phoenix, mapped by an archaeologist; the map was published in 1929. The irrigation system was likely abandoned because of drought. Later many of the canals were reused by EuroAmerican settlers (see page 205).

Below, top. Pueblo house ruin at Acoma, New Mexico, near the mesa city of the same name.

Below, bottom. A Navajo hogan, a primary winter dwelling made of logs and earth. There are numerous variations on this design.

with small plots of squash, beans, and corn usually supported by irrigation, some of which was extensive (MAP 8, *above*). A large group of people—the Anasazi—lived in cliff dwellings for added protection. A vast system of twelve villages connected by roads centered on the Chaco Canyon of New Mexico lasted until the thirteenth century, when severe drought forced a dispersion into smaller, more sustainable groups. Considerable evidence of the once elaborate adobe buildings of pueblo-dwelling peoples remains today all over the Southwest.

The Native peoples' territory waxed and waned with their relative power compared with the groups next to them. Some were pushed into more marginal lands, such as into the mountains, by more aggressive neighbors. Some of the Plains Indians obtained horses from the Spanish in the 1600s, a development

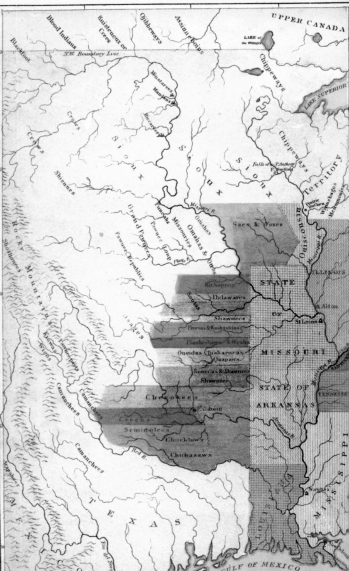

MAP 9 (*right*).
Artist George Catlin, who traveled the West in 1831 and 1832, created this map in 1840 showing the distribution of Indian tribes on the Great Plains. The map also shows the locations of eastern Indians relocated to the West in the 1830s, the forced exodus dubbed the Trail of Tears (see page 147). A similar map by George Catlin is MAP 303, *page 146*.

U. STATES' INDIAN FRONTIER IN 1840.
Shewing the Positions of the Tribes that have been removed west of the Mississippi

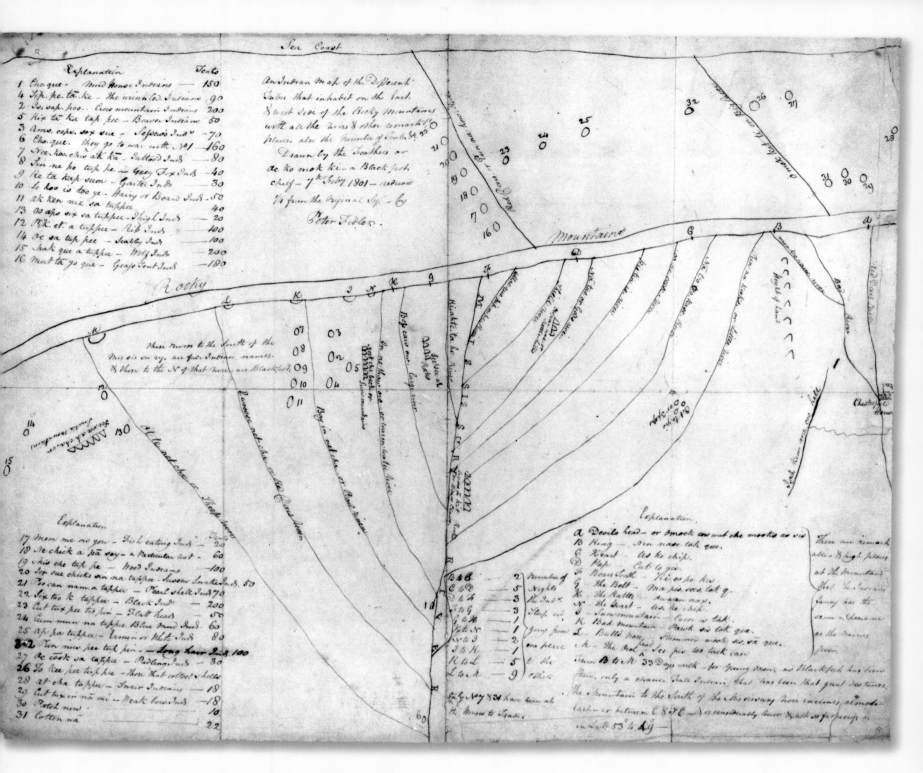

Map 10 (*above*).

that made them more powerful than those who did not. A notable example, the Comanche, remained feared by other Indians and EuroAmericans alike right up to the 1870s. The introduction of guns, this time from French or British sources, also had the effect of changing the power balance.

The conflict with EuroAmericans as the latter tried to take over the land the Indians had lived off for centuries was perhaps inevitable given the culture of greed, free land, and a feeling of God-given entitlement possessed by settlers, miners, and military of the time. Yet much can be attributed to improper and inconsistent protection of Indian rights. As a result, the American West—completely unlike the Canadian West just to the north—was the scene of a long series of Indian Wars and atrocities lasting into the last decade of the nineteenth century.

Native groups often had an extremely good notion of where they were in relation both to natural features, such as rivers, mountains, and pasturelands, and to other Native groups. But because their maps were ephemeral in nature, drawn on bark with charcoal or simply marked on the ground with a stick, few have survived. Those that did are usually those transcribed by early explorers onto a more preservable medium, such as paper.

This famous map, drawn with west at the top, shows the Upper Missouri and all its tributaries and some of what lay beyond the Rocky Mountains, the latter represented by the double line across the page. The map was copied onto paper by Peter Fidler, a Hudson's Bay Company explorer and trader, and it appears in his journal for 7 February 1801. The map information came from a Blackfoot chief, Ac ko mok ki, probably from a map he had scratched on the ground. The Missouri is the central vertical line, on the eastern (bottom) side of the mountains. Indian populations are represented by circles and numbers, which reference the number of tents shown in the lists. Fidler has recorded an extensive key. This map demonstrates the extensive geographic knowledge of Ac ko mok ki, well beyond the regions in which he likely traveled himself. Hence the information must have been derived from others, who probably conveyed it via temporary maps, drawn on the ground, that he would have had to commit to memory.

This map has another special significance in that the information was incorporated into a map carried by Meriwether Lewis and William Clark on their epic trek to the mouth of the Columbia in 1804–06. The Hudson's Bay Company supplied information to commercial mapmaker Aaron Arrowsmith, in London, and his maps were copied by Nicholas King onto the map carried by Lewis and Clark.

Between the Rocky Mountains and the Pacific Coast, the latter shown by the line at the extreme top of the page, two other rivers are depicted. These have been variously interpreted as the Columbia, the Snake, or the Fraser rivers, but once again credible information has traveled hundreds of miles across the mountain chain to be ultimately received by Ac ko mok ki. Coupled with George Vancouver's survey of the Pacific Coast in 1792 (and in particular the survey of the Columbia as far as today's Portland by his second-in-command, William Broughton), this information gave Lewis and Clark the confidence to believe that there was a river flowing to the Pacific from the western slope of the Rockies.

A West before the West

Europeans imagined the West long before they had ever seen it. In the years following the discovery of America by Christopher Columbus and John Cabot, most mapmakers depicted their East Coast landfalls as eastern extremities of Asia, with the result that America as we know it was not shown at all (MAP 11, *below*). It took the quantum leap of Martin Waldseemüller and Matthias Ringmann in 1507 to first show North America as a separate continent, and in so doing they had to invent a west coast (MAP 12 and MAP 13, *below, bottom*). Invent, we think, for there seems no evidence of actual exploration that might yield this information, and yet there is no doubt the depiction of a western coast was uncannily prescient, even accurate. Unless some new evidence surfaces, we may never know if it had a basis in fact.

Once a continent was formed in the European mind, cartographers felt compelled to fill it with something, notwithstanding the fact that they had no actual information at all. Imaginary inhabitants—human, animal, and plant—were enrolled to do the job (MAP 14, *right*). The West thus existed on maps drawn in Europe several years before even small parts of it appeared on maps as the result of exploration.

MAP 11 (*left, top*).
The West—indeed, the North American continent—is nowhere to be seen in this 1506 map by Giovanni Contarini. The peninsula at top is part of Asia, extending east to John Cabot's discoveries in Newfoundland, while south of it are the islands of Cuba and Hispaniola found by Christopher Columbus; to the west is Japan.

MAP 12 (*left, bottom*) and MAP 13 (*below*).
The very first depiction of the West Coast, created by default when Martin Waldseemüller and Matthias Ringmann drew their famous world map in 1507. MAP 12 is from the main map, and MAP 13 is from a smaller version of the world map on a different projection that sits astride the main map. The latter, in particular, suggests that a west coast was just a lucky guess, given that it is shown as a straight line, but a more accurate depiction of the west coast of South America has led to speculation about unrecorded voyages of exploration. There is also some argument about the date of the map, though the dispute mainly concerns the date of this printing rather than the date the map was originally drawn. Europeans first saw the Pacific Ocean in 1513; the Spaniard Vasco Núñez de Balboa first saw what he called the South Sea when he crossed the isthmus of Panama where it trends east–west and came to an ocean on its southern side. As far as we know, it took another seven years before Europeans sailed on the new ocean, when Ferdinand Magellan exited his eponymous strait in 1520 and named the unusually storm-free ocean the Pacific.

On the main map the West Coast is labeled *Terra Vlteri' Incognita*, unknown land. This map now resides in the Library of Congress, in a special argon-filled high-security case. The map includes the word *America* (in South America), its first use on any document, and has led the map to be dubbed "America's birth certificate."

MAP 14 (*right*).
It is perhaps just as well we can recognize an inverted Florida on this 1550 map of the western part of North America by the French mapmaker Pierre Desceliers, for without it we would have a harder time determining what region it depicts. The West Coast is shown at right, disappearing behind an elaborate margin. The West is inhabited with flamingos and pygmies and other flights of Desceliers' (or more likely his assistants') imaginations. The result, nevertheless, is a beautiful map and a work of art.

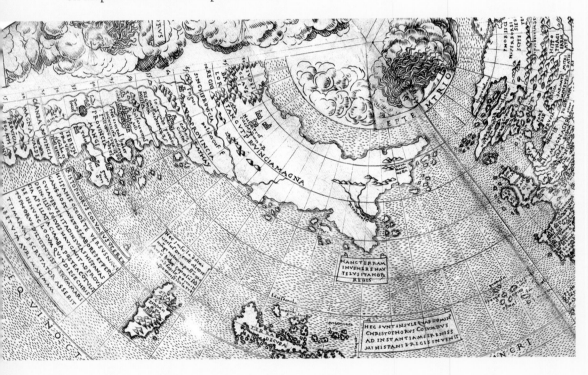

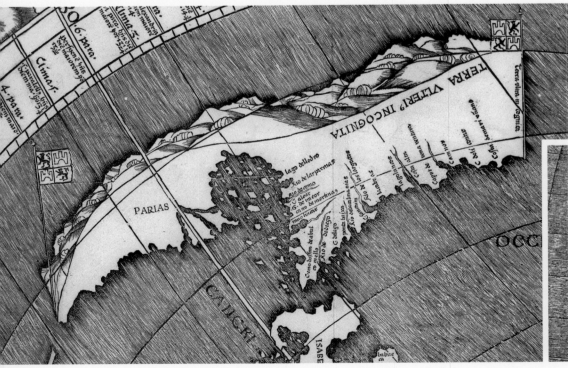

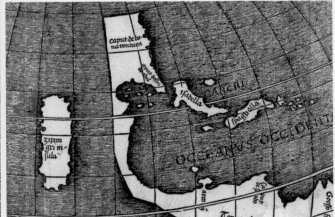

SEVEN CITIES OF GOLD

Above.
A restored Spanish helmet, displayed at the Coronado State Monument, Bernalillo, New Mexico.

Map 15 (*below*).
This beautiful manuscript portolan map shows what the Spanish knew of the West by about 1544. The Gulf of California, shown north to its termination, is unnamed but colored red, reflecting the name it was given by Francisco de Ulloa: the Mar Vermijo—the Vermilion Sea.

The search for wealth was to drive much of the early Spanish effort to explore the West. Gold and other precious metals were first on the list, with slaves as another possible source of wealth if gold was lacking. Later, Spanish missionaries would comb the West searching for souls to convert, but throughout the Spanish period religion provided much of the moral justification in the European mind for what was really exploitation.

The Caribbean islands and South America kept the Spanish interested during the first decade or so following Columbus. By 1510 they had made a settlement at Panama. In 1513 Vasco Núñez de Balboa crossed the isthmus and saw the Pacific Ocean. And in 1519 the Aztec empire in Mexico was invaded, and conquered by 1521, leading to the establishment of New Spain, the epicenter from which the American West would later be colonized. Also in 1519, Juan Ponce de León invaded Florida, looking for yet another form of wealth—a fountain of youth—and the same year Alonzo Álvarez de Pineda sailed along the Gulf Coast, showing that Florida was connected to New Spain and that there was no passage from the Gulf of Mexico to the Pacific.

In 1528 Pánfilo de Narváez, who had been appointed governor of Florida, then the huge territory stretching right along the Gulf Coast, landed on the west coast of the Florida peninsula with four hundred conquistadors, intent on finding gold in his new domain. He made what was to be a fatal mistake by sending his ships away. The Indians picked him and his men off one by one. The survivors moved north and, near today's Tallahassee, constructed small boats in which they hoped to float west along the coast to Spanish settlements at the Pánuco River in New Spain. Most were drowned, but a few survivors washed up on the shore near today's Galveston, including Narváez's second-in-command, Alvar Núñez Cabeza de Vaca.

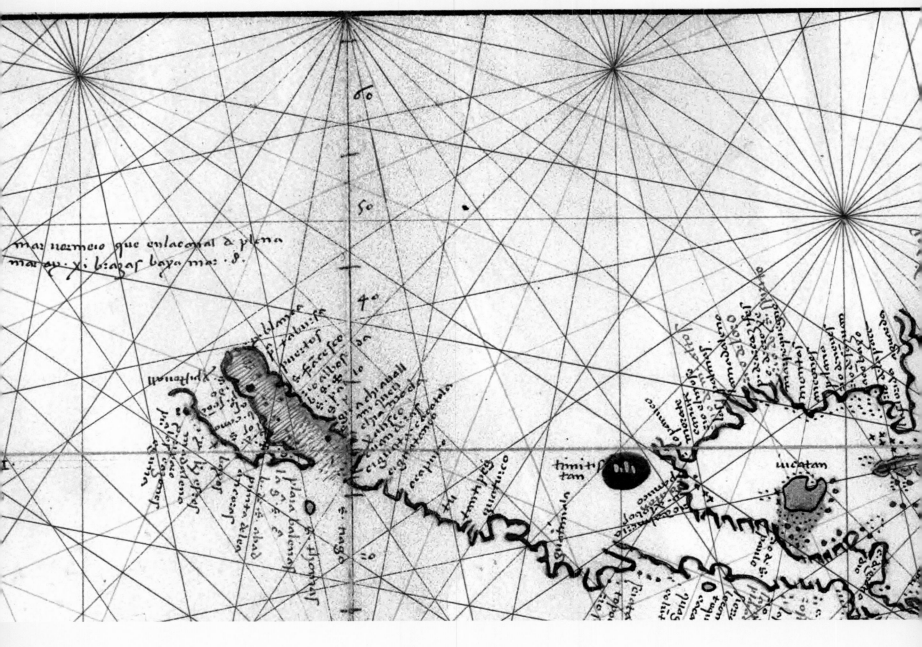

He and three others, including a black slave, Estéban (or Estebanico), lived with several Indian tribes as their slaves for four years, following them in their wanderings all over the Southwest. Then, in 1534, they managed to coordinate an escape. The four fled north and west, keeping away from the coast, where they expected to find hostile Indians. Aided by interior Indians, many of whom considered Estéban a god because of his blackness, they found their way toward the Gulf of California where, in April 1536, they were found by Spanish slave hunters.

In Mexico City, Cabeza de Vaca delighted the viceroy with the stories of his adventures. The viceroy, Antonio de Mendoza, was especially interested in his account of the large pueblos that he had encountered, for in his mind such large cities equated with wealth—and what could that mean but gold? He organized a further reconnaissance, and Estéban was dispatched to report. He sent back a story of seven large cities in a land called Cibola—in fact Zuni pueblos.

About this time, the sadistic conquistador Hernando de Soto received a royal contract to "conquer, pacify, and populate" the vast area of Florida as then defined, and he arrived in the Caribbean in 1538 with seven hundred followers. Between 1539 and 1541 he would range over the South and Southwest, brutalizing the Native peoples in an attempt to find gold at any cost (MAP 16, *right*). He did find

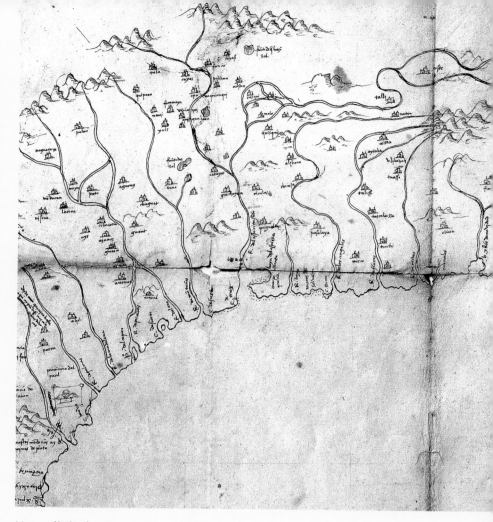

MAP 16 (*right*).
The nonpeninsula part of the region that was then considered Spanish Florida is depicted on this pen-and-ink map by Alonso de Santa Cruz. It was completed about 1544 using reports from the survivors of Hernando de Soto's expedition and shows locations of Indian villages and rivers flowing to the gulf. At center is the *R. del Espiritu Santo*, the Mississippi.

MAP 17 (*below*).
The fabled Seven Cities of Cibola—the seven cities of gold—are fancifully depicted on this 1578 map by Sicilian mapmaker Joan Martines. The southern coast appears to reflect information from the 1542 voyage of Juan Rodríguez Cabrillo. Note the large island of Japan shown in mid-ocean.

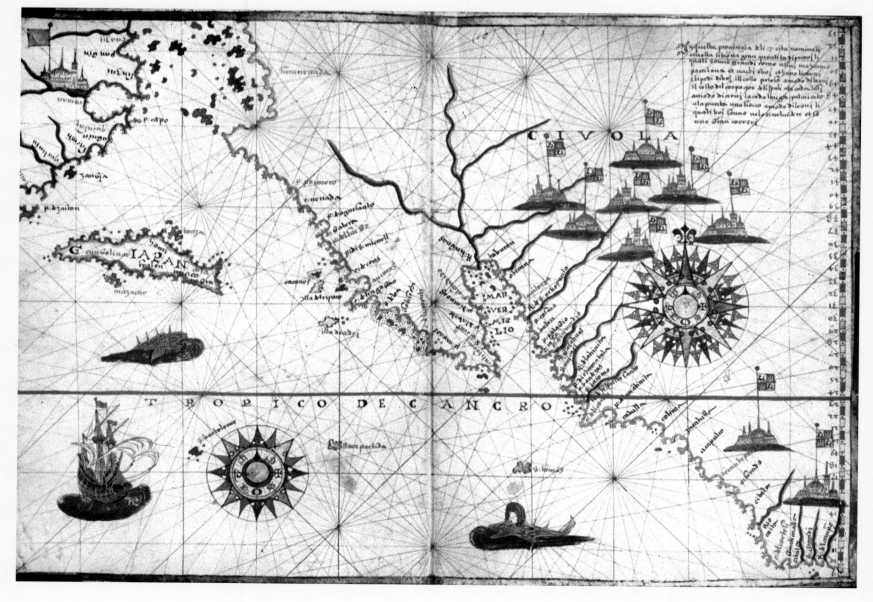

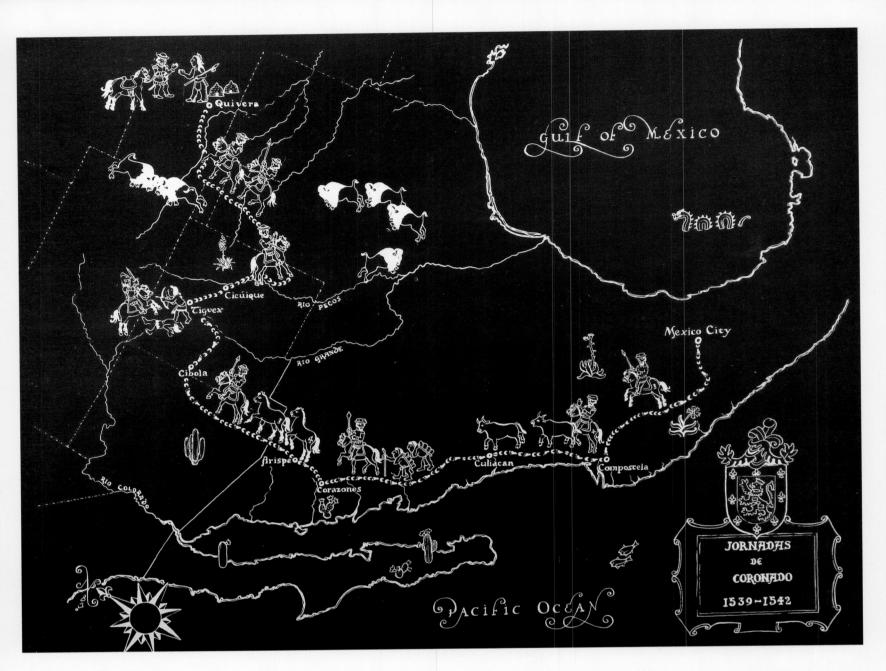

MAP 18 (*above*).
This map shows Francisco Vázquez de Coronado's route to *Quivera*. It is engraved on a brass plate at the Coronado State Monument at the pueblo of Kuau'a, Bernalillo, New Mexico, a location thought to have been one of Coronado's camps in 1540.

MAP 19 (*below*).
A good deal of artistic license is required for this 1931 gas company road map of Kansas. The cover shows Coronado, straight off his ship somehow and presumably in the middle of Kansas, about to discover Quivira.

and cross the Mississippi, the Spanish Rio del Espiritu (or Spiritu) Santo, but his expedition was a failure. Just over three hundred of his men survived, but de Soto did not.

Viceroy Mendoza, spurred on by the notion that de Soto might discover the seven cities before him and also concerned about the intentions of another rival, Hernán Cortés, organized an army under the governor of New Galicia (a province of northern New Spain), Francisco Vázquez de Coronado, to locate—and loot—the seven cities. Coronado marched north with 330 of his men and a thousand Native allies in February 1540.

Coronado, of course, found not cities of gold but modest mud habitations. He and his men fought with Native groups when the latter defended themselves. He dealt with his adversaries in what, sadly, seems to have been the typically brutal Spanish fashion at this time. But he did search quite thoroughly, and covered a lot of ground, by sending out small exploration parties.

One of these, led by García López de Cárdenas, found the Grand Canyon. They were the first Europeans to see it. Another party, sent north and east to the edge of the Great Plains, interviewed an Indian who described a city of gold called Quivira. Coronado immediately marched his main army to the location of Quivira, near today's Kansas City, but found only villages of mud and thatch. Clearly the riches of the Aztec or Inca empires were not going to be found to the north of New Spain. One thing Coronado did find were vast herds of buffalo (American bison). He also noted how the Native peoples used everything the buffalo provided.

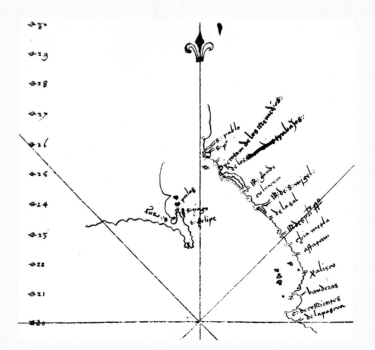

Map 20 (*left, top*).
Baja California. This is the first map of the peninsula, drawn by Hernán Cortés in 1535 as part of a legal document.

Map 21 (*left, center*).
Printed in a 1770 history of New Spain is this map, which shows the routes of Cortés to and from the Bahía de la Paz. The name *California* is prominent but was likely added by the eighteenth-century engraver.

Map 22 (*left, bottom*).
Considered to be the origin of the first, short-lived conception of California as an island (see pages 22–23), this map was drawn by Alonso de Santa Cruz, the Spanish royal cartographer, in 1542. A narrow channel separates the tip of Baja from the continent. Cortés himself appears to have thought Baja to be an island in this fashion. The inscription at its southern tip reads (in Spanish): "the island which the Marques de Valle [Cortés] discovered." Apart from names around the Gulf of Mexico, most of the rest of the West is covered with space-filling illustrations. Note that the West Coast north of Baja is not defined. The map was drawn in gores to be cut out and pasted onto a globe.

Map 23 (*below*).
This portion of the famous 1544 world map by Sebastian Cabot incorporates information from the voyage of Francisco de Ulloa, dispatched by Cortés in 1539. Most of Baja California is now defined, as in the complete coast of the Gulf of California. The map clearly indicates that Ulloa considered Baja a peninsula.

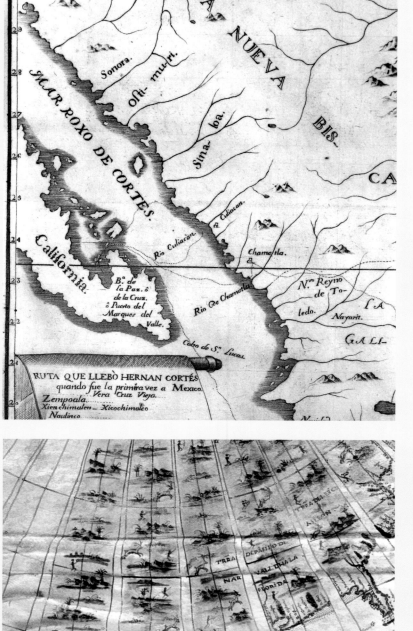

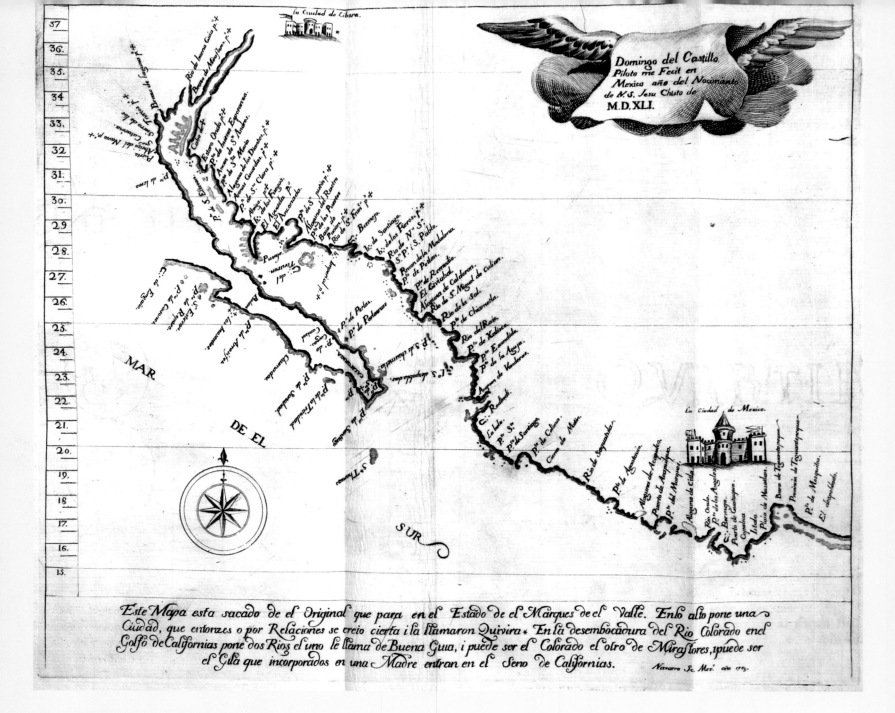

Este Mapa esta sacado de el Original que para en el Estado de el Marques de el Valle. En lo alto pone una Ciudad, que entonzes o por Relaciones se creio cierta i la llamaron Quivira. En la desembocadura del Rio Colorado en el Golfo de Californias pone dos Rios el uno le llama de Buena Guia, i puede ser el Colorado el otro de Miraflores, i puede ser el Gila que incorporados en una Madre entran en el Seno de Californias. Navarro Sc. Mei: año 1769.

MAP 24 (*above*).

This map, published in a 1770 history of New Spain, is thought to be a copy of a map drawn in 1541 by Domingo del Castillo, Hernando de Alarcón's pilot. He may also have been with Ulloa. Alarcón's *Rio de buena Guia*, the Colorado, is shown emptying into the head of the gulf. Much has been made of the fact that this map also carries the name *California* (on the lower part of the Baja peninsula) but this is likely simply an addition by the engraver in 1770. The reference in the caption to the *Marques de el Valle* is to Cortés, who was given the title Marquis of the Valley of the Oaxaca in recognition of his achievements conquering Mexico.

While these various Spanish probes into the interior were being carried out, others were searching north along the coast. In theory, sailing in a ship ought to have been easier than trekking overland, but owing to perverse winds and currents on the West Coast, not to mention fog, cold, rough seas, and a lack of decent harbors for refuge, mariners soon found out that this was not necessarily the case.

In 1533 an expedition sent out by Hernán Cortés, the conqueror of the Aztec empire, found the southern tip of Baja California, which they believed to be an island (MAP 21 and MAP 22, *previous page*). A settlement at Santa Cruz, on the site of today's La Paz, was created as a base for a search for pearls in the Gulf of California (MAP 21, *previous page*). In 1539 Cortés sent out an expedition led by Francisco de Ulloa to seek out new sources of wealth. Ulloa sailed to the head of the Gulf and determined that Baja was not an island, a fact that was later totally overlooked. The following year Cortés's rival, Viceroy Mendoza, sent out another maritime expedition. Hernando de Alarcón was sent north with the principal mission of

resupplying the Coronado expedition. Alarcón entered the Colorado River and dragged his boats upriver for ninety miles before coming to the conclusion that he was not going to find Coronado. Alarcón's Rio de Buena Guia, his name for the Colorado, is shown on MAP 24, *above*.

Viceroy Mendoza was also keenly interested in obtaining wealth from farther afield, and in 1542 he dispatched two expeditions, one across the Pacific to the Spice Islands and one up the West Coast. For the latter he enlisted one of his most experienced men, Juan Rodríguez Cabrillo, giving him instructions to find a passage then thought to lead back to the Atlantic—the fabled Northwest Passage. Cabrillo found an excellent harbor he called San Miguel—today's San Diego—but farther north was forced by the winds to sail offshore. Returning to the Channel Islands off Los Angeles to overwinter, Cabrillo died, and the expedition was taken over by his second-in-command, Bartolemé Ferrer (or Ferrelo). Making a valiant effort to carry out Mendoza's instructions, Ferrer got as far north as Cape Blanco in February 1543 before deciding there was no practical strait.

After Ferrer, no Spanish ships sailed north for almost sixty years. By the beginning of the seventeenth century the galleon route from the Philippines to New Spain was well established, and since this route usually entailed a final leg of the voyage down the West Coast, finding harbors that the galleon could use if distressed, which it often was after its long voyage across the Pacific, became critical.

In 1602 Sebastián Vizcaíno, a merchant involved in the galleon trade, sailed north in search of harbors. He found Cabrillo's San Miguel

OCEANO SETENTRIONALE

CIRCVLO ARTICO

TERRA INCOCNITA

GOLFO DI TONZA

MAR DELA CHINA

LE SETE CITA

TROPERA PRO

Map 25 (*above*).
North America is firmly attached to Asia in this map, drawn about 1565. The Seven Cities of Cibola are shown, and the large river discovered by Alarcón flows from the interior of Asia. Baja California peninsula is particularly prominent in this view.

Map 26 (*right*).
One of the first maps to show geography from the Cabrillo voyage was this 1555 map by Venetian cartographer Giacomo Gastaldi. Of special note is the *Sierra Nevadas*, a snow-capped range of high mountains. Although referring to the Coast Range south of Monterey, not the range today called the Sierra Nevada, the name does originate from Cabrillo. The California peninsula is curiously foreshortened; the *I. de Cedri* (Isla Cedros) is shown near its tip. *Cibola* is also named. This map also includes information from the Coronado expedition; *Quivira, Axa, Cicuich,* and *Tiguas* were Coronado's names for Native settlements.

again, renaming it San Diego (Map 30, *page 21*), and also found Monterey Bay and Drake's Bay, behind Point Reyes, which he also named. Vizcaíno mapped the West Coast as far north as Cape Mendocino in some detail, though his map was not published by the secrecy-obsessed Spanish government for another two hundred years (Map 29, *page 21*).

During the expedition, one of the ships in Vizcaíno's little fleet, commanded by Martín de Aguilar, had become separated from the others in a storm and was blown northward.

Map 27 (*right*).
One of the earliest representations of a Northwest Passage, which could be reached on the Pacific side by sailing north up the west coast of North America, was this set of globe gores. The gores were produced about 1530 for a globe depicted behind three ambassadors in a painting by Hans Holbein in 1533; the globe has hence gained the name Ambassadors' Globe. The globe has disappeared, alas, but the geography it showed has been preserved and is shown here. In this early depiction is the motivation for sailing north: a shortcut back to Europe. But the continuing coast could also be followed west, it was thought, thus providing a sailing route to the riches of the Orient.

Here he discovered a large river, which *could* have been the Columbia; he named it the Rio Santa Iñez. Aguilar's name showed up on numerous maps of the West for two centuries afterward at the entrance to a Northwest Passage, a strait, or the mouth of the mythical River of the West (see, for example, Map 42, *page 25*, and Map 103, *page 58*).

Despite Vizcaíno's meticulous mapping of the West Coast, but likely abetted by the lack of publication of his maps, the popular view of the West well into the eighteenth century often included a

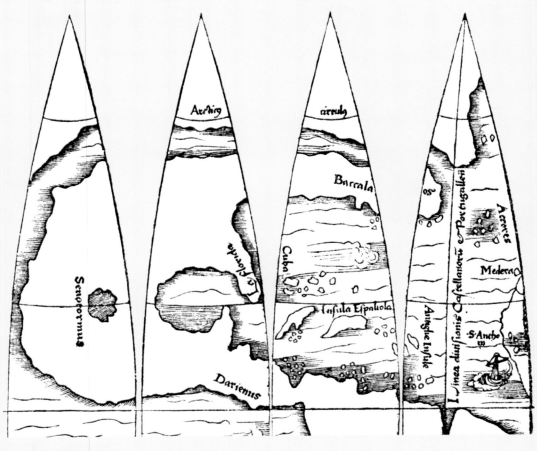

Map 28 (*below*).
An early mixture of sparse fact with what was otherwise fantasy in the map of the West. The Northwest Passage was well shown in this 1570 world map published by Abraham Ortelius in his atlas *Theatrum Orbis Terrarum*—"Theater of the World." The West looms large as *America Sive India Nova*—America or New India. The Seven Cities of Cibola dominate the Southwest. *Quivira* has been moved nearer the coast, while to the north is the mythical land of *Anian*, a name that originated in Ania, a Chinese province mentioned in a 1559 edition of Marco Polo's travels.

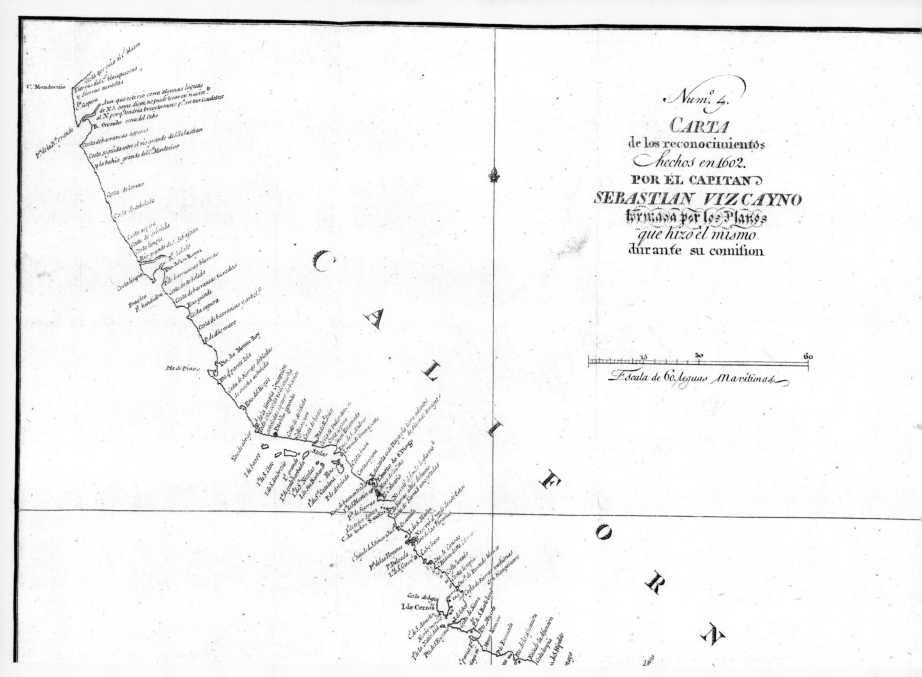

Num.º 4.

CARTA
de los reconocimientos
hechos en 1602.
POR EL CAPITAN
SEBASTIAN VIZCAYNO
formada por los Planos
que hizo el mismo
durante su comifion

Escala de 60 leguas Maritimas.

MAP 29 (above).

The Spanish kept the results of Sebastián Vizcaíno's voyage secret from the rest of the world for two hundred years. In 1802, concerned that its claims to the Northwest were being eroded by the incursions of Britain's George Vancouver (see page 60), the Spanish government published the *Relación,* an account of all Spanish voyages to the region. Vizcaíno's summary map, shown here, was finally engraved and revealed and shows his mapping of the West Coast as far north as Cape Mendocino.

MAP 30 (left).

Detailed maps of the sections of the coast were drawn by Fray Antonio de la Ascension, a Barefoot Carmelite priest with the Vizcaíno expedition. Here is his sketch map of San Diego Bay. The bay to the immediate north is Mission Bay.

MAP 31 (right).

This map by Abraham Ortelius, published, like MAP 28, in 1570, is another fine artistic representation of the West. Mapmakers seemed to have no problem creating quite different interpretations of geography they were largely only guessing at anyway. Again, a number of cities are shown in the Southwest, but not all those on MAP 28 are present here.

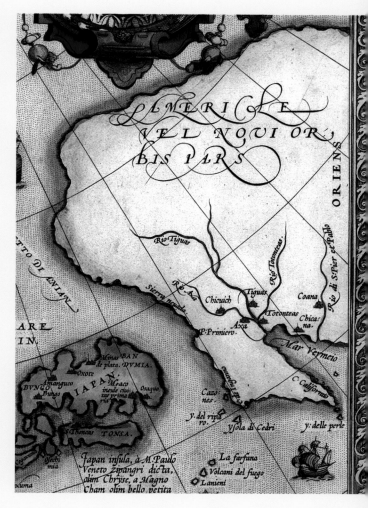

depiction of California as a large island, not just Baja separated from the mainland by a narrow channel, as it had been in its first incarnation (Map 22, *page 17*).

The concept, ironically, originated with Fray Antonio de la Ascension, who had been with Vizcaíno and had drawn sketch maps of harbors (Map 30, *previous page*). Ascension noted, correctly, the apparent lack of large rivers along the coast, a feature caused by the topography of the Central Valley of California and the fact that the two principal rivers, the San Joaquin and the Sacramento, flow parallel to the coast, exiting together into San Francisco Bay, the entrance to which was not found until 1772. Ascension concluded that the preponderance of small rivers was due to the fact that they were flowing from an island.

Fray Ascension's concept was first published on the title page of a history book in 1622 (Map 32, *above right*) and was extensively copied thereafter.

At the end of the seventeenth century, a wide-ranging Jesuit missionary, Fray Eusebio Kino, reached the confluence of the Colorado and Gila rivers and realized that he was north of the Gulf of California. In 1701 and 1702 he went down the Colorado to the head of the gulf, and from that location it was clear that there was land to the north, not water. He wrote a report to his superiors in which he concluded that Baja California was a peninsula. His map (Map 36, *far right*), included in his report, was reprinted in several languages.

Kino's map should have put an end to the myth of California as an island, but it did not. Only the most progressive mapmakers paid attention to this new information. In 1746 another Jesuit, Fray Fernando Consag, reached the head of the Gulf of California in a canoe, again proving that it terminated and that Baja was a peninsula. Finally, in an unusual royal intervention into mapmaking, the king of Spain, Ferdinand VI, issued a royal decree that stated "California is not an island," and this, it seems, did finally put an end to the island myth. Soon after, the land route to Alta California became an important route for Spanish colonizers (see page 37).

Map 33 (*left*).
Part of Englishman Henry Briggs's famous map *The North part of America*, published in 1625. This was the first published map to repeat Ascension's view of California as an island.

Map 34 (*below*).
There are probably a few hundred different maps that depict California as an island, but none is more beautiful than this example, drawn around the middle of the seventeenth century by Dutch cartographer Joan Vinckeboons.

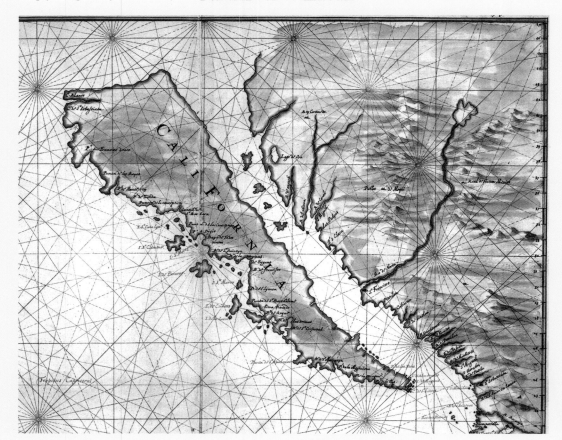

Map 32 (*left, top*).

The first publication of a map that showed California as an island appears to be this illustration from the title page of Antonio de Herrera y Tordesillas's *Description de las Indias Occidentales*, which appeared in 1622. This map was drawn by Fray Antonio de la Ascension, who had been with Vizcaíno in 1602 and originated the island concept its second time around.

Map 35 (*right*).

The actual shape of the island California varied depending on the mapmaker, although some similarities are apparent. This map represents a further variation and comes from one published by French mapmaker Nicolas Sanson in 1657. This edition was published in 1683.

Map 36 (*below*).

This is the French edition of Fray Eusebio Kino's seminal map, finally showing California attached to the rest of the continent via a land connection across the head of the Gulf of California.

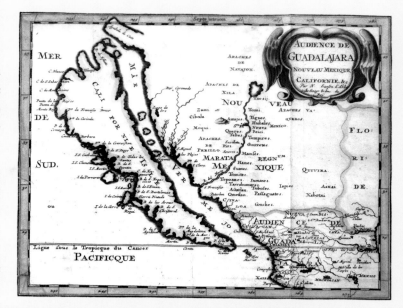

An English Interloper

The early EuroAmerican history of the West is exclusively the domain of Spain, with the sole exception of a short interlude that occurred in 1579 when the famous English buccaneer, Francis Drake, visited the West Coast. Its significance partly lies in the ongoing English, then British, interest in the region and the claims it later enabled, as well as the political geography of western North America that it can be said to have fostered (see page 84).

Drake arrived on the West Coast in 1579, on one leg of his voyage of plunder that would become a circumnavigation of the world, loaded with gold and silver captured from the Manila galleon and thinking the Spanish hot on his trail. He had heard of the rumored Northwest Passage and wanted to find its western entrance to facilitate a quick run back to England. To this end he sailed north—how far is unclear—before deciding, in the bitter cold, that he was not going to find it. He urgently needed to repair his ship, and for this task he found a secluded bay somewhere—probably, but by no means certainly, Drake's Bay at Point Reyes—to careen his ship.

While there Drake and his men encountered the local Miwok Indians, and somehow a ceremony took place in which Drake was "crowned" by the Miwok chief, an act that was likely a courtesy but that was conveniently transformed in the minds of some into a surrender of the entire West to Britain (Map 42, *right, bottom*). Britain used claims such as these in the negotiation of the forty-ninth

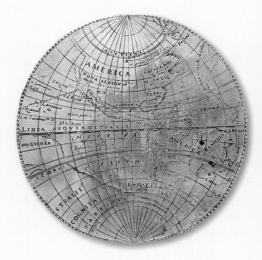

Map 40 (*above*).
A silver medal made in Holland in 1589 by Michael Mercator commemorated Drake's circumnavigation, the second ever (after Ferdinand Magellan/Juan Sebastián del Cano, 1519–22), and the first by an English navigator. Again Drake's track north in the Pacific is not well defined.

Map 37 (*right*).
Part of a world map by Dutch mapmaker Joducus Hondius, originally produced in 1589; this is the 1595 edition. The track of Drake up the West Coast is indicated, petering out between 40° and 50° N, perhaps reflecting an erasure on the original it was copied from.

Map 38 (*right, inset*).
Also from the 1595 Hondius map is this little chart of *Portus Novæ Albionis*, the harbor where Drake careened his ship and the subject of endless debates as to its location. All the modern evidence points to Drake's Bay at Point Reyes, California.

Map 39 (*below*).
In 1581, only a year after his return to England, French mapmaker Nicola van Sype published a world map depicting Drake's circumnavigation. Here Drake's track to the north conveniently disappears behind an image of a ship. *Nova Albio[n]* is now shown covering the West north of *Nova Hispanie* (New Spain), even though this is a French map.

parallel boundary as late as 1846. To bolster the notion that sovereignty could be bestowed on Drake by the Miwok, the account of the voyage, *The World Encompassed,* is careful to state that "the Spaniards never had any dealing, or so much as set a foote in this country"—which, no doubt, was true for that central or northern California location in 1579.

The question of how far north Drake reached before turning back has sparked entire speculative books. Some claim he reached the Alaska Panhandle, and much is made of the extreme cold he encountered, but this is common in the North Pacific even in the summer. He likely reached about 42° or 43° N. His return route seems to have been deliberately falsified in order to worry the Spanish into thinking he must have found the Northwest Passage. Drake did arrive in England just the next year, after a quick voyage west around the southern tip of Africa, and his swiftness added to the Spanish concern that he had returned through the passage.

Other than the ongoing sovereignty issue, Drake's impact on the West was but ephemeral. All but two hundred years would pass before Britain would again show interest in the West Coast.

Map 41 (*right*).
The first map to note Drake's visit to the West Coast was this map with a bizarrely shaped California and a wide Northwest Passage across the top of North America. It was produced by the English promoter of the Northwest Passage, Michael Lok. At the north end of the West Coast are the words *Anglorum 1580*—Lok could not even get the date right. Note also a depiction of Cabrillo's *Sierre Nevada,* and even *Quiviri* on the north coast.

Map 42 (*below*).
The West remains *New Albion* as late as 1768, the date of this map. Albion was an old name for England. Note also the caption *So named by Sr. Francis Drake to whom the Country was surrendred by the King in 1578 [1579],* referring to the ceremony in which Drake was "crowned" by the Miwok chief but which many in Britain deliberately interpreted as a prima facie British claim to the Northwest. Other features of interest include the prominent *River of the West* (see page 55) and the *Opening discover'd by Martin D'Aguilar in 1603* (see page 20).

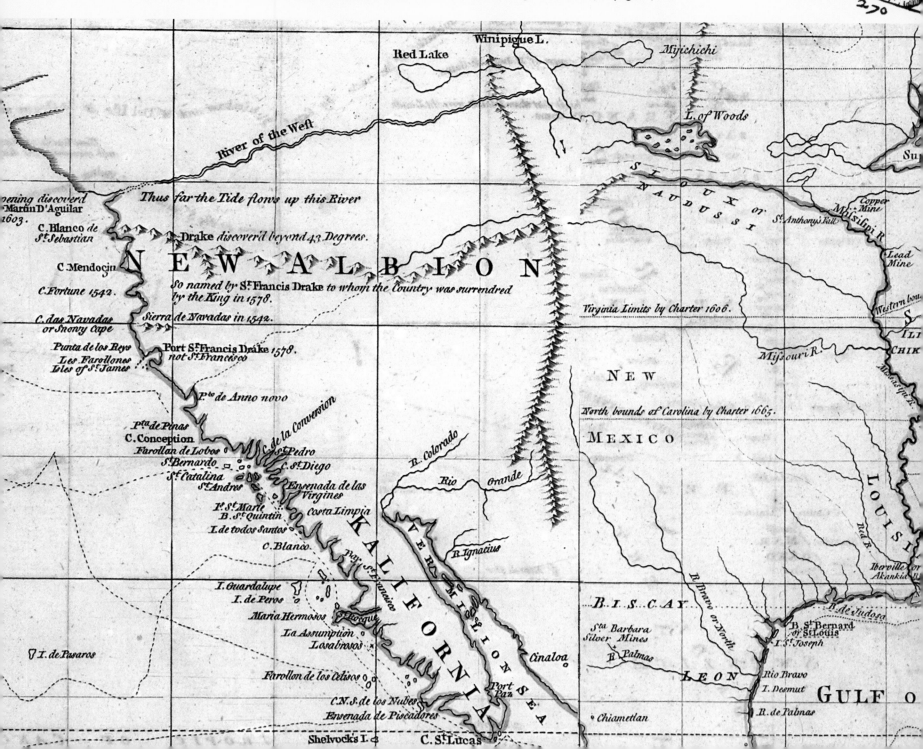

The Northern Provinces of New Spain

Entering the eighteenth century, Spain slowly turned its hand from the raw search for gold to colonization of the northern borders of New Spain as a way of producing other forms of wealth. The motive—officially at least—was religious; the Natives were to be converted but also brought into a subjugation that would ultimately serve the mother country. Spain developed the presidio and mission system, where presidios, or forts, would secure areas militarily where necessary, and missions would secure their inhabitants' loyalty through conversion to Roman Catholicism. As areas were stabilized, villas, or chartered towns, might also be established. This pacification system proved workable for two centuries, first in New Mexico (which included the area of today's Arizona), then in Texas, and finally in California.

The gentler handling of the Indians did not start off well, however, for its first practitioner, Juan de Oñate, was censured, fined, and banished for his overly harsh treatment of Indians. Even recently, Native groups protested when a statue of Oñate was unveiled in El Paso.

All attempts at colonization had to be licensed by the government and better respect human rights, a doctrine called the Ordinances for New Discoveries decreed by the Spanish king in 1573. In 1590 Gaspar Castaño de Sosa, lieutenant-governor of the province of Nuevo León, tried to colonize New Mexico without a license and found himself arrested by an armed party dispatched by the viceroy. Juan de Oñate was licensed in 1595 to colonize the region and become the first governor of Spanish New Mexico. In 1598 he set out with six hundred soldier-colonists, with some women and eight Franciscan priests, moving up the Rio Grande, stopping at a pueblo he named San Juan Bautista, near the confluence of the Rio Chama (twenty-five miles north of Santa Fe). It was the first Spanish settlement in New Mexico. Two years later the settlement was moved across the river and renamed San Gabriel.

The Spanish were dependent at first on supplies from the pueblos. On a foray around the new province some of Oñate's men demanded food from the Acoma pueblo, which sits atop a 357-foot-high sandstone mesa in a uniquely defensible position. They were refused, and attacked, with much loss of Spanish lives. Determined to assert his authority Oñate then sent a larger army against the Acoma. By arranging a clever feint attack at one side of the mesa, the army managed to scale the mesa and decisively defeat the Acoma. Hundreds were killed. At a trial of captives Oñate is said to have ordered the left feet of males over twenty-five cut off and all the women and children to be enslaved. By so doing he hoped to send a message to all

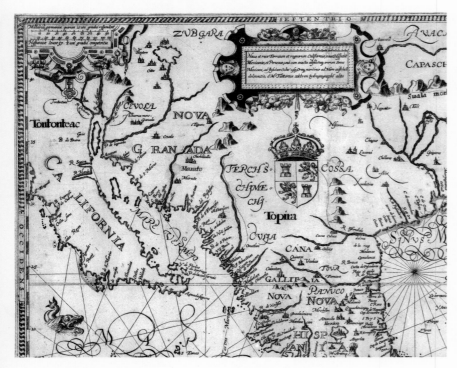

MAP 43 (*above*).
New Spain depicted on a 1600 map, just prior to the period of northward expansion that would see Spanish settlement in New Mexico, Arizona, and Texas. *Cevola* (Cibola) is shown near the head of the Gulf of California, the *R. de Spiritus Santos*—the Mississippi—is at right, but only the lower reaches of the Rio del Norte—the Rio Grande—are shown, unnamed. This was one of the earliest maps to name *California.* The Gulf of California is *Mare Vermejo*—the Vermilion Sea.

Below.
The Spanish Mission San Xavier del Bac, founded near Tucson in 1699 (the present building was completed in 1797), shown in an 1897 photograph.

Top right.
Motif from a 1940 map drawn by Bob Goldwaters showing Spanish missions in Arizona.

Map 44 (*right*).
This sketch map by Enrico Martínez shows Juan de Oñate's search for Quivira in 1601. Quivira is shown as *Pueblo del nuevo describimento* at top right, a location about twenty-five miles northwest of modern Wichita, Kansas. The *rio del robrodal* is today's Arkansas River. The more populated region at top left is the valley of the Rio Grande, shown as the *rio del norte*, where the Spanish would establish Santa Fe a few years later. The *Rio salada* is the Pecos River, and the *Rio de la madalena* is the Canadian River.

Map 45 (*below*).
Santa Fe, the capital of the Spanish province of New Mexico, founded in 1610. Here it is shown in a 1766–67 map by military surveyor José de Urrutia. Note the main irrigation canal *Acequia Para Regadio* at the base of the hills to the north. The original plan of Santa Fe has been lost.

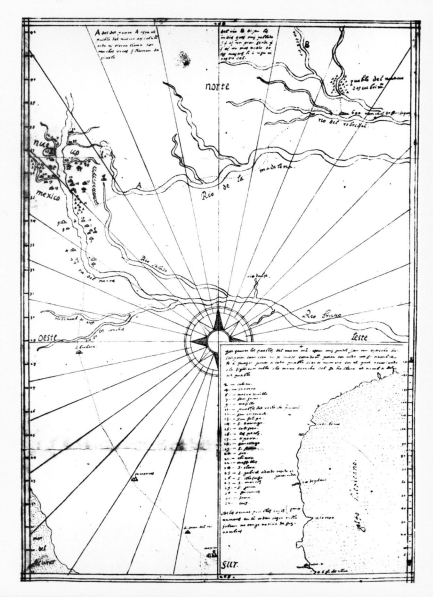

the Indians of the region. But the sentence went beyond the new government guidelines for dealing with such matters and ensured his later censure. Yet there is actually no evidence that the more brutal sentences were ever carried out.

Stories of great Indian cities of gold to the east across the Plains continued to interest Oñate, and in June 1601 he led seventy men in search of Quivira, reaching a Native village near today's Wichita, Kansas, before, as others who had preceded him, deciding that the city was an illusion (Map 44, *right*). In 1604–05, with the idea that his colony would benefit from a Pacific port, Oñate led another expedition, this time west, down the Colorado River to the Gulf of California.

Oñate was recalled to New Spain in 1608, but before he left he had planned a villa to be called San Francisco. Instead, his colonists had by 1607 or 1608 begun to build a town at a site south of San Gabriel they called Santa Fe. The new governor, Pedro de Peralta, accepted the new site, and in 1610 Santa Fe became the second-oldest European town to be established in what is now the United States (after St. Augustine, Florida, established in 1565).

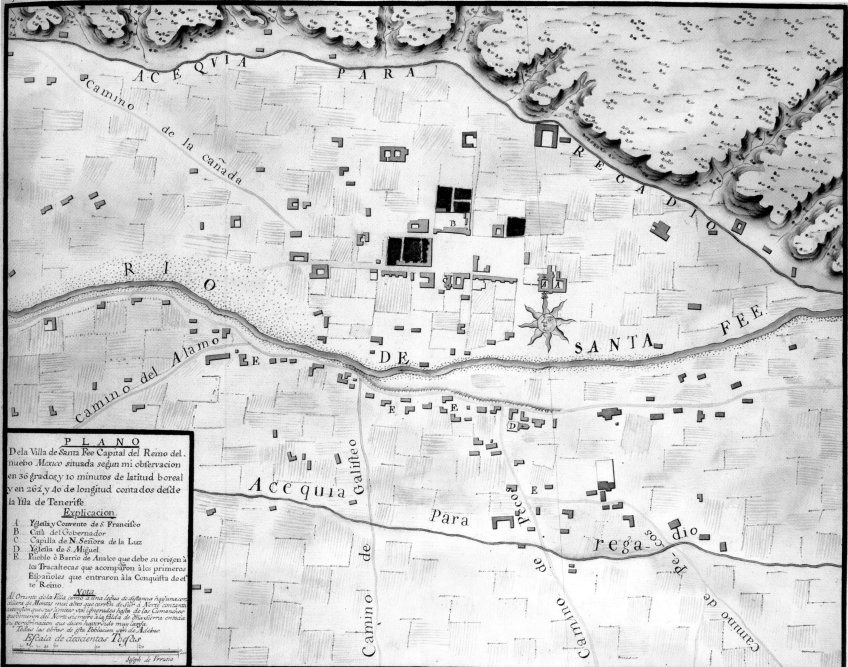

MAP 46 (above).
Spanish expeditions onto the Great Plains, including those of Coronado and Oñate, noted the vast herds of buffalo, shown on this 1685 map as *Tract of Land full of Wild Bulls*. The Rio Grande is shown flowing from a large lake. *S Fe als New Mexico* and *Acoma* are recorded on this relatively undetailed English map.

MAP 47 (right).
Much more information appears on this map by Venetian mapmaker Vincenzo Coronelli, originally published in 1688; this version is a later edition. The information found its way to the French through the ex-governor of New Mexico Diego Dionisio de Peñalosa (1661–64), who, after running afoul of the Inquisition and fleeing to Europe, offered to assist the French king Louis XIV in an invasion of Spanish territories. Note that this map now shows *el Passo* (Ciudad Juárez–El Paso) at the bend in the *Rio del Norte* (Rio Grande). *Acoma* is pictorially depicted atop its mesa.

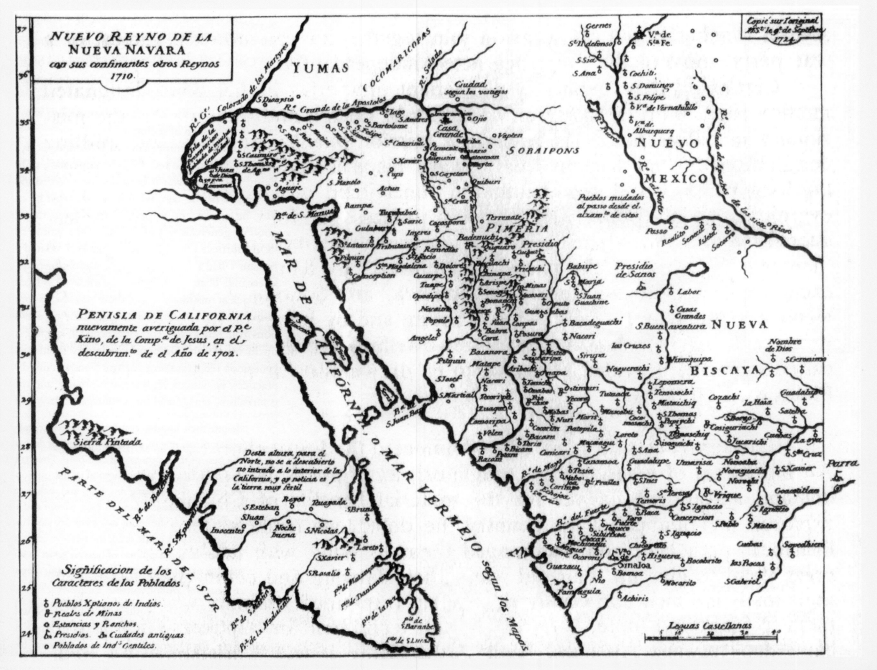

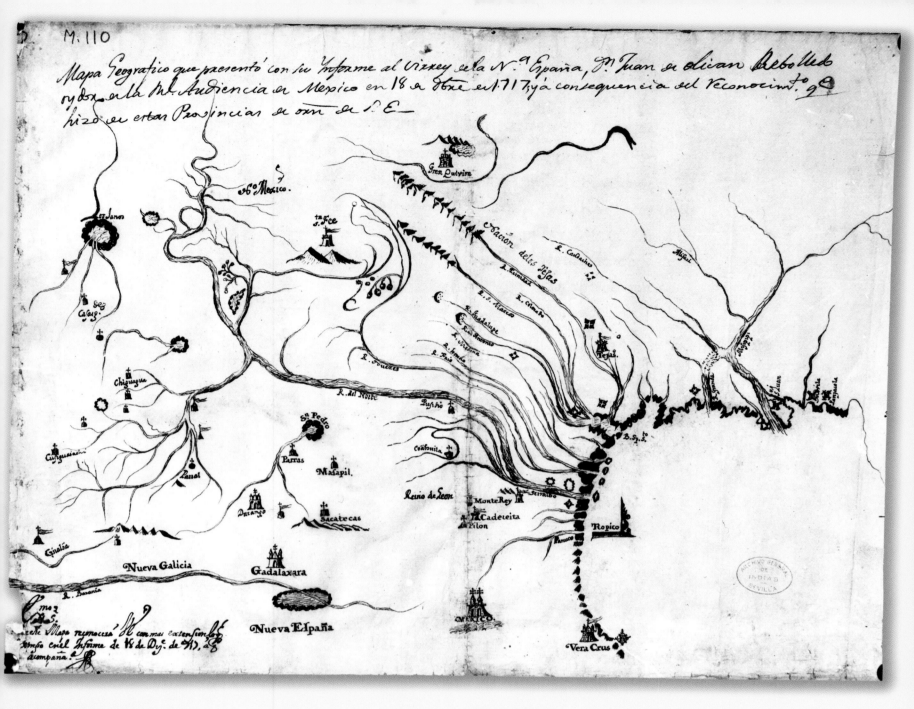

Mapa Geografico que presentó con su Informe al Virrey de la N.ª España, D.ⁿ Juan de Olivan Rebolledo y dⁿ de la M.ª Audiencia de Mexico en 18 de Dbre en 1717, y a consequencia del Reconocimⁱ.ᵗᵒ qᵉ hizo en estas Provincias de ordn de S.E.

Map 48 (*left, bottom*).

This was the last map made by Eusebio Kino, in 1710. It shows not only the lands bordering the Gulf of California—including Baja California as a peninsula, of course—but also New Mexico, a region Kino never visited himself. In the valley of the *R. del Norte* (the Rio Grande) is *Vª. de Alburquerq*, the villa (town) of Alburquerque (now Albuquerque). The map documents the religious motive of the Spanish government in the colonization of the northern provinces and indicates the considerable number of missions (all marked by ⊙) founded in the century between 1610 and 1710.

Slowly new missions were founded across the Southwest. A particularly large complex was built on the Pecos River in the 1620s. And in 1668 an important mission, the Mission Nuestra Señora de Guadalupe, was completed at El Paso del Norte; it survives today in Mexican Ciudad Juárez, across the river from El Paso, Texas. In 1706 the Villa de Alburquerque de San Francisco Xavier del Bosque—today Albuquerque—was founded, named after the Duque de Alburquerque, then viceroy, and the governor's saint.

For many years there was an ongoing struggle between the Franciscans and the Jesuits to establish missions and spread their version of Catholicism. In the early years the Franciscans had the upper hand, but after 1687, largely owing to the efforts of Eusebio Kino, the Jesuits established twenty missions in the northwest, plus another twenty in Baja California. Kino's final map (Map 48, *left*), made just before he died in 1711, showed them all.

The tenuous Spanish hold on its New Mexico province was broken in 1680 when the Spanish tried to crack down on non-Christian rituals, sparking an Indian revolt led by Popé. Churches burned; priests were

Map 49 (*above*).

A map presented by military advisor Juan Manuel de Oliván Rebolledo, along with his report, to the Marqués de Valero, viceroy of New Spain, in 1717. Much of the information shown on the map was derived from the French trader Louis Juchereau de Saint-Denis. In his report, Oliván Rebolledo recommended a series of forts to protect New Mexico against incursions upriver from the Gulf of Mexico, hence the emphasis here on the river systems.

Below.
A typical southwestern adobe mission, looking much the same today as it would have four centuries ago. This is St. Anne Mission, in Acoma, New Mexico.

killed, and the Spanish population retreated in terror to Santa Fe, then evacuated south to El Paso. About two thousand people moved en masse. Popé set himself up as the new ruler of New Mexico but was unable to control stepped-up Apache raids, and when a Spanish military expedition in 1692 attempted to retake Santa Fe, it met with little resistance, and Spanish rule was quickly reinstated.

The Spanish at this time were becoming increasingly concerned about a new threat—the French. René-Robert Cavelier, Sieur de La Salle, had journeyed down the Mississippi River to its mouth in 1682 and by 1685 was trying to establish a colony at Matagorda Bay, Texas. He even ascended three hundred miles up the Rio Grande. This was a menace the Spanish could not ignore, and they had some success in containing the threat, but the French established a firm foothold in the Mississippi Valley, effectively cutting the Spanish territories in East Florida off from those in Texas (see page 50).

In 1690 San Francisco de los Tejas, the first mission in Texas, was set up on the upper Neches River among the Hasanai—for whom the Spanish word was *Tejas* or, in Castilian Spanish, *Texas*; this is the origin of the name. Rising opposition from the Hasanai led to the mission's abandonment in 1693.

Both local French and Spanish settlers wanted to trade, since doing so was to their mutual benefit, but the authorities in Mexico City did not approve. French trader Louis Juchereau de Saint-Denis reached the Rio Grande in 1714, leading the Spanish authorities to reconsider their strategy (MAP 49, *previous page*). Two years later they sent Domingo Ramón and a group of about seventy-five north to found a colony in East Texas, the first Spanish settlement in Texas other than missions. With them was Saint-Denis, who had ingratiated himself with the viceroy and married a Spanish woman. The Neches mission was reestablished as Nuestro Padre San Francisco de los Tejas, and several other missions were also established.

At this time the French built a fort at Natchitoches (now in Louisiana), and the Spanish countered by building two more missions just west of the French outpost. Then in 1718 the French founded New Orleans as a commercial trading center.

To supply the increasingly remote missions built to counter the French, in 1718 a new governor of Texas, Martín de Alarcón, set up a mission on the San Antonio River, San Antonio de Valero, named after the viceroy, the Marqués de Valero; the chapel of this mission would later

MAP 50.
Francisco Álvarez Barreiro's 1729 map was a good attempt at a comprehensive map of the Spanish northern provinces, with most of the information gained from actual field observation, though not all locations are correct. The Gulf Coast is at right; the *Rio del Norte*, the Rio Grande, flows down the middle of the map; and at left is the Gulf of California. The *Rio Colorado* is shown joining the *Rio Gila* and then flowing into the gulf at about 34° N (the head of the gulf is actually at about 32° N), but the sea is incorrectly shown continuing farther north, presumably indicating that Barreiro had not seen Eusebio Kino's map (MAP 36, *page 23*) and still thought California was an island. At center is *Vᵃ de Sᵗᵃ Fée* and *Alburquerque; Sⁿ Antonio* is on the *Rio de San Antonio* (which flows into the *Rio de Medina*, right, center); and *Adaes* is shown at the right margin.

be called the Alamo. Alarcón also constructed a presidio, San Antonio de Béjar, and chartered a villa, Béjar, later San Antonio (MAP 488, *page 212*).

The same year, the War of the Quadruple Alliance (1718–20) broke out in Europe, and Spain was defeated by Britain, France, Austria, and the Netherlands. During this period the French regained control of East Texas, but at war's end a new viceroy, the Marqués de San Miguel de Aguayo,

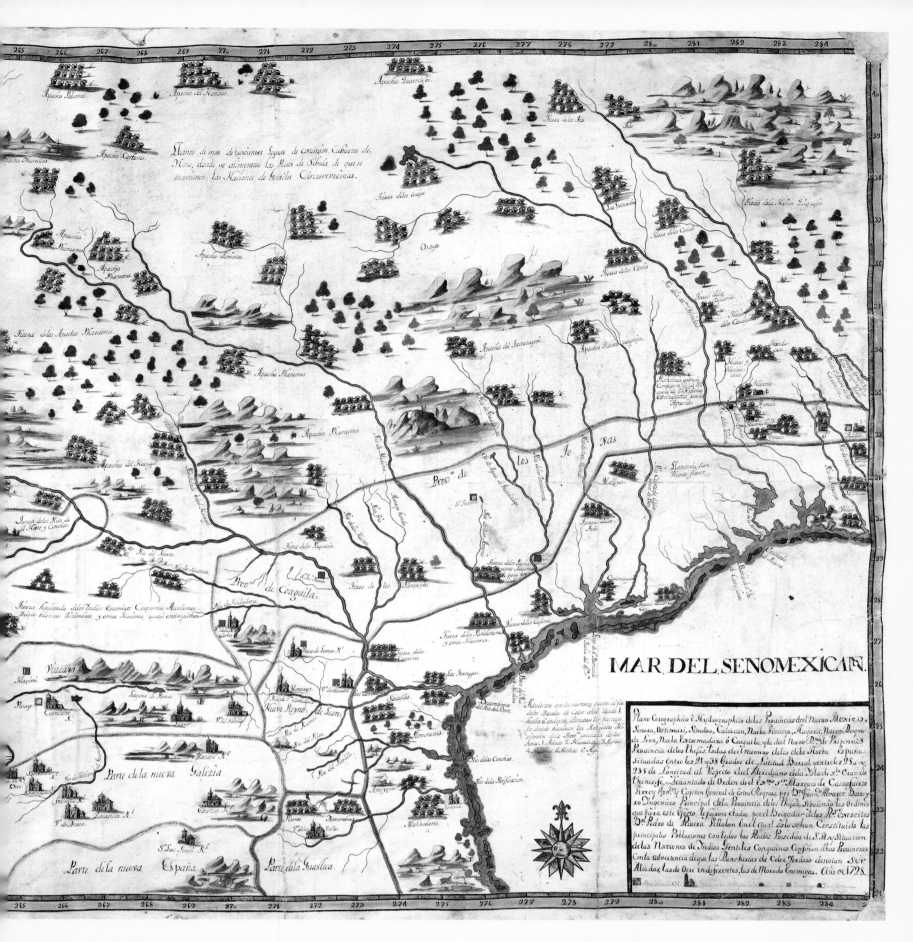

set out to reoccupy Texas, building a new presidio, Nuestra Señora del Pilar de Los Adaes, just twelve miles west of Natchitoches. This fort was the capital of Texas until the French ceded Louisiana to Spain in 1762 to avoid losing it to Britain.

The war also raised concerns about a French incursion into New Mexico, and the Spanish drew up plans to build a presidio to the east, on the Plains. In 1720 the governor ordered Pedro de Villasur to search among the Pawnee villages along the Platte River (in what is now eastern Nebraska) to root out Frenchmen believed to be hiding there, perhaps poised to attack New Mexico. At the confluence of the Platte and Loup rivers, Villasur's small army of forty-five Spaniards and sixty Pueblo Indians was annihilated by a large band of Pawnee and Oto. The massacre ended Spanish ambitions of expansion onto the Plains.

The Spanish authorities were at this time in any case becoming increasing concerned about the cost of maintaining a Spanish empire of sorts north of New Spain. From 1724 to 1728 the inspector general, Pedro de Rivera y Villalón, made a grand tour covering eight thousand miles. He produced a report recommending economies, and subsequently the garrison strengths of a number of presidios, including Santa Fe, were reduced. Rivera's tour did increase Spanish knowledge of the West, however, for with him was his cartographer and military engineer, Francisco Álvarez Barreiro, who produced a number of maps, such as MAP 50, *above*.

The greatest enemy of the Spanish at this time was not in fact the French but the Indians, especially the Comanche and the Apache; the latter regularly attacked San Antonio. Peace with the Apache in 1749 just increased the enmity of the Comanche.

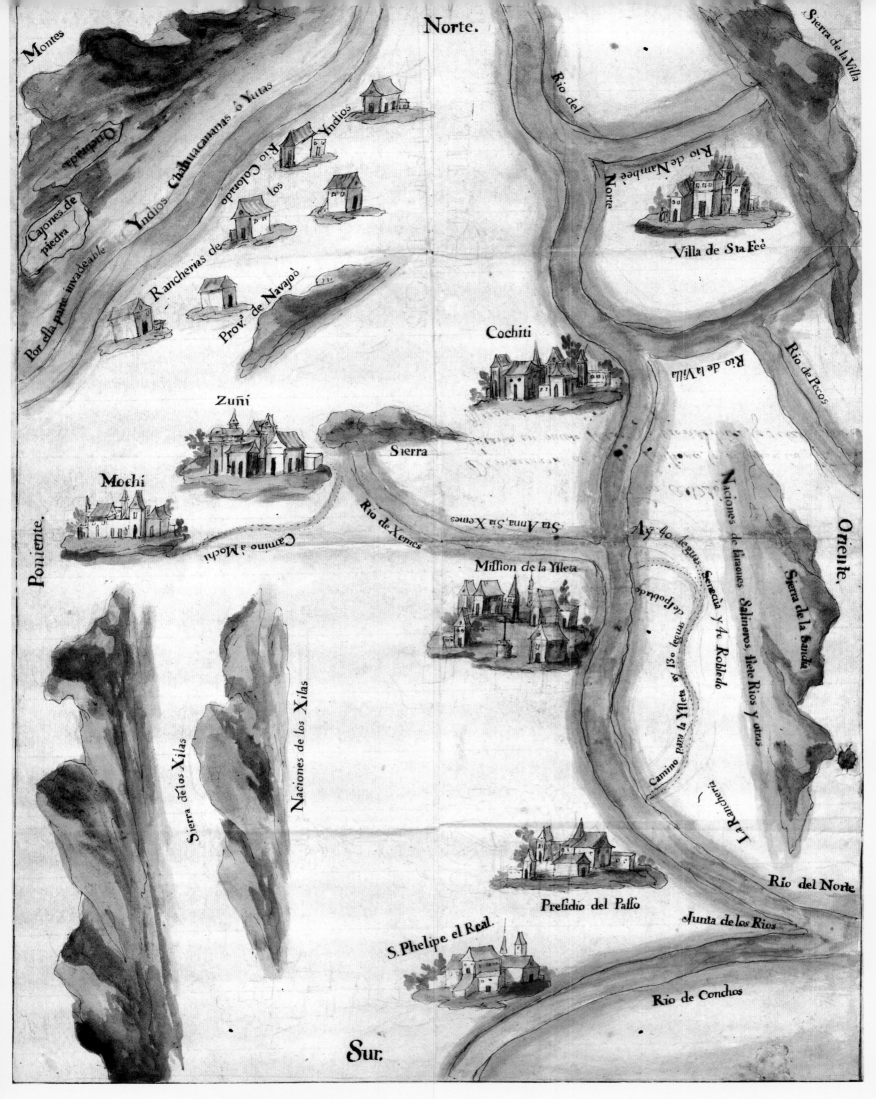

Norte.

Montes

Sierra de la Villa

Quebrada

Cajones de piedra

Por ella para. invadeable

Yndios. Chahuacananas. ó Yutas

Rio Colorado

los

Yndios

Rancherias de

Prov.ª de Navajoo

Rio del Norte

Rio de Nambee

Rio de Nambee

Villa de Sta Feé

Cochiti

Zuñi

Sierra

Rio de la Villa

Rio de Pecos

Mochi

Rio de Xemes

Sta Anna. Sta Xemes

Camino a Mochi

Poniente.

Naciones de faraones Salineros. flete Rios y otras

Oriente.

Ay 40 leguas

Sienega y A. Robledo

del poblado

Million de la Ylleta

Camino para la Ylleta ay 130 leguas

Sierra de la Sandia

Sierra de los Xilas

Naciones de los Xilas

La Rancheria

Rio del Norte

Presidio del Passo

Junta de los Rios

S. Phelipe el Real.

Rio de Conchos

Sur.

MAP 51.

This rather nicely illustrated map, drawn in 1746, depicts the rivers, roads, missions, and settlements of Spanish New Mexico, along with Indian pueblos shown in exactly the same distinctly European fashion. One gets the feeling that the mapmaker had not visited the region: the map gives the impression of a river-laced land, when this could hardly be further from the truth. Then again, per-

haps the dominance of the rivers reflects their importance. The *Rio Colorado* is at top left, and the *Villa de Sta Feé* (Santa Fe) is at top right; the *Rio del Norte* (Rio Grande) flows at center right, and the *Presidio del Passo* is at the *Junta de los Rios* in what is today Mexican Ciudad Juárez, across the river from El Paso. The *Rio de Conchos* is today the main river of the Mexican state of Chihuahua.

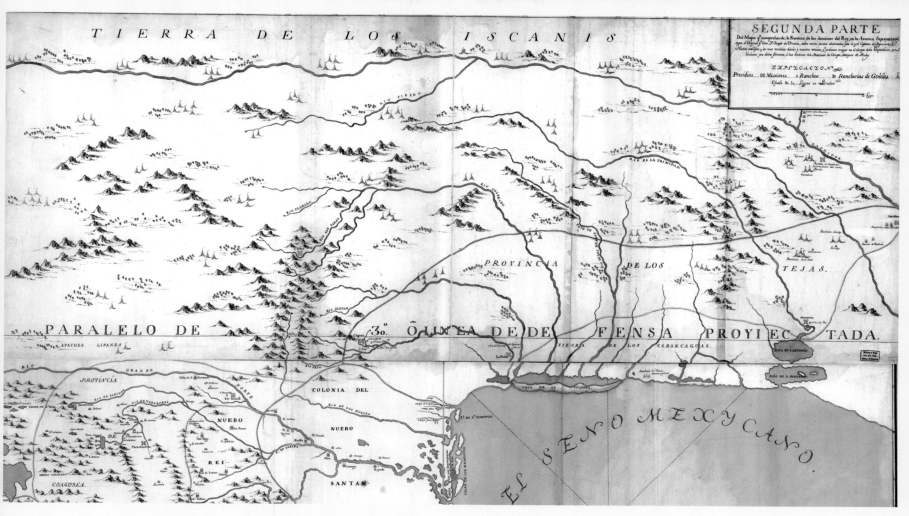

TIERRA DE LOS ISCANIS

SEGUNDA PARTE
Del Mapa g⁰ comprehende, la Frontera de los dominios del Rey, en la America Septentrional
EXPLICACION
Presidios, Misiones o Ranchos Rancherias de Gentiles

PROVINCIA DE LOS TEJAS.

PARALELO DE 30. LÍNEA DE DEFENSA PROIECTADA.

PROVINCIA

COLONIA DEL

NUEBO

NUEBO

REI

SANTAN

COAGUILA

EL SENO MEXICANO

Map 52 (*above*).
A huge four-sheet summary map of the entire Southwest was drawn up in 1769 by José de Urrutia and reflected his artistic method of depicting missions, presidios, and Native settlements, the latter reasonably depicted as tents, though flying flags in European battle–style. Shown are the two eastern sheets, covering Texas and not altogether joining correctly along the Gulf Coast. *Los Adais* (Adaes) is at the right-hand margin, *Sⁿ Antonio* at center left. The east Texas presidios Rubí recommended for closure are also shown.

Map 53 (*below*).
A section of the first (northwestern) sheet of José de Urrutia's map depicted six grand cities, not seven, just to the west of Santa Fe, on mountaintops near a river called the *Rio de Nabajo*. This name likely refers to Navajo settlements, but their precise location—as is fitting given their history—is confusing, since the Gila River and Santa Fe areas are in fact separated by at least a hundred miles on the north–south plane, not at the same latitude as shown here, and the river here is more likely the Colorado rather than the Gila.

By 1762 it was clear that France would lose the Seven Years' War against Britain, and before signing a treaty with Britain in 1763 France signed the Treaty of Fontainebleau with Spain, ceding all claims west of the Mississippi. As a result of this massive gift, Spanish territory was now in direct contact with that of Britain. Spain reassessed its policy toward the northern provinces and in 1766 dispatched the Marqués de Rubí on a grand tour of the frontier, charged with assessing the strengths and weaknesses of the Spanish position and recommending new policy for the changed situation. With him went Nicolás de Lafora, engineer, and Lieutenant José de Urrutia, both of whom engaged in mapmaking, making beautiful if not always totally accurate maps. Urrutia drew detailed plans of each of the presidios they visited, as well as maps of the settlements and their surroundings. Map 45, *page 27,* is his map of Santa Fe, and Map 55, *overleaf,* is his map of El Paso, both of which are invaluable records of the Spanish era.

OS ∙ PROVINCIA DE

RIO DE NABAJO

MOOVI

Oraibe.

Mansanabi

Joncoba-bai

Pueblos de Gualpe

Coninas

Aguambi.

Cuma

Following a familiar pattern, Rubí's report recommended economies, and the East Texas presidios were abandoned as no longer necessary and the number of soldiers reduced. At the same time he recommended an increase in military activity against the Comanche, a proposition entirely infeasible with reduced troop numbers. Rubí also recommended a cordon of uniformly spaced presidios from the Gulf of Mexico to the Gulf of California to protect New Spain, although presidios at Santa Fe and San Antonio were to remain as outposts. This recommendation overlooked the fact that Indians usually raided settlements rather than attacking heavily fortified positions.

MAP 54 (above).
From the first sheet of Urrutia's map is the *Tierra de los Papagos* (land of the Papagos, today the Tohono O'odham), the area roughly covered by today's state of Arizona. The presidio at *Tubac* is shown near the bottom edge of the map. Just to the north is *S. Xabier del Pac*, the mission of San Xavier del Bac, founded in 1699 (see also photograph, *page 26*), and *teuson*, today Tucson. The settlements of the Yuma, who in 1781 would annihilate a detachment of soldiers and the explorer Francisco Garcés, are shown along the lower Colorado.

MAP 55 (below).
José de Urrutia's map of El Paso, drawn in 1766. A is the presidio, such as it was (it consisted at this time of just a captain's house and a guardhouse); B is the church and mission. The surrounding irrigated fields are shown; the two *Acequia* are irrigation channels.

MAP 56 (right).
Urrutia's superb map of the northern Rio Grande Valley, with numerous Spanish settlements and Indian pueblos beautifully depicted, though with his usual artistic license. Note *Acoma* to the west of *Alburquerque*.

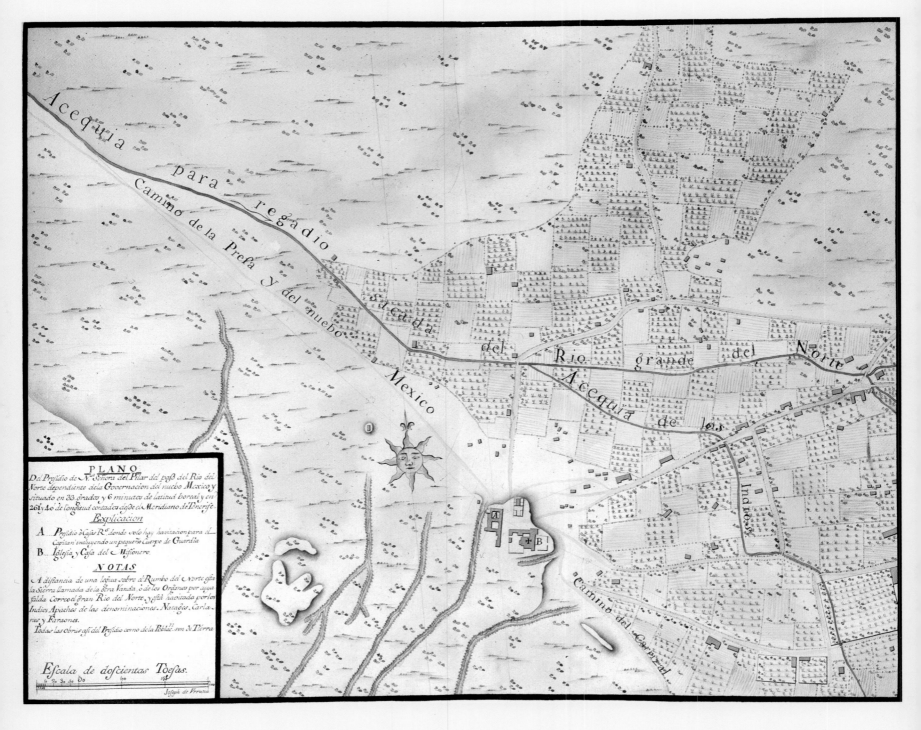

Pecuries

Embudo

Sª Barbara

Ojo Caliente

Rio ariba

Trampa

Abiquiu

Sª Cruz

Chimaio

R. DE MORA.

Sª Clara

S. Juan

Chimaio

CIA

LLE DE PIEDRA LVMBRE

pajuqu

Vrambe

S. Yldefonso

tesugue

PROVIN

Sª Feé.

DE NU

Alamo

Galisteo

Peos

S. domingo

EVO

Nemes

Cochia

R. DE LAS GALLINAS.

ME

chia

S. Felipe

Bernalillo

O

R. DEL PECHO.

S. Ana

Sandia

Las Huertas.

R. PUERCO.

Alameda Chiliti

X

I

Atrisco

Alburquerque.

Cebolleta

Pajarito

Laredo

Ysleta

Valencia

Puara

R. SALADO.

Laguna

Nª Sepora.

Honcara

toquigue

Salinas

Acoma.

S. Gabriel

Abo.

de las Nutrias.

SIERRA CUMAN

SIERRA DE LOS LADRONES.

CO

A

ALAMILLO.

SIERRA OBSCURA.

Socorros.

S. Pasqual.

PRO

tra Christobal.

Ojos de Amaya

Aleman

SIERRA DEL MUERTO.

Perxillo

SIERRA DE SIETE RIOS.

JORNADA DEL MUERTO

HOAGANOS

S. Diego.

DE DOS

SIERRA BLANCA.

Bernardo.

Robles

CORDILLERA

PASO DEL RIO DEL NORTE.

S. Lorenzo.

ZERRO DEL AYRE.

Seneca

RRA FLORIDA

Socoro

Caldas

Ysleta

Tiburcio.

VINCI

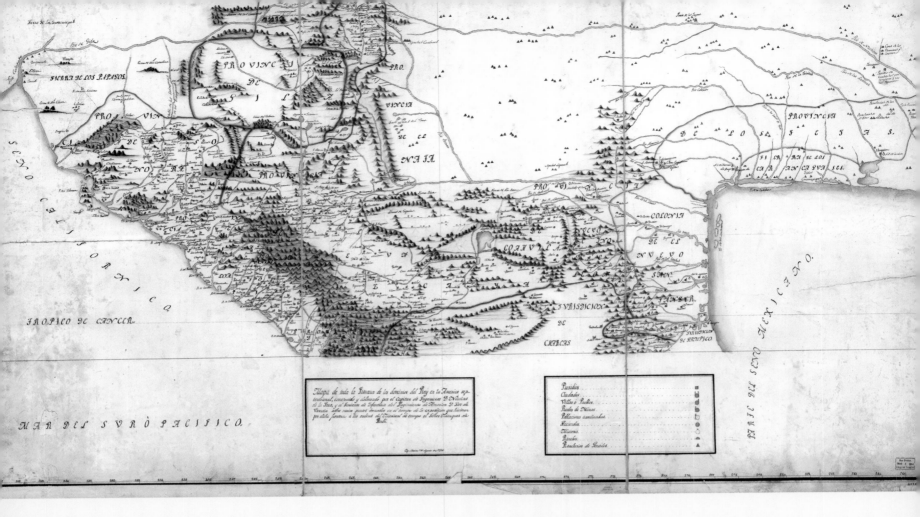

Map 57 (*above*).

This is a single-sheet copy of José de Urrutia's great map of the West, attributed to 1771, and to Nicolás de Lafora, Rubí's military engineer; no doubt Lafora and Urrutia collaborated in making most of the expedition's maps. This copy, done in 1816, shows an interestingly different cartographic style to the four-sheet map. Note the key at bottom.

Below.

The Palace of the Governors in Santa Fe, as it is today. This seat of the Spanish government of New Mexico grew from a building begun by governor Pedro de Peralta around 1610, when Santa Fe itself was founded. This National Historic Landmark is today the oldest continuously occupied building in the United States. In the nineteenth century modifications were made to the building to add a classical-style colonnade to make it look more impressive, but in 1913 renovations began to revert the architecture back to near-original adobe form; its style is described now as Pueblo Revival. It has been the home of the New Mexico History Museum, which houses the Segesser Hide Paintings, enormous depictions of the massacre of Pedro de Villasur by the Pawnee and Oto in 1720 (see page 31). In 2009 the museum is scheduled to move into a new building being constructed on an adjacent site. Native and other vendors sell local arts and crafts along the colonnade.

Spain's imperial policy in North America underwent a change from 1765 on, becoming much more expansionist and aggressive. This development was largely due to José de Gálvez, who in 1765 was appointed *visitador general* (inspector general) to New Spain, with power above the viceroy in some matters; in 1776 he became secretary of the Indies, a position from whence he continued to direct Spain's expansionist policies.

For Spain was becoming increasingly concerned about what it viewed as incursions into its territory, especially by Russia and Britain. Following Vitus Bering in 1741 (see page 56), the Spanish imagined Russians everywhere; in 1759 a book called *Muscovites in California* was published, and several more warned of an impending British discovery of the Northwest Passage. British commodore George Anson had sacked a city in Peru in 1741 and captured the Manila galleon in 1743; in 1764 Commodore John Byron was sent to search for the passage, and although he got nowhere near it, this fact was unknown to the Spanish at the time. And after 1763 the British were also expected to push westward from their new boundary on the Mississippi. "There is no doubt," Gálvez wrote in 1768, "the English are very

close to our towns of New Mexico and not very far from the west coast of this continent." This sentiment does much to explain Spanish moves over the next thirty years.

In 1767 the Spanish king, Carlos III, decided to expel the Jesuits from Spain and its colonies, following the same move by Portugal in 1759 and France in 1764. The intention seems to have been to eliminate a wealthy order that stood in the way of secular reforms. Gálvez used the Jesuit purge to begin implementing a grand strategy to colonize Alta (Upper) California and thus, he hoped, preempt other nations on the western edge of the Spanish dominions.

Gálvez supported Rubí's proposal for a cordon of defensive presidios but also aimed to defend the frontier by expanding beyond it. He planned to secure the interior provinces with a new independent military government, strengthen Spanish presence in Baja California, and establish a new colonial outpost on Monterey Bay far to the north, a bay described by Sebastian Vizcaíno in glowing terms as long ago as 1602 (see pages 19–21).

Gálvez enlisted a veteran army commander, Gaspar de Portolá, to expel the Jesuits from Baja California. They were replaced by Franciscans, led by Father Junípero Serra. Gálvez, Serra, Portolá, and the viceroy, Carlos Francisco de Croix, came up with the campaign plan to colonize Alta California, a plan confirmed by royal order in January 1768.

The campaign was named the Sacred Expedition in recognition of the significance of the mission. Three parties were to be sent north, two by land and one by sea; in this way the Spanish hoped success would be assured. The three were to meet at San Diego Bay, but by the time they all arrived one ship had been lost and half the men in the land expeditions had died.

Portolá was not to be stopped, however, marching north with the fittest men he could find. With him went Franciscan Juan Crespi; Serra stayed behind and on 16 July 1769 founded the first of many missions in Alta California, San Diego de Alcalá.

At the beginning of October, Portolá reached Monterey Bay but, because of Vizcaíno's overly rosy description, was unsure that he had reached the right place. He therefore sent a small party to search farther north. On 1 November 1769 an advance party led by Sergeant José Ortega came to the crest of a hill and saw before them a vast expanse of water, later to be called the Bahía de San Francisco—San Francisco Bay. It would prove to be far more useful than Monterey Bay ever could have been.

Portolá returned to San Diego but later realized that he had indeed reached Monterey Bay. Since he had a royal order to occupy this bay, in June

MAP 58 (*below*).
A map of Spanish New Mexico drawn about 1770. There were by this time four Spanish villas. In the north is the *Villa d[e] Sta Cruz* (de la Cañada), established in 1695; the *Villa de Sta Feè* (1610); and *Alburquerque*, established 1706. In the south the mission of *El Passo* on the now Mexican side of the *Rio del Norte* (Rio Grande) is shown. This is also the location of a presidio and the fourth villa, that of El Paso, established in 1680 by refugees from the Pueblo Revolt and by 1765 boasting a population of over 2,600. *Acoma* and other Native pueblos are also shown.

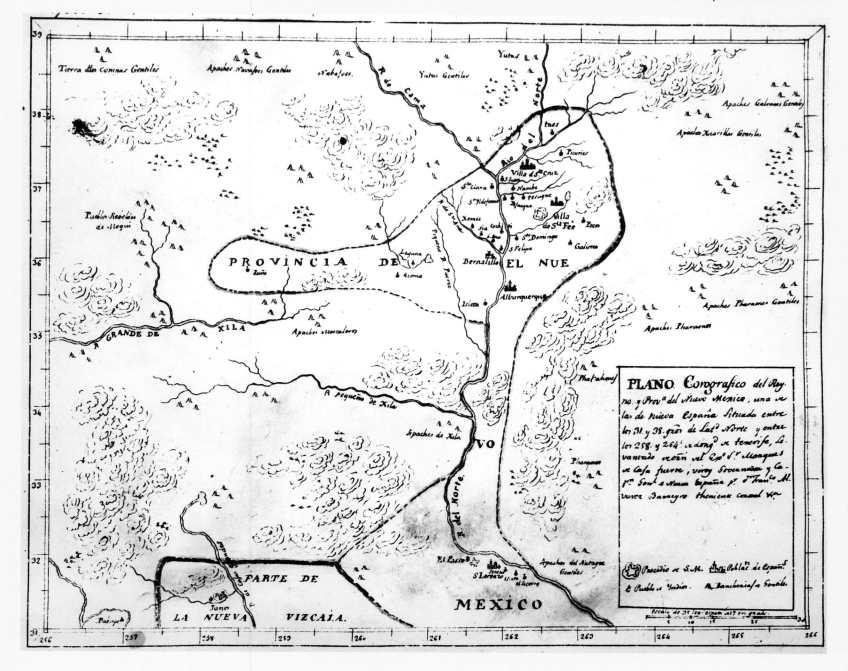

1770 he returned and established a settlement there. Another mission was founded, the second of a string of missions Serra would create along the southern California coast.

In 1772 a party under Lieutenant Pedro Fages, which included Juan Crespi, explored from Monterey north along the eastern shore of San Francisco Bay. The entrance to the bay was finally discovered, by looking outward. They also found the outlet of the San Joaquin and Sacramento rivers, and Fages explored far enough east to realize that they ran in the Central Valley. Crespi drew the first map of the complete bay from observation (MAP 60, *below, bottom*).

The Spanish also dispatched several expeditions by sea far to the north, instructing them to seek out any Russian

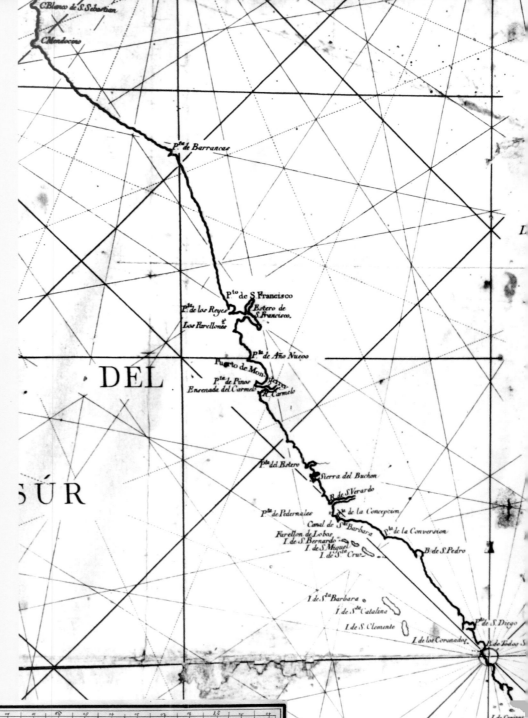

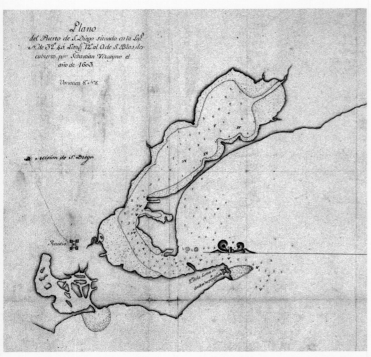

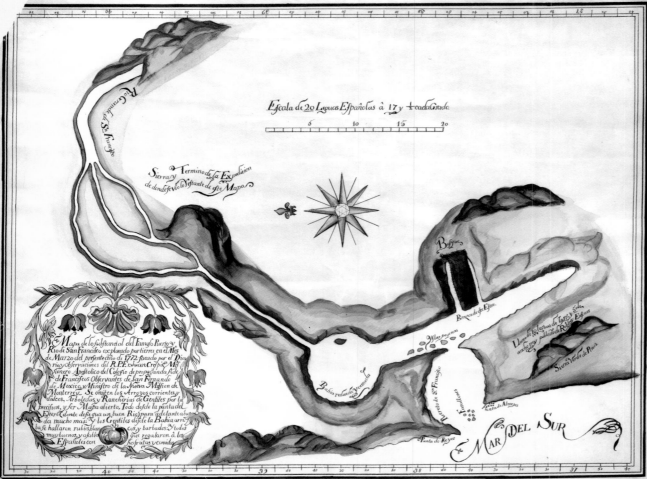

MAP 59 (*left, top*).
San Diego Bay on a Spanish map dated 1779. The *Presidio* is shown, as is the *Mision de S. Diego*, eight miles up the San Diego River.

MAP 60 (*left, bottom*).
Juan Crespi's 1772 map of San Francisco Bay, the first to show the bay complete and from exploration.

MAP 61 (*above*).
Army engineer Miguel Costansó, who was with the Portolá expedition in 1769 and with the Ortega group that first saw San Francisco Bay, drew this map of the California coast the following year. It was the first printed map to show the bay—*Estero de S. Francisco*, although at this time only part of it had been seen; the location of the entrance was a guess. Manuscript versions of this map both with and without San Francisco Bay are known to exist, the former only recently discovered.

Carta Reducida
del Océano Asiático ó Mar del Sur que contiene la Costa de la California comprehendida desde el Puerto de Monterrey, hta la Punta de S.ta Maria Magdalena hecha segun
las observaciones y Demarcaciones del Alferez de Fragata
de la R.l Armada y Primer Piloto de este Departamento
D.n Juan Pérez por D.n Josef de Cañizares

Map 62 (*right*).

Discovered deep in the U.S. National Archives in the 1980s was this beautiful manuscript map showing the coast discovered by Juan Pérez in 1774. The map was drawn the following year by José de Cañizares and uses a delightful picture method to show what the coastline at various points looked like from the sea. Monterey Bay is shown at bottom, with a not very well-delineated San Francisco Bay immediately to the north. Halfway up the coast is *Cerro de Sta Rosalia*, Mount Olympus, on Washington's Olympic Peninsula. Vancouver Island is not distinguished from the mainland, and neither are the Queen Charlotte Islands, the tip of which is near the top margin; this is the farthest north that Pérez reached. The land reaching down from the top map border is the southernmost tip of the Alaska Panhandle. How this important and apparently unique map found its way into the U.S. National Archives is still unknown. It is the first map of the West Coast north of San Francisco drawn from exploration rather than from imagination.

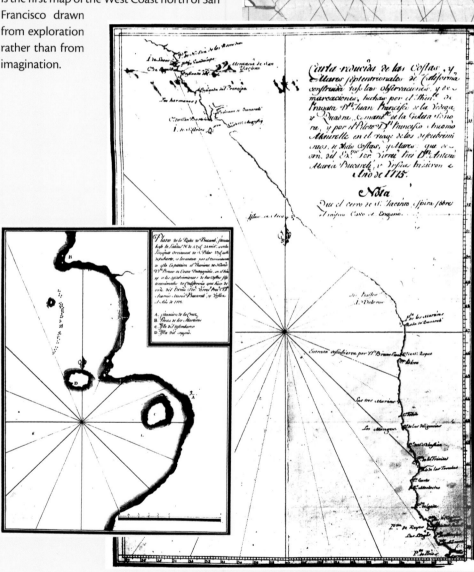

Map 63 (*above*).

This map documents the voyage of Juan Francisco de la Bodega y Quadra to Alaska in 1775. The coast is well defined north to Oregon, where Bruno de Hezeta and Bodega y Quadra sailed together, and, in the northern part, to the Alaska Panhandle, sailed by Bodega y Quadra alone. Between them is the coast roughly corresponding to that of today's west coast of Canada, sketchily defined because Bodega y Quadra was sailing well offshore here. This map is the first of the Alaska Panhandle.

Map 64 (*above, inset*).

Cape Elizabeth on the coast of Washington, mapped in 1775 by Hezeta. This is the first map of any part of Washington drawn from exploration. *B* is where some of Hezeta's men were killed.

trespassers and to perform acts of possession wherever they made a landfall. In 1774 a new viceroy, Antonio María de Bucareli y Ursúa, sent Juan Pérez north with a single ship; he made it as far as the northern tip of the Queen Charlotte Islands before turning back. He had been instructed to sail to 60° N but reached 54° 40′ N. The latitude he reached was later used as the farthest point of Spanish claims and would eventually define the location of the southern tip of the Alaska Panhandle.

The following year another expedition was dispatched, also ordered to sail to 60° N. There were three ships, one of which, under Juan de Ayala, sailed only to Monterey with supplies. Ayala became the first to sail into San Francisco Bay (see overleaf); the remaining ships, one under Bruno de Hezeta, with Juan Pérez demoted to first officer, and the other, only thirty-eight feet long, under Juan Francisco de la Bodega y Quadra, continued north.

In July 1775 the ships anchored off Cape Elizabeth (now in Washington State), where men were murdered when they went ashore to fill water casks (Map 64, *previous page*). At about 50° N, in a storm, the ships were separated. Hezeta returned south along the coast because his men were falling ill—Pérez was one of those who died—discovering and mapping the entrance to the Columbia River, though he thought it was a bay.

Bodega y Quadra, however, was determined to carry out his orders and, braving heavy seas in his diminutive ship, made it to 58° N after making a landfall near today's Sitka, Alaska. His map (Map 63, *previous page*) shows considerable detail of the Alaskan coast. But he found no Russians.

Meanwhile, the Spanish were intent on consolidating their settlement of Alta California and establishing a more extensive military presence as a buffer to the northern frontier. In 1774 Juan Bautista de Anza, commander of the presidio at Tubac and a veteran soldier sometimes referred to as "the last conquistador" for his role, marched north with thirty men to confirm that there was a viable land link to California. With Anza was the Franciscan Francisco Tomás Garcés, from Mission San Xavier del Bac, near Tucson, who was an experienced desert explorer. Despite Garcés's experience, Anza became lost, and two months passed before they struggled into the new mission of San Gabriel Arcángel. (Established in 1771 at Montebello, it was moved to San Gabriel in 1776; both locations are within what is now Los Angeles.)

Nevertheless, his expedition had demonstrated the California land link existed, and the next year viceroy Bucareli ordered Anza north once more. Garcés again accompanied Anza, but the viceroy had requested that

Garcés try to find a route from Monterey to Santa Fe, so he struck out on his own on an extensive interior traverse, finding the Grand Canyon for the first time since the Coronado expedition in 1540. He was prevented from reaching New Mexico by uncooperative Hopi, but his trek did improve Spanish knowledge of the geography of the interior (Map 66, *right,* and Map 69, *overleaf*).

Also with Anza was another Franciscan, Pedro Font, whose maps and diary have given us a detailed account of the 1775–76 Anza expedition. Anza had with him 240 people, including settlers and 29 women. He began the trek with 695 horses and 355 head of cattle. The intention was, as Bucareli had ordered, colonization. Anza arrived at San Francisco at the end of March 1776. Here he built a presidio to guard this newfound and important harbor; he also selected the site for a mission.

At the same time that Garcés was trying to find a route from California to Santa Fe, two other Franciscans, Francisco Atanasio Domínguez and Silvestre Vélez de Escalante, were preparing to set out from Santa Fe to find a route to the coast. Escalante had traveled west in 1775 but, like Garcés, had been stopped by the Hopi. Now he was trying again, but although Domínguez and Escalante made an impressive tour of the Southwest, they were unable to find a route to the coast. With them were eight

Map 65 (*below*).
The route of Francisco Tomás Garcés in 1776. Garcés was with Anza on both his expeditions but on the second left to search the interior for Indians to convert. He reached the Central Valley and the San Joaquin River, here *R. S. Felipe*, before turning east to the Colorado River. He was the first European since García López de Cárdenas of the Coronado expedition in 1540 to see the Grand Canyon. Pedro Font is referred to in the cartouche. Font was also with Anza but remained with him north to San Francisco Bay.

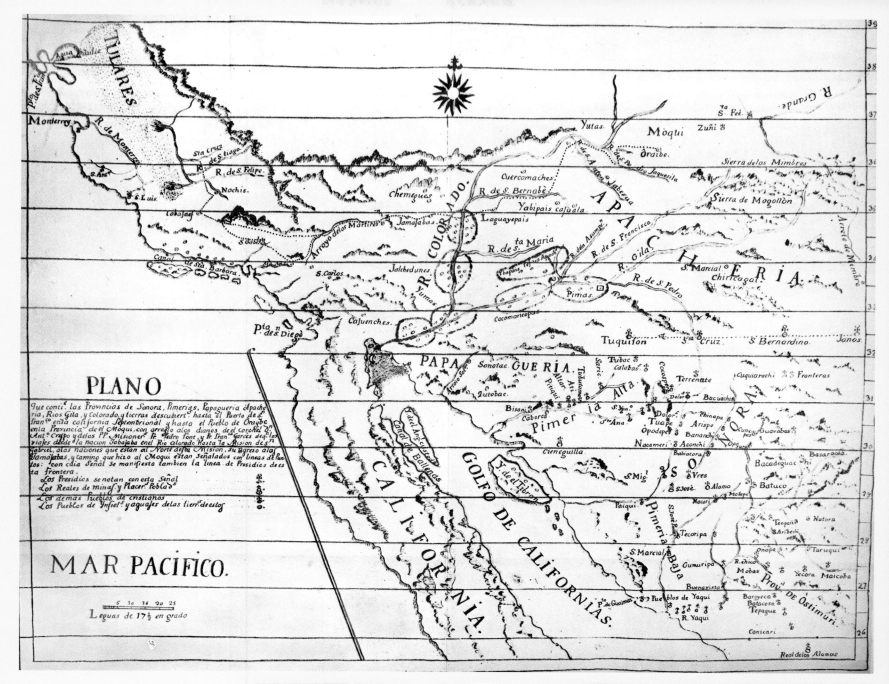

PLANO

Que conti.ᵉ las Provincias de Sonora, Pimeria, Papagueria Apache
ria, y en la california Rios Gila, y Colorado, y tierras descubiert.ᵃ hasta el Puerto de S.
fran en la california Septentrional y hasta el Pueblo de Oraybe
en la Provincia del Moqui, con arreglo a los diarios del Capp.ⁿ
Ant.ᵒ crespo y de los PP. Misioner.ˢ fr. Pedro font, y fr. fran.ᶜᵒ garcés des de los
riajes desde la nacion Jabajaba en el Rio colorado hasta la Mision de S.
Gabriel, a las naciones que estan al Norte desta Mision, su regreso a los
Jamajabas, y camino que hizo al Moqui estan señalados con lineas de pun-
tos; con cuia Señal se manifiesta tambien la linea de Presidios de es-
ta frontera.
   Los Presidios se notan con esta Señal
   Los Reales de mina.ˢ y Placer.ˢ Pobla.ᵈᵒ
   Los demas Pueblos de cristianos
   Los Pueblos de Infiel.ˢ y aguajes de las tierr.ˢ de estos

MAR PACIFICO.

Leguas de 17½ en grado

Map 66 (above).
Francisco Garcés's map of his travels in the interior Southwest in 1776, from his diary. This map marks the position of the Sierra Nevada and the Central Valley but does not name them. *Tulares* (marshland) marks the delta of the San Joaquin and Sacramento rivers. The locations of presidios and Indian *Infiel*ˢ and Spanish *cristianos* pueblos are shown (see key). The *R. Colorado* is now reasonably well defined, but the *R. Gila* is still erroneously shown reaching east almost to the *R. Grande*. The complicated river system at the southern end of the Central Valley is partly defined.

Map 67 (right).
Juan Bautista de Anza's second march to Alta California in 1775–76, shown on a map from the diary of the Franciscan Pedro Font. Anza's presidio at Tubac is at *14*, otherwise unnamed. *S[an] Miguel* was a presidio and villa farther south. This map by Font appears to be the first to name the Sierra Nevada in their approximately correct position, both east of San Francisco Bay and north of Los Angeles. However, *sierra nevada* simply means "snowy range" in Spanish.

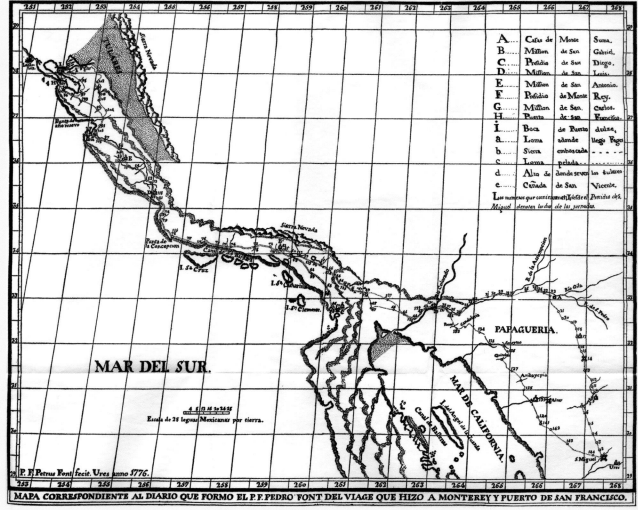

MAPA CORRESPONDIENTE AL DIARIO QUE FORMO EL P. F. PEDRO FONT DEL VIAGE QUE HIZO A MONTEREY Y PUERTO DE SAN FRANCISCO.

Map 68 (right).

This 1777 map by Pedro Font shows the Bay Area in some detail. *Monte Rey* (Monterey) is at bottom. The Central Valley is clearly depicted with *Tulares*, the marshlands of the lower Sacramento and San Joaquin rivers, and the *Sierra Neva adas[?]* at top right. The map also commemorates Bodega y Quadra's voyage to Alaska in 1775; his ship, the tiny *Goleta Sonora*, has been drawn just offshore. *Goleta* is a Spanish word for a schooner.

Map 69 (below).

This fine map of San Francisco Bay is a presentation copy of a 1775 map made by José de Cañizares. *1* is the presidio, and *2* is Mission San Francisco de Asís (Mission Dolores).

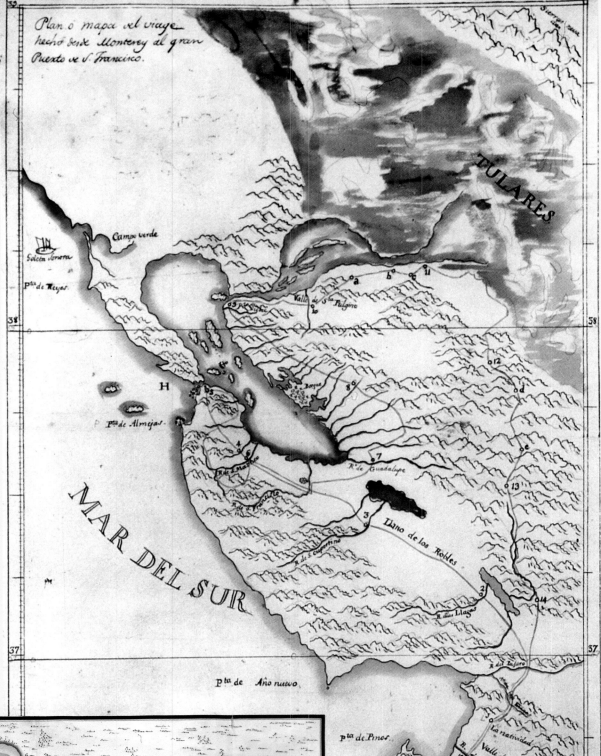

others, including Bernardo Miera y Pacheco, a military mapmaker who made a map of their trek (Map 70, *far right*).

Domínguez and Escalante left Santa Fe in July 1776 (unaware, no doubt, of the revolution beginning far to the east) and followed the Rio Grande north, finding an ancient Anasazi site before turning westward, finding Utah Lake, and learning from the Indians about the even larger Great Salt Lake to the north. Then they turned south

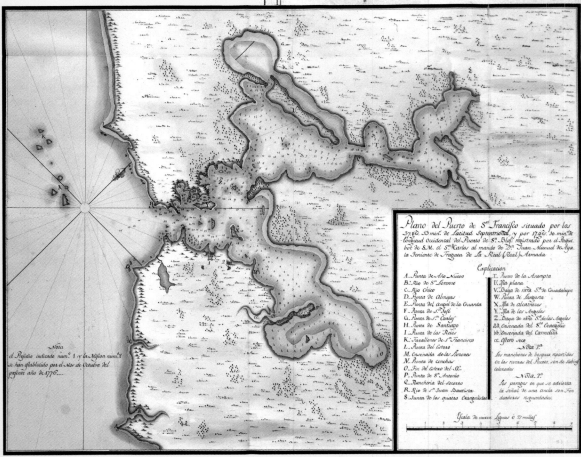

to cross the parched land of southwestern Utah, part of which is today named the Escalante Desert. Here, because they were running low on food and water, they decided to turn back to Santa Fe.

But now the Colorado River blocked their way. They searched for two weeks before they were able to find a place to cross. This location was later named the Crossing of the Fathers; it is now submerged beneath the Lake Powell Reservoir in Glen Canyon. They arrived back in Santa Fe on 2 January 1777, having covered 1,800 miles of country mostly heretofore unknown to Europeans. Miera drew a nonexistent large river, the Buenaventura, flowing into a lake (Map 70, *right, top*); this would be interpreted by later generations of mapmakers as a major river that

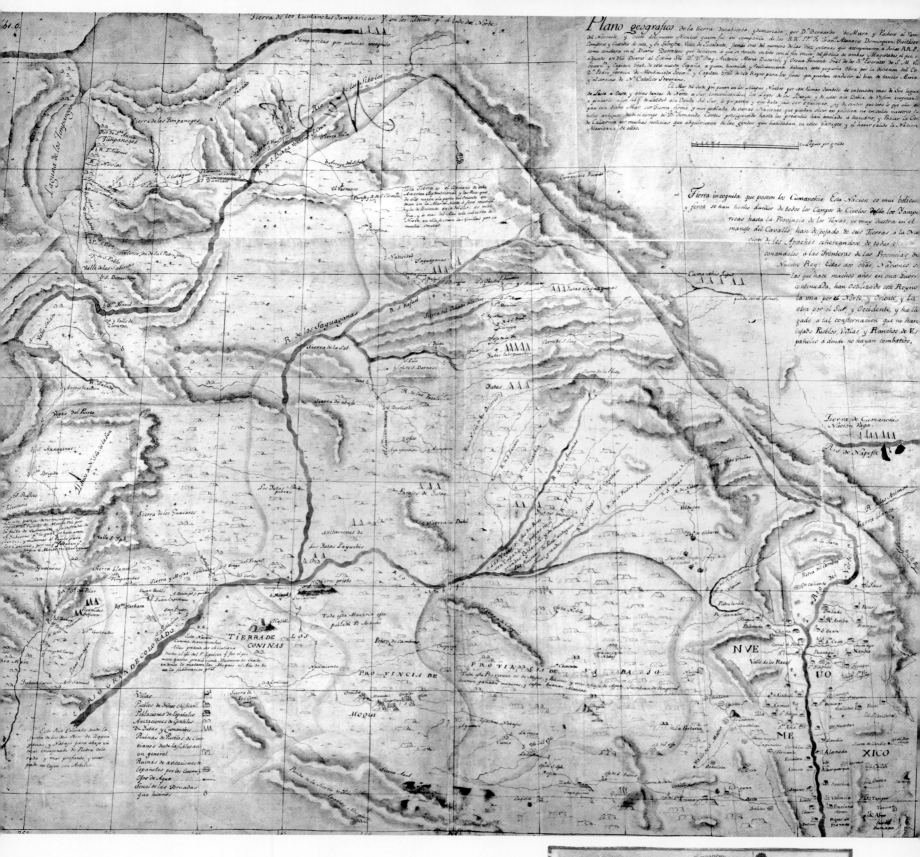

MAP 70 (above).
A map of the travels of Domínguez and Escalante drawn by Bernardo Miera y Pacheco, the map-maker who accompanied them. The *Rio Del Norte* and *Sta Fee Capital* (Santa Fe) are at bottom right. The line of mountains to the north is the Continental Divide; the headwaters of two rivers flowing east are shown. *Laguna de los Timpangos* is a combination of the Great Salt Lake and Utah Lake. South of it is another lake, the *Laguna de Miera*, now the dry Sevier Lake. Miera has shown a river flowing into it called the *R. de S[an] Buena ventura*. This river would show up on some later maps as one flowing from a large interior lake or the Rocky Mountains to the Pacific (for example, MAP 82, *page 49*). It is in fact the Green River, which flows into the upper Colorado River, here labeled *R. de los Saguaganas*. Farther downstream it becomes *El Rio Gran de Colorado*. The Crossing of the Fathers, where Domínguez and Escalante crossed the Colorado, is here at *Concepcion*, just below the confluence of the *R. de los Saguaganas* and *Rio de Nabajo* (the San Juan River). The steps they carved into the canyon wall were visible until submerged by the building of the Glen Canyon Dam.

MAP 71 (right).
This is another version of the map depicting the trek of Domínguez and Escalante, of unknown origin, from the Library of Congress collection. It appears to be a copy made in 1777. Their route is perhaps more clearly shown on this map.

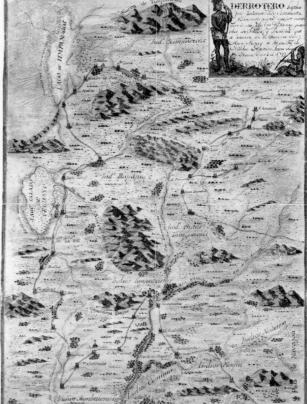

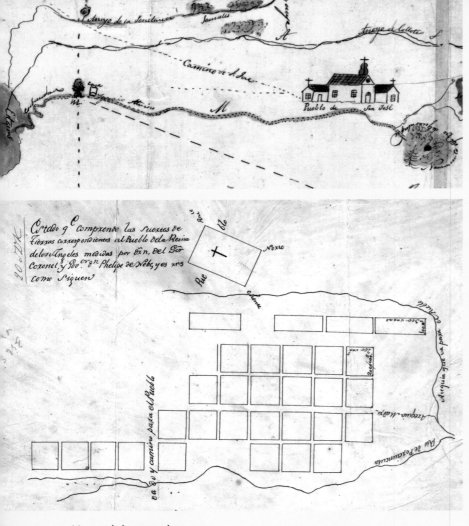

flowed from the Rocky Mountains to the Pacific. The river was a product of wishful thinking; if it had existed, it would have provided a convenient highway west. Nevertheless, Domínguez and Escalante's expedition added significantly to Spanish knowledge of the interior; their map was the first to show—*almost* from exploration—the Great Salt Lake.

Spain created three incorporated settlements in Alta California: San José de Guadalupe (San Jose) in 1777 (MAP 72, *left*); Nuestra Señora la Reyna de los Angeles del Río de Porciúncula (Los Angeles), nine miles southwest of the San Gabriel mission in 1781 (MAP 73, *left*); and the Villa de Branciforte, created in 1797 at Santa Cruz as a sort of retirement residence for soldiers. The latter failed because all soldiers wanted to do when they ended their service was leave California for good.

MAP 74 (*right*).
San Antonio in 1780. The church (*1*) and public buildings (*2*) front a public square at center. The plan is a square—compact and thus defensible.

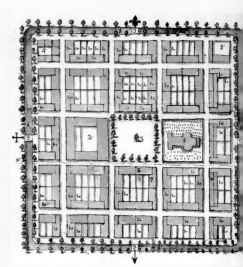

MAP 75 (*below*).
This 1782 Spanish summary map of the Southwest shows exploration routes for the fifteen years previous. Note that San Francisco Bay is shown. The map also shows the first extrapolation of a river (in the form of a disconnected section) flowing from the Rockies to the Pacific, deduced from Domínguez and Escalante's explorations and Miera's map (MAP 70, *previous page*).

MAP 72 (*above, top*).
The *Pueblo de San José* pictorially depicted on a later map from the 1840s.

MAP 73 (*above*).
The pueblo at Los Angeles, established in 1781. This map shows the central plaza and the surrounding farmlands but not the house lots. The Los Angeles River and irrigation ditches are also shown.

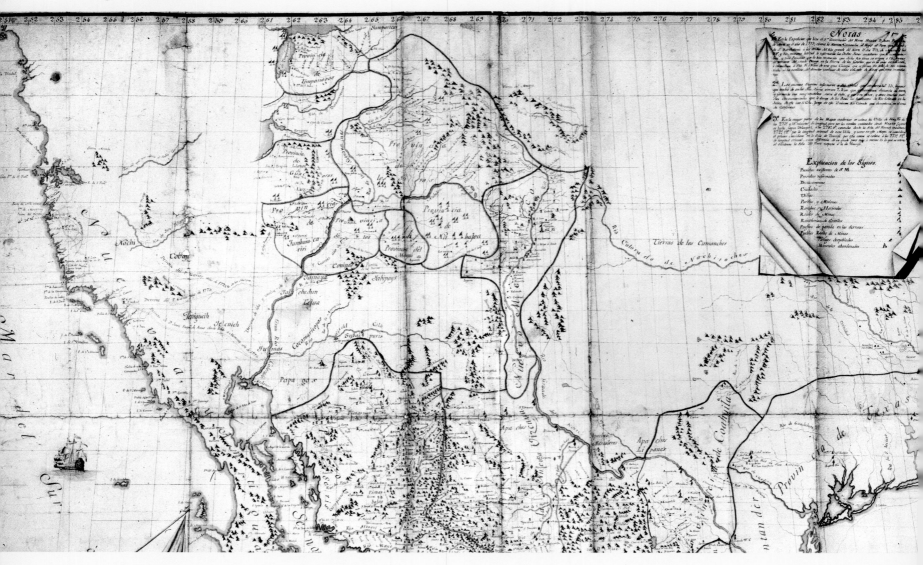

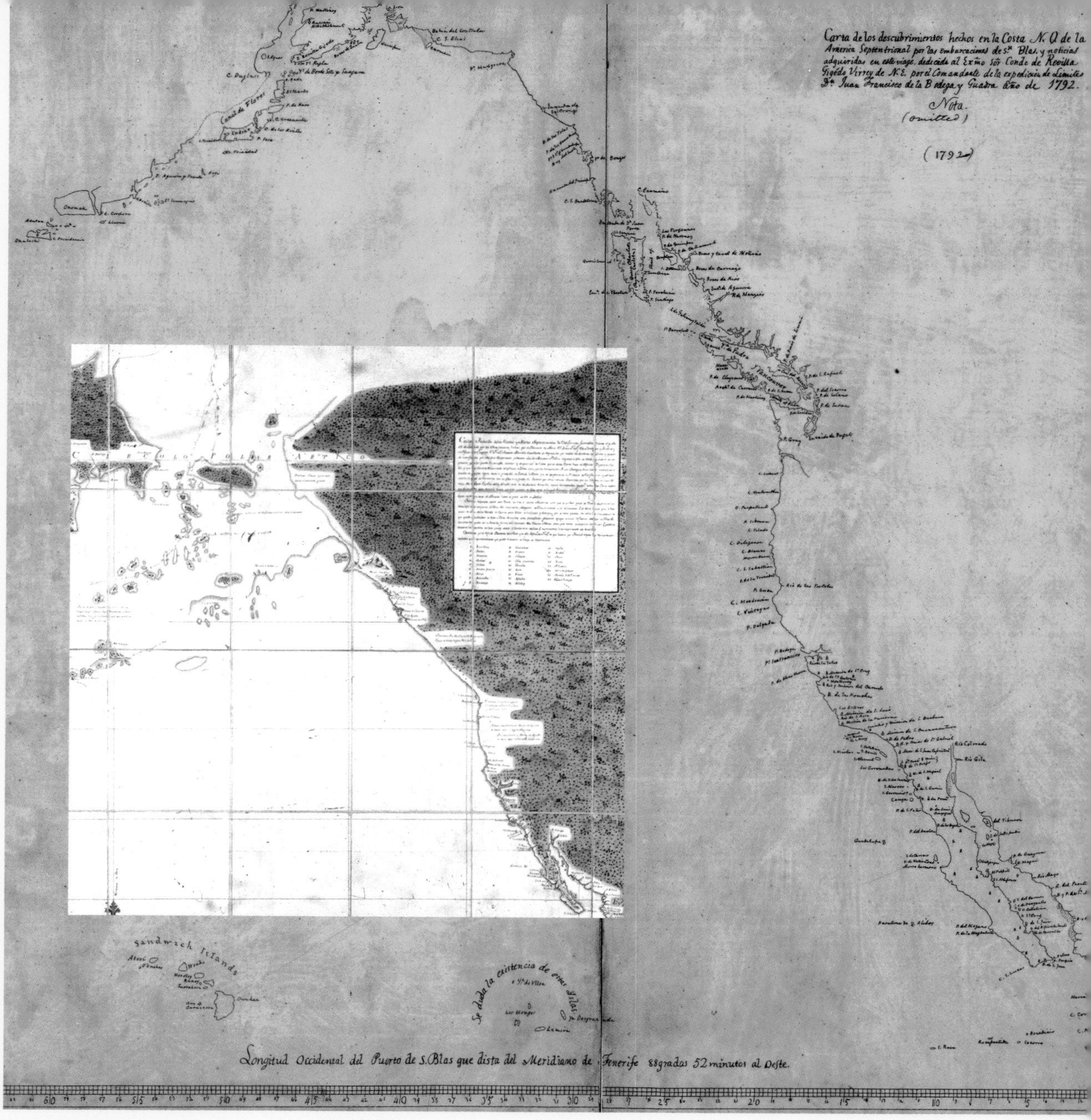

The American War for Independence gave Spain a chance to drive Britain out of Florida; an unusually aggressive commander, Bernardo de Gálvez, defeated the British well enough that both West and East Florida became Spanish possessions by the 1783 treaty ending the war. Because of the eastern thrust, in 1776 Gálvez instructed the viceroy to halt further exploration on the Pacific Coast, only to promptly reverse himself when he heard that James Cook had sailed on his third voyage to search for the Northwest Passage. In 1779 Ignacio de Arteaga was dispatched with two ships, 205 men, fourteen cannon and fifteen swivel guns with orders to intercept and stop Cook. He reached Afognak Island, near Kodiak, before bad weather and death and illness of his men caused him to turn back. He extended Spanish knowledge of Alaska but did not find Cook.

The supposed threat from Cook having passed, Spain again ignored the Northwest Coast until concern over incursions by Russian, British, and now some American fur traders searching for sea otters in the wake of the discovery by Cook's men that their pelts could be sold for huge sums in Canton. The period 1788–92 saw a flurry of Spanish maritime exploration on the Northwest Coast, made ever more urgent when Spain learned of the dispatch of Britain's George Vancouver to search, once more, for a Northwest Passage.

Esteban José Martínez (who had been with Pérez in 1774) and Gonzalo López de Haro were dispatched to Alaska in 1788. They reached as far west as Unalaska Island, in the Aleutians. This was the farthest the Spanish ever reached. Martínez did encounter a Russian fur trader at Unalaska, Potap Zaikov, but far from expelling him from this supposed Spanish territory, he tried to outdrink him! It seems that Zaikov liked Spanish brandy as much as Martínez appreciated Russian vodka.

Yet Martínez recommended to the viceroy that a base be established at Nootka Sound, on Vancouver Island, to forestall the Russian advance south to California. In 1789 this suggestion was implemented, despite the fact that Nootka was already occupied by British fur traders; one trader, William Douglas, was arrested by Martínez for "having anchored in Spanish domain without a license," though he was later released. Another British trader, James Colnett, was arrested with his ship, which a Spanish crew sailed back to New Spain. Colnett's arrest provoked an international incident. Spain, now weakened by events in Europe, was forced to sign the Nootka Treaty in 1790, in which Spain agreed to share the Northwest Coast with Britain; it left unresolved the question of the northern boundary of California but for the first time recognized that occupation was required to claim ownership of territory rather than merely carrying out acts of possession and then leaving, which is what Spain had done for hundreds of years.

Spain engaged in a few more voyages to the Northwest, desperately seeking to ensure that no Northwest Passage would be discovered. Francisco Eliza made a base at Nootka in 1790 and sent Salvador Fidalgo to Alaska and Manuel Quimper into the Strait of Juan de Fuca. Further explorations in 1791

MAP 76 (*above, inset*) and MAP 77 (*above*).

These two maps dramatically demonstrate the improvement in Spanish geographical knowledge, especially that of Alaska, between 1779 (MAP 76) and the end of 1792 (MAP 77). MAP 76 incorporates information from the voyage of Ignacio de Arteaga in 1779, together with that from Russian sources, which for a brief period portrayed Alaska as an island (see MAP 104, *page 58*). Note that no information from James Cook's voyage was yet available. MAP 77 is essentially the final Spanish map of the West Coast explorations, incorporating information from the voyage of Esteban José Martinez and Gonzalo López de Haro to Alaska in 1788 and also that of Salvador Fidalgo in 1790. In addition there is 1791 information from Alejandro Malaspina's circumnavigation, Jacinto Caamaño's Alaska voyage in 1792, and that of Dionisio Alcalá Galiano and Cayetano Valdés y Flores round Vancouver Island the same year. Only then, as Spain gave up its aspirations to extend its American empire to the northwest, could there be any certainty that there was no Northwest Passage at a navigable latitude.

defined southern Vancouver Island and the northwest Washington–southwestern British Columbia coast, though Puget Sound was missed. The same year Alejandro Malaspina visited Alaska as part of a grand scientific circumnavigation planned to redeem Spanish glory thought lost to Britain's James Cook. In 1792, the final year of Spanish coastal exploration, Juan Francisco de la Bodega y Quadra, now a senior officer, was at Nootka. He sent Dionisio Alcalá Galiano and Cayetano Valdés y Flores around Vancouver Island—they cooperated with George Vancouver on the way—and Jacinto Caamaño was sent north to Clarence Strait, the Inside Passage of the Alaska Panhandle, which he initially thought was the long-sought Northwest Passage.

And then it was all over. Declining as a world power, Spain never again sent exploring expeditions north, giving up on Alaska and effectively anything north of San Francisco.

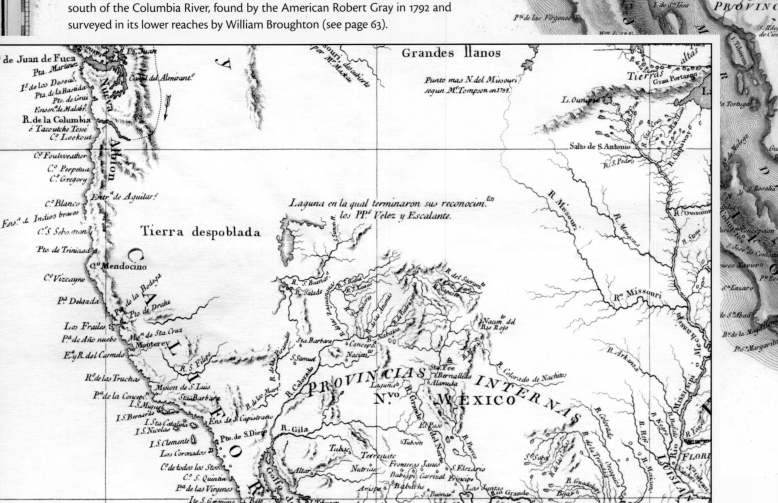

Map 78 (*below*).

Engraved for an 1802 Spanish geography, this map displays the maximum extent of the northern provinces of New Spain and the farthest extent of Spanish knowledge beyond that, largely due to the explorations of Domínguez and Escalante in 1776–77. The Great Basin west of Escalante's lake is *Tierra despoblada*, unpopulated land. Note that their *R. S. Buenav^a* (Buenaventura) shown flowing into the lake to the south (actually the dry Sevier Lake) is partially continued in a disconnected section flowing toward San Francisco Bay. The latter is shown not by that name but as *Pto. de Drake*, an early attribution of the bay as the one Francis Drake visited in 1579 (see page 24). *Californias* traverses Alta and Baja California. The area now covered by Arizona, New Mexico, and Texas is *Provincias Internas N.^vo Mexico* (Internal Provinces of New Mexico). *Sta. Fee, El Paso,* and *Bejar* (San Antonio) are shown but, surprisingly, not Alburquerque. Quite a concession on a Spanish map, *Nueva Albion* is shown on the coast north and south of the Columbia River, found by the American Robert Gray in 1792 and surveyed in its lower reaches by William Broughton (see page 63).

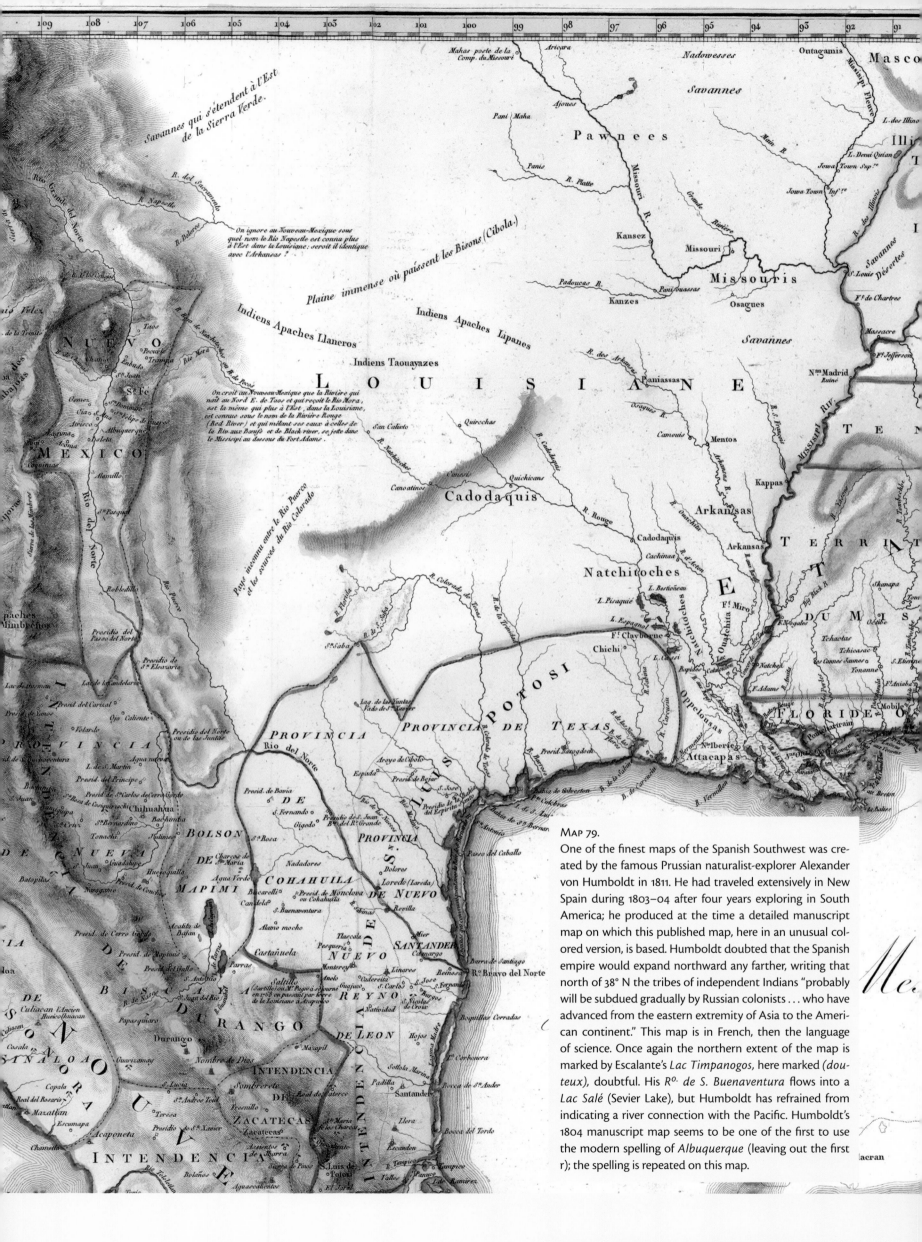

Savannes qui s'étendent à l'Est de la Sierra Verde.

On ignore au Nouveau-Mexique sous quel nom le Rio Napestle est connu plus à l'Est dans la Louisiane; seroit il identique avec l'Arkansas ?

Plaine immense où paissent les Bisons (Cibola.)

Indiens Apaches Llaneros

Indiens Apaches Lipanes

Indiens Taouayazes

On croit au Nouveau-Mexique que la Rivière qui naît au Nord E. de Taos et qui reçoit le Rio Mora, est la même qui plus à l'Est, dans la Louisiane, est connue sous le nom de la Rivière Rouge (Red. River) et qui mêlant ses eaux à celles de la Rio. aux Bœufs et de Black river, se jette dans le Missisipi au dessous du Fort Adams.

Pays inconnu entre le Rio Puerco et les sources du Rio Colorado.

L O U I S I A N E

Pawnees

Missouris

Savannes

Cadodaquis

Natchitoches

Arkansas

N U E V O

M E X I C O

PROVINCIA DE TEXAS

S. LUIS POTOSI

PROVINCIA DE COHAHUILA

PROVINCIA DE NUEVA BISCAYA

PROVINCIA DE NUEVO SANTANDER

NUEVO REYNO DE LEON

BOLSON DE MAPIMI

DURANGO

INTENDENCIA DE ZACATECAS

S O N O R A

S I N A L O A

FLORIDE

Map 79.

One of the finest maps of the Spanish Southwest was created by the famous Prussian naturalist-explorer Alexander von Humboldt in 1811. He had traveled extensively in New Spain during 1803–04 after four years exploring in South America; he produced at the time a detailed manuscript map on which this published map, here in an unusual colored version, is based. Humboldt doubted that the Spanish empire would expand northward any farther, writing that north of 38° N the tribes of independent Indians "probably will be subdued gradually by Russian colonists . . . who have advanced from the eastern extremity of Asia to the American continent." This map is in French, then the language of science. Once again the northern extent of the map is marked by Escalante's *Lac Timpanogos*, here marked (*douteux*), doubtful. His *Rº. de S. Buenaventura* flows into a *Lac Salé* (Sevier Lake), but Humboldt has refrained from indicating a river connection with the Pacific. Humboldt's 1804 manuscript map seems to be one of the first to use the modern spelling of *Albuquerque* (leaving out the first r); the spelling is repeated on this map.

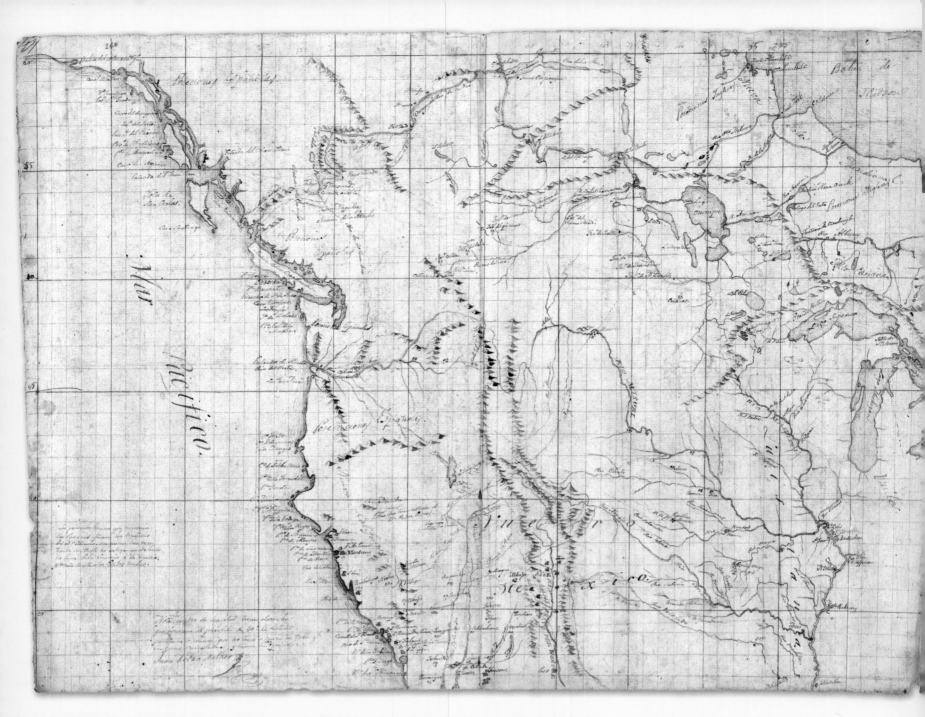

Map 80 (above).

One of the last Spanish maps of the West was this detailed one drawn by Juan Pedro Walker about 1817. It shows that the Spanish knew quite a lot about the geography of the West. They had not at this time given up claims to the territory farther north. Some areas, notably the Great Basin, show more detail than was available on any other map of the time. Walker had traveled extensively and incorporated information he had gathered into maps that combined all the available geographical intelligence of the period. Yet despite this knowledge, Spain was certainly the territorial loser in the negotiations for the 1819 Transcontinental Treaty.

Map 81 (left).

In a sense the final Spanish map of California, drawn in 1823, just after Spanish rule had ended, by José María Narváez, a naval chartmaker, explorer, and veteran of several expeditions to the Northwest. Narváez made this map after delivering the emissary of the new Mexican government to Monterey in 1822. There is a suggestion of a Central Valley here, with two chains of mountains, and the *Rio de S. Felipe*, which is the southern end of the San Joaquin, is shown. Another river, the hoped-for river connecting the Great Salt Lake with the Pacific, is shown at

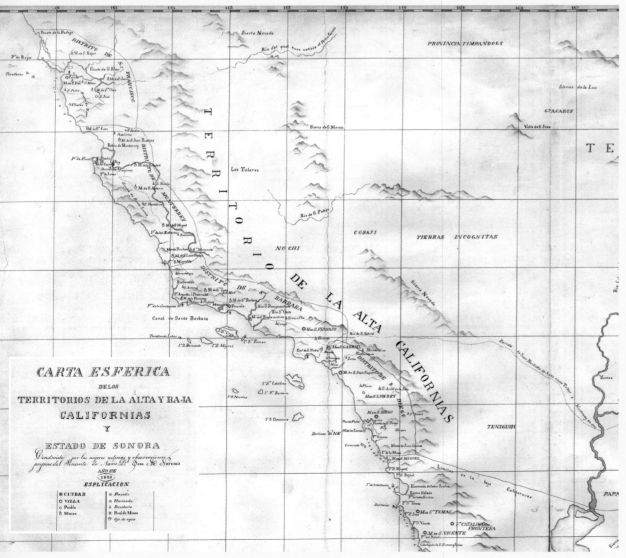

MAP 82 (*above*).
The boundary between American and Spanish territory agreed to in the Transcontinental Treaty of 1819. The 42° N line, which today forms the northern boundary of California, Nevada, and Utah, is accurately shown, as is the line along the Sabine River, today the boundary between Louisiana and Texas, but the boundary up the Red and Arkansas rivers (connected south to north along the 100° W meridian) is incorrect because the courses of those rivers are inaccurately shown, as they had been on the 1818 map by John Melish that had been used to negotiate the treaty. A later and more accurate rendering of the agreed-upon boundary is shown as **MAP 383**, *page 180*, with which this map may be compared.

The Spanish did explore the interior of Alta California a little more, though most expeditions were to search for possible mission sites. Army officer Gabriel Moraga and Franciscan Pedro Muñoz in 1806 left Mission San Bautista, crossed the San Joaquin River, and traversed the Central Valley from the Mokelumne River south to the end of the valley. They found Tejon Pass and continued south to the mission in the San Fernando Valley. Two years later Moraga explored the Central Valley to the north, probing the rivers flowing into the Sacramento from the Sierra Nevada and reaching a point about fifteen miles north of Colusa. Two years later, after again exploring in the Central Valley for mission sites, he visited the Russian settlement at Bodega Bay to report on these now materialized Russian incursions (see page 75). The first recorded navigation of the Sacramento River was in 1811, by Franciscan Ramón Abella, searching again for mission sites but this time by water. Most of the further Spanish forays into the Central Valley were to round up Indians who had escaped from missions. A major roundup of runaways occurred in 1815 when army detachments under Juan Ortega

and José Dolores Pico combed the southern end of the Central Valley. The names of the Sacramento and San Joaquin rivers did not appear on maps until 1824, however, and even then they were drawn from a verbal report by a French mapmaker (MAP 80, *left, top*).

Spain was on the decline as a world power, a course hastened by Napoleon's removal of the Bourbon king of Spain in 1808, replacing him with his brother, Joseph Bonaparte. Spain had so many problems in Europe that it was unable to focus on its North American dominions. The United States took advantage of Spain's weakening position to negotiate, in 1819, the Transcontinental Treaty, officially the Treaty of Amity, Settlement and Limits Between the United States of America and His Catholic Majesty, also called the Adams-Onís Treaty after its two principal negotiators, John Quincy Adams, the U.S. secretary of state, and Luís de Onís, Spanish minister in the United States.

This treaty was a diplomatic victory for the United States, which was able to secure access to the Pacific, inheriting all Spanish claims north of 42° N. The treaty also attempted to define the western boundary of the United States, which would stand until the Mexican War in 1846 (MAP 82, *above*). It was also significant in that it was used to derive boundaries between numerous later American states (see page 180 and MAP 383, *page 180*).

Spain's power in North America was completely usurped only two years later, when the Mexican War for Independence, which had been raging on and off since 1810, finally resulted in the creation of Mexico. Spain's policy of keeping out American trade was reversed overnight, and Americans became welcome at Santa Fe (see page 76). But Mexico was no stronger than Spain, and it would only hold on to its northern territories for another twenty-five years before the United States wrested them away (see page 87).

OTHER NATIONS EXPLORE THE WEST

FRANCE IN THE WEST

France arrived in the West south via the Mississippi in two exploratory pushes, by Louis Jolliet and Jesuit Jacques Marquette as far as the Arkansas River in 1673 (MAP 90, *page 53*), and by René-Robert Cavelier, Sieur de La Salle, to its mouth in 1682. Only thirty-six years later France had established a city, New Orleans, near the river's mouth, and French-held territory had driven a wedge though that claimed by Spain, separating West and East Florida from Texas.

La Salle was back before long, attempting to establish a colony, his Fort Saint Louis on Matagorda Bay, after he could not find the Mississippi again when he arrived by ship—four ships and three hundred men. While searching for the Mississippi he ascended the Rio Grande for three hundred miles. Fort Saint Louis was the French intrusion that caused the viceroy of New Spain to send out an expedition to eradicate it (see page 30).

But France was to stay, at least for a while. Other explorers improved knowledge of first Texas and later the Great Plains while seeking to trade with Indians and to find a trade route to New Mexico itself.

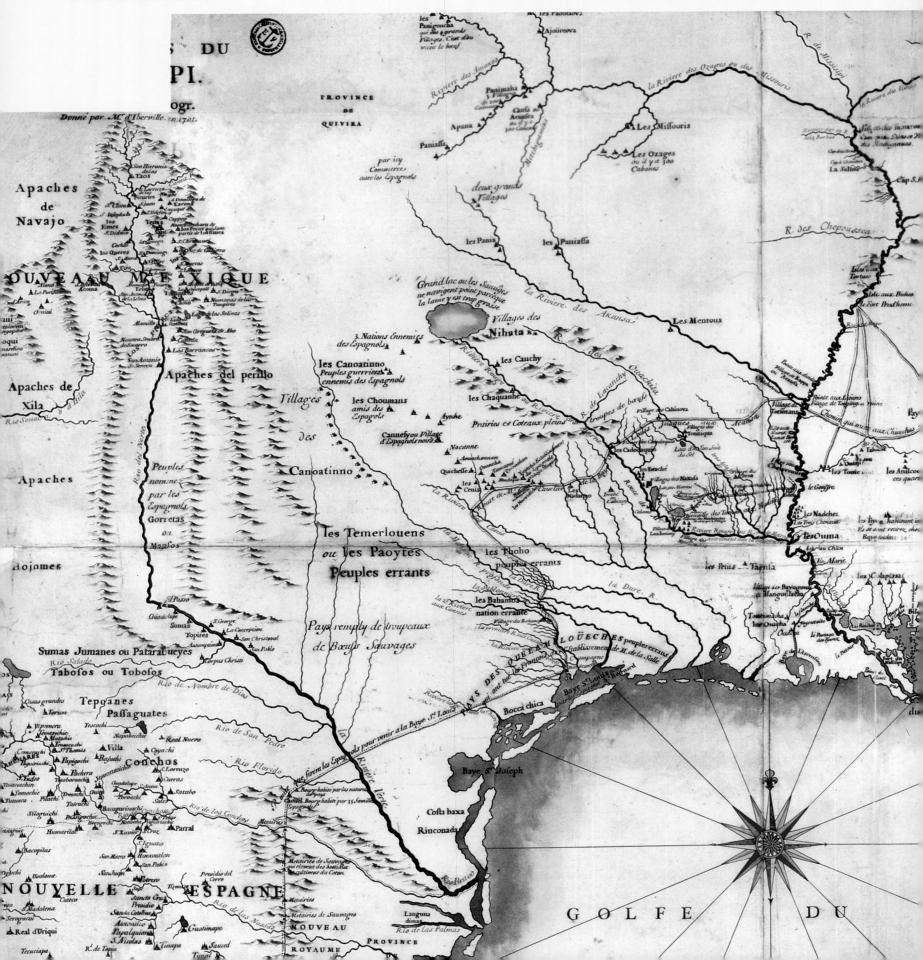

In 1700 Jean-Baptiste Le Moyne, Sieur de Bienville, and Louis Juchereau de Saint-Denis explored inland as far as Oklahoma, and Saint-Denis ascended the Red River for several hundred miles; the following year he explored the area between the Red and Ouachita rivers. The information, taken to France, was used by the famous geographer Guillaume De L'Isle to compile a map synthesizing it all (Map 83, below, left).

Commissioned to locate a trade route to New Spain, Saint-Denis established a post at Natchitoches, on the Red River, in 1713, and from there set out overland to the southwest, crossing all of Texas and arriving at the Spanish presidio of San Juan Bautista, on the Rio Grande. Here he was promptly arrested and taken to Mexico City, where he surprised the viceroy with his knowledge of what he considered Spanish Texas (Map 49, page 29). As a matter of expediency, Saint-Denis joined forces with Spain and accompanied an expedition to settle eastern Texas—as a buffer against the French (see page 30). Saint-Denis's route is shown on De L'Isle's 1718 map (Map 85, below, right).

In 1712–14, Étienne de Véniard, later Sieur de Bourgmont and then a deserter from Fort Cadillac at Detroit, lived among the Missouri Indians and gained a good knowledge of the Missouri River. The written information was used in 1716 by Guillaume De L'Isle to compile a detailed map of the river between the Mississippi and the Platte (Map 88, page 53).

To pave the way for French trade with the Indians of the lower Missouri, Bienville, now governor of Louisiana and ensconced in the newly established New Orleans, dispatched Claude-Charles du Tisné, who found himself halted by hostile Pawnee (Panis on the French maps) beyond the head of the Osage River at today's Chelsea, Oklahoma. The Pawnee also stopped Jean-Baptiste Bénard, Sieur de La Harpe, who had been sent via a different route, up the Red River above Natchitoches. He traveled overland to the Arkansas River and ranged up and down that river. His notes were used to create two artistic maps—one of Texas and the eastern Plains (Map 86, page 52) and one of much of the West (Map 87, page 52), the latter with information from many other sources.

Bourgmont was enlisted again for another expedition in 1720, ordered to build alliances with the fearsome Padouca (Comanche) and find a trade route to Santa Fe. The Spanish had other ideas, however; it was at this time that the governor of New Mexico dispatched Pedro de Villasur and a small army on his abortive mission to counter reports of French intrusion (see page 31).

Bourgmont, given the grandiose title of Commandant of the Missouri River, established a base he called Fort D'Orleans on the Missouri River in 1723 (Map 89, page 53). From

Map 83 (left).

This superb manuscript map, drawn in 1701 by French geographer Guillaume De L'Isle, was state-of-the-art at the time. It incorporated not only the latest French discoveries but also information gleaned from Spanish and English sources; at left the Rio Grande and the Spanish settlements in New Mexico are prominent, based on information given to the French by the Spanish turncoat Diego Peñalosa, briefly governor of New Mexico (1661–63), who hoped to induce the French to attack the upper Rio Grande settlements. Much of the rest of the information on the map was brought back to France in 1701 by Pierre Le Moyne, Sieur D'Iberville, and the map also shows the explorations of Bienville and Saint-Denis in 1700–01. *La Riviere de Ozagesou ou des Missouris* is the Missouri River, *La Riviere des Akansa* is the Arkansas River, and *Riviere Rouge* is the Red.

Map 84 (right, top).

The hydrographer of New France, Jean-Baptiste-Louis Franquelin, based in Québec, drew this map from one, now lost, given to him by La Salle. The course of the Mississippi reflects La Salle's broken compass and thus shows the river diverting more than five hundred miles into the West and perhaps being confused with the lower Rio Grande.

Map 85 (right, bottom).

The western half of Guillaume De L'Isle's seminal 1718 *Carte de la Louisianne*. The French claim traverses the continent west to Spanish New Mexico. The river systems are all there, their lower courses explored but their upper courses generally incorrect, being based only on Indian report. Of note is the course of the Missouri, plotted by De L'Isle himself from explorer Bourgmont's notes (Map 88, page 53), though beyond Bourgmont's ascent it also relies on Indian information.

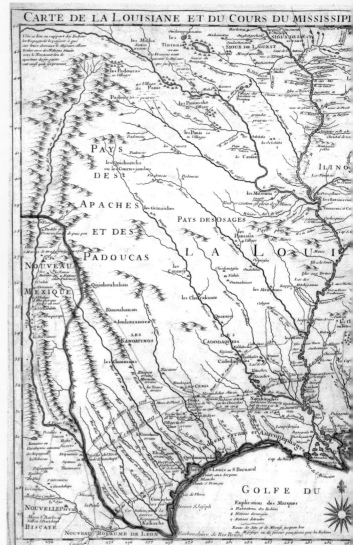

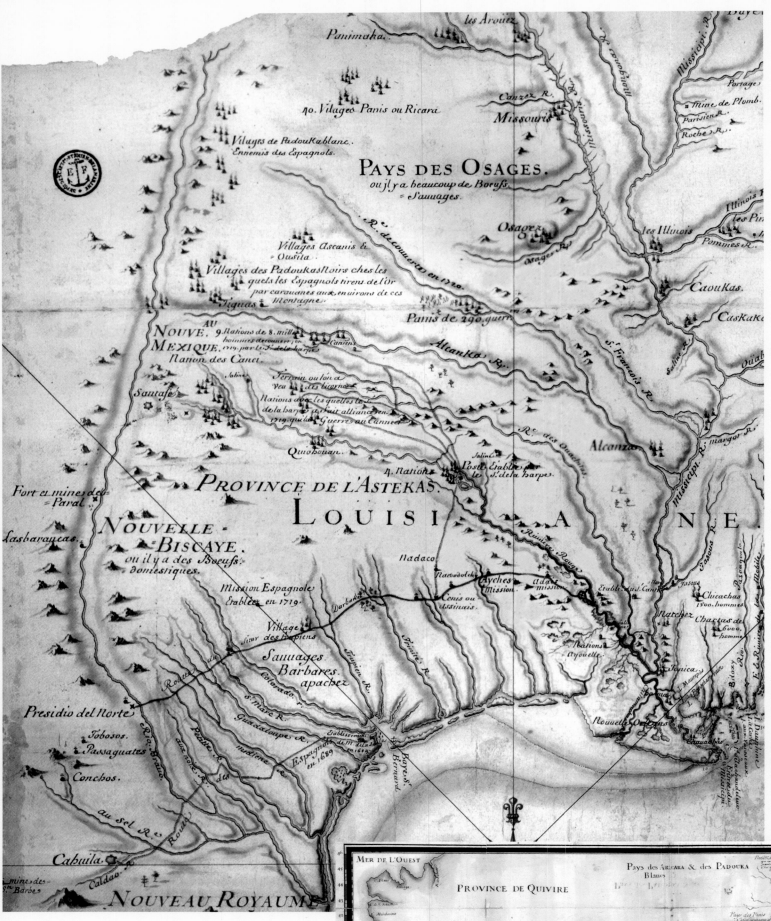

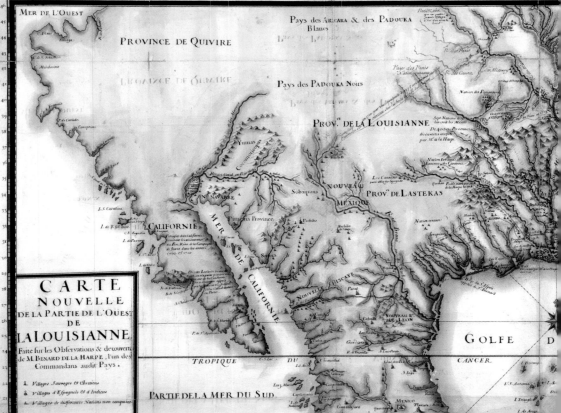

Map 86 (*above*) and Map 87 (*right*).

These two maps were drawn to illustrate the discoveries of La Harpe from 1718 to 1721 up the Red River but incorporate much other information from French sources. On Map 86 is the *Missouris R.*; on Map 87 it is the *R du Missoury*. La Harpe's travels up the Red River and overland to the Arkansas River are shown on Map 87 as a red line leading to land *découvertes [discovered] en 1718 [sic, 1719] par Mr. de la Harpe*. Also shown is the route of Pedro de Villasur's *300 Espanols* (300 Spaniards) in 1720, soldiers from Santa Fe searching for Bourgmont or other French intruders onto what the Spanish considered their domain. Villasur's men were massacred by Pawnee and Oto (see page 31) without ever encountering a Frenchman.

MAP 89 (*right*).

In the winter of 1723–24 Bourgmont built a fort on the banks of the Missouri, about seventy-five miles east of today's Kansas City. His elaborate plan of his establishment, shown here, was likely more sophisticated than the structure itself; indeed, the map may have been exaggerated to impress colonial officials in France—Bourgmont had been appointed "Commandant of the Missouri River" after all—or it may have shown what was intended rather than what was actually built. Called Fort D'Orleans, it was not a success and was abandoned in 1728. The site has never been found and was likely obliterated by a shifting river.

Some of the letters and numerals, according to the key: *A* the commandant's house; *B* officers' quarters; *C* chapel; *D* blacksmith's house; *E* forge; *F* chaplain's house; *G* storekeeper's house; *H* store; *I* guardhouse; *K* drummer's house; *L* laundry; *O* barracks; *Q* powder magazine; *R* embrasures for cannon; *1* Bourgmont's house; *2* poultry house; *3* oven; *4* ice house; *5* big garden; *6* yard; *7* little garden; *8* store; *9* field of tobacco; *10* kitchen garden; *18* parade ground; *19* pond; *20* island; *21* prairie; *22* big hills two leagues from the fort; *23* road from the river to the fort; *24* 15-foot embankment.

MAP 88 (*above*).

The French geographer Guillaume De L'Isle, ever on the lookout for new information to use on his maps, used the written journal of Bourgmont's ascent of the Missouri in 1714 to construct this detailed map of the river two years later. It was the first reasonably accurate map of the Missouri drawn from exploration. The map extends from the Mississippi, at bottom right, to the Platte, at top left. Note the *Village des Missouris* near the map's midpoint. The rather strange shape of this map results from the addition of extra pieces of paper at both ends, presumably when De L'Isle realized his map was not going to fit on the original sheet.

MAP 90 (*above*).

French explorers Louis Jolliet and Jacques Marquette noticed the Missouri as they passed its mouth in their pathfinding trip down the Mississippi in 1673. The short *Pekittan8i* (Pekitanoui, the silt-laden Muddy River) is the Missouri; this river, they were told, led to a western ocean (yet it flowed *into* the Mississippi). This map is the very earliest in a series of explorers' maps culminating with those of Lewis and Clark 132 years later that would finally extend knowledge of the river to its source.

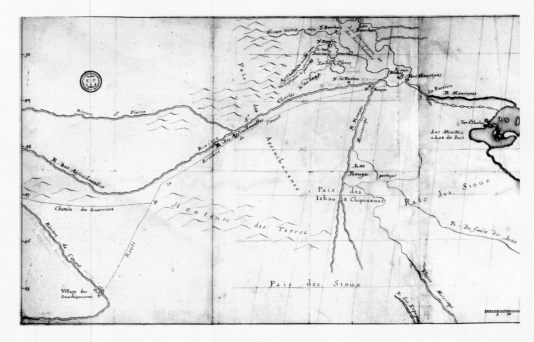

here Bourgmont, often accompanied by hundreds of Kansa Indians, ranged westward, ascending the Kansas River and southward toward the Arkansas River on the Great Plains. Bourgmont did establish Indian alliances, but they did not last, French presence being unsustainable in this westernmost pale of the French Empire. Fort D'Orleans was abandoned in 1728.

Another French excursion onto the Great Plains came from an entirely different direction—the north. Fur trader Pierre Gaultier de Varennes et de La Vérendrye, together with various sons and nephews, had been exploring westward from Lake Superior and Lake Winnipeg as part of a fur-trade monopoly he had negotiated with the governor of New France at Québec.

He was entranced by Indian reports of a River of the West, flowing all the way to the Pacific. One of these reports seems to have been of the Missouri, despite the fact that it would have been flowing the wrong way. It was shown on a map drawn by his nephew in 1733 (MAP 91, *above*) and reached by La Vérendrye himself at the Mandan villages the following year. In 1742–43, La Vérendrye's two sons, Louis-Joseph and François (known as the Chevalier), set off to search for the River of the West, ranging west perhaps into northern Wyoming and to the Black Hills of western South Dakota, and certainly to a place near today's Pierre, South Dakota, where a lead plate claiming possession of the land for Louis XV was found in 1913; it appears to be genuine.

Santa Fe was finally reached in 1739 by the French trading brothers Pierre and Paul Mallet, crossing the Plains from a point on the Missouri now in northeastern Nebraska. They were welcomed despite it being illegal for Spanish citizens to trade with the French. The Mallets made their way back to New Orleans the following year via the Pecos, Canadian, and Arkansas rivers and realized that they provided a better route to Santa Fe than the Missouri. They had found the Santa Fe Trail, which would later become one of the major routes west.

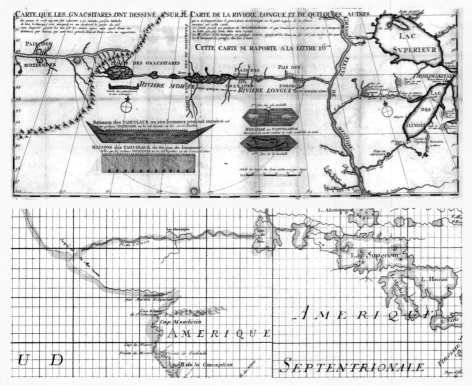

MAP 91 (*above, top*).
This map by Christophe Dufrost de La Jemerais was drawn in 1733, with the notations in red added in 1742. In the bottom left corner is the *Riviere de l'ouest*—River of the West—thought to be a depiction of the Missouri, with the *Village de Ouachipouanes* being the Mandan villages at the Great Bend of that river. This is where La Vérendrye is considered to have reached in 1738. At right is Lake Superior, at center is Lake of the Woods (now at the intersection of Ontario, Manitoba, and Minnesota), and *Lac Rouge* is Red Lake, Minnesota; at top is Lake Winnipeg.

MAP 92 (*above*).
La Vérendrye drew one of the more bizarre maps of the unknown West in 1737 to send to the governor of New France to demonstrate his progress in exploration and support his request for a further trading monopoly. Here a major river is shown flowing from Lake Winnipeg to the west (north is approximately the top left corner of the map) to a *Mer Inconnuë*—Unknown Sea—complete with a totally fictitious *Ville* (town) at its mouth. Quite how La Vérendrye thought this great river flowed across the mountain range shown is unclear. The body of water at the bottom right edge (again complete with *Ville*) is conceivably intended to be the Gulf of California, or it could have been derived from the Great Salt Lake.

MAP 93 (*above, top*).
The map that likely started the myth of the River of the West was this map of the Long River by Baron de Lahontan, published in his book in 1703. Lahontan claimed to have journeyed up this river, which was met at a watershed by another, westward-flowing river.

MAP 94 (*above*).
Isaac Brouckner's 1749 map shows a River of the West flowing from Lake of the Woods to the Pacific at the location of the Strait of Juan de Fuca.

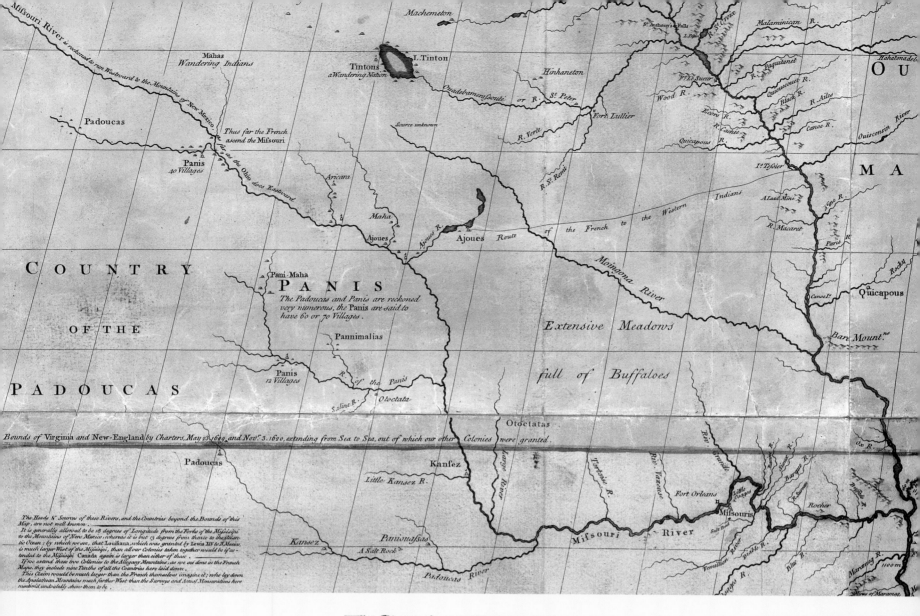

A RIVER TO THE WEST

One of the enduring early myths about the West was that there was a large river flowing to the Pacific from some height of land in the center of the continent, which in turn could be reached by ascending a similar river flowing eastward. The whole theory was bound up in the eighteenth-century notion of geographical balance—that features in one place had to be mirrored by similar geography elsewhere. As the Missouri River became known, this river was assumed to be the eastward-flowing stream required by the theory, first espoused in 1703 in an enormously popular and influential book by Louis Armand de Lom d'Arce, Baron de Lahontan (MAP 93, *left*).

This was the river sought by Bourgmont and by La Vérendrye (MAP 92, *left*); depicted on maps as a Buenaventura River; and sought by later explorers such as Jonathan Carver, who did not travel very far west but whose map (MAP 96, *right*) was also published in an influential book that went through thirty editions in several languages. Explorers long had a tendency to interpret their discoveries in light of what they expected to find, and, of course, as with the best fiction, the river did have some basis in fact—the Columbia. However, as Lewis and Clark were to find, it would not be an easy portage to its headwaters from those of the Missouri (see page 67).

MAP 95 (*above, top*).
The Missouri as known to the British by 1755 is shown on this map by John Mitchell. A later edition of this map, unchanged, was used to negotiate the Treaty of Paris in 1783, ending the Revolutionary War, and gave rise to later problems because the Mississippi, used as a boundary, was depicted rising much farther north than it really does.

MAP 96 (*above*).
A plain River of the West is shown on Jonathan Carver's map, published in his 1778 book. The river flows to the Pacific at the entrance *Discovered by Aguilar* (see page 19). Carver's book was a major bestseller, and thus his geographical ideas gained more exposure than they perhaps deserved. This is the book that many credit with the origin of the word *Oregon*.

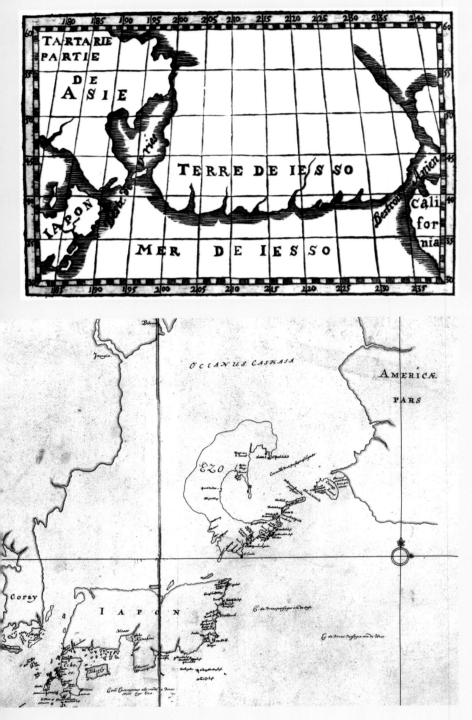

A Great Land to the East

At the same time that French explorers were tentatively probing west, another of the great powers, Russia, was doing the same from the other direction. Its interest was Alaska, first found by Mikhail Gvozdev in 1732. Uncertain knowledge of Russian activity to the north was what drove Spain, in moments of imperial paranoia, to send its ships to drive them out.

Another myth of the eighteenth century was that of the land of Jesso (with various other spellings), stretching across the North Pacific (MAP 97, *left*), a fantasy that originated in 1643 when the Dutch East India Company's Maerten Vries saw the western coast of one of the Kuril Islands and assumed it was a continent. It appeared on his map as Compagnies Land and soon on other Dutch maps as *Americæ Pars*—part of America (MAP 98, *left*).

In 1648 a fur trader, Semen Dezhnev, sailed right around the eastern extremity of Siberia, thus proving that Asia and America were not joined. The voyage was apparently forgotten by 1728, when the Russian tsar, Peter the Great, dispatched a hired Danish captain, Vitus Bering, to determine where America was and if Asia was connected to it. Bering sailed through the strait that now bears his name but did not see the Alaskan mainland. That was left to Mikhail Gvozdev four years later; he saw a coast east of the Diomede Islands but could not reach it (MAP 99, *below, left*).

A large-scale expedition was then organized to discover America, but such was the speed of the Russian bureaucracy and the state of communication with Siberia that two ships, captained by Vitus Bering and Aleksei Chirikov, did not sail from Kamchatka for another thirteen years. The pair spent time looking for an apocryphal Gama Land, then thought to be located in mid-ocean, when the ships became separated, and thus they made two separate landfalls on the coast of the Alaska Panhandle. Chirikov made a landfall at Baker Island, off the west coast of Prince of Wales Island, on 15 July 1741,

MAP 99 (*below, left*).
Mikhail Gvozdev's map of his sighting of the coast of Alaska—the first actual sighting of America by the Russians—in 1732. The map shows Siberia, to the left; Cape Prince of Wales, Alaska, to the right; and the Diomede Islands, in the Bering Strait, between them.

MAP 100 (*below*).
This map, drawn by French geographer Joseph-Nicolas De L'Isle in 1730, shows all that was known about the North Pacific and the American West and was intended to guide Vitus Bering on his voyage to the West Coast. Because of numerous delays, the voyage did not occur for another eleven years.

MAP 97 (*above, top*).
The *Terre de Iesso*—Land of Jesso—faces California across the Strait of Anian and fills most of the North Pacific on this 1702 map.

MAP 98 (*above*).
Drawn the year after Maerten Vries's discovery of his Compagnies Land (named for his employer, the Dutch East India Company), this map appeared in the Netherlands showing the land as *Americæ Pars*—part of America. The similarity with reality, as shown on MAP 99 (*below*), is striking; the geography was merely displaced thousands of miles across the Pacific.

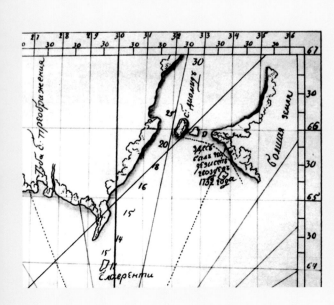

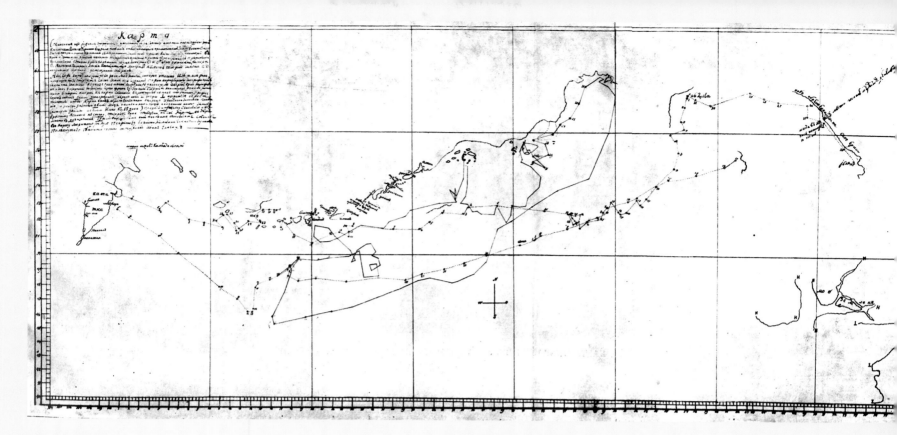

MAP 101 (*above*).

Aleksei Chirikov's pilot, Ivan Elagin, drew this chart of their 1741 voyage after they returned to Russia the following year. The track of Chirikov's ship, *Sviatoi Pavel* (St. Paul), is shown, and that of Vitus Bering's ship, the *Sviatoi Petr* (St. Peter), is also drawn, with parts of the coast where sighted. Both tracks show the outward journey and the return. There are two coasts shown in different positions at right, the first the result of dead reckoning on the outbound voyage and the second the result from the return.

MAP 102 (*below*).

The track of Bering is depicted on this map drawn by his surviving lieutenant, Sven Waxell, in 1742. Bering's landfall at Kayak Island, in sight of Mount St. Elias, is shown at top right; the Kamchatka Peninsula, and the starting point of the voyage, is at left. There is also an illustration, in the box close to Kamchatka, of a sea cow (described and documented in detail by Bering's naturalist, the famous Georg Steller) above a fur seal and sea lion. At right is an illustration of a Native hunter in a *baidarka*, a skin-covered kayak on a frame of driftwood and bone.

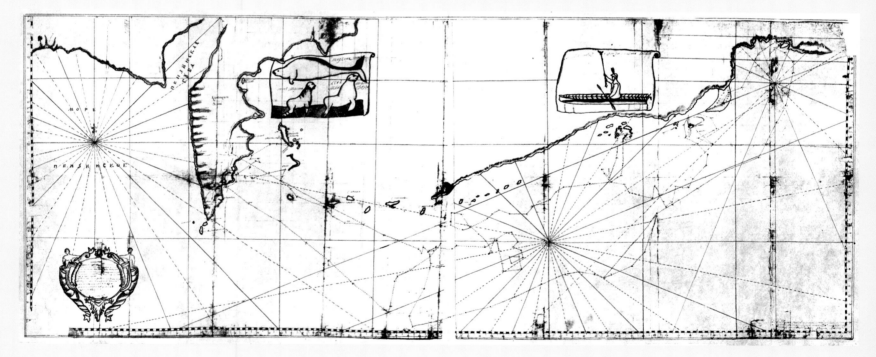

but he lost both his boats when one was sent to find an anchorage and the other sent to look for the first—it is presumed that they were attacked by local Tlingit—and thus could not land. So Chirikov sailed back to Kamchatka, sighting a number of coastlines along the Aleutian chain on the way (MAP 101, *above, top*).

Bering made his landfall a few days later farther to the north at what is now Kayak Island, within sight of Mount St. Elias, which he named. He feared (rightly, if what we think happened to Chirikov is correct) for the safety of his ship and so allowed his men only ten hours ashore, much to the chagrin of his naturalist, Georg Steller, who was forced to carry out research in ten hours that should have taken weeks. Steller is known for his description of the now-extinct sea cow, his pioneering descriptions of the various types of salmon, and a host of other scientific achievements.

Bering also returned along the Aleutian chain, and the map of his voyage shows that they were thought to be a continuous coast rather than islands (MAP 102, *above*). Bering took so long to return, however, that his men suffered from scurvy, and, as he tried to land, the ship was wrecked. The men were washed up on what was later named Bering Island, only 110 miles from the coast of Kamchatka—and safety. Here, over the winter, Bering and many of his men succumbed to the scurvy and to the cold. Some survivors made it back to Kamchatka the following spring in a boat constructed from the wreckage of his ship.

Bering and Chirikov's mapping of the coast of Alaska and the Aleutians as a continuous coastline led to the production of maps that for over thirty years showed Alaska as a huge peninsula jutting out toward Asia (MAP 103, *overleaf*).

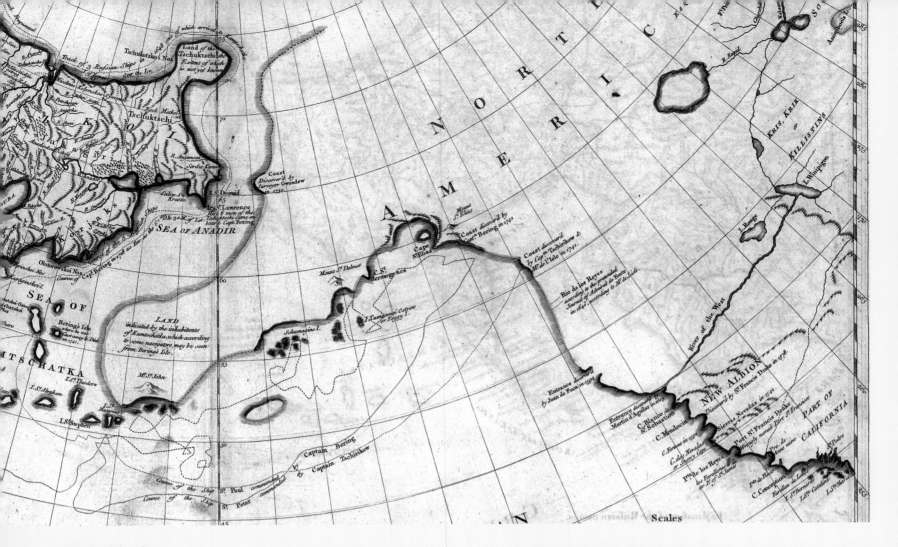

Map 103 (above).
This map, which originated with one of the Bering expedition scientists, Gerhard Müller, was published in 1768. It shows Alaska the way it was assumed to be after the voyages of Bering and Chirikov. The sightings of coasts along the Aleutian chain have been joined to form a continuous coastline; this demonstrates that it is unwise to construct a map by joining the dots! The tracks of Bering's and Chirikov's ships are shown together with the landfall of each. Note also the *River of the West* flowing straight from *L. Winipigon* (Lake Winnipeg) to the Pacific. Much of the West is shown as *New Albion*—the map is a British edition.

Map 104 (below).
A Russian map from about 1773, showing Alaska as an island. This followed the voyage of Ivan Synd in 1764. Bering's and Chirikov's tracks are now correctly shown as hopping from island to island, but Synd's report of many islands has been taken too far.

After Bering, a progression of Russian fur traders pushed slowly ever farther east, with their activities—and supposed activities—keeping the Spanish authorities awake at night. After the British sent Commodore John Byron to the Pacific in 1762, Catherine the Great sent a naval officer, Ivan Synd, into the Bering Sea. Synd reported finding many islands, but the information was misinterpreted, with the result that now Alaska was depicted as a mass of islands (**Map 104**, *below, left*). It was not until 1779 that a Russian map showed the Aleutians correctly as a chain of islands, and it took Britain's James Cook to define continental Alaska correctly (see overleaf).

The fur trade was consolidated in 1799 under the Russian-American Company, led by Grigorii Shelikov. The company first had its base on Kodiak Island, but in 1804 it was moved to Novo Archangel'sk—Sitka—under a new manager, Alexandr Baranov. Under his aegis Fort Ross was founded in California in 1812 (see page 75). In 1821 the tsar issued an edict, called a *ukase*, which claimed Russian sovereignty south to 51° N, but it soon became obvious that this was too bold to hold, and in 1824 Russia signed a treaty with the United States (and the following year with Britain) that abandoned Russian claims below 54° 40′ N, the southernmost limit of today's panhandle of Alaska. The British treaty also established 141° W as the eastern limit of Russian territory, the modern Alaska–Canada boundary.

Map 105 (right).
Carried and disparaged by Captain James Cook in 1778, this map by Jacob von Stählin was published in a book in 1774, using then current Russian information. It is notable not only because it gave Cook so much trouble (see overleaf) but also because it is the first printed map to name *Alaschka*—Alaska.

The Sea of the West

In the eighteenth century, well before the basic outline of the West was known, yet another myth surfaced from time to time, showing up in what are perhaps some of the most artistically superb yet geographically absurd maps of the West ever produced.

The Sea of the West, another product of the necessary exploration optimism that salvation was just over the next horizon, may have originated partly in exaggerated Native reports of large lakes, which seemed to Indians to be exactly the western sea that explorers were inquiring about.

The existence of such a sea seemed to be demonstrated by an account published by Samuel Purchas in his *Purchas His Pilgrimes* in 1625. A Spanish ship with the Greek pilot Juan de Fuca aboard was said to have entered a strait at 47° N and sailed around in an inland sea for twenty days. Here, then, was that inland sea depicted on maps. No record of any such voyage has ever been found, but neither has it been disproved; the inland sea could have been the Strait of Georgia and the entrance today's Strait of Juan de Fuca, the latter named by fur trader Charles Barkley in 1787 after after our erstwhile pilot, who Barkley assumed was its original discoverer.

Map 106 (*right, top*), Map 107 (*below, left*), and Map 108 (*below, right*). Various depictions of a Sea of the West shown on maps by Jean Janvier in 1762 (Map 106); Jean Covens and Corneille Mortier about 1780 (Map 107); and Jean Nolin in 1783 (Map 108). In one case the sea stretches east well beyond the 100th meridian. These maps also show another geographical myth popular at the time—that of a strait forming a Northwest Passage said to have been discovered by a Spanish admiral, Bartolemew de Fonte, in 1640. An account of his voyage was published in a British magazine called *Memoirs for the Curious* in 1708 and was later used by promoters of voyages to find a Northwest Passage. These maps just predate the 1784 publication of the account of James Cook's third voyage, which finally showed this charming geography to be a total fiction.

CHARTING THE WEST COAST

In response to the Russian and Spanish voyages to the Northwest, Britain in 1776 dispatched its most famous navigator, Captain James Cook, on his third and final voyage and charged him with determining whether a Northwest Passage existed through the continent in temperate latitudes north of 65° N. (The British knew at this time there could be no passage south of that latitude because of the as yet unpublished explorations of Hudson's Bay Company explorer Samuel Hearne.) Cook's mapping of the entire peninsula of mainland Alaska north to 70°44´ in 1778 proved that no such passage existed (MAP 109, *below*). His accurate maps, published in 1784, suddenly brought Alaska onto the world map in more or less its true form.

Cook's crews also discovered that considerable profits were to be made in Canton, China, from the sale of sea otter pelts obtained on the Northwest Coast, and as a result a succession of fur traders, both British and American, appeared on the coast in the decades after Cook's voyage, often adding many details to the map of the coast as they made sure they could find their way back to a lucrative spot the following season.

In 1785, just a year after Cook's work had been published, the French, not to be outdone, dispatched an around-the-world scientific expedition of their own, led by naval officer Jean-François Galaup, Comte de La Pérouse. He reached Alaska in 1787 and then sailed south along the West Coast, mapping as he went (MAP 112, *right*).

La Pérouse and his ships were later lost in the South Pacific, but not before depositing copies of his maps with the British at Port Jackson (Sydney), Australia. The French Revolution then intervened, and his maps were not published until 1797, by which time they had been superseded by the detailed mapping of another British naval officer, Captain George Vancouver.

After Cook, lingering doubts still existed as to possible passages through the continent, and the Spanish were making what turned out to be a last-ditch effort to find one. This doubt especially manifested itself at Cook's River, Alaska, now Cook Inlet, on which Anchorage now stands, because Cook had not explored the inlet to its end. Over three seasons, 1792–94, Vancouver explored and mapped the coast from Washington—where he was the first to find and map Puget Sound (MAP 114, *far right, bottom*)—north to Cook Inlet. The latter was given special attention, resulting in a change of name from Cook's River to Cook's Inlet when Van-

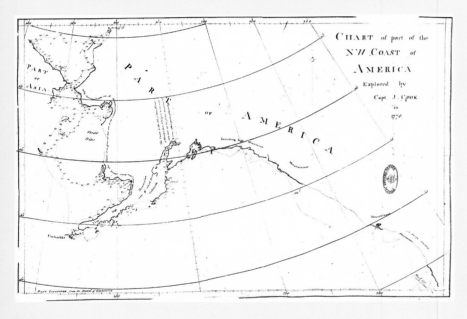

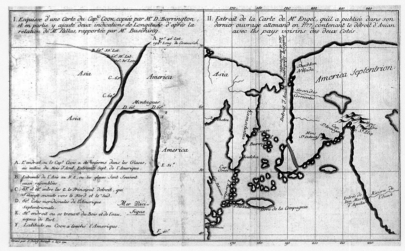

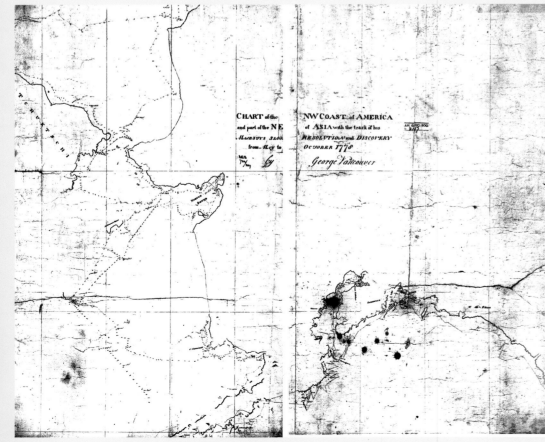

MAP 109 (*above, left*).
The first map to summarize James Cook's exploration and first accurate definition of the mainland peninsula of Alaska was this pen-and-ink manuscript, enclosed in a letter to the Admiralty given to Russian traders on Unalaska on 20 October 1778. It arrived in London on 6 March 1780.

MAP 110 (*above, right*).
These two very rough approximations of a map of Alaska were included in a 1781 book that tried to beat Cook's book to the press. These maps were drawn, one assumes, from textual description only, leaked from one of Cook's crew. Their claim to fame is that they were apparently the first maps of Cook's third voyage to be published.

MAP 111 (*left*).
George Vancouver was a young midshipman (a trainee officer) with Cook. He produced this map of Alaska onboard ship in 1778, at the same time that Cook was producing his maps. Vancouver went on to chart the Northwest Coast in detail over three seasons, 1792–94, including the coast of Alaska as far west as Cook Inlet, shown but not named on this map. When he first mapped the inlet, Cook thought it might end in a river that penetrated inland to the Great Slave Lake and thus named it Cook's River; Vancouver proved it was a dead end and changed the name to its present Cook Inlet. The city of Anchorage now stands on the inlet.

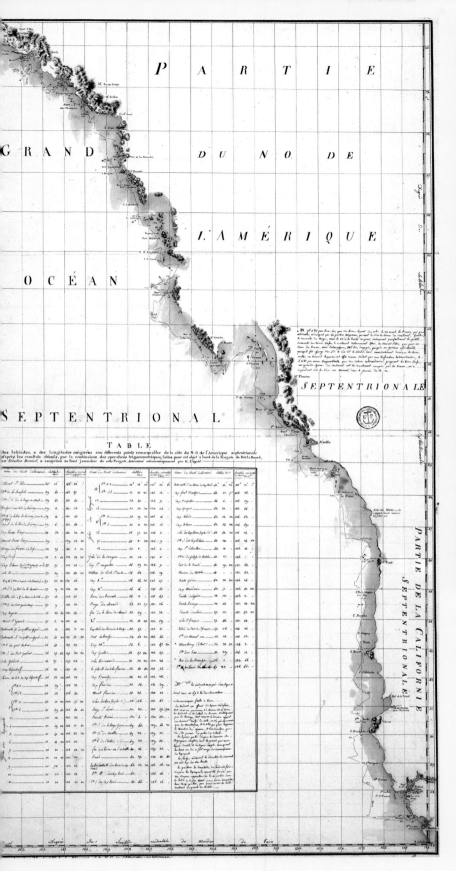

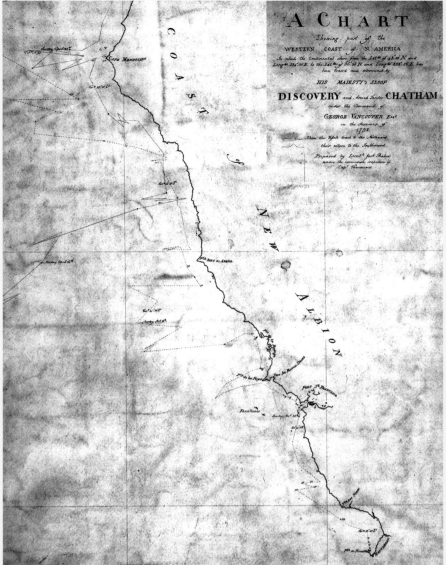

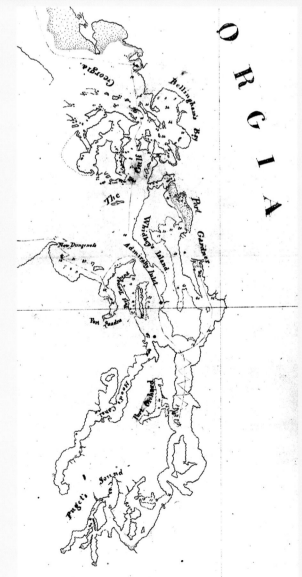

MAP 112 (*above*).
The West Coast as mapped by Joseph Dagelet and Gérault-Sébastien Bernizet, two of La Pérouse's officers, in 1787. San Francisco Bay and Monterey Harbor are at bottom, *Nootka* is at the midpoint, and *Mont St. Elie* (Mt. St. Elias) is at top. Islands of the Alaska Panhandle, the Queen Charlottes, and Vancouver Island are not distinguished from the mainland coast. The printing of this map was delayed by La Pérouse's demise and the French Revolution, and the map was not published until 1797, just in time to be eclipsed by George Vancouver's work, published the following year.

MAP 113 (*above*).
George Vancouver's first map of the West Coast—predictably labeled the *Coast of New Albion*. The map was drawn late in 1792 .

MAP 114 (*right*).
Vancouver was the first to find Puget Sound and to chart it. The inlet was named after Peter Puget, the officer in charge of its survey. The name was originally applied to only the southernmost reaches, as shown on this map; Vancouver intended *Admiralty Inlet* to apply to most of the sound. *Port Orchard* was named after Harry Orchard, clerk of Vancouver's ship *Discovery*. To the north, *Bellingham Bay* was named after naval store-keeper William Bellingham.

couver proved it a dead end. Vancouver's mapping finally demonstrated beyond any reasonable doubt that no Northwest Passage existed in temperate latitudes. His detailed mapping of the intricate coastline of Washington, British Columbia, and the Alaska Panhandle has rarely been matched by anyone else, anywhere else. Vancouver's maps were so accurate that they were in active use for more than fifty years.

These coastal voyages of the closing years of the eighteenth century finally defined the West. Cook measured his longitude with accuracy and was the first to use the newly invented chronometer for on-board measurement of longitude. Through his efforts the width of the North American continent was itself defined.

THE ROAD TO MANIFEST DESTINY

When the United States was created, the rest of the North American continent was claimed—though not occupied—by four European nations—Britain, Spain, France, and Russia—and there is little doubt that had some of these nations possessed the will at the right moment of time, the sovereignty of the United States, and especially the West, might have looked a great deal different from what it does today. But a mixture of political foresight, military muscle, and perhaps pure luck was to ensure that the United States would occupy much of the continent, including Alaska.

The transition from a nation entirely east of the Mississippi in 1783 to one stretching to the West Coast took place in a remarkably short time; eighty-four years later the territorial process was essentially completed by the addition of Alaska, and within another twenty-three the western "frontier" was generally considered to have disappeared.

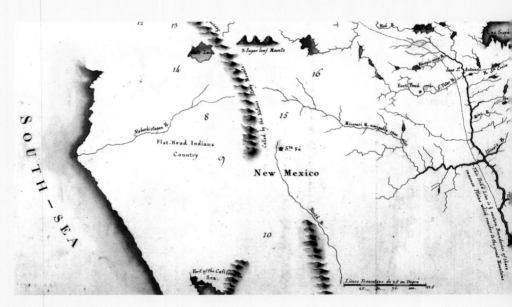

MAP 115 (above, right).
Little detail of the West is displayed on this map presented to Congress by Connecticut fur trade explorer Peter Pond in 1785. Well illustrated is the notion that the Missouri reached west to a narrow and easily surmountable single range of mountains, only to be mirrored on the other side by a river flowing straight to the Pacific. In addition the *North R.* (the Rio Grande) flows south from the same general height of land.

MAP 116 (below).
Here the *Oregan, or R. of the West* flows but a short distance from the *Rocky Mountains* to the Pacific in *Unknown Country*. The latter's few details contrast with the dense network of streams depicted east of the mountains, including a *River Missouri* that conveniently flows right through the Rockies, rising very close to the *Oregan. The Grand Detour* on the Missouri (in South Dakota) was a long meander of the river later measured by Lewis and Clark to be two thousand feet across its neck but thirty miles around. This simplistic view of the lay of the rivers and mountains of the West lured explorers upriver in the years before Lewis and Clark. This map is a copy of one drawn by Spanish surveyor general of Louisiana Antoine Soulard and was actually carried by Meriwether Lewis in 1804–06; the hole is the result of wear and tear from being carried folded in his pocket.

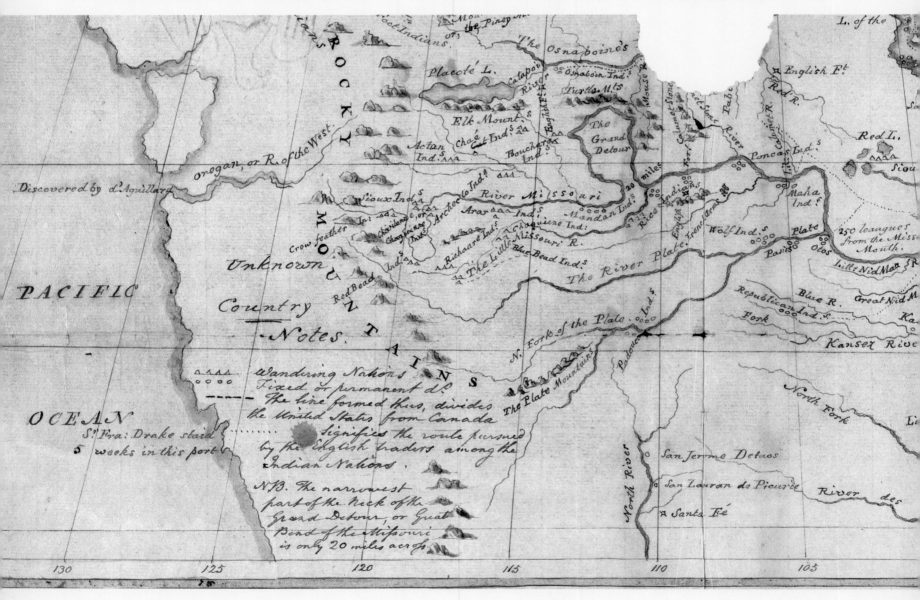

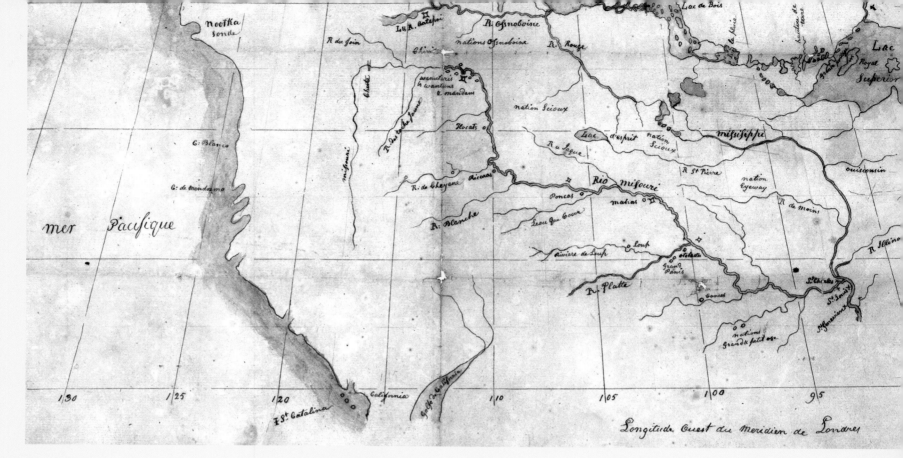

Map 117 (*above*).
The river systems of the West were beginning to be unraveled as the eighteenth century drew to a close, but this map shows them far too close to the West Coast—alluringly so, in fact. This Spanish map, in French, was drawn in 1795. The Missouri is clearly thought to be the main river route west. Some information as to its course comes from the expedition of James Mackay and John Evans (see next page).

Map 118 (*right*) and **Map 119** (*below*).
The mouth of the important Columbia River had remained undiscovered by EuroAmericans, owing in no small measure to the presence of a long bar across the river's entrance. Martín de Aguilar had in 1603 reported an "entrada" that could have been the Columbia, but his crew had been too weak to continue to explore it (see page 20). Bruno de Hezeta had in 1775 even mapped the bay into which the river empties, without finding the river itself (see page 40). It was left to an American captain, Robert Gray, in 1792, to finally find the elusive river, naming it Columbia's River after his ship, the *Columbia Rediva*. Gray mapped only the wide part of the river immediately behind the bar, and **Map 118** is a copy of that map given to George Vancouver. North is to the left. Later in 1792 Vancouver sent his second-in-command, William Broughton, to map the river. His ship, the *Chatham*, could more easily cross the bar than Vancouver's principal ship, *Discovery*. Broughton surveyed the Columbia to *Point Vancouver*, opposite the location of today's Portland. His map was incorporated into Vancouver's published plate in 1798; the Columbia detail is shown here as **Map 119**. The fact that Gray beat Vancouver to the Columbia became one of the American claims to the region when the location of the international boundary was being negotiated in 1845–46.

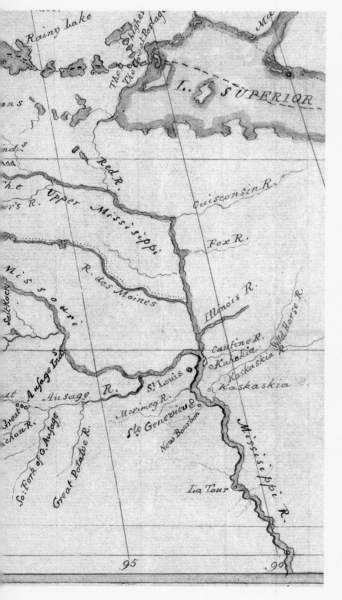

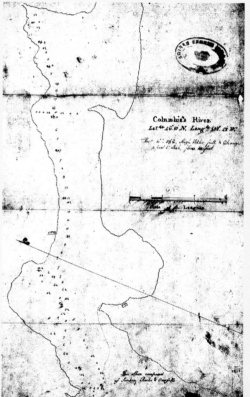

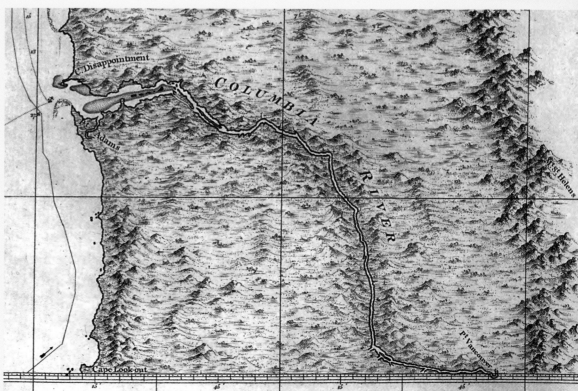

Before Lewis & Clark

Even while Spain held undisputed sway over Louisiana, American fur traders advanced up the Missouri. In 1793 Jacques Clamorgan, a St. Louis merchant, obtained a monopoly from the Spanish government and formed the Company of Explorers of the Upper Missouri, usually known simply as the Missouri Company.

The company dispatched Jean Baptiste Truteau the following year, but he only got as far as the present North Dakota–South Dakota boundary. Then in 1795 the Missouri Company employed James Mackay, an ex-Nor'Wester, (employee of the North West Company) and John Thomas Evans, a seeker of a tribe of supposed lost Welsh Indians he thought might be the Mandan. They established Fort Charles (near today's Sioux City, Iowa) but were prevented by Teton Sioux from ascending the river further.

Over the winter, Mackay and Evans concocted a grand plan by which they would find a passage to India for the Missouri Company by following the Missouri to its source, cross what they anticipated to be an easy portage—they had been looking at the map then available—and find a river flowing to the Pacific. Evans set out the following spring and reached the Mandan villages at the Great Bend, where he abandoned this dream after coming into conflict

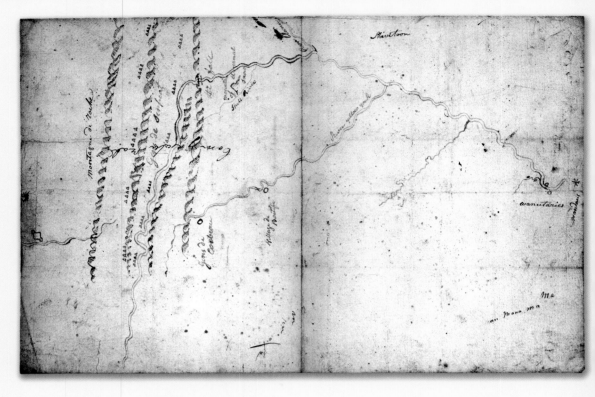

MAP 120 (*above*).
John Evans's 1797 map of the country upstream from the Mandan villages at the Great Bend of the Missouri. This information was completely derived from Indian sources. For the first time multiple ranges of mountains appear; perhaps it was not going to be as easy to reach the Pacific as had been imagined. As a result of this information Evans decided not to attempt to reach the Pacific. The westernmost range is the *montagne de roche*—"rocky mountain."

MAP 121 (*below*).
British mapmaker Aaron Arrowsmith created a series of maps, all titled *A Map Exhibiting All the New Discoveries in the Interior Parts of North America*, over several decades, each updated with the latest information available to him. The maps are important because of this sequence and also because Arrowsmith did not speculate, except, as here, to interpret Indian reports with clearly tentative dashed lines. This map shows the then presumed route of the Missouri from the single-ranged Rocky Mountains and the extension eastward of the lower Columbia already mapped by George Vancouver—*The Indians say they sleep 8 Nights in descending this River to the Sea.* This is the edition from 1802.

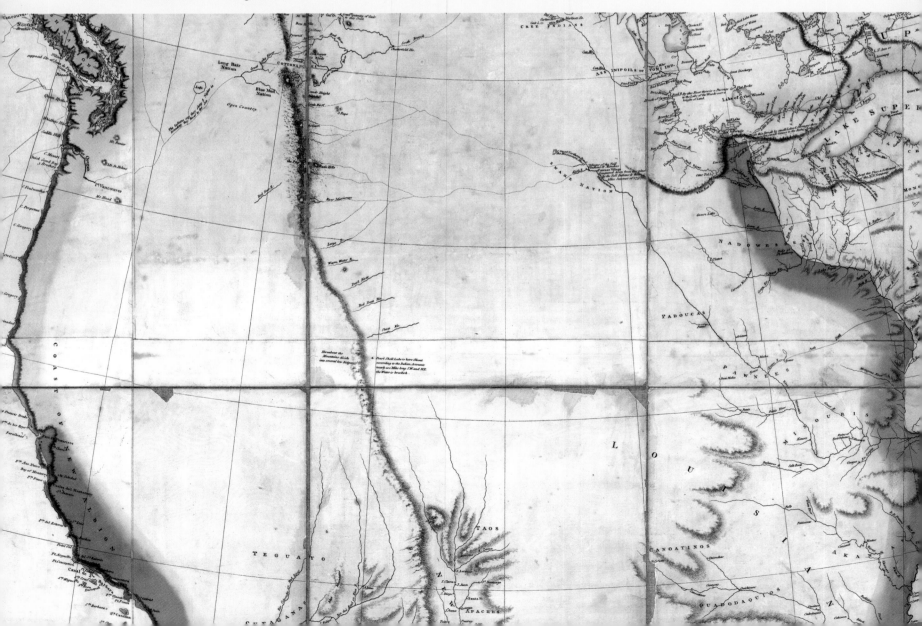

Map 122 (*right*).

This map was drawn in 1798 and shows the course of the Missouri between the *Yellow Stone River* at top left and Fort St. Charles, near today's Sioux City, at bottom right. Known for many years as the Indian Office map, it was likely drawn by James Mackay of the Missouri Company. The map incorporates information from his expedition with John Evans up the river (when they founded Fort St. Charles) in 1795 and includes information gained from Evans's expedition the following year. This map was carried to the Pacific by Lewis and Clark in 1804–06.

Map 123 (*right, center*).

By the time of Lewis and Clark, British fur traders were also familiar with the region around the Great Bend of the Missouri. This map was made by North West Company surveyor David Thompson in 1798. Today this entire section of the river is submerged under the artificial Lake Sakakawea.

Map 124 (*right, bottom*).

All sides were unclear about what had been acquired in the Louisiana Purchase of 1803. This map, published the same year, shows a very poor understanding of the geography of the West, with Louisiana the area in red. This ignorance was why the expeditions sent out by Thomas Jefferson were needed.

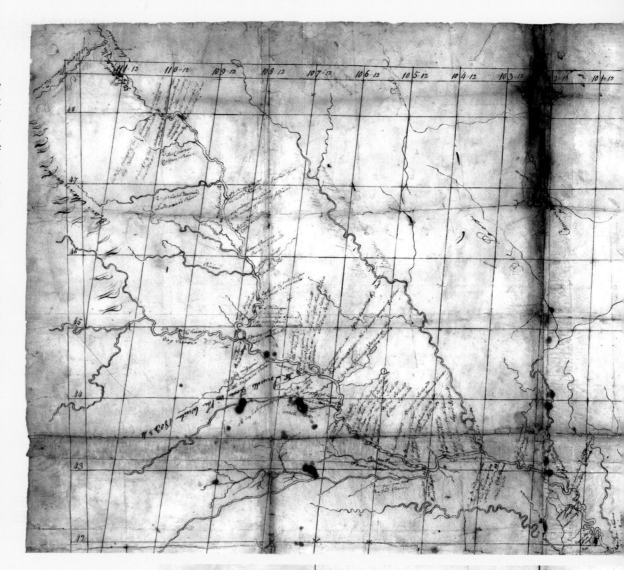

with North West Company traders and gaining new information from the Mandan about the distance to the mountains. Map 120, *left, top*, was drawn by Evans using this information and shows graphically what he discovered—that there were multiple mountain ranges to cross rather than the single easy range he had envisaged.

The maps made by fur traders such as Evans helped mapmakers such as Aaron Arrowsmith and Nicholas King create maps with the latest geographical information that would soon be useful to Meriwether Lewis and William Clark, whom President Thomas Jefferson enlisted in 1803 to mount a military expedition to find a route to the Pacific.

THE LOUISIANA PURCHASE

For in 1803 it had unexpectedly become more urgent that the United States gain knowledge of Louisiana; a commercial imperative turned into a national one. The French had regained the territory from Spain in 1800 by the secret (third) Treaty of San Ildefonso, signed by Spain under duress from Napoleon in Europe. The French had lost Hispaniola to a slave uprising led by François-Dominique Toussaint L'Ouverture, and Louisiana, with which they had intended to supply Hispaniola, was now of little use to them. Hence Napoleon, shelving any ideas of a resurgent French empire, resolved to sell it to the United States to keep it out of the hands of his enemy, Britain.

James Monroe and Robert R. Livingston, sent to Paris by Jefferson to try to negotiate the purchase of New Orleans for $10 million, were dumbfounded to be offered all of Louisiana for $15 million but quickly accepted. At the stroke of a pen the United States acquired half of the current West—something over 800,000 square miles—for less than four cents an acre. The exact figures are elusive because the extent of the territory purchased was not known properly by either side, though Napoleon may have had a better idea than the Americans (Map 125, *overleaf*).

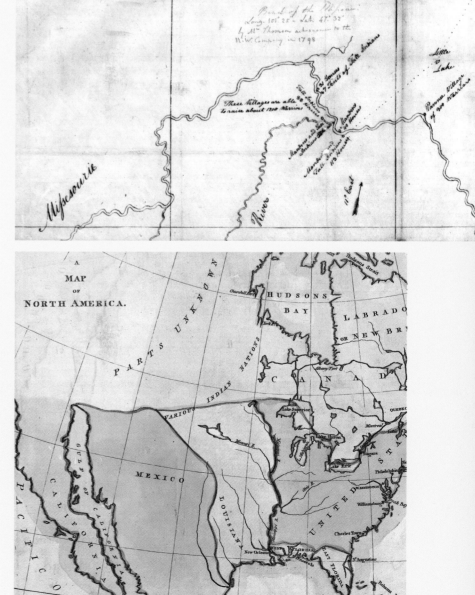

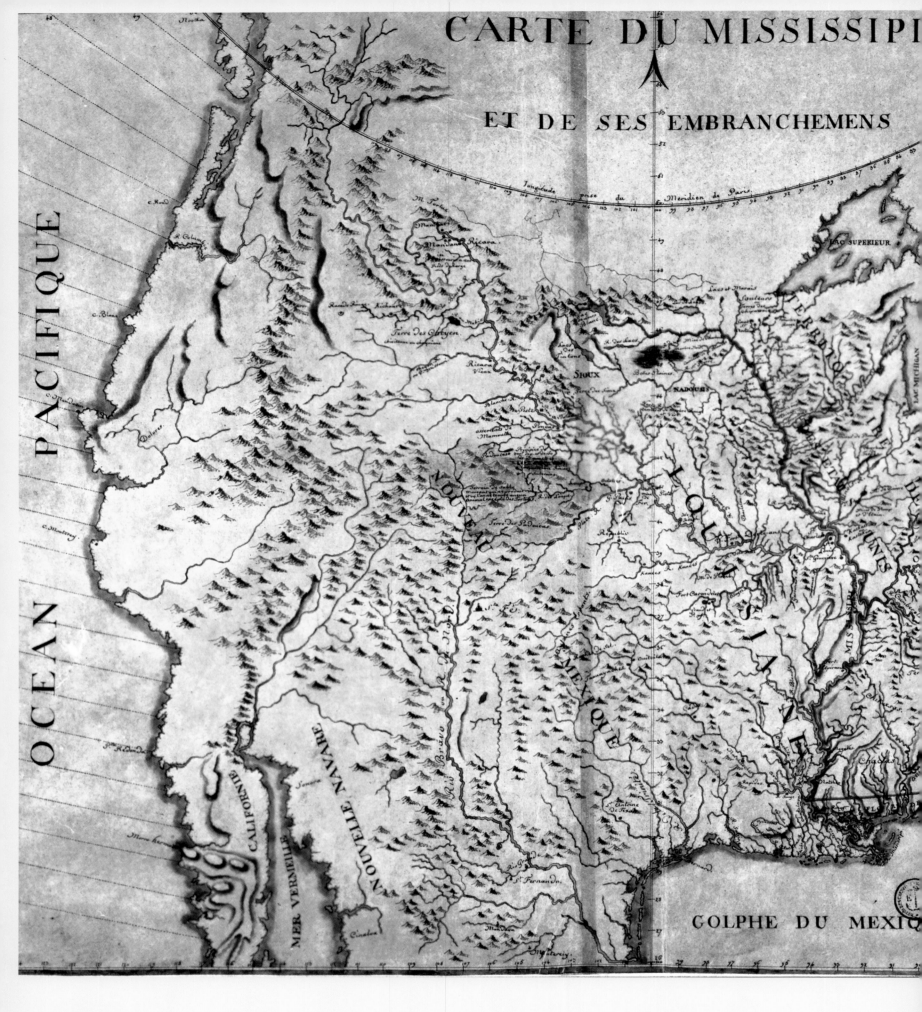

CARTE DU MISSISSIPI

ET DE SES EMBRANCHEMENS

MAP 125.

This very interesting but somewhat confused view of the West was created by a widely traveled merchant and sometime mayor of New Orleans, James Pitot, in 1802. Nevertheless, it represents quite well the knowledge of the West immediately prior to Lewis and Clark. In the north, the Great Bend of the Missouri is prominent, but the river is shown rising far to the northwest in what is today the Canadian province of British Columbia, and the Columbia River is shown extending inland not much farther than the point to which it was surveyed by Vancouver. In the Northwest the mountains are still depicted as a single range; the Missouri cleverly avoids flowing directly over them, Pitot seemingly being at least aware of the laws of physics. The other major rivers shown are the Rio Grande and the Colorado, both correctly flowing south. What must be San Francisco Bay is shown as a simple inlet with a short river flowing into it. The coast reflects the surveys of Vancouver but does not reproduce them very well, as if Pitot were drawing from memory. Some of the information incorporated in this map came from an associate in New Orleans, an architect-engineer named Barthelemy Lafon. The map was taken to France by Pitot in 1802 and may have been used by the French officials at the time of the Louisiana Purchase; Napoleon may have had a better idea of what he sold than Jefferson had of what America had bought. The map is now held at the French naval archives in Vincennes, France.

OCIAN IN VIEW

The Louisiana Purchase was dated 30 April 1803, was signed on 2 April, and reached Washington on 14 July. Jefferson already had a plan for an expedition to find a route to the Pacific. In 1793, as a member of the august American Philosophical Society, he had drawn up instructions for a French botanist, André Michaux, to find the shortest route of communication between the U.S. & the Pacific Ocean." Michaux had subsequently become suspected as a spy, so the expedition had not taken place, but Jefferson's instructions to Lewis and Clark were virtually identical. And even before the Louisiana Purchase Jefferson was considering such an expedition again, becoming worried about British intentions after reading Alexander Mackenzie's 1802 account of his first overland crossing of the continent in 1792–93. Mackenzie's book had recommended that the North West Company establish fur trade ports on the Pacific Coast.

Jefferson selected his personal secretary, Meriwether Lewis, to lead the expedition, soon termed the Corps of Discovery—a military unit with a military objective. Lewis gave co-command to his friend William Clark. With twenty-five men and five tons of food and other supplies, Clark left St. Louis on 14 May 1804 in a fifty-five-foot-long keelboat and two pirogues—large dugout canoes with sails. He was joined by Lewis, traveling overland, at St. Charles six days later.

By late October the expedition had reached the Mandan villages at the Great Bend of the Missouri, a thousand miles from St. Charles, and here they overwintered. On 7 April 1805 they started west once more. Native information and the maps they had with them proved invaluable. After a decision at a fork in the river, Lewis and Clark knew they were on the right stream when they encountered the Great Falls of the Missouri (MAP 126, *right, top*).

When they reached the Rockies, they were able to purchase horses from wary Shoshone after Sacagawea, Shoshone wife of Toussaint Charbonneau, a fur trader guiding the expedition, was recognized as a chief's sister. But the going was tough. Reaching the crest of the Continental Divide, Lewis hoped to see a mighty river flowing westward but instead saw more ranges of mountains—the Bitterroot Range—which they crossed through Lemhi Pass. Snow fell, food ran short, and a horse was killed and eaten. "The difficulty of passing [these] emence mountains [has] dampened the Spirits of the party," wrote Clark.

After eleven days, they reached a friendly Nez Percé village on the Weippe Prairie, near the

MAP 128 (*right*).
Cape Disappointment and the north shore of the mouth of the Columbia River, drawn by Clark in his journal on 19 November 1805.

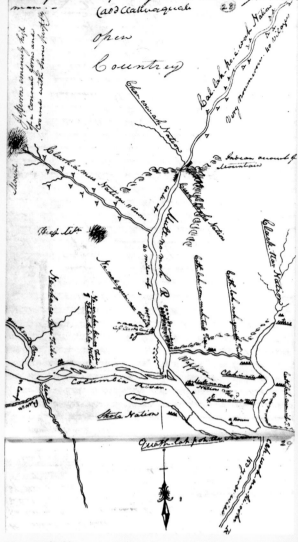

MAP 126 (*left*).
It took the Corps of Discovery a month to portage around the Great Falls of the Missouri and the associated rapids, shown here in William Clark's journal dated 4 July 1805. Power projects have submerged much of the area shown, near today's Great Falls, Montana.

MAP 127 (*above*).
The *Mult-no-mah R* is the Willamette River at today's Portland, Oregon. Meriwether Lewis drew this map, which has south at the top, on 3 April 1806, on the return journey. He used information given to William Clark *by an old and inteligent Indian.*

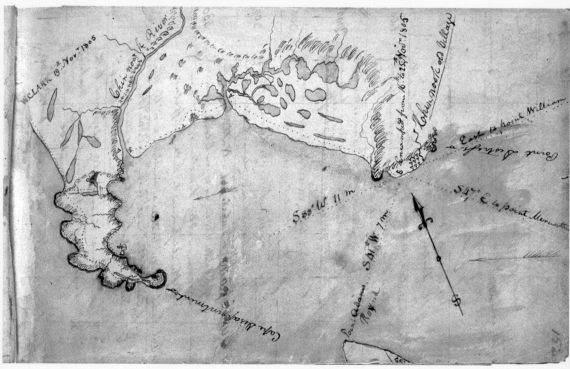

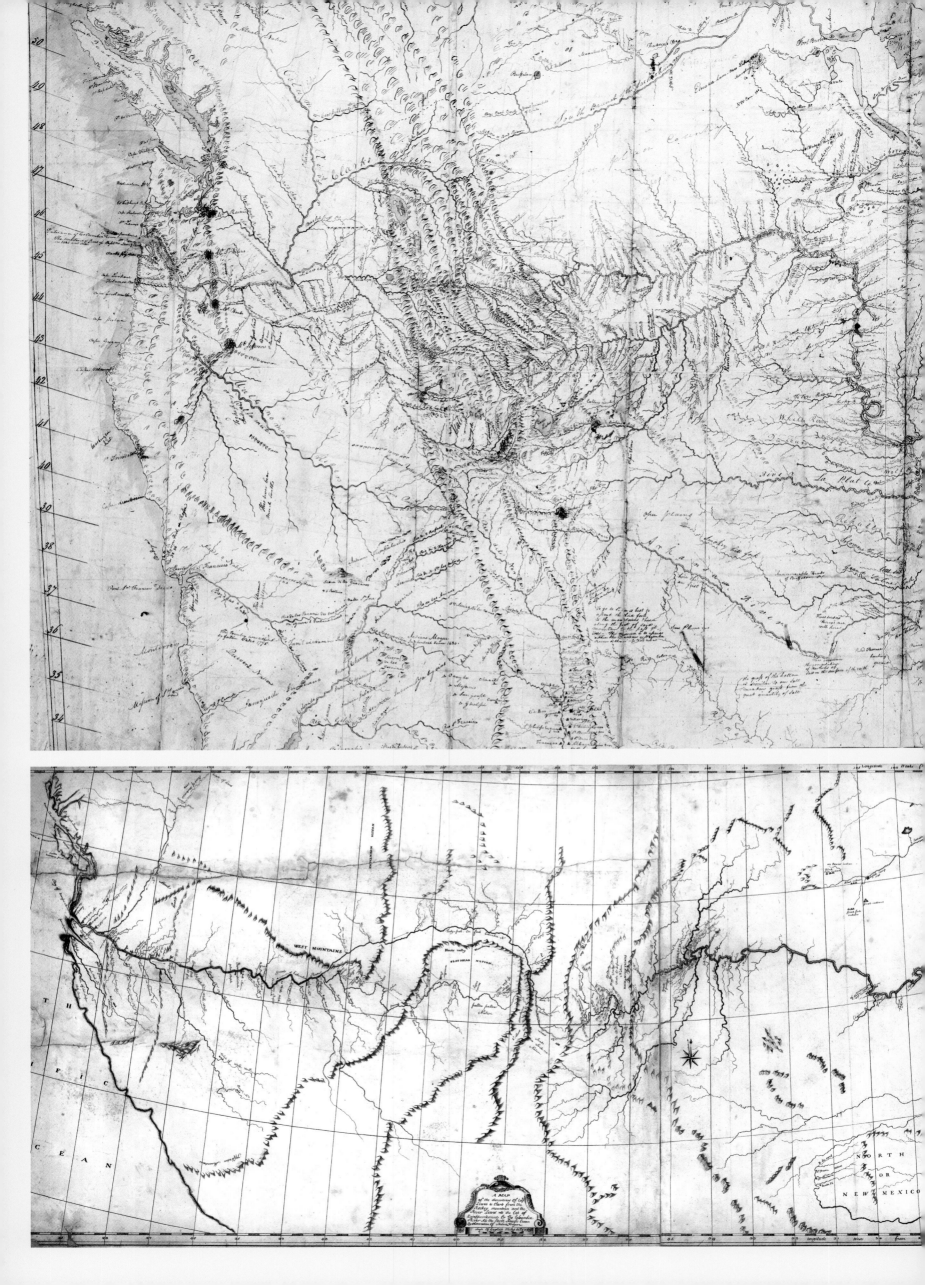

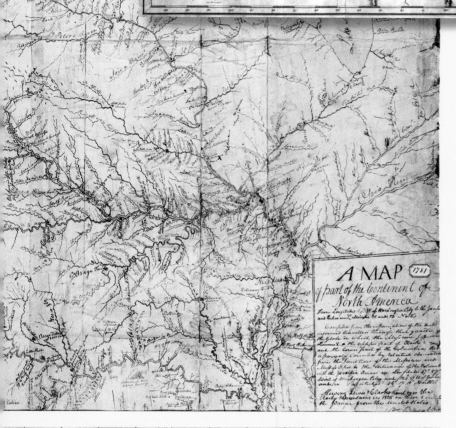

Clearwater River, in today's Idaho. And finally, here was a river flowing west. They borrowed canoes and floated down first the Clearwater, then the Snake, and then, on 16 October, the Columbia. On 7 November, still twenty miles from the sea, Clark recorded in his field book the famous line: "Ocian in view! O! The joy." They had made it. After exploring the Columbia estuary, on 3 December both Lewis and Clark found themselves suitable trees and carved inscriptions on them. Clark, in emulation of his hero Alexander Mackenzie, carved the words "Capt. William Clark December 3rd 1805. By Land. U. States in 1804–1805."

The Corps made a camp they called Fort Clatsop from logs just south of today's Astoria, Oregon, and settled in for the winter, Clark using the time to construct a large map from his field sketches. "We now discover," wrote Clark, "that we have found the most practicable and navigable passage across the Continent of North America." But it was not true. They had found a route, but it was barely practical. The dream of a passage to India was finally laid to rest.

The return journey was easier and faster; they split up so as to explore several different routes. They reached St. Louis, where they had been given up as dead, on 23 September 1806.

MAP 129 (above, left).
William Clark's map of the West, which incorporates much Indian information as well as that from the expedition. The original Lewis and Clark map was updated until 1810 by Clark, who was for a time superintendent of Indian affairs for Louisiana, based in St. Louis. Although the information from the Lewis and Clark expedition is generally correct, some of the additions are not—notably the location of the headwaters of the *Rio del Norte* (Rio Grande), far west and north of their true position. This information came from Corps of Discovery member George Drouillard (see MAP 132, overleaf).

MAP 130 (left).
One of the members of the Corps of Discovery, Private Robert Frazer (or Frazier), kept a journal, as several others did, and on his return announced his intention to publish a book about the expedition. He never did; his journal was lost, but his map survived. The map is not as accurate as that of Lewis or Clark but is a fair representation of the courses of the Missouri and the Columbia. It was likely drawn in 1807.

MAP 131 (above).
The engraved final summary map of the Lewis and Clark expedition, published in 1814 in the two-volume account of the expedition edited by Nicholas Biddle. The map was copied from one by Clark by engraver and mapmaker Samuel Lewis—no relation to Meriwether. Here at last was a widely available, comprehensive, and reasonably accurate map of the northern and hitherto incompletely known part of the West.

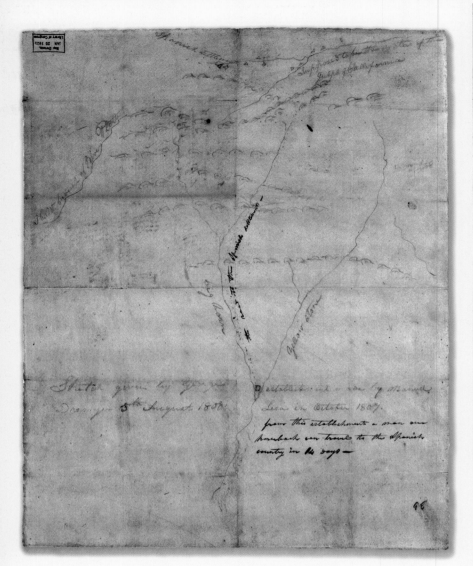

Map 132 (*above*).
This map was drawn by George Drouillard in 1808. It shows Fort Raymond (unnamed) as the *establishment made by Manuel Lisa in October 1807* at the confluence of the *Yellow stone* River and the *Big Horn* River. Note that the map has south at the top. At Fort Raymond, a likely later addition, in ink, notes that *from this establishment a man on horseback can travel to the Spanish country in 14 days*, and likewise *The road to the Spanish settlements* is noted along the *Big Horn*. At top the *Spanish settlements* are shown. Drouillard tried to find a route to Santa Fe in 1808.

THE GREAT AMERICAN DESERT

Even before Lewis and Clark returned, fur traders were following in their wake. St. Louis merchant Manuel Lisa ascended the river in 1807 and built a post at the forks of the Yellowstone and Bighorn rivers that he called Fort Raymond. From here John Colter, who had been with Lewis and Clark, explored to the south, finding sulfurous geysers and tar pits on the Shoshone River, soon dubbed by other traders "Colter's Hell." Colter became the first EuroAmerican to find what is now Yellowstone National Park.

Another Corps member, George Drouillard, tried to find a route to Santa Fe, which he was convinced lay not far to the south. His erroneous map (Map 132, *above*) was used by Clark to update his large map of the West (Map 129, *previous page*), introducing errors to that.

When Lewis and Clark were dispatched, Thomas Jefferson had also sent out others to explore possible boundaries of Louisiana. Surveyor William Dunbar was sent up the Ouachita River and on to the Ozark Plateau. With him was George Hunter, a naturalist, one of the first scientists in a government-sponsored exploration of the West. Thomas Freeman, accompanied by naturalist Peter Custis, explored the Red River, but they were stopped by a Spanish force under Francisco Viana, who had orders to intercept American incursions into what the Spanish saw as their territory.

In 1806 another expedition was dispatched up the Red River, led by army officer Zebulon Montgomery Pike. He was sent not by Jefferson but by General James Wilkinson, governor of Louisiana and a double agent for the Spanish and an independent Louisiana. In concert with Aaron Burr, Jefferson's first-term vice president, Wilkinson wanted to set up a republic between the territories of the United States and Spain in much the same way as the Republic of Texas was created later. With Pike he hoped to create an international incident that would allow Burr's private troops to take over New Orleans.

Wilkinson informed the Spanish that Pike was coming, and troops were sent out to find and capture him. Pike managed to explore a good deal of the Kansas and Arkansas rivers into what is today eastern Colorado, finding the peak that would be named after him (Map 133, *above*). Spanish troops located Pike in the Rio Grande valley and arrested him, despite his protestations that he thought he was on the Red River—and therefore not trespassing on Spanish territory. Pike was later released, and in 1810 he published an influential account of his adventures, with Map 133, in which he stated that the Great Plains were sandy deserts, "tracts of many leagues . . . on which not a speck of vegetable matter existed." The powerful idea of the Great American Desert was born. Pike thought this beneficial in that it would tend to confine Americans to their own country.

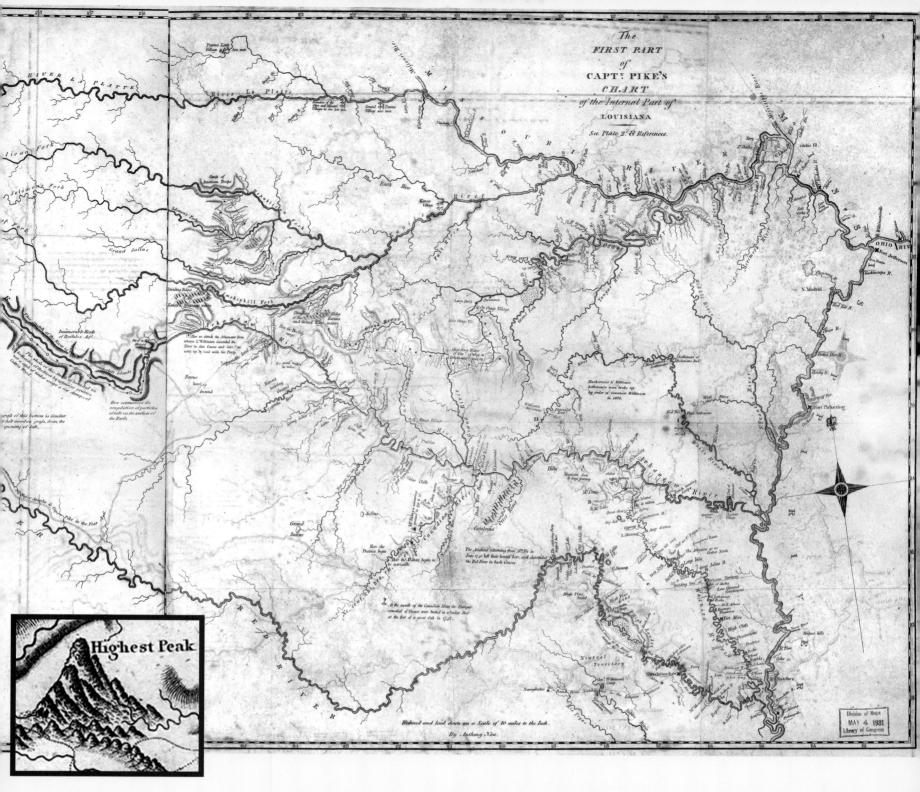

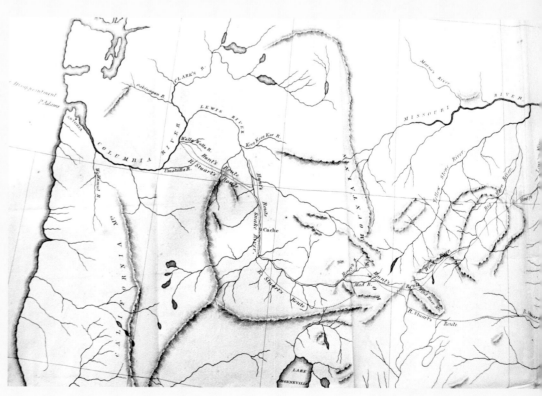

Map 133 (*above and inset*).

A composite of two sheets, this is Zebulon Pike's map of the West. As well as mapping his own expedition, Pike added information from several other sources, including the mapping of part of the Red and Ouachita rivers by William Dunbar and Thomas Freeman, sent out by Thomas Jefferson to explore Louisiana at the same time as Lewis and Clark. They are referenced on the key at bottom left. Note, at extreme left, the *Head Waters of California*. The inset shows, enlarged, the first mapping of Pikes Peak, then unnamed. At left is the wide valley of the *Rio del Norte,* the upper Rio Grande, that Pike told the Spanish he thought was the Red River. *Sta. Fee* is shown. *Innumerable Herds of Buffalos* are shown in the Arkansas River valley. This map, together with that of Lewis and Clark (which had not been published at the time Pike's appeared in 1810), now displayed the river framework of the Great Plains between the Rockies and the Mississippi with reasonable accuracy.

Map 134 (*right*).

A map of the routes of Astorians Wilson Price Hunt, going west in 1811–12, and Robert Stuart, going east in 1813. South Pass, round the southern end of the *Wind River Mts.*, is shown but not named; this important route west was discovered by Stuart. The map is from the book *Astoria,* by Washington Irving, commissioned by John Jacob Astor and published in 1836.

MAP 135 (*above and inset left*).
This is John Robinson's large, detailed, important, and extremely rare map of the American West, published in 1819. Robinson had accompanied Zebulon Pike in 1808 and used his own observations in compiling this map, adding information from all other sources available to him. And there is much detailed information on this map. The northern part of the map is very similar to the published Lewis and Clark map (MAP 131, *page 69*), but *Colter's route in 1807* and *Manuels Fort in 1807* have been added. Just east of the *Laguna de Timpanogos* is the notation *The most Northern point discovered by the Spaniards in the Interior* (at 41° 12´N), and the map is right up-to-date with the depiction of the *Western Limits of the United States According to the Late Treaty*. There are lighter details, too: at *Passo* (El Paso) is the note *Excellent wines made here.* Robinson's landmark map was used as a source by other mapmakers for many years. *Pikes Mountain* is shown enlarged on the inset and represents the first naming of Pikes Peak, the name Robinson himself bestowed.

The river that Lewis and Clark found on the other side of the Rockies soon attracted the attention of fur traders. Another of Manuel Lisa's men, Andrew Henry, in 1810 briefly established the first American trading post west of the Continental Divide, on a tributary of the Snake River, Henrys Fork.

In 1808 entrepreneur John Jacob Astor formed the American Fur Company (and its subsidiary the Pacific Fur Company for its northwest operations) and planned to establish a post at the mouth of the Columbia to ship furs out, far easier and more economical than packing them back down the Missouri. This was exactly the plan first suggested by Alexander Mackenzie for the rival North West Company.

Astor's ship the *Tonquin* arrived at the mouth of the Columbia in March 1811, and his men established Fort Astoria on the south bank. It was only just in time, for the North West Company's David Thompson also arrived at Astoria in July 1811. Astor also dispatched a land expedition, led by Wilson Price Hunt, which left St. Louis in the spring of 1811, arriving at Fort Astoria in January 1812 after a harrowing trek in which Hunt discovered Union Pass across the Continental Divide, at the north end of the Wind River Range. A return overland party led by Robert Stuart, who had arrived on the *Tonquin,* left Fort Astoria in June 1812 and, taking a new route around

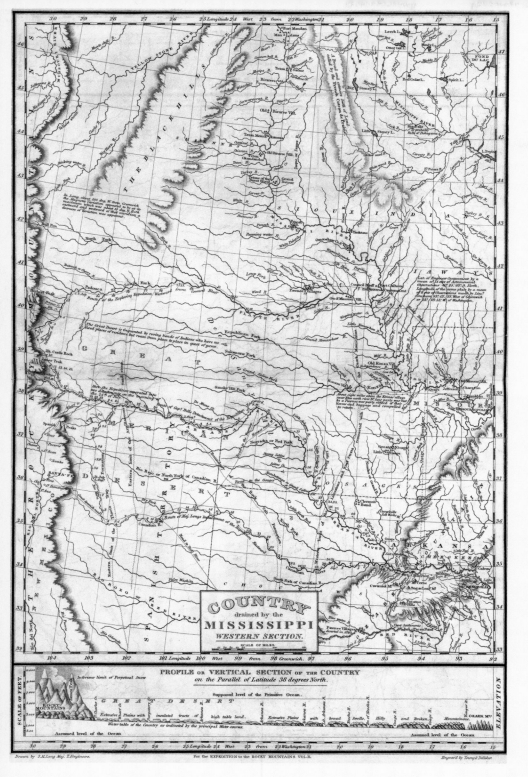

Map 136 (*left*).
Stephen Long's map of the Great Plains, published in 1823. Over what is today western Kansas and Oklahoma and eastern Colorado are emblazoned the words *Great American Desert*, a concept originated by Pike but often attributed only to Long. This map reinforced the desert idea and was influential for fifty years; migrants would pass through the area but not settle it. At the time the description was not really a myth, though it has since been written of as such; the technology available in the mid-nineteenth century would not have allowed farming in this treeless area of low rainfall. At the time of its publication and for several decades thereafter, Long's map was easily the finest map of the Trans-Mississippi West. Note, on the left margin, *James' Peak*. This is Pikes Peak, here named after Edwin James, who in 1820 became the first to climb the mountain. Note, lower on the left margin, *Santa-Fe* at the end of the *Great Spanish road*.

Map 137 (*right*).
This was the manuscript version of Long's map, drawn in 1820 or 1821. The words *Great Desert* on this map were transformed into the grander *Great American Desert* on the published version.

Map 138 (*right, bottom*).
The geographical extent of the United States on this 1835 map illustrates the American view; the Oregon Country was at that time officially a region of "joint occupancy" with Britain. The forty-ninth parallel boundary west to the Rocky Mountains had been agreed upon in 1818, and the 42° N boundary of California and the boundary with New Mexico by the Transcontinental Treaty with Spain the following year (see page 49).

the southern end of the Wind River Range to avoid Indians, found South Pass. This pass, particularly significant because it was passable by wagons, later became part of the Oregon Trail. Both Hunt's and Stuart's routes are shown on Map 134, *page 71.*

Astor did not keep Fort Astoria for long. The War of 1812 intervened. In September 1813 John McTavish of the North West Company arrived with eight canoes and a letter telling Astor's men that a British frigate was en route with orders to seize the fort. The American traders therefore accepted McTavish's offer to purchase the fort. Yet when the British corvette *Racoon* did finally appear, its captain insisted on ceremonially seizing the fort. That was a mistake, for the United States later used the fact of seizure rather than sale to claim American sovereignty to the Oregon Country.

The Corps of Topographical Engineers of the U.S. Army was founded in 1818 and was to explore and map the West for decades. One of its first members was Stephen Harriman Long, who was involved in a disastrous large-scale expedition, with over a thousand men, up the Missouri to the Platte in 1819. So many became ill that the mandate for the expedition was changed to a smaller-scale one; Long was to explore southwest up the Platte to the Arkansas and Red rivers, toward Spanish territory. The Army was learning that in the West, where resources could be scarce, small parties were preferable to large.

Long had with him engineers, soldiers, naturalists, a geologist, and a painter and during 1820 explored up the Platte and Arkansas. He found and mapped the headwaters of the Canadian River and distinguished them from those of the Red River, but he lost his scientific papers to deserters. Long is often considered to have originated the idea

of the Great American Desert, which he named and placed prominently on his map (Map 136, *above, left*). His map was influential for several decades. The region Long explored almost immediately assumed greater importance with the opening of Santa Fe to trade following the Mexican Revolution (see page 76).

With the establishment of the Nor'Westers at Fort Astoria (which became Fort George), and their new headquarters at Fort Vancouver (now Vancouver, Washington) in 1825–26, British fur traders battled their American counterparts until the mid-1830s, by which time the fur trade was in general decline.

Mountain Men

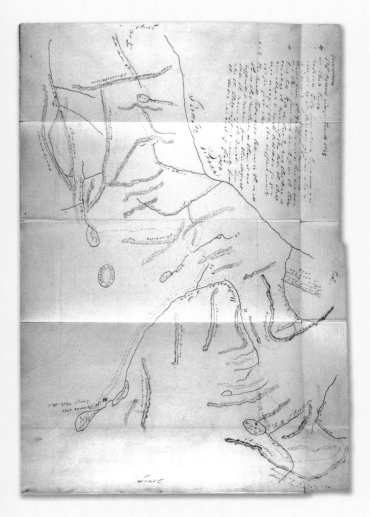

The North West Company merged with the Hudson's Bay Company in 1821, and its energetic governor, George Simpson, formulated a plan to keep American trappers out of the Snake River country by overtrapping, creating a so-called fur desert. In charge of this operation was Peter Skene Ogden, whose subsequent forays all over the Northwest increased knowledge of the interior considerably; many of his discoveries found their way onto maps by Aaron Arrowsmith and French mapmaker Adrien Brué, despite the fact that most of Ogden's original maps were lost. One of Ogden's maps that survived (Map 139, *left*) was perhaps his most significant, illustrating his fifth expedition, in which he found the important Humboldt River Valley, later to become a link in the California Trail.

The American fur trappers and traders, many of whom began their careers by answering a newspaper advertisement placed by William Ashley and Andrew Henry, were a tough lot, well deserving of their popular moniker: mountain men. South Pass was rediscovered in 1823, and Jim Bridger found the Great Salt Lake in 1825, perhaps at the same time as Ogden or Étienne Provost, a trapper from Taos. But the most famous of all the mountain men was Jedediah Strong Smith, who between 1823 and 1831 crisscrossed the West. In 1826 he explored west from the Great Salt Lake looking for the mythical Buenaventura River. The same year he went down the Sevier River of central Utah, the Virgin River, and the Colorado before setting out across the Mojave Desert—still looking for the Buenaventura—reaching the San Joaquin Valley. The following year he crossed the Sierra Nevada, going east through Ebbetts Pass and undertaking an epic crossing of the Great Basin in thirty-two days, surprising his fellow trappers at their annual rendezvous on the Bear River in Utah. Only ten days later he set out again, retracing his path down the Colorado and across the Mojave, where he was attacked by Indians, who killed ten of his men.

Map 139 (*above*).
Peter Skene Ogden's map of his fifth expedition, in 1828–29, oriented with north approximately at top. Fort Walla Walla, Ogden's starting point, is at top, and the Snake River is at top and center right. At left, bottom, the Humboldt River flows across the Great Basin to Humboldt Lake in the Carson Sink area. At this location are the words (here upside down) *280 Indian seen Camp attacked*. The Humboldt was the nearest thing to a Buenaventura River (see page 42) that actually existed, but of course it ended before reaching the Sierra Nevada, reflecting the fact that the Great Basin is a closed drainage area. The Humboldt Valley later became part of the California Trail. After Ogden's fifth and sixth expeditions (the latter in 1829–30), the British gradually withdrew north.

Map 140 (*below*).
This map by Adrien Brué, published in 1839, shows various *Route[s] de Smith*—routes of Jedediah Smith.

In California he was arrested on orders from the Mexican governor, who thought him a spy. Smith escaped north to San Francisco Bay by ship, then headed farther north along the Sacramento and along the coast to the Umpqua River, learning that the Multnomah River—the Willamette—was just to the north. On the Umpqua, in July 1828, he was again attacked by Indians; this time fourteen of his men perished. Smith and three others escaped north and sought sanctuary at the Hudson's Bay Company post at Fort Vancouver. Despite the best efforts of Governor Simpson, Smith's reports made it clear the region was very suitable for settlement. Within twenty years, American settlers would pour into the Oregon Country.

RUSSIA IN CALIFORNIA

The Americans were not the only ones interested in the West Coast; the Russian-American Company, headquartered at Novo Archangel'sk (Sitka), also cast a covetous eye on the region to the south as a possible source of food to supply its northern posts.

After extensive reconnaissance, the Russians built temporary structures at Bodega Bay in 1809, as a base from which Aleut hunters in kayaks were sent out to hunt sea otters. In 1812 the Russians purchased land farther up the coast—so as to be more remote from Spanish settlements—from the local Kashaya Indians. Here they built a stockaded post that they named *Rossiia*—Russia—which quickly became known to others as Fort Ross.

Although ordered to remove the Russians in 1819, the commandant of the San Francisco presidio refused, saying he lacked the military strength. But new missions at San Rafael and Solano were established in 1817 and 1823 as supposed buffers against further Russian encroachments. The little Russian colony in fact never did very well, owing mainly to its isolation; the

Map 141 (*right, top*).
A Russian map of the northern California coast in 1817. Fort Ross is at the top, Bodega Bay at center, and Tomales Point, at the entrance to Tomales Bay, at bottom.

Map 142 (*right, center inset*).
A plan of Fort Ross, also drawn in 1817. *A* is the fort itself, with the blockhouses at the top left and bottom right. Other polygons are gardens, some with habitations, mainly along the stream flowing into Ross Cove. The serrated-type lines represent the edges of an otherwise reasonably flat coastal terrace.

Map 143 (*right, bottom*).
This French map dated 1845 shows *Étabt. Russe* (Russian Establishment) as if a separate country in California. *Ross* is marked on the coast.

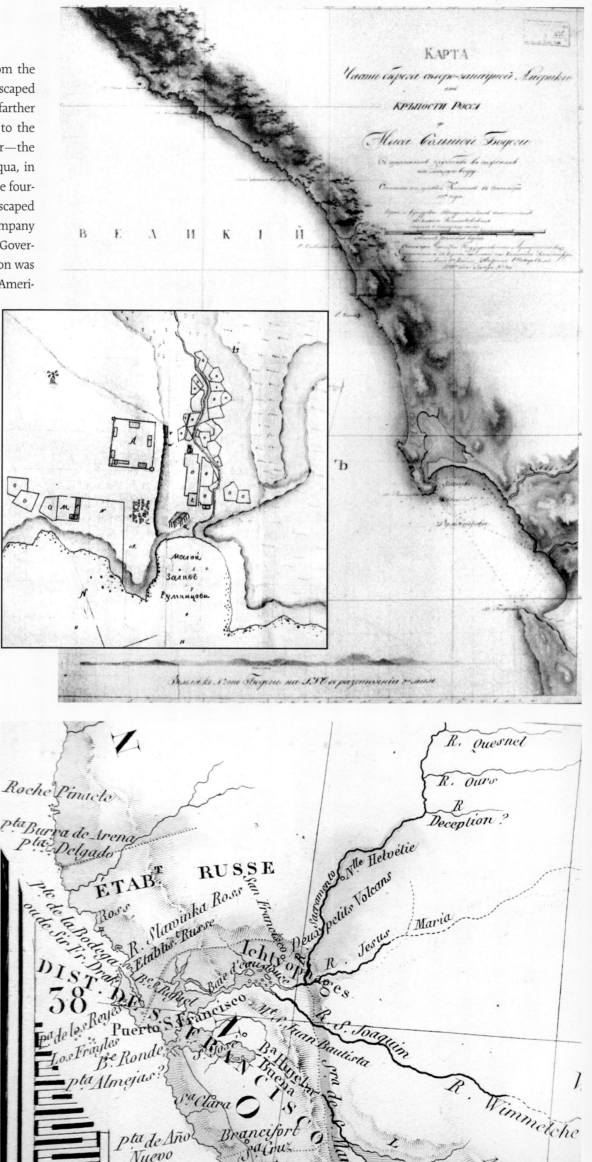

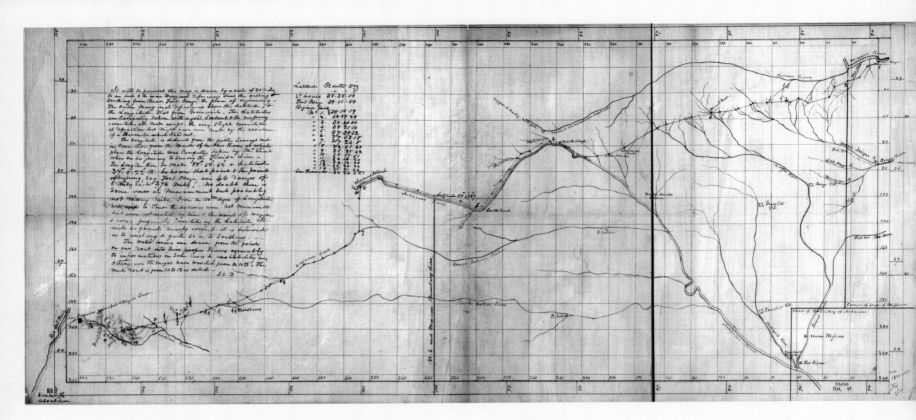

Russians were never a threat because they numbered at most four hundred, including their Aleut hunters.

Eventually the fort became so unprofitable that in 1841 the Russian-American Company sold everything movable to entrepreneur and colonist John Augustus Sutter, and he moved cattle, buildings, and a schooner to his rancho at Fort Sutter, in today's Sacramento.

THE MEXICAN WEST

In 1821 Mexican revolutionaries finally succeeded in toppling the Spanish regime in New Spain, and the country became Mexico. The Mexican government was much more open to trade than the Spanish had been, and a long line of traders began to frequent Santa Fe. William Becknell, who led a trading party there in 1821, expected problems but was one of the first to find the new welcome.

The route from the Missouri to Santa Fe, the Santa Fe Trail, crossing the region so recently mapped by Stephen Long (see page 73), became the principal trading route; President James Monroe soon ordered it surveyed and mapped (MAP 144, *above*).

Life in the Mexican West was not much different from that under Spanish rule. In Alta California, pueblo status was granted in 1834 to the settlements that had grown up around the presidios at San Francisco, Santa Barbara, San Diego, Monterey, and Sonoma. The documentation was not always what it should have been, leading to later problems after the American takeover; the pueblo lands surrounding San Francisco, for example, were not confirmed until 1884. Those of San Diego took until 1874.

The Mexican government stepped up the Spanish policy of granting land to favored applicants in its frontier provinces. Some huge land grants

MAP 145 (*right*).
Spanish explorer and mapmaker José María Narváez continued to work in Mexico after the revolution and in 1830 updated his 1823 map of Spanish California (MAP 81, *page 48*). For the first time the Central Valley is clearly depicted between the coast ranges and the Sierra Nevada, although it is shown as a closed basin; the Sacramento and San Joaquin are but short streams. Narváez should have known better because by this time those rivers had been explored inland much farther than he indicates. A large area of *Cienagas*, or marshland, is shown covering the entire northern side of the Central Valley. The *Establecimiento Ruso*, Fort Ross, is in the top left corner. Missions, presidios, and other settlements are also shown. At top right is a population table listing a total of 23,676 for all Alta California.

MAP 144 (*above*).
Soon after Mexico took over New Mexico and allowed trade with the United States, President James Monroe commissioned Joseph Brown to survey the Santa Fe Trail. This is Brown's map, drawn in 1825. Clearly Brown did not survey all the way to Santa Fe, for at bottom left, the city is marked with the words *Santa Fe about here*. Indeed, he shows it at 105° W when it is actually at 106° W. At top right is the *Missouri* and *Fort Osage* (just east of today's Kansas City), the starting point for the trail, which meets the *Arkansas River* near the middle of the map, then cuts south to *Simarron Creek* (the Cimarron River, a more southerly branch of the Arkansas) at about 101° W, before cutting across the headwaters of the *Canadian River* and crossing the *Divid'g Ridge* (between Mississippi and Rio Grande waters) to *San Fernando* and the *Rio del Norte*, at bottom left.

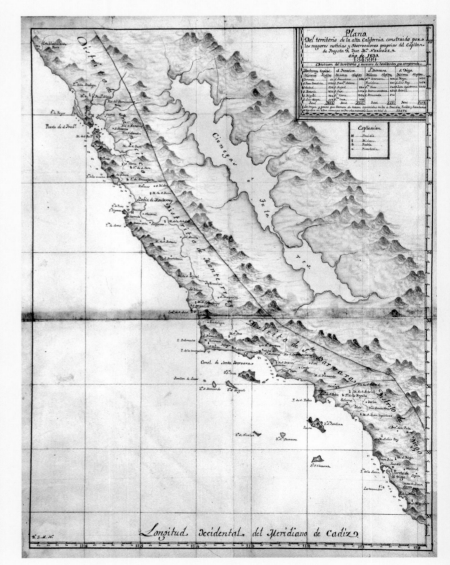

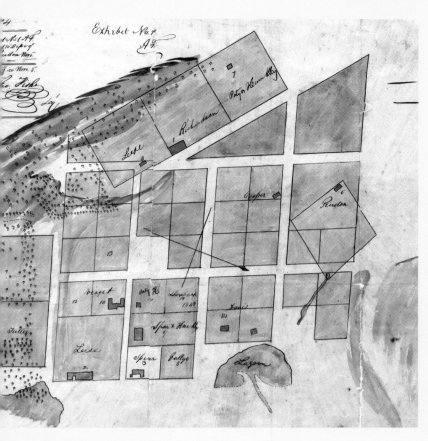

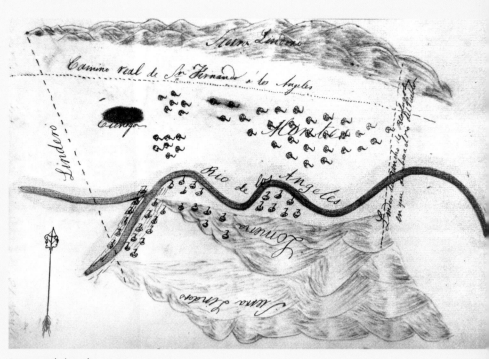

Map 146 (*above*).

The Mexican settlement of Yerba Buena was surveyed in 1839 by Jean Jacques Vioget, a Swiss engineer and resident. William Richardson, an Englishman, settled here in 1835, trading with visiting ships. Town lots were sold from 1836. North is to the right; the bottom street (unnamed) on this map is Montgomery Street, then on the waterfront.

Map 147 (*above*).

Rancho Providencia, just over four thousand acres in the San Fernando Valley, was granted to Vicente de la Ossa in 1843. The area now forms the southwestern part of the city of Burbank, within the Los Angeles metropolitan area. The *Rio de los Angeles* runs through the grant. The *Camino real de San Fernando a los Angeles* is now followed by the San Fernando Road and part of Interstate 5.

Map 148 (*below*).

Rancho San Miguelito de Trinidad, 22,135 acres in southern Monterey County, California, was granted to Lieutenant José Rafael Gonzalez, a veteran of the Mexican revolutionary war, in 1842. This map of the rancho is perhaps the most artistic of all the Mexican land claim maps, the *diseños*.

MAP OF
THE
SANGRE DE CRISTO GRANT.

SITUATE IN

SAN LUIS VALLE,

COLORADO TERRITORY.

R. FISHER, CIVIL ENG.   SCALE OF MILES   ○ DENOTES PUEBLO

were made during the Mexican period. The idea was to encourage the growth of a population loyal to Mexico in the regions where there might be expansionist pressure from its neighbor, the United States. Owners were expected to improve their land, patrol its boundaries, and defend it against any foreign attack. But the ownership of land carried with it considerable social status. Mexican land grants were usually defined in terms of geographical features: a mountaintop, a river, and so on, and often in less than exact terms. Often no surveyor was available, and so applicants might provide their own rough sketch map, called a *diseño,* to show the area they wished to claim. These created boundary definition problems in many cases after the more exact American system of land tenure took over. The United States agreed to honor existing land holdings, and the maps were needed for the legal process—but then were preserved as legal documents. Thus in California there exist a few hundred of these *diseños* that document the Mexican West in a way nothing else does (MAP 147 and MAP 148, *previous page*).

The Mexican government also marked out lands north and east of Santa Fe for land grants, as it tried to create a population buffer near the new American boundary. Lands east of the Sangre de Cristo Mountains and in the headwaters of the Rio Grande were granted between 1833 and 1843, although most of the earlier attempts at settlement failed because of attacks by Navajo or Ute. Two large grants in New Mexico and what is now southern Colorado are illustrated here (MAP 149, *left,* and MAP 150, *right*). In some places the rights of early Mexican settlers, guaranteed by the Treaty of Guadalupe Hidalgo (see page 91) came into conflict with later American owners, a conflict that has not entirely been resolved today.

MAP 150 (*right*).
The *Maxwell Land Grant* has a history so complex and convoluted that entire books have been written about it and it has been used in case studies of the conflict between Mexican and later American property rights. Once again, the map shown here is later than the original grant and includes lands added to the property up to 1870. The map was drawn up to promote railways (shown in red) through the grant, which is, in the northwestern part, adjacent to the Sangre de Cristo Grant. The Maxwell Grant was one of the largest grants, totaling over 1.7 million acres. The land was originally granted by Governor Armijo to Carlos Beaubien and Guadalupe Miranda in 1841 after receiving a petition in which the pair promised to develop the property and grow, among other crops, sugar beet. But not much was done. Later Beaubien's son-in-law, Lucien Maxwell, took over running the estate and expended far more effort building up its business, driving herds of sheep to California, growing crops where none had grown before, and raising 15,000 head of cattle. In 1864 Maxwell bought out the other heirs and co-owners. In 1866, gold was discovered on Baldy Mountain, further increasing Maxwell's wealth, but he invested in an irrigation scheme that did not work properly, invested in a bank that failed, and invested in the Texas & Pacific Railway, which had financing difficulties (see pages 131 and 133). Maxwell sold his interest in the grant in 1870, and the land was rapidly sold twice more, ending up in the hands of a Dutch enterprise that tried to aggressively market the land to new settlers, overriding any claims of existing settlers, who were technically squatters. Enlisting the help of influential Santa Fe lawyers, the so-called Santa Fe Ring used often dubious methods to try to force settlers off the land. The resulting melee, dubbed the Colfax County War, featured gunmen, vigilantes, and shoot-outs, and quite a few people were killed. It was the Wild West at its wildest.

Elizabeth Town was founded in 1867 to service gold mines near *Baldy Mt.,* all shown on the map. The settlement declined rapidly after 1917, when the mines closed. *Maxwell,* now incorporated into *Cimarron,* was the first town with this name in New Mexico; today's Maxwell, farther east, is the third town to have the name. Springer, on today's Interstate 25, was the second. Lucien Maxwell named *Virginia City* after one of his daughters. Note the *Telegraph and Gt. Southern Overland Mail Route.*

Left. The San Luis Valley, looking east to the Sangre de Cristo Mountains.

MAP 149 (*above*).
The *Sangre de Cristo Grant* covered a huge area east of the Upper Rio Grande, including the San Luis Valley, principally in what is now Colorado but with the southern part in New Mexico. This is a later map, dating from 1882, which delineated the estate of the Colorado Freehold Land Association, which represented only the portion of the grant in Colorado Territory. A company called the Colorado Freehold Land and Emigration Company had been formed in the Netherlands in 1869 to purchase the northern part of the grant. The original grant, well over one million acres, was given by New Mexico governor Manuel Armijo to Stephen Luis Lee and Narciso Beaubien in a document dated 27 December 1843, but both were killed in the Taos Revolt in 1847 (see page 88). Narciso Beaubien's father, Carlos, leased the site for Fort Massachusetts, later known as *Fort Garland* (shown at top, center), to the U.S. Army in 1852. The Beaubien family was recognized as the owner by the U.S. government in 1860. A later owner, territorial governor William Gilpin, divided the estate in half so that it could be sold, but there was little recognition of the rights of existing settlers, and litigation continues to this day. A recent case pitted the common land rights of original settlers against a landowner who wished to fence in his land. Interestingly, the settlement of San Luis (near *Culebra*) is not specifically named on this map, possibly because the later European owners, for whom this map was drawn, failed even in 1882 to recognize the existing rights of its inhabitants. San Luis was settled in April 1851 by fifty families brought in by Beaubien and is today the oldest surviving settlement in Colorado. The first irrigation project in Colorado, the San Luis People's Ditch, was dug here in 1852.

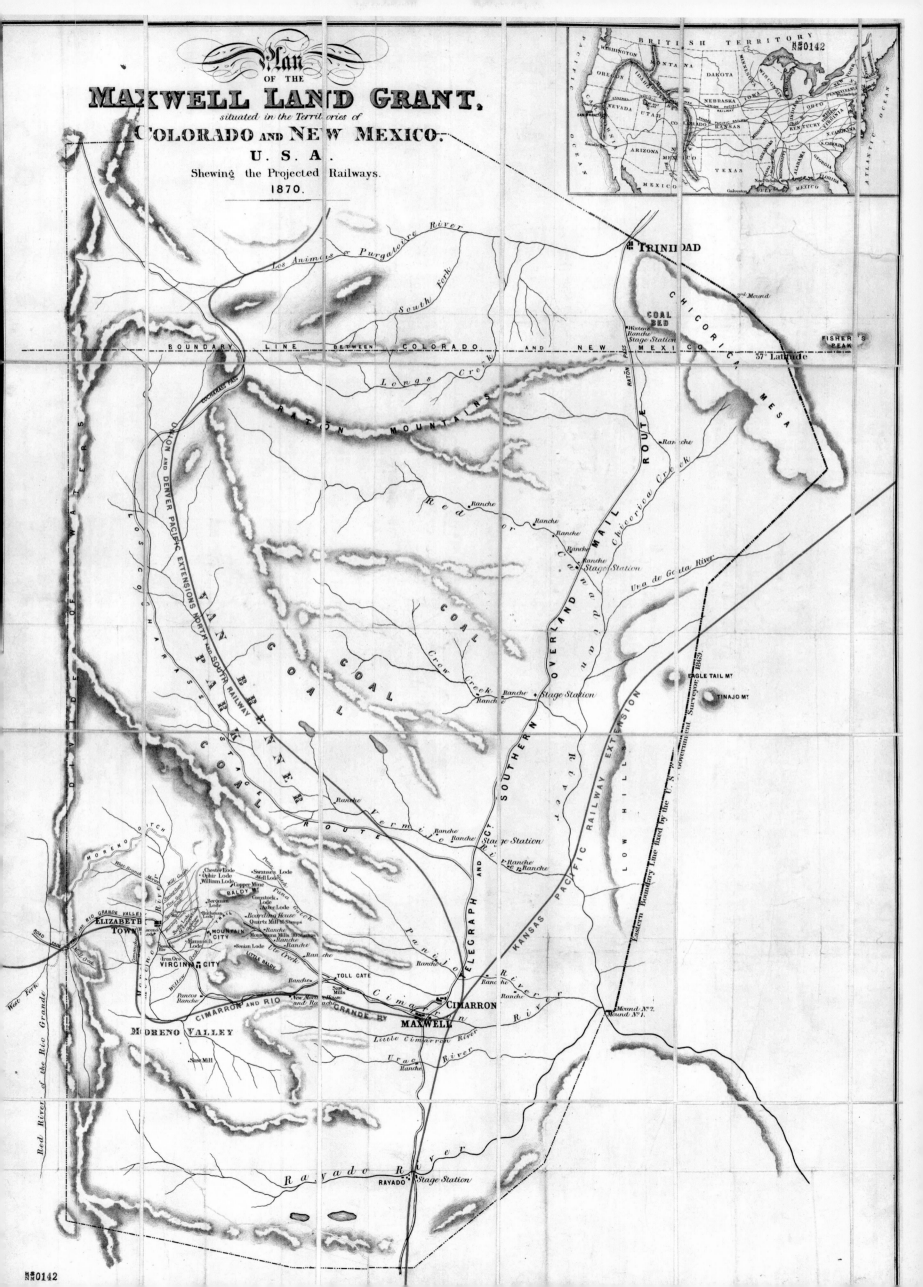

Even larger land grants were also made in the Spanish province of Tejas. Although the concept originated with the Spanish, most were made during the early Mexican era. Spain, and Mexico, could not persuade its own citizens to move to the relatively dangerous and inhospitable frontier of Texas and so made the decision—a very poor one, perhaps, in the light of later history—to encourage foreign immigration. Land was granted to empresarios who would be responsible for settling and supervising colonists.

EuroAmericans were attracted to Texas by that ongoing western prize—the lure of cheap land. Many pioneers expected that one day the United States would annex Texas and that this development would result in windfall profits for them. Some were fugitives from defaulted farm loans.

In 1820 Moses Austin, an Arkansas merchant, was granted 200,000 acres in return for his promise to settle three hundred families. He died before he could take up the grant, but his son, Stephen Fuller Austin, did take it up and even managed to get it expanded. He was the first of about twenty empresarios granted land in Texas over the next dozen years. Empresarios did not own the land directly but, acting as intermediaries, could allocate it to their settlers; the state gave land to the empresarios personally in proportion to the number of settlers they brought in. Many empresarios formed land companies to facilitate the attraction of settlers. Colonists were sup-

posed to be Catholic and were required to become Mexican citizens, but many failed to do so. After 1830 Mexico thought better of its immigration policy and halted further immigration to Texas. Despite the prohibition, Austin managed to obtain an exemption from the new law and even gain its repeal three years later. But the prohibition gave the colonists the idea that they might be better off without the restrictions of Mexican law.

THE REPUBLIC OF TEXAS

At a convention in San Felipe in 1833, the colonists drew up a proposed new constitution for Tejas as a separate Mexican state, persuading a reluctant Stephen Austin to take it to Mexico City. There Austin found himself clapped in jail for supposed treason, fanning flames of revolution back home. Austin was released in July 1835 and returned to a Texas on the brink of revolt. A ragtag Texian (American Texan) army, ill-disciplined but nonetheless determined, was assembled, and it managed to capture San Antonio de Béxar, the capital, in December.

The Texians took control of the Alamo, a mission established in 1718 and used as a fortress since 1803. By February 1836 volunteers had reinforced the Alamo garrison, now led by William Barret Travis. The Texian success was short-lived, however, for the Mexican president, Antonio López de Santa Anna, was determined to teach them a lesson; he assembled a six thousand–strong army and marched on the Alamo. Although the Texian side was growing in strength, its principal army, led by Samuel Houston, was not yet in a position to break through the sizable Mexican force.

The attack on the Alamo (MAP 154, *overleaf*) on 6 March is the stuff of legend; about 250 defenders—including the famous American frontiersman Davy Crockett—bravely tried to fend off the overwhelming Mexican army and died almost to a man for their yet unborn nation. For Santa Anna, determined to wipe out any revolt against his authority, and thinking he had found a way to prevent American intervention, had at the end of 1835 passed a decree that stated that all foreigners taken in arms against the government would be treated as pirates and shot.

This brutal policy was also implemented later in March when nearly 340 Texian prisoners, captured after battles at Refugio on

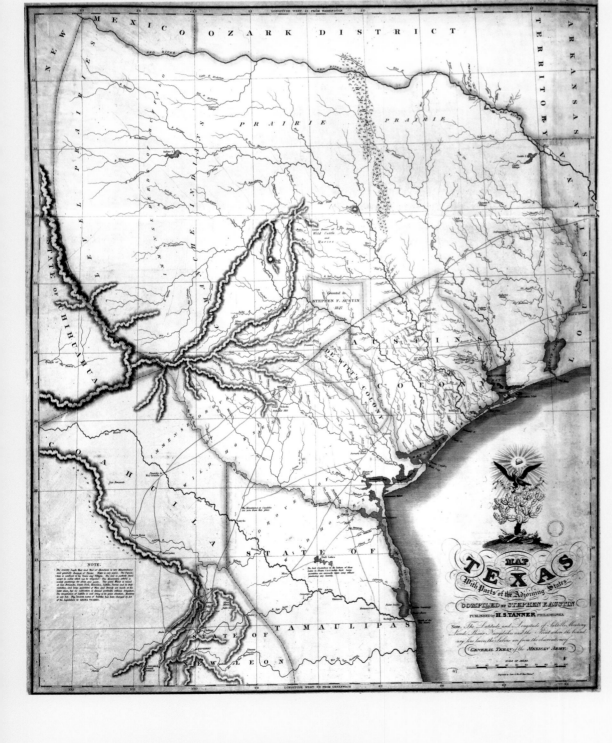

MAP 151 (*left*).
This map, published by commercial mapmaker Henry S. Tanner in 1830, used information compiled by Stephen Austin. It shows the land *Granted to Stephen F. Austin 1827* and *Austins Colony*. Land granted in 1825 to Green DeWitt, from Missouri, is shown as *De Witt's Colony*. The Mexican province of Tejas extends south to the Nueces River, with the *State of Coahuila* and *State of Tamaulipas* south of it. The northwestern part of *Texas* is *Level Prairie* and has the notations *Comanche Indians* and *Immense Herds of Buffalo*.

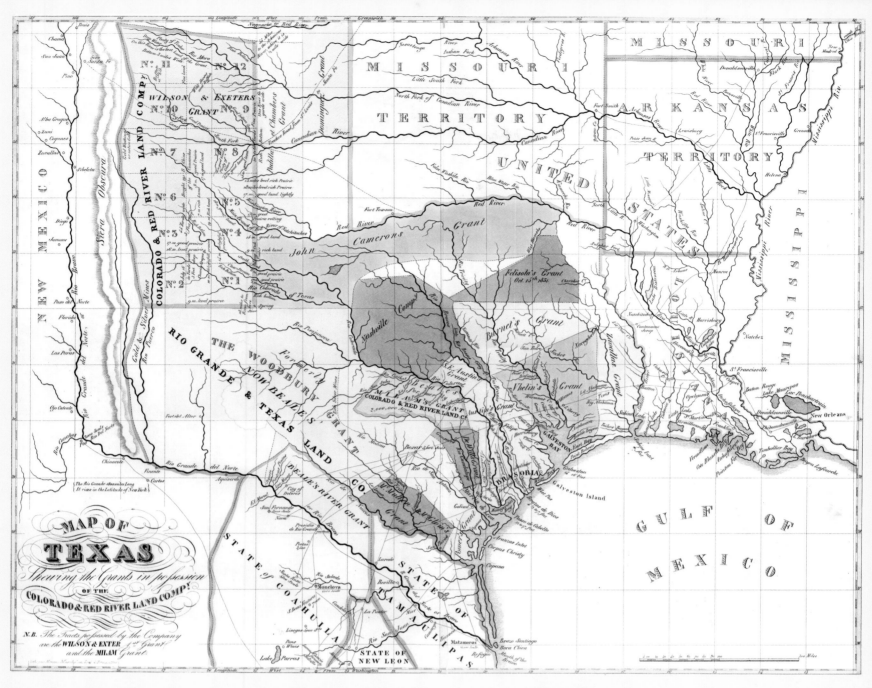

MAP OF TEXAS

Shewing the Grants in possession

OF THE

COLORADO & RED RIVER LAND COMP.Y

N.B. *The Tracts possessed by the Company are the* WILSON & EXETER *Grant and the* MILAM *Grant.*

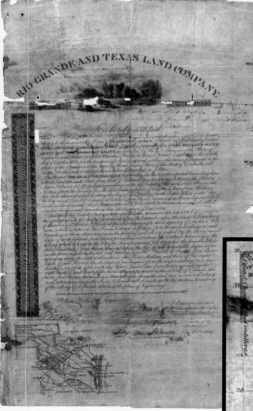

MAP 153 (*left and below*).

This document, complete with map at bottom left (enlarged below), is a regranting of lands in a grant to a prospective settler. The original grants of the tracts shown as *The Woodbury Grant* and *Beales's River Grant* were from the Mexican state of Coahuila and Texas to John Charles Beales and the appropriately named James Grant and dated 9 October 1832. This document is from another company John Beales was involved with, the Rio Grande and Texas Land Company. It conveyed one thousand acres of the grant lands to Roger G. Little two years later, on 21 August 1834.

MAP 152 (*above*).

Speculative land companies purchased some of the Texan land grants with the intention of reselling them to settlers at a profit. This *Map of Texas Shewing the Grants in Possession of the Colorado & Red River Land Comp.y*, was drawn up and attached to a share certificate for one of the investors in this land speculation company. Two tracts belonging to the company are both shown in red. This land company had been sold land by John Charles Beales, an English physician who had married the widow of Richard Exeter. Exeter had joined with Mexico City merchant Stephen Wilson in an 1826 land grant (known as the Wilson and Exeter Land Grant) that had included a third of the territory of today's state of New Mexico. Part of this grant was sold to the Colorado and Red River Company and is here also marked *Wilson & Exeters Grant. Milam's Grant*, also purchased by the company, was originally granted to Benjamin R. Milam in 1826. The map also shows the lands of the *Rio Grande & Texas Land Co.* (MAP 153, left). North of *S.E. [sic] Austin's Grant* is that of the *Nashville Comp.y*, a group of investors from Nashville, Tennessee, who called themselves the Texas Association. Stephen Austin's loose translation of their petition to the Mexican government resulted in a grant made out to the Nashville Company. Such was the inexactitude of Mexican land grants.

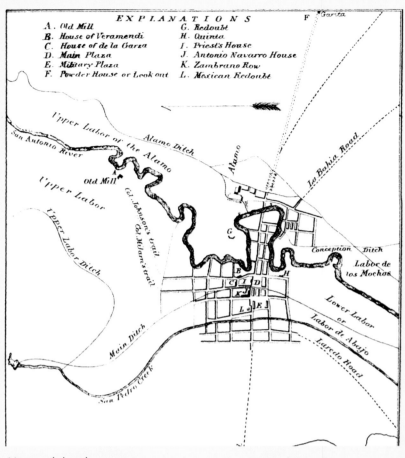

MAP 154 (above).
The *Alamo* and the surrounding area, shown in a map of San Antonio drawn in 1855 for a history of Texas. Note the irrigation ditches.

MAP 155 (below).
One of the very few eyewitness maps of the critical Battle of San Jacinto, this was drawn by James Monroe Hill in 1897. At the time of the battle, Hill served in the First Regiment, Texas Volunteers. *Houstons Encampment* is at left, backed by *Buffalow Bayou,* which flows into the San Jacinto River, at top. At left center is *Houston line of march* and at center the site of the *Battle.*

14 March and Coleto Creek five days later, were shot at Goliad after being led to believe they would be set free. The Goliad Massacre, as it came to be called, would only strengthen the resolve of the Texians—and ensure that in the future they would fight to the death. Santa Anna would come to regret his brutality.

On 19 April 1836 Santa Anna's army found the 910-strong Texian army led by Sam Houston at a place on the San Jacinto River fifteen miles east of today's downtown Houston. Santa Anna thought that the Texians, with their backs to the river, were trapped, and so, expecting reinforcements, he decided to wait until the next day. Skirmishes began, however, and in one of these Private Mirabeau Buonaparte Lamar rescued two surrounded Texians. The next day he was promoted to colonel and placed in charge of the cavalry.

Santa Anna's reinforcements duly arrived, and the Mexicans now numbered about 1,300, but still he delayed. Houston seized the opportunity, leading a surprise attack on the overconfident Santa Anna during the Mexicans' siesta that afternoon. To cries of "Remember the Alamo" and "Remember Goliad," it took less than twenty minutes of fierce fighting to ensure the freedom of Texas. It was a bloodbath, with the Texians in a retaliatory mood. Houston tried but could not control his men. "Gentlemen, I applaud your bravery but damn your manners!" he is reputed to have shouted.

Santa Anna had slipped away once it became apparent that the battle was lost but was discovered later during a roundup of stragglers, dressed as a private. One might have thought Santa Anna would have been roughly treated, even slaughtered on the spot, given what he was responsible for, but Houston was in command again and traded Santa Anna's life for the removal of all troops from Texas and a treaty recognizing Texas's independence. The first condition was carried out; the second was not. Santa Anna would show up again ten years later, this time pitted against the United States (see page 89).

Stephen Austin had in the interim approached the United States with the proposal that Texas join the Union as a state, only to be rebuffed, a victim

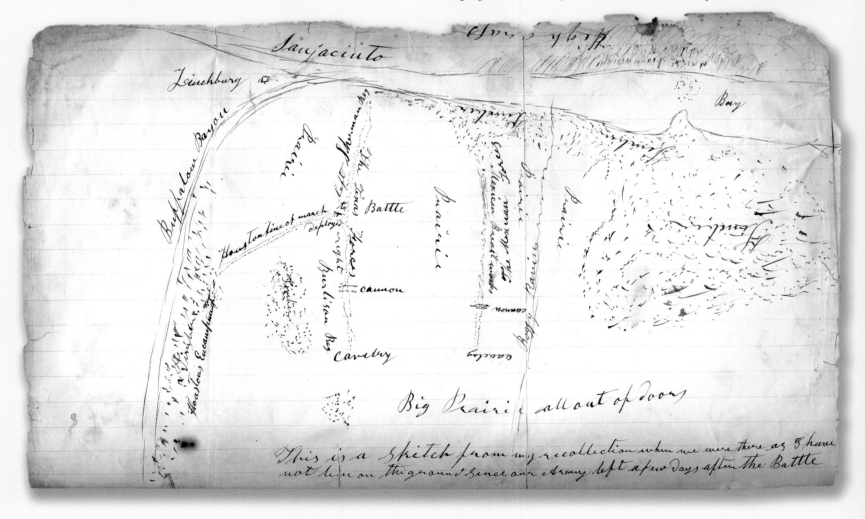

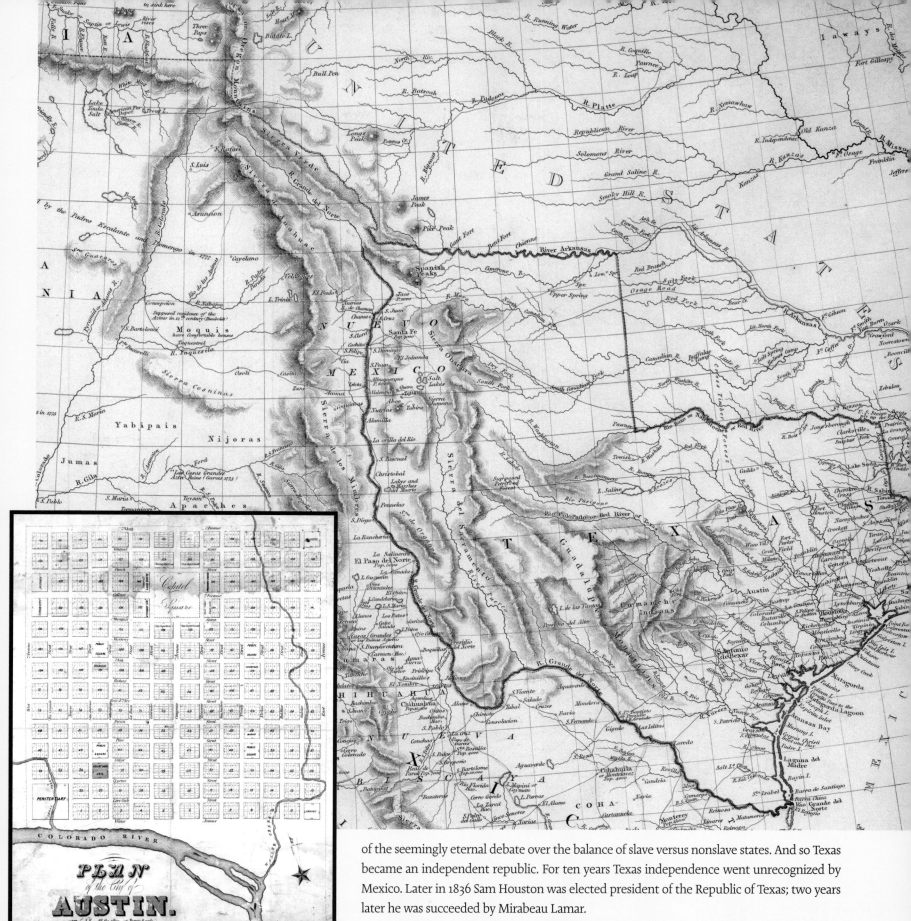

MAP 156 (*above, top*).
The Republic of Texas in 1842. Note the boundary in the northwest, following the assumed line according to the Transcontinental Treaty of 1819 and including much of New Mexico. Once Texas joined the United States the federal government would compensate Texas for lost land as part of a boundary readjustment (see page 182). Note that the southern boundary, never recognized by Mexico, is the *R. Grande del Norte* rather than the *R. Nueces* farther north.

MAP 157 (*above, inset*).
The small settlement of Waterloo was renamed in 1839, and a much larger capital for the republic was laid out, named Austin in honor of Stephen Austin.

of the seemingly eternal debate over the balance of slave versus nonslave states. And so Texas became an independent republic. For ten years Texas independence went unrecognized by Mexico. Later in 1836 Sam Houston was elected president of the Republic of Texas; two years later he was succeeded by Mirabeau Lamar.

Lamar is perhaps best known for his prosecution of war against the Indians. The Cherokee were driven to Arkansas in 1839, and in 1840 the Comanche were defeated at Plum Creek, twenty miles south of Austin, and then pursued to their villages in what is now northern New Mexico.

Sam Houston favored annexation with the United States, while Lamar was for an independent republic. When Houston was reelected in 1841, he directed his secretary of state, Anson Jones, to work for annexation or, failing that, a recognition of the republic by Mexico. In November 1844 the expansionist American president James Polk was elected. One of his platforms was the annexation of Texas, but before he took office, the retiring president, John Tyler, signed the bill authorizing the admission of Texas. Three months later, through a British diplomat, Charles Elliot, Mexico guaranteed Texas independence. (Britain thought an independent Texas to be in its own interest.) Jones, since September 1844 president of Texas, put the two options to a vote, and annexation won. On 29 December 1845 Texas became the twenty-eighth state of the United States.

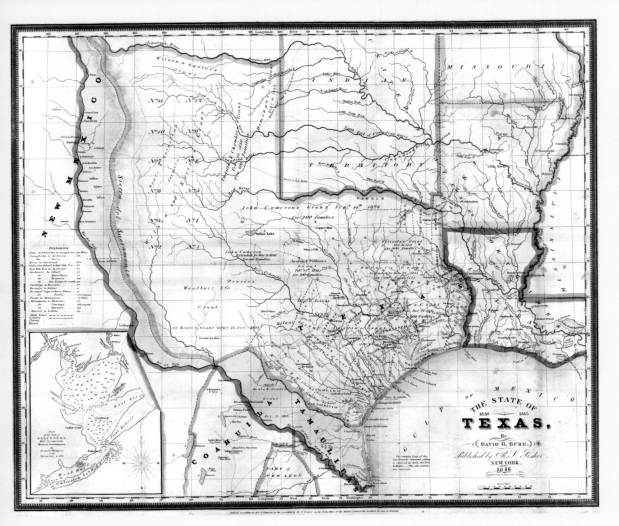

During the republican period, land continued to be granted. Four empresario contracts were established with the Texas government between 1841 and 1844. Bounty grants for military service during the Texas Revolution were issued at the rate of 320 acres for every three months of service. In addition land was granted for fighting in specific battles—640 acres per battle—and between 1838 and 1842 for guarding the new border with Mexico. Over 6.5 million acres of land were dispensed in this fashion.

THE OREGON QUESTION

In the Northwest after 1819, when Spain had retreated south of the 42° N line, the northern boundary of today's California, the United States did not gain clear title, for Britain still claimed Oregon. A convention the previous year had established a boundary between the United States and British territory along the forty-ninth parallel, but only as far west as the Rockies. West of that point the Oregon Country, which consisted of most of today's Canadian province of British Columbia as well as the Pacific Northwest, was designated an area of joint occupancy—one in which the citizens of both countries were free to live until such time as a boundary might be agreed upon (MAP 160, right).

In 1838 expansionist senator Lewis Linn of Missouri introduced a bill to annex Oregon, and a map attached to the document showed

MAP 158 (*above*).
The 1846 edition of the first map of Texas depicted as a state of the United States. As with many commercial maps at this time, it is an updated version of a series of previous maps drawn by David Burr, who later became official geographer to the U.S. Senate. The base map was quite out of date, showing only Mexican land grants and not those from the Republic of Texas. Disputed territory between the Rio Grande (here *Rio Grande del Norte or Rio Bravo*) and the Nueces River (here *River Nuces*) is shown in yellow. It would take the upcoming war with Mexico to resolve the ownership of this disputed strip in favor of the United States. A crossed-swords symbol and the word *Alamo 1836* depict the site of the battle—but incorrectly on the Rio Grande.

MAP 159 (*below*).
Attached to Senator Lewis Linn's bill to occupy Oregon in 1838 was this map by Washington Hood, boldly entitled *United States Territory of Oregon*. The details had been copied from a British map published in 1832.

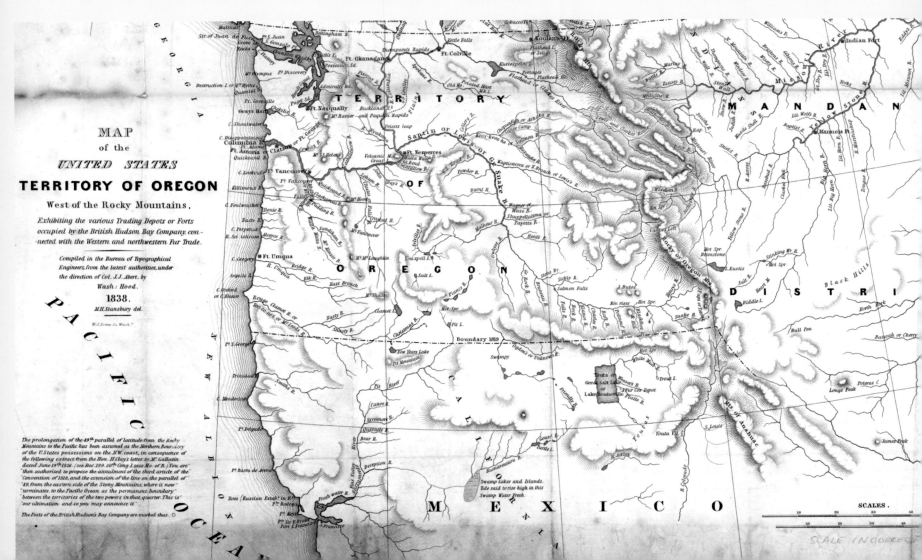

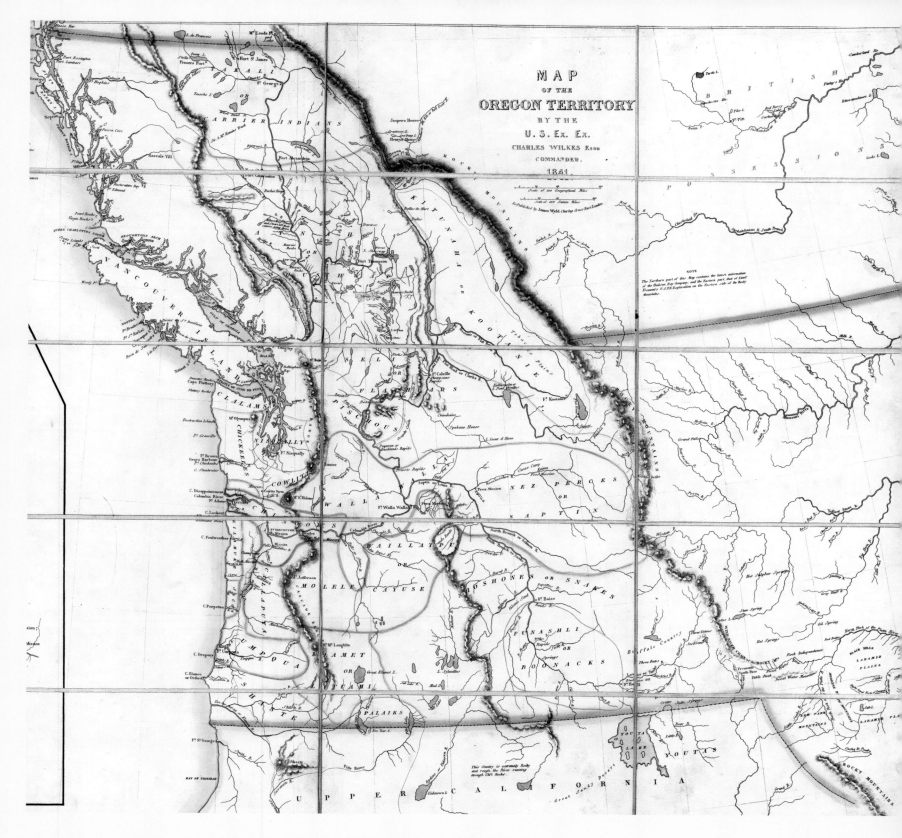

MAP OF THE OREGON TERRITORY BY THE U. S. Ex. Ex. CHARLES WILKES Esqr COMMANDER. 1841

the forty-ninth parallel extended west through Vancouver Island to the Pacific (MAP 159, *left*). Linn's bill was not able to garner enough support to pass.

Ultimately it was the increasing flow of emigrants to Oregon (see page 95) that focused American attention on the boundary issue. The only Britons that lived in the region were those involved in the fur trade, most employed by the Hudson's Bay Company based at Fort Vancouver. Indeed, Senator John C. Calhoun remarked in 1843 that the United States government should pursue a policy of "wise and masterly inactivity" in order to let settlement determine the eventual boundary.

The issue was picked up by expansionist Democrats in 1844, who called for both annexation of Texas and "the whole" of Oregon. James Polk was elected president in November 1844—taking office in March 1845—on an aggressive platform of annexation. And at this time, New York journalist John L. O'Sullivan coined the term "Manifest Destiny"—really a useful label for the sentiments of the times—to define America's right to the West to the exclusion of other powers.

The die was cast. Not only was Texas annexed but war begun with Mexico—a war that would gain the United States most of the West. And

MAP 160 (*above*).

The United States Exploring Expedition (1838–42), led by Charles Wilkes, was a naval scientific voyage around the world, a belated American answer to the voyages of Britain's James Cook, Spain's Alejandro Malaspina, France's Comte de La Pérouse, and Russia's Urei Lisianski. One of the objectives of the expedition was to examine the resources of the Oregon Country, which was reached on the final leg of the voyage in 1841. The report of the expedition, published in 1844, was a major influence on American policy in the region. One of the expedition's ships, the *Peacock*, had floundered trying to cross the bar at the mouth of the Columbia, and the need for a better harbor was apparent; one was found in Puget Sound, farther north. The United States became unwilling to agree to any boundary resolution that did not include Puget Sound. This map, also published in 1844, by British mapmaker James Wyld, is a direct copy of Wilkes's map,

a treaty was hammered out with Britain to divide the Oregon Country at the forty-ninth parallel, except on Vancouver Island. British foreign secretary George Hamilton-Gordon, Earl of Aberdeen, saw little value for Britain in Oregon except for the interests of the Hudson's Bay Company, which was allowed continued navigation on the Columbia. The United States seemed to be becoming increasingly willing to commit to military activ-

ity to enforce its claims—and was about to in Mexico—and Aberdeen did not want to have to deal with that. The rallying cry "Fifty-four-forty or fight" (54° 40´ N, the southern tip of Alaska) appeared in the American press in January 1846. Aberdeen quickly worked out a deal with the American minister in Britain, Louis McLane, sending it to the United States, where British minister Richard Pakenham and Secretary of State James Buchanan drew up the formal Oregon Treaty, which was ratified by the Senate on 18 June 1846. America now stretched from Atlantic to Pacific.

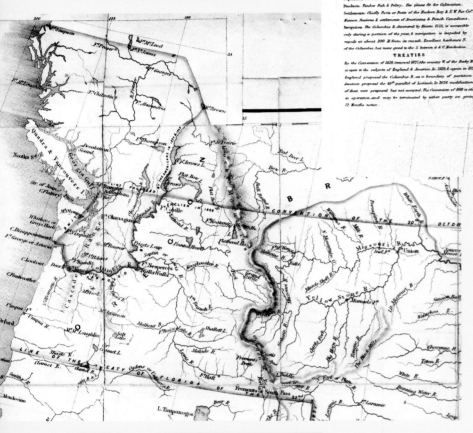

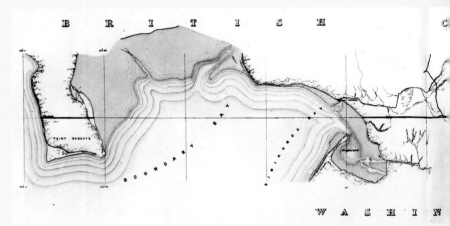

MAP 161 (*right, top*).
A British map published in 1846 to summarize the "Oregon Question"—the dispute over the Oregon Country. A thin red line delineates the American proposal for an extension of the forty-ninth parallel boundary to the Pacific, dissecting Vancouver Island. This division was especially unacceptable to the Hudson's Bay Company, which, seeing the writing on the wall, had established a new fort on the island (Fort Victoria, in 1843) that would, in 1849, become its new headquarters, replacing the lost Fort Vancouver on the Columbia.

MAP 162 (*above, left*).
Various boundary proposals and claims shown on a map by James Wyld in 1845. Had Britain held its resolve, the red boundary, down the Columbia (originally proposed by Britain in 1826), might well have been agreed to by the American side, as few settlers were at that time living north of the river. One British proposal (in 1844) was to allow the United States to have the detached territory of the Olympic Peninsula, separated here by a green line, allowing Britain to keep Puget Sound, a proposal clearly unsatisfactory to the American negotiators following Charles Wilkes's report.

MAP 163 (*above, right*).
A detailed survey of the boundary was not attempted until 1858. Here the surveyed line crosses *Semiahmoo Bay* and *Boundary Bay* in northwestern Washington. The boundary cut off Point Roberts, which to this day remains an island of the American West only reachable through Canada.

MAP 164 (*left*).
The Oregon Treaty stated that the boundary would follow the "middle of the Channel" in southern Georgia Strait, but it was not until 1872, following arbitration by the emperor of Germany, that the boundary was fixed to include the San Juan Islands as part of the United States. For twelve years prior to that, British and American army detachments faced each other on San Juan Island. Here the three possible boundaries are shown; the westernmost is the one that was selected.

AN AMERICAN WEST

Mexico had sworn that American annexation of Texas would lead to war and in the summer of 1845 looked set to make good its word. President James Polk could not have asked for a better pretext, ordering General Zachary Taylor and an army of 3,500 men to the Rio Grande. A formal declaration of war came much later, on 13 May 1846, only after hostilities had commenced.

The war was won in California first. Secret plans for the seizure of ports and an organized revolt of settlers were preempted by the arrival in California in January 1846 of the explorer John Charles Frémont, bent on glory. He raised the American flag near Monterey before retreating to the Oregon borderlands, where he heard of the Bear Flag Revolt, an uprising of American settlers. He rushed back and assumed leadership of the rebels. The U.S. Pacific Squadron, acting on its previous orders, seized Monterey and San Francisco. Its commander, Commodore Robert Field Stockton, who seems to have been as much in search of personal glory as Frémont, joined in an uneasy liaison with the latter and set off to take Los Angeles and San Diego. On 17 August 1846 Stockton announced the American annexation of California and proclaimed himself governor.

Meanwhile, Polk dispatched Colonel Stephen Watts Kearny with about 1,600 men—what would become known as the Army of the West—from Fort Leavenworth, on the Missouri, west to take New Mexico. They traveled on a variation of the Santa Fe Trail via Bent's Fort, on the Arkansas, and were guided by Josiah Gregg's new map of the Great Plains (Map 201, *page 105*). New Mexico governor Manuel Armijo amassed his troops

Map 167 (*below*).
An American copy of a map captured from Mexican general Mariano Arista at the Battle of Resaca de la Palma on 9 May 1846. It shows the area around the lower reaches of the Rio Grande (*Rio Bravo del Norte*). *Matamoros* is on the river's southern side, with the American *Fort Brown* opposite it. The battles at *Palo Alto* and *Resaca del Palma* are shown, both locations straddling the road between *San Isabel* and *Matamoros*; they were fought on 8 and 9 May 1846, respectively. Up the coast is *Fort Polk*, the American supply point.

Map 165 (*right*).
Both sides claimed victory at the Battle of San Pasqual, north of San Diego. The battle was fought between the Mexicans and the arriving American contingent under Colonel Stephen Watts Kearny on 6 December 1846. Twenty-two Americans were killed.

Map 166 (*below*).
One of the two battles for Los Angeles, the battle on the plain of La Mesa, often called the *Battle of Los Angeles*, was fought on 9 January 1847, and the action was recorded by topographical engineer William Hemsley Emory, one of Kearny's officers, and published in a later report.

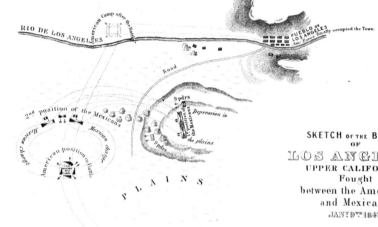

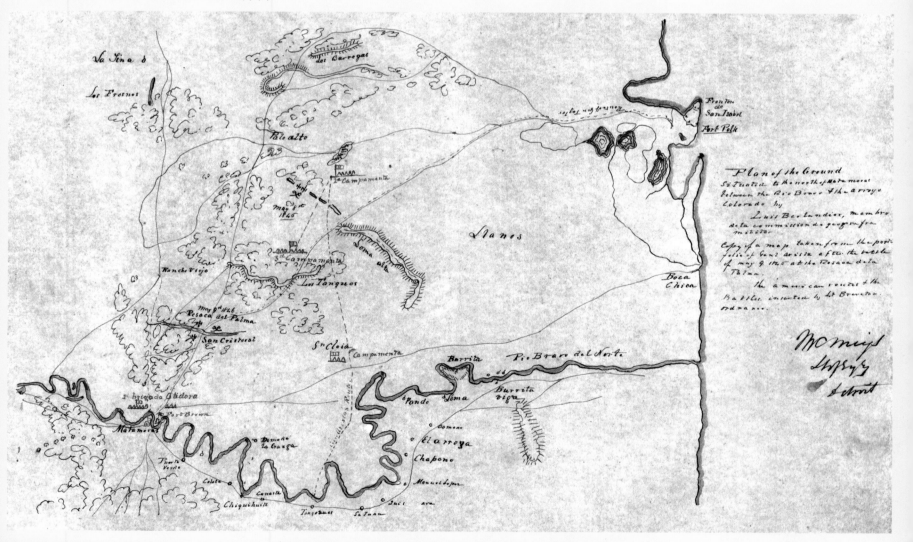

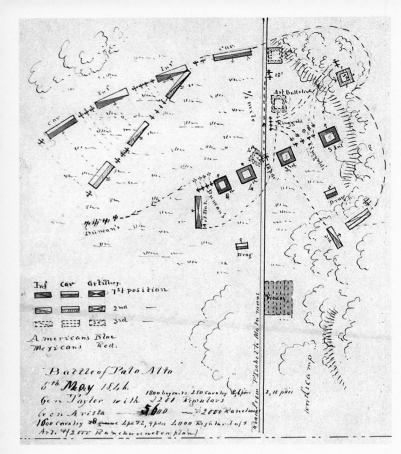

The *Battle of Palo Alto*, Texas, fought 8 May 1846, with the American army winning the day despite being outnumbered 2,228 to 4,000; the map says 5,600, but this figure is thought to be overstated. Zachary Taylor's leadership and modern weaponry aided the victory. Five Americans were killed and forty-three wounded; Mexican losses were sevenfold. American positions are shown in blue and Mexican positions in red.

but declined to fight, possibly because of a large bribe that passed from American trader James Magoffin to Armijo. Magoffin, acting for the U.S. government, secretly visited Armijo in the days before Kearny's arrival. Armijo fled south to El Paso. Kearny entered Santa Fe unopposed on 18 August 1846 and proclaimed the American annexation of New Mexico. As ordered, he then set about making the transition to American rule as seamless as possible.

Kearny received news of the fall of California and so, thinking he would not need an army, sent most of his men south to join Zachary Taylor in Texas. He then proceeded west with about a hundred men.

A short-lived rebellion against American rule took place in January 1847, beginning in Taos, when many who had accepted office under the United States were killed, including Charles Bent, the new governor of New Mexico. The Taos Revolt, as it is known, was quickly suppressed, and the principal perpetrators were hanged in the plaza at Santa Fe.

Kearny, meanwhile, likely thought he should have taken more men to California. Some *Californios* (California-born Mexicans) who had originally supported the American takeover changed their minds, and both Kearny and Stockton found they had more of a fight on their hands than they had bargained for. As Kearny neared San Diego, he attacked a smaller force of *Californios* at San Pasqual on 6 December 1846 but nearly lost the fight; twenty-two of his men were killed (Map 165, *previous page*). He was rescued by two hundred of Stockton's men marching out from San Diego.

Stockton and Kearny combined their forces and marched north to retake Los Angeles, engaging the Mexicans at the San Gabriel River on 8 January 1847 and on the plain of La Mesa the next day (Map 166, *previous page*), driving the Mexicans away. On 10 January Los Angeles was reoccupied. Frémont, arriving from the north with four hundred men, encountered the Mexican force a few miles north of Los Angeles on 13 January and persuaded their leader, José María Flores, to surrender. With the surrender document, the Treaty of Cahuenga, California was finally and permanently American.

Kearny, Stockton, and Frémont, however, bickered about who was really in charge. Kearny had orders from Polk to set up a civil government, but Stockton refused to turn

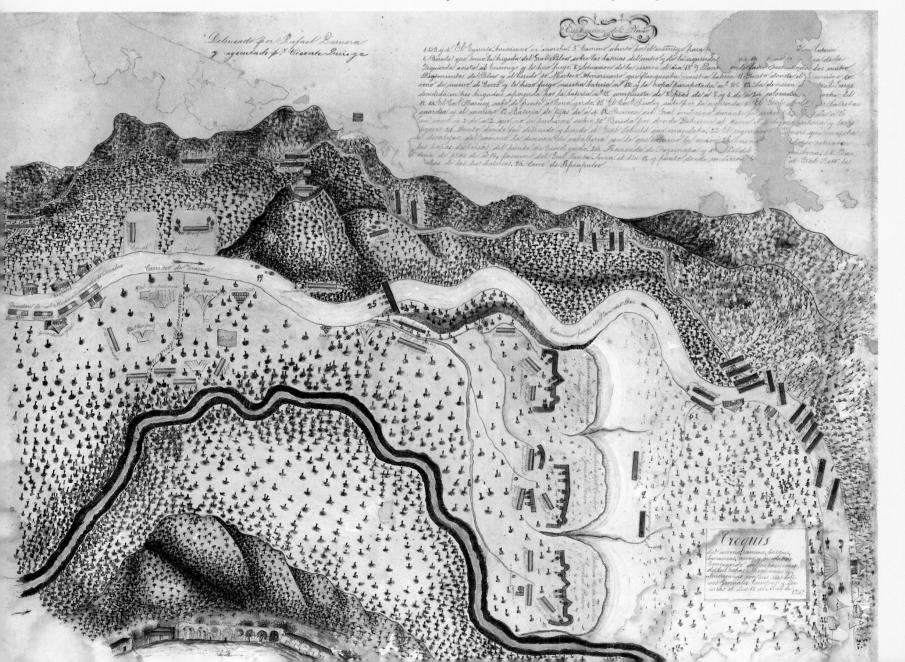

over command and appointed Frémont governor. Then Colonel Richard Mason arrived to take over from Stockton, and he immediately accepted Kearny's orders. Frémont found himself without authority and was ordered back east with Kearny, who then arrested and court-martialed him. President Polk could not allow this affront to happen to a man so central to the American success and remanded his sentence of dismissal from the Army. Frémont, outraged, resigned anyway.

In Texas, General Zachary Taylor received orders in the spring of 1846 to advance to the Rio Grande. There, opposite Matamoros, the army built a fort. A skirmish resulting from a Mexican foray across the river allowed President Polk to declare that "by the act of the Republic of Mexico, a state of war exists." Yet even before Polk issued that statement the war had begun in earnest. Mexican general Mariano Arista crossed the Rio Grande, intending to cut off Taylor's supply line from the coast at Fort Polk (MAP 167, *page 87*). Taylor found himself cornered, and on 8 May 1846 2,228 Americans fought 4,000 Mexicans at a place called Palo Alto. Despite the Americans' numerical disadvantage, modern warfare methods and Taylor's leadership gave them the victory (MAP 168, *left*). A further engagement the next day at a narrow ravine called the Resaca de la Palma produced another American victory. A few days later, the American army crossed the Rio Grande.

Taylor then marched his army to Monterrey, two hundred miles west. But 1,500 died of dysentery and yellow fever just getting there. The city was fortified, and the Mexicans thought it impregnable. But once again the Americans triumphed, though it took three days of bloody building-to-building fighting. So intense was the fighting that cannon had to be loaded and the fuse lit before being hauled with ropes into the middle of the street; to attempt to reload in the open was to invite sudden death.

Taylor became a hero—too much for Polk, who was convinced—correctly—that Taylor had his eyes on the presidency. Many of Taylor's men were ordered to join a new army being assembled by General Winfield Scott.

Taylor moved his remaining army, now mainly volunteers, to Saltillo to face a new Mexican army led by the old Texan nemesis vanquished at San Jacinto, Antonio López de Santa Anna. Taylor was joined by more volunteers under General John E. Wool, who marched south from San Antonio. The Battle of Buena Vista, fought 22–23 February 1847, was remarkable: six thousand American volunteers defeated a twenty thousand–strong Mexican army.

The last northern Mexican battle was at the Rio Sacramento, near Chihuahua, where another volunteer force, led by General Alexander Doniphan (detached from Kearny's army at Santa Fe and marching to meet Taylor) defeated the Mexicans once more. With this coup de grace, Mexican resistance in the north collapsed.

The final campaign of the war took place deep within Mexico and ended with the capture of the capital itself. Peace terms offered by Polk after Monterrey had been spurned by Santa Anna, and so a plan to take Mexico City had been devised. An army of over ten thousand men under General Winfield Scott landed near the heavily fortified coastal city of Veracruz on 9 March 1847 and laid siege to the city, which fell at the end of the month. Overcoming considerable logistical problems, the army moved inland, meeting a blockade by the Mexican army under Santa Anna at Cerro Gordo, where the road climbed out of the lowland plain. Despite being outnumbered and despite having to fight an enemy entrenched above them, the Americans won the day (MAP 169, *left, bottom*).

The city of Puebla, only fifty miles from the capital, was occupied on 15 May. In July Commodore Matthew Perry took a contingent of over a thousand marines up the Grijalva River to capture Villahermosa (called Tabasco by the Americans), a source of supply for Santa Anna's army.

By now the Mexicans were falling back and desperate. At Churubusco, a fortified town today within the urban area of Mexico City, the Mexicans made a stand, and on 20 August Scott once again prevailed despite again being outnumbered. Santa Anna lost a third of his army—four thousand killed or wounded and three thousand taken prisoner. Santa Anna at this point requested a truce but kept breaking it to reinforce his position.

Closing in on Mexico City, Scott ordered General William Jenkins Worth (after whom Fort Worth, Texas, is named) to take Molino del Rey (King's Mill), a group of buildings where cannon were being cast, just west of the city, guarding the two western causeways into the capital, and shown on MAP 170, *below*. A night attack on 8 September succeeded in destroying the foundry but was a disaster, with massive losses on both sides.

MAP 169 (*left*).
This excellent Mexican map shows the Battle of Cerro Gordo, west of Veracruz, Mexico, fought on 18 April 1847. The Mexican army, at left, blocked the *Camino de Veracruz*, the road from Veracruz to Mexico City, where it passed through mountainous terrain with narrow ravines. Santa Anna positioned his army with its cannon trained on the only way up the narrow valley. The Americans were outnumbered, but Scott's army nevertheless won the day in a stunning victory that gained the Americans access to the Mexican highlands.

MAP 170 (*right*).
The final assault on Mexico City is depicted in this map. The cannon foundry at *Molina del Rey* and the fortress of *Chapultepec* are at left center, as are the *H^d.Q^trs.* of *Genl. Worth* and *H^d.Q^trs.* of *Genl. Scott*; the *Chapultepec Causeway* leads to the *Garita*, one of the gates to the city, at right.

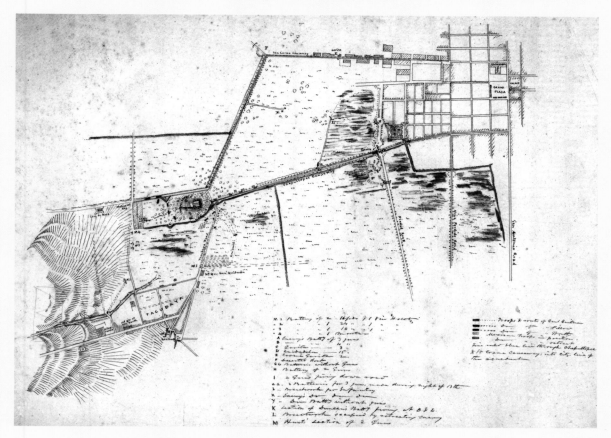

MAP 171 (*above*).
The actual map used by Nicholas Trist while negotiating the Treaty of Guadalupe Hidalgo, ratified by the United States on 10 March 1848 and now in the National Archives. About 600,000 square miles of Mexican territory were ceded to the United States. The map was of the United States of Mexico and was published in 1847 by American John Disturnell. The positions of the Rio Grande and El Paso are inaccurate, errors that led to boundary definition problems later, problems largely solved by the Gadsden Purchase, finalized in 1854 (see pages 182–83).

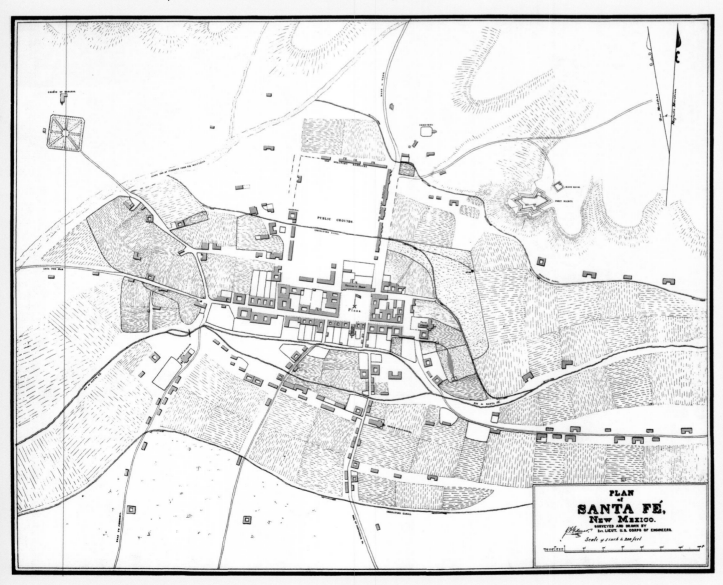

MAP 172 (*left*).
This superbly detailed map of *Santa Fé* was surveyed and drawn by Army engineer Lieutenant J.F. Gilmer in 1846, after the American takeover. The *Rio de Santa Fé*, a tributary of the Rio Grande, flows through the center of town, flanked on either side by an *Irrigating Canal*. On the higher ground overlooking the town is the castellated American *Fort Marcy*, with an outlying *Blockhouse*. At top left is an unnamed recreation park, or alameda. Adobe buildings—made from bricks of clay and sand—surround the central *Plaza*, overlooked by the *Governor's House* (the Palace of the Governors; see page 36). Much of this plan of Santa Fe remains today, with considerable additions, of course, a fact that is in no small part due to the decision of the Atchison, Topeka & Santa Fe Railway to bypass the settlement, creating a station instead at Lamy, a few miles to the southeast.

MAP 173 (*above*).
The new boundary between the United States and Mexico is shown on this commercial map published in 1848. Apart from the boundary on the Rio Grande and across the northern end of the Baja peninsula, which was easy to define, the boundary is still somewhat indefinite, reflecting the sketchy geographical knowledge of both sides to the Treaty of Guadalupe Hidalgo and the less than exact mapping of features on John Disturnell's map (MAP 171, *left, top*) used at the time. The still-disputed boundary would be finally settled by the Gadsden Purchase in 1853–54 with the acquisition of yet more Mexican territory (see page 183), which the United States coveted because it included the Gila Valley, a potential route for a railroad. *Upper or New California* stretches across the West as far as today's Colorado; to the north is the new territory of *Oregon*.

The final assault on the capital was through the fortress of Chapultepec, where it was least expected, since the route was so well fortified. A feint attack from the south was arranged; Santa Anna fell for the ruse and positioned his armies to repel an attack from the south. The fortress of Chapultepec was bombarded for a whole day and assaulted the next morning, falling in only an hour after vicious hand-to-hand fighting and despite a valiant defense by nine hundred military cadets whose heroism is still honored in Mexico today.

The final assault wave followed. Sheer force of numbers allowed the American army to surge up the causeway leading to the gates of the city, notwithstanding a defense by fifteen hundred Mexican cavalry. Santa Anna, once again, had been bested by Scott. By nightfall on 13 September the Americans were within the city, and by morning they had consolidated their position; Santa Anna and his remaining army fled.

Negotiations began for a peace treaty with a new Mexican government put together after Santa Anna's flight. American negotiator Nicholas Trist concluded the Treaty of Guadalupe Hidalgo (named after the village just north of the capital where it was concluded), signed on 2 February 1848 and ratified by the U.S. Senate on 10 March. With it the United States gained half of Texas and ended the dispute over the rest, and it also acquired the vast area now covered by the states of California, Nevada, Utah, some of Colorado, and most of Arizona and New Mexico.

With the recently acquired Oregon Territory (see page 84) the United States had in only two years gained almost all of the western half of the West and a Pacific coastline two thousand miles long. For the United States, Manifest Destiny had been achieved. Ironically for Mexico, it lost the West at the very same moment the territory acquired new value, at least in EuroAmerican eyes: gold was discovered in California in January 1848.

THE RUSH WEST

Even before the West was fully theirs, a few Americans rolled west intent on settlement, seemingly sure in their hearts that the West would someday belong to the United States. First came missionaries, then colonists. After 1846, when the West was truly American, the trickle became a flood, encouraged almost immediately by reports of untold wealth—gold had been found in California, the first of many discoveries of mineral wealth throughout the West.

OREGON AND THE OREGON TRAIL

Oregon was the destination of some of the first American settlers, largely because Oregon was outside Mexican territory and officially a region of joint occupancy with Britain; the principal hazard here was not Mexicans but Indians.

Hall Jackson Kelley, a Boston school principal, had been interested in Oregon since 1818. In 1829 he chartered the American Society for Encouraging the Settlement of the Oregon Territory, publishing the following year a book, *A Geographical Sketch of That Part of North America Called Oregon,* to inspire and instruct potential colonists. In 1831 he assembled several hundred of the would-be emigrants, who were to go with him to Oregon in the company of Nathaniel Wyeth, a Massachusetts merchant. Wyeth intended to start a business enterprise on the Columbia closely modeled on that of John Jacob Astor twenty years earlier, a business built around fur and fish—specifically salmon—but he left without Kelley when the latter seemed to be taking too long to get organized. Traveling by boat up the Mississippi, Wyeth joined the expedition of Benjamin Louis Eulalie de Bonneville, which was probably the first to traverse the route that would become known as the Oregon Trail. But Wyeth's business in Oregon was not successful, as his supply ship was wrecked. Wyeth tried again in 1834, traveling west in the company of missionary Jason Lee and famous naturalist Thomas

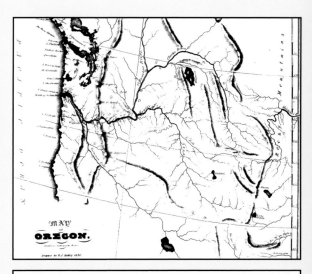

MAP 175 (*above, top*).
What appears to be the first printed map of the Oregon Country alone appeared in Hall Kelley's *Geographical Sketch of That Part of North America Called Oregon,* published in 1830.

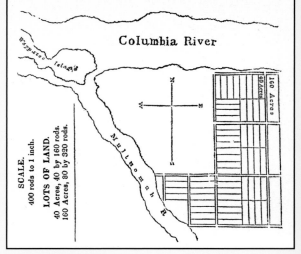

MAP 176 (*above*).
This map was published in the *Geographical Sketch* and also in *A General Circular to All Persons of Good Character Who Wish to Emigrate to the Oregon Territory,* published the next year by Kelley's American Society for Encouraging the Settlement of the Oregon Territory. It shows a proposed settlement at the confluence of the *Multnomah R* (Willamette) and the *Columbia River,* on land that is today Kelley Point Park in Portland. Nathaniel Wyeth tried to establish his Fort William on Sauvie Island, *Wappatoo Island* on this map.

MAP 174 (*across page and continuing overleaf*).
In 1846 Charles Preuss, Frémont's accompanying mapmaker, produced a large-scale sectional map of the entire Oregon Trail from Westport (now part of Kansas City), on the Missouri, to Fort Walla Walla, on the Columbia. It was in seven sections, here digitally stitched together, and was intended to be used by wagon trains heading west. Congress ordered an amazing ten thousand copies to facilitate migration to Oregon.

Nuttall. This time Wyeth founded a fur-trading post at Fort Hall (in today's Idaho) and a salmon cannery at Fort William, on Sauvie Island (Wappatoo Island on Kelley's map (MAP 176, *left*)). But neither prospered, owing to the Hudson's Bay Company's tight control of the market; Wyeth could find but few Indians willing to trade. He returned east, disillusioned.

Between 1832 and 1835 Bonneville covered much ground in the West and was the first to take loaded wagons across South Pass, thus showing that the route would be suitable for later emigrant wagons. Bonneville was an officer on leave from the U.S. Army who some think was spying for the American government but was more likely in search of adventure and a fortune. He also ran afoul of the Hudson's Bay Company, which would not let him proceed west of Fort Walla Walla, perhaps not surprising considering that he was financed by Astor himself. Bonneville did, however, build a trading post on the Green River. In 1834 one of Bonneville's associates, Joseph Red-deford Walker, ranging farther south, found a crossing of the Sierra Nevada into California—Walker Pass—another route that would be followed by later emigrants.

Hall Kelley's book was widely influential—luring settlers west with promises of not only bountiful crops but also fat and healthy babies—but his own expedition to Oregon, which finally left Boston in 1833, was a failure. At New Orleans most of his party of would-be emigrants deserted him. With a few loyalists Kelley crossed Mexico and reached California, traveling north to Oregon by horse in the company of Ewing Young, a fur trader who settled in the Willamette Valley. Kelley was unlucky enough to become ill with malaria while in the Umpqua Valley. When he finally reached Fort Vancouver he was made less than welcome by the Hudson's Bay Company's chief factor, John McLoughlin. Discouraged and ill, Kelley found his way back to Boston in 1835.

In 1831 four Nez Percé had traveled to St. Louis to visit William Clark, then with the Bureau of Indian Affairs. The Nez Percé were thought to have asked for information on the Christian religion—though the request likely was misunderstood in translation—and this resulted in several missionaries being sent to Oregon. The first was Jason Lee, a Methodist; he established a mission in the Willamette Valley, northwest of today's Salem. In 1835 the American Board of Commissioners for Foreign Missions, an interdenominational group, sent an exploratory party to Oregon led by Samuel Parker. With him was Marcus Whitman.

In 1836 Parker was not accepted for further missionary work after he returned east with mission site recommendations, but Whitman was, although he was required to marry. He and his new wife, Narcissa, accompanied by missionaries Henry and Eliza Spalding, rode wagons along the future Oregon Trail in 1836.

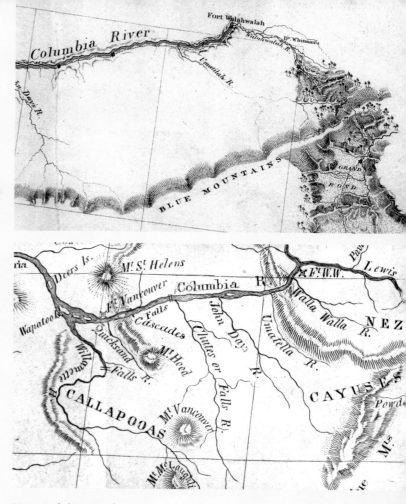

MAP 177 (*above, top*).
John Charles Frémont's map of 1844, depicting his travels over the previous three years, showed *D^r. Whitman's* mission on the *Walahwalah R.* upstream of the Hudson's Bay Company's *Fort Walahwalah.* Note that the original Fort Walla Walla, or Fort Nez Pérces, was on the Columbia at today's Wallula; the current Fort Walla Walla, in the city of the same name, was a U.S. military fort built in 1856.

MAP 178 (*above*).
The Hudson's Bay Company's *F^t. W.W.* (Walla Walla) and *F^t. Vancouver* are depicted on this 1838 map of Oregon by missionary Samuel Parker. The Multnomah River is now shown as the *Willamette R.* The Willamette Valley was to prove to be the destination of choice for most of the early emigrants to Oregon.

MAP 174 (*continued*).
The mission of *D^r. Whitman's* is also shown on this map, on the *Wallah-Wallah River*, at extreme left. Near the center of this two-page section of the map is *Fort Hall*, established by Nathaniel Wyeth in 1834 and named after a financial backer, Henry Hall. The fort was sold to the Hudson's Bay Company in 1837.

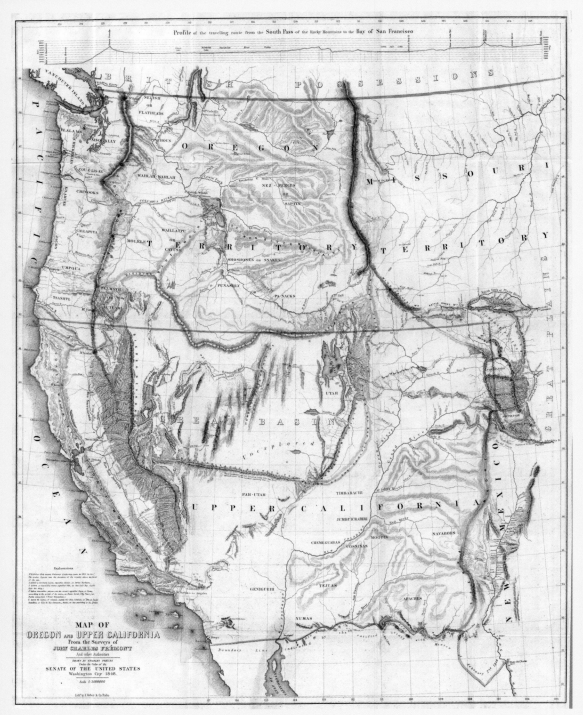

MAP OF
OREGON AND UPPER CALIFORNIA
From the Surveys of
JOHN CHARLES FRÉMONT
And other Authorities
DRAWN BY CHARLES PREUSS
Under the Order of the
SENATE OF THE UNITED STATES
Washington City 1848
Scale 1:3000000

Profile of the travelling route from the South Pass of the Rocky Mountains to the Bay of San Francisco

MAP 179 (*left*).

This excellent map of the West, by far the most up-to-date at the time, was drawn by Charles Preuss and published in 1848. It incorporates all of the previous Frémont surveys and the Oregon surveys of Charles Wilkes's U.S. Exploring Expedition (MAP 160, *page 85*). Note, too, that the new southern and northern boundaries of the United States are now shown. The remaining unknown large areas are principally in the Great Basin, in previously Mexican territory.

The Spaldings set up their mission near today's Lewiston, Idaho; the Whitmans in the Walla Walla Valley (MAP 177, *previous page*).

The story of the Whitman Massacre, as it was called, is well known. The missionaries tried to make farmers of the nomadic Cayuse Indians, which was one cause for dissent, but emigrants using the Oregon Trail also brought diseases with them. A measles outbreak in 1847 was the last straw, for the Indians saw emigrants recovering while half of their own people died; an event they construed as some sort of deliberate attack. Marcus and Narcissa Whitman and eleven others were murdered by the Cayuse on 29 November 1847; sixty others were taken hostage and were ransomed by the Hudson's Bay Company a month later.

The Willamette Valley attracted most settlers. In 1837 John McLoughlin of the Hudson's Bay Company joined with Ewing Young and Jason Lee to bring cattle north from California, the start of Oregon's cattle industry. Young died in 1841 without leaving a will and without heirs; the subsequent disputes highlighted the need for some sort of government. In February and March 1843, various meetings were held at what had emerged as a settlement center, Champoeg, now a state park between Salem and Oregon City, to discuss the control of wolves, which were troublesome to the valley livestock farmers. From these meetings came a decision to form a provisional government and petition the federal government to annex Oregon.

TOPOGRAPHICAL MAP
OF THE
ROAD FROM MISSOURI TO OREGON
COMMENCING AT THE MOUTH OF THE KANSAS IN THE MISSOURI RIVER
AND ENDING AT THE MOUTH OF THE WALLAH WALLAH IN THE COLUMBIA
In VII Sections
SECTION II
From the field notes and journal of Capt. J.C. Frémont.
and from sketches and notes made on the ground by his assistant Charles Preuss
By order of the Senate of the United States
SCALE: 10 MILES TO THE INCH

TOPOGRAPHICAL MAP
OF THE
ROAD FROM MISSOURI TO OREGON
COMMENCING AT THE MOUTH OF THE KANSAS IN THE MISSOURI RIVER
AND ENDING AT THE MOUTH OF THE WALLAH WALLAH IN THE COLUMBIA
In VII Sections
SECTION I
From the field notes and journal of Capt. J.C. Frémont.
and from sketches and notes made on the ground by his assistant Charles Preuss
By order of the Senate of the United States
SCALE: 10 MILES TO THE INCH

Meteorological Observations

MAP 174 (*continued from overleaf*).

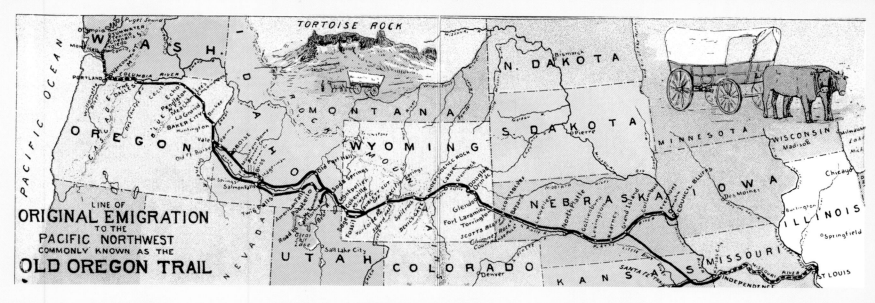

The situation was resolved in 1846 with a treaty defining the new international boundary west of the Rockies (see page 84) and the organization of Oregon Territory in August 1848. Hall Kelley's dream had become a reality.

By this time colonists were streaming into Oregon along the Oregon Trail, a route suitable for wagons from the Missouri to Oregon across South Pass. Between 1842 and 1844 Army topographical engineer John Charles Frémont, who was to play an important role in the acquisition of California (see page 87), mapped routes west, producing in 1848 the finest map of the West to date (MAP 179, *left*). That his maps were so accurate was principally due to his mapmaker, Charles Preuss, who carefully computed astronomical positions and pioneered the use of the barometer for determining elevations. In 1846 Preuss created a seven-section large-scale map of the Oregon Trail, which became the guide carried by most emigrant wagon trains (MAP 174, *across pages 92–94*). The map contained a myriad of notes with such important information as where to find water and where to pasture livestock. Congress ordered ten thousand copies for distribution to emigrants to facilitate the peopling of the Northwest.

MAP 180 (*above*).
Few people did more to memorialize the Oregon Trail than Ezra Meeker, a pioneer who went west in 1852. Meeker published this map in 1907. In 1906, by then a successful Puget Sound businessman, Meeker decided that the trail had been unjustly forgotten, and he devoted a good deal of effort over the next two decades promoting it. He traveled the Oregon Trail twice in a covered wagon pulled by an ox-team, in 1906 continuing to Washington, D.C., to meet President Theodore Roosevelt. In 1916 he traveled the trail in an automobile. In 1924, at the age of ninety-four, he flew over the trail in an open-cockpit plane, again continuing on to Washington, where he presented President Calvin Coolidge with a plan to make the trail a national highway.

MAP 181 (*below*).
Jesuit missionary Pierre-Jean De Smet, the original Blackrobe, explored widely in the West, helping Native peoples wherever he could, often acting as a mediator between warring tribes. De Smet and his fellow missionaries founded several missions in the Pacific Northwest, and this is part of a map he drew (his initials are at the bottom) about 1846, covering what is today northeastern Washington, northern Idaho, and eastern Montana. In 1841 De Smet founded the *Ste. Marie* Mission, thirty miles north of present-day Missoula, Montana; it is shown at bottom right. Locations of Native groups and missions are shown. The *Riv: Okinakane* (Okanogan River) is at left. The *Fleuve de la Colombie* (Columbia River) flows from the north to meet it at bottom left. The river across the bottom is the *Spokane*; where De Smet has noted the *Spokans* is the site of the future city of Spokane; farther east is the location of the *Coeurs d'Alenes*. De Smet also noted the competition: *Mission protestante*, also on the Spokane River. De Smet gathered his information not only from his own extensive travels but also from Native sources, and his map demonstrates a considerable working knowledge of the region, even if it is not always entirely accurate.

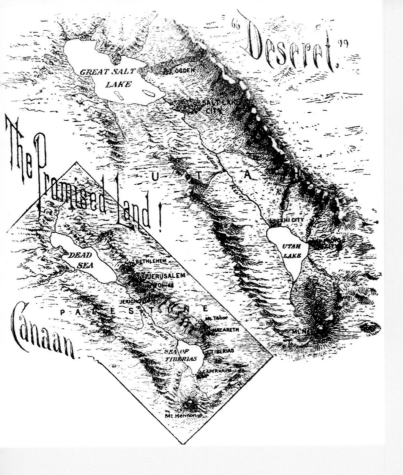

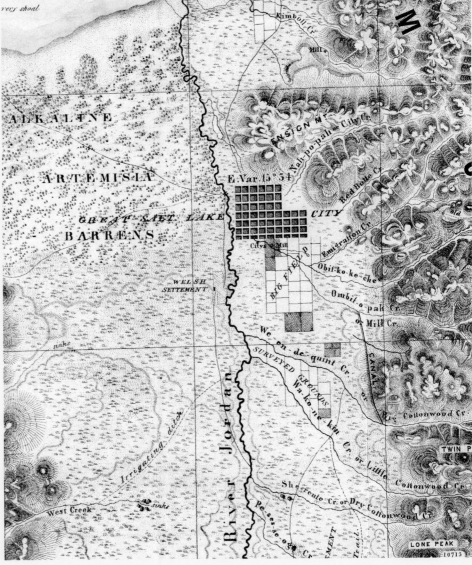

The Mormon Trek

The Oregon Trail was the route used for the most part by another group of emigrants—the Mormons. The Mormon Trail left the Oregon Trail at Fort Bridger, about ninety miles east of the Great Salt Lake, before heading southwest to the valley of the Utah River.

Members of the Church of Jesus Christ of Latter-day Saints, founded in 1830 by Joseph Smith in upstate New York, had been persecuted from the beginning, moving to Kirtland, Ohio, in 1831, and to Missouri over the next eight years, where they faced determined and violent opposition. Smith then moved his followers to Commerce, Illinois, renaming it Nauvoo. But the hostility persisted, and continuing violence led to Smith's death in 1844. Brigham Young assumed the Mormon leadership, and it was he who, two years later, made the decision to move west.

In 1846 Mormons moved to Winter Quarters (now Florence, Nebraska, a suburb of Omaha), and on 5 April 1847 a vanguard group, with Young at its head, headed west, with the main body of Mormons not far behind. On 24 July Young came within sight of the Great Salt Lake, and he decided this was the place he would settle and reestablish his church.

MAP 182 (*above, left*).
Deseret, the Mormon homeland, bears a remarkable resemblance to *Canaan*, with both hailed as *The Promised Land* in this rather clever 1896 map, which appeared in a brochure published by the Denver & Rio Grande Western Railroad. The similarity was enhanced by drawing the inset map with south at the top.

MAP 183 (*above*).
Howard Stansbury, a topographical engineer, was ordered to map the Great Salt Lake with his assistant, John Gunnison, in 1849, and report on the Mormon settlements. His map, not published until 1852, shows *Great Salt Lake City* and a surrounding agricultural area, with a number of all-important *Irrigating ditch[es]*. The Utah River was renamed the Western Jordan River in 1847 by the Mormons, and here the *River Jordan* (Jordan River) flows through the settlement region from the freshwater Utah Lake to the Great Salt Lake.

MAP 184 (*below*).
The South Pass–to–Great Salt Lake segment of the California Trail, also the Mormon Trail, is shown in this map published in 1849 by T.H. Jefferson, who had previously traveled to California along the route. Note that the map is oriented with north to the top right corner. The *Utah R.* is at left; *Fort Bridger* is at approximate center, with the Oregon Trail, marked *Road to Fort Hall*, diverging north. The *Great South Pass of the Rocky M*ts, the (Wind River) *Mountains*, and the headwaters of the *Sweet Water River* are at right, where there is also the notation *Last Buffalo seen here*. The map, in four sheets, is now extremely rare, with only five extant copies.

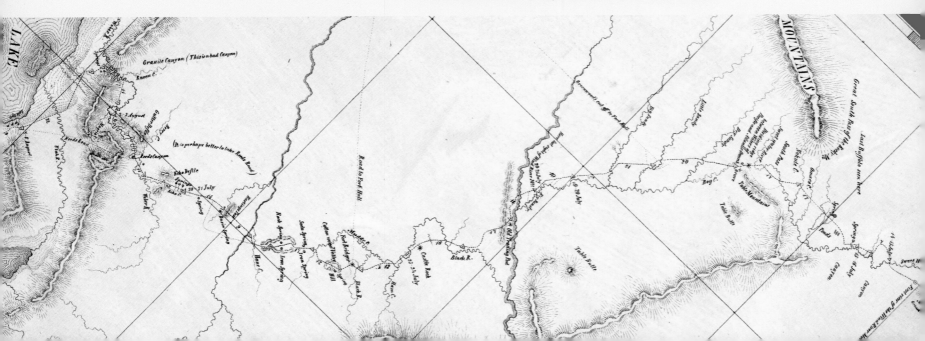

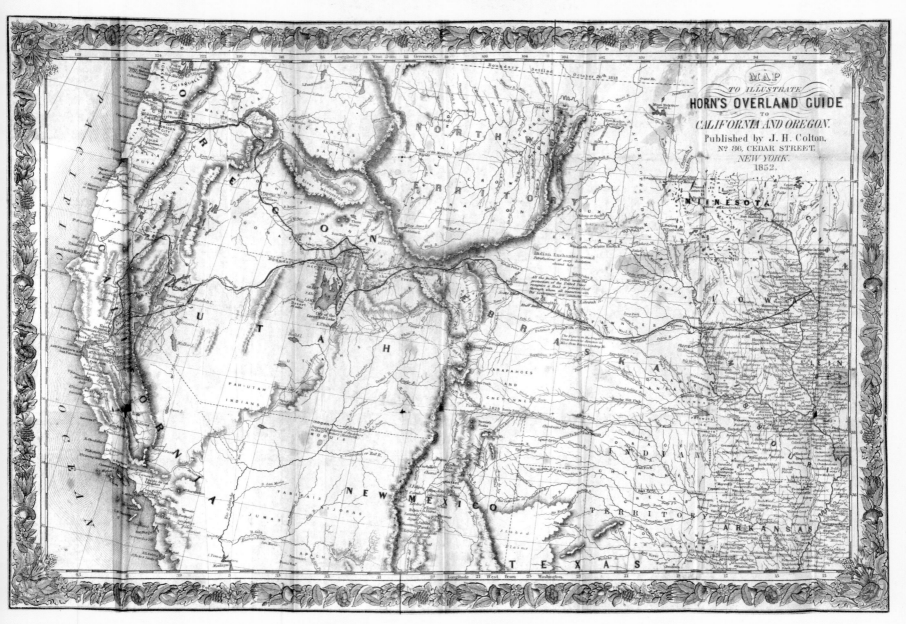

Map 185 (*above*).
Some of the trails to Oregon, California, and the Great Salt Lake, together with some of the alternative routings, are shown on this 1852 map from a publication called *Horn's Overland Guide.* The book was written by Hosea B. Horn, who had traveled to California in 1850 and was considered the best guide to the Oregon Trail route west available at the time. "No one should venture across the desert without it," effused the *New York Observer* in a March 1852 review. The California Trail is shown here leaving the Oregon Trail just before Fort Hall, then heading southwest to the Humboldt River.

Map 186 (*below*).
The western part of the Mormon migration of 1846–47 is depicted in this pictorial map created in 1899. Although the route shown here as far west as *Fort Bridger* was essentially identical to that of the Oregon and California trails, no mention is made of these. The route is up the *North Platte* River, then up the *Sweetwater* to South Pass. Landmarks such as *Chimney Rock* and *Scott's Bluffs* are illustrated. Also shown is *Ft. Laramie*, established in the 1830s by fur traders and made into an army fort in 1849 to protect travelers on the emigrant trail.

Young selected a site for a settlement—Great Salt Lake City—and it was laid out on a wide north–south and east–west grid (Map 183, *above left*). Although the area was distinctly arid, it possessed rivers flowing from the mountains and a freshwater lake, Utah Lake, to provide water for irrigation. Every year after settlement, until the coming of the railroad in 1869, Mormons trekked along the Mormon Trail, mostly the same route as the Oregon Trail as far as Fort Bridger, where the Mormon Trail diverged for the last miles to Salt Lake City.

The California Trail is a name collectively applied to several variations on the route to California. The most usually followed route left the Oregon Trail near Fort Hall, but some migrants tried to follow a shorter route around the southern end of the Great Salt

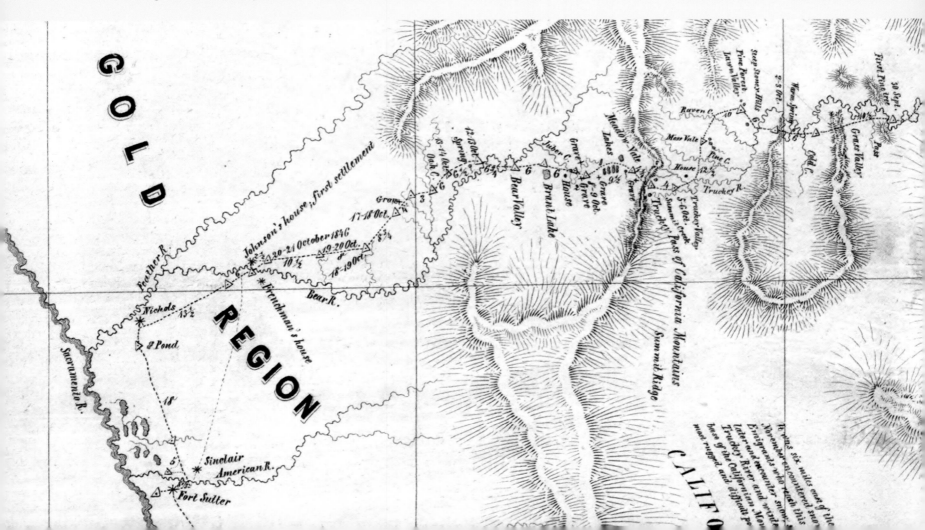

The fearful long drive 83 Miles — no grass nor water

sali wel

To accomplish the long drive grass & water must be carried from Hope Wells and the journey performed night and day making short & regular camps. Not more then five waggons should go in company and the cattle should be continually guarded.

Long Drive   35 Miles

Lake before heading out across the desert; this was the Hastings Cutoff, recommended by Lansford Hastings in an 1845 book, *The Emigrant's Guide to Oregon and California.* Many wished they had not followed it. Part of the desert portion of this route is shown on T.H. Jefferson's map (MAP 187, *above*), complete with dire warnings about the lack of water.

One of the first emigrant parties on the California Trail was that of John Bidwell and John Bartleson in 1841; they were forced to abandon their wagons in the desert. In 1844 the Stephens-Townsend-Murphy party, led by Elisha Stephens, became the first to successfully maneuver their wagons across the Sierra Nevada, via Donner Pass, named later for the ill-fated Donner party that became stuck in the Sierra snows in the fall of 1846 after being delayed in the desert following the Hastings Cutoff route; thirty-nine out of eighty-seven died in an epic made more famous because some of the survivors ate the dead bodies of their companions.

Exact figures are difficult to find, but between 1840 and the coming of the railroad in 1869, certainly more than 350,000, and perhaps as many as half a million, people followed the emigrant trails west, looking for a better life on the other side of the mountains. The migration created the West.

CALIFORNIA GOLD

The United States had acquired the West by 1848, but the seminal event that jump-started the peopling of the West was the discovery of gold on the American River. It was found on 23 January 1848, just ten days before the Mexican government formally signed the treaty ceding the region to the United States.

Gold was found on the land of John Augustus Sutter, an immigrant who had been granted the land by Mexico in 1841 and had set up Sutter's

MAP 187 (*above*).
The fearful long drive 83 Miles no grass nor water faced intrepid emigrants on the southern California Trail route following the Hastings Cutoff around the southern end of the Great Salt Lake, visible at extreme right. The text on Jefferson's 1849 map warned of what was necessary to cross the waterless desert successfully.

MAP 188 (*below*).
The westernmost section of Jefferson's four-section map shows the route across the Sierra Nevada and the descent into California's Central Valley, ending at John Sutter's fort, today Sacramento.

Fort, in what is today Sacramento, as a base for his agricultural empire; the fort is shown on MAP 188, *below,* and MAP 189, *right.*

James Marshall, a millwright and employee of Sutter's, found gold in the tailrace of a mill forty miles above Sutter's Fort on the South Fork of the American River. By March the San Francisco *Californian* announced that "gold has been found in every part of the country." And indeed it had. Soon three-quarters of the city's population had flocked to the gold fields—so many that the newspaper went out of business for lack of subscribers.

The gold rush was to prove hard on many businesses, which could not compete with the vast sums some found—or thought they would find—in the goldfields. Even the military had problems. "The struggle between right and six dollars a month and wrong and $75 a day is rather a severe one," wrote military governor Richard Mason in a report to the War Department. Between July 1848 and the end of 1849 the Army of Northern California lost 716 men to desertion, over half its strength. The Navy took to "much cruising" to prevent sailors from jumping ship.

By August 1848 reports of the gold find began to appear in eastern newspapers. By the end of the year gold fever had hit the nation. Ships

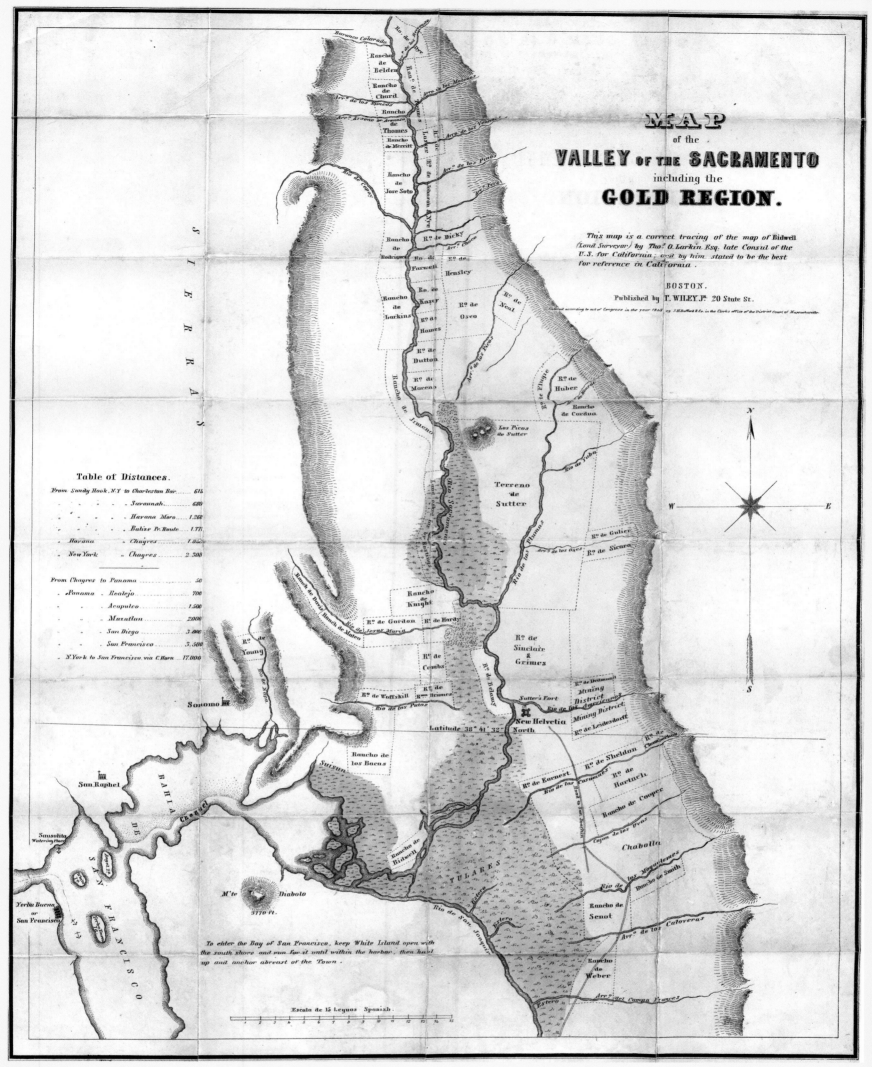

MAP
of the
VALLEY OF THE SACRAMENTO
including the
GOLD REGION.

This map is a correct tracing of the map of Bidwell
(Land Surveyor) by Thos. O. Larkin Esq. late Consul of the
U.S. for California; and by him stated to be the best
for reference in California.

BOSTON.
Published by T. WILEY Jr. 20 State St.

Map 189.

An 1848 map of the lower Sacramento River valley copied by Thomas Oliver Larkin, entrepreneur and late American consul at Monterey, from a map drawn by John Bidwell, then Sutter's principal assistant. Much of the eastern valley has optimistically been colored gold, yet the map does not actually show the region where most of the gold had been found, higher up the valleys of the rivers flowing from the Sierra Nevada. *Sutter's Fort* is shown at the junction of the *Rio de*

los Americanos (American River) at *New Helvetia* (New Switzerland), Sutter's name for his rancho. John Sutter was ruined by the gold rush, being unable to find men willing to work for wages. Bidwell went on to become a successful businessman, then a U.S. congressman, and later ran unsuccessfully for both California governor and president of the United States.

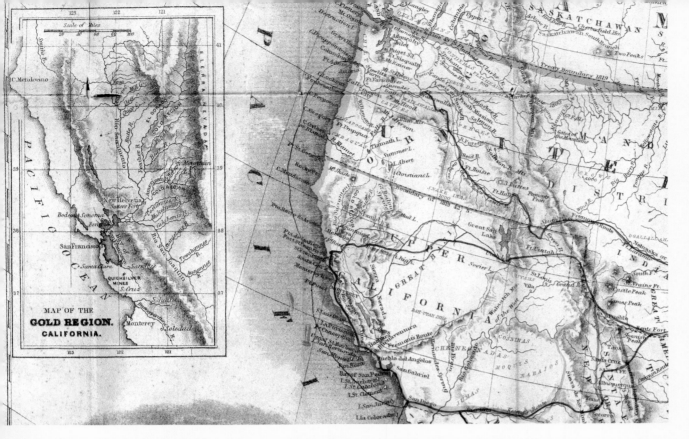

MAP OF THE
GOLD REGION.
CALIFORNIA.

MAP OF THE GOLD REGIONS OF CALIFORNIA.
Showing the Routes via Chagres and Panama, Cape Horn, &c.

were chartered and overland treks planned. Maps and information about the overland trails sold for a premium, and many more were rushed into print. St. Louis assumed new importance as a staging post for the West. The stream of fortune seekers, self-styled Argonauts later dubbed "California Forty-niners," swelled and poured west. It is thought that 70,000 made it to California in 1849 alone, despite the fact that the year was wetter than usual on the plains and swollen rivers often could not be crossed. In 1850, 45,000 trekked along the California Trail. Most, 40,000 in 1849, arrived by sea. Between 1848 and 1851 36,000 of those arriving by ship had crossed the Panamanian isthmus or Mexico and taken a ship north from West Coast ports—often with great difficulty and expense.

Most of the easily accessible placer gold had been found by 1853, and miners resorted to hydraulic mining, an environmentally disastrous method of washing out gold-bearing gravel deposits with high-powered jets of water, a practice later banned. This method required more capital, and many individual miners became employees of larger concerns.

MAP 190 (*left, top*).
Commercial mapmaker J.H. Colton published this rather attractive map in 1849 to show the location of the new California gold discoveries and the routes to them. The connection of the California Trail to the Oregon Trail near Fort Hall is surprisingly not indicated, despite the fact that it was one of the most popular routes.

MAP 191 (*left*).
An interesting broadsheet published in 1849 to a ready market anxious for information on the gold discoveries. The map at left shows the location of the goldfields within Upper or New California, the territory just acquired from Mexico, while the map at right shows the principal sea routes available: round the Horn; to the isthmus of Panama; and to Vera Cruz, on the east coast of Mexico, the latter two also requiring a dangerous trek across land to reach the Pacific and an uncertain further voyage north. Parties of forty or fifty are recommended to help prevent attack by bandits.

IMPORTANT DIRECTIONS
TO PERSONS EMIGRATING TO
CALIFORNIA.

DESCRIPTION OF CALIFORNIA,
OR THE NEW
GOLD REGION.

ROUTE via CHAGRES and PANAMA.

ROUTE BY CAPE HORN.

ANOTHER ROUTE.

Map 192 (*right*).
San Francisco was the West's first city, retaining its dominance until the rise of Los Angeles in the next century. This is a map of the Bay Area, complete with a view of the city, published in Germany in 1854.

Map 193 (*below, center*).
Barely qualifying as a map is this evocative 1851 view of San Francisco in the gold rush days, based on the sketches of a visiting Englishman. The harbor is crammed with ships that brought gold seekers to the city and were then abandoned when the crew deserted to try their luck in the goldfields as well. Many ships were hauled up onto the mud flats along the San Francisco waterfront and covered over to make instant warehouses or stores.

Map 194 (*below*).
A superb promotional bird's-eye map of Virginia City, published in 1861, complete with views of all the subscribing businesses around the perimeter. Virginia City, Nevada, is perhaps the most famous of all the western mining boomtowns, appearing in 1859 following the discovery of gold and silver at the equally famous Comstock Lode. The settlement had close to 30,000 inhabitants at its peak.

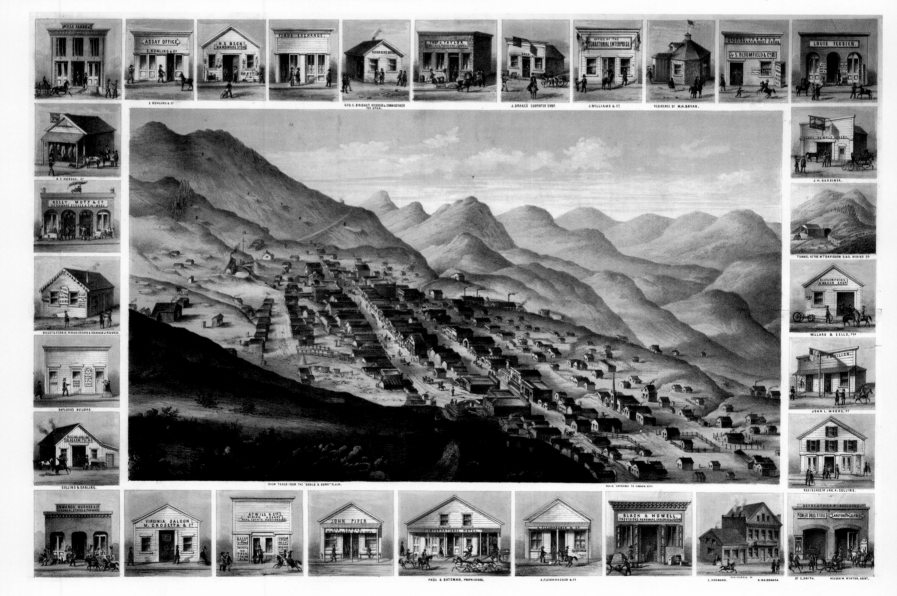

The California Gold Rush was essentially over by 1855, but many of those who had rushed to the goldfields stayed in California, settling down to other more mundane, but sustainable, livelihoods. The gold rush brought the new American acquisition, California, dramatically to the attention of the world, assuring its prosperity from its very beginning. Settlers lured not by gold but by agricultural prospects and a forgiving climate would continue the migration west. California became a state in 1850 (see page 182) and was connected to the rest of the nation by a railroad within twenty years.

THE COMSTOCK LODE

The promise of easy wealth would long continue to draw men west. Hardly was the California Gold Rush over when rumors began to circulate about other fabulous gold strikes throughout the West—in today's Nevada, in Arizona, in Colorado, in Montana and Idaho, and in British Columbia.

Probably the most famous of these was the Comstock Lode, which, as well as being a major gold source, was the first major American deposit of silver ore to be discovered. Between 1859 and 1878 the Comstock Lode yielded $400 million in silver and gold—worth more than $400 billion today—and played a huge role in financing the growth of San Francisco as well as Nevada. The wealth brought Nevada into the Union as a state in 1864, even without the normal population numbers, so important was it in financing the Union armies in the Civil War.

Gold production in Nevada had spilled over from the California fields in 1850 after a company of Mormon emigrants found gold near Dayton; the emigrants abandoned their find because they anticipated finding even more in California!

The details of the discovery of the Comstock Lode are disputed. The initial discovery is attributed to two veterans of the California Gold Rush, the brothers Ethan Allen and Hosea Ballou Grosh, in 1857. Hosea died from tetanus after injuring his foot, but Ethan, taking with him samples and maps, set out to raise capital in San Francisco, only to be caught in Sierra snows, dying after gruesome amputation of his limbs to prevent gangrene. Their cabin and lands were taken over by Henry Comstock, who, when miners Pat McLaughlin and Peter O'Reilly found silver ore at Gold Hill,

MAP 195 (*above*).
Gold Hill, the site of the first gold find, and *Virginia City*, also shown in bird's-eye views in MAP 194, *previous page*, and MAP 199, *overleaf*. At top is *Site of American City*, the area that became American Flat. At one time this community was growing so fast its residents petitioned to have the state legislature moved there, but it failed when the gold and silver ran out, and nothing remains but the ruins of later mills that were built to extract minerals from the tailings. This map is from 1864.

MAP 196 (*below*).
The main Comstock Lode is shown in yellow on this 1865 map. *Gold Hill* Mine, site of the first find, is at center left, just below the "D" of the larger words *Gold Hill*, applied to the immediate district. *The Comstock Ledge* is covered with mine workings, shown with the mine name or that of its owner.

MAP 197 (*right, top*).
An 1862 map of the Washoe silver region. Shown are *Virginia City* and *Gold Hill*, connected by the straight line of the *Comstock Lead* (center left). *Dayton* (bottom right); *American Flat* (bottom, center); several settlements that are now ghost towns, such as *Silver City*; and numerous mines are named. Note also, at right, the *Immigrant Road*.

MAP 198 (*right, bottom*).
Central Nevada is littered with silver mines on this 1866 map. At center top is Humboldt Lake and the *Proposed Route Central Pacific Rail Road*, which would be completed in 1869.

immediately filed a claim on the adjacent land. Gold Hill Mine was not on the main lode, as can be seen on MAP 196, *below*. Another version of the story has Comstock persuading McLaughlin and O'Reilly that their find was on his land and making him a partner, together with two of his friends, Manny Penrod and James Finney. The latter went by the moniker

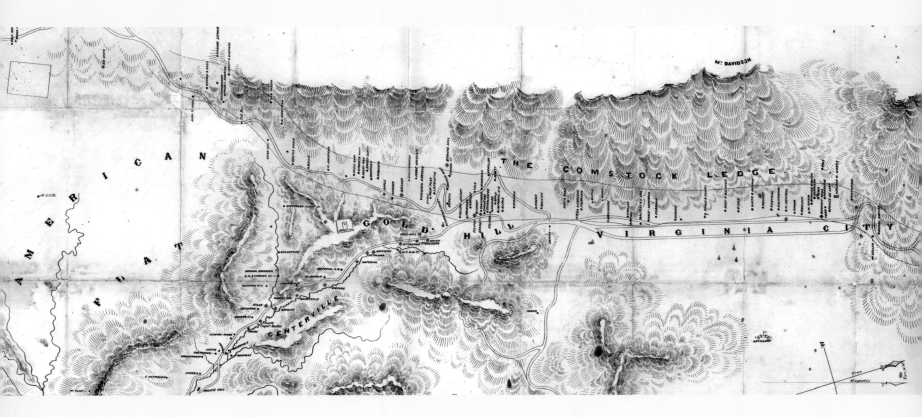

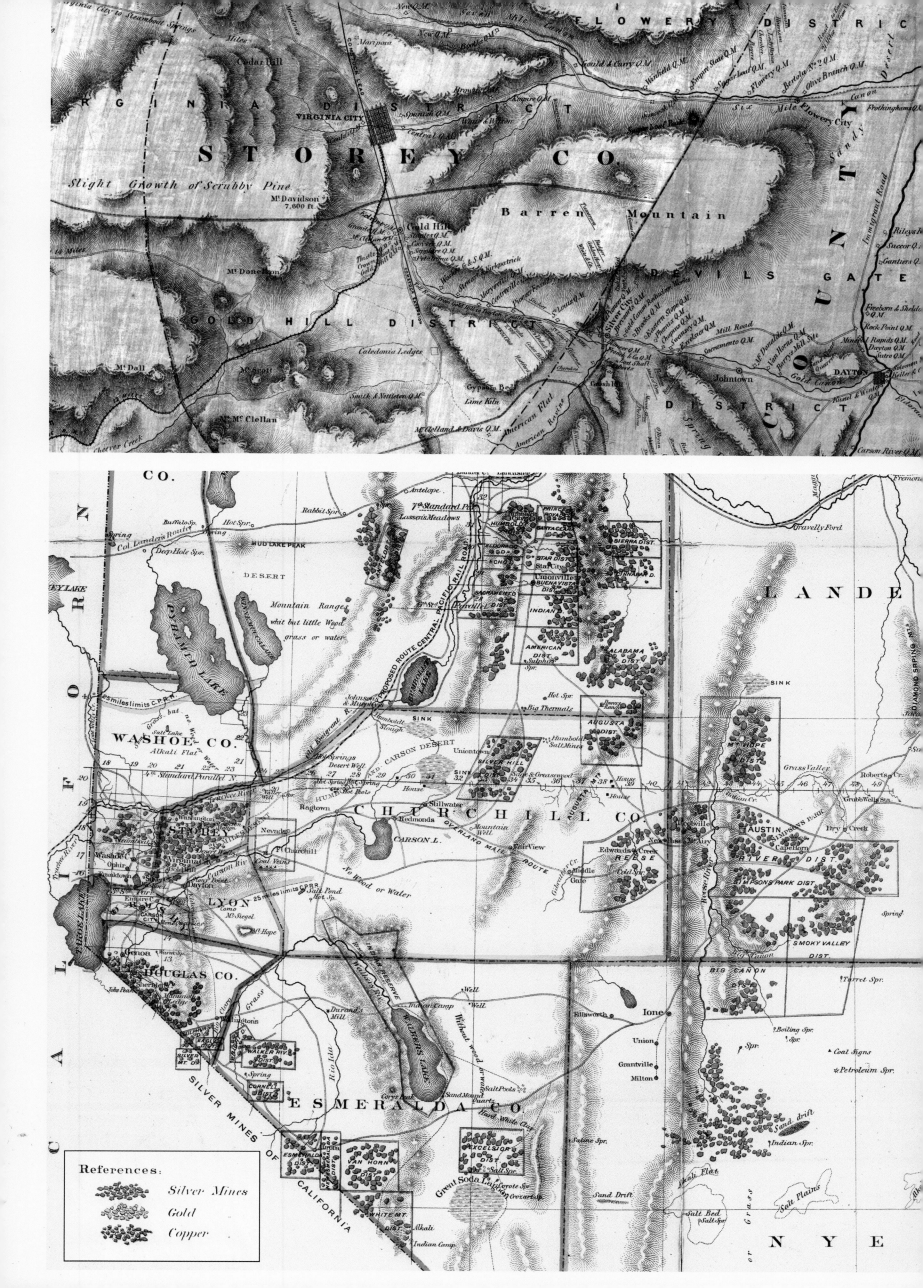

BIRDS EYE VIEW OF
VIRGINIA CITY
STOREY COUNTY, NEVADA.
1875

MAP 199 (*left*).
A superb bird's-eye-view map of Virginia City at its prime in 1875. A decade later it would be all but abandoned.

MAP 200 (*below*).
This wonderful 1875 map plots all the claims in and around the Comstock Lode. At top is a section of the lode, showing the many mine shafts. Also shown is the line of the Sutro Tunnel, built to drain all the mine workings, for, despite a lack of water above ground, below ground flooding was a constant problem. Adolph Sutro came up with the idea of running a drain tunnel under the workings from the lowest possible point. Such a tunnel could also be used to more easily remove the ore. A four-mile-long tunnel, about 1,900 feet deep, sixteen feet high, and twelve feet wide, was dug out from the valley near Dayton. Construction began in 1869 but took eight years to complete, and by that time most of the ore above the tunnel had already been removed, and ore now had to be brought up to the tunnel. The tunnel can be seen in the section, drawn two years before its completion. Nevertheless, it did make life easier for the miners; although little ore was removed through it, it greatly improved the drainage. But it was rather a major project for what proved to be a very short life span.

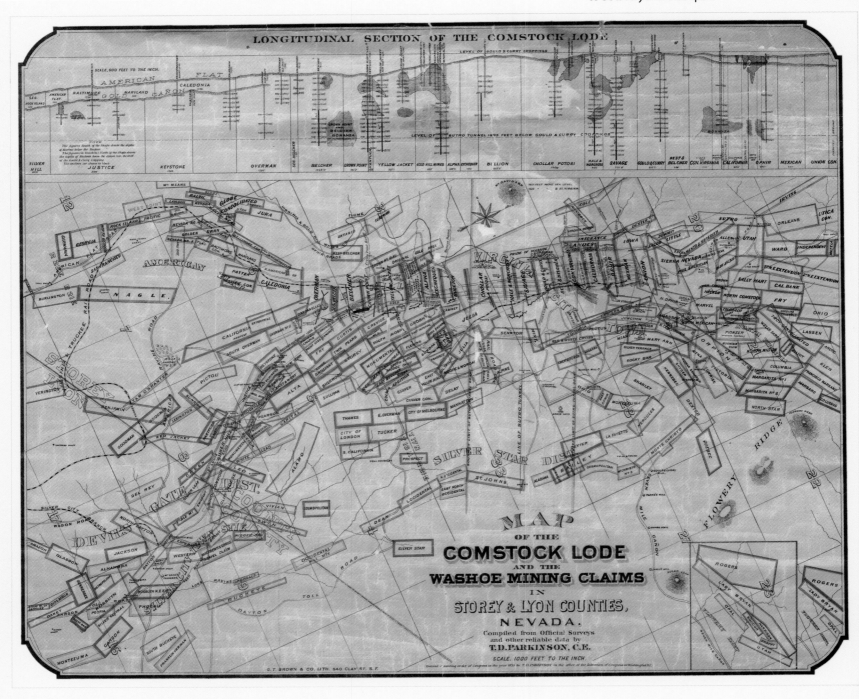

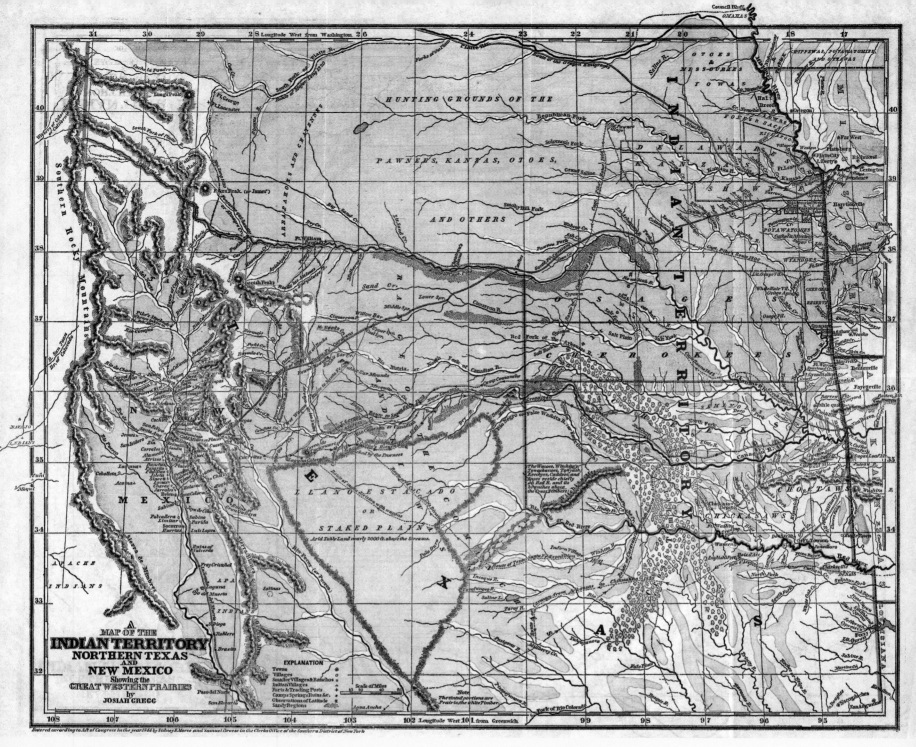

A MAP OF THE
INDIAN TERRITORY
NORTHERN TEXAS
AND
NEW MEXICO
Showing the
GREAT WESTERN PRAIRIES
by
JOSIAH GREGG

Map 201 (*above*).

Any good map available was pressed into service to aid gold seekers crossing the Plains in 1859 to the Pike's Peak goldfields. One was Josiah Gregg's map of the Great Plains, published in 1844 in his influential book *The Commerce of the Prairies,* known for its advancement of the myth that "rain follows the plow"—that cultivation will of itself create rainfall by increasing evaporation (see page 160). Gregg's theories may have been erroneous, but his map was excellent. The map was used by Stephen Watts Kearny and his Army of the West on their way to annex New Mexico in 1846 (see page 87).

Map 202 (*right*).

This 1836 map was reprinted in 1861 to give senators and congressmen an idea of the routes to Pike's Peak. The *Route of the Dragoons under the command of Col. Dodge in 1835* refers to the expedition of Henry Dodge to make a peace with the Comanche following the latter's attacks on emigrant Indians. *Bent's Trading House* is Bent's Fort, constructed in 1833 by traders Charles Bent, his brother William, and Ceran St. Vrain. The fort had fourteen-foot-high adobe walls. Charles Bent was killed in the Taos Revolt (see page 88) while governor of New Mexico in January 1847. *Pike's Peak,* in the region that would spark a short-lived gold rush in 1859, is at left. The *Arkansas River* is here the *United States Boundary.* The *Western Territory* is today Kansas, Colorado, and Nebraska. Map 304, *page 147,* appeared in the same 1836 Senate document as this map.

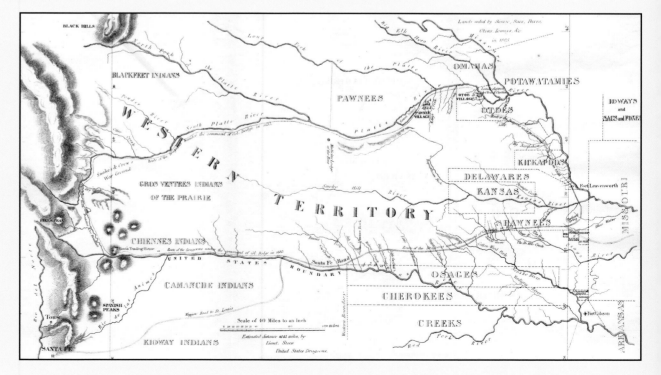

"Old Virginny" and lent his name to the instant town that appeared on the site, Virginia City. At any rate, Comstock seems to have got the better of the others, buying them out and ensuring that his name would be the one that would live on for posterity.

The Comstock Lode was one of the richest sources of silver and gold ever found. By June 1860 Virginia City had over ten thousand inhabitants; by October, it had 154 businesses, including eight law offices and six physicians, who were needed to attend to miners who were poisoned by the drinking water, which contained arsenic.

Fortunes were made and lost, many by staking claims and buying and selling them rather than mining. By the 1870s claims were consolidated by larger companies with the capital to buy the heavy equipment needed to mine the remaining ore, deep underground. The peak year for production was 1877, but the Comstock was largely exhausted only three years later.

GOLD AND SILVER

Not all gold or silver discoveries were as lucrative as the Comstock. In 1859 the Pike's Peak Gold Rush began, and although the gold find turned out to be much less significant than in California. All the same, the rush produced an influx of EuroAmericans, many of whom stayed. The rapid population growth led, in 1861, to the creation of Colorado Territory. Prior to 1859 the central Rockies had been sparsely populated, the domain of fur traders such as Charles Bent and Ceran St. Vrain, who established trading forts such as Bent's Fort, on the Arkansas, in 1833, and Fort St. Vrain, on the South Platte, in 1837.

Gold had been found as early as 1850 in streams flowing out of the Rockies to the South Platte River, and a small group from New Mexico had obtained gold there in 1857. But it was William Green Russell, who had previously found gold in Georgia and California, who set off a rush. In July 1858 he found gold where Dry Creek entered the South Platte, now the city of Englewood, in the metro Denver urban area.

The Pike's Peak Gold Rush produced as many paper cities as gold finds, even before it really got started. Prospectors from Lawrence, Kansas, already in the region, were attracted to Russell's find, building cabins to winter at a place they christened Montana City. Anticipating a demand, some of them built cabins and claimed a site they called St. Charles. Later that year Russell organized yet another town he called Auraria. A veteran town promoter, William Larimer, arrived on the scene in November, staking out a town to be called Highland. On 22 November 1858 Larimer and others organized the Denver City Town Company, naming it after the governor of Kansas Territory, James Denver. (Unknown to the promoters was the fact that Denver had resigned a few weeks earlier.) All these sites would later be amalgamated into the city of Denver (see page 206).

The real gold rush materialized the following year, with forty or fifty thousand gold seekers streaming across the Plains and ascending rivers and creeks into the Rockies. In May a vial containing eighty dollars' worth of gold was displayed in Denver—gold found a week earlier on Clear Creek, west of Denver and near another new town, Golden City. The towns, such as they were, emptied as gold fever seized the country. That year a quarter million dollars' worth of gold was obtained, both panned from placer deposits and mined from quartz ores.

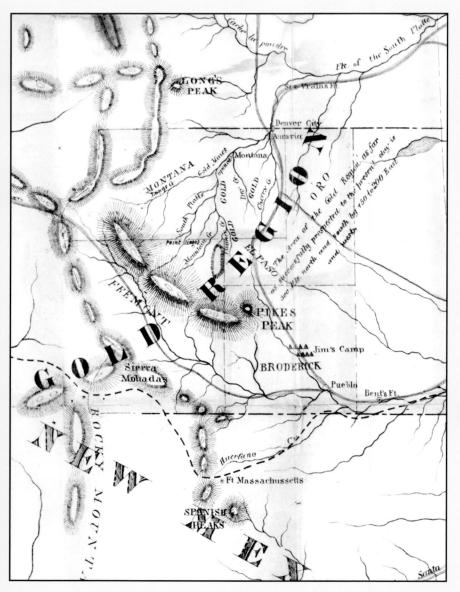

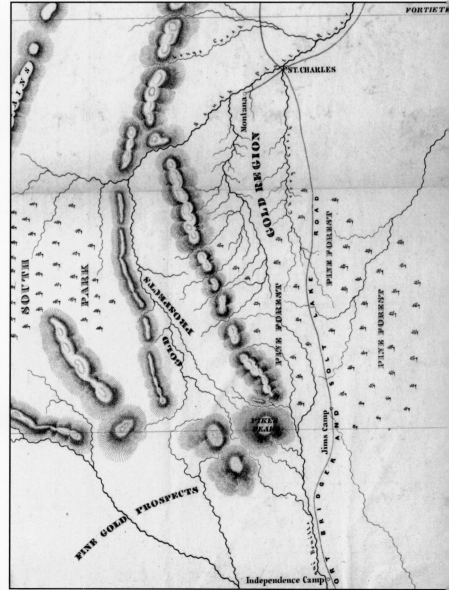

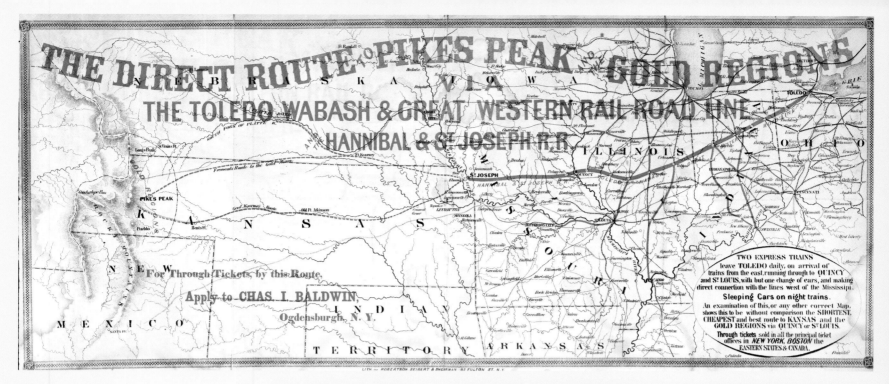

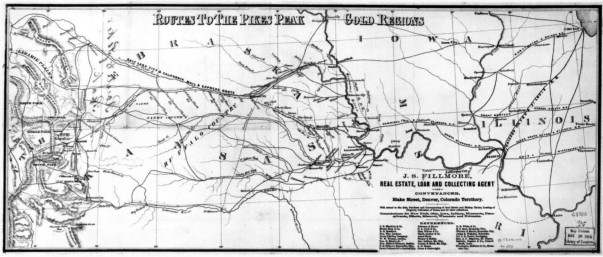

Map 203 (far left).
This 1859 map shows both *Denver City* and *Auraria* and the network of streams along the upper South Platte River marked *Gold* and *Gold mines opened*. *Dry Cr[eek]* was one of the first places gold was found, in July 1858. *Montana* City is shown; it consisted of a few cabins built by a contingent of gold seekers from Lawrence, Kansas.

Map 204 (left).
Maps showed what their creators or commissioners wanted to show. Here, on another map of the gold regions dated 1859, the settlement of *St. Charles* is shown but not the competing towns of Denver and Auraria, which are shown on Map 203 to the exclusion of St. Charles.

Map 205 (above) and Map 206 (right, above).
As with the California Gold Rush, numerous maps and guidebooks were hurried into print to take advantage of the sudden demand. These two maps show competing routes. Map 205, published in 1859, was clearly drawn in a particular hurry to advertise the two railroads, as the routes lead to *Pike's Peak* rather than to the area in which gold had been found up to that time. The Hannibal & St. Joseph Railroad was completed in 1859 and made St. Joseph, Missouri, for a time the westernmost point connected by rail to the east.

Map 207 (right).
Not long after the influx of settlers came demands for territorial status. Various names were proposed for a territory to be carved out of western Kansas and eastern Utah, such as Jefferson (for which a territorial government was even elected), Idaho, and, as here, *Colona*. The region would achieve territorial status as Colorado in 1861. See page 184.

Map 208 (below).
The extent of Kansas at the time is clearly shown in this map, published in 1862. The *Gold Regions* are shown at left, with the settlements of *Denver City*, *Auraria*, and *Montana*.

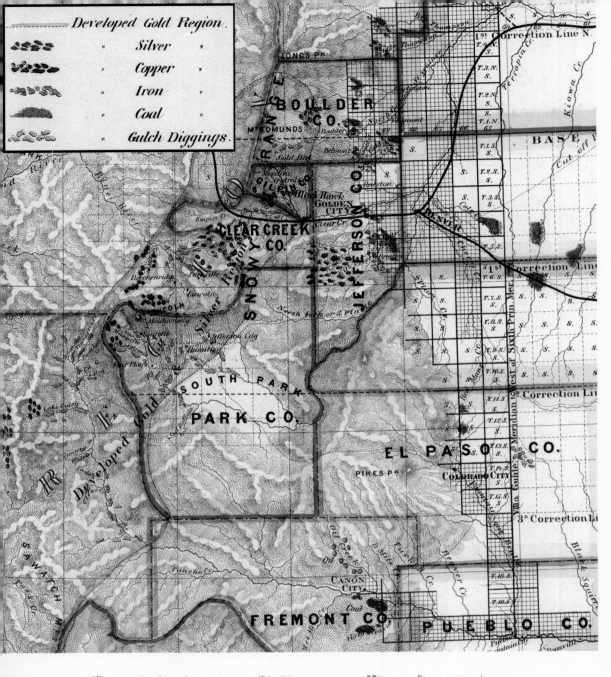

Developed Gold Region.
Silver
Copper
Iron
Coal
Gulch Diggings.

MAP 209 (*left*).

All manner of minerals had been discovered in Colorado by 1866, as this map from that year shows. Note especially the numerous coal deposits east of *Denver*. The *Developed Gold & Silver Region* covers a large area of the mountains. The rail lines shown are projected tracks; it would be 1870 before the Kansas Pacific and Denver Pacific lines were completed into the city (see page 122).

MAP 210 (*below, left*).

This 1866 map produced, like MAP 209, by the United States Land Office, shows the location of known gold, silver, and copper deposits in Arizona Territory and New Mexico Territory. The color key is shown *below*. The United States gained extensive deposits of silver and gold with the territory it acquired in 1853–54 with the Gadsden Purchase, all those shown in the southern part of Arizona. See also MAP 395, *page 183*.

MAP 211 (*below, right*).

Mining districts, organized when significant mineral finds were made, are shown as they existed in 1865 in the new Arizona Territory. Some of the settlements shown, for example *La Paz*, are today ghost towns. (See also MAP 599, *page 259*, a modern marker for the ghost town of Chloride, also in this region.) Henry Wickenburg's *Vulture Mine* is shown in the *Wickenburg Dist.*, northwest of the confluence of the *Gila River* and the *Rio Salado* (Salt River), the location of today's Phoenix. To the north is the U.S. Army's *Ft. Whipple* and the territorial capital, *Prescott*, a mining town established in 1863. The town was chosen as the capital to be far removed from Confederate sympathizers in the south; the capital moved to Tucson after the Civil War, in 1867, and then to the newcomer, Phoenix, in 1889.

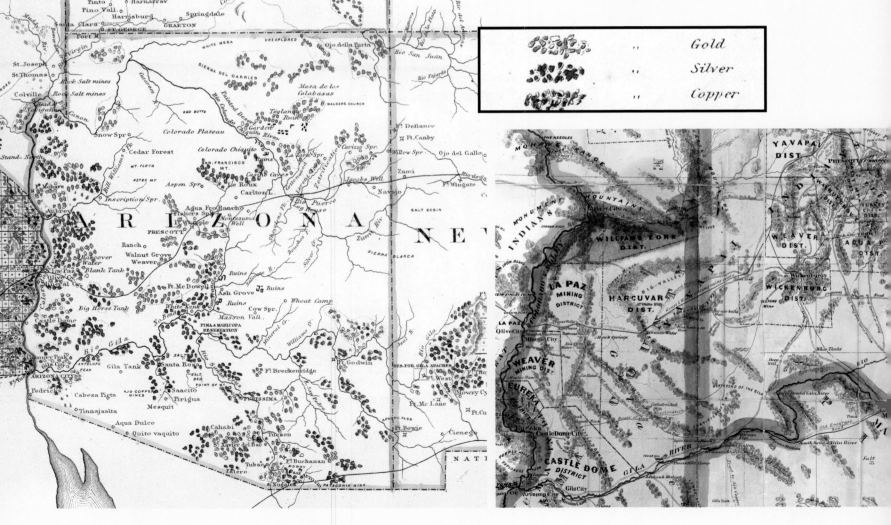

Gold
Silver
Copper

MAP 212 (*right*).
Another part of the 1866 U.S. Land Office map, showing mineral deposits in eastern Washington Territory, Idaho Territory, and Montana Territory. The key is the same as for **MAP 210**, with the addition of coal deposits, in dark blue, found on the Green River in southeastern Idaho, close to modern-day coal workings in the Powder River Basin of Wyoming (see **MAP 586**, *page 254*). The dotted line running into *Virginia City* from the east is the line of the Bozeman Trail (though this trail goes to Yankton, in Dakota Territory). The solid line is the northern route proposed in the Pacific Railroad Surveys of 1853–56 (see page 114). **MAP 210** and this map demonstrate the extensive nature of gold and silver mining in the West at this time.

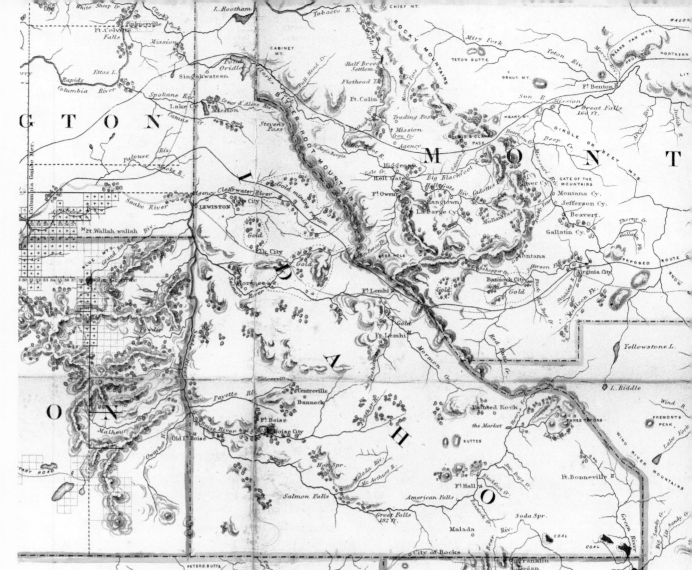

As had happened in Nevada, the easily obtainable gold was soon gone, and deep-rock mining, requiring more capital, was required. Nevertheless, gold worth some $3 million a year was mined in Colorado between 1860 and 1864. Further mineral wealth was to be found in Colorado but would await a second boom after silver was found near Leadville in 1874 (see page 138).

Gold was found in 1857 on the Gila River in New Mexico, and many other finds followed. One of the most famous was that of Henry Wickenburg, an Austrian prospector who in 1863 found what became the Vulture Mine; this created the town of Wickenburg, northwest of Phoenix (**MAP 211**, *left*). Arizona is today littered with ghost towns from this era.

Gold and silver were also discovered in the Northwest, where an influx of miners led to the creation of Idaho Territory in 1863 and Montana Territory, a subdivision of the former, in 1864 (**MAP 213**, *right*). It also resulted in the building of the Bozeman Trail from the Oregon Trail near Fort Laramie to Virginia City (Montana), location of the first gold discovery in 1863 and the territorial capital in 1865, when it had ten thousand inhabitants. A series of forts were built along the Bozeman Trail to try to prevent depredations by Lakota, led by Red Cloud, upset at the intrusion of miners and settlers into their prime hunting territory (see page 150). Unfortunately for the Indians, the lure of easy wealth was going to ensure that EuroAmericans would keep coming west, regardless of the danger.

MAP 213 (*right*).
Part of a detailed map of gold and silver workings in the southern part of the new territory of Montana in 1865. Mine names have been inked in on a printed base map. The white area at bottom is Idaho Territory; note the *Mormon Fort*. The white square at bottom right is part of what would become Yellowstone National Park, in Wyoming. Near its northwest corner is *Virginia City*, territorial capital and western terminus of the Bozeman Trail. This trail was located in 1863 by John Bozeman, and in 1864 he led about two thousand settlers along it to Montana.

Map OF THE TERRITORY OF MONTANA WITH PORTIONS OF THE ADJOINING TERRITORIES.

Showing the Gulch or Placer Diggings actually worked, and Districts where Quartz (Gold & Silver) Lodes have been discovered to January 1st 1865

Drawn by W. W. de Lacy, for the use of THE FIRST LEGISLATURE OF MONTANA.

War in the West

Three armed conflicts occurred in the West in the nineteenth century, other than Indian wars, which are considered separately (see page 146). All were civil wars, pitting American against American. The first was the Mormon War, or Utah War, which took place between May 1857 and July 1858; the second was "Bleeding Kansas," between 1856 and 1859, over the slave status of the new territory; and the third the western battles of the Civil War, which, although serious, were but skirmishes compared with the carnage of the eastern killing fields.

What could be thought of as the West's own civil war was an armed confrontation between Mormons and the U.S. Army. At the time prejudice persisted against Mormons, especially with regard to their practice of polygamy and the appointment of church officials to civil positions. A number federal officials, including judges, deserted their posts in Utah, claiming that they feared for their safety. An incoming president, James Buchanan, in 1857 determined to bring the Mormons into line by establishing a larger military presence in the territory and replacing governor Brigham Young with a non-Mormon. The approach of a 2,500-strong federal army panicked the Mormons, who were used to persecution, into mounting a defense, and the Mormon militia—the Nauvoo Legion—blocked the passes into the valley of the Great Salt Lake.

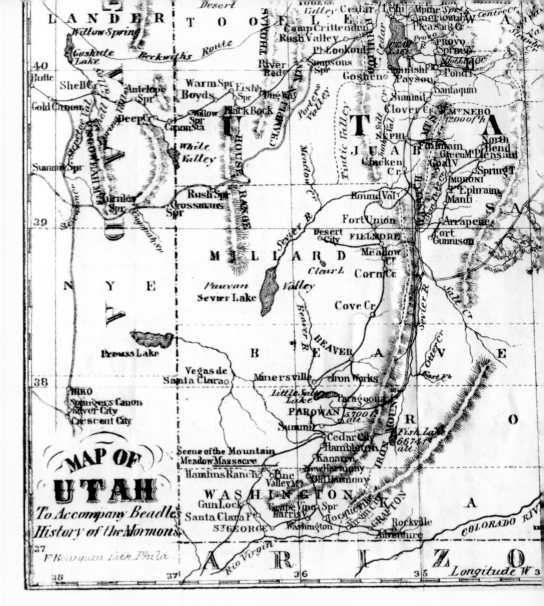

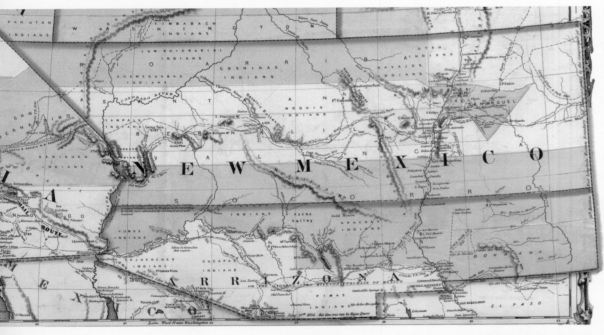

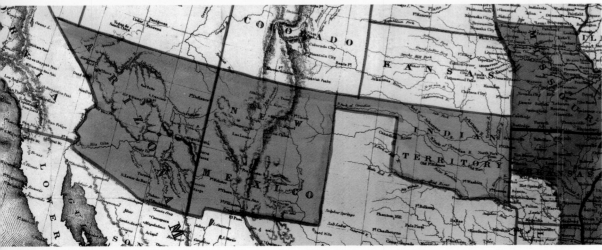

Map 214 (*above*).
A lack of understanding of their different religion meant that the Mormons always seemed to have enemies. Such people had driven them west in 1847. This map is from a biased anti-Mormon so-called exposé published in 1870 called *Life in Utah; or the Mysteries and Crimes of Mormonism*, by a journalist, J.H. Beadle. It seems to be the only map from the period that locates the *Scene of the Mountain Meadow Massacre*, near *Hamlins Ranch*, in the southwestern corner of the territory.

Map 215 (*left, top*).
In March 1861, Confederate sympathizers met at Mesilla and declared Arizona, the southern part of New Mexico, as shown on this map, a separate Confederate territory. The longitudinal shape was due to two factors: most Southern sympathizers were in the south, and the Confederate government had designs on southern California. Arizona, as shown in this 1862 commercial map, was confirmed as a Confederate territory by President Jefferson Davis in February 1862.

Map 216 (*left, bottom*).
In February 1863 U.S. President Abraham Lincoln signed an act creating a Union Arizona Territory, deliberately dividing New Mexico with a north–south line to thwart Confederate designs on California. In any case the Confederates did not continue to contest the Southwest as they were unable to follow up on their earlier military successes. This 1864 map shows "territory in possession of the Union" and depicts the new Union Arizona Territory, complete with what is now the southern tip of Nevada.

On 11 September 1857 local militia led by John D. Lee, together with some Paiute allies, ambushed a party of California-bound emigrants in southwestern Utah in an infamous incident that has not been properly explained even today. One hundred and twenty emigrants, including women and children, surrendered after a short siege, only to be killed by their attackers. The location of this sorry episode, later dubbed the Mountain Meadows Massacre, is shown on MAP 214, *left*.

Other than this incident the Mormon War produced only skirmishes with the U.S. Army, and a conclusion to the hostilities was negotiated in July 1858. The Army was allowed to set up bases, Brigham Young stepped down as governor, and Mormons were pardoned of rebellion. Only one person was ever convicted in connection with the Mountain Meadows Massacre: John D. Lee was executed at the site of his crime nearly twenty years later.

Kansas was the scene of much violence in the period leading up to the Civil War, all of which was a precursor to that conflict. The Kansas–Nebraska Act of 1854, which created those two territories, incorporated the principle of "popular sovereignty," whereby the territorial population could decide whether or not to allow slavery. Settlers from Missouri, an adjacent slave state, and from southern states poured into Kansas with the intention of voting for slavery, while organizations in the north funded settlers to move to Kansas to vote against it. Antislavery zealot John Brown also went to Kansas. The result, inevitably, was violence. Confrontations in "Bleeding Kansas" (a name coined by New York newspaperman Horace Greeley) led to over fifty deaths between 1856 and 1859.

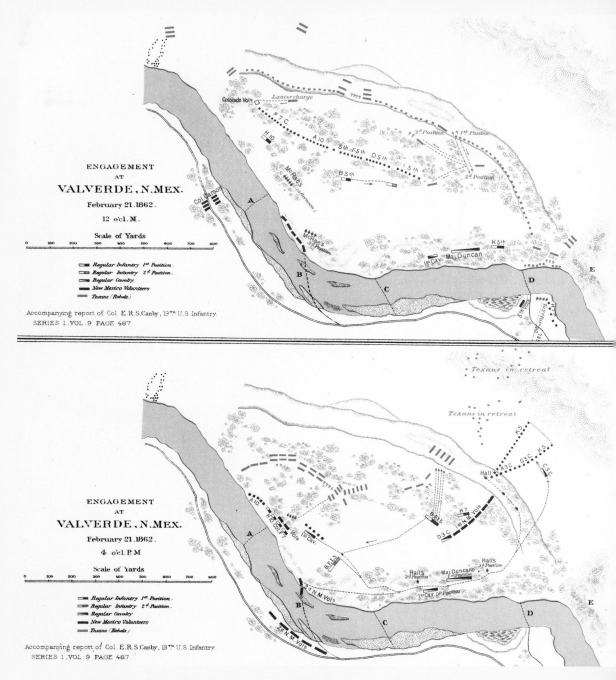

MAP 217 (*above, top*) and MAP 218 (*above*).
These two maps illustrate the Battle of Valverde, fought on the banks of the Rio Grande on 21 February 1862. Confederate troops—Texan volunteers—are indicated in red, while Union forces are in blue. MAP 217 and MAP 218 show the battle in detail at noon and 4 PM, respectively. These maps are from the official atlas of the Civil War, published in 1895.

Then came the Civil War, fought over the same issues. In Kansas, Confederate William Quantrill led 450 men on a murderous raid on the Union center of Lawrence on 21 August 1863, killing at least 150 men and burning most of the town. Later that year Quantrill and his men ambushed a Union military wagon train at Baxter Springs, Kansas, and after obtaining the Union surrender, massacred over a hundred soldiers.

As the Union was threatened in the East, western forts were abandoned to redeploy soldiers. In 1861 Texan colonel John R. Baylor saw an opportunity and raised a 250-strong army of volunteers to attack Fort Fillmore, across the border from El Paso. Despite boasting a garrison of seven hundred, the fort's commander panicked, and the fort was abandoned on Baylor's approach.

The following year, as part of a Confederate strategy to take California, an army under Henry Hopkins Sibley, with about three thousand men, moved north to take Fort Union, on the Santa Fe Trail, but the fort commander, Colonel Edward R.S. Canby, reinforced Fort Craig, to the south, on the Confederate line of advance. Canby's army, swollen with volunteers, including cavalry under Colonel Christopher "Kit" Carson, numbered about four thousand. On 21 February 1862 the two forces clashed at the Battle

of Valverde (MAP 217 and MAP 218, *above*). Sibley is generally considered to have won the day, although Canby destroyed half of the Confederate supply train and retained possession of Fort Craig.

Sibley clearly thought he was winning, for he moved north and, not bothering with Fort Union, took Albuquerque and Santa Fe. Then, however, thirteen hundred volunteers organized by the governor of the new Colorado Territory, William Gilpin, marched to Canby's aid. On 28 March the two forces met at Glorieta Pass, east of Santa Fe. Major John Chivington (of more later; see page 149) led an attack on Sibley's supply train, destroying seventy-three wagons and killing all his horses. Without them, Sibley could not prevail, and he retreated to Texas.

There were other minor skirmishes in the West, notably what is considered by some to have been the westernmost battle of the Civil War, at Picacho Pass, fifty miles northwest of Tucson, on 15 April 1862; but here only thirteen Union Californians fought ten New Mexican Confederates.

But the Civil War did spur the resolve of the Union to unify the country under its banner, and to this end President Abraham Lincoln authorized the building of the transcontinental railroad, an event that in the longer term would have a much greater effect on the West.

LINKING THE WEST

BY STAGE AND WAGON AND PONY EXPRESS

1861

TODAY

With thousands of people in the West, and more arriving every day, an urgent need for communications arose—with families back east, with each other, and with suppliers. The first requirement was for mail, and this need was initially satisfied in California by private individuals such as Alexander Todd, a miner who gave up looking for gold because of poor health and in 1849 signed up miners for his service—sorting through mail dumped at a post office after arriving by sea to San Francisco and delivering it to the gold workings. Todd charged an ounce of gold dust for each letter and made more money from the gold rush than many of the miners.

To carry people and supplies, however, several stagecoach lines were organized. In 1854 competing lines merged to form the California Stage Company, which quickly grew to control most of the stagecoach lines in California and north to Oregon. By 1856 it was the largest such operation in the United States, with routes totaling over two thousand miles.

Still there was no regular service connecting the West with the East. In 1856 a petition signed by 75,000 Californians pushed Congress to agree to award a mail contract to a transcontinental service. Sectional factions argued about the route, and in 1857 the postmaster general, a southerner, decided on a southern route from Tipton, Missouri, to San Francisco via El Paso and Fort Yuma and awarded the lucrative mail contract to John Butterfield, one of the

Above and right.
Two covers from the same Union Pacific travel brochure in 1931, showing western travel in *1861*, the stagecoach, and *today*—that is, 1931. Interestingly, the second cover shows two planes as well as the train; in 1931 this new form of transportation was clearly not considered a threat to long-distance trains.

MAP 219 (*below*).
The principal stagecoach routes in the West are depicted on this rare 1867 map produced by the U.S. Post Office two years before the railroad would preempt the central route. The routes connect main nodes of population—typically mining centers—and also military forts.

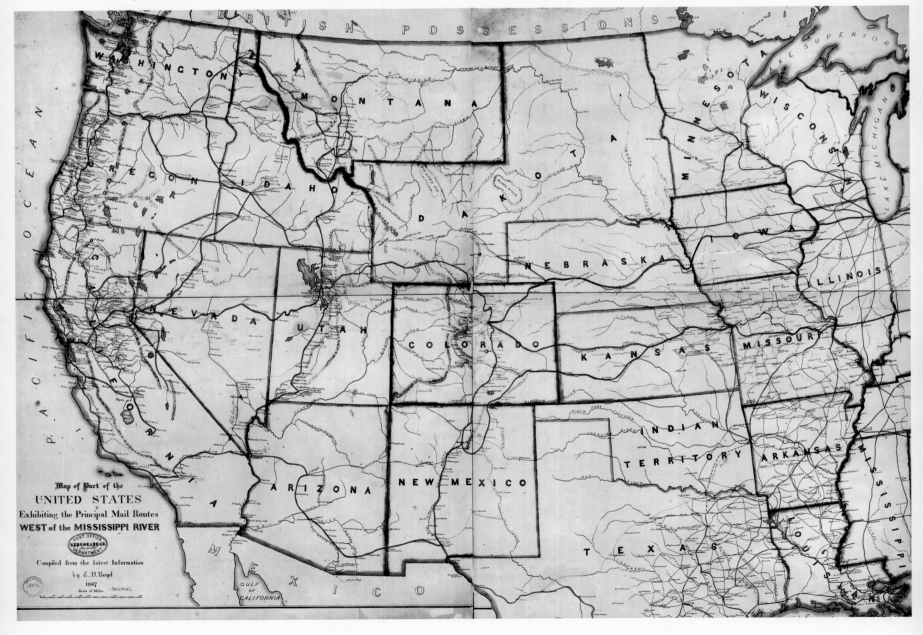

Map of Part of the
UNITED STATES
Exhibiting the Principal Mail Routes
WEST of the MISSISSIPPI RIVER

Compiled from the latest Information
by E.D.Boyd
1867

Map 220 (above, left and right).
Two extracts from an 1860 map name two mail routes: the *Overland Express Route* along the South Platte River north of *Denver* and the *Salt Lake City & California Mail & Express Route* along the North Platte west of Omaha. The former also shows *St. Vrains Fort*, the trading fort set up by Ceran St. Vrain in 1833. This map also shows a *Cut Off* to Denver. One of the critical factors that allowed the infant Denver to succeed over its several competing neighbors was that it won the first stagecoach connection; in its day this achievement was as important as winning a railroad connection would be later.

Map 221 (right, center top).
In the wake of the unrest in Utah (see page 110), in 1859 Topographical Engineer Captain James H. Simpson was ordered to survey better wagon routes to Utah. This is part of his map of the Great Basin delineating a better route that he had found across the Kobeh Valley, one of the many dry valleys that alternate with minor mountain ranges across the basin. The route, part of the Central Overland Trail, is marked *Practicable for wagon's [sic]*. His new route shortened the distance from San Francisco to the East by 250 miles and was, as Simpson wrote, "at once adopted by the overland mail, the pony-express, and the telegraph."

Map 222 (right, center).
The West has no telegraph lines at all according to this 1858 map, whereas the area east of the Mississippi has a reasonably dense network. The transcontinental telegraph line would be completed three years later.

Map 223 (right, center bottom).
The transcontinental telegraph—the green line—is already shown completed on this 1855 map, which shows the approximate route it would take in 1861.

Map 224 (below).
The legendary Pony Express was so short-lived that few, if any, contemporary maps were made of its route. This beautifully illustrated map is a poster issued by the American Pioneer Trails Association in 1960 to mark the centennial of the beginning of the Pony Express, though it was originally published in 1951 by Union Pacific. The western scenes are paintings by artist William Henry Jackson, most of which are in the collection of the National Parks Service at Scott's Bluff, on the Oregon Trail. Forty-four of the over 150 waystations are marked. These were placed every ten miles or so—the distance over which a horse could maintain a gallop.

PONY EXPRESS ROUTE APRIL 3, 1860 – OCTOBER 24, 1861.

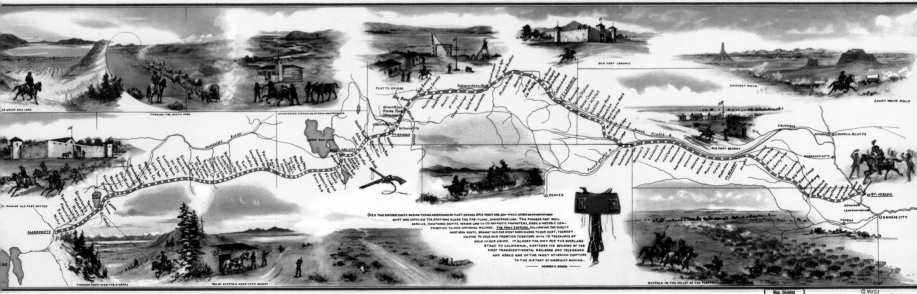

ISSUED BY THE AMERICAN PIONEER TRAILS ASSOCIATION IN COMMEMORATION OF THE PONY EXPRESS CENTENNIAL ★ APRIL 3, 1960 – OCTOBER 24, 1961

founders of American Express. He was financed by two of the other founders, Henry Wells and William Fargo, who in 1852 had set up an express company—a combined bank and transportation company—in California, the renowned Wells Fargo. Butterfield set up two hundred relay or swing stations—where horses were changed—and home stations—where drivers were changed and meals provided. The entire trip took twenty-four or twenty-five days. Butterfield Overland Mail operated from 1858 to 1861, when service was interrupted by the Civil War.

To profit from the U.S. Army's need for supplies to be delivered to its network of western forts, a wagon freight company, Russell, Majors & Waddell, was organized in 1854 and soon emerged as the predominant company. In 1855 twenty separate wagon trains were dispatched, five hundred wagons carrying 2.5 million pounds of freight west across the Plains. The wagon trains were highly structured, moving with military precision with hundreds of men, covering about fifteen miles a day.

Russell, Majors & Waddell thought 1857 would increase its profits, as the Army geared up for the Mormon War (see page 110), but the wagon trains became the victim of guerilla attacks by Mormons, and the Army did not follow through with its promise of reimbursement. William Russell came up with a scheme to ship supplies to the new Pike's Peak gold-mining region, and to Salt Lake City, then to California, creating the Central Overland, California and Pike's Peak Express and a new central overland stage route. The 1,913-mile-long journey took three weeks and had 153 stations about twelve miles apart—a costly business. From the beginning it was uneconomic without a mail contract, and the company initials quickly became popularly known as "Clean Out of Cash and Poor Pay."

Russell then devised a new scheme to win a mail contract. He created the famed but short-lived Pony Express, using single riders on a relay of fast horses, and a network of relay (swing) and home stations, just like the stagecoach but taking shortcuts on lesser trails and covering the almost two thousand miles from St. Joseph, Missouri, where the westernmost rail lines ended, to Sacramento, California, in just ten days (MAP 224, *previous page*). It was a dangerous business. The company advertised for "young, skinny, wiry fellows, not over eighteen. Must be expert riders, willing to risk death daily. Orphans preferred. Wages $25 per week."

The Pony Express lasted from April 1860 to October 1861, when it was put out of business by the completion of the transcontinental telegraph. In a few years, communication with the West Coast had been cut from twenty-five days to a few minutes. Stages and wagons remained, since they transported people and goods, not just information.

The Russell, Majors & Waddell empire was forced into bankruptcy by the ruthless Ben Holladay, who took over the company in 1861 and for a while held a virtual monopoly on freight and passenger service between Salt Lake City and the Missouri. Holladay owned 20,000 vehicles that worked over 2,670 miles of routes, employed 15,000 people, and crushed potential competitors mercilessly. In 1866 he sold out to Wells Fargo, which was able to adapt its business to the coming railroad by providing security cars on trains and developing a network of feeder stagecoach routes. A considerable network of stagecoach and wagon routes remained in the West (MAP 219, *page 112*), but most were eventually put out of business by the railroad.

SURVEYING A RAILROAD

A transcontinental railroad had been proposed as early as the 1840s, but it was not until 1852 that Congress approved a comprehensive survey of possible routes, to be carried out under the direction of the secretary of war, Jefferson Davis, later the first and only president of the Confederate States of America. These were the Pacific Railroad Surveys.

Three principal general routes were surveyed and mapped. A northern route (MAP 225, *below, left*), surveyed under Isaac I. Stevens, the new governor of Washington Territory, and carried out by Captain George B. McClellan, later a Civil War general, was considered dubious, since Stevens wanted to promote the Northwest, and the route was later resurveyed by a civilian engineer hired by the Washington territorial legislature. A survey of a central route (MAP 227, *right, top*) was begun by topographical engineer Captain John Gunnison, but he was killed by Indians at Sevier Lake in Utah. The survey was continued by Lieutenant E.G. Beckwith. Ironically, despite the fact that it was the central route over which the first rail link would be built, Beckwith's survey was largely ignored because he was unable to

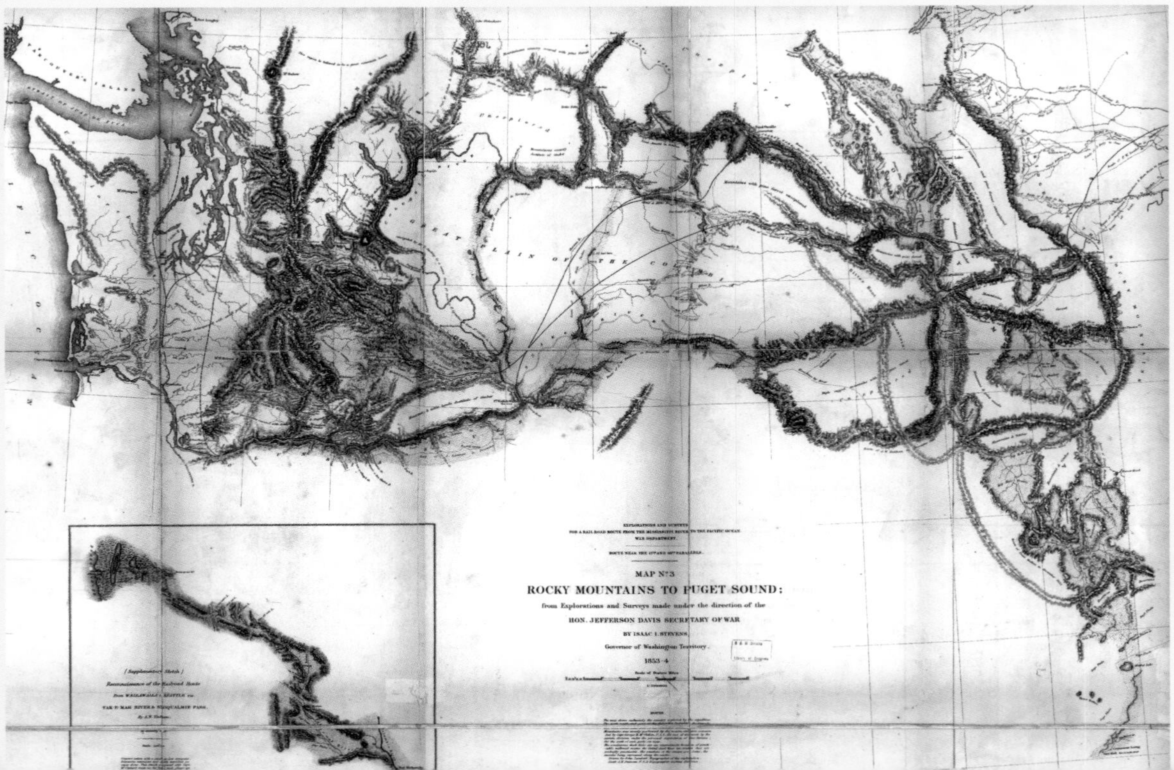

MAP 225 (*below, left*).
The westernmost sheet of the survey of the northern route produced by Isaac Stevens and George McClellan. Puget Sound is at left.

MAP 226 (*below, right*).
The survey of a southern route carried out by Amiel Weeks Whipple and Joseph Christmas Ives in 1853 and 1854. *Albuquerque* is at right, *Los Angeles* at left.

MAP N?3
ROCKY MOUNTAINS TO PUGET SOUND:
from Explorations and Surveys made under the direction of the
HON. JEFFERSON DAVIS SECRETARY OF WAR
BY ISAAC I. STEVENS
Governor of Washington Territory.
1853–4

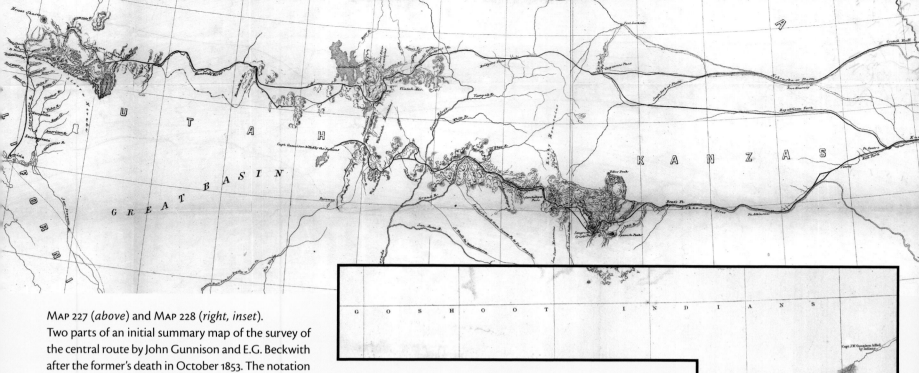

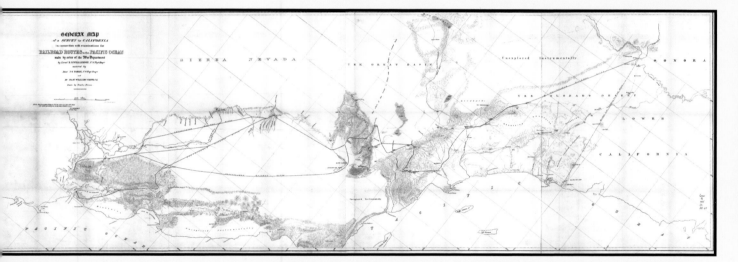

Map 227 (*above*) and Map 228 (*right, inset*).
Two parts of an initial summary map of the survey of
the central route by John Gunnison and E.G. Beckwith
after the former's death in October 1853. The notation
Capt Gunnison killed by the Indians can be seen near Sevier Lake in Utah. The route entered the Central Valley of California at
the headwaters of the Sacramento River before going south to San Francisco Bay. Map 228 is one of the more detailed maps of
the Gunnison-Beckwith survey and reflects the animosity between EuroAmericans and Indians. Not only is there the notation
about *Capt. J.W. Gunnison killed by Indians*, just north of Sevier Lake, but the cartographer, F.W. von Egloffstein, has written
Goshoot Indians in the blank area north and west of the lake, perhaps as a result of this incident.

Map 229 (*left*).
Robert Williamson's
1853 survey of po-
tential north–south
railroad routes in
California, to connect
either San Francisco
or Los Angeles with
the endpoints of the
southern or central
routes, respectively.
North is at left.

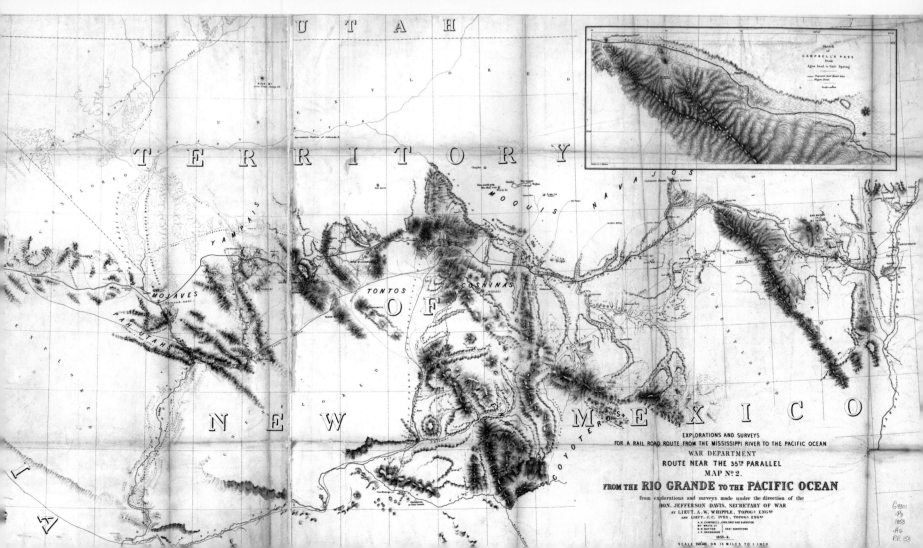

Map 230 (left).
Topographical engineer Lieutenant Gouverneur K. Warren compiled the Pacific Railroad Surveys into several summary maps such as this one, drawn in 1857. On it he has superimposed the state and territorial boundaries existing at the time.

Map 231 (below).
Theodore Judah's map of the Sacramento Valley Railroad, which actually ran up the American River from Sacramento to Folsom, at top, at the location of *Negro Bar.* Construction of the line began in February 1855, and the first train ran the full length a year later. Judah could see the possibilities of continuing the line to create a railroad to the East.

President Abraham Lincoln, who had previously been a railroad lawyer, was a strong proponent of a transcontinental line and, despite the distraction of the Civil War, brought the process to fruition. The first Pacific Railroad Act was passed by Congress in 1862, creating the Union Pacific Railroad and authorizing it to build west to meet the Central Pacific, which was to build east. Financing was critical. The government awarded the railroads five alternate sections (square miles) on each side of the track for every mile laid and purchased railroad

calculate cost estimates. A southern route (Map 226, *previous page*) was surveyed by topographical engineers Amiel Weeks Whipple and Joseph Christmas Ives. Congress decided in 1854 that Whipple's survey was not far enough south—given the Gadsden Purchase of 1853–54, which added considerably to the territory of the United States in this region (see page 182). So another survey, led by Lieutenant John G. Parke and Lieutenant John Pope, mapped a possible route that used the valley of the Gila River. In addition to the lateral surveys of the West, Lieutenant Robert S. Williamson was commissioned to survey north–south routes within California and north to the Columbia in Oregon—routes that might connect with whatever east–west route was chosen to serve the whole coast (Map 229, *previous page*).

Analysis of the surveys produced a recommendation for the southern route, but sectional interests in this period just prior to the Civil War would not allow for the congressional authorization of any one route, and with the war the scheme was temporarily shelved until the North alone, and Abraham Lincoln in particular, revived the scheme in 1861, easily choosing the central route. The surveys did, however, vastly increase American knowledge of the West, and they were published in several large illustrated tomes that included reports by specialists on scientific subjects. It was the first major Army survey of the West, but it would not be the last.

A Transcontinental Railroad

Theodore Dehone Judah, a young New York railroad engineer, went to California in 1854 to supervise the construction of the Sacramento Valley Railroad, a line from Sacramento up the American River valley toward the mining districts of the Sierra (Map 231, *right*). His experience with this line led to aspirations for its continuation east to create a transcontinental line. In 1860 he surveyed a route across the Sierra Nevada and the following year, with four Sacramento merchants—Leland Stanford, Collis P. Huntington, Charles Crocker, and Mark Hopkins—founded the Central Pacific Railroad to build such a link.

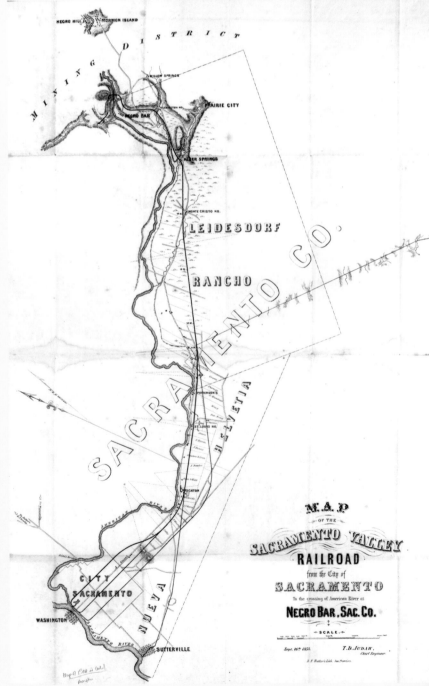

bonds, the money for which would be paid out as the work progressed. The act was amended in 1864 to award ten sections of land on each side of the track. This amendment led the railroad, especially its vice president, Thomas Durant, to demand route changes where more money could be made from the change. Such a demand caused the railroad's first chief engineer, Peter Dey (Map 233, *below*), to resign. Durant also set up a financing and supply business called the Credit Mobilier, the main purpose of which seems to have been to ensure that the principal investors would make money from the construction even if the railroad itself failed.

In February 1866 the Casement brothers, John ("Jack") and Dan, were put in charge of track-laying operations, and in May Grenville Mellen Dodge took over from Dey as chief engineer. All were Civil War veteran officers, and toiling for them were thousands of workers, most fresh from the war themselves, who were used to taking orders and working with military precision under sometimes difficult circumstances. And it was a military-style operation. Surveyors placed stakes indicating the route, graders followed many miles behind, and then tracklayers laid the sleepers and

Map 232 (*above*).

This undated map, thought to have been created in 1859 or 1860, shows in red a *Proposed Union Pacific Rail Road Route* following more or less the line of the central route of the Pacific Railroad Surveys, south of the Great Salt Lake. It also shows a *Central Pacific Rail Road Route* following in the West the route that the line would be completed over in 1869, but on the Plains the survey follows the North Platte rather than the South Platte. The latter is shown here as the Union Pacific route, and it is the route that was actually built. A red flag marks the 100° W meridian, the point at which a Union Pacific train would be photographed in 1866 when the line reached that far west (see photo, *overleaf*).

Map 233 (*below*).

Various initial routes west from the Missouri considered by Peter Dey, the Union Pacific chief engineer. The twenty-three miles west of Omaha shown as *Union Pacific Rail Road* had already been graded at a cost of $100,000 when Thomas Durant insisted that the line be moved to follow a route down Mud Creek, unnamed on this map but shown immediately south of Omaha, and *West Papillion Creek*, creating a loop nine miles longer than Dey's route. Durant wanted to do this to collect another 115,000 acres of land grants and $144,000 in subsidy. Dey reluctantly resigned in December 1864 because he could not endorse such chicanery.

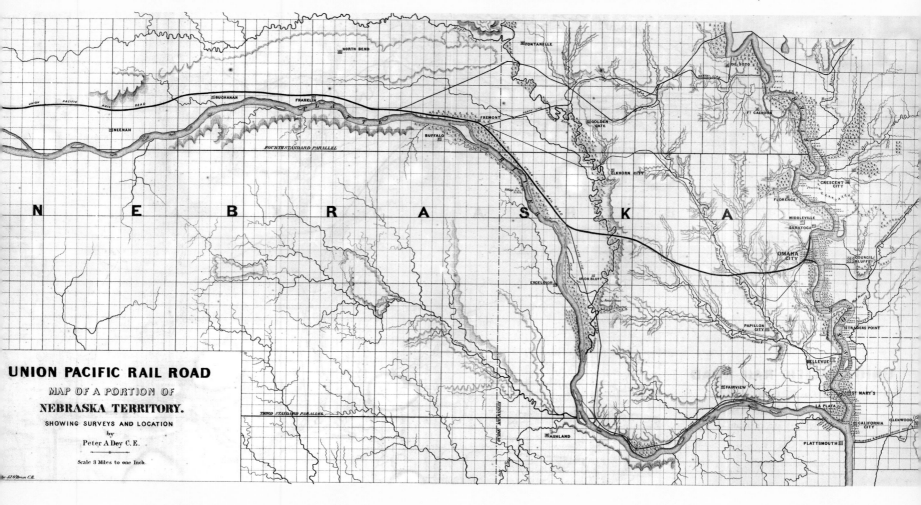

UNION PACIFIC RAIL ROAD
MAP OF A PORTION OF
NEBRASKA TERRITORY.
SHOWING SURVEYS AND LOCATION
by
Peter A Dey C.E.
Scale 3 Miles to one Inch.

MAP 234 (*above, top*).
This 1866 map from the United States Land Office shows a *Proposed Route Central Pacific R.R.* in the west and the proposed *Middle Route of Pacific R.R.* on the Plains. Farther east is the *Omaha Br. Union Pacific R.R.* It reflects the fact that in 1866 the plans, if not the aspirations, of the Central Pacific were ahead of those of the Union Pacific. The *Middle Route* is that taken from the Pacific Railroad Surveys. The Central Pacific's route is shown south of the Great Salt Lake.

MAP 235 (*above*).
This heavily damaged manuscript is Theodore Judah's original map of the route he planned for the Central Pacific across the Sierra Nevada—shown as a red line—and filed with the secretary of the interior on 30 June 1862. Abraham Lincoln signed the Pacific Railroad Bill the day after. *Sacramento* can just be made out among the damage at lower left; *Big Truckee Meadows* and the Truckee River Valley are at right. The railroad was built almost exactly along Judah's planned route.

rails. It was a production-line method that got the job done. By November 1867 the track had reached Cheyenne, and the Continental Divide was crossed the following summer. By 1869 the track was in Utah, reaching Ogden on 7 March.

Simultaneously the Central Pacific built the line east over the Sierra. A workforce totaling ten thousand, including seven thousand Chinese workers, was supervised by Charles Crocker. A young engineer, Lewis Clement, designed and supervised the construction of the 1,659-foot-long Summit Tunnel, hewn out from east and west and also in both directions from a shaft dug in the middle; the latter

MAP 236 (*below*).
The Union Pacific's own summary map of its surveys, used for the construction of the transcontinental line. The survey goes as far west as the Humboldt Valley, beyond Promontory Point north of the Great Salt Lake, where the railroad finally connected with the Central Pacific. Until 1869 it was unknown where the two railroads would meet. The line west of the Great Salt Lake follows the route along which the Union Pacific laid two hundred miles of track, parallel with that of the Central Pacific going in the opposite direction.

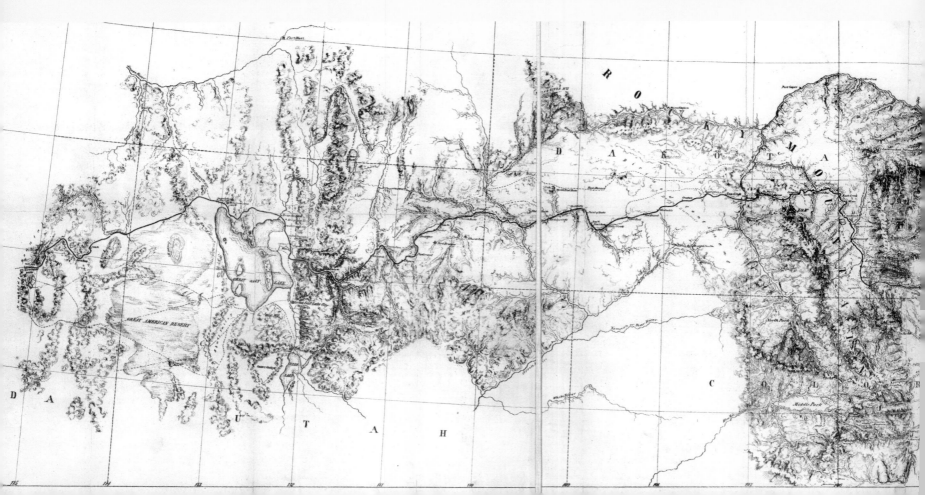

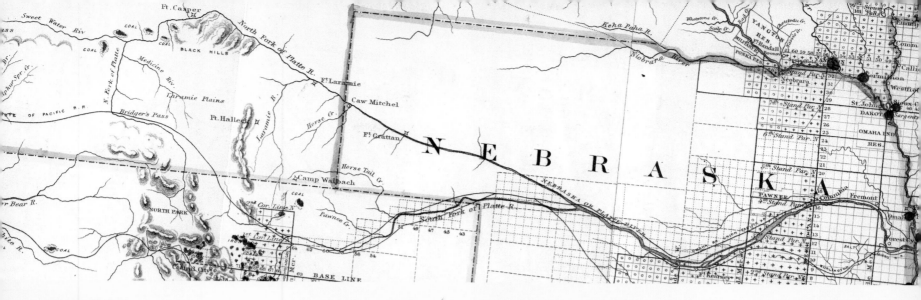

Map 237 (*below*).

This magazine cartoon map was published as the transcontinental line was completed in 1869. Mr. United States had good reason to smile at the successful completion of this massive engineering project. The artist, however, seems to have forgotten that the Central Pacific was responsible for almost 40 percent of the line, track laid over the most difficult terrain.

was accessed by an elevator cage powered by a steam engine made from parts cannibalized from a locomotive. It was a tremendous achievement; his four separate borings were out by only two inches when they met. Bad weather also necessitated that fifty miles of snowsheds be built; they were also designed by Clement.

Even while the tunnel was under construction, locomotives and materials had been hauled over the mountains so that work could progress from the Truckee Valley back to the summit. In the final months the Central Pacific and Union Pacific were laying duplicate track in Utah, driven by the subsidies.

In the end Congress had to dictate a meeting place, and it selected Promontory Point, north of the Great Salt Lake. On 10 May 1869 the two railroads

Above. Directors of the Union Pacific gather for a photograph on the 100° W meridian in October 1866 to mark the completion of the track west to this point. The location is now Cozad, Nebraska.

were joined, with Leland Stanford driving the last spike, and the transcontinental line was a reality. The Union Pacific had laid 1,060 miles of track and the Central Pacific 690, over considerably more challenging terrain.

The transcontinental railroad connected California and Oregon to the other states and began the process of truly opening the West. Other lines would follow. The railroad created many towns and cities itself—cities such as Cheyenne, Wyoming; Laramie, Wyoming; and Reno, Nevada, the latter named after a Civil War general, Jesse Reno, whose name Crocker reputedly drew from a hat. But the railroad, more than any other single factor, although coupled with other enabling factors such as the passage of the Homestead Act in 1862 (see page 156), was responsible for the peopling of the West, its settlement by EuroAmericans anxious for cheap land and a new life.

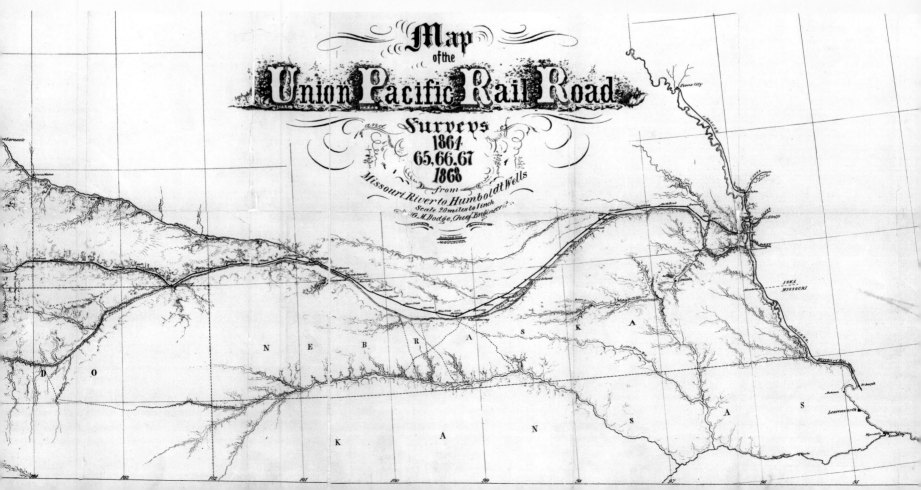

OPENING THE WEST

In the almost fifty years after the completion of the first transcontinental line, the expansion of the railroad network was almost single-handedly responsible for opening the West to mass EuroAmerican settlement.

The Union Pacific and Central Pacific railroads had been granted vast swathes of public lands to enable them to raise capital to complete their lines. Now it was time to begin to recoup the considerable investment that had been required and that would continue to be needed to maintain and run the railroad. Maps such as MAP 238, *below,* were used to advertise and keep track of the land for sale, sold in the convenient quarter-section format devised nearly a century earlier (see page 156).

The success of the Union Pacific drove many investors to railroads, and even before the first transcontinental line was complete, other railroads were under construction, though not until 1883 was a second transcontinental, the Northern Pacific, completed. The practice of granting federal lands to railroads ended in 1871, but land granted to railroads chartered by that date was still available to them or their successors decades later.

MAP 238 (*below*).
Union Pacific and all the other railways built with the aid of land grants lost no time in trying to sell off their land, both to raise money but also to populate the trackside with potential customers for the railroad. This is a typical railroad sales map. It shows lands still for sale in 1904—the sections shaded gray—in Nebraska and Colorado. Easy terms were available, noted below the map title.

MAP 239 (*right, top*).
Another Union Pacific map, this one rather more artistically presented, probably used to generate tourist traffic as well as being useful for land sales and other business. It is a bird's-eye map of the Great Plains section of the railroad and is dated 1890. Railroad lines are in red. *Denver* is at bottom left, *Cheyenne* at top left, and the *Missouri* at right. Across the top is the *Platte River* with the Union Pacific main line, and at bottom is the *Kansas River* and its tributaries, with *Topeka* at bottom right, and the old Kansas Pacific main line, acquired by Union Pacific in 1880. *Kansas [City]* is in the extreme bottom right corner. Note that the map carefully excludes the main line of Union Pacific's competitor, the Atchison, Topeka & Santa Fe, just to the south, and does not show it at all between *Atchison* and *Topeka*, at right.

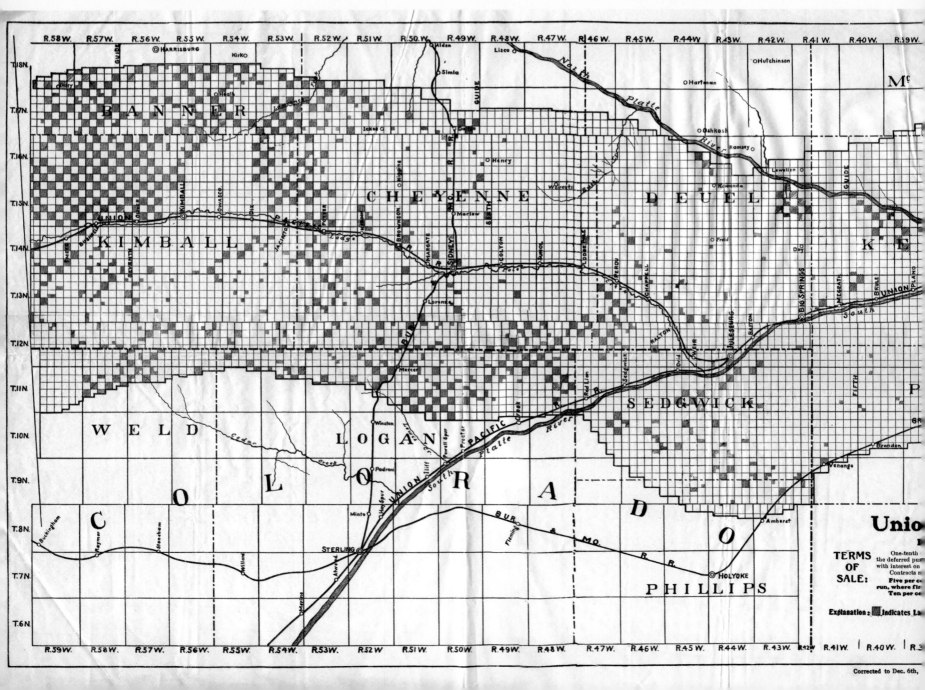

Map 240 (*right, center*).

This interesting "Map of the Middle States" was part of a Union Pacific promotional package aimed at German immigrants or investors and was published about 1878. It promotes *The Great Central Belt of Population, Commerce and Wealth* not only in the East but right across the United States, conveniently along the route of the Union Pacific.

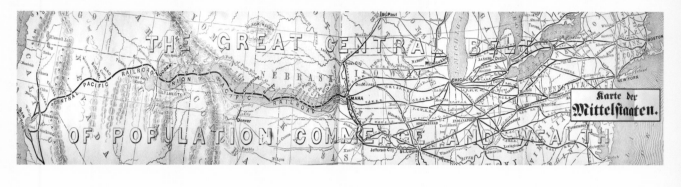

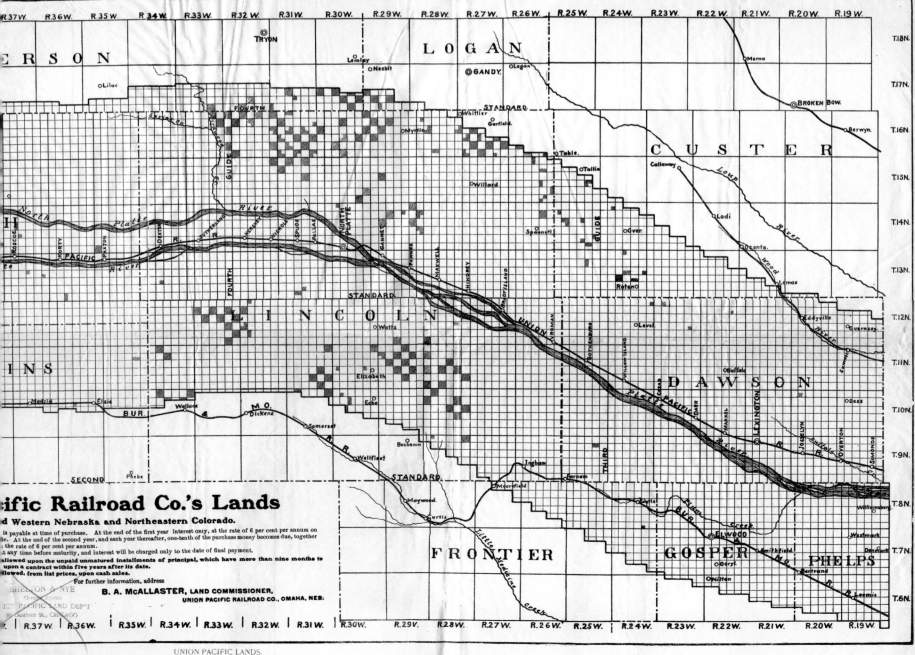

ific Railroad Co.'s Lands

d Western Nebraska and Northeastern Colorado.

is payable at time of purchase. At the end of the first year interest only, at the rate of 6 per cent per annum on
e. At the end of the second year, and each year thereafter, one-tenth of the purchase money becomes due, together
the rate of 6 per cent per annum.
t any time before maturity, and interest will be charged only to the date of final payment.
lowed upon the unpaid unmatured installments of principal, which have more than nine months to
upon a contract within five years after its date.
lowed, from list prices, upon cash sales.
For further information, address

B. A. McALLASTER, LAND COMMISSIONER,
UNION PACIFIC RAILROAD CO., OMAHA, NEB.

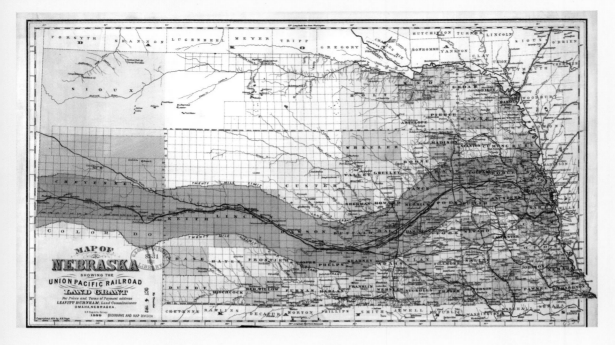

MAP 241 (*left, top*).
Lands granted to the Union Pacific in Nebraska are shown in this 1880 map. However, the map exaggerates the amount of land granted; it was not all the land in the green zone but alternate sections only.

MAP 242 (*left, center*).
Samuel Bowles's 1869 book *Our New West*—new because of the coming of the railroad—contained this map, which, in addition to the *Union Pacific R.R.* and *[Central] Pacific R.R.*, shows a number of other *Unfinished Rail Roads*, including several transcontinental railroads already in the planning stages, including the *Northern Pacific R.R.* and the *Southern Pacific R.R.*, following broadly the routes recommended by the Pacific Railroad Surveys of the previous decade. Note also the *Old Stage Road*, the first to be put out of business by a railroad.

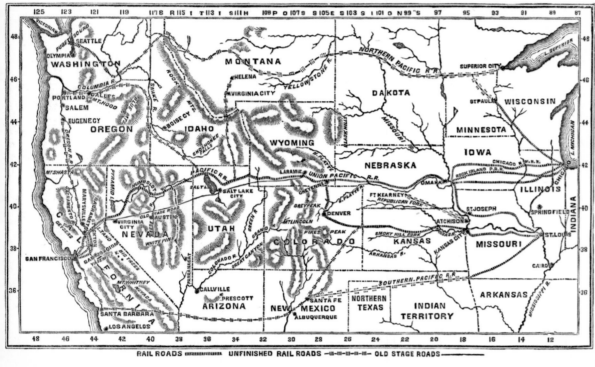

MAP TO ACCOMPANY "OUR NEW WEST" BY SAMUEL BOWLES.

THE KANSAS PACIFIC

One of the first new lines was a feeder to the Union Pacific. The Denver Pacific Railway and Telegraph Company was incorporated by Denver businessmen in November 1867 with the objective of linking their city to the Union Pacific at Cheyenne. They began construction in May 1868, moving quickly to ensure that they beat rival investors at Golden City who had formed the Colorado, Clear Creek and Pacific Railway with the same intention. The first train from Cheyenne pulled into Denver on 24 June 1870. The line was soon absorbed into the Kansas Pacific system (MAP 245, *right, bottom*).

Two months later the first train arrived in the city from Kansas City on the just-completed Kansas Pacific Railway. This company began life in 1855 as the Leavenworth, Pawnee & Western and changed its name in 1863 to the Union Pacific Railway Company, Eastern Division (despite having no connection with the original Union Pacific). It had plans to build to the Pacific, complete, of course, with land grants, all authorized in the same Pacific Railway Act of 1862 that had authorized the Union Pacific transcontinental line. Construction started at Wyandotte, Kansas—now Kansas City—in September 1863, and a line to Lawrence was completed by April the next year. But the murder of the railroad's principal, Samuel Hallett, slowed progress.

Once the other Union Pacific had reached the 100° W meridian the Union Pacific Eastern Division saw that it could not win the race to the West Coast and changed its objective to Denver. Abilene was reached in March 1867 and Salina in April. Then progress was slowed by repeated Indian attacks incited by the Sand Creek Massacre of 1864 (see page 149). The Army had to be called in to guard construction workers.

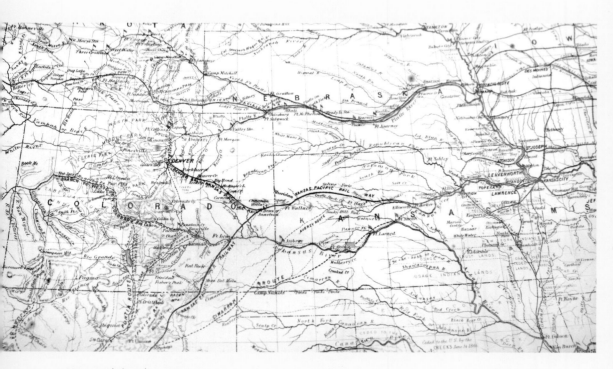

MAP 243 (*above*).
Part of a large map published in 1868 or 1869 showing the surveys for the Kansas Pacific, not only following the route over which it was built but also dipping down into New Mexico where it followed a route to the Pacific coast. This route was not built beyond *Ft. Lyon*, at Las Animas.

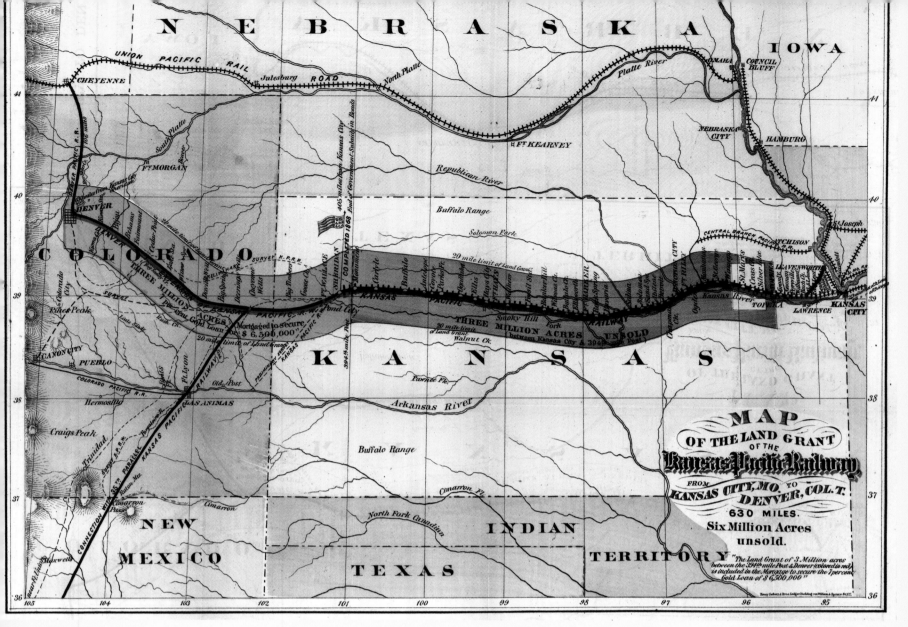

Map 244 (above).
An advertising map for Kansas Pacific lands: *Six Million Acres unsold.* The lands colored red were those mortgaged by the railroad to secure a $6.5 million loan for construction. Again, only alternate sections were actually railroad property. Note the *Connection with 35th Parallel,* the proposed line to the Pacific.

Map 245 (below).
A map of the Kansas Pacific Railway about 1872. Note again the proposed extension of the subsidiary *Arkansas Val[ley] R.R.* beyond U.S. Army post *Ft. Lyon.* This was the "Pacific" pretension of the Kansas Pacific, but it never reached beyond Fort Lyon, at Las Animas.

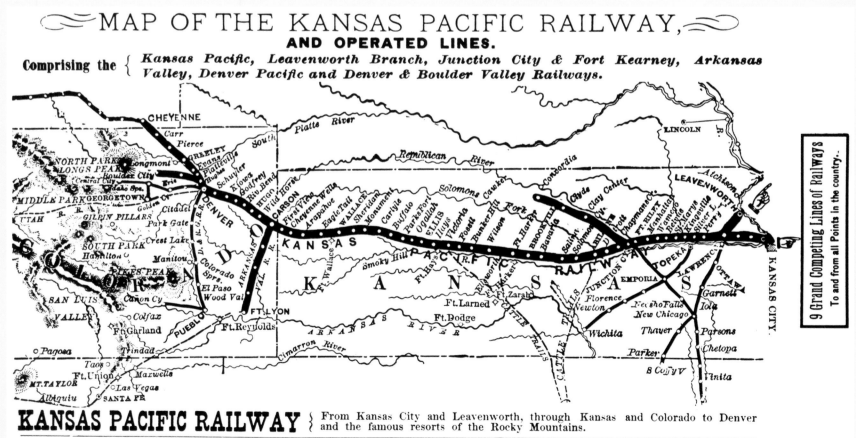

MAP OF THE KANSAS PACIFIC RAILWAY,
AND OPERATED LINES.

Comprising the { *Kansas Pacific, Leavenworth Branch, Junction City & Fort Kearney, Arkansas Valley, Denver Pacific and Denver & Boulder Valley Railways.*

KANSAS PACIFIC RAILWAY { From Kansas City and Leavenworth, through Kansas and Colorado to Denver and the famous resorts of the Rocky Mountains.

Splendid Mountain Scenery, Pike's Peak, Gray's Peak, Perpetual Snow, Good Hotels, Pure Air, Crystal Streams, Beautiful Cascades, Hot and Cold Soda Springs, Sulphur and Chalybeate Springs; Gold, Silver, Copper, Lead, Iron and Coal Mines; Pleasant days with Cool nights.

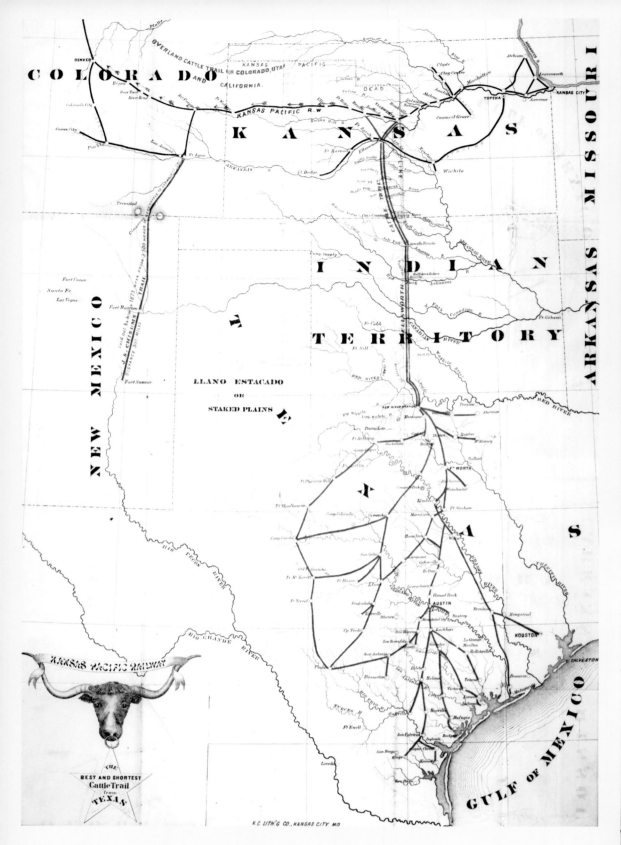

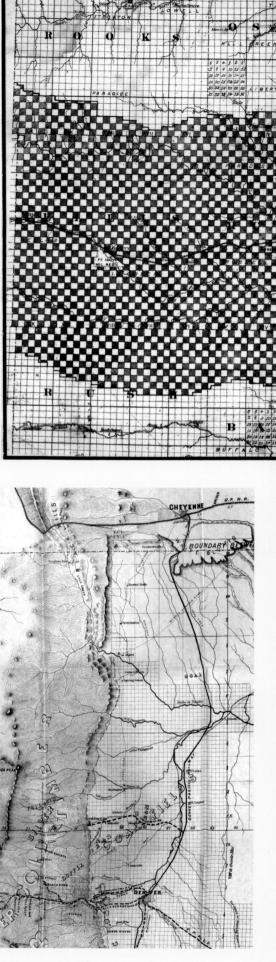

Map 246 (*above*).
The Kansas Pacific's ill-fated promotion of the *Ellsworth Cattle Trail* from Texas used this 1873 map. The trail crosses the Santa Fe line west of *Newton* (just north of *Wichita*), the trailhead promoted by that competitor railroad. After the Civil War Texas had huge cattle herds, and the North needed beef, but no railroads yet served Texas. Hence cattle were taken north in great cattle drives to the railheads of Kansas.

Then the railroad ran out of money, and the railhead remained at Sheridan for almost a year, during which time the town became infamous for its lawlessness. (Sheridan, the location of which is shown on Map 245, *previous page,* no longer exists.) When work resumed, the railroad had again gained transcontinental aspirations and changed its name to the Kansas Pacific Railway Company. After the railroad also built east from Denver to meet the oncoming track from Kansas City, the last spike was driven on 15 August 1870, near Strasburg, Colorado.

The Kansas Pacific never reached its eponymous destination, though the Arkansas Valley Railway, a subsidiary, took off in the right direction (Map 244 and Map 245, *previous page*). This branch, in 1878, would gain the dubious distinction of becoming the first in Colorado to be fully abandoned.

The Kansas Pacific joined with the Denver Pacific in 1870. This line was correctly the first completed continuous transcontinental line, by virtue of a bridge across the Missouri; the Union Pacific route, when completed, required a steamboat ferry across that river.

Map 247 (*above*).
The proposed line of the *Denver Pacific Railway* between *Denver* and *Cheyenne* is shown on this 1868 map. The dashed line of the *U.P.Ry.E.D.* (Union Pacific Railway Eastern Division, later the Kansas Pacific) runs into Denver from the southeast. At right, halfway between Denver and Cheyenne, is *Latham*. This was a stagecoach station on the Overland Trail and the site where the Union Colony of Colorado, Greeley, would be created in 1870 (see page 158).

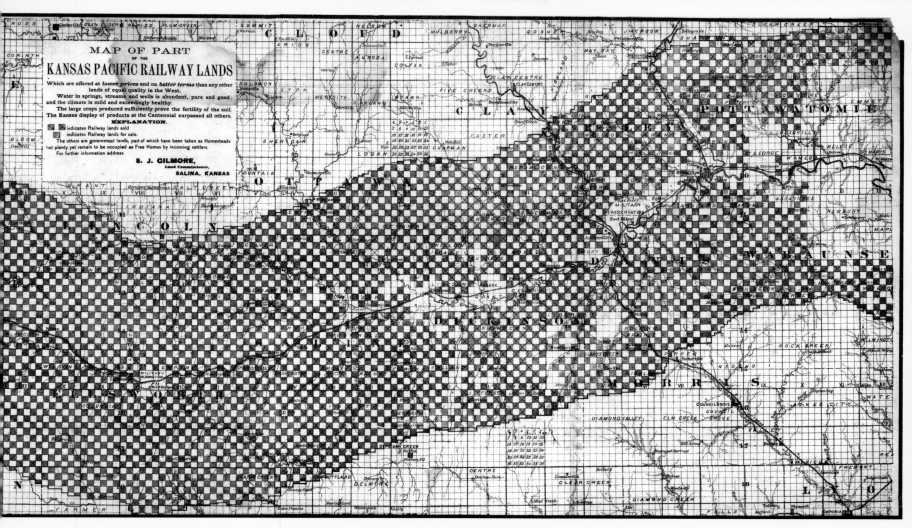

The railroads allowed ranchers to transport their cattle to market far more easily than before, and the Kansas Pacific in 1867 established Abilene as a transfer point for cattle from Texas, at the endpoint of a trail scouted by Jesse Chisholm that became known as the Chisholm Trail. Abilene became infamous for its lawlessness. For a short time in 1871 the town's marshal was the famous James Butler "Wild Bill" Hickok. In 1871 the competing railroad, the Atchison, Topeka & Santa Fe Railway (always more simply known as the Santa Fe) reached the Chisholm Trail, cutting off the Kansas Pacific's business. The latter fought back, promoting other trailheads such as Ellsworth (MAP 246, *far left*). But no rancher wanted to drive his cattle farther than he needed to, and the Santa Fe won that fight. The Kansas Pacific survived, however, and in 1880 became part of the Union Pacific system.

THE OREGON SHORT LINE

When the Southern Pacific was completed in 1883, the Central Pacific, then part of the latter railroad, began diverting traffic to its new southern line, away from Union Pacific's connection. Realizing early that this might happen, Union Pacific in 1881 began constructing the Oregon Short Line to connect with the line of the Oregon Railway and Navigation Company,

MAP 248 (*above*).
The Kansas Pacific was the first of the western railroads to fully exploit a boom in population growth caused by the availability of free or cheap land after the Civil War. The railroad began selling its land grant property in 1868, selling 111,000 acres in that year alone, a figure that multiplied four times the following year as the population frontier moved west onto the Great Plains. This map shows the Kansas Pacific's land sales situation in 1876. It illustrates well the checkerboard pattern of sections, where railroad grant land intersperses with public lands. The part of Kansas shown is between *Ellis*, on the left, and *St. Marys* (just west of *Topeka*), on the right. *Ellsworth* is immediately below the map title, while farther east are *Salina* and *Abilene*. A promotional bird's-eye map of Abilene is shown as MAP 482, *page 209*.

MAP 249 (*below, left*).
The Union Pacific and its connecting lines shown on an 1875 map. The dashed *Oregon Branch* is the Oregon Short Line, which would be constructed between 1881 and 1884 to connect with the line of the Oregon Railway and Navigation Company's line along the Columbia River.

MAP 250 (*below*).
The Union Pacific in 1880. That year the railroad acquired the Kansas Pacific, and that line, together with the belt of land grants of both, are depicted on this map. Union Pacific now served Denver directly and had two connecting points with the eastern system—Omaha and Kansas City.

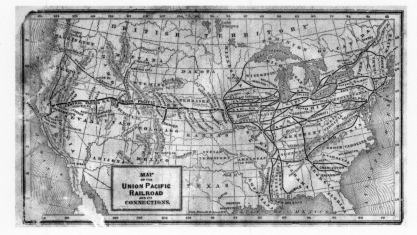

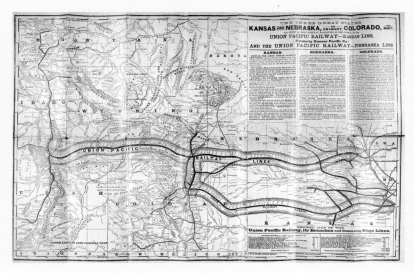

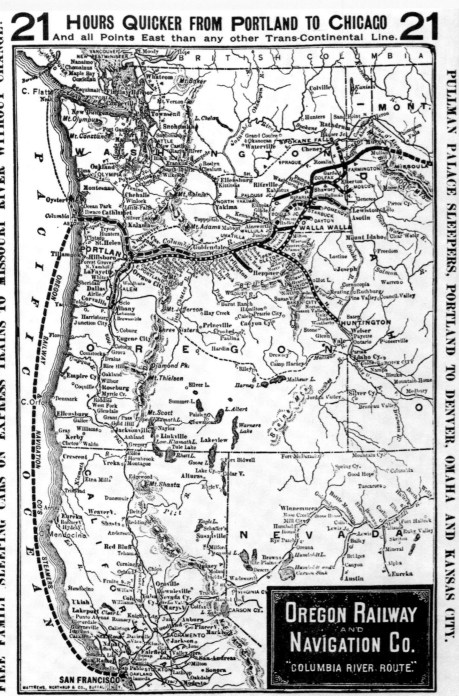

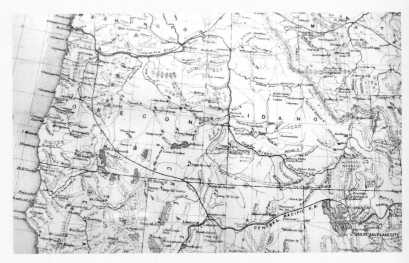

with which it had a running rights agreement, on the Columbia River. The Oregon Railway and Navigation Company began life as the Oregon Portage Railroad, operating around rapids on the Columbia between Bonneville and Cascade Locks in 1862. By 1884, when it connected with the Short Line at Huntington, on the Snake River at the Idaho–Oregon boundary, it had over six hundred miles of track (Map 251, *left*). The Short Line, which left the main line at Granger, Wyoming Territory, was so named because it was the shortest practicable route between the Union Pacific line and the Columbia. Union Pacific acquired its desired exclusive outlet to the West Coast in 1898, when it purchased the Columbia line.

A NORTHWEST LINK

A northern transcontinental line, the Northern Pacific Railroad, had been chartered in 1864 to build from Lake Superior to the Pacific Northwest; it received its land grants at the same time: twenty sections of land for each mile built in a state and double that in western territories. Construction began in 1870, financed by banker Jay Cooke, and by 1873 the line had reached Bismarck, on the Missouri in Dakota Territory. The railroad named Bismarck after the German chancellor, Otto von Bismarck, unifier of Germany and victor of

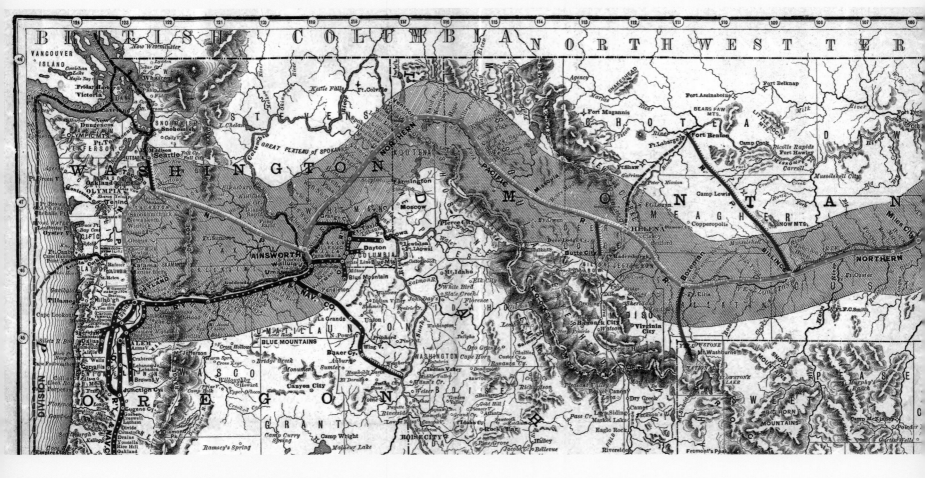

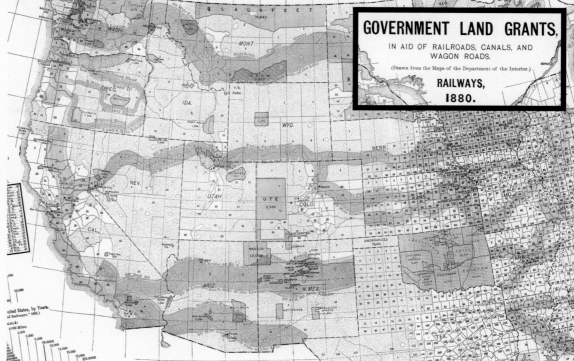

Map 251 (*far left, top*).
The Oregon Railway and Navigation Company's routes, about 1891. Note the connection at *Huntington* with the Union Pacific's Oregon Short Line.

Map 252 (*left*).
The originally planned route by which the central route would connect with the Pacific Northwest ran from the Central Pacific line at a point in the Humboldt River valley to Portland and is shown on this map from 1868 or 1869. The Union Pacific, however, wanted a line more under its control and so opted for a connection to the Columbia leaving its own line at Granger, Wyoming—the Oregon Short Line.

Map 253 (*below, bottom*).
The Northern Pacific issued this map of its system in 1882, the year before it was completed to the Pacific Northwest by connecting with the tracks of the Oregon Railway and Navigation Company at *Wallula Jc [Junction]*. The more direct line to Puget Sound at *Tacoma*, across south-central Washington (through *Yakima*), shown on the map starting at *Ainsworth*, would not be completed until 1887.

Map 255 (*below*).
The 1870 plan for the transcontinental Northern Pacific, shown in red, from Lake Superior to the Columbia. The line as surveyed and built would prove to be considerably less straight.

Map 254 (*above*).
The extent of federal land grants to the railroads was misrepresented for many years. This is a typical map that visually exaggerates the extent of the grants. In reality only alternate sections were granted, and grants excluded any lands already owned. In California and New Mexico, in particular, large tracts were already alienated by Mexican grants (see page 76). The original exaggerated map appeared in 1878, published by the Department of the Interior, which perhaps should have known better. This map is from the statistical atlas of the 1880 census, published in 1883. Some of the land in Oregon is military road land grant, for construction of a wagon road. Note that grants are not shown in Texas, where they were a state function.

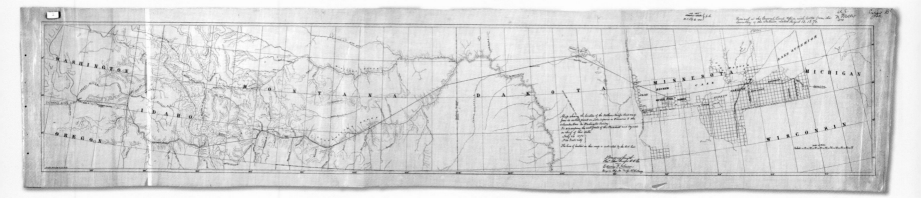

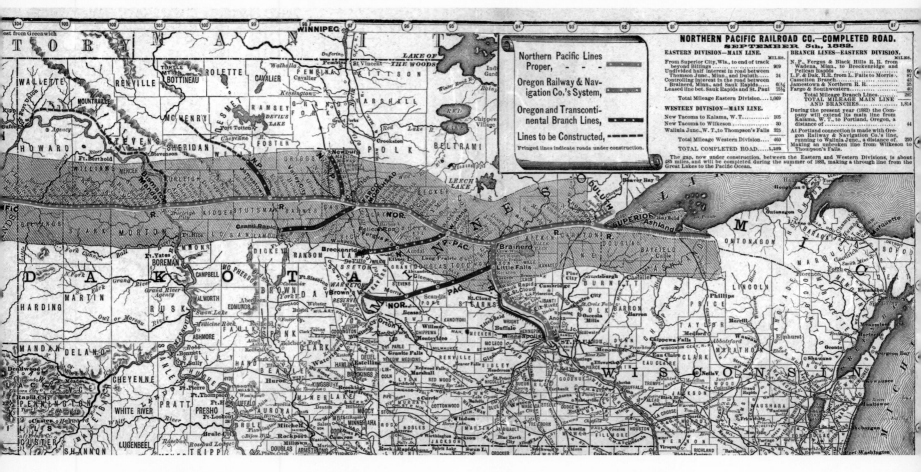

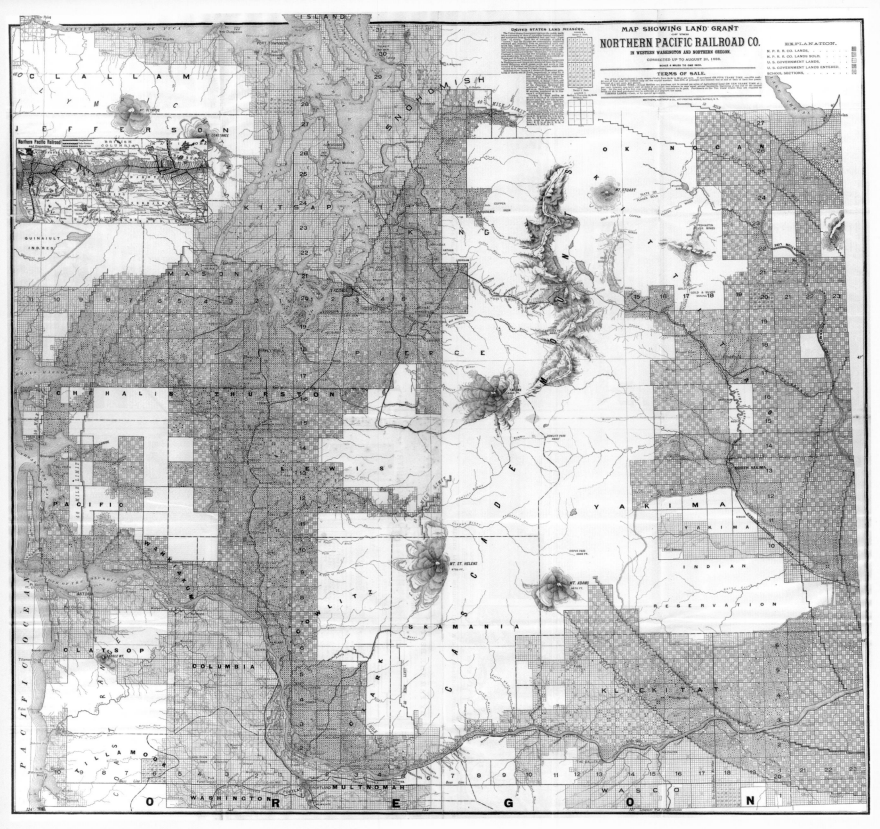

Map 256 (above), Map 257 (below), and Map 258 (right, top).

These maps were used to market the Northern Pacific's land grant. Map 256 dates from 1888 and shows the whole map used in western Washington; Map 257 is part of an 1895 map of the area around Bismarck, then in Dakota Territory; and Map 257 is a detail of the adjacent sheet to the east of Map 256 but dated 1891. The key displayed on Map 258 is valid on all three maps. Not only did the railroad show its own lands for sale and those that had already sold, but it also showed federal lands, including those "entered" (that is, taken up for preemption, subject to residency and other requirements).

On Map 256, *Tacoma* and *Puget Sound* are at top left. Note how the limit of the land grant is reached. The Columbia River, with the Oregon Railway and Nav-

igation line, runs along the bottom of the map. Map 257 shows *Bismarck* and the Missouri (green line) at center. As it approached Bismarck, the Northern Pacific switched its route to throw off land speculators. After the railroad arrived the new town experienced a land boom, with lots selling for as much as $8,000. Map 258 shows a detail of the land grant maps around Spokane Falls, since 1889 in the state of Washington; the city in 1891 dropped the "Falls" part of its name to become Spokane.

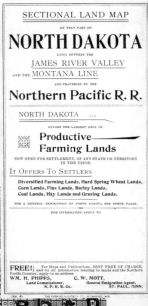

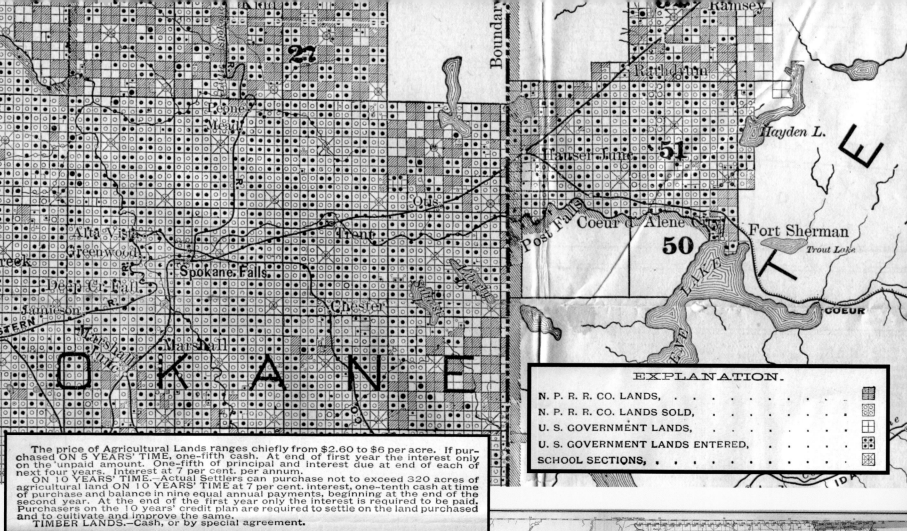

The price of Agricultural Lands ranges chiefly from $2.60 to $6 per acre. If purchased ON 5 YEARS' TIME, one-fifth cash. At end of first year the interest only on the unpaid amount. One-fifth of principal and interest due at end of each of next four years. Interest at 7 per cent. per annum.
ON 10 YEARS' TIME.—Actual Settlers can purchase not to exceed 320 acres of agricultural land ON 10 YEARS' TIME at 7 per cent. interest, one-tenth cash at time of purchase and balance in nine equal annual payments, beginning at the end of the second year. At the end of the first year only the interest is required to be paid. Purchasers on the 10 years' credit plan are required to settle on the land purchased and to cultivate and improve the same.
TIMBER LANDS.—Cash, or by special agreement.

the recent Franco-Prussian War in Europe, as the Northern Pacific had opened European offices the year before to encourage German immigration to its lands.

Tacoma, on Puget Sound, was selected as the Pacific terminus, and a 110-mile-long line from Kalama, on the Columbia, was completed in 1873.

Trouble lay ahead. Jay Cooke was badly affected by a financial crisis in 1873, and by 1875 the Northern Pacific was bankrupt. The company was reorganized by Frederick Billings, one of the directors, but in 1881 Henry Villard, at the head of a group of European investors, took over the company, reigniting the push for a transcontinental line. On 8 September 1883 the last spike was driven at Gold Creek, in western Montana. The trans-

MAP 259 (right, center).
Other railroads acquired land grants in the 1860s. One was the Burlington and Missouri River Railroad, chartered as early as 1852. The railroad began operations, in Iowa, in 1856, and was acquired by the Chicago, Burlington and Quincy Railroad in 1872, another line that aspired to transcontinental status but ultimately reached only as far as Billings, Montana. The railroad did, however, in 1882 complete the first direct line from Chicago to Denver, using, in part, the line of the Burlington and Missouri shown here. This 1876 map dates from a period when the subsidiary was still using its original name west of its namesake river.

MAP 260 (right, bottom).
An 1882 map shows the just-completed direct line from Chicago running straight to Denver.

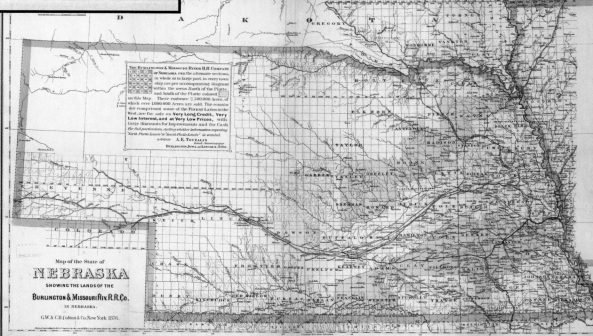

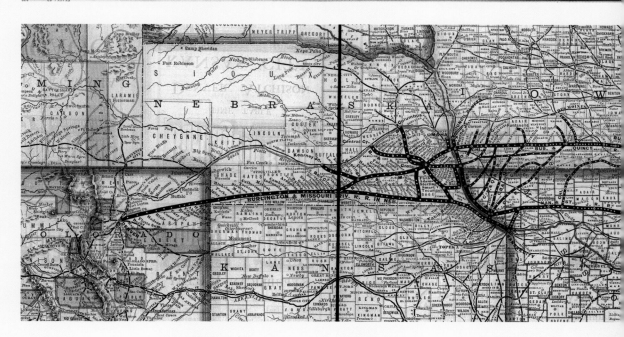

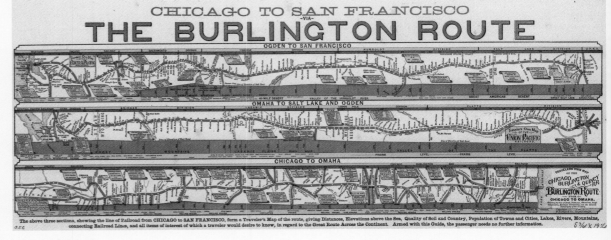

continental link was completed, thanks to a connection with the Oregon Railway and Navigation line at Wallula Junction, on the Columbia. This line allowed through trains to East Portland, then, via ferries across the Willamette at Portland and across the Columbia at Kalama, on to Tacoma.

The Northern Pacific finally completed its own line to Tacoma, through south-central Washington, in 1887. A route was found across the Cascades at Stampede Pass, and by 1886 only a seventy-seven-mile gap remained, but the summit required the completion of the nearly two-mile-long Stampede Tunnel. The work was given to contractor Nelson Bennett, who took a chance on a contract that would have seen him lose money if the tunnel were not completed on time; he completed the work with just seven days to spare in May 1888. In the interim, trains had used an eight-mile-long switchback, which took them over an hour to traverse.

The Northern Pacific aggressively marketed its land grant, as the maps on pages 128–29 attest. The railroad created many towns and cities, such as Bismarck, Billings, and Spokane. The latter, reached in 1881 from the west and before 1891 named Spokane Falls (and shown as such on MAP 258, *previous page*) would have its growth doubly reinforced by the arrival in 1892 of another transcontinental line, the Great Northern, completed the following year.

MAP 261 (*above*).
The Chicago, Burlington and Quincy, universally known as the Burlington, advertised through service via Union Pacific connections in this colorful 1879 strip route map.

SOUTHERN LINES

The "Big Four" of the Central Pacific—Leland Stanford, Collis Huntington, Mark Hopkins, and Charles Crocker—created another railroad, the Southern Pacific, with the intention of building lines within California that would connect with, and feed, their transcontinental creation. However, they soon tired of feeding business onto a competitor's lines, those of the Union Pacific, and so set about planning a transcontinental line of their own.

Even before the transcontinental line was complete, the four had acquired a sizeable network of rail lines in central California. They built to the north, up the Sacramento Valley, buying and connecting with the Oregon and California Railroad, which had built south from Portland. A connection between Ashland and Redding was made in 1887.

By 1876 the Southern Pacific had reached Los Angeles, a difficult line made possible by the ingenuity of engineer William F. Hood, who devised the Tehachapi Loop, a complete 360 degrees that took the railroad over the Tehachapi Mountains at the southern end of the Central Valley. Hood realized that he had plenty of room to maneuver at the base of the incline but almost none at the top, and so he started at the top and worked down, thus locating the optimal position for the beginning of the ascent on the valley floor. No one had thought to do it that way before. The line also required the nearly three-mile-long San Fernando Tunnel to enter the Los Angeles Basin, where a network of lines had already been acquired.

MAP 262 (*left*).
A Northern Pacific poster dating from about 1880, when the railroad was promoting its lands in Dakota Territory and Montana Territory. At the bottom is a map of the completed transcontinental system.

MAP 263 (*right*).
Published by commercial mapmaker Rand McNally in 1879, this map shows more or less correctly the extent of the Southern Pacific as it was by that year. To the north the line has reached Redding, named after Benjamin B. Redding, Central Pacific land agent and sometime mayor of Sacramento. It would be extended into Oregon to meet the Oregon and California Railroad in 1887. To the south a line is shown across Arizona and New Mexico territories to El Paso, which the mapmaker has erroneously placed in Mexico. This line would connect with the Texas & Pacific in 1881, eighty miles east of El Paso, at Sierra Blanca, Texas, to create a second transcontinental route.

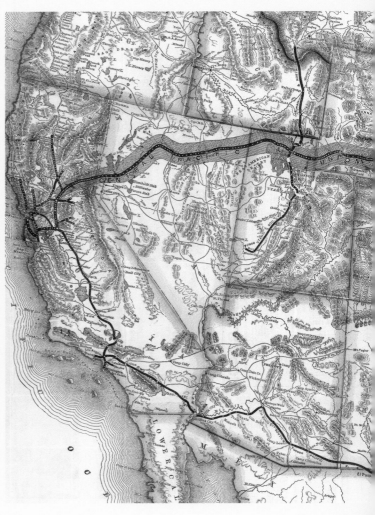

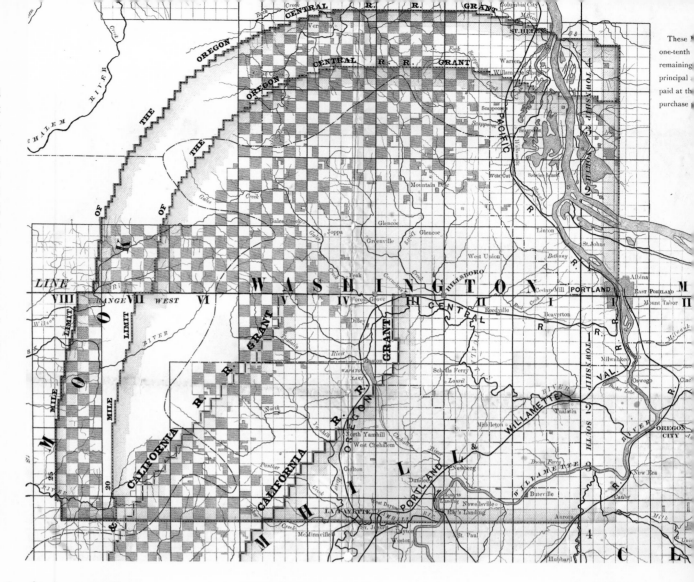

Map 264 (*right*).
The Oregon Central Railroad rushed a line twenty miles south from East Portland to completion in December 1869, thus entitling the company to a land grant, shown here on a map from about 1887. The limits are shown in red and orange. This is the "east side" line, shown running through Oregon City. The map also depicts the land grant of the "west side" line, the Oregon and California Railroad, with its limits in yellow. Ben Holladay, the onetime stagecoach and wagon company operator (see page 114) managed to gain control of both railroads, and the Oregon and California extended the line south to Roseburg by the end of 1872. Holladay sold out to Henry Villard (who acquired the Northern Pacific the same year) and German bondholders in 1881, and construction reached Ashland, Oregon, in 1884. The Southern Pacific acquired the line in 1887, and the connection to Redding was completed the same year. The original Oregon and California grant had unusually contained the stipulation that the land be sold only to actual settlers, in parcels with a maximum size of 160 acres and at a maximum price of $2.50 per acre. The Southern Pacific acquired the Oregon and California in 1887 and later sold off land, especially timberland, in larger parcels and higher prices, thus violating the congressional stipulation. This breach led to protracted litigation, which in 1915 was decided in favor of the Southern Pacific. Congress, however, was having none of it and passed a law confiscating over two million acres of the railroad's unsold land, the largest single revocation of a railroad land grant.

Map 265 (*right*).
The original aspirations of the Texas & Pacific Railway are shown on this interesting 1877 map. A transcontinental line is shown running from Texas to San Diego. This was the route usurped by the Southern Pacific. Other lines completed (cross-hatched) and projected (dashed) are shown. This map appeared in a guide to the mineral wealth of the Southwest. The author, Alexander Anderson, extolled the virtues of the Southwest and contrasted them with the "cold and barren" region through which the Northern Pacific must pass. He pointed out the strategic value of the line to the U.S. Army, to protect people and property from "the barbarous Apache Indians" and noted that the region is without heavy snows. He also thought the line would facilitate the development of gold and silver mining and turn western Texas, New Mexico, and Arizona "into as wonderful a wheat region as has California."

Then the Southern Pacific turned its attention to a transcontinental line. Its potential rival, the Texas & Pacific, had lines in Texas, a land grant from the state right across Texas to El Paso, and a federal land grant for a line across the Southwest to Yuma and on to San Diego. A Southern Pacific line from Los Angeles to Yuma was completed in 1876, and a bridge built across the Colorado the following year. The Texas & Pacific could not have chosen a more difficult Pacific terminus than San Diego;

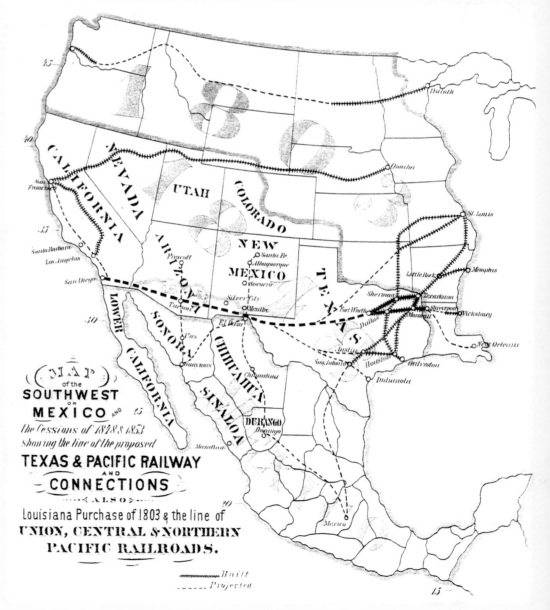

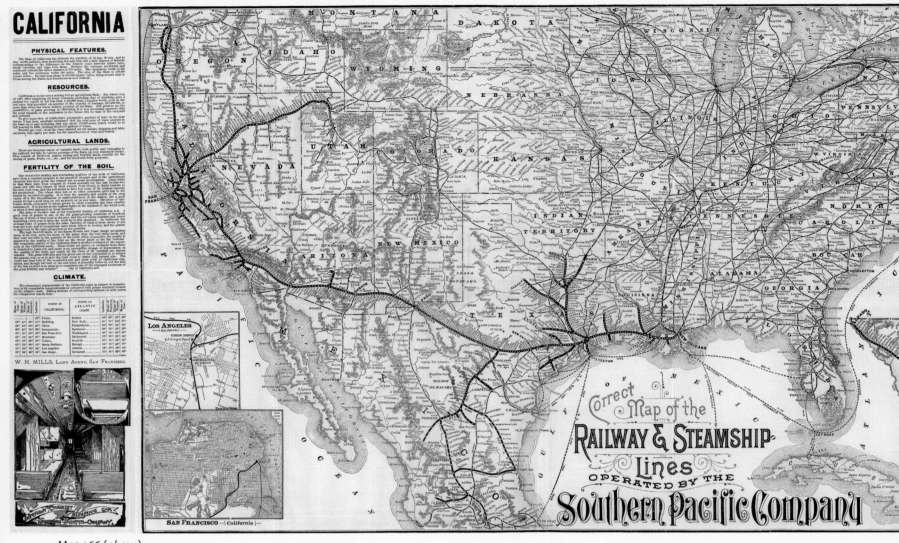

Map 266 (*above*).

A fine map of the Southern Pacific rail network as it was in 1892. The railroad purchased lines reaching into Mexico, here the *Mex[ico] Int[ernational] R.R.* East of *El Paso* is *Sierra Blanca*, at the end of the track laid by the Texas & Pacific.

Map 267 (*below*).

This interesting bird's-eye-like map of Texas displays little drawings of towns and cities. The front and back covers of this folding map are at *right*. The International and Great Northern Railroad was created in 1873 by the merger of two smaller systems and was purchased by Jay Gould in 1880. In 1956 the system became part of the Missouri Pacific.

Productions on the International & Great Northern Railroad

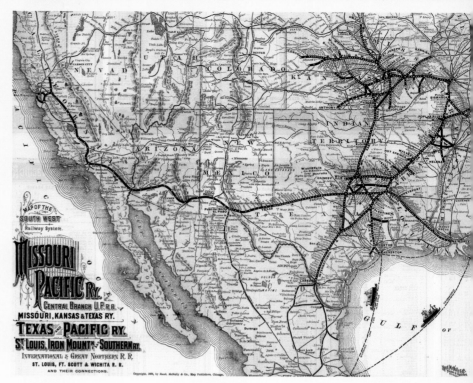

railroad access was such that one line that was completed, the San Diego and Arizona Railway in 1919, detoured into Mexico to achieve its objective. The Texas & Pacific began constructing the line east from San Diego and had graded for ten miles when news arrived of the stock market crash of September 1873, and all worked stopped. The Texas & Pacific failed, not to be revived until 1879, when financier Jay Gould took over.

The Southern Pacific, in the spirit of the times, decided to proceed anyway, and in 1879 construction began on a line east, using the designated and surveyed route of the Texas & Pacific, without federal subsidies or a land grant. The track was completed to Tucson by March 1880 and by February 1881 was at Deming, New Mexico. Here, by prior agreement, an Atchison, Topeka & Santa Fe line from the Arkansas Valley connected, and the first through train from the Middle West arrived in California in March—a second transcontinental link.

MAP 268 (*above, left*).
The Texas & Pacific Railway in 1873, with the state land grant across central Texas to El Paso. The grant was never finalized because the line was not finished within the required time.

MAP 269 (*above, right*).
The Missouri Pacific was another land grant railroad, but it was one that never reached farther west than Kansas with its own lines, relying instead on links through the Texas & Pacific and the Southern Pacific to be able to advertise a route to the West Coast. This map was published in 1886.

MAP 270 (*below*).
The Atchison, Topeka & Santa Fe Railroad advertised its land grant for sale with this 1872 map, although at this time the line only reached as far as *Ft. Larned*, in the Arkansas Valley. A million acres are being offered for sale at $2 to $8 per acre, with eleven years to pay.

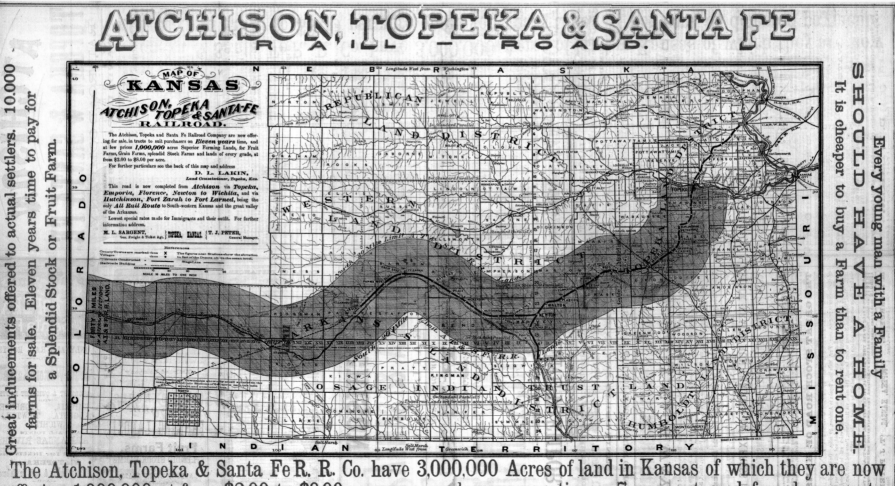

The Southern Pacific arrived in El Paso in May 1881 and quickly continued beyond, seizing the only pass into the city from the east. At this point Collis Huntington was able to more or less force Jay Gould to link their lines; a connecting last spike was driven at Sierra Blanca, eighty miles southeast of El Paso, on 15 December 1881. Henceforth the Texas & Pacific would have to use the Southern Pacific line to enter El Paso.

By connecting to lines in Texas already controlled by Huntington, the Southern Pacific was completed to both Houston and New Orleans. The whole route was soon christened the Sunset Route by the Southern Pacific's marketing department. In February 1883 the first trains ran between San Francisco and New Orleans.

In 1888 another transcontinental line was completed, this one by the Atchison, Topeka & Santa Fe Railroad, known and marketed as the Santa Fe. This railroad, chartered in 1859, was given a three-million-acre land grant in 1863 in Kansas to construct a line from Atchison to the Colorado border. Parts of the grant are shown on MAP 270, *previous page*, and MAP 271, *below*. The railroad built beyond Kansas without a land grant, reaching Pueblo, Colorado, in 1876. Two years later the railroad outwitted its rival, the Denver & Rio Grande, to secure the vital Raton Pass into New Mexico. This led to a confrontation the same year when the Santa Fe attempted to build a line

MAP 271 (*below*).
A Santa Fe land marketing broadsheet promoting lands in the Arkansas River valley as far west as Syracuse, Kansas, in 1876. Every fact that could be pressed into service to entice the potential settler is here.

to the new silver mines at Leadville, Colorado (see page 138); after many legal struggles, the Denver & Rio Grande won that battle.

William Barstow Strong (after whom Barstow, California, is named) became president of the Santa Fe in 1881 and vastly expanded the railroad's horizons by acquiring the Atlantic & Pacific Railroad, which possessed land grants for a projected line to the West Coast across northern New Mexico and Arizona (MAP 272, *right*). By 1888 the Santa Fe had completed the line and now possessed its own route into California, though from Needles to Mohave it leased track built by the Southern Pacific.

MORE TRANSCONTINENTALS

There were three relative latecomers to the American transcontinental game: the Great Northern, which completed a line to Seattle in 1892; the Western Pacific, a subsidiary of the Denver & Rio Grande, which arrived in Oakland in 1909; and the Chicago, Milwaukee & St. Paul, which built to Seattle and was also completed in 1909.

Canadian James Jerome Hill, arguably the most successful of all the railroad builders, controlled the St. Paul, Minneapolis & Manitoba Railway in Minnesota and had built a line north to Winnipeg. To tap the agricultural potential of the Plains in 1886 he extended this line to Minot, Dakota Territory. (MAP 357, *page 171*, shows the effort to market such lands to immigrants.) Then, with an eye on Montana Territory's mineral wealth, in early

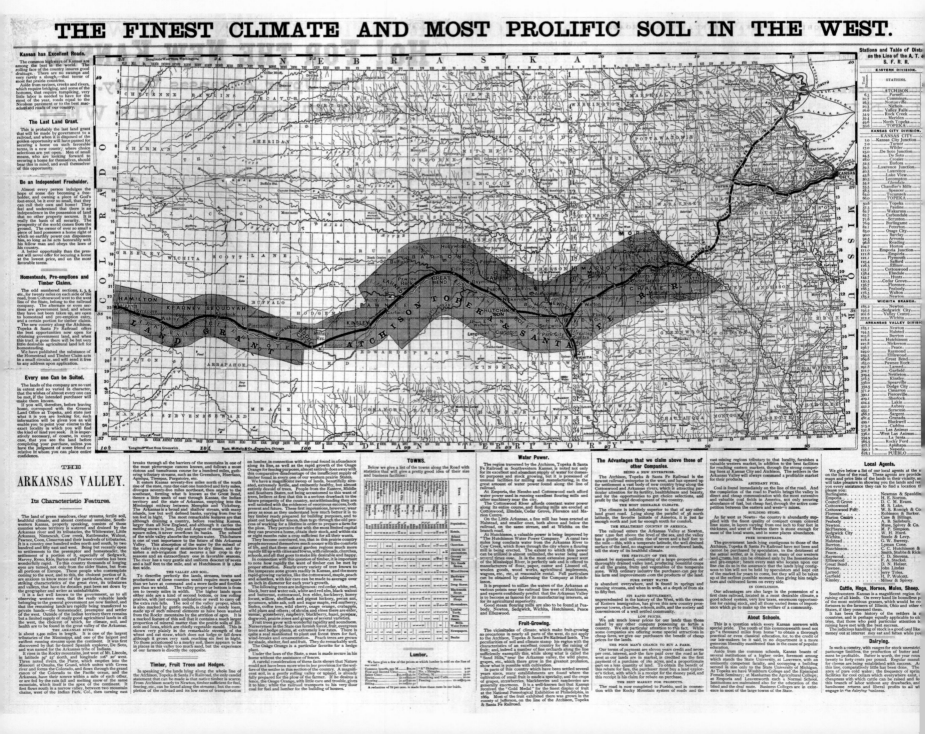

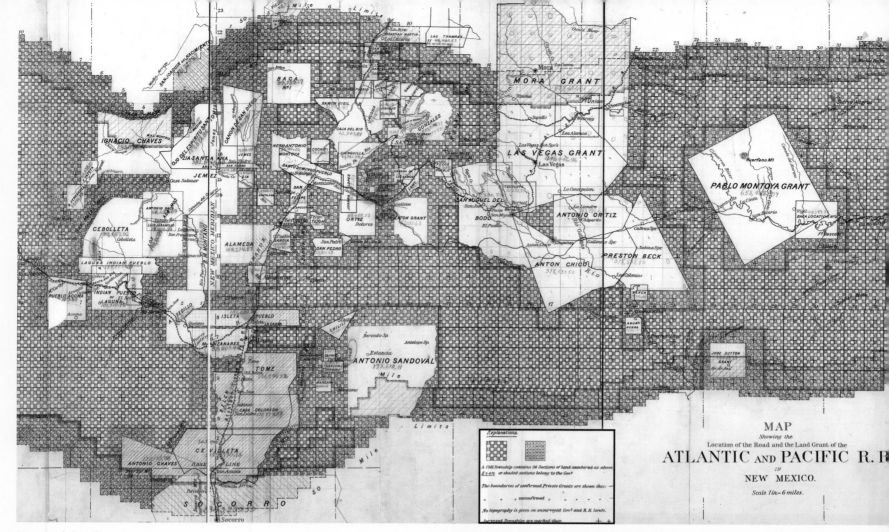

Inside the map (lower right):

MAP
Showing the
Location of the Road and the Land Grant of the
ATLANTIC AND PACIFIC R. R
IN
NEW MEXICO.
Scale 1in = 6 miles.

MAP 272 (*above*).

The Santa Fe acquired the land grant of the Atlantic & Pacific Railroad along with a controlling interest in 1881, and until 1897 the railroad operated as a subsidiary of the Santa Fe. This 1883 map depicting the grant shows very well the omission of previously owned or granted lands, in this case the earlier Mexican land grants (see page 76). So what might appear visually as a huge swathe of land either side of the line on a smaller-scale map loses close to half of its area on a map at this scale. Much of the remainder shown on this map was desert.

MAP 273 (*below, left, center*) and **MAP 274** (*below, right*).

An 1884 map of the Santa Fe system, MAP 273, shows the line from the Arkansas Valley seamlessly joined to the Southern Pacific line at Deming, New Mexico, where it connected in 1883. It also shows the line of its subsidiary, the Atlantic & Pacific, connecting to Southern Pacific track in California, at Needles, despite the fact that the transcontinental line was not completed until 1888. MAP 274 shows the Santa Fe system in 1904. Now the Southern Pacific transcontinental line is hardly shown—just a very thin line—as the Santa Fe attempts to preferentially market its own main line. From it, the branch that on the 1884 map was depicted as serving only Prescott, Arizona, extends to Phoenix, reflecting the growth of the latter at the expense of the former as mining activity declined. Despite the railroad's name, the city of Santa Fe was not served by the railroad's main line but by a short branch, which can be seen on both maps.

MAP 275 (*below*).

The Texas & Pacific route across Texas after its connection to the Southern Pacific line at Sierra Blanca for the last few miles into El Paso. This map dates from 1903.

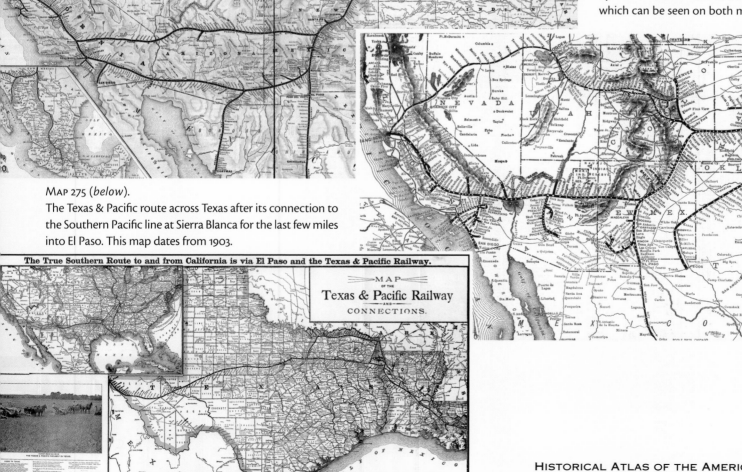

The True Southern Route to and from California is via El Paso and the Texas & Pacific Railway.

MAP
OF THE
Texas & Pacific Railway
AND
CONNECTIONS.

1887 he managed to obtain congressional permission to build through the Indian lands of northern Montana. Some 643 miles of track were laid to Hill's high standards that year, west to Great Falls, where the Montana Central Railroad—which Hill helped finance—linked with Butte and Helena.

In 1889 Hill consolidated his railroad holdings as the Great Northern Railway and made the decision to continue to the Pacific, selecting Seattle as his terminus. But there was a problem: no suitable pass over the Rocky Mountains had yet been found between the passes used by the Northern Pacific to the south and the Canadian Pacific to the north. Luckily, Hill had an excellent locating engineer, John F. Stevens, who—in a December 1889 snowstorm—found the Marias Pass, which had quite reasonable grades, and this is what the railroad used to continue west. Fortuitously the pass was at the southern end of what would become Glacier National Park, which would in later years prove to be an income generator for the line.

Engineer Charles Haskell, sent by Stevens, located and surveyed Stevens Pass through the Cascades and named it after his boss. Here Hill for the first time ordered speed rather than quality: a series of switchbacks, necessitating multiple reversing over twelve miles, were constructed as a temporary expedient; these were replaced by a tunnel completed in 1900 (MAP 277, *right*).

The last spike of the Great Northern was driven in the Cascades on 6 January 1893, and the first transcontinental train arrived in Seattle in June. The Great Northern was the first transcontinental line to be completed without subsidy or land grant and was very likely the best built of all, for Hill was in the business for the long term and judged that maintenance costs would eventually catch up with his competitors. In particular, he knew that the Northern Pacific had been hastily and poorly built. Later in 1893 the stock market crashed, and a recession set in. Soon the Northern Pacific was in financial trouble, largely because of its high maintenance costs, and was acquired by banker J. Pierpont Morgan, who was allied with Hill.

Hill never missed an opportunity to gain business for his line. In addition to allowing many small farms to be established throughout the route, Hill was responsible for attracting pioneer apple grower Julius Beebe to Washington; the latter's crop eventually filled many eastbound Great Northern freight trains. Hill also interested his friend, lumberman Frederick Weyerhaeuser, in the Northwest, beginning a considerable timber industry.

The Chicago, Milwaukee & St. Paul—later renamed the Chicago, Milwaukee, St. Paul & Pacific Railroad and marketed as the Milwaukee Road—was completed as a transcontinental extension into Puget Sound in May 1909. Though deliberately very well constructed, the line met its demise in 1977, with the Pacific Extension abandoned in 1980; it is now a public trail with the rail right-of-way preserved for potential future use. The Milwaukee was noteworthy for its pioneering use of main line electrification, though with two disconnected sections—from Harlowton, Montana, to Avery, Idaho; and from Othello, Washington, to Tacoma (with electrification completed in 1917) and Seattle (electrified ten years later). Electrified lines totaled 656 miles.

MAP 276 (*right*).
James J. Hill plots his new line to the Pacific in this magazine cartoon from 1889. Many people thought Hill mad to contemplate yet another transcontinental, especially one so close to the rival Northern Pacific, but Hill's scheme succeeded, and his railroad prospered even where others failed.

MAP 277 (*below*).
The (first) Cascade Tunnel and the switchbacks it replaced are shown on this map of the Stevens Pass area published in 1900, the year the tunnel was completed. The series of switchbacks is interesting and rarely mapped—railroads did not want to advertise the fact that they were necessary, and presumably the Great Northern only permitted their depiction here because they were about to be replaced. The 2.6-mile-long tunnel had smoke problems because it was still sloped and was replaced by a second tunnel, 7.8 miles long, in 1929.

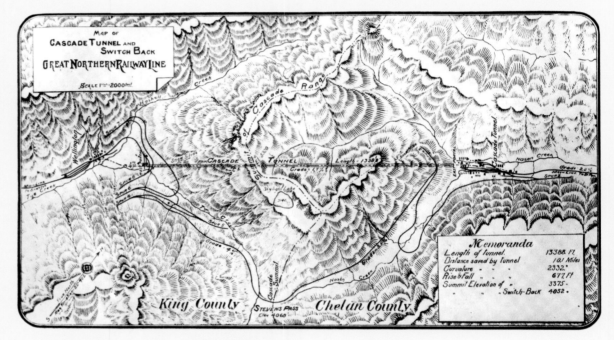

MAP 278 (*below*).
A scheme for a direct route west from Denver is shown on this 1892 map, the Denver, Apex & Western Railway to Salt Lake City, through a tunnel at the Continental Divide called the Atlantic–Pacific Tunnel, for which a company was formed in 1885 and shares issued (inset). The scheme did not succeed, but a similar one, for the Denver and Salt Lake Railroad, through the more than six-mile-long Moffat Tunnel (slightly to the south of this proposed tunnel), was completed in 1927. The tunnel was named for David Moffat, the Denver businessman who originated the idea of a directly westward tunnel.

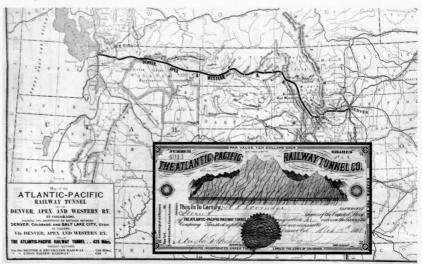

Coast to Coast Map
of the
Denver & Rio Grande Railroad
and the
Western Pacific Railway
and connections.

The last U.S. transcontinental line was that of the Western Pacific, which was completed from Salt Lake City to Oakland in November 1909. The road was owned by the Denver & Rio Grande Western, which had combined with the Denver & Rio Grande in 1901. The latter line had been shut off from its original Pacific aspirations when the Santa Fe captured Raton Pass. Although the Denver & Rio Grande had completed a line from Pueblo to Salt Lake City through Grand Junction in 1883, it still had to deliver up passengers and freight to other railroads—Union Pacific and Southern Pacific (the Central Pacific having been effectively absorbed into its larger offspring in 1885).

The transcontinental railroads transformed the West, allowing settlers to arrive in volume, to keep in contact with the places they had left, and to ship their produce or their products or the vast resources of the West to markets back East. And they would open up the West to tourism on a grand scale as Easterners saw photographs of the natural wonders of the West and wanted to see them for themselves. But by allowing the fast transport of the U.S. Army, as well as swarms of land-hungry settlers, they also foreboded the end of a way of life for Native peoples.

MAP 279 (*above*).
The Western Pacific Railroad, completed in 1909 and using a route south of the Great Salt Lake, connected with its sister system, the Denver & Rio Grande, in Salt Lake City. This map was published in 1912.

MAP 280 (*right*).
Although produced by the Union Pacific and highlighting its own line, this 1900 map of the West also shows most of the other lines in existence by that time. The only transcontinental line that is not on the map is the Western Pacific, shown separately in MAP 279, *above*.

The railroads also facilitated the development of the West by allowing settlers in remote areas access to a full range of retail and farming goods delivered to them by mail-order companies, bringing comfort hitherto impossible when the nearest store might be twenty miles away or more. One company was at the forefront of this revolution: Montgomery Ward. Based in Chicago, the company was the brainchild of Aaron Montgomery Ward, who recognized a need and moved to fulfil it, mailing out his first catalog, a paltry one-page list, in 1872. Ward disdained the normal rule of *caveat emptor*—let the buyer beware—and promised refunds on any goods found to be unsatisfactory. In this way he was able to overcome the initial resistance of homesteaders to an unknown company in faraway Chicago. Ward's business spread west with settlement and with the railroad, along with those of later competitors such as Sears, Roebuck and Company, which began trading in 1893.

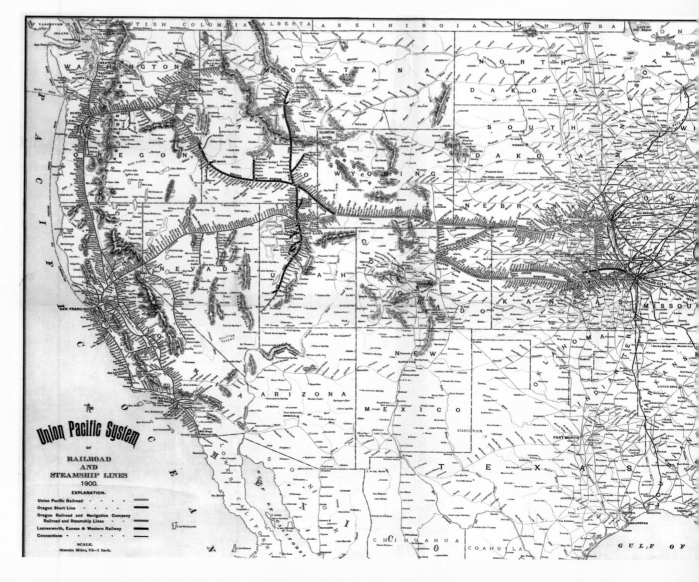

The
Union Pacific System
OF
RAILROAD
AND
STEAMSHIP LINES
1900.
EXPLANATION.

Union Pacific Railroad	
Oregon Short Line	
Oregon Railroad and Navigation Company Railroad and Steamship Lines	
Leavenworth, Kansas & Western Railway	
Connections	

SCALE
Statute Miles, 75=1 Inch.

A Mineral Bonanza

In the early years of western mining, anything that was not gold or silver tended to be overlooked or even regarded as a nuisance. That all changed when the realization dawned that fortunes could also be made with other metals, such as copper or zinc, often found with gold and silver and initially discarded. And the West proved to be rich in many different minerals.

In addition, new chemical processes were invented in the late nineteenth century that permitted much more gold to be extracted from its ores, and suddenly companies that were sitting on what they had thought were piles of waste now set to reprocessing them, often making more money than they had with the original mining.

Railroads developed networks designed to service these heavy mineral extractive industries. Sometimes the terrain was so difficult that narrow-gauge track was used. The Denver & Rio Grande, turned back from its transcontinental aspirations when the Santa Fe built across Raton Pass, instead developed a network of such lines to service the mines in the mountains of Colorado. Railroads, of course, the new mines, and just about any industry requiring power at this time now used steam, generated with coal. And so finding and developing some of the numerous coalfields in the West linked in with a developing industrial web and an expanding western economy.

In the Leadville area, a hundred miles west of Denver, gold had been found in California Gulch in 1860 but had all but run out after two years. Then, in 1874 a prospector named Will Stevens, reworking the depleted diggings, wondered about the underlying black sand and rock; when he had it assayed it proved to be a lead carbonate ore rich in silver. Leadville was created in 1877 when the news finally leaked out, and a new boom began. By 1880 the area had produced $12 million in silver. When the extraction of silver slowed, new deposits of copper and zinc were found and fueled economic activity for many more years. This story was repeated, to a lesser extent, perhaps, in many locations in the West.

In Butte, Montana, the Anaconda Mine produced silver from 1875 to 1881. The red metal found with it was deemed a nuisance. The mine was sold for seventy thousand dollars in 1881, as the silver output declined. The new owners soon found a massive vein of almost solid copper, and so a copper smelter was built, which produced huge quantities of copper

Map 281 (below).

Georgetown, Colorado, forty miles west of Denver, was founded in 1859 during the Pike's Peak Gold Rush by two prospectors, George and David Griffith; the town was named after George. Silver was found nearby in 1864, but the town's greatest growth took place in the 1880s, when, with over ten thousand inhabitants, it rivaled Leadville, and its citizens even tried briefly to wrest the state capital from Denver. The town dwindled after the 1893 financial collapse. This superb bird's-eye-view map was published in 1874 to assist with the promotion of the town.

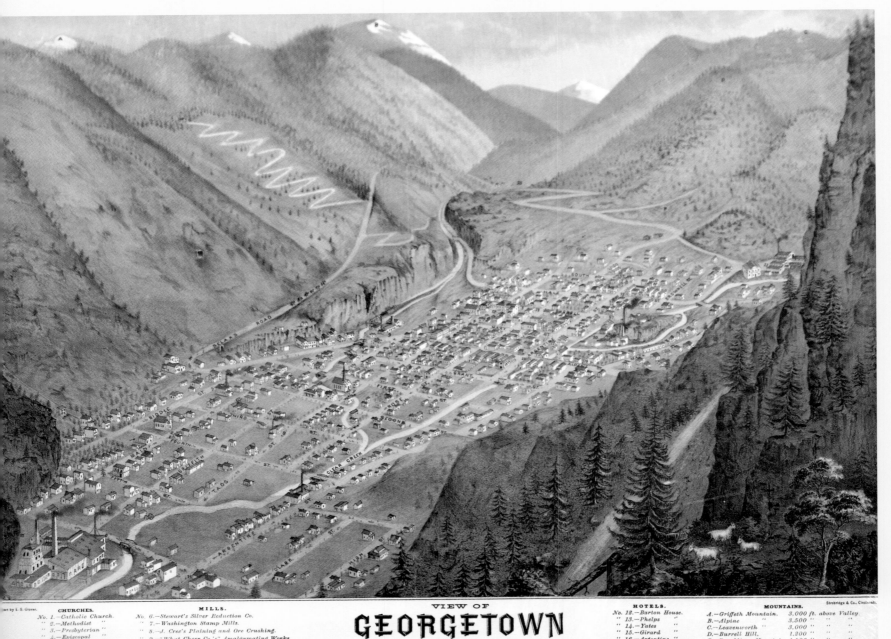

CHURCHES.	MILLS.		VIEW OF	HOTELS.	MOUNTAINS.

No. 1.—Catholic Church.
  " 2.—Methodist   "
  " 3.—Presbyterian   "
  " 4.—Episcopal   "
  " 5.—Congregational.

No. 6.—Stewart's Silver Reduction Co.
  " 7.—Washington Stamp Mills.
  " 8.—J. Cree's Plaining and Ore Crushing.
  " 9.—"What Cheer Co.'s" Amalgamating Works.
  " 10.—G. W. Hall & Co.s Plain'g & Ore Crush'g "
  " 11.—Crosby's Amalgamating Works.

GEORGETOWN
COLORADO, 1874.

No. 12.—Barton House.
  " 13.—Phelps   "
  " 14.—Yates   "
  " 15.—Girard   "
  " 16.—Argentine   "

A.—Griffeth Mountain. 3,000 ft. above Valley
B.—Alpine   3,500 "
C.—Leavenworth   3,000 "
D.—Burrell Hill.   1,200 "
E.—Republican Mountain. 1,500 "

No. 19.—Office Colorado Miner, A. Cree, Propr.

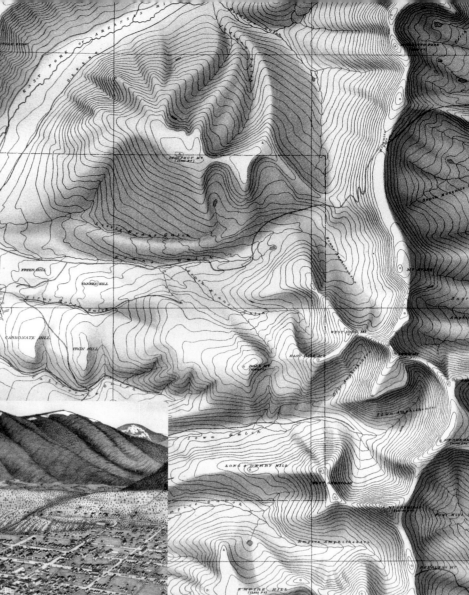

Map 282 (*right*).
An *Atlas of Leadville*, published by the U.S. Geological Survey in 1886, included a number of very nicely drawn topographic maps such as this one. *Leadville* is at left.

Map 283 (*below, center*).
This bird's-eye map of Leadville was published in 1879. The view is from Stray Horse Gulch, also shown on MAP 281 and MAP 284.

Map 284 (*below, bottom left*).
The complex underground network of tunnels and shafts is depicted on this geological map detail showing the silver mines of Fryer Hill, above and close to Leadville. The map is from the 1886 *Atlas of Leadville*. A two-dimensional map has a hard time depicting this essentially three-dimensional feature.

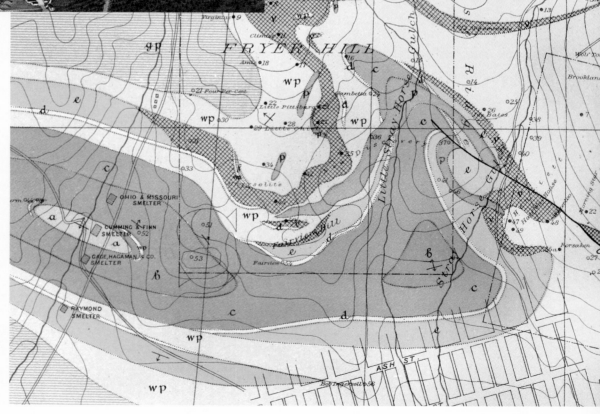

Map 285 (*below*).
Also from the 1886 *Atlas of Leadville* is this map of the geology near the town. Many mine entrances are shown (black dots), and some are named. Several smelters are shown and named.

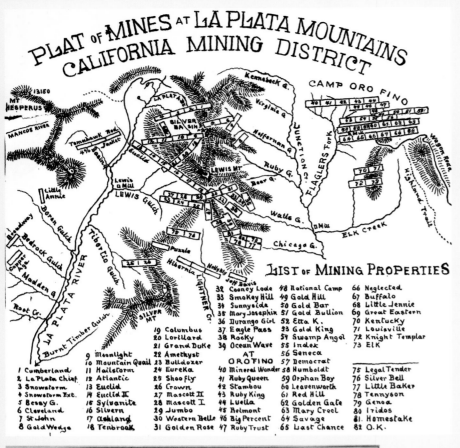

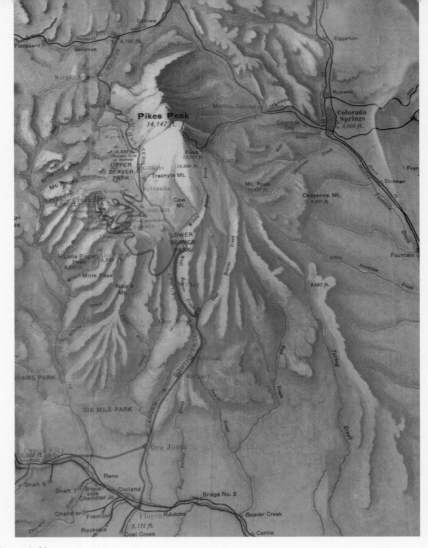

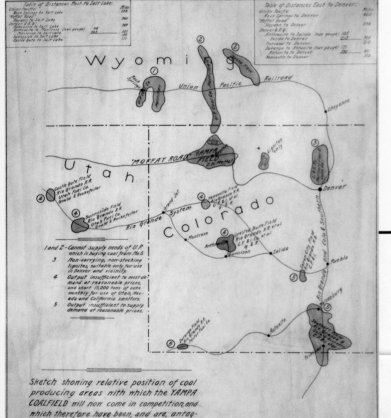

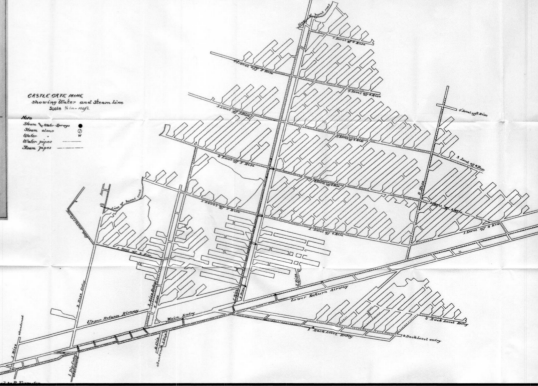

Map 286 (above, left).
This 1893 map shows the claims at the *California Mining District*, a few miles northwest of Durango, in the southwest corner of Colorado. Many of the mining camps in this more remote region of Colorado were tied together by toll roads.

Map 287 (above).
The 1899 proposed lines of the *Denver & Southwestern Railway* into the *Cripple Creek* mining district shown on an unusual shaded topographic base. The convoluted routes are clearly shown.

Map 288 (above).
Coalfields of *Colorado* and parts of *Utah* and *Wyoming* are shown on this 1903 map, produced to promote a proposed new field, the *Yampa Field*, west of Denver and served by the *Moffat Road*, a railroad intended to connect Denver with Salt Lake City but that failed. This route eventually used the Moffat Tunnel, completed in 1928 across the Continental Divide west of Denver (see Map 278, page 136).

Map 289 (above, right).
An unusual map of the underground pattern of tunnels and galleries in the Castle Gate coal mine in Utah, about ninety miles southeast of Salt Lake City, in 1890. The mine opened in 1886 after the Denver & Rio Grande Western Railroad built a line over the Wasatch Plateau in Utah. The mine supplied high-grade coal for locomotives. The Castle Gate Mine was the scene of a massive explosion in March 1924 that killed all 171 men working in the mine at the time. It was the second-worst mining disaster in Utah; the worst was that at the Winter Quarters Mine, at Scofield, a few miles west of Castle Gate, in 1900. There an explosion killed 200 men. Thousands of miners died in the myriad mines of the West, but coal mines were some of the most dangerous because of the explosive nature of coal dust.

to be shipped back East, finding an emerging market for electric and telephone cables. By 1892 the Anaconda Mine was producing 100 million pounds of copper each year and was the largest single source of copper in the world.

New gold was found on the Coeur d'Alene River in Idaho in 1883, causing five thousand gold seekers to descend on the region (Map 292, *overleaf*). Two years later silver was found on the south fork of the river. Like many mining areas in the West, the silver could only be obtained by hard-rock mining that necessitated the use of heavy equipment and required a great deal of capital, and so mining quickly passed into the hands of companies large enough to handle it. Nevertheless, the large labor force required

Map 290 (*right*).
Completed and proposed railroads (see key) are shown on this 1873 map of Colorado, produced only four years after the completion of the first transcontinental railroad, shown at top. The map also shows the location of resources—gold, silver, coal, and timber.

Map 291 (*below*).
The Great Gold Belt of Colorado is the focus of this promotional map published in 1908. The tables at left tell the story—$23.5 million worth of gold mined in Colorado in 1906, and $13.4 million of silver—in both cases the highest production of any state. The message to investors is clear—put your money into a proven area.

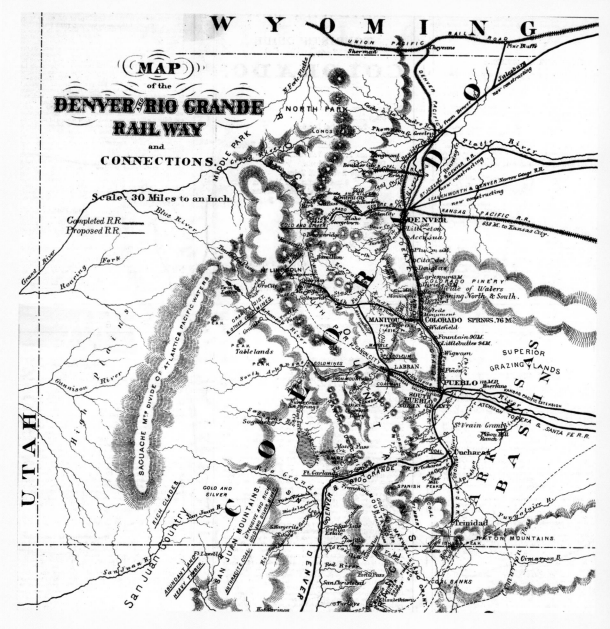

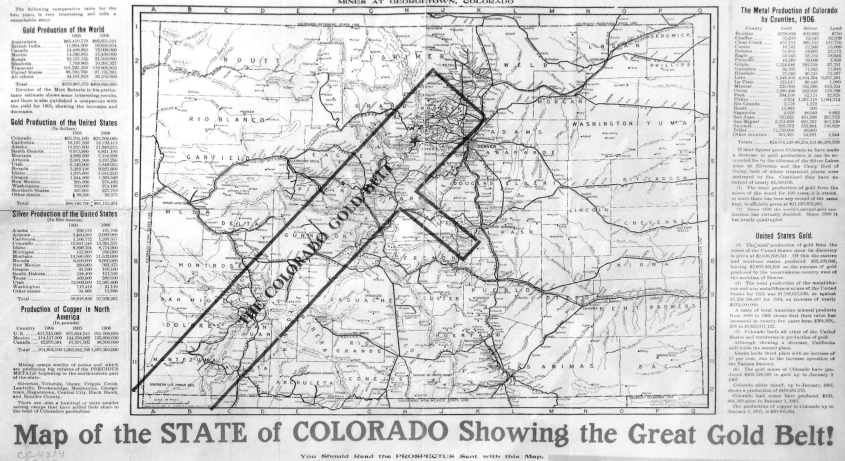

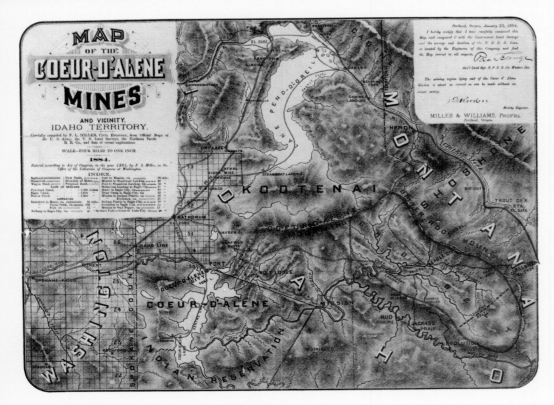

provided jobs for many immigrants. One of Idaho's silver mines, the Sunshine Mine, near Kellogg, continued production for many decades, ultimately yielding more silver than the much more famous Comstock Lode in Nevada (see page 102). In 1985 the Coeur d'Alene silver mines produced their billionth ounce of silver and claimed the largest silver production in the world.

Such accolades were used early on in Arizona and Nevada; MAP 295, *right, bottom,* published in 1907, claims the *Greatest Mineral Belt in the World.* Arizona, in particular, benefited from the new cyanidation process to recover silver or gold coated with sulfur compounds that could not be extracted previously. One location that used the new method was at Chloride, in western Arizona, remembered on a roadside marker, shown as MAP 599, *page 259.*

The silver-mining industry of the West was boosted by the Sherman Silver Purchase Act of 1890, which required the federal government to buy huge quantities of silver each month. But the boom did not last long. The plan backfired, contributing to the Panic of 1893 and a subsequent slowing of the economy; the act was repealed that year.

Nevertheless, the mineral resources of the West were such that they continued to attract settlers but increasingly as workers to man industrial extraction and refining works, creating employment but not immediate riches.

MAP 292 (*above*).
The Coeur d'Alene mining area on an 1884 map. Routes to the mines are shown in red, both by *stage* and *steamboat.* The recently completed *N.P.R.R.*—the Northern Pacific—vastly improved outside access to this region; its track is shown curving in a long arc across the top of this map. Note the surveyed sections in eastern *Washington* and north of *Coeur D'Alene City.*

MAP 293 (*below*).
The complex and, in their time, rich mining claims at *Tonopah City,* Nevada, are shown on this 1902 map, complete with a photograph of Jim Butler, the man who in 1900 discovered the first gold at this location—the *Mizpah* Lode, shown at center on the map—while chasing his burro, which had strayed. The advertisements around this map attest to the fleeting but once substantial settlement.

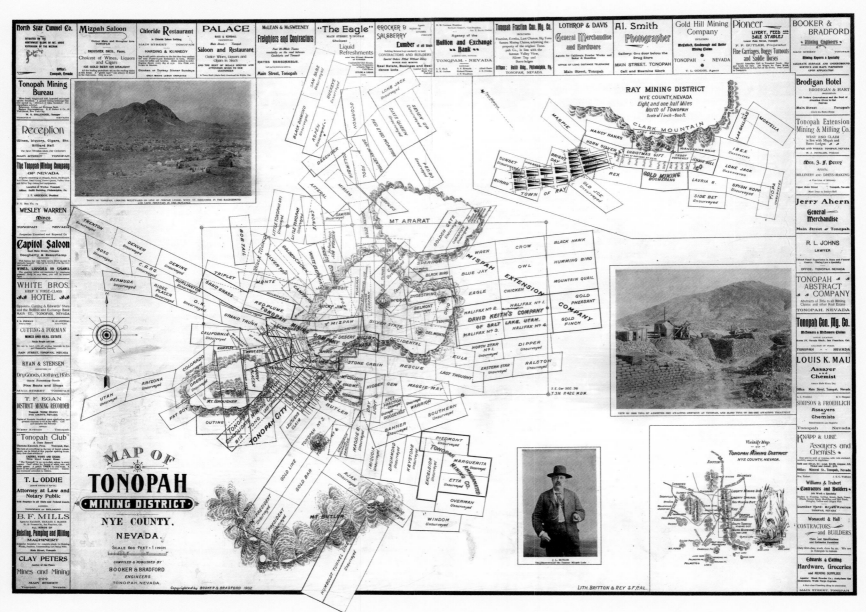

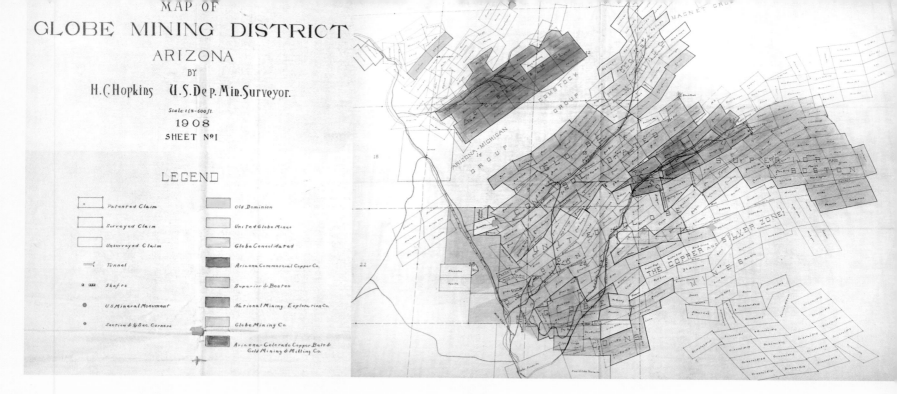

MAP OF
GLOBE MINING DISTRICT
ARIZONA
BY
H. C. Hopkins U.S. Dep. Min. Surveyor.

Scale 1in=600 ft.
1908
SHEET No 1

LEGEND

MAP 294 (above).

Claims cover the map north of Globe, Arizona (*Globe Townsite* is outlined at bottom), in this 1908 federal government map. The *Globe Mining District*, in its time one of the richest mineral districts in the United States, is about ninety miles east of Phoenix. The townsite of Globe City was laid out in 1876 following discoveries of silver in the area. Gold had been found earlier but not in major quantities. In 1873 the Apache had been driven from the immediate mining region by the U.S.

Army under General George Crook, and the Globe Mining District was removed from the San Carlos Apache Indian Reservation. By 1881 there was more interest in the significant copper deposits of the area than there was in silver. A Swiss mining engineer was brought in, and a copper mining industry was established. By 1908, as might be deduced from this map, claims were largely in the hands of companies rather than individuals. Mining continues to this day.

MAP 295 (right).

Similar in intent to MAP 290, *page 141,* this map depicts the *Greatest Mineral Belt in the World* extending from Nevada into Arizona. This map was published in 1907 by the promoters of a new mine at Kingman, Arizona. The company was also in the business of selling mining properties elsewhere in the region.

MAP 296 (below).

This ingenious map depicted the *Bullfrog Mining District* in 1907. It appeared in a newspaper, the *Bullfrog Miner,* in Beatty, Nevada, shown as the heart of the mining district—and the frog. Railroads, both existing and hoped-for, are shown as arteries.

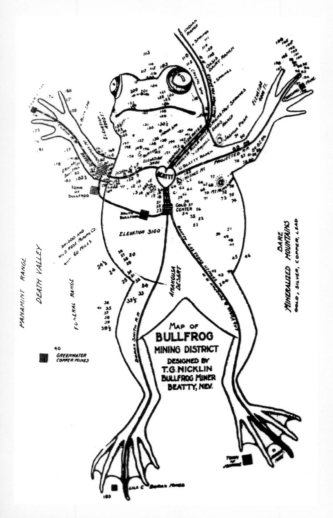

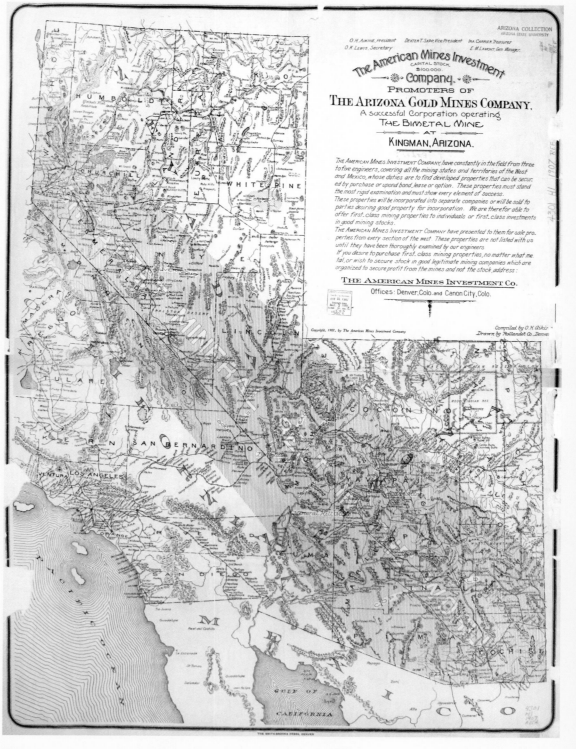

MAP 297 (above).
This 1906 map reveals a sea of oil wells across downtown Los Angeles. The belt of producing oil wells—shown as black dots—extends right across downtown to the *Los Angeles [River]* at right. Many people literally had oil wells in their backyards. By the 1920s local ordinances sometimes required an oil derrick to be covered on the side it faced a dwelling to protect the house from a potential gusher.

LIQUID GOLD

The other mineral resource that the West would come to produce in quantity found its real value in the twentieth century, after the automobile became mass produced. The American oil industry had been born in Ohio in 1859 but produced mainly kerosene, used for lighting, replacing whale oil and candles.

Drilling for oil was taking place in both California and Texas by the end of the nineteenth century; the McKittrick-Cymeric field, shown on MAP 298, *right*, was producing oil by 1887. But the oil find that is generally considered to have been the beginning of the modern oil industry was the one at Spindletop, just south of Beaumont, Texas, in 1901. Here a hill that had long been suspected of having oil underneath it, because of sulfur springs and bubbling natural gas seepages, was being drilled in the closing years of the 1890s, yet without success. Then, on 10 January 1901, Anthony Lucas, financed by James Guffey, whose company name is all over the Spindletop map (MAP 301, *far right, bottom*) found oil at 1,139 feet. The Lucas Gusher, as it was called, blew oil over 150 feet into the air at a rate of 100,000 barrels a day, and it took nine days before it could be brought under control. Beaumont became a boomtown overnight, its population tripling to 30,000 in three months as speculators rushed in to stake claims everywhere.

The promise of wealth soon evaporated, and the Spindletop wells produced only 10,000 barrels a day by 1904. It was not until 1925 that a new reservoir of oil was struck at 2,500 feet, a find that sparked a second boom, with 72 million barrels of oil being produced over the next ten years. When the oil finally ran out the field was mined for sulfur, completing the devastation of the landscape.

Oil was subsequently found in many locations across the West, but especially in California. From 1905 to 1928 the state was the largest oil-producing region in the United States. A big oil find took place in 1921 at Signal Hill, at Long Beach, California. Here Shell's Alamitos #1 well began a new oil boom in southern California. By 1923 Signal Hill was producing 259,000 barrels of oil a day. In 1924 the area incorporated itself to prevent Long Beach from taxing its oil; today the small city remains completely surrounded by Long Beach.

In 1968 oil was found at Prudhoe Bay in Alaska, in quantities that eclipsed all previous finds, and today the state produces more oil than California and Texas combined (see page 250).

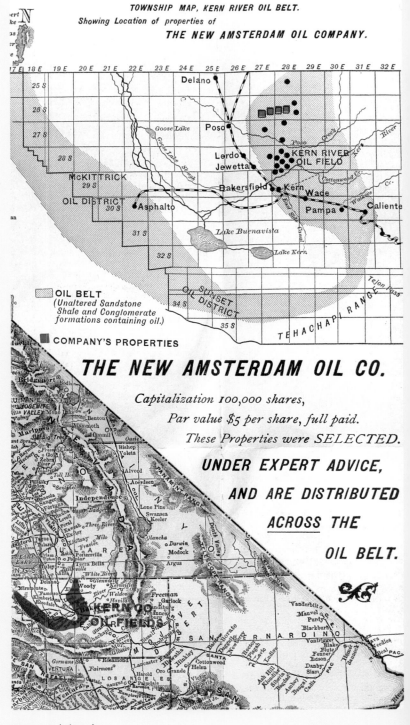

TOWNSHIP MAP, KERN RIVER OIL BELT.
Showing Location of properties of
THE NEW AMSTERDAM OIL COMPANY.

OIL BELT
(Unaltered Sandstone Shale and Conglomerate formations containing oil.)

COMPANY'S PROPERTIES

THE NEW AMSTERDAM OIL CO.

Capitalization 100,000 shares,
Par value $5 per share, full paid.
These Properties were SELECTED.

UNDER EXPERT ADVICE,

AND ARE DISTRIBUTED

ACROSS THE

OIL BELT.

MAP 298 (above).
The New Amsterdam Oil Company issued a prospectus in 1901 addressed to potential investors, which included this map of Kern County Oil Fields, about eighty miles north of Los Angeles. The map also shows the *McKittrick Oil District*, where drilling had begun as early as 1887.

Below. The Spindletop Oil Field, at Beaumont, Texas, in 1902, the year after oil was first discovered there.

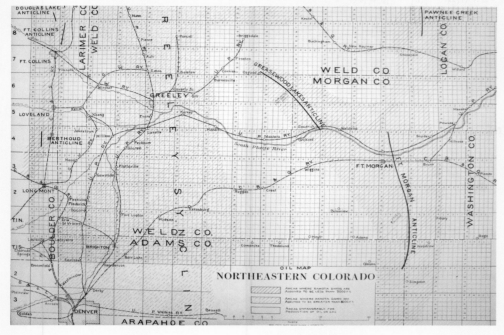

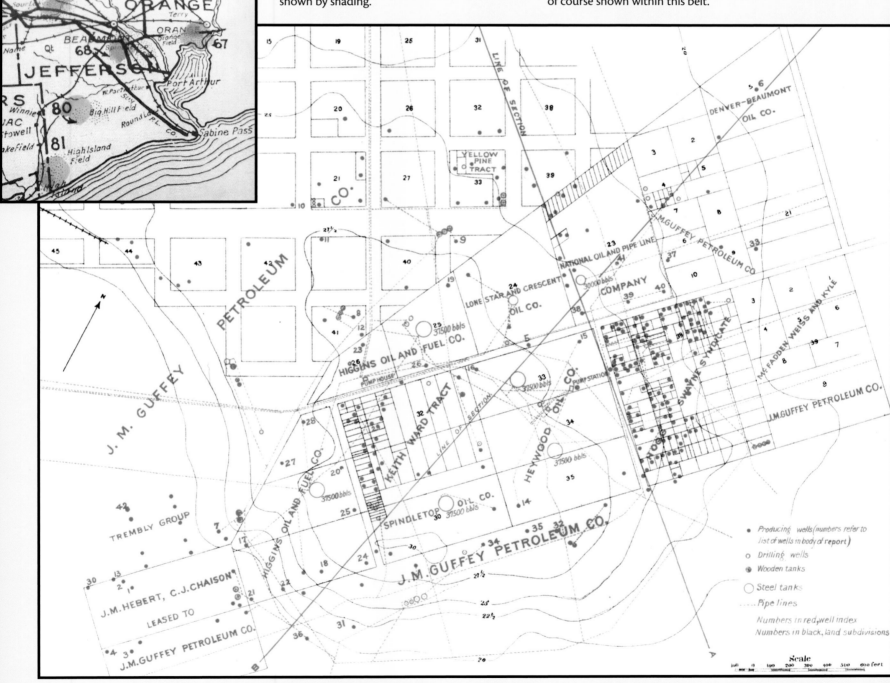

MAP 299 (above).

An oil prospecting map of northeast Colorado, dating from the 1930s. *Denver* is at bottom left. Anticlines are shown. These are arched underground rock formations that often trap oil underneath them. In this region the Dakota Sands were the oil-bearing sediment, so the areas where these were assumed to exist at two depths are shown by shading.

MAP 300 (above).

Drawn to aid the sale of oil lands in 1919, this map and bird's-eye view advanced the idea that there was an oil belt from Pennsylvania to Texas; the lands for sale, marked in red, are of course shown within this belt.

MAP 301 (above) and MAP 302 (inset).

There were only a few wells being drilled but still many producing wells at Spindletop by 1906, the date the U.S. Geological Survey published this map. Notice the claims of *J.M. Guffey*, the company of one of the major financiers of the drilling here. On the inset map, which was drawn in 1930, *Spindletop Field* is at 68, just south of *Beaumont*.

An Unequal Fight

As the many attractions of the West enticed EuroAmericans, so were the traditional lands of the Indian encroached upon. Although tribes had always fought among each other for the best territories, the ultimately unequal battle with the newcomers would lead to an irrevocable loss of Indian lands. Fight as the Indians might, the resources and arsenal of the settlers and the U.S. Army were such that they could not win. Not only did EuroAmericans take the Indians' land, they also killed their principal food source, the buffalo, en masse, forcing Indians to adopt Western ways or die.

Some of the first encroachers onto western Indian territory were not, however, EuroAmericans but eastern Indians, forcibly relocated from their lands in the South coveted by settlers. In 1830 President Andrew Jackson signed the Indian Removal Act, which exiled Indians then occupying land wanted by settlers to the lands of the Louisiana Purchase west of the

Above. This illustration, *Combat between a Kiowa and a Comanche*, was drawn by an eleven-year-old Comanche boy. It appeared in an 1890 *Census Report on Indians*, published in 1894. The two tribes were in fact often allies against both settlers and other tribes.

MAP 303 (*below*).
Artist George Catlin visited the West in 1831 and 1832 and drew this map a year later. It shows the locations of various Indian groups using his own information and that derived from others; the result is an important record available from no other source. The black dots show the distribution of buffalo herds.

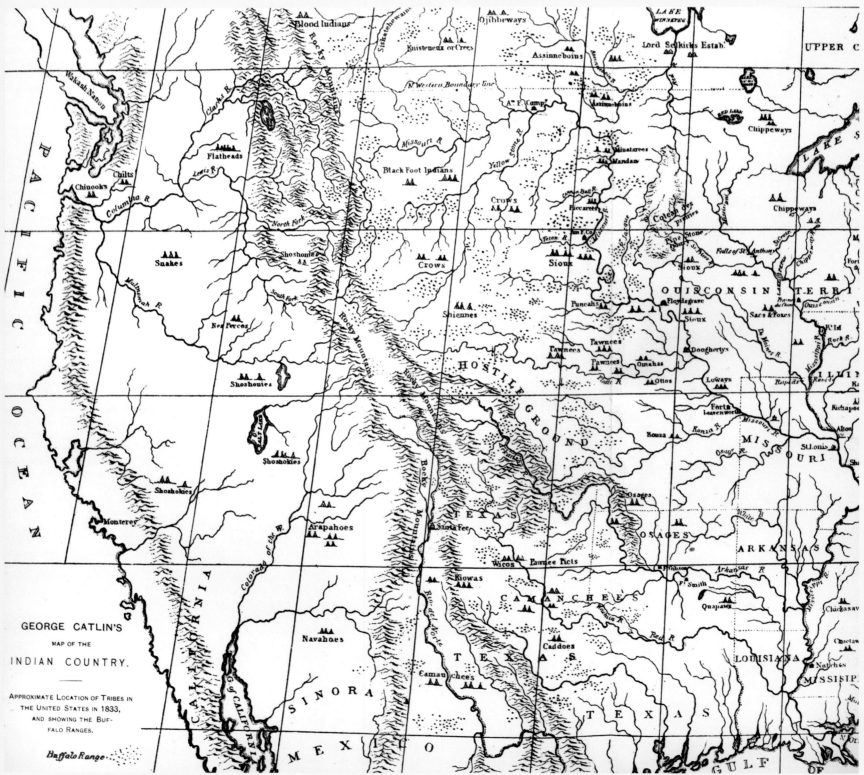

GEORGE CATLIN'S
MAP OF THE
INDIAN COUNTRY.

APPROXIMATE LOCATION OF TRIBES IN
THE UNITED STATES IN 1833,
AND SHOWING THE BUF-
FALO RANGES.

Buffalo Range

Mississippi. Most of the land they were allocated was taken from Plains Indians such as the Kansa and the Osage. The land allocations are shown in MAP 304, *right.* The Cherokee, who initially resisted the move but were undermined by factions that signed a treaty for removal, left for the West in 1838. The removal of Indians west is popularly known as the Trail of Tears.

The movement of EuroAmericans west was already causing friction with the Indians by 1851, and that year an attempt was made to maintain peace and, in particular, stop Indian attacks on wagon trains moving west along the Oregon Trail. Indian agent Thomas Fitzpatrick and superintendent of Indian affairs Colonel David Mitchell brought together some ten thousand Sioux, Cheyenne, Arapaho, Assiniboine, Mandan, Hidatsa, Arikara, and Shoshone at Fort Laramie in September 1851. Also

MAP 304 (*right*).
A federal government map from 1836, which shows the lands allocated to *Emigrant Indians.* The map covers the area of today's states of Oklahoma, Kansas, and Nebraska. Note the *Santa Fe Road* across the center of the map. Land and population tables are at right. See also MAP 202, *page 105.*

MAP 305 (*below*).
Confining Indians to areas smaller than their initial reservations became a pattern followed everywhere. This War Department map lists lands ceded as the result of treaties that year. It is signed and dated *5 September 1854* by the *Indian Office, Washington.* One entry from the list is typical: *The Miamies cede all their country to the U.S. excepting 70,000 acres and* one section for school purposes. Citizens not allowed to settle on their land until they have made their selection. The Miamis' 325,000-acre reservation is shown outlined in red adjacent to the Missouri boundary at bottom right. They lost almost 80 percent of it in 1854.

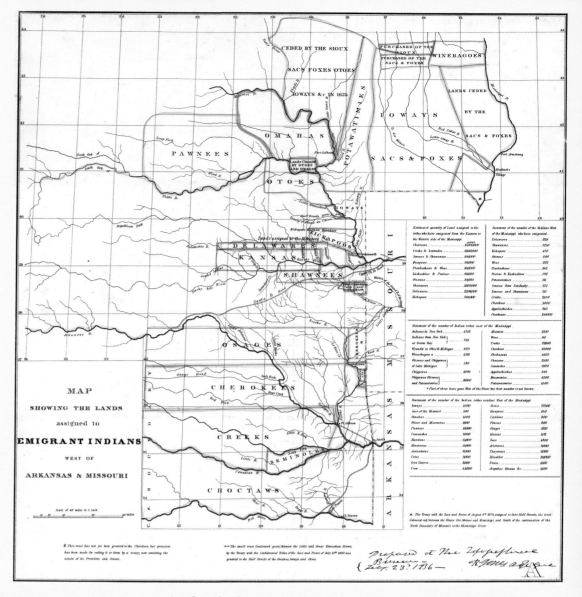

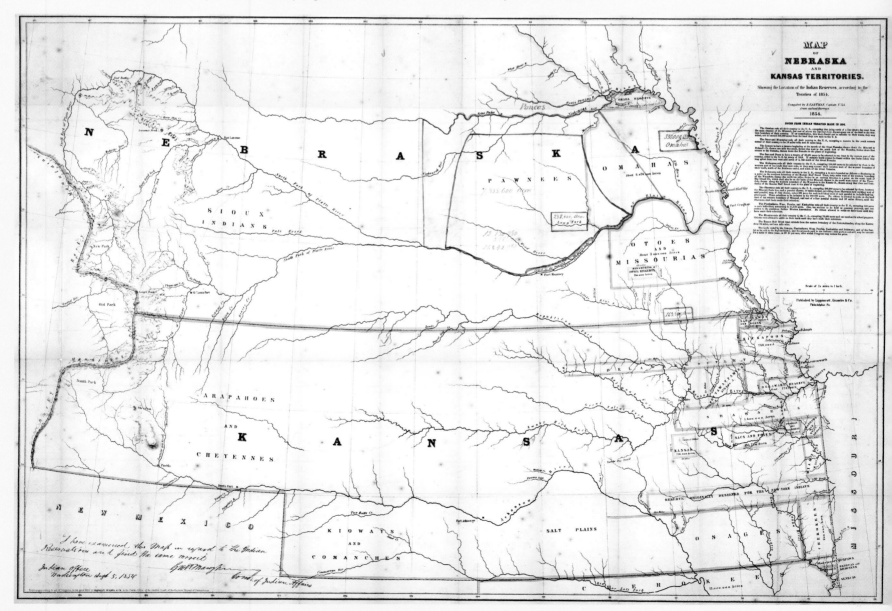

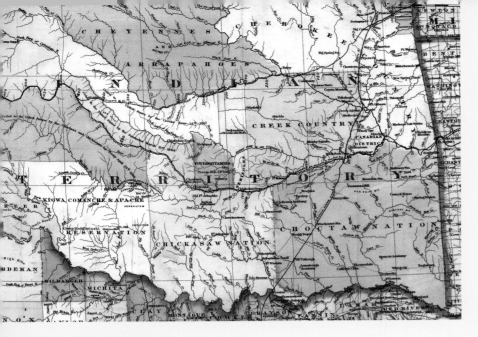

Map 306 (*above*).
This 1872 map shows Indian reservation lands covering all of *Indian Territory*, now the state of Oklahoma.

Map 307 (*below*).
The map drawn by Father Pierre-Jean De Smet to document the areas reserved for each tribe under the 1851 Treaty of Fort Laramie. The map was drawn in St. Louis late in the year. It has a note that it was presented to *Col. D.D. Mitchell by P.J. de Smet, Soc. Jes.* On the north branch of the Platte is *Fort Laramie,* depicted by a dot (at the center of the map). On the western boundary of *Sioux or Dacotah Territory* are the *Black Hills.* In the top margin is a picture of *Big Robber, Crow Chief.* The southern part of *Blackfoot Territory* contains a *Great Volcanic Reg. about 100 miles in [extent?] now in a state of eruption.* This is an early reference to the geysers of Yellowstone National Park.

present was the Jesuit Father Pierre-Jean De Smet, known as Blackrobe, who was trusted by most of the Indians. Pawnee, Comanche, and Kiowa refused to attend.

The resulting (first) Treaty of Fort Laramie allocated lands to each of the tribes, confining them to those areas in return for annuities and presents. Eleven chiefs were taken to visit Washington, D.C.; the idea seems to have been to awe them with a sense of overwhelming power of the government and was a policy followed time and time again. De Smet drew up a detailed map showing the treaty land allocations (Map 307, *below*).

It did not take long for the treaty to be broken. In August 1854 a brevet second lieutenant, John Grattan, led twenty-nine men to punish a Brulé Sioux who had shot a cow. Grattan and his men were wiped out after finding themselves up against four thousand Sioux. It was dubbed the Grattan Massacre by the press. The following year the Army moved to punish the offenders, and Brigadier General William Selby Harney led a force along the North Platte, killing eighty-six Brulé Sioux at the Battle of Bluewater Creek, also known as the Battle of Ash Hollow. The engagement was dubbed by some the Harney Massacre, for Harney had his men fire into caves where Sioux had taken refuge, with the result that women and children were killed. This sort of revenge and counter-revenge was to characterize the Indian Wars of the next several decades.

In 1862 Dakota Sioux living along the Minnesota River in southwest Minnesota did not receive their annual government annuity and, taking advantage of the fact that many soldiers had been transferred to fight in

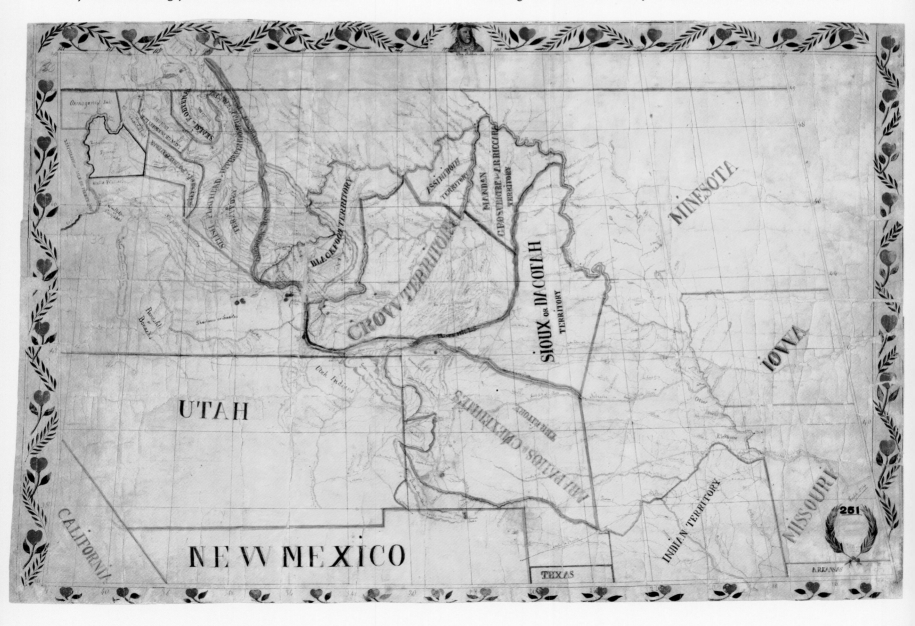

the Civil War, besieged the Army's Fort Ridgely, burned the town of New Ulm, and killed eight hundred settlers. Thirty thousand more abandoned their farms in panic. When federal help finally arrived, a 1,600-strong militia was organized at Mankato and fought with the federal troops against the Dakota at Wood Lake. Many Dakota were killed; two thousand were taken captive, and thirty-eight were hanged, the largest mass execution in American history. The Minnesota reservation was abolished, and 1,600 Sioux moved to a reservation farther west.

Also during the Civil War came one of the most infamous incidents of the Indian Wars. A group of about 550 Cheyenne and Arapaho, led by Cheyenne chief Black Kettle, had surrendered after signing a treaty and agreeing to move to what is now Oklahoma. Yet, on 29 November 1864, they were attacked at their encampment on Sand Creek, on the Plains in eastern Colorado Territory. Cavalry and other troops under Colonel John Chivington cut down 150 men, women, and children as they attempted to escape. Chivington was investigated by Congress for this action but escaped prosecution because of a general amnesty following the Civil War.

Chivington's massacre led to retaliatory Indian raids on isolated settlements, including, in 1867, attacks on crews building the Union Pacific Eastern Division (later Kansas Pacific) line between Kansas City and Denver (see page 122).

Black Kettle and his Cheyenne moved to Oklahoma, but history seemed to repeat itself. At dawn on 27 November 1868, on the banks of the Washita River in western Oklahoma, they were attacked by federal troops looking to retaliate for Indian raids. The troops were commanded by a man whose name would become synonymous with the western Indian Wars—Lieutenant Colonel George Armstrong Custer. Black Kettle died along with forty of his people as they tried to surrender. Custer avoided censure because women and children were not killed. Custer escaped as

Map 308 (below).
Part of a large and detailed map of the Black Hills prepared after George Custer's foray in 1874 in which gold was found along *French Cr[eek]*, shown flowing into the *South Fork of Cheyenne* near the bottom of this map. His report triggered a gold rush into the region, considered sacred by the Dakota.

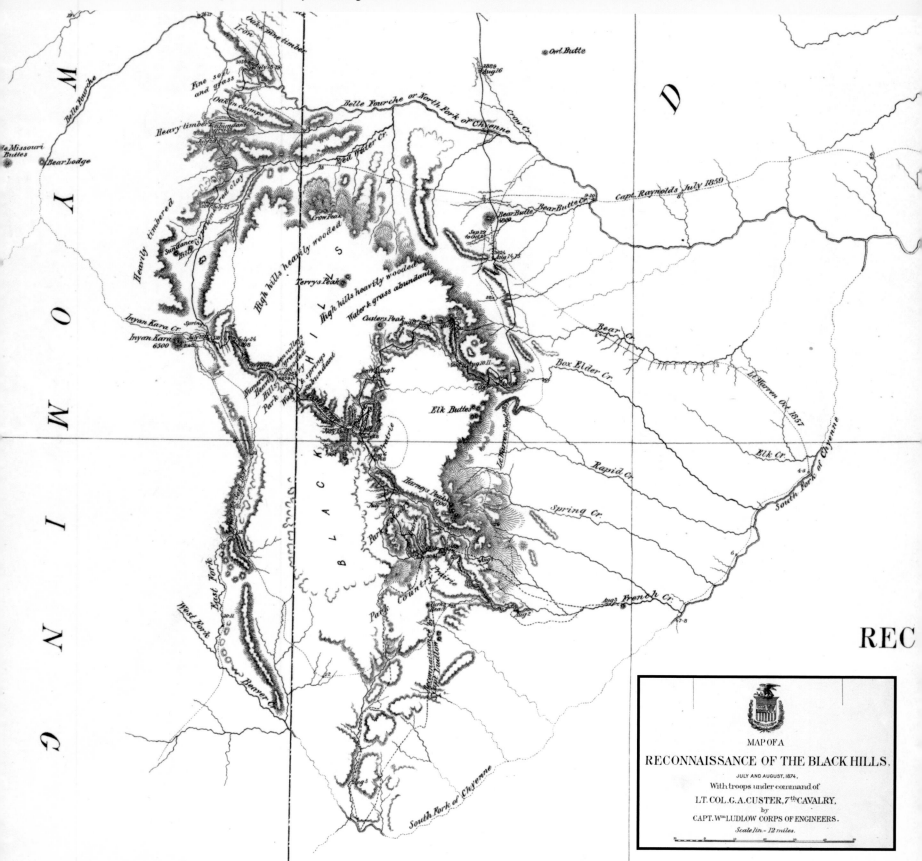

MAP OF A
RECONNAISSANCE OF THE BLACK HILLS,
JULY AND AUGUST, 1874,
With troops under command of
LT. COL. G. A. CUSTER, 7TH CAVALRY,
by
CAPT. WM LUDLOW CORPS OF ENGINEERS.
Scale 1 in. - 12 miles.

eight thousand Arapaho, Kiowa, and Cheyenne camped nearby moved to the rescue. The incident probably emboldened Custer to the idea of success (from his point of view) even against overwhelming Indian numbers. The conceit would prove his downfall eight years later.

In the Southwest, Chiricahua Apache under their chief, Cochise, rampaged across the country in 1861 attacking settlers, murdering 150; this violence was in retaliation for the probably incorrect arrest of his family by the Army, who thought he was responsible for kidnapping a young boy. This was not a good time to act insensitively and enrage the Indians, as the forts were depleted of their garrisons, transferred to fight in the Civil War. This was also the time the Confederacy was invading the Southwest (see page 110). In 1862 eighteen hundred Union troops were dispatched from California. Ambushed by seven hundred Apache under Cochise and another chief, Mangas Coloradas, the federal troops quickly turned the tables with two howitzer field artillery guns.

Navajo also took advantage of the Civil War to step up raids against settlers and Pueblo Indians. In 1863–64 Colonel Christopher "Kit" Carson led a force of about four hundred against the Navajo, invading their stronghold at the Canyon de Chelly in northeastern Arizona Territory. Three thousand Navajo were captured and marched to Fort Sumner before being sent back to a reservation created around the Canyon de Chelly.

Later that year Carson was sent to punish Kiowa and Comanche that had been attacking wagon trains on the Santa Fe Trail. With 350 volunteers and 75 Ute he found himself up against a thousand Kiowa and Comanche at Adobe Walls, an abandoned trading post near the Canadian River in the Texas Panhandle. Two howitzers were all that saved Carson that time.

In 1866 Lakota Sioux chief Makhpyia-luta—Red Cloud—began attacking U.S. Army troops attempting to secure the Bozeman Trail to the new mining districts of Montana (see page 109). On 21 December Captain William J. Fetterman and eighty men were lured into an ambush by one of Red Cloud's warriors, Tasunka Witko—Crazy Horse—and all were killed. The following year Red Cloud set out with a thousand warriors to attack Fort Phil Kearny, on the Bozeman Trail, but met thirty-one soldiers on a work detail under Captain James Powell, who managed, against all odds, to hold off the Lakota attackers, by firing for many hours from an oval of wagon boxes lined with sheet iron, until relief arrived. This incident is known as the Wagon Box Fight. Red Cloud was persuaded to make peace, on terms favorable to the Lakota; in 1868 the government concluded a second treaty of Fort Laramie, making huge concessions. A large Lakota reservation was established, centered on the Black Hills, without any military supervision; the Powder River was reserved as a hunting ground, and all EuroAmericans were forbidden to enter either area.

But this concession did not last very long. Rumor had it that there was gold in the Black Hills, and in the wake of the financial Panic of 1873 gold seekers illegally began searching there. In 1874 Custer was sent into the Black Hills to investigate, finding gold himself along the banks of French Creek (MAP 308, *previous page*). His report made matters worse, as it triggered a full-scale gold rush. The resulting Lakota attacks led to a government order to report to various Indian agencies, an order they ignored. The Army was then ordered to round them up, and in the spring of 1876 a coordinated military campaign was launched.

A three-pronged offensive was planned. Brigadier General George Crook approached from the south, Colonel John Gibbon from the west, and Brigadier General Alfred H. Terry from the east. With Terry was Custer, leading six hundred of his Seventh Cavalry. Crook, with about a thousand soldiers and 262 Shoshone and Crow, was attacked by about 1,500 Lakota, led by Crazy Horse, on 17 June

MAP 309 (*below*).
It is not surprising considering the outcome, but there are few contemporary maps illustrating the Battle of the Little Bighorn, fought on 25 June 1876. This one was drawn five days after the battle by Lieutenant Robert Patterson Hughes, an aide-de-camp of the expedition commander Alfred Terry. The map is oriented to be the same as MAP 310, *right, top*, with north to the top left. Hughes enclosed the map in a letter to his wife, a letter that supports the view that Custer acted rashly by engaging his adversary before help arrived and by splitting his men into three groups despite the odds. The Lakota and Cheyenne encampment is at bottom center, below (west) of the Little Bighorn River, with the arrow to the right of it being the direction of the initial attack led by Marcus Reno. Custer's route is thought to be the dashed line above (east of) the river, while the site of the "Last Stand" is at top left. The defense of Reno and Frederick Benteen is at right center top.

Below.
Sitting Bull, a Sioux chief and spiritual leader, widely credited as the strategist behind the Indian victory at the Little Bighorn. Sitting Bull was killed in 1890 by Indian police sent to arrest him shortly before the massacre at Wounded Knee.

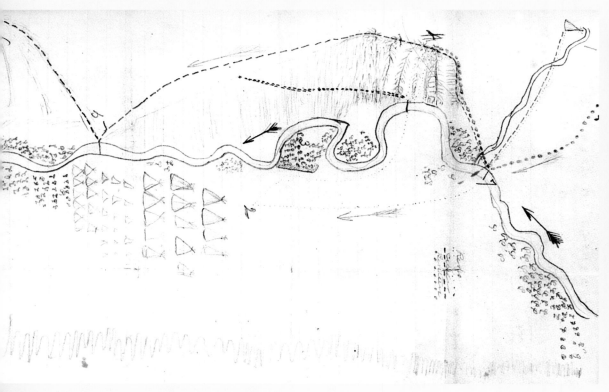

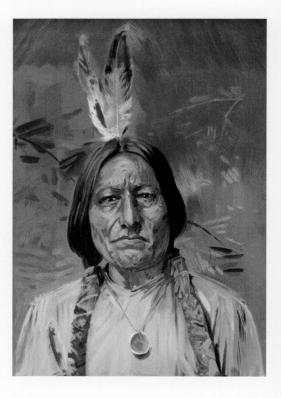

1876 at Rosebud Creek, one of the south bank tributaries of the Yellow-stone River in southern Montana. Wave after wave of Sioux descended on Crook's men, and had it not been for the support of his Indian allies the result would certainly have been disaster. Crook was lucky to escape alive, for Crazy Horse had perhaps another 2,500 warriors concealed in the hills. With fifty-six severely wounded men, Crook retreated in disarray.

Terry, meanwhile, ordered Custer and his six hundred cavalry to pursue the Lakota who had attacked Crook; Terry, like Crook and everyone else, had grossly underestimated their adversary's strength. On the morn-ing of 25 June Custer neared a large Lakota and Cheyenne village on the Little Bighorn River—called the Greasy Grass River by the Lakota—anoth-er of the Yellowstone's tributaries. The vainglorious Custer made the fatal error of deciding to attack without waiting for Terry's main column or that of Gibbon, either again completely misunderstanding the Indian strength or somehow believing that his cavalry were so superior and better trained that they could beat them anyway. We shall never know.

Custer split his men into three groups. Major Marcus Reno took 150 men to attack the encampment directly; 125 men under Captain Frederick Benteen were sent to the south to cover the supposed route of escapees; and Custer led a frontal attack with just over 200 men. Reno was surprised to find himself up against hundreds of warriors; after retreating he man-aged to link up with Benteen, and the two companies repelled waves of Indian attacks into the next day, when the Lakota and Cheyenne slipped quietly away. Custer was not as lucky. Surrounded, his men were finally overwhelmed by a surprise charge led by Crazy Horse, and all perished. Of course, few details are known for sure. "Custer's Last Stand" passed into western myth, the subject of countless books and movies, the story of-ten embellished and glorified. Only relatively recently has the Indian view been taken into consideration. Known as the Custer Battlefield National Monument since 1946, the site's name was changed to the Little Bighorn Battlefield National Monument in 1991, and memorials to Lakota and Cheyenne casualties in the battle were added in 1999.

Despite this setback, the Army's relentless pursuit of the Indians was not abandoned, and with weapons such as Gatling guns and howitzers against them, in the long term the Indians did not stand a chance. Within

MAP 310 (above).
A map of the Battle of the Little Bighorn painted from memory by White Bird, a Northern Cheyenne, on muslin, about 1895. It is oriented as MAP 309, with which it should be compared. The emphasis here is on the actual fighting: the Last Stand is at left and the Reno-Benteen defense at right, while Reno's initial attack on the encampment is across the river, to the right of the tents.

MAP 311 (below).
The region southeast of *Lewiston,* Idaho Territory, where young warriors of the Nez Percé went on a rampage in 1877, prompting the flight of the tribe, led by Chief Joseph. The key indicates *Ranches burnt.*

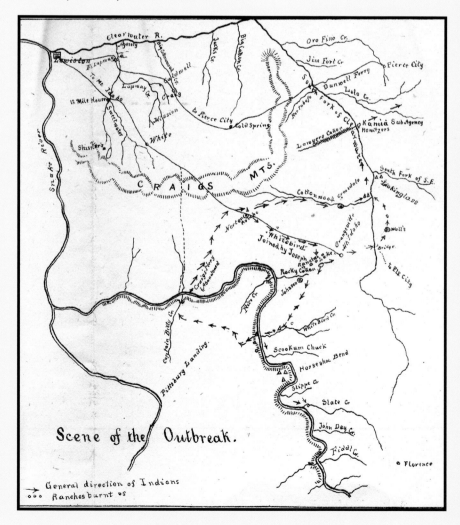

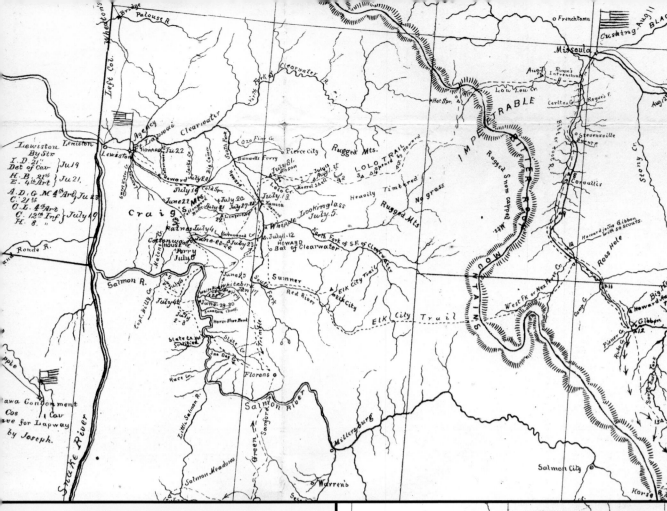

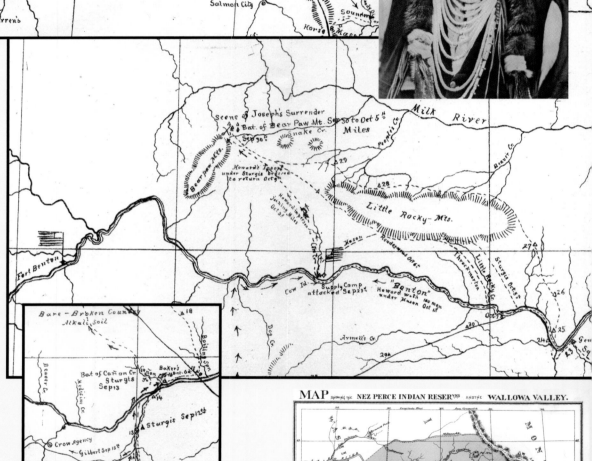

Below.
Chief Joseph, leader of the Nez Percé, in a classic photograph taken by the eminent recorder of the Indian way of life in the West, Edward Curtis.

Map 312 (*in three parts, above and right*).
The U.S. Army published a report on the 1877 pursuit of Chief Joseph and the Nez Percé later in the year. It included a large and detailed map; for clarity several enlarged parts of it are displayed here.

Younger warriors went on a rampage on hearing that they had to move (Map 311, *previous page*). Joseph returned from hunting to find the part of the army of Indian agent Brigadier General Oliver O. Howard attacking his main camp. The Nez Percé won that conflict, called the Battle of *Whitebird* Canyon (on the Salmon River south of Lewiston), but Joseph knew more soldiers would come. Over the next four months he led his entire tribe—women and children and even livestock—in an attempt to escape, first to their allies, the Crow, and then to Canada. They held off Howard and his Gatling guns and howitzers at the *Bat[tle] of Clearwater* Creek on 11–12 July. On 27 July they bypassed a blockade by a detachment from Fort *Missoula* set up by Captain Charles Rawn; *Rawn's Intrenching* is shown just south of the fort. As they headed east along the *Bitterroot Mountains*, they fought a series of battles, all against numerically superior U.S. troops: Big Hole on 9 August; Camas Creek on 18 August, and *Cañon [Canyon] Creek* on 13 September. Then, heading north, the Nez Percé crossed the Missouri at *Cow I[slan]d* on 25 September and attacked an Army depot there to acquire food and supplies. After Canyon Creek Howard was desperate and was being censured by his superiors for failing to catch Joseph, so he enlisted the help of Colonel Nelson Miles, and it was Miles's troops that finally caught up with the Nez Percé and defeated them, only forty miles from the Canadian border at the *Bat[tle] of Bear Paw M[oun]t[ain]* on 30 September. Joseph surrendered to Howard and Miles on 5 October with an eloquent farewell to the Indian way of life: "I am tired; my heart is sick and sad. From where the sun now stands I will fight no more forever."

Lewiston is at top left on the top map, and the *Bitterroot Mountains* diagonally bisect this map portion. On the middle map the large river, unnamed on this portion, is the Missouri. Just to the north is the *Scene of Joseph's Surrender* at *Bear Paw Mt.* The bottom map segment shows the site of the Battle of Canyon Creek; the river, again unnamed on this portion, is the Yellowstone.

Map 313 (*right, bottom*).
This 1877 government map shows why the Nez Percé were upset. They had agreed to a large reservation, shown in red, in 1855, only to see it much reduced in 1865—the area in blue. Chief Joseph claimed the entire reservation but especially the area between the *Grand[e] Ronde River* and the *Snake*, shown in yellow. When the U.S. Army was sent to enforce the move to the small reservation in 1877, the Nez Percé refused to cooperate.

Map 314 (*right*).
In 1889 the U.S. National Museum published a report by William Hornaday entitled *The Extermination of the American Bison*, which included this summary map showing the ranges of bison (buffalo) at various dates (see key at top right). It demonstrated the dramatic reduction in range since the coming of EuroAmericans. With it went the Indians' food supply. After 1883 all that was left were the pathetically small numbers of animals shown in the tiny blue circles—10, 20, and 25—with 550 in Canada.

Below.
Hunting Buffalo, an 1870 painting by noted western artist George Catlin, who also drew **Map 303**, *page 146.* Catlin was much admired in Europe, but when he presented his paintings to Congress in 1838 they were rejected.

a year Crazy Horse was defeated at nearby Wolf Mountain, and most of the Lakota and Cheyenne surrendered and were sent to reservations that would become ever smaller.

In southern Oregon and northern California in 1872–73 fewer than sixty Modoc warriors battled nearly a thousand U.S. Army troops in a series of skirmishes known as the Modoc War, which erupted when the government attempted to move the Modoc to a reservation. Their wily leader, Kientpoos—known to settlers as Captain Jack—led the Modoc through six months of resistance among the lava beds of Tule Lake. Kientpoos killed General Edward Canby at a parley in April 1873 and after the Modoc surrender was hanged for the offense. Canby became the only American general killed in the Indian Wars.

The so-called Red River War was fought in 1874–75 in the Texas Panhandle between the Army and Comanche and other tribes bitter from the erosion of reservations and the violation of an earlier treaty. The Comanche leader, Quanah Parker, was the son of Cynthia Ann Parker, a settler's daughter who had been captured by the Comanche when she was nine. Quanah gave up the struggle in 1875 and moved to a reservation in Oklahoma; he became an elder statesman of sorts, skillfully protecting Comanche interests and riding—with Geronimo—in Theodore Roosevelt's inaugural parade in 1905.

Map 315 (*above*).
Herds of Buffalo are featured across the Plains north of *Austin*, Texas, on this 1844 map.

The most famous escape from the U.S. Army was that of the Nez Percé of Idaho in 1877, led by Hin-mah-too-yah-lat-kekht, better known as Chief Joseph. Their flight is detailed and described on **Map 312**, *left.*

The longest struggle, however, was that of the Apache of the Southwest under their even more famous chief, Goyaalé—Geronimo. The Apache were involved in skirmishes after being ordered onto a reservation in 1862, but it was not until 1886 that Geronimo surrendered. That year, with thirty-eight warriors, he evaded five thousand U.S. troops and the Mexican army for almost a year before finally surrendering—with possible conditions that are still debated—to General Nelson Miles at Skeleton Canyon, Arizona.

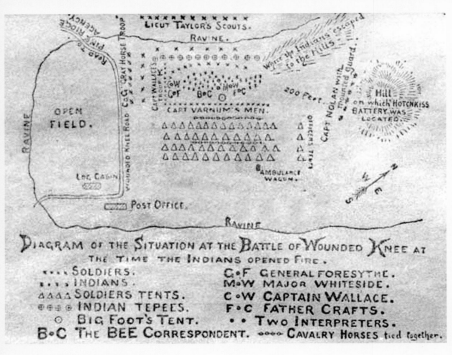

MAP 316 (above).
A contemporary sketch map of the *Battle of Wounded Knee*. Although called a battle here, it was in reality a massacre; most of the U.S. Army's casualties were inflicted by its own men, what today would euphemistically be termed "friendly fire."

MAP 317 (below, bottom).
The *Cherokee Outlet Lands*, a tract of land in today's northern Oklahoma west of the Arkansas River often called the Cherokee Strip. Nearly 7 million acres were available, having been purchased by the federal government from the Cherokee for $7 million. *Tulsa* is at right. *Below* is a photograph of the chaotic start of the Cherokee Strip Land Run in 1893.

MAP 318 (below, right).
This 1866 U.S. Land Office map shows what happened to many Indian groups across the West. The Yankton Cession of 1858 removed the Yankton (Santee) Sioux from the area labeled *Indian Title Extinguished* and confined them to the much smaller *Yankton Reserve*, across the Missouri River from *Ft. Rendall* and the *Military Reservation*. Unusually, in this case, poor demand from EuroAmerican settlers for the land—due to drought, grasshoppers, and Indian attacks—led to its restoration to the Sioux in 1867. Two years later, however, demand from settlers moving to Dakota had increased, and the restoration order was rescinded.

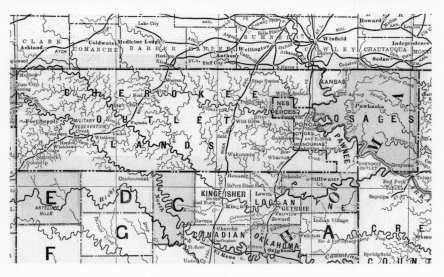

As the days of the western "frontier" were drawing to a close came the event often depicted as the final chapter in the demise of the Indian in the West—the infamous massacre at Wounded Knee.

In 1889 a promise of some miraculous Indian redemption had come from Nevada, where a young Paiute mystic named Wovoka claimed to have visited the spirit world and been told of the coming disappearance of the white man and the return of the buffalo. Ironically, as it would turn out, Wovoka's dream demanded no violence, just dancing. To a downtrodden Indian population, these ideas, soon dubbed the Ghost Dance religion by EuroAmericans, offered a way to salvation, and they spread like wildfire.

On the northern Plains, Indian agent James McLaughlin decided that Sitting Bull was responsible for the unrest, though in fact Sitting Bull was skeptical of the new religion. Nevertheless, rumors spread, and both sides became wary. In December 1890 General Nelson Miles arranged for a party of forty Sioux police to arrest Sitting Bull, and in the melee surrounding the attempt, Sitting Bull was killed.

Matters rapidly deteriorated after the revered chief was gone. Sitting Bull's followers joined up with other Sioux under Big Foot. The Army had already marked him as a threat and moved to arrest him. Big Foot surrendered and was ordered to move his 350 followers to Wounded Knee Creek, where they set up camp surrounded by about 470 heavily armed U.S. Army troops. When, in the frigid morning of 29 December 1890, the Army moved to disarm the Indians, a medicine man began to perform the ghost dance, and an Indian fired his gun into the air, to calamitous effect, for at this the nervous soldiers opened fire, even firing their new Hotchkiss guns—early machine guns—into the tents when women and children emerged. Big Foot and about 180 of his followers died that cold day, as did the Indian dreams of salvation.

Wounded Knee became the site of a seventy-one-day standoff in 1973 between authorities and militant members of the American Indian Movement, an organization set up to protect Indian civil rights.

Many Indians were sent to reservations in what was called Indian Territory, now the state of Oklahoma, but even there their land was desired by EuroAmericans. Many of the eastern Indians who had been

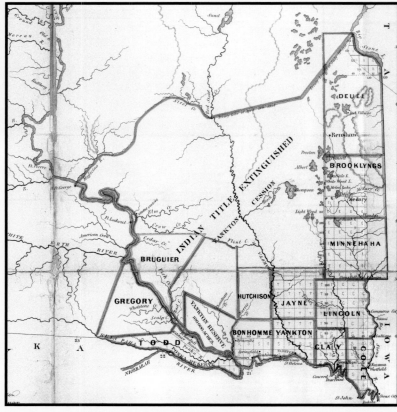

settled there in the 1830s had supported the Confederacy during the Civil War and as a result suffered a forced sale of much of their land. EuroAmericans settled on this land beginning in 1889 with a series of land runs—mad races from the boundaries of the land to see who could stake a claim—and retain—land first. A run to the so-called Unassigned Lands (in central Oklahoma) took place in April 1889, and one to the Cherokee Outlet (MAP 317, *far left, bottom*) in September 1893. Tent cities sprung up across the Plains, and in 1890 Oklahoma Territory was created.

One of the most devastating effects of EuroAmerican settlement on the Plains was the destruction of the great herds of buffalo—American bison—that once formed the backbone of Indian survival and way of life (MAP 314, *page 153*). During the 1870s hunters slaughtered buffalo indiscriminately at the rate of more than a million a year; by 1883 virtually none were left. Without them the Indians were forced to adopt a more sedentary—and EuroAmerican—existence.

Forced onto reservations, the Indians found that no matter what they agreed to, whatever land they had allowed themselves to be confined to was soon coveted by EuroAmerican settlers. The reservations were reduced in size or removed altogether, with the result that the area occupied by Indians was dramatically reduced (MAP 319, *above, right,* and MAP 320, *below*). A modern comparison is MAP 602, *pages 260–61*.

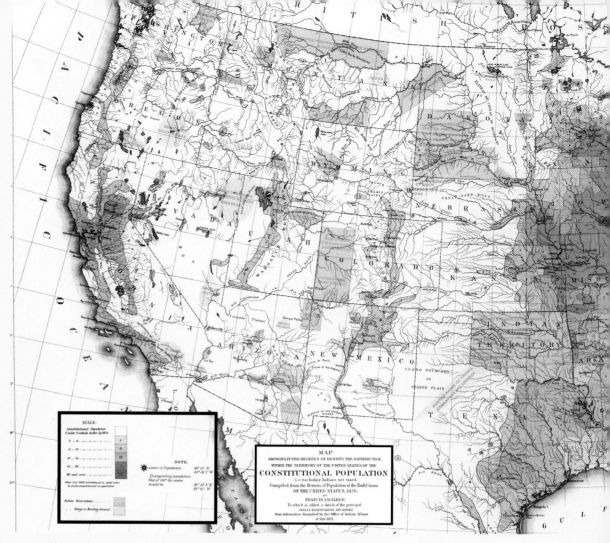

MAP 319 (*above*).
Quite extensive areas of *Indian Reservations* and *Range or Hunting Ground* (two shades of yellow—see key) set aside for exclusive Indian use are shown on this 1870 census map, published in 1874. The map also shows density of non-Indian population (shades of gray), still quite peripheral except for the valleys of the Rio Grande and the Great Salt Lake. All of Indian Territory—Oklahoma without the panhandle—and huge tracts in Dakota, Nebraska, Colorado, and Montana are still in Indian hands.

MAP 320 (*below*).
Another government map showing Indian reservations in the West, this one dated 1923. Reservation area has been dramatically reduced. Gray areas are said to be former reservations, but not all are shown.

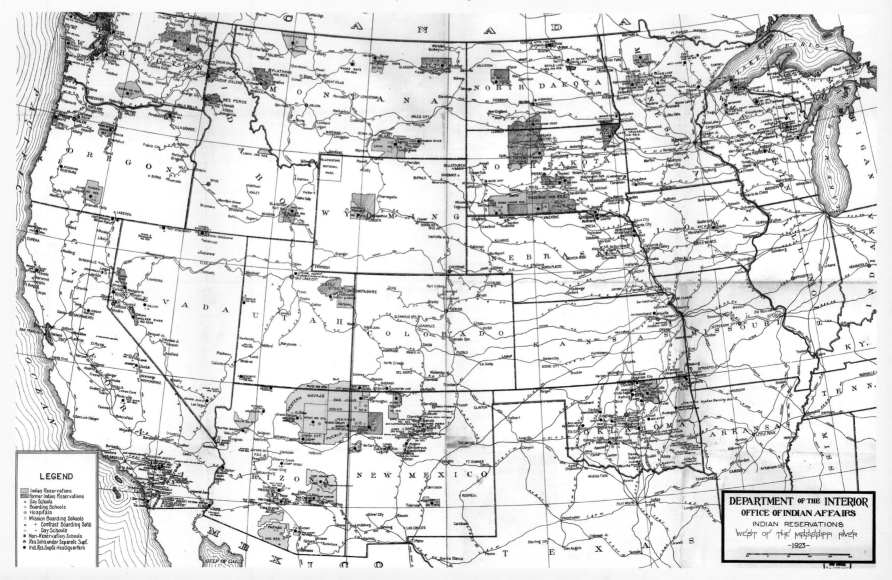

SETTLING AND WATERING THE WEST

SUBDIVIDING THE LAND

The public lands of almost the entire West were subdivided using a method first defined by the Land Ordinance of 1785, as passed by the Continental Congress of the United States. The system was first applied by surveyor Thomas Hutchins in Ohio beginning in September that year (MAP 321, *below*). This Public Land Survey System would be followed for over a century as settlement advanced ever farther west. Land was to be divided first into parcels six miles square, called townships. Each thirty-six-square-mile block would in turn be divided into one-square-mile sections, each with 640 acres. Certain sections would be reserved for schools, public buildings, and, at first, veterans of the War for Independence. The rest would then be sold at auction for a minimum bid of $1 per acre, or $640 per section. This simple and orderly system today defines the map of the West.

Congress was very interested in promoting the settlement of the West. In 1850 it passed the Donation Land Claim Act, which applied to the Oregon Territory—then the entire Pacific Northwest—to jump-start the colonization of the recently acquired region. The act, which became law in September 1850, gave 160 acres—a quarter-section—to single males and twice that to a married couple, if they settled before the end of the year. Settlers had to live on the land and cultivate it for four years. From 1851 to 1854, half this amount could be granted. After that, land was sold at $1.25 per acre. Some 7,437 patents were issued under this act granting free land to Oregon settlers.

The Donation Land Claim Act was the forerunner of the Homestead Act, signed by President Abraham Lincoln on 20 May 1862. This act liberalized the requirements of the Preemption Act of 1841, which had permitted low-cost sale of public land to settlers and had been widely used in Kansas and Nebraska territories. Now 160 acres could be claimed for free if the applicant lived on the land for five years and built a dwelling.

An astonishing 1.6 million homesteads on 270 million acres were granted to individuals during the long life of the Homestead Act. It amounted to 11 percent of all the land in the United States. The last land taken up under the act was in Alaska as late as 1988.

In 1862 Lincoln also signed the Morrill Land-Grant Colleges Act, which granted land to state governments to fund agricultural and technical colleges; 17.4 million acres were granted under this act.

Whether the land was free or not, farmers had to be able to protect their land against intrusion from animals, especially on the Plains, where cattle often roamed free. Fences were expensive to build in a region where there was little wood, but Joseph Glidden's invention of barbed wire in 1874 revolutionized fencing. Now only two wires, easily installed by untrained hands, allowed huge areas to be enclosed in an economic and practical fashion. The new fences led to many struggles between farmers and free-range ranchers. Barbed wire soon became such a desired commodity

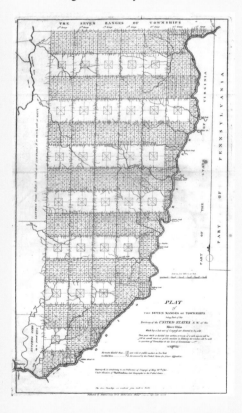

MAP 321 (*left*).
Thomas Hutchins's map of *The Seven Ranges of Townships* in Ohio, which he surveyed using the new land-subdivision method beginning in 1785. Today a stone marker in East Liverpool, Ohio, marks "The Point of Beginning" (it is at top right on this map) for a survey that ultimately reached across the West to the Pacific Ocean and continued in Alaska, though not in Hawaii, which had another system left over from the days in which it was a kingdom.

MAP 322 (*below*).
The Public Land Survey System did not cover areas already surveyed under some other system, even if the original system was far less accurate. This was the case in New Mexico, where Mexican land grants from the 1830s and 1840s covered many areas (see page 76). This 1879 U.S. General Land Office map depicts the Mexican grants along with the new land surveys in the upper Rio Grande region between Albuquerque and Santa Fe.

Below, left.
An early advertisement for Joseph Glidden's barbed wire.

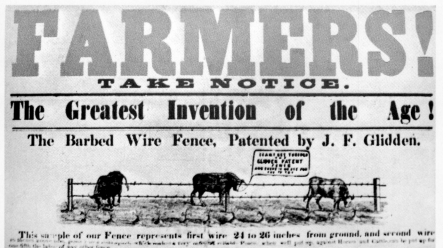

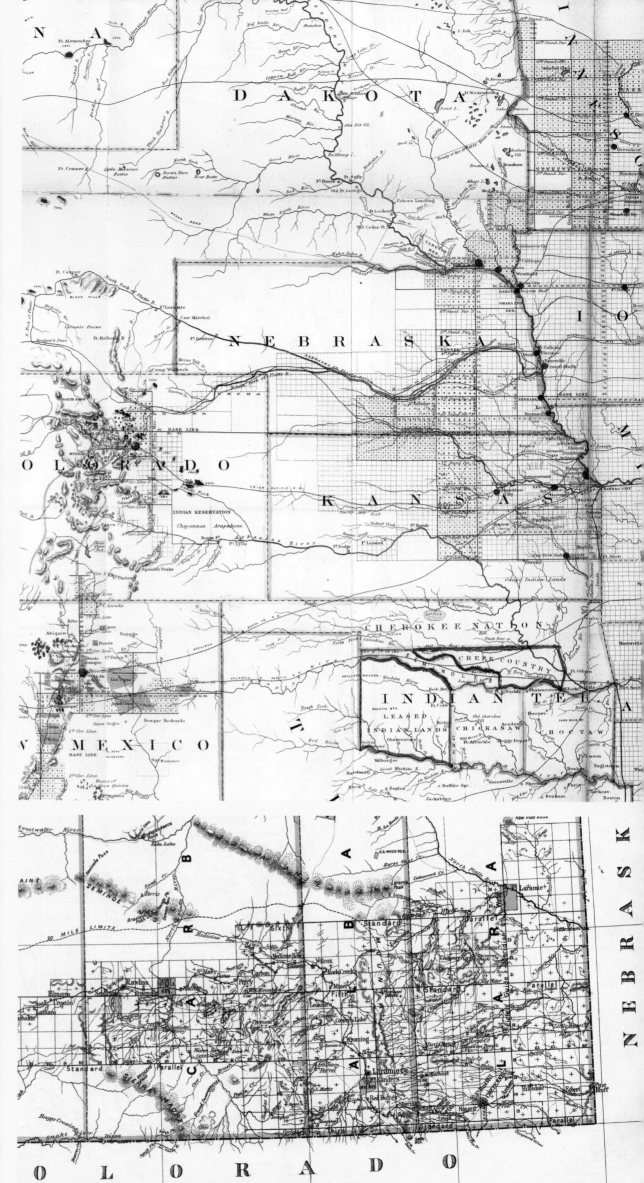

FREE HOMESTEADS FOR THE MILLION.

America stands alone among the nations of the world in the benificence of her laws for the acquisition of land by all who wish to obtain it. Every man can become his own landlord, if he so desires. Eevery head of a family, widow, single man or woman of the age of twenty-one years, who is a citizen of the United States, or who has declared his or her intention of becoming so, can enter upon eighty acres of GOVERNMENT land within the forty mile limits of our Railroad grant, or one hundred and sixty acres outside said limits, and after a continuous residence upon it and cultivation for five years, an absolute title to the land will be given by the United States Government, at a total cost of about nine dollars on eighty acres, or eighteen dollars on one hundred and sixty acres.

Any soldier or sailor who served during the Rebellion not less than ninety days, and was honorably discharged, can homestead one hundred and sixty acres, either within or outside of the forty mile limits of our Land grant, and his terms of service will be deducted from the five years' residence required upon the land, but in any event he must reside *one year* upon it. Thus, if he served three years, he would have to reside upon the land two years, and in the event of his having served four or five years, *one* year's residence would be necessary.

A soldier or sailor has the privilege of filing application for homestead upon the land through an agent or attorney, and need not for six months commence actual settlement upon it. Absence from a homestead at any time, for more than six months, works a forfeiture of right to the land.

PRE-EMPTION.

Any person qualified under the Homestead Laws can pre-empt one hundred and sixty acres of Government land within the limits of our Railroad grant, and after an actual residence upon and cultivation of same for at least six months, can obtain title by payment of $2.50 per acre, or, if outside the limits, $1.25 per acre. It is imperative, however, that the person so pre-empting shall (with his family, if any) reside upon the land. The cultivation of a few acres is sufficient. The same person, after having complied with the requirements of the laws of pre-emption, can homestead eighty acres within the Railroad grant, or one hundred and sixty acres outside the limits. In this way, a soldier or sailor can secure *three hundred and twenty acres* within the limits; and it is open to the *world at large* or *any* man to acquire his two hundred and forty acres.

that prices were kept artificially high by monopolistic trusts, a situation finally broken by the mail-order company Montgomery Ward in 1892. The company purchased wire outright and then resold it at fair prices beyond the control of the trusts.

Map 323 (*right, top*).
In this 1866 U.S. Land Office map, the Public Land Survey System is reaching west from the Missouri River, over the previously unsurveyed Plains toward islands of subdivided land along the Front Range in Colorado Territory and in northeastern New Mexico Territory. Just the southeastern corner of Dakota Territory has been subdivided. The building of the transcontinental railroad was at this time beginning to make southern Nebraska Territory more accessible; here the railroad would plat its own land grant for sale (see Map 238, *pages 120–21*).

Map 324 (*right, bottom*).
The plat of townships is expanding west and north from the southeastern corner of Wyoming Territory, away from Cheyenne and Laramie on this 1879 U.S. General Land Office map. Wyoming Territory was created in 1868.

Above.
The procedure for obtaining free land under the Homestead Act is explained in a brochure issued by the Kansas Pacific Railway in 1874.

A Western Utopia

The West opened up many new possibilities for a new beginning, and more than a few took advantage of it. A number of communities were created where emigrants came together to overcome the sometimes formidable obstacles to success. One of these settlements was the Union Colony of Colorado, at the confluence of the Cache la Poudre River with the South Platte, today Greeley, northeast of Denver. Here Nathan Meeker, one-time agricultural editor of the *New York Tribune,* launched a community with utopian ideals. The colony was encouraged and financed by Horace Greeley, the newspaper's owner, most famous for popularizing the catchphrase "Go West, Young Man." He had long thought that western settlement might be the answer to the crowded slums of eastern

cities, was a supporter of the transcontinental railroad, and continued the work of reformer George Evans in advancing the cause of the Homestead Act, passed in 1862.

Greeley and Meeker wanted more than just a colony—they wanted a model one, an ideal. In particular, it was to be teetotal. An irrigation system was to be developed communally, benefiting all; the colony was intended as a good investment as well as a new place to live. Each family paid $155 toward land purchase—mostly from the Denver Pacific Railway—and improvements. Some 442 settlers paid up to join the new colony, and they all arrived in Colorado in the spring of 1870.

By their joint efforts, the colonists quickly dug irrigation ditches and built the beginnings of a town. And here something apparently unique was also built: a fifty-mile-long fence around the whole community, to keep the herds of cattle grazed nearby from entering their fields. It was never quite finished and needed a constant sentry to guard its openings. The town flourished, and the Union Colony's name soon changed to Greeley to honor its benefactor.

Other communities based on cooperative effort and sometimes utopian ideals copied the Greeley model. These included Evans, just south of Greeley and today part of its urban area, where the St. Louis–Western Colony was established and named after George Evans, its promoter (Map 329, *right, bottom*); Fort Collins, an existing military post but settled as a town in 1872 by some of the officers of the Union Colony; and the Chicago-Colorado Colony at Longmont, north of Denver, in 1871 (Map 330, *far right, bottom*). Both of the latter towns followed the Greeley model almost to the letter.

Map 325 (*left*).
A bird's-eye promotional map of a well-established Greeley in 1882. One of the principal canals leaves the Cache la Poudre River, at top center, crosses under the railroad, and enters the town, turning through two right angles before arriving at the control gate at bottom, just left of the *Oasis Hotel* inset. Some of the streets named after trees can be seen. Meeker had the idea that the streets could be named after trees, and their namesakes could be planted along them, hence making them instantly recognizable and saving the cost of street signs! The cross streets were named after presidents, so presumably they would have required signs.

Above, left.
One of the first photographs of Greeley, appropriately enough of a just-completed irrigation ditch, flowing down the center of one of the deliberately wide streets of the community. This is the Main Street Lateral, looking east along 8th Street, on 4 July 1870. Signs advertising a drug store, a meat market, and a bakery can just be seen at left.

Map 326 (*below*).
The irrigation ditches down the middle of streets were not particularly successful, but the wide streets, designed to accommodate a turning wagon and team, were later found suitable for streetcar and interurban lines, as can be seen here on a 1910 map of Greeley.

OASIS HOTEL

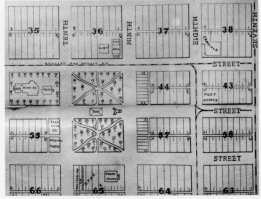

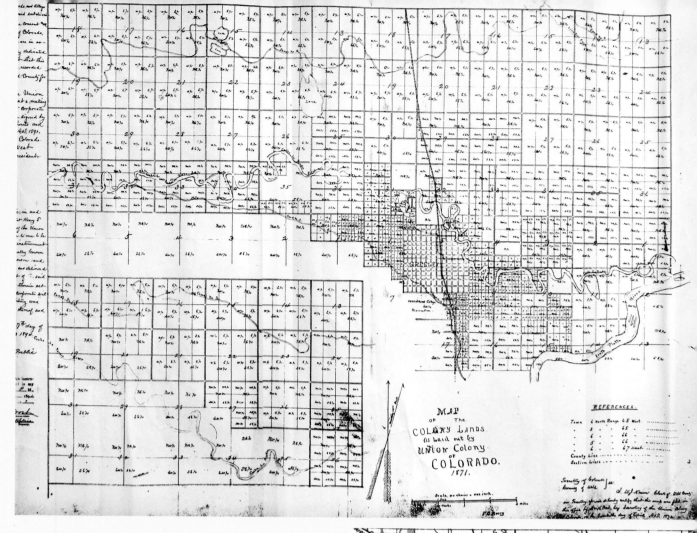

MAP 327 (*right*).
The subdivision map of the Union Colony of Colorado, dated 1871. The inset map is a continuation west. Here the irrigation canal seen in MAP 325 can be traced from where it leaves the Cache la Poudre River, at left center, through part of the townsite before exiting at bottom, flowing toward the South Platte. The Denver Pacific rail line passes through the center of the townsite. Meeker and Greeley knew how important the railroad would be to the colony's long-term viability and deliberately chose a site on a railroad, even purchasing land from it. They were right; Greeley grew into a thriving center for the surrounding agricultural region. Land was reserved for an agricultural college and can be seen immediately south of the townsite, but a year later the college was moved to Fort Collins, the town's clone-turned-competitor established a few miles away.

Left. Nathan Meeker's adobe house still stands today in Greeley.

MAP 328 (*right*).
This 1897 map of the Greeley area also shows *Ft Collins*, established two years after Greeley and following the same principles. Also shown, farther east along the South Platte, is the *Tennessee Colony,* yet another attempt to copy Greeley's example; it was populated by emigrants from Tennessee. This colony, however, did not thrive and is nowhere to be found today.

MAP 329 (*below*).
The community of *Evans,* just south of Greeley, still survives as part of the latter's urban area. Lands belonging to its founders, the *Saint Louis Western Colony,* are marked west and northwest of the townsite. The river is the South Platte. The map dates from 1915.

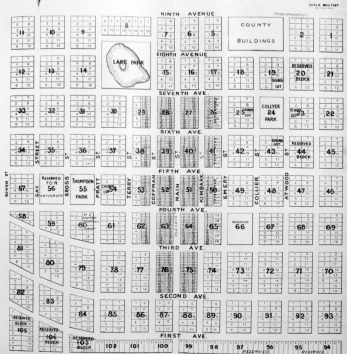

MAP 330 (*below*).
A further Greeley clone was at Longmont (a name derived from explorer Stephen Long; see page 73), where a group of emigrants from Chicago settled, calling themselves the *Chicago Colorado Colony.* Note the block at left, center, *Reserved for University.*

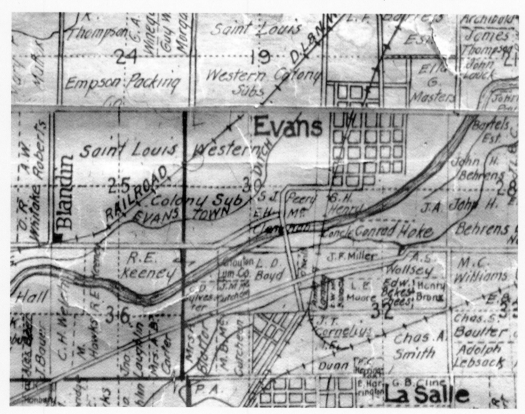

RECLAIMING THE DRY LANDS

Much of the West would never have been available for agriculture without the import of water, but much of the land is excellent for cultivation given that one missing ingredient—water.

In the early days all land east of the Pacific coastlands was passed over as containing unusable desert—the Great American Desert of explorers Zebulon Pike and Stephen Long. The myth then developed that if the Plains were cultivated, rain would come—rain follows the plow; the idea found voice in Josiah Gregg's influential book, *The Commerce of the Prairies,* published in 1844 (see page 105). Might not cultivation "contribute to the multiplication of showers?" he wondered. He even thought planting "shady groves" might affect the seasons.

More scientific heads ultimately prevailed, and the reality of the dry West was famously documented in John Wesley Powell's *Report on the Lands of the Arid Region of the United States,* published in 1878 (see page 178). Powell's very influential work was the forerunner of the multitude of schemes that have reclaimed huge areas of the West. He advocated using cooperative irrigation, regulating grazing and farming for the good of all, and revising the rectangular quarter-section Homestead Act system of land subdivision to accommodate water supply requirements.

The Desert Land Act, passed the year before Powell's work was published, did not allow the Public Land Survey System to be modified but did offer a larger area, a whole section—one square mile—to anyone willing to pay $1.25 per acre and irrigate it within three years. In 1894 the Carey Act allowed private companies to invest in irrigation systems and profit from the sale of water.

But the federal law that had the most effect and lasting benefit to the West was the Reclamation Act of 1902, which funded irrigation projects with monies from the sale of land. It was sponsored by Representative Francis G. Newlands of Nevada and is often referred to

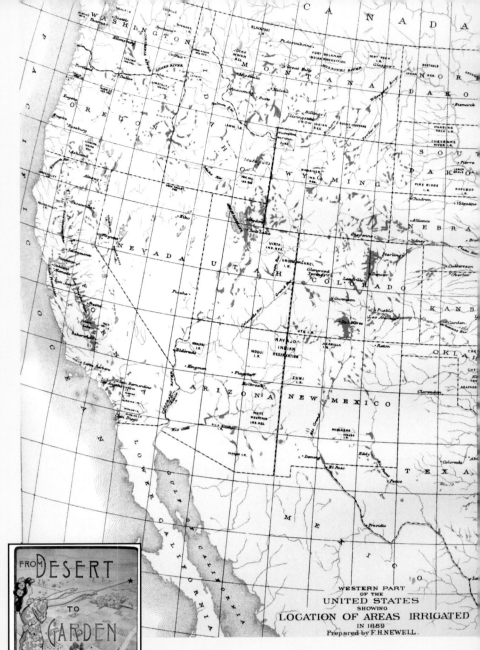

MAP 331 (*above*).
The extent of irrigated lands in the West in 1889, shown on a map from the 1890 census. Even by this early date there are hundreds of separate projects, located anywhere there was fertile soil and an easily diverted river. Most were small projects, however.

MAP 332 (*left*).
An irrigation map of part of the upper Rio Grande Valley in southern Colorado around *Antonito* displays an extensive system of irrigation channels along the *Rio Conejos,* which flows into the *Rio Grande,* at right. Note the *Sangre de Cristo Grant,* at right (see page 78).

MAP 333 (*below*).
This map of irrigated areas in the southeastern corner of Wyoming Territory in 1889 shows many small localized projects. *Cheyenne* and *Laramie* are at bottom.

Center. A booklet published in 1902 by the magazine *California Homeseeker* promoted irrigation: *From Desert to Garden, From Worthlessness to Wealth.*

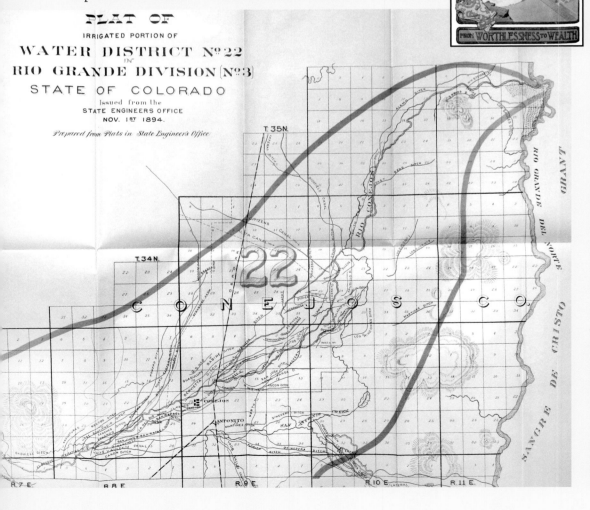

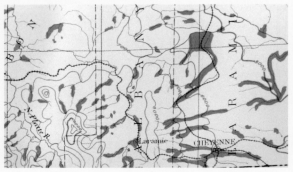

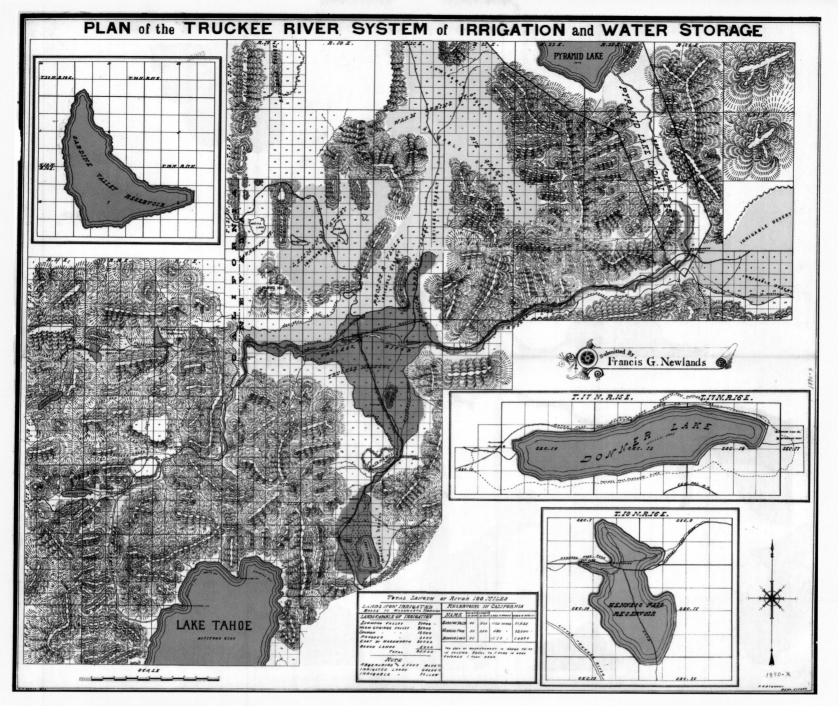

PLAN of the TRUCKEE RIVER SYSTEM of IRRIGATION and WATER STORAGE

Submitted By Francis G. Newlands

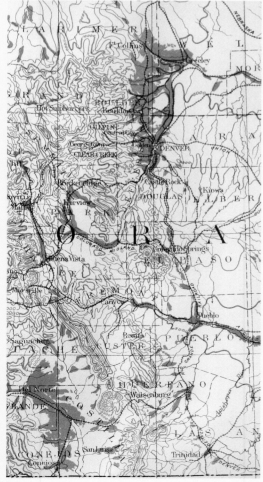

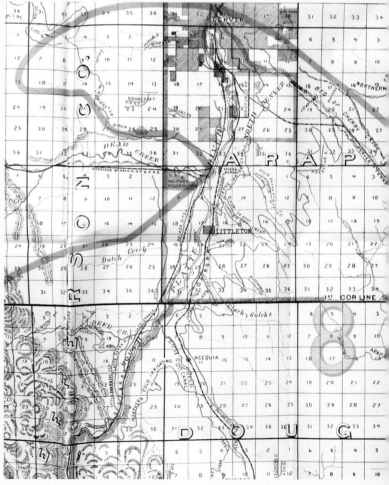

MAP 334 (*above*).
With Francis G. Newlands's name on it, this map illustrates a detailed proposal for a scheme to irrigate 95,000 acres in the Truckee Valley, east of Reno, in 1890. Newlands's 1902 Reclamation Act would eventually permit some 206,000 acres in the valleys of the Truckee and Carson rivers to be irrigated.

MAP 335 (*left*).
Irrigated lands in Colorado are shown on this 1889 map and reveal two of the most extensive areas of irrigation at that time: the upper Rio Grande and the area between *Denver* and *Ft. Collins* between the Front Range and the South Platte River. The upper Rio Grande was the scene of the first irrigation scheme in Colorado, the San Luis People's Ditch, constructed in 1852.

MAP 336 (*right*).
Shown in red, irrigation channels following the contours of the land are depicted in this 1894 map of the *South Platte* south of *Denver*, shown at top. The built-up area of metro Denver now extends just south of *Littleton*.

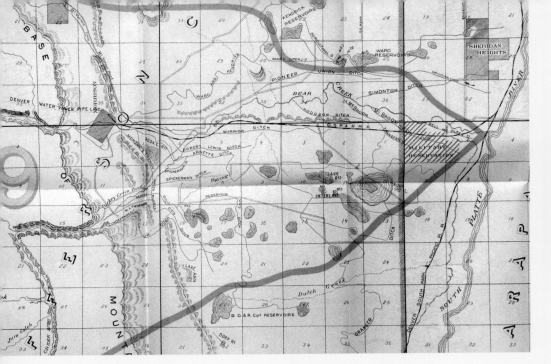

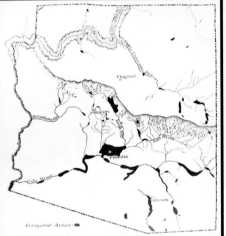

MAP 337 (*above*).
Another 1894 map of the irrigation systems around Denver, this one to the west between *Morrison*, at left, and today's *Sheridan* and Englewood, on the *South Platte*, at right. Almost the entire area is now metro Denver.

MAP 339 (*left, center*).
The annual report of the governor of Arizona Territory in 1901 contained this map showing irrigated lands in the territory, principally on the Salt and Gila rivers around Phoenix. Note the canyon of the Colorado, at top, its western part now filled by the largest irrigation reservoir of all—Lake Mead, behind the Hoover Dam, completed in 1935 (see page 238).

MAP 340 (*below*).
A 1908 real estate promoter's map touts the *Salt River Project* in Arizona. The project, one of the U.S. Reclamation Service's first, involved construction of the Theodore *Roosevelt Dam*, shown in the inset photo. The dam was completed in 1911, along with the *Granite Reef Diversion Dam*, noted on this map northeast of *Mesa*, then a separate city, now part of metro *Phoenix*.

MAP 338 (*above*).
The Minidoka Dam on the Snake River in Idaho was completed in 1906 and was the first of seven dams for the Minidoka Project. The town of *Minidoka* is noted on the map. This graphic and map commemorated the completion of the *American Falls Dam*, also on the Snake, in 1927. The dam necessitated relocating the town of American Falls, beginning in 1923 using the powers of eminent domain that were given to the secretary of the interior by the 1902 Reclamation Act. In 1973 the concrete in this dam was found to be dangerously deteriorated, and a replacement dam, just downriver, was completed in 1978.

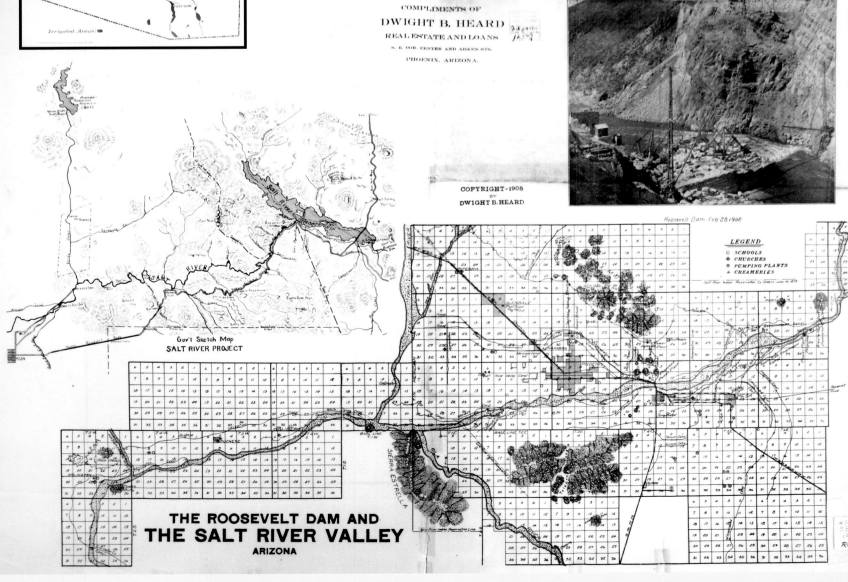

COMPLIMENTS OF
DWIGHT B. HEARD
REAL ESTATE AND LOANS
S. E. COR. CENTER AND ADAMS STS.
PHOENIX, ARIZONA

COPYRIGHT—1908
BY
DWIGHT B. HEARD

Gov't Sketch Map
SALT RIVER PROJECT

LEGEND
○ SCHOOLS
⊕ CHURCHES
◆ PUMPING PLANTS
✦ CREAMERIES

THE ROOSEVELT DAM AND
THE SALT RIVER VALLEY
ARIZONA

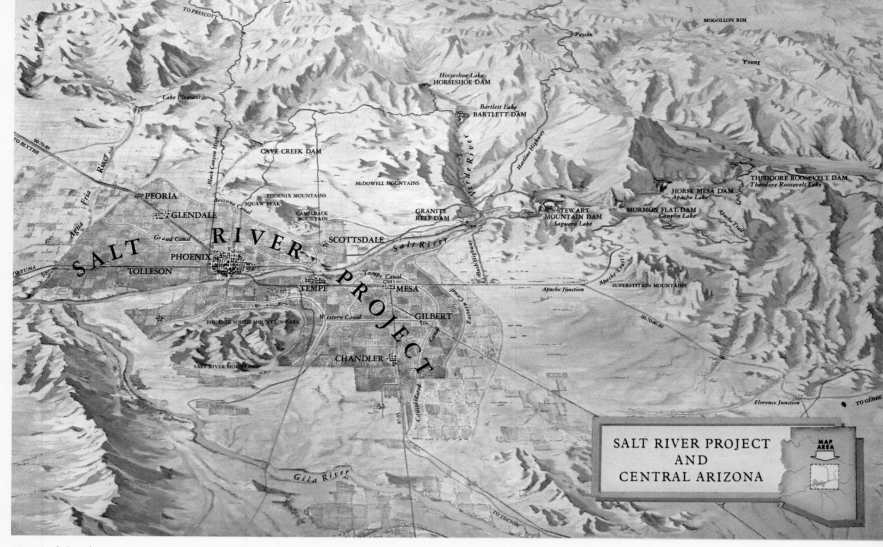

MAP 341 (*above*).
A painted bird's-eye map of the numerous dams of the *Salt River Project* dating from the late 1940s. The *Theodore Roosevelt Dam* and lake are at right. A series of other dams create further reservoirs on the Salt below it: the *Horse Mesa,* completed in 1927; *Mormon Flat* (1925); and *Stewart Mountain* (1930). Several other dams are shown on other rivers. *Bartlett Dam* was completed on the *Verde River* in 1939. The *Horseshoe Dam* was not completed until 1946, a private project of mining company Phelps Dodge; to the west, *Cave Creek Dam* was completed in 1923 to control flash floods and was superseded in the late 1970s by the Cave Buttes Dam a little farther downstream. Preexisting canals that were used by the Salt River Project are also shown. One is the *Arizona Canal,* built in 1886 and 1887 and purchased for the project by the Department of the Interior in 1906. In recent years metro Phoenix has sprawled over much of the irrigated land shown in this map. See also MAP 584, *page 253.*

MAP 342 (*below*).
Another excellent bird's-eye-style map, though harder to read, of the lands irrigated by the *Salt River Project,* shown in 1934.

as the Newlands Reclamation Act. Never has a bill's sponsor had a more appropriate name. Using powers authorized by the act, the secretary of the interior created the United States Reclamation Service (after 1923 the Bureau of Reclamation) later in 1902.

The Reclamation Service immediately began its work. One of its first projects was the one that Newlands himself advanced, in the Truckee-Carson area of his home state, where 206,000 acres would eventually be irrigated (MAP 334, *page 161*). Other early projects included the Salt River Project of Arizona (182,000 acres; MAP 340, *left,* MAP 341, *above,* and MAP 342, *below*); the Minidoka Project on the Snake River in Idaho (219,500 acres; MAP 338, *left, top*); and the Milk River Project in Montana (219,000 acres).

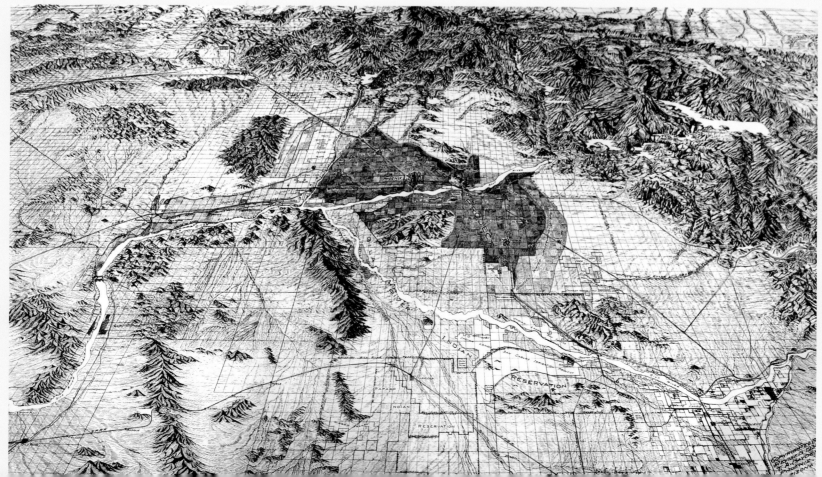

The long march from an arid region to an agriculturally productive one had begun. By the late 1980s, when the Bureau of Reclamation reported that "the arid West essentially has been reclaimed," over six hundred dams had been constructed and were providing water for a stunning 10 million acres—15,625 square miles.

There had been a side benefit not actually mentioned in the 1902 act—the generation of electricity. Something like 40 billion kilowatt-hours are generated each year, and it is this power, with the water itself, that allowed the growth of the urban West, although sometimes urban areas competed with agricultural uses for the resource. This battle was exemplified by the conflict between the city of Los Angeles and the farmers of the distant Owens Valley over an incipient Reclamation Service project in the early years of the twentieth century (see page 194).

A typical example of a reclamation project is that of the Umatilla, which created over 36,000 acres of fertile agricultural land in northeastern Oregon between 1903 and 1927. The maps and illustrations on this page, the latter done in classic period style, are from a 1910 booklet published by the Umatilla Project Development League, a local booster group, and issued with the help of the Oregon Railroad and Navigation Company, which stood ready to ship the region's produce.

Left.
The cover of the 1910 booklet published by the Umatilla Project Development League, with superb artwork of an Indian in classical garb releasing water to irrigate the land. Unfortunately, the irrigation led to the destruction of the Indian salmon fishery on the Umatilla River. *Hermiston* was incorporated in July 1907 and its name chosen from a novel popular at the time: Robert Louis Stevenson's *Weir of Hermiston.* Hence this personification of the weir was used to illustrate the league's promotional literature.

MAP 343 (*below*).
An excellent bird's-eye map of the Umatilla Project, looking east over the new city of *Hermiston.* The *Columbia River* is at left, flowing toward the viewer, and the *Umatilla River* flows across the bottom of the map into the Columbia. Cold Springs Reservoir, labeled simply *U.S. Reservoir,* is at center, and behind it are the dry hills of eastern Oregon, the *Blue Mountains.*

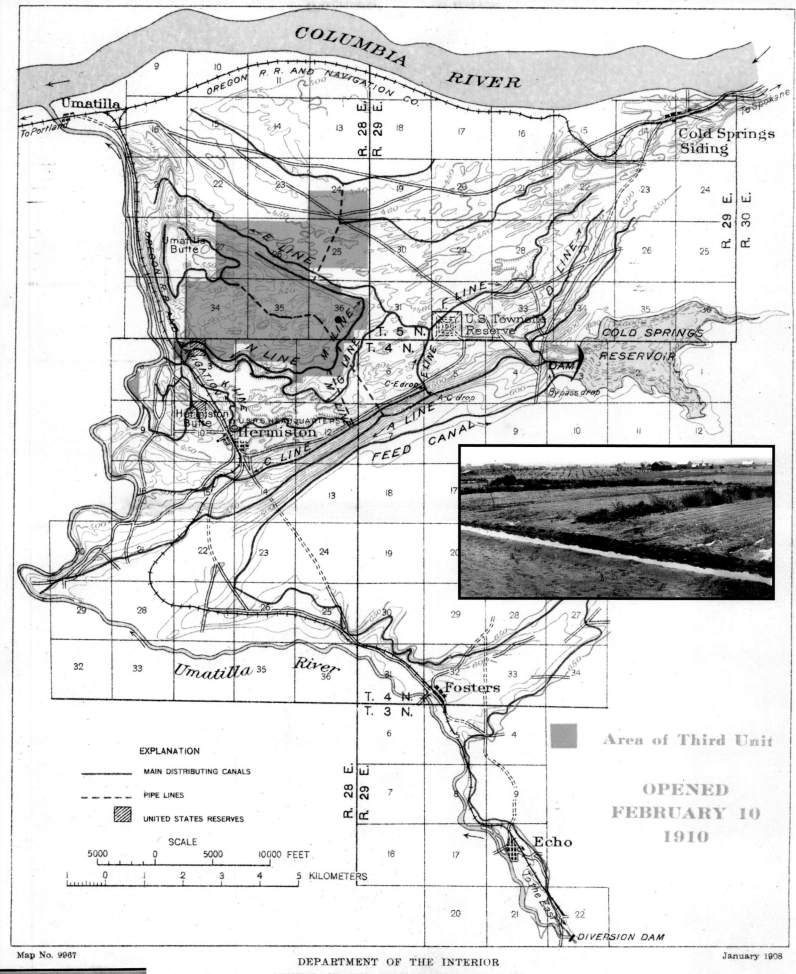

Map No. 9967

DEPARTMENT OF THE INTERIOR
UNITED STATES RECLAMATION SERVICE

January 1908

UMATILLA PROJECT-EAST BRANCH-OREGON

GENERAL MAP

REPRINT JANUARY 1910

MAP 344.

The topography of the region dictated, as it always did, where water might be stored. This Reclamation Service map shows the *Feed Canal* leaving the *Umatilla River* at the *Diversion Dam* at bottom, flowing into the *Cold Springs Reservoir*, which began to fill after the dam was completed in 1908. Then a series of distribution canals or ditches, labeled *A Line* through *N Line*, takes the water to the lands around the city of *Hermiston*. Note the line of the *Oregon R.R. and Navigation Co.* along the banks of the Columbia, at top. The inset photo, from the promotional booklet, shows an irrigation ditch, cleared land, and beyond it a young orchard near Hermiston.

Left. The back cover of the Umatilla Project Development League 1910 booklet was equally well designed, featuring some of the hoped-for bounty of the irrigated land: apples and grapes to supplant sagebrush.

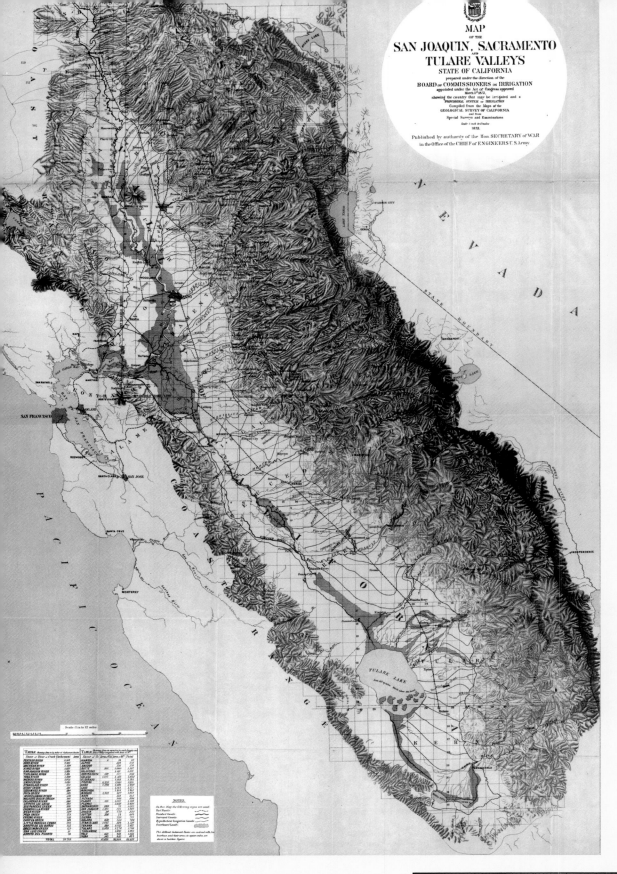

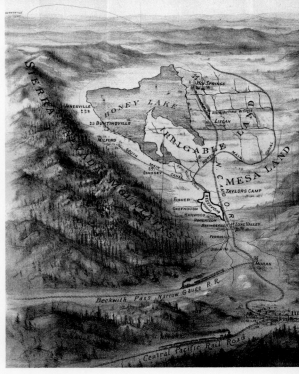

MAP 345 (*left*).

The California Board of Commissioners on Irrigation published this map of potentially irrigable lands in the Central Valley in 1873. It also shows proposed and completed irrigation channels such as the *Finished Canal*, the Kings Canal west of the San Joaquin River. The gray area denotes "overflowed lands"—that is, lands subject to flooding, especially in the delta region. These lands today have been reclaimed and provide some of the most fertile land in the state. Note also *Tulare Lake, Buena Vista L.*, and *Kern L.*, all now long disappeared under fertile fields.

MAP 346 (*above*).

Honey Lake, just across the California state line north of Reno, formed a natural reservoir that the Honey Lake Valley Land and Water Company tapped to water the surrounding *Irrigable Land*. This 1891 "semi-bird's-eye" map shows the plan, a smaller-scale scheme typical of a number in the West where a water body existed.

MAP 347 (*below*).

Buena Vista Lake and *Kern Lake* are also shown in this 1877 map of the southern part of the Central Valley, showing the irrigation channels that distribute the waters of the Kern River south of Bakersfield. Colonel Thomas Baker moved to this area in 1863 to begin reclaiming the frequently flooded land.

Nowhere were the conditions for irrigated agriculture more favorable than in California. Fertile soils of the Central Valley lay adjacent to rivers pouring from the Sierra Nevada; all that was required was a water distribution system. Slowly the area covered by irrigation expanded, though in more recent years much reclaimed land has been lost again to urban sprawl.

The first large-scale irrigation project in California created the forty-mile-long Kings River Canal west of the San Joaquin River in 1873; it is shown on MAP 345, *above*. By the 1920s, as ground water became depleted, planners recognized that the Central Valley required a coordinated plan. The Central Valley Project was authorized in 1933 but delayed because of the Depression. The Bureau of Reclamation (the renamed U.S. Reclamation Service) took over the project in 1935 and implemented an integrated flood

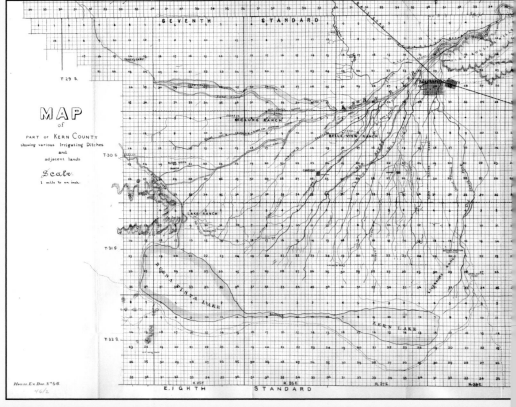

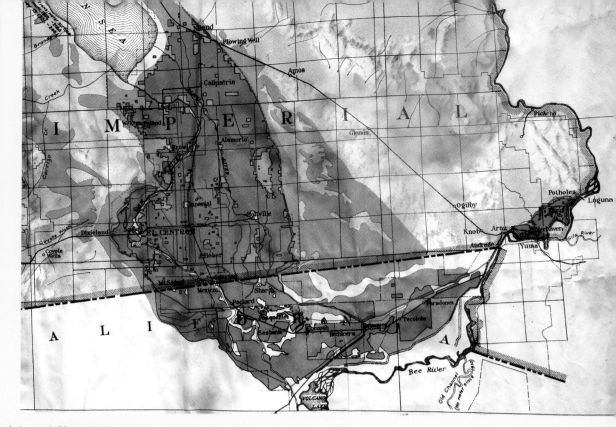

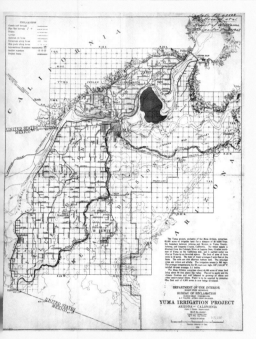

MAP 348 (*above, left*) and MAP 349 (*above*).

An important early irrigated region was that of the Imperial Valley, a former extension of the Gulf of California. The California Development Company cut the Alamo Canal from the Colorado, through Mexico, in 1900–02. In December 1904 a sudden flood overwhelmed a bypass channel cut to deal with silting, and by April 1905 all the water of the Colorado flowed into the Imperial Valley, creating a large inland lake, the Salton Sea, and it was not until February 1907 that the Southern Pacific managed to dump enough rock to divert the river once again to the Gulf of California. By 1920 400,000 acres were being irrigated in the Imperial Valley and a range of crops produced. A canal on American soil—the All-American Canal—was completed in 1940. MAP 348 was part of a 1907 investor's information package. MAP 349 is part of a four-sheet map showing irrigated areas of California in 1920, published two years later by the U.S. Department of Agriculture. Green areas are irrigated; brown are other potential agricultural areas. The Alamo Canal can be seen running through Mexico on its way to the Imperial Valley. The Salton Sea is at top left. The Yuma Irrigation Project is at right.

MAP 350 (*left*).

The *Yuma Irrigation Project* shown on a 1924 map by the recently renamed U.S. Bureau of Reclamation.

MAP 351 (*below*).

Another part of the 1922 U.S. Department of Agriculture map shows the Los Angeles Basin. It is striking how virtually the entire 1920 irrigated area has since disappeared, inundated by a sea of concrete and asphalt.

THE LANDS OF UTAH

DENVER AND RIO GRANDE RAILROAD

control, power generation, and irrigation plan after long delays, this time caused by World War II. The project's principal components were the Shasta Dam, on the Sacramento River in northern California, completed in 1945; the Friant Dam, on the San Joaquin, completed in 1945, which diverts water into the Friant-Kern Canal, completed in 1949; and the Delta-Mendota Canal, completed in 1951, down the west side of the San Joaquin Valley.

The California State Water Project, authorized in 1960, uses the California Aqueduct to transport water from the Oroville Dam on the Feather River in the north to the Los Angeles Basin in the south. The project featured a number of pumping stations, and the aqueduct included a two-thousand-foot lift over the Tehachapi Mountains. The project is an integrated one: urban and industrial uses take 70 percent of the water and agriculture the remaining 30 percent.

With this project and others California now has about 8 million acres of irrigated land. Aqueducts principally supplying urban areas are considered on pages 191, 194, and 240–41.

On the Great Plains, the experience of the Dust Bowl years of the 1930s led to a vast increase in so-called deep-well irrigation, where water is obtained from fossil sources often over 200 feet deep. Nebraska now has about 6 million acres of land irrigated in this manner, and Texas has 4.5 million. The total irrigated land in the West now amounts to about 37 million acres, which produce some $32 billion worth of crops every year. Irrigation is largely responsible for the well-known foods Americans now take for granted, from Idaho potatoes to Sunkist oranges (see page 225).

Map 352 (left, top).
The Denver & Rio Grande Railroad published this brochure in 1915 to attract settlers to Utah.

Map 353 (left, bottom).
A system of irrigation channels is well developed around Utah Lake in this 1899 federal government map. The key distinguishes between private and government-owned land.

Map 354 (below).
A map in the 1915 Denver & Rio Grande brochure emphasizes fertile land for both homeseekers and investors.

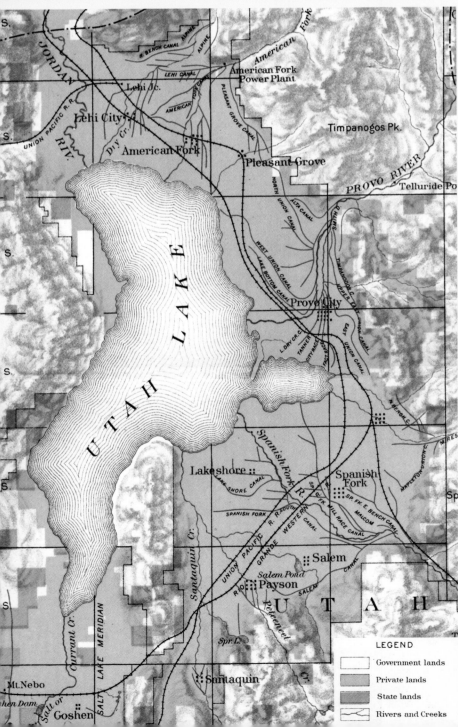

LEGEND

☐ Government lands
☐ Private lands
☐ State lands
〰 Rivers and Creeks

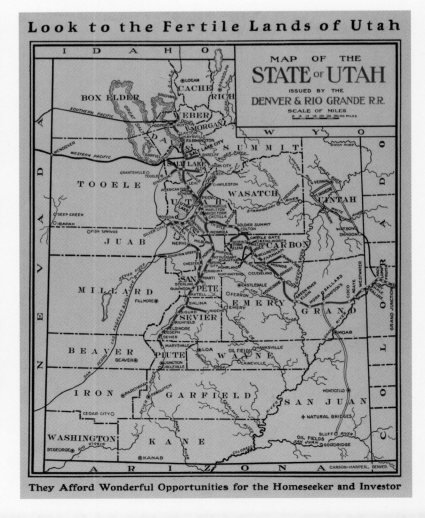

Look to the Fertile Lands of Utah

MAP OF THE
STATE OF UTAH
ISSUED BY THE
DENVER & RIO GRANDE R.R.
SCALE OF MILES

They Afford Wonderful Opportunities for the Homeseeker and Investor

Selling the West to Settlers

At first the railroads, and then the territorial and state governments, had a vested interest in selling their land grants or populating their jurisdictions and thus increasing the tax base. A myriad of creative ways were found to lure the settler west.

When the lure was gold and the attraction the promise of quick riches, no advertising was needed, but although free or cheap land held obvious attractions for many, it required often backbreaking work to achieve success, and so a little encouragement was in order.

Some railroads were particularly good at it. The Southern Pacific funded California booster organizations, exhibited at agricultural and other exhibitions and expositions all over the East and in Europe, enlisted famous writers to extol the virtues of the land, and published *Sunset* magazine as its very own advertising vehicle; the latter served the dual purpose of promoting tourism as well (see page 214). Newspapers often reprinted *Sunset* articles. It all filled trains. And of course, like most railroads, the company issued booklets and brochures containing all the information a potential settler might want to know. In one year, 1910, the Southern Pacific paid for over half a million informational booklets published by towns and cities along its lines. The railroad also supported scientific research aimed at widening the crops that might be grown in a region.

The railroad's rival, the Northern Pacific, had similar programs to encourage traffic on its lines and sales of its land. One region it successfully

Map 355 *(below, right)*.
A superb advertising poster map-image from 1911 cleverly shows money being plowed from the soil atop a map of Montana. The Chicago, Milwaukee & St. Paul Railway created a subsidiary, the Chicago, Milwaukee & Puget Sound Railway, to build the third transcontinental into the Northwest. It was completed between Mobridge, South Dakota, and Seattle in 1909. By the mid-1920s the innovative railroad electrified 600 miles of the new line, but the railroad never prospered, going bankrupt several times. In 1927 the two lines were merged and reincorporated as the Chicago, Milwaukee, St. Paul & Pacific Railroad and officially became the "Milwaukee Road." In 1977 the company went bankrupt for the last time, and thousands of miles of line were simply abandoned.

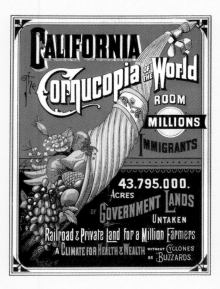

Above.
A superb 1883 poster with a cornucopia of fruits, published by the Southern Pacific's immigration office in Chicago. It advertises nearly 44 million acres of *untaken* government lands and emphasizes the climate—*without cyclones or blizzards.* The latter phrase was designed to attract settlers already established on the Plains.

Below.
This settlers' booklet with information about Oregon was published in 1923.

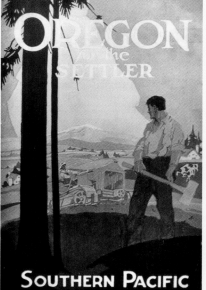

promoted over a long period was Dakota Territory, from where its lines had extended to the Pacific in 1883. The line had reached Bismarck, Dakota Territory, in 1873, and the company lost no time promoting its newly acquired land grant.

In 1874 some directors partnered with an expert Minnesota wheat grower named Oliver Dalrymple, who, on a massive, nearly flat holding of 11,250 acres, applied the latest mechanized cultivation techniques to harvest a bumper crop. It was perhaps the first application of so-called corporate farming methods that would one day become the norm on the Great Plains. Dalrymple used mechanical seeders, steam-powered threshing machines, and self-binding reapers, with hundreds of seasonally employed men and even more horses, and he made a huge profit that the Northern Pacific of course immediately used in its marketing efforts.

The demonstration paid off. Five years later virtually all the land was sold, mainly to eastern investors and syndicates out to make a killing. Many huge farms were established in the region. The boom finally ended when, in the late 1880s and early 1890s, a series of droughts quickly rationalized

Map 356 (below).
In 1883, the Northern Pacific issued this map, complete with a train illustration featuring *Pullman and Dining Cars*. In that year the railroad was completed to the Pacific, but on the Columbia route, not on the line across the Cascades, as shown; the latter would be completed in 1887 (see page 130).

Above. A traveling agricultural exhibition railroad car helped the Northern Pacific sell its lands in 1895.

Right. A Northern Pacific advertisement touts *Lands! Millions and Millions of Acres* in 1883.

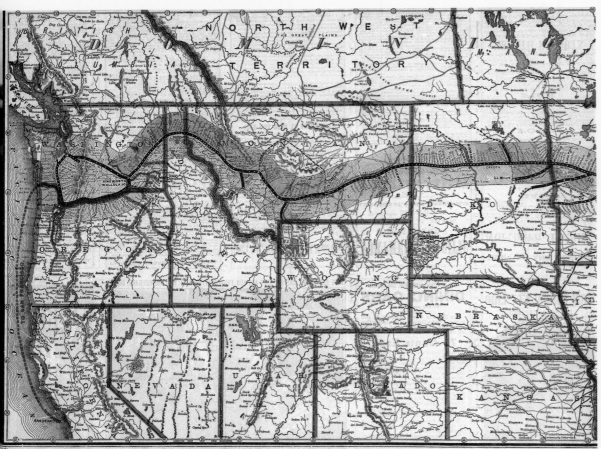

This is our Pacific Express, with Pullman and Dining Cars attac
running through to Portland wit

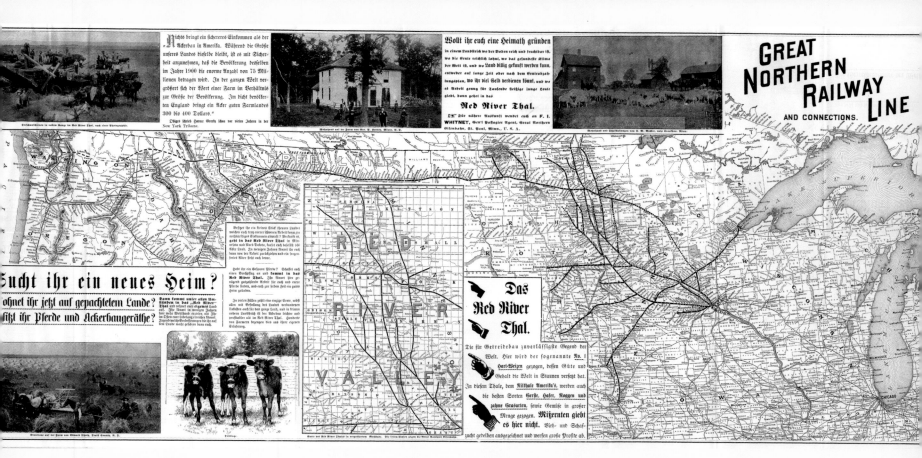

MAP 357 (*above*).

When the Great Northern Railway built its transcontinental line, it too promoted the agricultural wealth of the northern West to potential European colonists. This 1892 map was published for use in Germany.

MAP 358 (*below*).

A fast as the railroads promoted their lands on the Great Plains, others drew attention to their drawbacks to promote their own properties. This rather beautiful 1896 bird's-eye map directs attention to Port Arthur, a new venture on the Gulf Coast by entrepreneur Arthur E. Stillwell, after whom it was named, and his rail line, the Kansas City, Pittsburgh & Gulf Railroad, renamed the following year as the Kansas City, Shreveport & Gulf Railway.

the overexuberance. Many of the large farms were subdivided and sold off to smaller-scale farmers. But the land was agriculturally developed, a population was installed, and the Northern Pacific had moved on to newer pastures farther west. In the 1880s the population of Dakota Territory increased to over half a million; that of neighboring Nebraska hit the one-million mark. Government lands, claimed under the Homestead Act, were taken up as well as railroad lands. And in 1889 the population increase led to the creation of two new states from Dakota Territory—North Dakota and South Dakota.

UNCLE SAM AND HIS SEARCH LIGHT.
LOOKING OVER THE "PORT ARTHUR ROUTE."

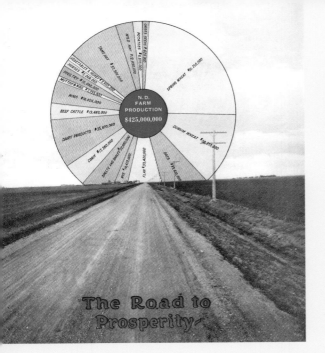

The Road to Prosperity

Left. The illustration from the inside front cover of the 1928 Northern Pacific booklet showed North Dakota as *The Road to Prosperity*, actually a 1924 view along the "Red Trail," which paralleled the main line, complete with farm production depicted as a rising sun. "It conveys," said the caption, "some idea of the nature of this immense agricultural country whose farming possibilities have been but scratched."

North Dakota
The Center of the North American Continent

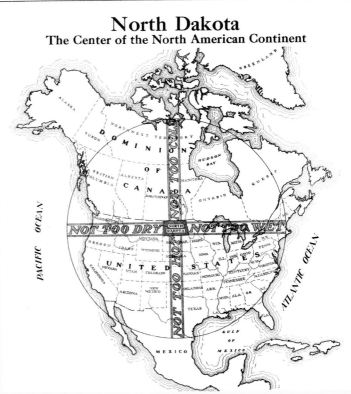

Map 359 (*above*).
This clever map depicts the location of North Dakota as the *Center of the North American Continent—not too hot, not too cold, not too wet,* and *not too dry—* a brilliant piece of marketing hype.

The Northern Pacific continued its marketing efforts, using all sorts of arguments to convince settlers—and investors—to buy its land and become its freight customers. In 1928 the railroad published a magnificent example of western railroad marketing literature, and a number of maps and other illustrations from it are shown on this page. Yet although it was an excellent example, it was by no means atypical; all the railroads did it to a greater or lesser extent. It was but one way in which settlers, farmers, colonists, emigrants—call them what you will—were induced to move to the West.

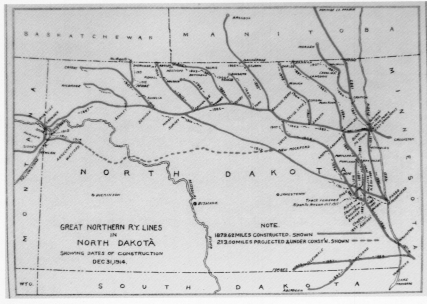

Map 360 (*above*).
The lines of competitor Great Northern Railway in *North Dakota* in 1914. The company, like the Northern Pacific, had by this time developed quite a network of branch lines to serve the agricultural communities of the northern Plains.

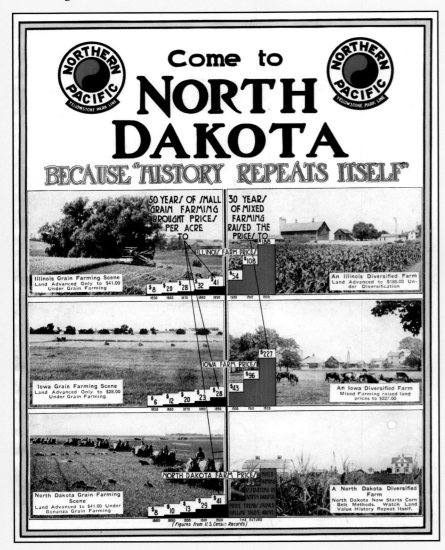

Come to NORTH DAKOTA
BECAUSE "HISTORY REPEATS ITSELF"

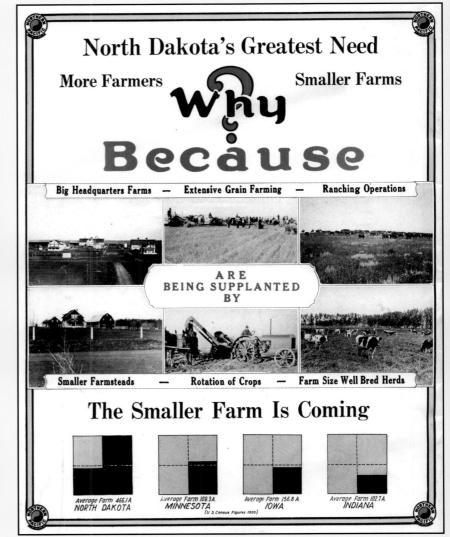

North Dakota's Greatest Need
More Farmers   Smaller Farms
Why Because

The Smaller Farm Is Coming

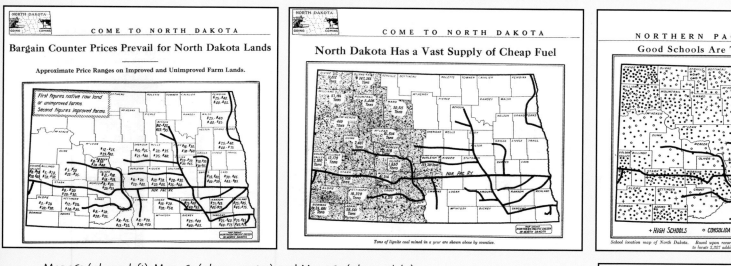

Bargain Counter Prices Prevail for North Dakota Lands

Approximate Price Ranges on Improved and Unimproved Farm Lands.

North Dakota Has a Vast Supply of Cheap Fuel

Tons of lignite coal mined in a year are shown above by counties.

NORTHERN PACIFIC RAILWAY

Good Schools Are The Rule in North Dakota

School location map of North Dakota. Based upon records of State Department of Public Instruction. No attempt has been made to locate 3,327 additional graded and one room schools.

+ HIGH SCHOOLS · o CONSOLIDATED SCHOOLS · • GRADE SCHOOLS

Map 362 (*above, left*), Map 363 (*above, center*), and Map 364 (*above, right*).

The Northern Pacific booklet contained numerous maps depicting various facts about North Dakota, all designed to sell the emigrant farmer on the region. These three show *bargain* prices for land, *cheap fuel* in the form of lignite coal, and *schools*. The latter map manages to make the state look like a veritable sea of education yet still does not include 3,327 *additional graded and one room schools*. All the maps, of course, have the Northern Pacific rail system overlaid.

Map 361 (*left, bottom, and far left, bottom*).

The front and back cover of the 1928 Northern Pacific booklet expounded the idea that one should invest in North Dakota land *because "history repeats itself"*—that is, because farms in Minnesota, Iowa, and Indiana were considerably smaller, on average, North Dakota farms could be expected to also become smaller over time, thus increasing their value per unit. The little schematic maps depict the notion that *The Smaller Farm Is Coming*, that soon the average farm size in North Dakota—then 466.1 acres—would reduce to somewhere near the 169.3 acres in Minnesota, the 156.8 acres in Iowa, or the 102.7 acres in Indiana, owing to more intensive use of the land. But history did not repeat itself. The average farm size in North Dakota by the 2002 Census of Agriculture was 1,283 acres, yet still only 340 acres in Minnesota, 350 acres in Iowa, and 250 acres in Minnesota. The fact was that the topography of the Great Plains lent itself to large-scale farming in 1928 and still does today. Yet in 1928 the argument that farms would get smaller seemed reasonable and no doubt sold some land.

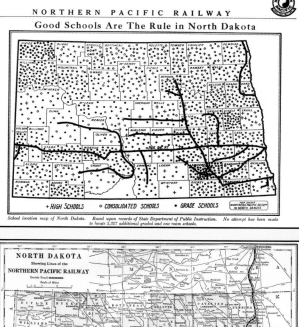

NORTH DAKOTA
Showing Lines of the
NORTHERN PACIFIC RAILWAY

Map 365 (*above*).

The 1928 Northern Pacific booklet also contained this detailed map of North Dakota with the branches of the railroad emphasized. Notice that all of the dead-end branches lead east—to markets.

Map 366 (*below*).

A general system map of the Northern Pacific was overlaid with marketing photographs showing planting suggestions: *sweet clover* for sheep and *corn* for hogs. Under the map are details of *What May be Taken in a Carload of Emigrant Movables*: they could include such items as *tools* and *agricultural implements, vehicles,* but not *motor vehicles*; also allowed were *fence posts, wire fencing,* and *lumber, shingles or one knocked-down portable house*. When shipment included *Ordinary Live Stock*, one man in charge would be carried free.

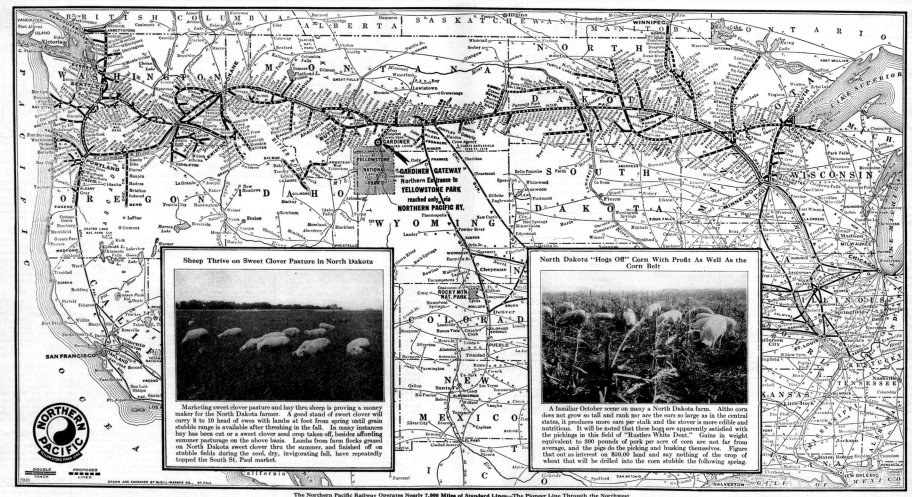

Sheep Thrive on Sweet Clover Pasture in North Dakota

Marketing sweet clover pasture and hay thru sheep is proving a money maker for the North Dakota farmer. A good stand of sweet clover will carry 5 to 10 head of ewes with lambs at foot from spring until grain stubble range is available after threshing in the fall. In many instances hay has been cut or a sweet clover seed crop taken off, besides affording summer pasturage on the above basis. Lambs from farm flocks grazed on North Dakota sweet clover thru the summer, and finished off on stubble fields during the cool, dry, invigorating fall, have repeatedly topped the South St. Paul market.

North Dakota "Hogs Off" Corn With Profit As Well As the Corn Belt

A familiar October scene on many a North Dakota farm. Altho corn does not grow so tall and rank nor are the ears so large as in the central states, it produces more ears per stalk and the stover is more edible and nutritious. It will be noted that these hogs are apparently satisfied with the pickings in this field of "Rustlers White Dent." Gains in weight equivalent to 300 pounds of pork per acre of corn are not far from average, and the pigs do the picking and husking themselves. Figure that out as interest on $50.00 land and say nothing of the crop of wheat that will be drilled into the corn stubble the following spring.

NORTHERN PACIFIC YELLOWSTONE PARK LINE

The Northern Pacific Railway Operates Nearly 7,000 Miles of Standard Lines—The Pioneer Line Through the Northwest

What May be Taken in a Carload of Emigrant Movables

The description "Emigrant Movables" will only include:
Second-hand (used) Household goods or Personal Effects, such as clothing, furniture or furnishings for residences, with not to exceed one Piano, but not including goods shipped for sale or speculation; Tools and other hand implements of calling; Second-hand (used) Agricultural Implements or Traction Engines; Second-hand (used) Vehicles, other than Motor Vehicles, Ambulances, Coaches, Hearses or similar vehicles; Fence Posts, Wire Fencing, Lumber, Shingles, or one knocked-down Portable House; Grain, Seed, Shrubbery or Trees, for planting; Feed for live stock and poultry while in transit, Live Poultry not exceeding five hundred (500) lbs. in weight; or Ordinary Live Stock as defined in classification, not exceeding ten (10) head; declaration of value on Ordinary

Live Stock not required; additional Ordinary Live Stock will be subject to the L. C. L. charges therefor as provided in classification.

Emigrant Movables rating will not apply on Matches or other inflammable or explosive articles, nor on Boats, Drugs, Paintings, Silverware, or Bric-a-brac of extraordinary value, nor on any articles intended for sale or speculation.

When shipment of Emigrant Movables includes Ordinary Live Stock as defined in classification, one man in charge will be carried free in the car with the shipment and the carrier's agent must require the execution of the Uniform Live Stock Contract. Additional man or men must pay full fare.

*On the Nor. Pac. Ry. one second-hand automobile may be included in a C. L. of Emigrant's Movables.

MINIMUM WEIGHTS

Minimum carload weight Sims, North Dakota, and east thereof is 24,000 lbs. per 36½ ft. car. West of Sims, North Dakota, and on the Killdeer and Mott branches, the minimum weight is 20,000 lbs. per 36½ ft. car. The minimum weight will vary with the length of car ordered.

The rules applied to shipments from points east of St. Paul will vary slightly, with respect to the minimum weight of carloads, articles permissible to constitute, etc., from those quoted in the foregoing. Full information will be furnished by addressing J. G. Morrison, G. F. A., Northern Pacific Ry., St. Paul, Minn., stating what shipment is to consist of, initial point of shipment, destination, etc.

The rates on Emigrant movables are conditional upon declaration by the shipper that the value of each article does not exceed 10 cents per pound. All freight charges must be prepaid or guaranteed.

LOCAL FREIGHT

If you have only a few hundred pounds to ship, you will get the best service if you ship them by local freight. Shipments of Emigrant movables by local freight must be indorsed by your local agent on bill of lading as follows: "Household goods, declared valuation 10 cents per pound."

Regulations for Shipping Live Stock Into North Dakota

North Dakota, as well as many other states, has certain rules and regulations covering the importation of Live Stock. These rules and regulations are continually changing and shippers should inform themselves regarding the various certificates, etc. required before stock can be imported into the state.

Science and Surveys

So much of the structural geology and geomorphology of the arid West lies open for examination that the region has played a large role in our understanding of the earth sciences. In addition the search for mineral wealth provided an early impetus; understanding of what lay under the surface of the earth could yield major rewards.

California's gold discoveries provided an early reason for a geological survey; the California Geological Survey was created in 1853, and a state geologist, Josiah Whitney, was appointed in 1860. Whitney was one of the first to advocate protecting the Yosemite Valley, now a national park.

The Pacific Railroad Surveys had included scientists, and several of the volumes the survey produced included detailed assessments of the geology and natural history of the West. Government attention turned to the idea of carrying out comprehensive surveys of the West to essentially conduct an inventory of its resources that could be exploited. A young geologist, Clarence King, was the first to advance the idea. He had worked with Whitney on the California Geological Survey, and today Kings Canyon National Park is named after him.

In 1867 King was appointed head of a new Geological and Geographical Exploration of the Fortieth Parallel, composed of civilians but sponsored by the Army. King spent six years crisscrossing the area shown on MAP 373, *page 177.* He found the first glacier to be discovered in the West—the Whitney Glacier on Mount Shasta. King and his scientists produced several important books detailing the economic geology of the West.

MAP 367 (*right*).
The first comprehensive geological map of the American West, compiled and published in 1857 by James Hall, a noted early stratigraphic geologist and paleontologist. Hall was able to visualize a general structure from local observations, an almost essential faculty for someone wanting to map the geology of the West as early as this. Hall gathered all known information, including that from William Blake in California (MAP 371, *page 177*) and William Emory, a topographical engineer responsible for several detailed surveys of the Southwest, including the Mexican boundary survey of 1857–59, and put them all together to create this pioneering map.

MAP 368 (*below*).
Upper California in 1841 as compiled by the first American round-the-world scientific expedition, the United States Exploring Expedition, led by Charles Wilkes. This map was published in 1844.

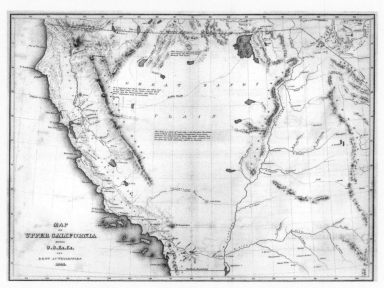

MAP
Illustrating the General Geological features
OF THE COUNTRY
WEST of the MISSISSIPPI RIVER.

Compiled from the surveys of W. H. Emory and
from the Pacific Railroad Surveys & other sources.

BY

Professor JAMES HALL,

ASSISTED BY

J. P. Lesley, Esq.

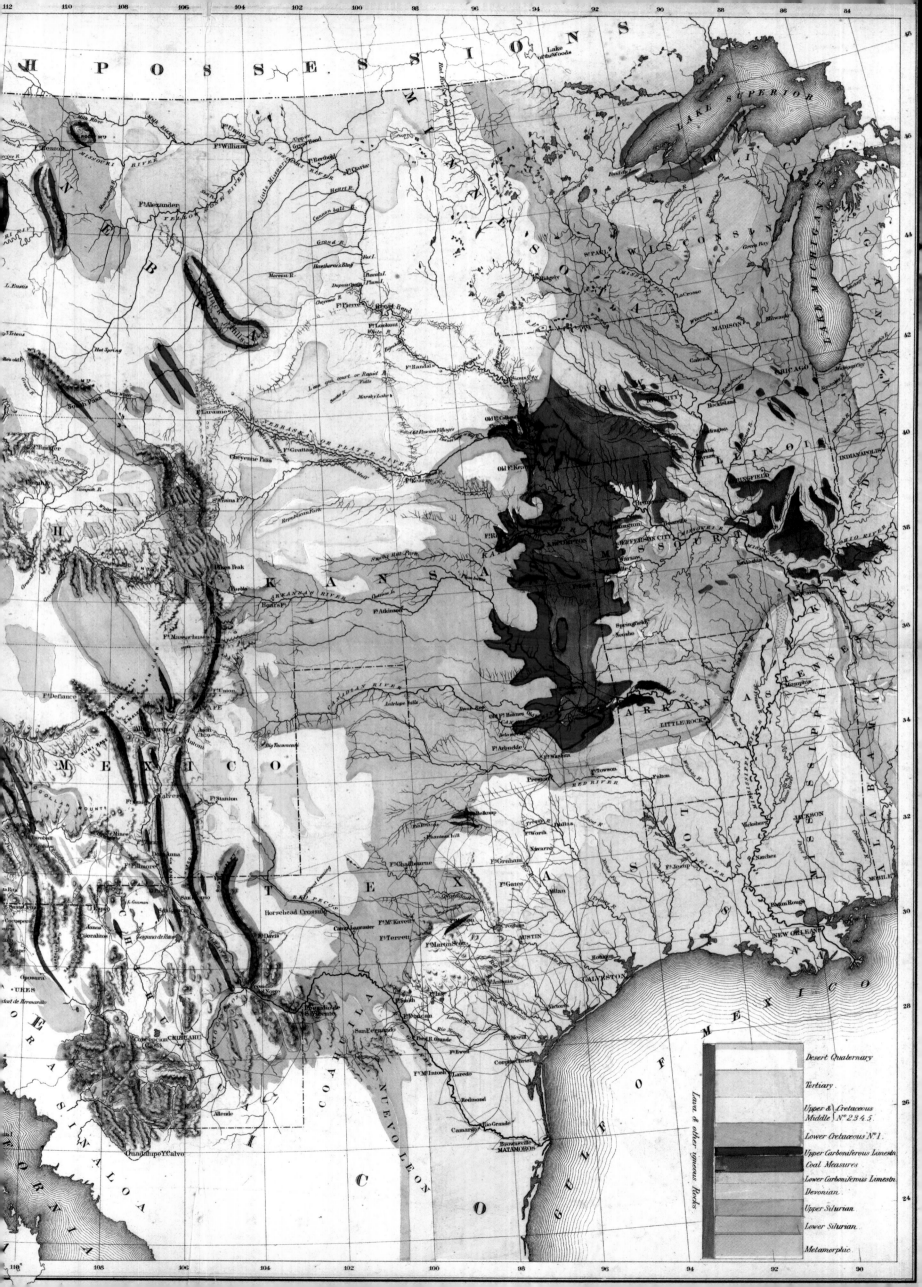

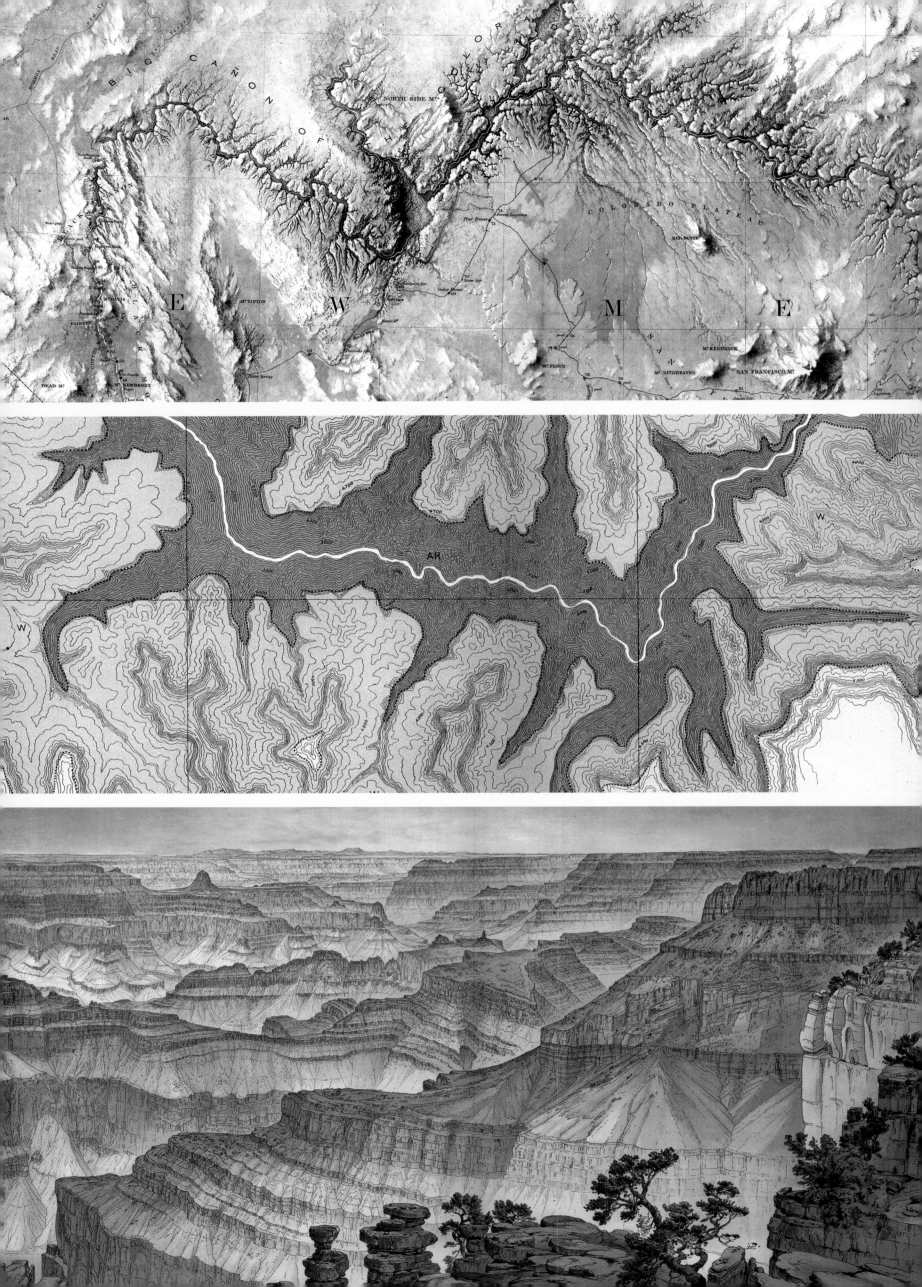

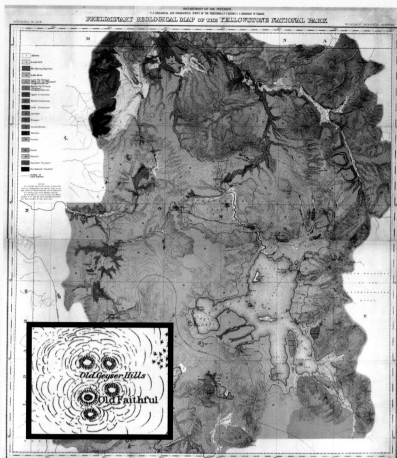

Map 369 (*left, top*).
Important for its first use of an innovative mapping technique using relief and shadow, still in use today, is this map of the Colorado and the Grand Canyon drawn in 1858 by topographer Frederick von Egloffstein, who was with topographical engineer Joseph Christmas Ives on his survey of the river in 1857–58. Ives was searching for a possible water route to Utah, which the Army desired during the Mormon War (see page 110).

Map 370 (*left, center*).
Stunning in its detail is this contour map of the Grand Canyon by Clarence Dutton, working for the new U.S. Geological Survey. It was published in 1882.

Left, bottom.
Also from Dutton's report was this much more famous engraving of the Grand Canyon, drawn by artist William Holmes, aided by a camera lucida.

Map 371 (*above, left*).
An early geological map of California produced by William Blake, who worked with Lieutenant Robert Williamson on the Pacific Railroad Surveys in the state. The map was published in 1855 in Williamson's report.

Map 372 (*above, right*).
Ferdinand Hayden's detailed geological map of what is now Yellowstone National Park, published in 1878. *Inset* is his map of the geysers, including *Old Faithful*.

Map 373 (*below, left*).
A progress report by George Wheeler in 1879 contained this map showing the *Area of Surveys by and under Lt. Wheeler* and *Geol. Exploration 40th Par. C. King*, Clarence King's survey of the fortieth parallel.

Map 374 (*below, right*).
A map of the Grand Canyon prepared by John Wesley Powell in 1873.

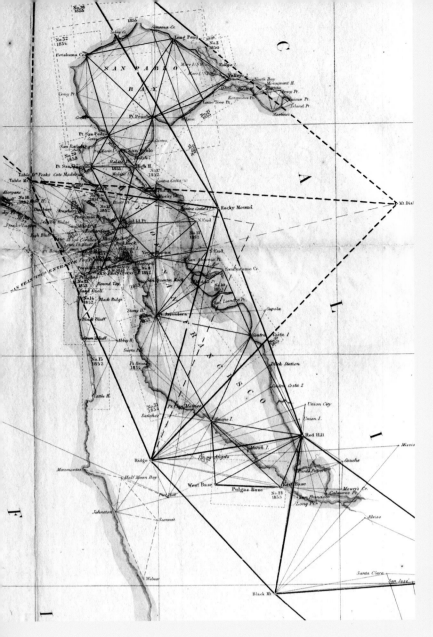

The U.S. Army's last major exploration of the West was that of Lieutenant George Montague Wheeler, who between 1867 and 1879 surveyed most of the remaining Southwest (MAP 373, *page 177*). His work added hugely to scientific knowledge of the region but was as much military in nature as purely scientific. He was, for example, to report on the "numbers, habits, and disposition" of the Indians—and not for anthropological reasons; the Army wanted to know whom it might be up against.

A better-known western exploration was that of John Wesley Powell, who descended the Colorado River to below the Grand Canyon in 1869. After an epic journey of more than a thousand miles he was idolized by the press, and Congress appointed him head of another survey, the Geographical and Topographical Survey of the Colorado River, which lasted two years. In 1872 he discovered the Escalante River, which today flows into Lake Powell behind the Glen Canyon Dam; it was the last river to be found in the contiguous United States. In 1878 Powell published his seminal *Report on the Lands of the Arid Region of the United States*, which was to have a profound effect on the planning of western development (see page 160). Powell also established the Bureau of Ethnology in 1879 to study Indian culture.

Exploration of the West at this time was downright competitive. The Department of the Interior appointed geologist Ferdinand V. Hayden to head the United States Geological and Geographical Survey of the Territories in 1869. Hayden's work in Wyoming led him to lobby for the establishment of Yellowstone as a national park; President Ulysses Grant set the area aside as a "public park or pleasuring ground" in 1872. The Department of the Interior then appointed Hayden to conduct a comprehensive survey of Colorado between 1873 and 1876. An unplanned overlap of work in Colorado in 1873 by Hayden's scientists and some sent by Wheeler began a process by which Congress rationalized the exploration of the West. In 1879 the teams were all brought together under the United States Geological Survey. Clarence King was its first director, and he was succeeded in 1881 by John Wesley Powell.

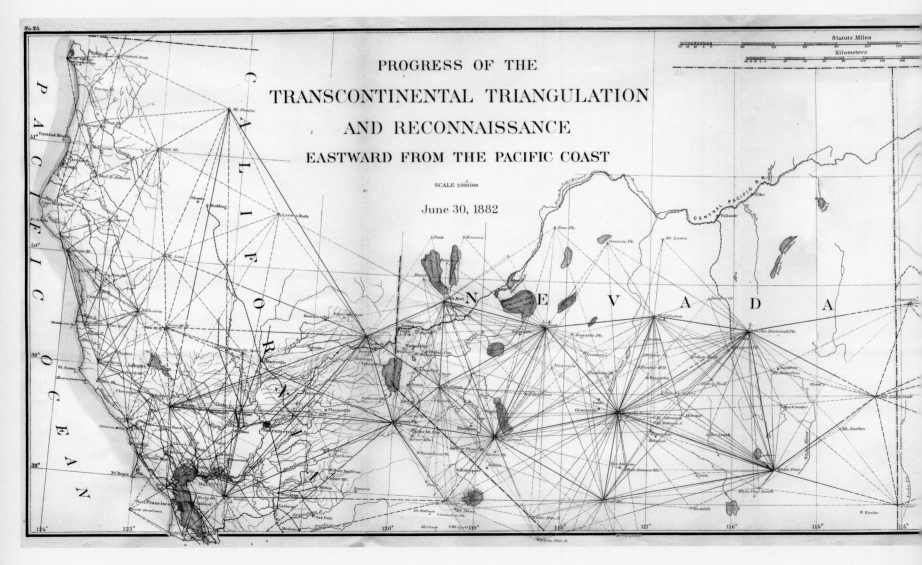

MAP 375 (*far left*).
With the California Gold Rush came many ships and a need to accurately map the coast. A progress report of the United States Coast Survey (USCS) in 1855 contained this map showing the triangulation of the San Francisco Bay region.

MAP 376 (*below*).
In 1871 the USCS was given the added responsibility of mapping the interior, and its name was changed to the U.S. Coast and Geodetic Survey (USCGS). Primary triangulation had been halted by the Civil War, but in 1871, Benjamin Peirce, third superintendent of the USCS (and then USCGS, 1867–74), obtained congressional authorization for the Transcontinental Arc, a network of triangulation connecting the coasts along the 39th parallel. It was perhaps the greatest surveying undertaking of its time. This map shows the progress of the triangulation eastward from the West Coast by 1882. Triangulation from the East has reached Colorado, but there is a gap between Colorado and Utah. The Transcontinental Arc was completed in 1900 and was the first measurement of the continent's width to exacting geodetic standards; the width of 4,224 kilometers (2,625 miles) was accurate to within 26 meters (85 feet). Peirce also began surveys in the newly acquired Alaska, beginning in the southeast. Note that the *Great American Desert* is shown on this map, but now it is confined to a truly desert region—that just west of the Great Salt Lake.

MAP 377 (*right*).
Pioneer climatologist Lorin Blodget's map of the average temperatures (red lines) and rainfall (shades of gray) in the United States, published in 1873. His map showed that there was enough rainfall to support agriculture on much of the Great Plains. However, exploiting that rainfall would have required water conservation techniques beyond those available at the time.

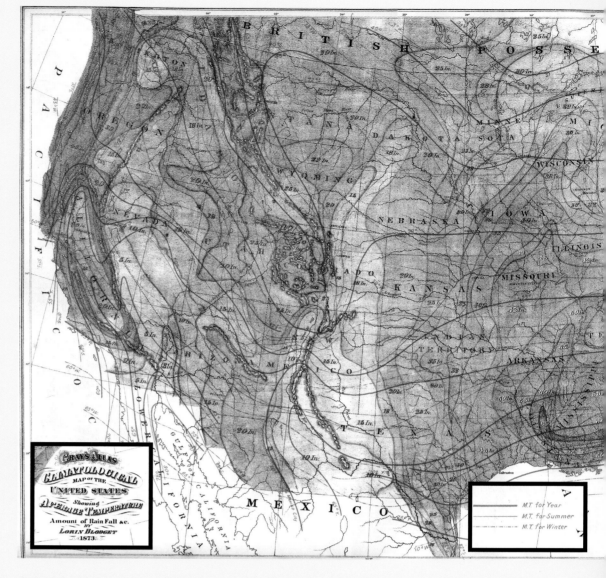

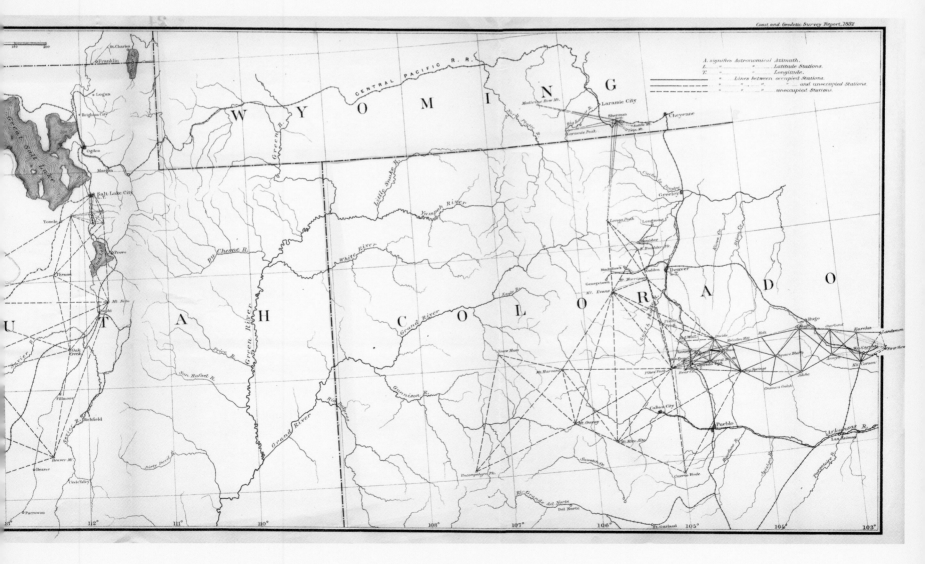

The Political Evolution of the West

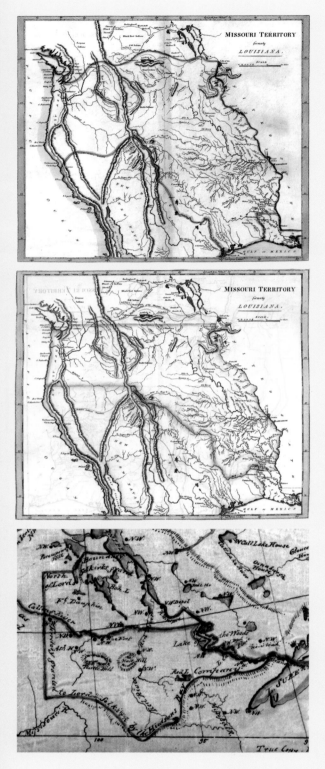

As the United States acquired the West and populated it, the region was progressively broken down into administrative areas—first unorganized territories, then organized ones, and finally states. And maps illustrate this process better than words.

When the Louisiana Purchase (see page 65) was first divided to create the state of Louisiana in 1812, the remainder was called Missouri Territory.

The Convention of 1818 between the United States and Britain was the last tidying-up of the War of 1812 and established the international boundary on the forty-ninth parallel as far west as the Rocky Mountains; beyond that the Oregon Country was left as an area of "joint occupancy" that would continue until 1846. This convention established the northern boundaries of today's Minnesota, North Dakota, and most of Montana.

In 1819 the Transcontinental Treaty between Spain and the United States (see page 49) established many boundaries that were later used as state boundaries (Map 383, *below*). These were the Sabine River and a projection north to the Red River (Texas/Louisiana and Arkansas); the Red River to 100° W (Texas/Oklahoma); 100° W to the Arkansas River (Texas Panhandle/Oklahoma); and the 42° N line of latitude (Oregon/Utah, Nevada, and California).

When Texas entered the Union in 1845, its boundaries were in dispute. In particular, the state claimed territory in what is today New Mexico and

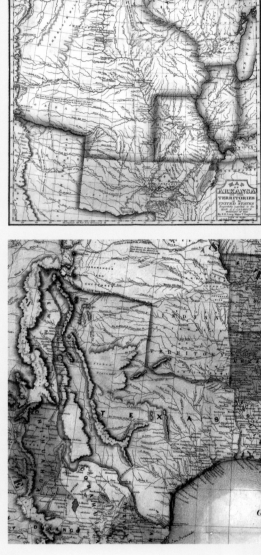

Map 378 (*above, top*) and Map 379 (*above, center*). *Missouri Territory* both before and after the 1818 convention setting the northern boundary, here erroneously shown straight through to the Pacific. Both maps are by the same mapmaker, Mathew Carey, and he has clearly just redrawn the boundaries on the same base map.

Map 380 (*above, bottom*).
Much of what is now North Dakota was claimed by the Hudson's Bay Company as land draining into Hudson Bay and as such was granted to Lord Selkirk in 1811 for his Red River Colony, the area around Winnipeg, Manitoba. This map shows the grant; an international boundary has also been drawn (dark red), but this is not the 1818 one, which is straight west of Lake of the Woods.

Map 381 (*right, top*).
This 1822 map shows the boundary with *Spanish Territory* as agreed in 1819 and *Arkansa[s]* territory, created in 1819 and including most of today's Oklahoma, which was separated in 1824 and 1828 before Arkansas became a state in 1836. The information on the map comes mainly from explorer Stephen Long.

Map 382 (*right, center*).
This 1850 map of Texas, created before the mapmaker had heard of or understood the terms of the Compromise of 1850 bill, shows the state extending to the Rio Grande north of Santa Fe, still a reduction from the original claim as shown on Map 384.

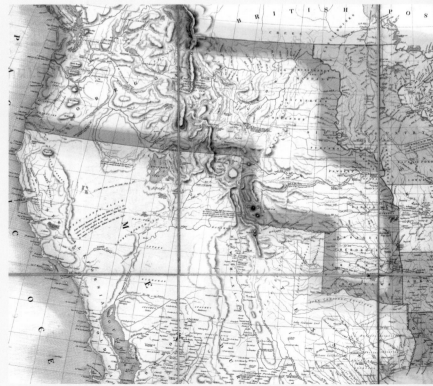

Map 383 (*above*).
The boundary agreed to in the Transcontinental Treaty of 1819 is well displayed on this map published twenty years later. Mexico is south of the yellow/green and red/green lines.

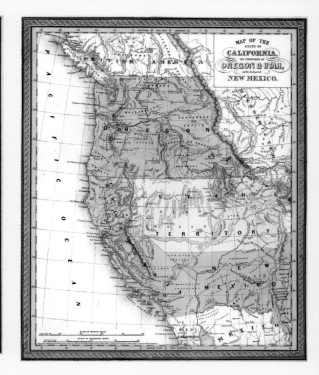

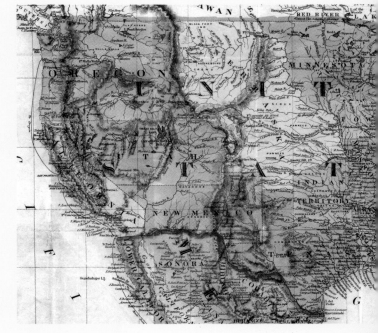

Map 384 (*top, left*), Map 385 (*top, center*), and Map 386 (*top, right*).
The three maps in this sequence from commercial mapmaker Samuel Augustus
Mitchell are dated 1846, 1849, and 1850, respectively.

Map 384. This map shows Texas with the boundaries claimed until 1850 extending north to 42° and
including part of New Mexico. Upper or New California (red) and New Mexico (yellow), the latter
shown as a thin strip of land along the Rio Grande, are still part of Mexico. To the north, the vast
Oregon straddles the forty-ninth parallel. A huge *Iowa* Territory extends onto the Plains north to
the international boundary; this would be truncated in December 1846 when Iowa became a state.
Between Iowa and Oregon lies *Missouri Territory.* To the south is *Indian Territory,* then extending
from Oklahoma to Colorado.

Map 385. *Upper or New California* is now American but unsubdivided. North of 42° is *Oregon* Territory, created the previous year and now separate from *British America*—today the Canadian province
of British Columbia.

Map 386. Now the previously Mexican territory is divided, under the Compromise of 1850, into the
State of *California* and *Utah Territory* and *New Mexico* Territory, both extending west to California.

Map 387 (*above, left*).
An interesting and rare German map published in 1850 that depicts the boundaries of the proposed
Mormon state of *Deseret,* including the southern part of what became California. The Mormons tried
to shape their proposal to exclude areas of immigrant population, so San Francisco and the Bay Area
were deliberately not included. A California prestate meeting, the Monterey Convention, rejected
boundaries for the state of California similar to those shown here for Deseret. One of the reasons was
that Mormons living in the Salt Lake area were not represented at the convention.

Map 388 (*above, right, center*).
An interpretation on a map published, in 1850, of the Mormon proposed state of *Deseret*. The map
seems to have been drawn after the boundaries of the state of California had been decided. Here
Deseret covers all of today's Utah, Nevada, and Arizona and extends east well into Colorado.

Map 389 (*above*).
This 1851 map shows the new state of *California* and the new
territories of *Oregon, Utah,* and *New Mexico,* together with
a massive, as yet unorganized *Nebraska,* organized *Minnesota* Territory, and *Indian Territory.*

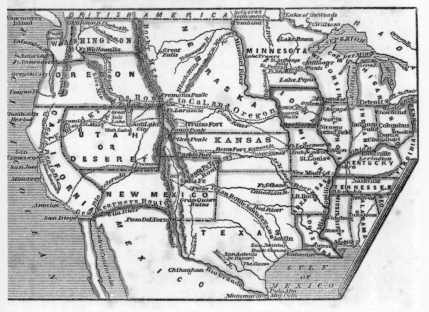

MAP 390 (*above*).
The political West in 1854. *Washington* Territory has been divided from *Oregon* Territory the previous year, and an organized *Nebraska* Territory and *Kansas* Territory have been created following the Kansas-Nebraska Act of the same year. *Minnesota* Territory stretches to the *Missouri*. Note the pre-Gadsden southern international boundary along the *Gila River* and the *Emigrants Route to Cal. and Oregon*. The name *Deseret* lives on four years after Utah Territory was created.

MAP 391 (*below*).
Various offers to purchase parts of Mexico were made in the period following the annexation of most of the West after the Mexican War. This map, drawn about 1853 (on an 1845 base map), depicts several proposals that would have added all of Baja California to the United States as well as substantial territory south of the Rio Grande. As it was, the Gadsden Purchase added to the United States approximately the area shown south to the straight, thinner red line on this map, increasing the area of what would become Arizona and New Mexico but not achieving access to the Gulf of California.

Colorado, north to 42°, all of which had been claimed by the Texas Republic in 1836; in 1841 Texas had even sent out the Texas Santa Fe Expedition in an unsuccessful attempt to confirm the region as part of Texas. New boundaries were agreed to as part of the Compromise of 1850; Texas ceded lands west of its current boundary in return for the federal assumption of $10 million in debt. The northern boundary was set at 36° 30´ as the Missouri Compromise of 1820 had disallowed slavery north of that line (except for Missouri) and Texas was a slave state. The resulting so-called Neutral Strip along the northern boundary of Texas was left with no formal territorial ownership until 1890, when it was assigned to the new Oklahoma Territory; today it is the Oklahoma Panhandle.

In January 1846 the United States and Britain agreed to divide up the Oregon Country by extending the northern international boundary along the forty-ninth parallel to the sea but with all of Vancouver Island going to Britain (see page 86). On 14 August 1848 the United States created the Oregon Territory, a large tract encompassing all of today's Washington, Oregon, Idaho, and parts of Montana and Wyoming.

Then came the Mexican War (see page 87), resulting in the Treaty of Guadalupe Hidalgo, signed 2 February 1848, and the American acquisition of most of the remaining West—the former Mexican Upper California and New Mexico. This region was subdivided by the terms of the Compromise of 1850. All federal–state relations at this time were pervaded by the struggle to maintain some sort of balance between slave and nonslave states, and the Compromise was a complex set of five bills that (among other things) admitted California as a nonslave state and created Utah and New Mexico territories without prohibition of slavery, that matter to be decided later. It also, as we have seen, decided the western boundary of Texas; here the idea was to exclude territory from a slave state.

In June 1854 President Franklin Pierce ratified the Gadsden Purchase, which added further to American territory in the Southwest. It was intended to allow for the easier construction of a southern transcontinental railroad. It was

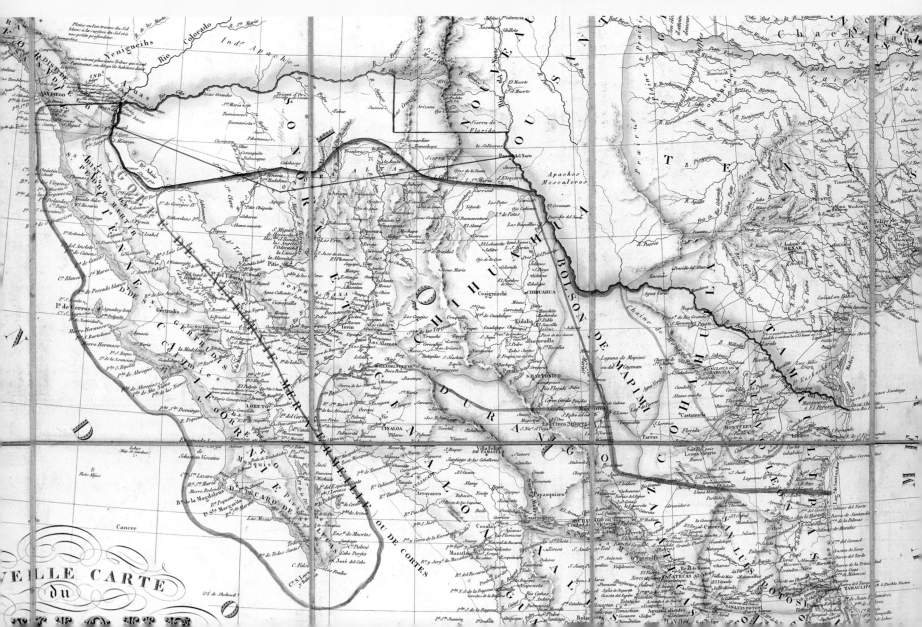

also intended to solve a border dispute that had erupted in the Mesilla Valley, west of El Paso. Mexico evicted American settlers and sent in the army in 1853. In December that year the American minister in Mexico City, James Gadsden, negotiated a solution with Mexican president Antonio López de Santa Anna—the same man whose life Sam Houston had spared on the battlefield at San Jacinto in 1836 (see page 82). For $10 million Gadsden purchased 29,670 more square miles to add to the United States—about 53 cents an acre.

The purchase did not entirely reduce border tensions, as many Mexicans were outraged that Santa Anna would sell off their country, and many Americans thought it only preliminary to eventual American ownership of much more of Mexico, especially all the border states and Baja California, as shown in an 1853 proposal (Map 391, left, bottom).

Map 392 (right).
The disputed territory of the Mesilla Valley, shown on a map that accompanied a report on the dispute in 1851. Disagreements had arisen because of inaccuracies in the map used to negotiate the Treaty of Guadalupe Hidalgo in 1848 (Map 171, page 90).

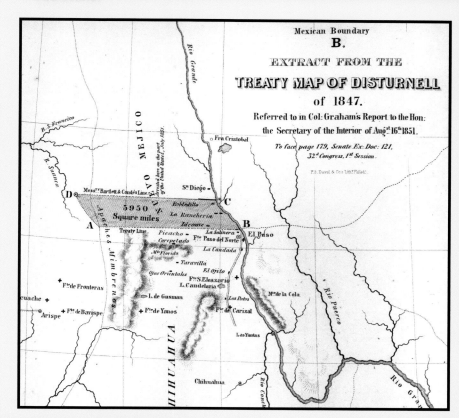

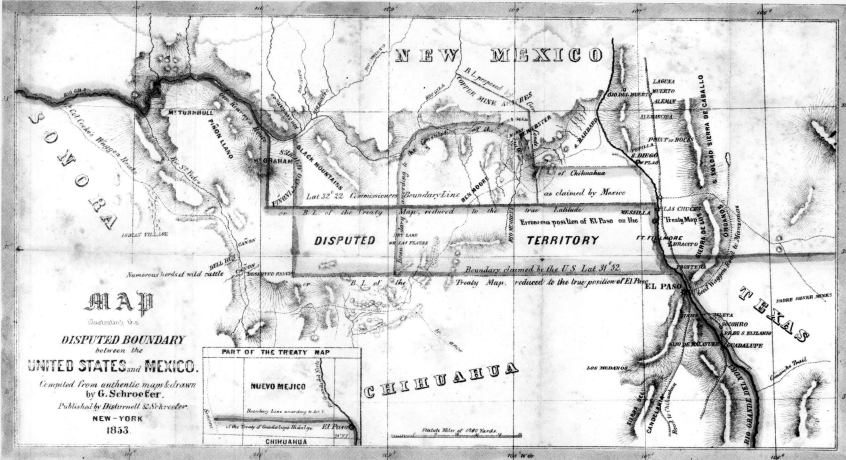

Map 393 (above).
The Mesilla Valley dispute. The treaty line as defined by latitude was not the same as the line defined by its intended location relative to El Paso, shown at right.

Map 394 (below, left).
A commercial map published in 1854 depicts the new boundary line and the territory gained by the United States by the Gadsden Purchase. The map also shows the projected Southern Route for Pacific Rail Road.

Map 395 (below, right).
Just as had happened in the newly acquired California, mineral wealth was found in the area of the Gadsden Purchase. This 1859 map shows the Silver Mines as now worked.

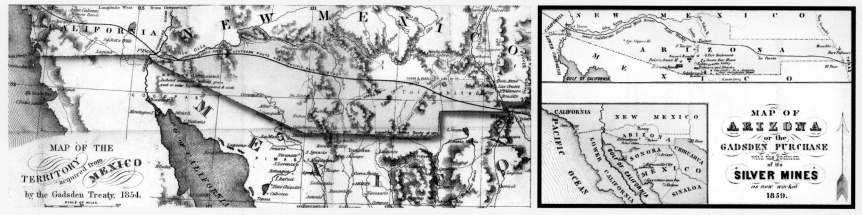

MAP 397 (above).
Kansas Territory, together with Indian Territory, later Oklahoma, on an 1857 map. Kansas stretches west into today's Colorado.

In 1854 the Kansas-Nebraska Act created Kansas and Nebraska as organized territories. This was an important act in that it also stated that the two territories, when admitted to the Union as states, "shall be received with or without slavery," the decision to be voted upon. This de facto repealed the Missouri Compromise of 1820, which had forbidden slavery north of 36° 30′. The act resulted in a sudden influx of settlers, both antislavery and proslavery, and the conflict known as "Bleeding Kansas" (see page 111), one of the precursors of the Civil War itself.

Once the Civil War began, the Union wanted to protect all the sources and potential sources of income it had—the major motivation behind the creation, in February and March 1861, of the new territories of Colorado, Dakota, and Nevada.

After the Pike's Peak Gold Rush (see page 106) miners unofficially organized the Territory of Jefferson, and an assembly, meeting between November 1859 and January 1860, had created twelve counties and incorporated the City of Denver, as well as adopted a civil and criminal code and passed laws

MAP 396 (above).
The organized territories of Kansas and Nebraska, created by the Kansas-Nebraska Act of 1854.

MAP 398 (below, center left) and MAP 399 (below, center right).
Nebraska Territory and adjoining Minnesota Territory in 1857.

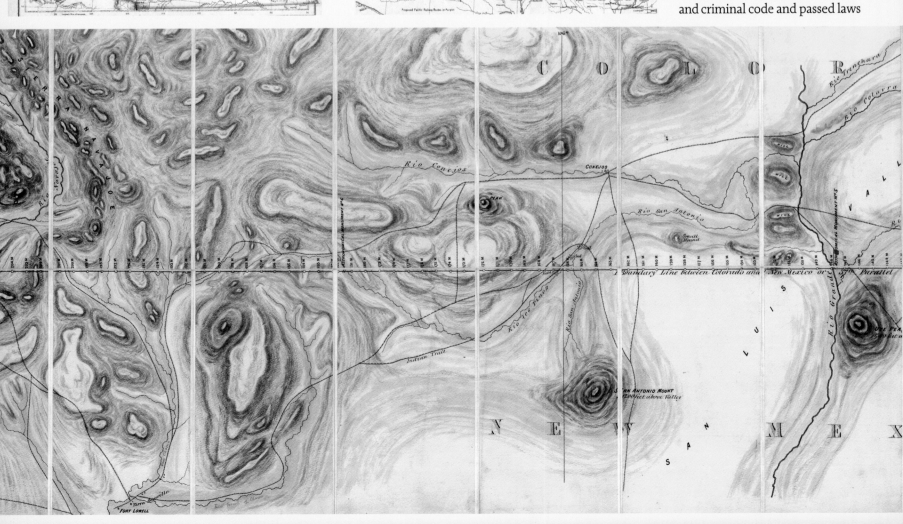

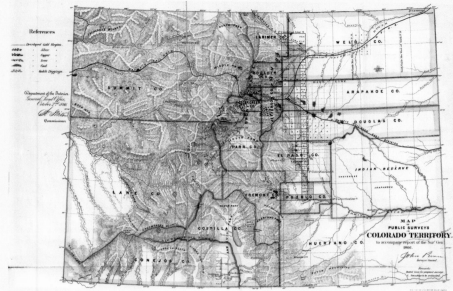

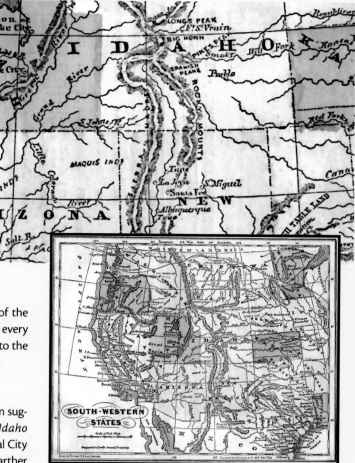

Map 401 (above).

Colorado Territory in 1866. Colorado was supposedly named because it was thought that the river of the same name rose in the region, but at that time it was called the *Grand River*, as shown on this map and every other map of the period. It took a resolution of Congress in 1921 to change the name of the Grand River to the Colorado, and at last the river arose in the state named after it.

Map 402 (detail, above, right, and right, inset).

Many maps got the changing political geography of the West wrong or marked placenames that had been suggested but never authorized. This interesting example is dated 1864: where Colorado was created, the name *Idaho* has been emblazoned across the map. This name was coined by Colorado territorial advocates at a Central City convention in 1860, but when Congress finally decided on territorial status Colorado prevailed as a name. Farther north, Dakota Territory, organized in 1861, is named *Chippewa Dacotah.* Chippewa was a name suggested earlier for this territory but not used.

Map 400 (below).

The creation of new territories required defining them on the ground, though much of this work was deferred until after the Civil War. The surveying of the boundary between Colorado and New Mexico well illustrates the difficulties this sometimes involved. This map shows a small part of that boundary from the 1868 survey. The portion shown is part of what was the northeast corner of New Mexico Territory, the Upper Rio Grande valley, as shown, for example on Map 409, *page 187*, now cut off at what was supposed to be 37° N. The Rio Grande is at approximate center. The surveyor, Ehud N. Darling, working for the U.S. General Land Office, did not fix the boundary correctly at 37° N but surveyed a boundary that was actually about a mile south of that line of latitude. In 1902–03 another surveyor, Howard Carpenter, also working for the General Land Office, resurveyed the boundary and, finding Darling's survey in error, destroyed many of his monuments and built his own. New Mexico sought to have the new, "correct" boundary confirmed in 1925, but the Supreme Court ruled that the boundary should stay were it was surveyed by Darling, as the state—then territory—had concurred with his original line. Carpenter's survey monuments were directed to be destroyed and the line of Darling's boundary resurveyed and remarked with monuments.

governing mineral and water resources. A rival group met at Golden and Central City in 1860 to propose a territory to be named Idaho (Map 402, *above*). Others used the name Colona (see Map 207, *page 107*). The federal government ignored petitions for territorial status until 28 February 1861, when, stung by the secession of the Southern states, including Texas, President James Buchanan, four days before the end of his term, signed the law creating Colorado Territory.

Two days later, Buchanan signed the law organizing Dakota Territory, encompassing a vast area of the Plains but also the new mining districts of what would become Montana and Idaho. Dakota Territory changed its shape frequently until 1868, when it reached the

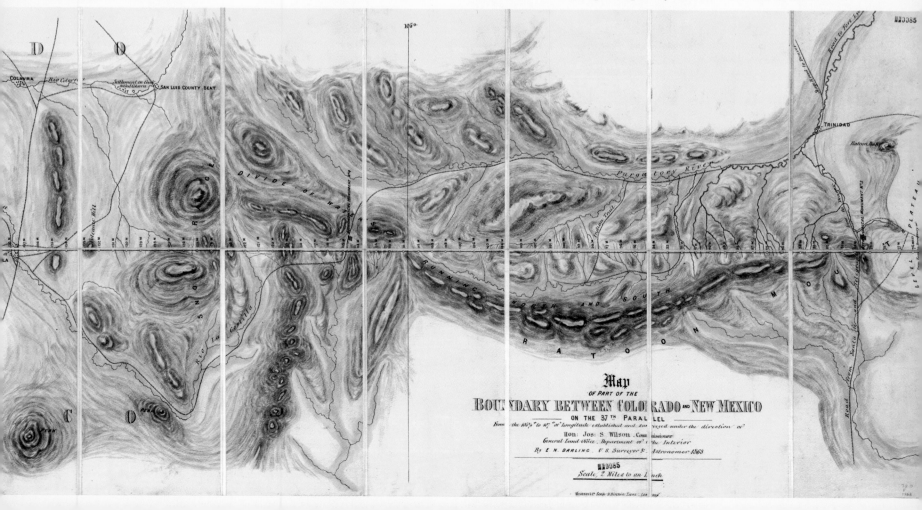

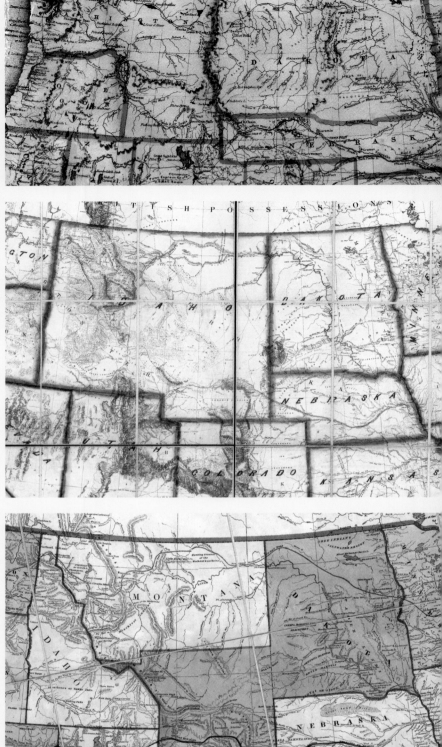

Map 403 (above).

The West in 1861. Mapmakers of this period had a difficult time keeping up with all the political changes to the West, many of which occurred in that year. *Oregon*, reduced in size, had become a state in 1859, leaving the remaining part of its territory to be added to Washington. The "long" *Arizona* shown is that proposed by a provisional government in Tucson in 1860; it would also be the shape of the short-lived Confederate state proclaimed in 1863. *Nevada* Territory, organized in 1861, is on this map but clearly as a revision to an earlier map edition where *Utah* stretched to *California*. The northern part of *Nebraska* Territory shown became Dakota Territory in 1861; the *Dakota* territory shown on this map is the unorganized part that existed before, created when Minnesota became a state in 1858. Colorado Territory is not shown but was also organized in 1861.

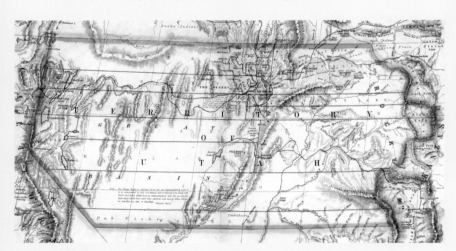

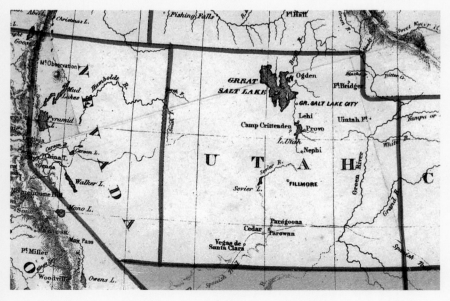

Map 404 (above, top), Map 405 (above, center), and Map 406 (above).

The changing face of Dakota Territory. Map 404 shows the territory as created in 1861, formed from the smaller, unorganized Dakota Territory (as on Map 403) and part of Nebraska Territory. In 1863 the large Idaho Territory was organized from the eastern part of Washington Territory and the western part of Dakota Territory, leaving the map as on Map 405. But the following year, with the organization of Montana Territory and a redefined Idaho, the southeastern quadrant of Idaho Territory was reattached to Dakota Territory (Map 406), giving Dakota a strange shape that lasted until 1868. In that year the western part of Dakota became Wyoming Territory, leaving Dakota as it would be until 1889 and its division into two states. Being a commercial mapmaker in these years of constant change must have been problematic.

Map 407 (left, center).

The *Territory of Utah* on an 1857 map. Utah stretches from today's Colorado west to Nevada.

Map 408 (left, bottom).

This 1864 map shows *Nevada* Territory as created in 1861 and as admitted as a state in 1864, with its eastern boundary at 115° W and missing the southern tip; an eastern strip of land nearly to 114° W and the southern tip were added in 1866.

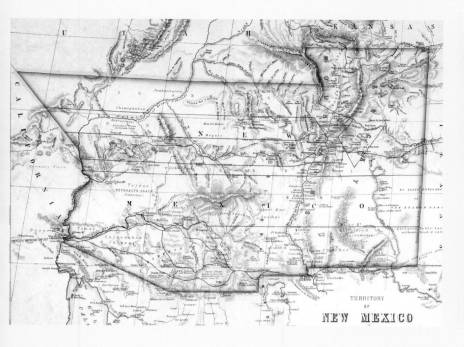

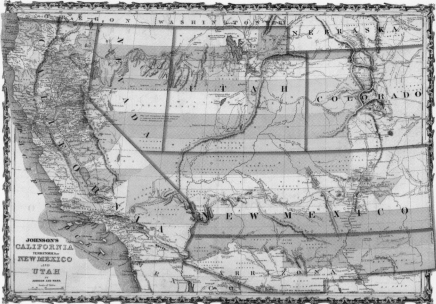

position and shape that would be divided into the two states of North and South Dakota in 1889 (MAP 404, MAP 405, and MAP 406, *left*).

Nevada Territory was created the same day. Although it still did not have the population usually required, the region's gold and silver mines tipped the scales. The Union's need for gold still applied three years later, when Nevada was made a state (MAP 408, *left, bottom*).

The Union Arizona Territory was created out of New Mexico Territory during the Civil War, but there had been briefly a Confederate Arizona, which divided New Mexico east–west. The reason for this "horizontal" division was twofold: most of the Confederate sympathizers lived around Tucson and Mesilla, in the south, and the Confederacy hoped to create a continuous swathe of territory to the Pacific (see MAP 215, *page 110*). The Union Arizona Territory, created in February 1863, was divided north–south from the rest of New Mexico Territory with the deliberate intention of foiling Confederate designs.

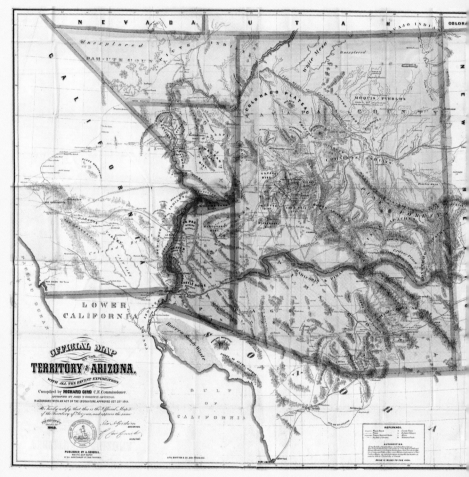

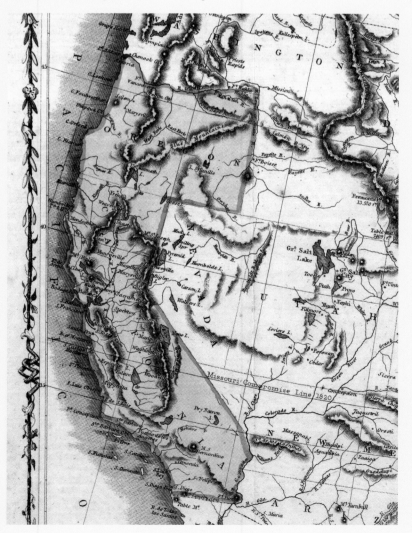

MAP 409 (*above, top left*).
New Mexico Territory in 1857. The northeastern projection above 37° N is well shown; this is the part lost to the new Colorado Territory in 1861. The northwestern tip is that part lost to the state of Nevada in 1866.

MAP 410 (*above, top right*).
This 1862 map depicts the Confederate *Arizona. Colorado* had now removed the northeastern part of *New Mexico,* but the northwestern tip is still part of the latter. *Nevada* is "thin"; it would gain territory on the east from *Utah* in 1866 along with a southern extension gained from Arizona.

MAP 411 (*above*).
Arizona Territory in 1865, complete with the portion west of the *Colorado River* lost to Nevada the following year. Note the several mining districts along the east bank of the Colorado.

MAP 412 (*left*).
On a map of American states published in 1861, a new "island" of California, this time with Oregon, stands out. For a long time the most populous regions of the West, California became a state in 1850 and Oregon in 1859.

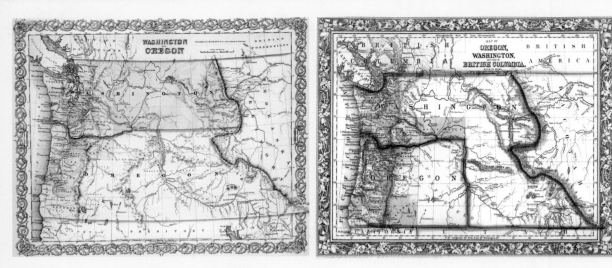

MAP 413 (*far left*).
Washington Territory and *Oregon* Territory as they were from 1853 to 1859.

MAP 414 (*left*).
Washington Territory and *Oregon* Territory in 1859, the year Oregon became a state, with a reduced size.

MAP 415 (*left, center top*).
Idaho Territory as it was for just over a year, between 4 March 1863 and 28 May 1864. The eastern half of Washington has become the western half of Idaho.

MAP 416 (*left, center bottom*).
The Pacific Northwest in 1864. A new *Idaho* Territory has been created west of the Rockies, while *Montana* Territory now covers what was most of the northern part of Idaho. The yellow area at center has now returned to *Dakota* Territory until 1868, when it would become Wyoming Territory.

In the Pacific Northwest, Washington Territory had been organized in 1853, with both that territory and Oregon Territory still extending east to the Rockies (MAP 413, *above, far left*). In 1859 Oregon was admitted as a state, but only after removing the eastern part of the territory from the application; this left an even larger Washington Territory (MAP 414, *above*). A very large Idaho Territory was created in 1863 (MAP 415, *left*) and then, the next year, split again to create both Montana Territory and an Idaho Territory similar in extent to the present state; these changes were to accommodate the increasing population of the mining districts of the northern Rocky Mountains. The remainder of the former large Idaho went back to Dakota Territory; in 1868 it would become Wyoming Territory (MAP 416, *left*).

Only Oklahoma and the remnant Indian Territory remained unorganized. Oklahoma was opened to EuroAmerican settlement by a series of land runs, beginning in 1889 (see pages 154–55), but the territory was not created until 1890. Between 1902 and 1905 the Indians of the Indian Territory unsuccessfully lobbied for a separate state to be called Sequoyah, but their efforts were ignored when Oklahoma became a state in 1907, by a merger of Oklahoma Territory and Indian Territory.

MAP 417 (*below*).
Oklahoma Territory, at left, created in 1890, with the remaining Indian Territory in 1892. Both lasted until 1907, when the state of Oklahoma combined the two, and, other than reservations that were getting smaller all the time (see page 155), no land remained of the once essentially complete Indian ownership of the West.

MAP 418 (*below, right*).
Where boundaries were defined as rivers there was an ongoing problem where rivers shifted their courses, as the meandering streams of the Plains were wont to do. Nowhere was this problem better illustrated than at the Red River, the boundary between Oklahoma (and its previous constituent area, the Indian Territory) and Texas. Here an 1895 U.S. Geological Survey map of the Red River documents the changes in the river's course. One of the major rivers of the West, the Rio Grande, also alters its course from time to time, and since many miles of it are an international boundary, a commission, now called the International Boundary and Water Commission, was created to deal with the fluctuating channels of the river. In 1963, in the largest settlement of its kind, Mexico gave the United States 437 acres and the United States gave Mexico a different 193 acres to end a long-standing dispute due to the Rio Grande changing its course near El Paso.

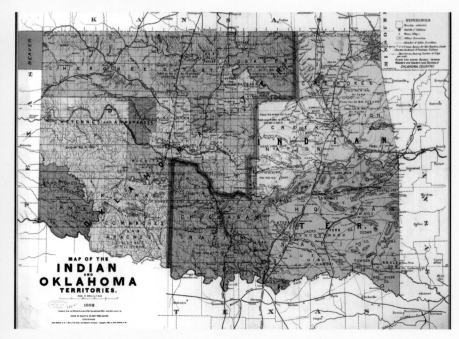

The last western frontier—if such a term still applied at all—moved beyond the lower forty-eight. The Kingdom of Hawaii was annexed in 1898, and Alaska, previously a mere administrative district, became a territory in 1912.

Americans had been interested in Alaska ever since the Russian-American Company made agreements with American fur traders to supply their outposts. A visit by Charles Wilkes and his United States Exploring Expedition in 1841 excited little American interest. By 1866 the Russian-American Company was almost bankrupt and appealed to the Russian government to save it. But the Russians did not save—they sold, offering Alaska to the United States to keep it out of the hands of Britain. Secretary of State William H. Seward, an expansionist, seized the opportunity, and Alaska was purchased on 30 March 1867—at four in the morning—for $7.2 million, a bargain at a little under two cents an acre. The official transfer took place at Novo Archangel'sk—now Sitka—on 18 October 1867.

MAP 419 (*above*).
A map of Alaska compiled by the U.S. Exploring Expedition in 1841. It includes information from Russian sources about the extent of the ice pack to the north. The *R. Youcon* (Yukon) is shown erroneously flowing north to the Arctic Ocean when it in reality flows in a big loop west to *Norton S[oun]d*.

MAP 420 (*right*).
This 1821 map by Russian naval officer Vasili Berkh shows his country's territory extending east to Hudson Bay. In 1825 the Russians signed a treaty with Britain establishing 141° W as the eastern boundary of Russian America, and it remains the Alaska–Canada boundary today.

MAP 421 (*below*).
A political change to the territorial extent of the West on a par with the Louisiana Purchase or the acquisition of Upper California and New Mexico was the purchase of Alaska from Russia in 1867. This is the map prepared by the U.S. Coast Survey for the Department of the Interior that year. *Inset* is the Treasury Warrant with which the purchase was finally paid. Note the "Paid By Treasurer U.S." stamp dated 1 August 1868.

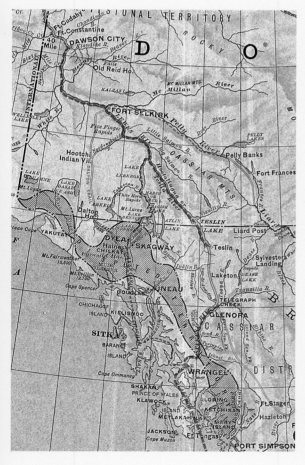

MAP 422 (*above*).
The area the United States had purchased from Russia was not exactly defined, and a dispute arose with Canada as to the location of the boundary in the Alaska Panhandle. It was settled by arbitration in 1903 after a British judge backed the American position, much to the disgust of the Canadians. This is a Canadian Pacific Steamships map depicting the area disputed.

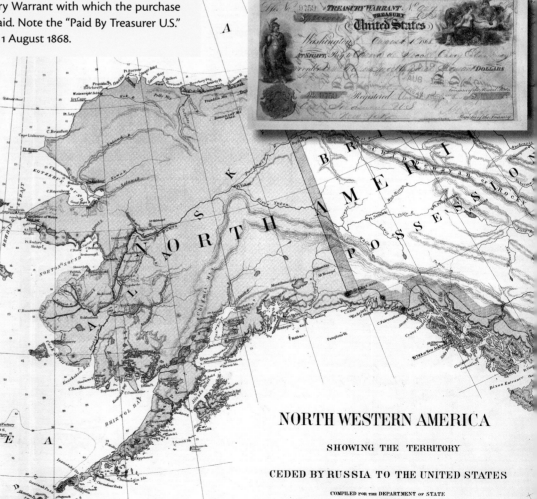

NORTH WESTERN AMERICA

SHOWING THE TERRITORY

CEDED BY RUSSIA TO THE UNITED STATES

COMPILED FOR THE DEPARTMENT OF STATE
at the
U.S. COAST SURVEY OFFICE
B. Peirce, Supt.
1867.

An Urban West

Nothing is more indicative of a nonfrontier society than the entirely artificial landscape of the modern city. By 1890, when, as some have postulated, the western frontier disappeared, the West had an already considerable network of urban places. Some arose from boom towns, servicing mineral discoveries, some were centers for a surrounding agrarian economy, and some were simply grown versions of an early settlement in a location too favored to abandon. One or two were harbors on a generally inhospitable West Coast. And more than a few were railroad towns, because the railroad, in the vast distances of the West, was an essential lifeline rival communities would fight each other for, and live or die by the results. This section examines the origins and history of the larger western cities and conglomerations, and a few smaller cities as well.

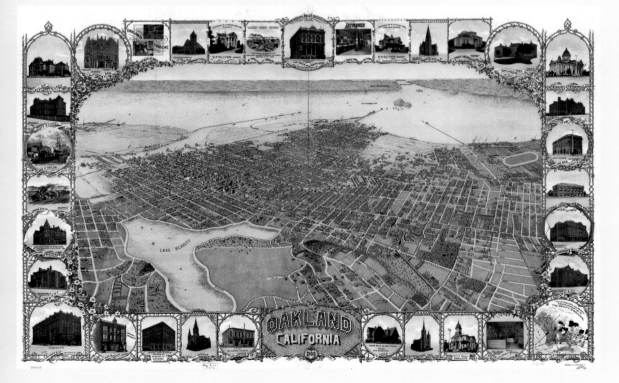

SAN FRANCISCO AND THE BAY AREA

San Francisco, of course, had its origins in the Spanish presidio and mission established on the bay in 1776 (see pages 40–42). A rare harbor, and one as spacious as San Francisco Bay, was destined for growth, and it came quickly during the gold rush. The influx of people, a shortage of buildings, and ship crews deserting led to ships being hauled up on the mudflats of Yerba Buena Cove and converted to warehouses (MAP 193, *page 101*); this began the process of land reclamation that has continued all around the Bay Area until modern times, when there has been a greater sensitivity to the ecological value of wetlands.

The railroad arrived in 1864 when the San Francisco and San Jose Railroad was completed between the two cities of its name. That line was soon acquired by the "Big Four's" Southern Pacific and connected to the Central Pacific, although the latter railroad moved its terminus from Sacramento to Oakland in 1869, providing a ferry across the Bay as a more convenient and direct connection to San Francisco.

Oakland had been incorporated in 1852, and for many decades the city promoted itself as a rival to San Francisco; a measure to create a consolidated metropolitan area with San Francisco at its center, on the ballot in 1912, was scuttled by Oakland politicians who saw no reason their city should not be the premier port of the Pacific Coast.

San Francisco's famous cable cars began service in 1873, the invention of Andrew Hallidie, owner of the California Wire Rope and Cable Company, and today survive as a tourist attraction.

The great earthquake and fire of 1906 strained San Francisco's resources to the utmost.

MAP 423 (*left, top*).
Because of San Francisco's early preeminence during the age when bird's-eye maps were popular, there are quite a few superb examples of such maps of the city. This one was published in 1868. Reclamation of the bay shoreline is already well underway, and a trestle, Long Bridge, has been constructed across Mission Bay, the original route to the Spanish Mission Dolores. Mission Bay would itself disappear, filled in, mainly with garbage, to create land for the railroad. Across the bay long wharves have been built at Oakland and Alameda.

MAP 424 (*left*).
The long wharves are also shown on this magnificent bird's-eye map of Oakland, looking west across the bay to San Francisco. In the foreground is *Lake Merritt*, donated to the city in 1867 by local resident Samuel Merritt. Although cut off from the bay by reclaimed land, it is connected by a channel and is still tidal. In 1869 Lake Merritt became the first national wildlife refuge in the United States.

MAP 425 (*left*).
San Jose, looking north, in 1875. Founded in 1777 as a Spanish pueblo, the city in 1850 became the first incorporated city in the new American state of California. Later it benefited from the founding in 1891 of Leland Stanford Junior University, better known as Stanford, twenty miles to the west. In recent decades the city has mushroomed, overtaking even San Francisco in population, with the growth of the computer industry in Silicon Valley.

The earthquake not only overturned stoves, starting the fire, but it also broke gas lines, which contributed to the fire's spread, and broke water lines, which prevented the fire from being contained. The resulting firestorm essentially burned itself out, with a little controversial help from the U.S. Army, which dynamited buildings in the fire's path. But San Francisco rebuilt at an amazing pace and in 1915 was able to host the Panama-Pacific International Exposition, which celebrated the opening of the Panama Canal but also highlighted the city's return to normality. A previously proposed urban development plan, developed by architect Daniel Burnham, was revived, and some of its proposals were brought to fruition—the Embarcadero, a waterfront boulevard; the Coit Tower atop Telegraph Hill; a neoclassical civic center; and some arterial thoroughfares.

MAP 427 (*below*).
The Exposition City—showing the *Panama Pacific Exposition* at top right—was fully recovered from the effects of the fire by 1912. This magnificent promotional bird's-eye map was published by the North American Press Association.

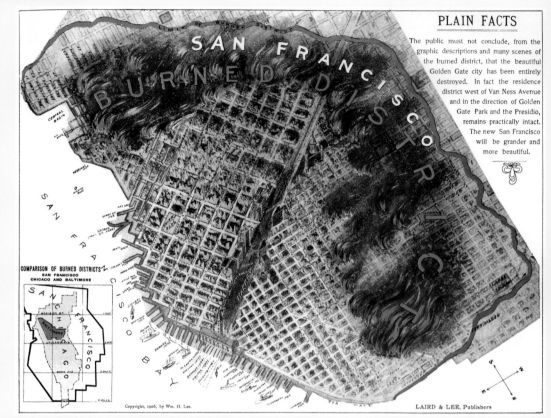

PLAIN FACTS

The public must not conclude, from the graphic descriptions and many scenes of the burned district, that the beautiful Golden Gate city has been entirely destroyed. In fact the residence district west of Van Ness Avenue and in the direction of Golden Gate Park and the Presidio, remains practically intact. The new San Francisco will be grander and more beautiful.

MAP 426 (*above*).
The 1906 San Francisco earthquake and fire were probably the world's first well-documented major disaster, as the city was home to numerous photographers who rushed out into the streets, photographing the fire even as it raged. A host of reports and books documenting the inferno answered the American and worldwide public need for information. Scientific reports led to revised building codes, but many books were in what one might politely call "popular" style. One such book was titled *The Doomed City—A Thrilling History of San Francisco's Destruction*, by Frank Thompson Searight. It contained this wonderful graphic map, which showed the coverage of the fire and also compared its area with previous disasters in other cities.

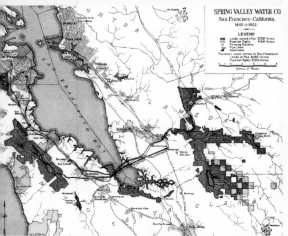

MAP 428 (*left*).
This 1922 map shows how San Francisco obtained its water from the East Bay. Spring Valley Water Company lines are in red. The city purchased the company in 1930.

MAP 429 (*right*).
When the Hetch Hetchy Aqueduct was under construction in 1930, this bird's-eye map was published to show its route.

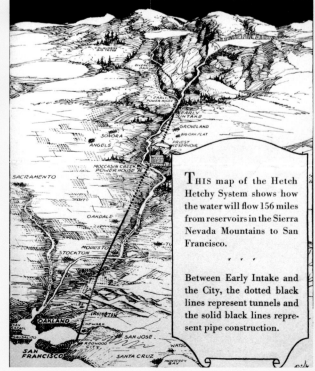

THIS map of the Hetch Hetchy System shows how the water will flow 156 miles from reservoirs in the Sierra Nevada Mountains to San Francisco.

Between Early Intake and the City, the dotted black lines represent tunnels and the solid black lines represent pipe construction.

Despite this success, San Francisco was never quite the preeminent center it once was, losing ground to the rising city to the south, Los Angeles. Between 1900 and 1930 San Francisco and the Bay Area more than doubled in size, but Los Angeles mushroomed tenfold.

As in many California and other western cities, water supply has always been an issue, more so for San Francisco because of its peninsular location. Water was piped from the East Bay area through a junction point named the Sunol Water Temple—its name reflecting its importance—but in 1910 the city had begun what would turn out to be a long process to obtain water from the Sierra Nevada. A dam was to be built in the Hetch Hetchy Valley in Yosemite National Park, and this proposal inflamed environmentalist John Muir to organize opposition, especially through the Sierra Club, which he had founded in 1892. The protests were to no avail, however, as the federal government granted San Francisco water rights to the valley in 1913. A dam was completed in 1923, but because of cost overruns and refinancings the Hetch Hetchy Aqueduct did not deliver its first water to San Francisco until 1934. The delays led the East Bay cities to construct their own Mokelumne Aqueduct from that river, well clear of the national park.

Los Angeles

Water was even more important for the growth of the urban area of the Los Angeles Basin, and twice the city built major aqueducts to bring water from faraway sources.

Los Angeles was another Spanish pueblo—El Pueblo de Nuestra Señora la Reyna de los Angeles del Río de Porciúncula—established in 1781.

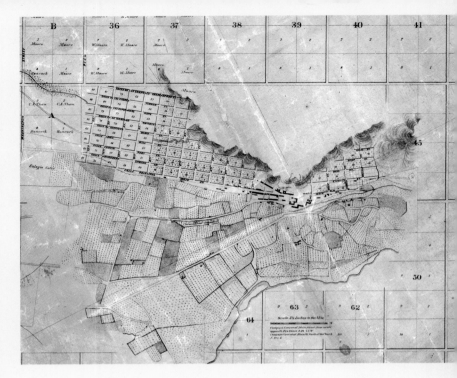

Map 430 (*above*).
A copy of the first survey of Los Angeles, made by Lieutenant Edward Otho Cresap Ord in 1849. The original pueblo, with existing buildings, is at center right. Agricultural lots are shown with dots, and some irrigation ditches are shown. First for agricultural and later for household and commercial use, water would prove to be critical to the city's expansion.

Map 431 (*below*).
Los Angeles in 1887, just before the major boom in real estate that took place that year. The view is over Elysian Park, looking south to the Palos Verdes and Catalina Island beyond. Illustrations of subscriber businesses and residents' houses line the top and bottom of the map in the typical bird's-eye style.

LOS ANGELES, CAL.
LOOKING SOUTH-WEST TO PACIFIC OCEAN
3-1887-E

Map 432 (*above*).
Los Angeles in 1894, at the end of the first major real estate boom, shown in an unusual double-view bird's-eye map. The Los Angeles River is at center on the top map, with the original townsite between it and the mountains. The bottom map, looking south, shows that the city would have ample room for expansion.

Map 433 (*below*).
A superb real estate sales map of *Hollywood*, laid out for sale by Harvey Henderson Wilcox in 1887. His wife, Daeida, thought up the name. Many such developments did not prosper, but Hollywood did. By 1900 it had five hundred residents. It incorporated in 1903 but joined Los Angeles in 1910 in order to share that city's water.

After the American takeover, the city fathers lost no time in getting a detailed survey made (Map 430, *above, left*) so that they could sell land to pay for the necessary confirmation of the land holdings of residents.

Beginning in the late nineteenth century, a series of real estate booms fueled the growth of the city. Oil was discovered at the beginning of the twentieth, and soon oil rigs dotted the city's landscape, even in residents' backyards (see Map 297, *page 144*). An extensive urban rail system, the Pacific Electric, began to cover the region in 1901 and was, at its peak, the largest electrically operated railway in the world. It would eventually lose out to another transportation system Los Angeles has become famous for—its road and freeway system (see page 248).

Los Angeles acquired a port at San Pedro in 1907 and connected it to the city by the acquisition of a long strip of land called the Shoestring Addition, shown on Map 435, *overleaf*. This map illustrates what Los Angeles did very well—grow by additions and annexations. And it was able to do this because it could offer the one thing every jurisdiction in Southern California had to have—water.

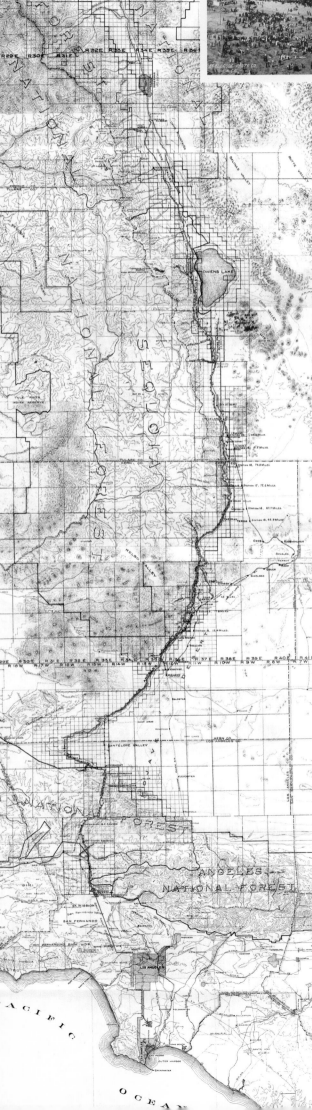

The plan to bring Los Angeles water from the Owens Valley, over 220 miles away, was the brainchild of municipal water engineer William Mulholland. It led to a battle over the water of the valley, which was slated to become a federal Reclamation Service irrigation project. The needs of the greater number of people—and voters—of the urban area of Los Angeles won out over the needs of the relatively few farmers of the Owens Valley.

MAP 434 (*left*).
A 1908 map of the entire Los Angeles Aqueduct, then under construction. The map was produced by the Los Angeles Department of Water and Power. The Owens Valley is at top. At the southern end are the two *Fernando Reservoirs*, and beyond them the first of several distribution pipelines, the *Projected Pipeline*, carries the water to *Los Angeles*. The Lower San Fernando Dam partially failed during an earthquake in 1971, and the reservoirs were drained. A new dam, the Los Angeles Dam, was constructed in 1975–76 three times stronger than the original two.

Above. Water cascades into the San Fernando Valley for the first time on 5 November 1913.

MAP 435 (*below*).
A great deal of the growth of the city of Los Angeles accrued from annexations, and most of those of jurisdictions anxious to avail themselves of Los Angeles's water. This is a 1916 annexation map, showing eighteen annexations to that date. The original Spanish grant, four leagues square, is the yellow square. The *Shoestring Addition* ties the city to its port at *San Pedro*. The *San Fernando Addition*, most of the San Fernando Valley, more than doubled the city's size in 1915. Note also the *City of Hollywood*, annexed in 1910. A table of annexations, with acreages and dates, is at bottom left.

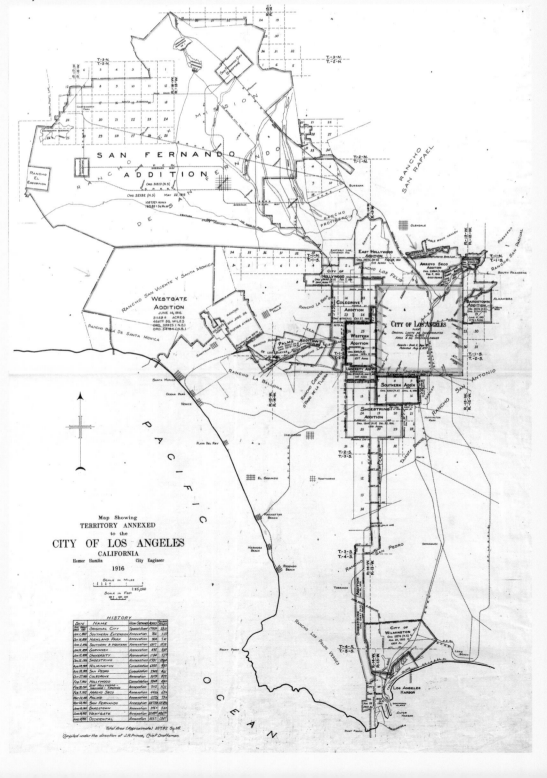

Construction began on the aqueduct in 1908. Some hundred thousand workers were employed fabricating, excavating, and laying the 223-mile-long, 12-foot-diameter pipe, and building two hydroelectric plants, and 170 miles of power lines. A railroad was built, as were 215 miles of roads. The aqueduct was completed in 1913 and gave the city of Los Angeles unprecedented power to annex its neighbors, for if they were not annexed, their access to the water was denied. Capacity was increased in 1940 with a forty-mile extension northward, and in 1970 another pipeline, on a similar route to the first, doubled the aqueduct's capacity. Los Angeles also built the Colorado Aqueduct, completed in 1939, to bring water from the Colorado (see page 241).

Mulholland's reputation suffered in 1928 when his St. Francis Dam, in the San Francisquito Canyon north of Saugus, collapsed, killing more than five hundred people. Only recently has it been shown that the cause was an ancient rockslide at one side of the dam; this was impossible to detect with the technology of the day.

MAP 436 (*right*).
This magnificent real estate sales map promoted a development in an area now part of Palm Springs and illustrates a clever promotion of the dry land of the eastern Los Angeles Basin. A veritable paradise awaits the purchaser: *Pure Mountain Water, Perfect Railroad Facilities, The Finest Oranges*, and *The Earliest Grapes; No Windstorms, No Frost*, and *Perpetual Summer*. The street plan includes *Good Luck Avenue*—in the shape of a horseshoe—and fruity avenues like *Mango* and *Banana, Date* and *Pine Apple*. Despite the extravagant promotion, the project failed, and little trace of the street pattern remains.

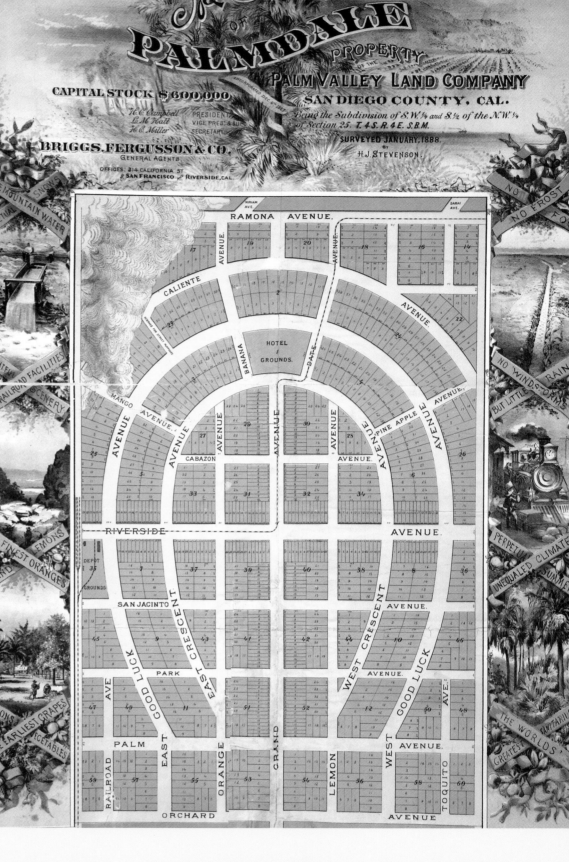

SAN DIEGO

San Diego, created as a Mexican pueblo in 1834, had grown up on the banks of the San Diego River downstream from the mission. In 1850 Andrew Gray, a boundary surveyor–turned–real estate speculator, teamed up with William Heath Davis, a San Francisco financier, to lay out New San Diego on San Diego Bay (MAP 437, *overleaf*). Davis brought in a shipment of prefabricated wooden houses from Maine and persuaded the U.S. Army to establish a barracks there. But the settlement was not a success; the wharf was rammed by a steamer and not repaired, and then it was ripped up for fuel by the troops stationed there in 1861–62. Many residents who had moved their houses from the first San Diego simply moved their houses back again. New San Diego all but disappeared.

In 1867 real estate entrepreneur Alonzo Erastus Horton arrived and saw immediately the potential San Diego held. He purchased 960 acres

adjacent to the original New San Diego for just $265—an area that today encompasses most of downtown San Diego (MAP 438, *overleaf*). To do that he had also to pay $10 to get an election held—to create trustees that could authorize the sale. Horton successfully promoted his new town in San Francisco so that by 1870 San Diego had a population of 2,300, with 915 occupied houses and 69 businesses.

The next requirement was a railroad, but this was slow in coming owing to the difficulty—and expense—of the topography of all possible routes into the town. The Texas & Pacific Railway was chartered in 1871 specifically to link San Diego to the East, and real estate boomed because of it, but the railroad failed, and it was not until 1885 that a link was finally made, by the California Southern, a Santa Fe subsidiary, which connected to existing lines.

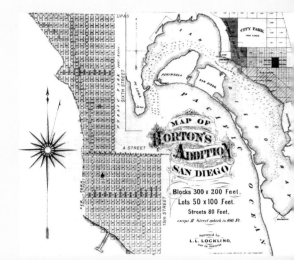

MAP 437 (*left*).
Andrew Gray's New San Diego, laid out in 1850.

MAP 438 (*right*).
Alonzo Horton's 1867 addition, which revitalized New San Diego. The inset map shows its position east and north of Gray's original town. Blocks were made short to create more corner lots, which sold for a higher price.

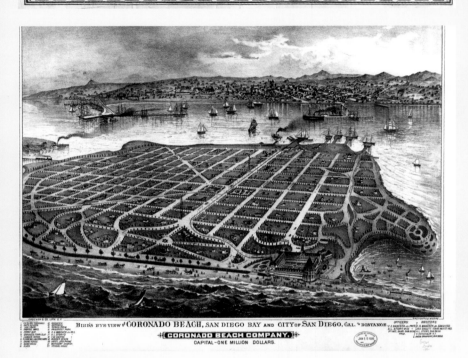

MAP 439 (*above*).
The Coronado Beach Company began developing land across the harbor as a resort community in 1886 and sold 350 lots in one day—13 November 1886—recouping its cost of purchasing the entire peninsula. Then the real estate boom collapsed. The company's world-famous Hotel del Coronado, shown at bottom right, still stands, and the subdivision is the city of Coronado.

MAP 440 (*above*).
San Diego, like most of the West Coast, anticipated great things from the opening of the Panama Canal in 1913. This postcard map from 1915 promotes the location of the city as the *First Port of Call*.

MAP 441 (*below, left*).
Sacramento in 1870. The Sacramento River is in the foreground, the American River in the background.

CENTRAL VALLEY CITIES

California's state capital, which now surrounds Sutter's Fort (see page 98), was laid out in 1850 by John Augustus Sutter's son in competition with Suttersville, a townsite laid out by his father. The survey was carried out by William Warner, an Army officer (MAP 442, *above, right*). The elder Sutter's site flooded more readily than the son's, and so the latter site prevailed.

Sacramento became the state capital in 1855 and thrived as the center of the agricultural region of the American and middle Sacramento valleys.

Most of the other cities of California's Central Valley began life when the Southern Pacific located a station there. The original plat of Fresno (MAP 446, *far right, bottom*) is typical. The station was constructed in 1872 as the railroad built its line south to Los Angeles. Fresno was incorporated as a city in 1895. A key agricultural center, it bills itself still as the "raisin capital of the world."

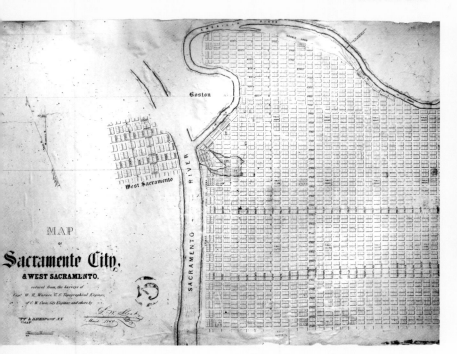

MAP 442 (*above*).
William Warner's plat of Sacramento, surveyed and drawn in 1850.

MAP 443 (*above*).
A black-and-white classical bird's-eye map of *Sacramento* in the 1890s. Businesses and residences border the map, crowned at center, top, with the state capitol.

MAP 444 (*below, center*).
Another superb promotional bird's-eye map, this one of *Fresno*, published in 1901. Note the rail line and depot, also shown in MAP 446, *below*.

MAP 445 (*left, bottom*).
Stockton in 1895. *Stockton Channel*, which connects the city with San Francisco Bay, is at left.

MAP 446 (*below*).
As with countless other western cities, Fresno had its beginnings as a townsite platted along a rail line. This 1886 map shows the Southern Pacific *Depot Grounds*.

Farther south, Bakersfield was founded in 1863 by Colonel Thomas Baker, who moved to the area to begin reclaiming the frequently flooded lands of the Kern River (see MAP 347, *page 166*). The 1901 bird's-eye map of the community (MAP 447, *overleaf*) is typical of the splendid promotional maps of the bird's-eye type as towns and cities competed among each other for regional preeminence.

Stockton (MAP 445, *left, bottom*), with water access to San Francisco Bay, was founded on a Mexican land grant in 1847 by Charles Weber, who had arrived in California with the Bartleson–Bidwell party in 1841. He initially named his city Tuleburg but changed it on incorporation to honor Commodore Robert F. Stockton.

Map 447 (*right*).
Yet another stunning promotional bird's-eye map of a Central Valley city; this is *Bakersfield* in 1901. The view is to the northeast. The map is full of interest. As the center of the *Kern River Oil District* (see Map 298, *page 144*) oil scenes dominate the surrounding cameos. The district is located at top left on the map. Also shown are the *Calloway Wier [sic] and Headgate*—part of the irrigation system—and a *Southern Pacific Oil Train*. The Southern Pacific depot is shown on the map at bottom left, complete with the locomotive roundhouse. Bakersfield was incorporated as a city in 1874, but then it reversed the incorporation two years later in order to rid itself of a city marshal. The city incorporated again in 1898. Kern City is now within the built-up area of Bakersfield, but the name was used for a retirement community built by Del Webb (see page 256) in the 1960s.

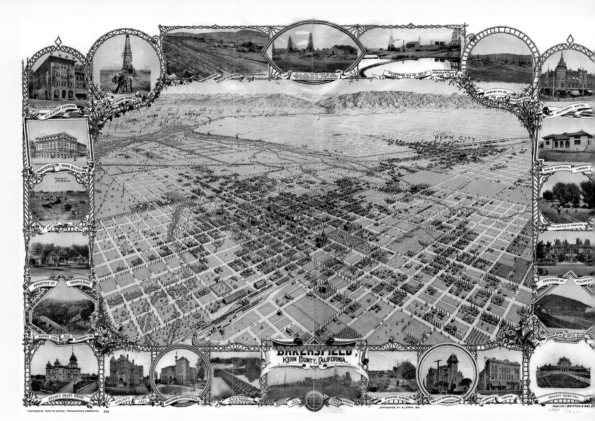

LAS VEGAS

At this one time brief Anasazi settlement, John Charles Frémont had noted the pure warm-water springs at a place the Spanish had named Las Vegas—the meadows—and put it on his map (Map 448, *right*). Mormon missionaries set up an adobe fort in the valley in 1855.

In 1902 James T. McWilliams surveyed the valley and filed a claim for eighty acres, on which, in late 1904, he laid out a townsite, anticipating the arrival of the San Pedro, Los Angeles & Salt Lake Railroad (Map 449, *right*), and his town soon boasted a motley selection of wood-frame and canvas houses, a hotel, and stores. But he had not reckoned with the railroad's founder, Montana Senator William A. Clark, who laid out another town—which he also named Las Vegas—on the east side of the line of track. Clark's Las Vegas Land and Water Company sold a few lots but, faced with overwhelming demand, decided to hold an auction instead. Three thousand people showed up for the auction; they were mainly investors from Los Angeles and Salt Lake to whom the company offered cheap rail tickets and a refund if they purchased a lot. Clark's townsite won the day, and many of McWilliams's residents—who had built their structures on skids—simply towed them across the tracks to the new site. Clark's victory was a classic in western land promotion.

The railroad, which was sold to the Union Pacific in 1921, provided a good job base for the town, but the building of the Boulder Dam in the 1930s (see page 238) gave the town a huge boost, and at a time when others were suffering. The era of casinos and the world-famous Las Vegas Strip began in 1942 when Los Angeles hotel owner Tom Hull built the first casino (with a hotel) after noticing how many tourists were passing the town; he decided to take advantage of the fact that a financially strapped Nevada had legalized gambling in 1931 to help its economy during the Depression.

Map 448 (*above*).
The spring and meadows at *Vegas* are noted on Frémont's 1848 map.

Map 449 (*right, center top*).
McWilliams's 1904 Las Vegas townsite, west of the line of the railroad, shown at right.

Map 450 (*right, center bottom*).
Clark's competing 1905 *Las Vegas Townsite*, now the city's downtown.

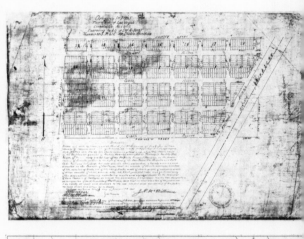

THE PACIFIC NORTHWEST

Oregon's principal city, Portland, grew up at the point on the Willamette River found to be the highest safe point for ocean-going ships. In 1843, using a land claim system set up by a provisional government in Oregon City, farther upstream, William Overton, an emigrant from Tennessee, filed a claim, giving his lawyer, Asa Lawrence Lovejoy, a half-interest in return for doing the filing and paying the fee. Thus did Lovejoy obtain half of what is now downtown Portland for twenty-five cents. The next year Overton moved on, selling his interest to Francis W. Pettygrove, a merchant, for fifty dollars' worth of supplies.

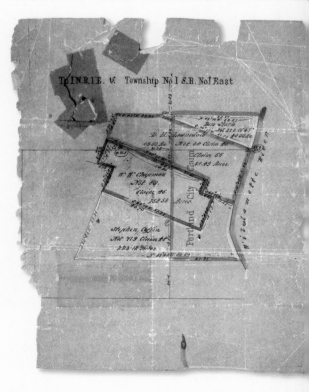

JAMES McI. WOOD,
REAL + ESTATE + AND + INVESTMENT + BROKER,
PORTLAND, OREGON.
1890.

Lovejoy and Pettygrove argued about a name for their town, and on the flip of a coin, the city-to-be became Portland instead of Boston. The advantages of Portland over competing townsites became increasingly apparent as trade grew after the international boundary was drawn in 1846.

Seattle, on Puget Sound, was another major city that began life as a land claim. Arthur A. Denny, Carson D. Boren, and William Bell claimed land on the east side of Elliott Bay in 1852 after first attempting to settle on the more exposed west side of the bay at Alki Point. They were soon joined by others, such as Henry L. Yesler, a lumberman from Portland who built a steam-powered sawmill. Seattle was named after the local Indian Chief Seattle.

Seattle, however, lost out to Tacoma, near the head of Puget Sound, in the competition to be the first Puget Sound railroad terminus. In 1873 the

BIRD'S EYE VIEW OF
SALEM, OREGON
FROM THE WEST, LOOKING EAST.
1876.

MAP 451 (left, bottom).
The ownership of Portland in 1850. The land ownership beyond Pettygrove and Lovejoy shown on this map is derived thus: Benjamin Stark purchased a half-interest from Lovejoy in 1845; his interest, though a smaller area, included most of the buildings. Pettygrove sold his half-interest in 1848, when he left for the goldfields of California, to Daniel H. *Lownsdale,* a tanner, for leather worth $5,000. Lownsdale in turn sold half of his interest to *Stephen Coffin,* an emigrant New Englander, for $6,000. In December 1849 Lownsdale and Coffin sold part of their land to William W. Chapman, an Oregon City lawyer. And so, as with countless other successful western townsites, the land was sequentially subdivided, increasing in value at each transaction.

MAP 452 (above).
A classic bird's-eye map of *Portland* in 1890. The view is to the east, over Portland toward East Portland across the Willamette River.

MAP 453 (right, center).
An 1876 bird's-eye map of *Salem,* the capital of Oregon, in the central Willamette Valley. Salem was first platted in 1850–51.

MAP 454 (below).
Seattle in 1878. In the foreground is Elliott Bay, part of Puget Sound; in the background is Lake Washington, with Lake Union to the left.

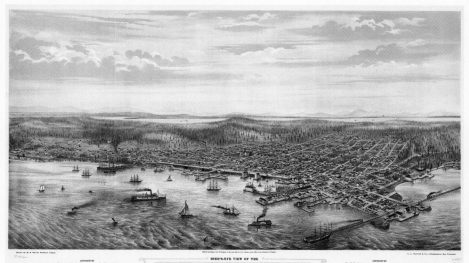

BIRD'S-EYE VIEW OF THE
CITY OF SEATTLE,
Puget Sound, Washington Territory, 1878.

Northern Pacific selected Commencement Bay as the terminus of its transcontinental line, and a line from Kalama, on the Columbia, was completed the same year. Because of this connecting line, Puget Sound and Portland were connected to a transcontinental link at the same time, in 1883, when the Northern Pacific connected to the Oregon Railway and Navigation line at Wallula Junction (see Map 253, *page 127*). Seattle was directly connected with the East in 1893 with the completion of the Great Northern Railway.

The railroad considerably boosted the prospects of Washington's largest interior city, Spokane (Map 458, *right*). Close to the site of the North West Company post, Spokane House, established in 1826, the city was connected to the west via the Northern Pacific in 1873 and to the East ten years later; and the Great Northern arrived in 1892. Incorporated as Spokane Falls in 1881, the city, like Seattle, suffered a devastating fire in 1889.

Farther west, Boise, the principal city of Idaho, began life as a center for the gold discoveries nearby and as a military establishment from where the U.S. Army could protect both the goldfields and the Oregon Trail from Indian attack. The Army selected the site as the location for a new Fort Boise in 1863, and the city was platted close by (Map 459, *right*).

Map 455 (*above*).
A superb bird's-eye map of Seattle in 1891, which emphasizes the downtown area as brick-built following a great fire two years earlier, the same year that Washington was admitted to the Union. The 6 June 1889 fire leveled sixty acres—more than thirty blocks of the city. Alki Point, first settled by Arthur Denny in 1851 and then abandoned, is at left. This map illustrates the positions of *Lake Washington* (the large lake at top right) and *Lake Union* (at left center). In 1917 (though not officially completed until 1934) a system of locks and channels joined the two lakes, permitting access to Lake Washington from Puget Sound. The idea had been around for some time; this map shows a narrow connection between the two lakes, the Montlake log canal, first cut in 1861 and enlarged in 1883. The shallow southern part of Elliott Bay (at bottom right) would eventually be filled in, using in part fill from the regrading of Seattle's downtown hills. *Great Northern* railroad track runs to the harbor from the north; the company would complete its direct transcontinental link to Seattle in 1893. Also visible are the three different street orientations of the city center, the result of three different original owners.

Map 456 (*below*).
This bird's-eye map of *Tacoma* in 1885 takes care to note that it is the western terminus of the Northern Pacific (*N.P.R.R.*) on Puget Sound. The harbor is depicted as alive with activity, a typical feature of this type of map.

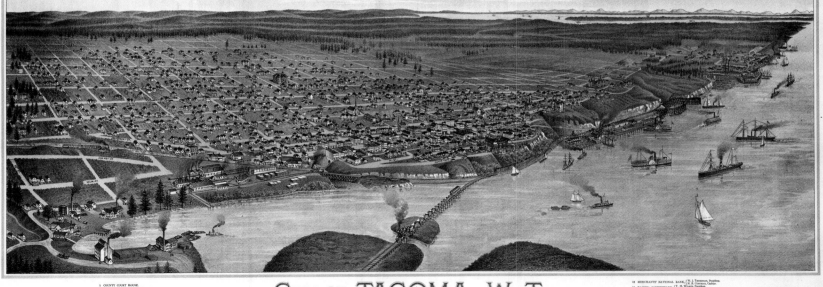

CITY OF TACOMA, W. T.
WESTERN TERMINUS OF N.P.R.R. PUGET SOUND.
1885.

TACOMA, WASHINGTON.
1893.

SPOKANE FALLS, W.T.
1884

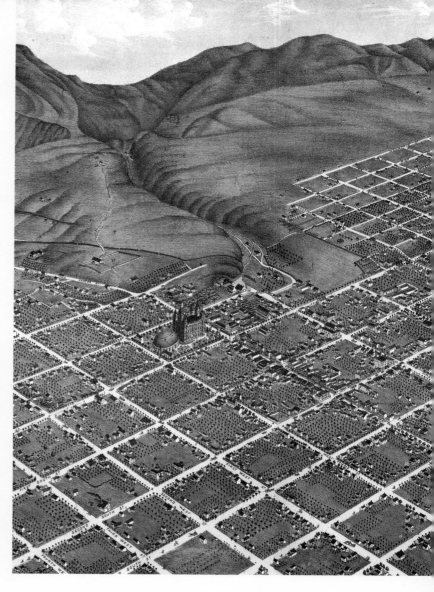

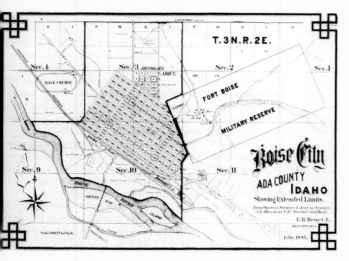

Map 457 (*above, top*).
Tacoma in an 1893 bird's-eye.

Map 458 (*above*).
Spokane Falls, today Spokane, Washington, in 1884.

Map 459 (*left*).
This 1865 map shows *Boissee City* (Boise) in the Snake River valley close to *Ft. Boisee;* the latter was the Hudson's Bay Company fort, while Boise was the U.S. Army site.

Map 460 (*left*).
Boise City in 1885, when the city limits were expanded. *Fort Boise Military Reserve* is adjacent.

Map 461 (*above, right*).
Detail of an 1870 bird's-eye map of Salt Lake City, showing the Mormon Temple and Tabernacle. The temple (*1*) was authorized by Brigham Young in 1847 but was not actually completed until about 1892; the tabernacle (*2*) was completed in 1867 and used a design that required few nails, since they were hard to obtain on a large scale. Wooden pegs and rawhide bindings were used instead.

Map 462 (*right*).
The fine cover of this 1915 advertising brochure depicted a bird's-eye view of *Salt Lake City* in that year and a somewhat stylized view of the Mormons descending in 1849 into the valley of the Great Salt Lake.

GARFIELD BEACH
REACHED ONLY BY THE UNION PACIFIC RY.

AMERICAN NATIONAL BANK
INTERIOR & EXTERIOR VIEW

PROGRESS BUILDING.

HOTEL ONTARIO.

SALT LAKE

75-696616.

PUBLIC BUILDINGS.	RAILROADS
1 The Temple.	17 U. P. Passenger Station.
2 The Tabernacle.	18 U. P. Freight Depot.
3 Assembly Hall.	19 U. P. Shops.
4 City Hall.	20 Rio Grande Western Passenger Station.
5 Capitol Building.	21 Rio Grande Western Freight Depot.
6 Post Office.	22 Rio Grande Western Shops.
7 Utah Exposition.	23 Utah & Nevada Passenger Station.
8 Court House.	24 Utah Central.
9 Fire Department.	25 Utah Central Freight Depot
10 Hospital of the Holy Cross.	
11 Industrial Home.	SCHOOLS.
12 Masonic Temple.	26 Rowland Hall.
13 Odd Fellows Hall.	27 Salt Lake Collegiate Institute.
HOTELS.	28 Salt Lake Acadamy and Hammond Hall.
14 The Cullen. S. G. Ewing, Prop'r.	29 Salt Lake Seminary.
15 The Ontario.	30 St. Mary's Seminary.
16 Hotel Knutsford.	31 Deseret University.
	32 Deaf and Dumb Institute.
	33 All Hallow's College.

SALT LAKE CITY

The religious beginnings of Salt Lake City are unique for a major western city. The site was selected by Brigham Young in July 1847 mainly because the valley was otherwise unsettled by EuroAmericans; avoiding the hostility that the Mormons had faced in their previous locations was an overriding criterion for Young. They had traveled beyond the boundaries of the United States only to find that the United States almost simultaneously expanded to include their chosen land (see page 96), and they

would come into conflict with the U.S. Army before long (see page 111). Denied statehood as Deseret, the Mormons had to be satisfied with the creation of Utah Territory in 1850. The state of Utah followed, in 1896, only after the Mormons promised not to practice polygamy.

The settlement of the Salt Lake valley depended from the beginning upon irrigation (see MAP 183, *page 96,* and MAP 353, *page 168*). When the first transcontinental railroad was completed in 1869, migration to the valley became much less arduous. One of the principal investors in the Union Pacific was none other than Brigham Young. The Mormon-

POPPERTON PLACE

H.WELLGE. SK.

ROUNDS
SOUTH WATER & FERRY STS. MILWAUKEE, WIS. U.S.A.
REAL ESTATE EXCHANGE.

WASATCH BUILDING.

MIDLAND INVESTMENT CO'S.
5 ACRE PLAT

AND

GRAND VIEW ADDITION

POPPERTON PLACE.

CITY, UTAH.

CHURCHES.

34 First Baptist.
35 First Congregational.
36 St. Mark's Cathedral. (Episcopal.)
37 St. Paul's Chapel. (Episcopal.)
38 Methodist Episcopal.
39 Presbyterian.
40 Reorganized Church of Jesus Christ of Latter Day
      Saints.
41 Phillips Congregational Church.
42 Westminster Presbyterian.
43 Swedish Evangelical. (Lutheran.)
44 First Skandanavian (M. E.)
45 St Mary Magdalen's. (Roman Catholic.)

SUBURBS AND PUBLIC PARKS.

48 Fort Douglas.
49 Garfield Beach.
50 8th Ward Square.
51 Old Fort Park.
52 Liberty Park.
53 Deseret Agricultural Society Driving Park.
54 Anderson Observatory.
55 City Reservoirs.

NEWSPAPERS.

56 The Herald.
57 The Tribune.
58 Evening Times.
59 The Deseret Evening News.

owned Utah Central Railroad, which connected Salt Lake City to the main line at Ogden, was completed in 1870.

An extensive streetcar system was built in Salt Lake City beginning in 1872, and the system was an early convert to electrification in 1889. The population of the entire valley, the so-called Wasatch Front urban area, which includes Ogden to the north (MAP 464, *overleaf*) and Provo to the south, now exceeds two million people.

MAP 463.

This magnificent bird's-eye map of Salt Lake City was published in 1891 and gives an excellent feel for the city's location adjacent to the *River Jordan* (at left) and the Great Salt Lake; the view is to the north. Part of the map's artistic appeal is due to the dramatic use of shade, apparently from clouds, although this has a deleterious effect on its usefulness as a map because some details are hard to see. But it was a real estate promotional map, and depicting an impressive city would sell land. Prominently depicted close to the mountains at the northern edge of the city are the Mormon Temple and Tabernacle, also shown in the cameo views at bottom center. The temple would have been close to completion by this date. To the north, the imposing building on the upland area is the Utah State capitol, actually not completed until 1915—nineteen years after Utah became a state and twenty-four years after this map was created.

Map 464 (*above, left*).
A beautifully engraved bird's-eye map of Ogden, published in 1875.

Map 465 (*above, right*).
Phoenix was so new that the engraver did not know how to spell the settlement's name on this 1879 map. *Phenix* is shown on the *Salt River* upstream of its confluence with the Gila on this 1879 map.

Map 466 (*left*).
The small city of Phoenix, a huge contrast to the metropolis of today, is showcased on this rather stunning bird's-eye from 1885, surrounded by views that emphasize water, verdant fields, and luxurious living. The view is to the northeast. Streets are named after presidents, with Washington and Jefferson at center. Later streets added new presidents ranging from Polk to Lincoln. The east–west streets retain their names today, but the north–south streets, which—as can been seen on this map—possessed much more western names, are now but soulless numbers.

Map 467 (*below*).
Today incorporated into the Phoenix metro area, *Tempe*, like Scottsdale and Mesa, was a separate settlement competing for growth with Phoenix itself. This bird's-eye, also beautifully executed, no doubt to rival that of Phoenix, was published to promote Tempe about 1888. The river is the Salt.

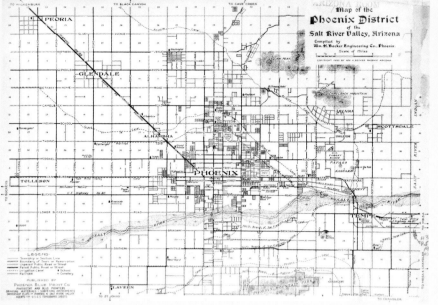

ARIZONA CAPITALS

When the first Arizona Territory was created—by the Confederate States of America in 1861—Tucson, a hotbed of Southern sympathizers, was selected as the capital. That capital, like Confederate Arizona, did not last long, owing to Union military victories in eastern New Mexico (see page 111).

When the Union created its Arizona Territory in 1863, Prescott, a mining center in the northern mountains—as far from Tucson as possible—was designated the territorial capital. Nevertheless, four years later Tucson managed to recapture the capital prize, keeping it for ten years until, in 1877, Prescott won it back again. Prescott retained its capital status for twelve years before losing it once more, but this time to an upstart Phoenix, which had not even been on the map when Arizona first became a territory.

Phoenix, as with all the surrounding settlements, owed its existence to the irrigation of the Salt River Valley, a rich agricultural area once watered and farmed by the Hohokam (see page 10). The ruins of these ancient ditches were noted by an ex–Confederate soldier, John William (Jack) Swilling, as he headed for the mining district to the north. In 1867 he created the Swilling Irrigating and Canal Company, hired unemployed miners and raised capital in Wickenburg, and began resuscitating the Hohokam system, cleaning out old ditches and building new ones. Phoenix, named for the mythical bird rising from the ashes, was born, and was incorporated in 1881. Other centers became established, notably Tempe, in 1871, and Mesa, in 1878.

In 1887 the Maricopa and Phoenix Railroad was completed, connecting both Tempe and Phoenix to the Southern Pacific main line. Phoenix had electric streetcars by 1893 and became the center for the Salt Valley Reclamation Project, one of the first irrigation projects to be carried out by the new U.S. Reclamation Service, created under the 1902 Newlands Reclamation Act (see pages 162–63). The advent of various forms of air conditioning beginning in the 1920s set the stage for today's metro Phoenix, with a population of over four million.

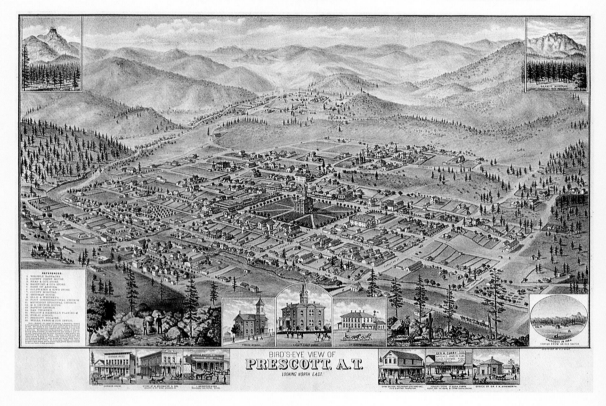

MAP 468 (*top left*).
Even in the 1930s *Phoenix* was a small town surrounded by irrigated areas, desert, and a few even smaller communities such as *Scottsdale* and *Tempe*.

MAP 469 (*top right*).
Tucson was a Spanish presidio and was acquired by the United States as part of the Gadsden Purchase of 1853–54. This 1877 map shows the small town north of the *San Xavier* Mission (see photo, *page 26*, and MAP 54, *page 34*).

MAP 470 (*above*).
A fine and detailed bird's-eye promotional map of *Prescott* published about 1885, during the city's second period as the capital of Arizona Territory.

ALBUQUERQUE

New Mexico's largest urban area, Albuquerque, was founded as the Spanish military outpost and villa of Alburquerque in 1706 (see page 29), on a site adjacent to the Rio Grande and the main route north to Santa Fe, the Camino Real.

In 1880 the Atchison, Topeka & Santa Fe Railroad reached the area but located its depot and yards two miles east of the old town. A community known as New Albuquerque grew up around the depot (MAP 471, *overleaf*), and this settlement was incorporated as the City of Albuquerque in 1891. The old town remained separate until 1920, when it was absorbed by the city.

DENVER

Denver was founded as a supply center for the goldfields of the Pike's Peak Gold Rush (see page 106) or, to be more exact, as several competing town-sites that were eventually merged (MAP 472, *left*). As the area had a low rainfall, water was brought from Rocky Mountain streams as early as 1867, when the twenty-four-mile-long Denver City Ditch was constructed from

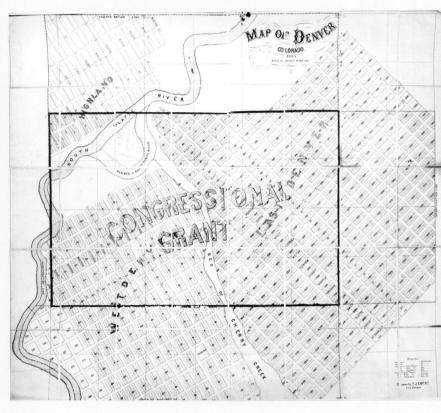

MAP 472 (*left*).
The *Congressional Grant,* 960 acres of what is now downtown Denver, was finally granted in 1864 for an official town development. It was superimposed on the already platted and somewhat settled *East Denver*—Denver City, originally St. Charles, the townsite of miners, claimed on 24 September 1858. William H. Larimer organized the Denver City Town Company here on 22 November 1858, naming the settlement Denver after James W. Denver, a governor of Kansas. The streets here roughly followed the line of the South Platte River. Across *Cherry Creek* is *West Denver*, originally Auraria, organized by William Green Russell on 1 November 1858, where the streets were laid out roughly parallel to Cherry Creek. To the north, across the South Platte, is *Highland*, also staked out by Larimer about the same time. The streets of today's downtown Denver retain this pattern within the Congressional Grant, the southeast corner of which is at today's Broadway and Colfax. The street pattern of Auraria is largely gone (except for 5th Street), swallowed up in larger institutional buildings.

MAP 473 (*below*).
Denver was a sizeable town by 1881, the date of this bird's-eye, seen in a view to the east. The river in the foreground is *Cherry Creek,* running into the *South Platte* at bottom left.

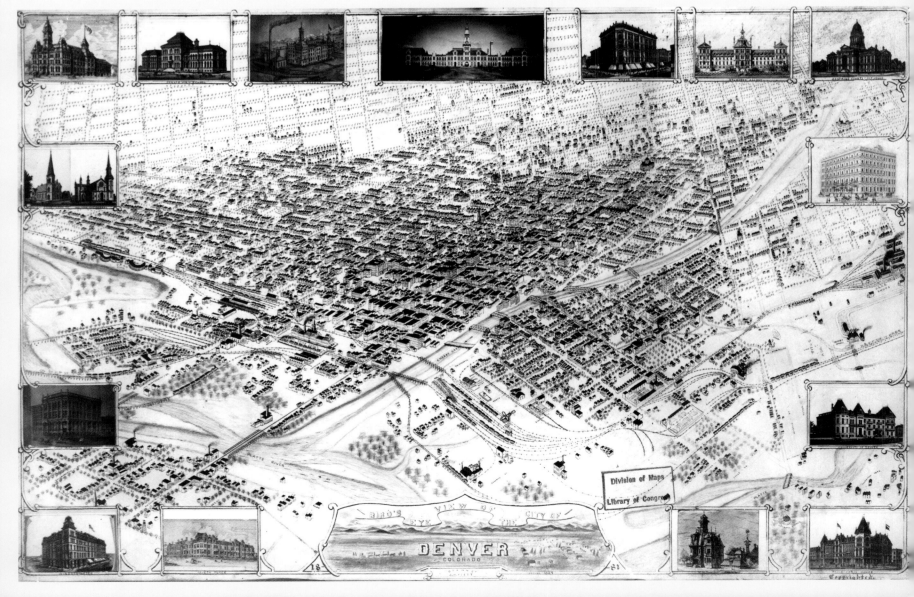

the South Platte Canyon. The High Line Canal was completed in 1882 but was found to have only a junior water right, so it could not be used in dry years. Artesian water was found in 1883, although that did not satisfy the city for long, and only when rival water companies merged to create the Denver Union Water Company did the city receive adequate water, helping fuel a population boom in the late 1880s.

Population growth was also aided by one of the most extensive streetcar systems in the West (Map 475, *right, center*), which began as a horse-drawn network in the 1870s and was largely superseded by electric or cable cars by the 1890s. The suburban growth that streetcars promoted was tempered in 1893 by the economic slowdown beginning that year.

Map 474 (*right, top*).
This excellent 1908 bird's-eye map of *Denver* also shows the different street patterns well.

Map 475 (*right*).
Street railways, and especially electric streetcars, were critical in facilitating the growth of cities before the coming of the automobile. This 1892 map of Denver shows an astonishing four different types of line: cable, electric, horse, and steam. Horse railways first appeared in the 1870s, allowing suburban growth for the first time. The Denver Tramway Company, established in 1886, acquired a franchise for cable or electric lines; the latter at first obtained their power from a slot between the rails; after animals and people kept stepping into the slot, it was abandoned in favor of overhead wires. By 1890 Denver had one of the most extensive cable networks of any American city.

Map 476 (*below, left*) and Map 477 (*below, right*).
An interesting pair of maps depicting the same area as a real estate promoter's bird's-eye and a more mundane street map. It is easy to see why bird's-eye maps sold real estate. The two maps were published only a year apart, the bird's-eye in 1888 and the street map in 1889. On Map 477 the *Subn. of Sheridan, Petersburg, Englewood,* and *Logandale* are platted as development subdivisions. Both maps show the location where gold was found in 1858, on Dry Creek where it enters the South Platte (see page 106). Petersburg, laid out in 1865, was in its time a "sin city," with the town hub being a notorious tavern. Logandale gets its name from nearby Fort Logan, built in 1888 and seen at left on Map 476. Sheridan, incorporated in 1890, and Englewood, incorporated in 1903, remain, much enlarged, as separate cities within the Denver metro area. Petersburg became part of Sheridan.

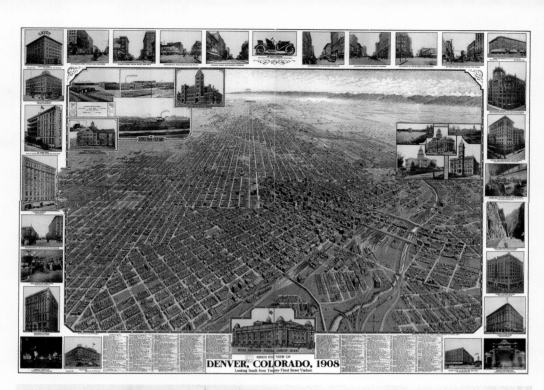

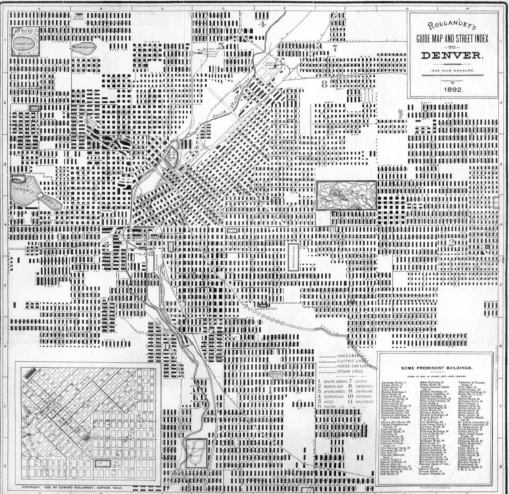

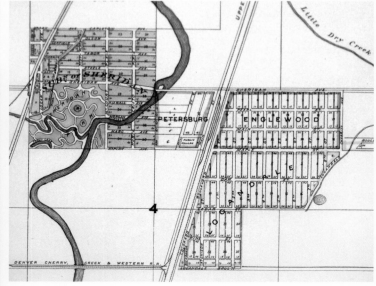

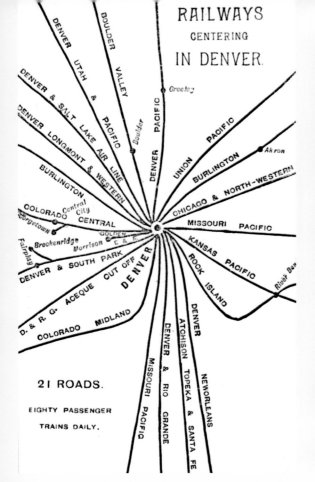

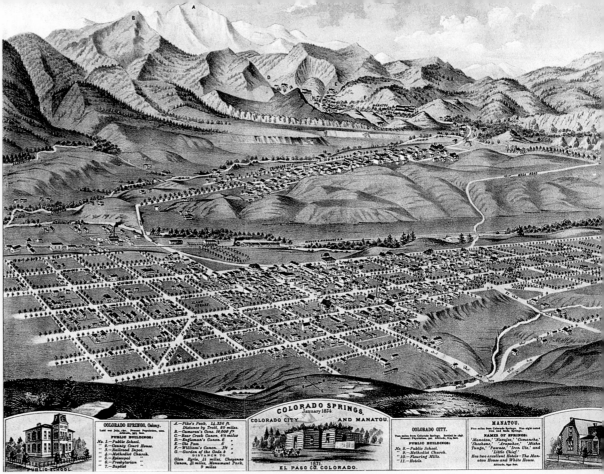

Map 478 (*above, left*).
A stylized 1891 advertising map showing all the railroads serving Denver, combining services through their own lines or trackage rights over others. The map made a convincing case for the city as a railroad hub.

Map 479 (*above, right*).
This particularly nicely engraved 1874 bird's-eye map shows Colorado Springs in the foreground while Colorado City is in the background.

Colorado Springs

Colorado City, an early competitor to Denver, also sprang to life following the Pike's Peak Gold Rush. Several men incorporated the Colorado City Town Company in August 1859 and began laying out a town on Fountain Creek, where they hoped it would be well positioned to supply the goldfields. Over the winter of 1859–60 a road was cut to the South Park mining area, and over two hundred houses and businesses were built on the townsite.

But the town's competitors built roads, too, and Colorado City did not thrive for long. However, it survived as an agricultural center until, in 1871,

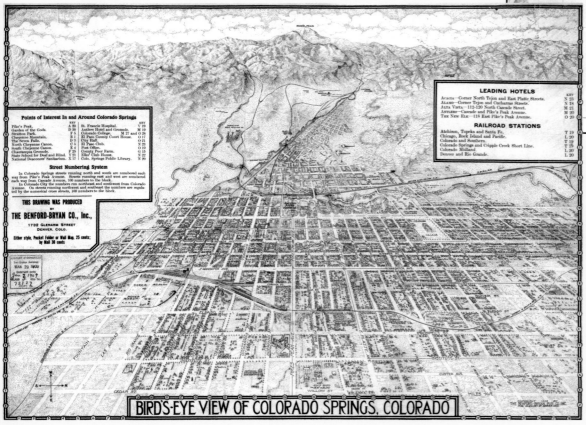

Map 480 (*above*).
Colorado City, founded in 1859 on Fountain Creek, here *Fontaine Qui Bouille* (boiling or bubbling fountain). The map dates from 1887 and shows the extensive *Colorado Midland Railway Yard and Shop Grounds*, including a semicircular roundhouse.

Map 481 (*left*).
Colorado Springs in 1909. Fountain Creek and Colorado City are in the background, below *Pike's Peak*. William Palmer's *Antler's Hotel Grounds* is at center, adjacent to his Denver & Rio Grande rail line.

General William Palmer founded the separate community of Colorado Springs—the name was originally intended to be the Fountain Colony—close by, with the intention of building a high-quality resort. Palmer, a retired Union cavalry commander, had worked on the Union Pacific transcontinental line and created the Denver & Rio Grande as a regional railroad to serve the Rocky Mountain region. He believed that the region was a healthy one that could attract both residents and tourists and had successfully promoted a new city at South Pueblo, farther south, on land he and his partners owned adjacent to Pueblo; the latter became an iron and steel center for the West.

In 1873 Palmer opened a resort hotel, the Antlers (MAP 481, *left, bottom*). Palmer's Colorado Springs Company advertised widely, and the city became a fashionable resort, managing to attract many affluent residents and tourists, including a significant number from Britain; British investors were putting money into many projects in the American West at this time. Palmer and his Colorado Springs were pioneers in the marketing of the West for pleasure (see page 214).

Colorado Springs is in modern times better known as a military center. Its first military base opened in 1942, the Air Force Academy was located there in 1954, and in 1963 the headquarters of the North American Aerospace Defense Command (NORAD) was constructed inside Cheyenne Mountain, in southwestern Colorado Springs.

THE GATEWAYS TO THE PLAINS

Several cities became in their times what might be termed gateways to the West, the points through which emigrants streamed on their way to a better life. The first was St. Louis, on the Mississippi, established by French settlers in 1763 and almost immediately lost to the Spanish but always remarkably tolerant of Americans, many of whom lived in the city. The city was the departure point for Lewis and Clark in 1804, the year the city became American as part of the Louisiana Purchase (see page 65). St. Louis grew in importance after 1817 as a transshipment point for Mississippi steamboats.

As the frontier moved west, other gateway cities grew up. St. Joseph, Missouri, flourished briefly as the western terminus of the Hannibal & St. Joseph Railroad, completed in 1859 and then the most westerly point of the eastern rail system—and the start point of the Pony Express (see pages 113–14).

MAP 482 (*below*).
Although hardly a major western city today, *Abilene*, Kansas, has an interesting and, one might say, typically western history of gunfights and outlaws during the period when the town was on the Kansas Pacific at the northern end of the Chisholm Trail, the cattle trail from Texas (see page 125). By 1895, the date of this bird's-eye map, created to promote the city as *The Future Capital of Kansas*, the city wanted to convey its solidarity and stateliness as a place of fine residences, upstanding citizens, and thriving industry, as are manifested in the cameo scenes around the map edge.

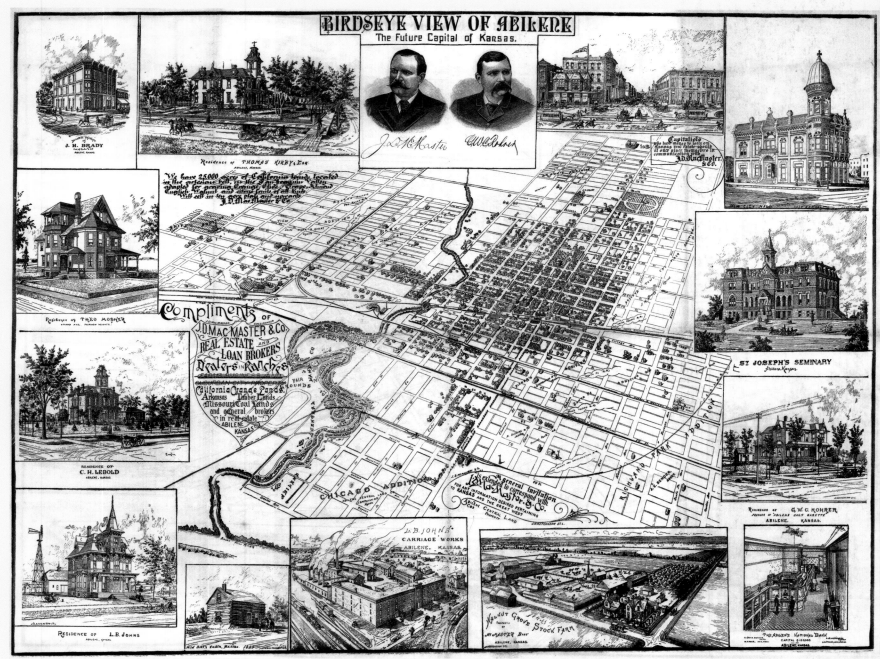

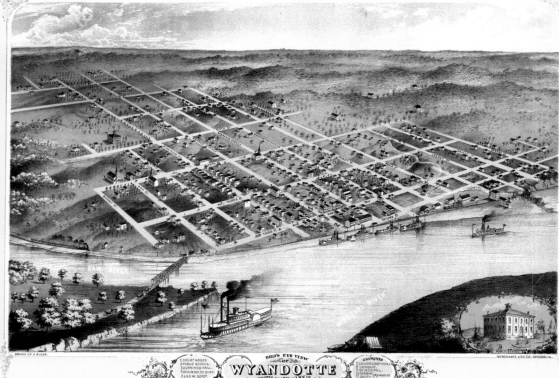

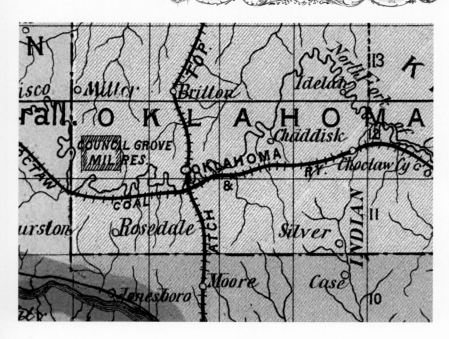

Map 483 (*left, top*).
Omaha, Nebraska, shown in an 1868 bird's-eye map, with Union Pacific trains front and center; this was, after all, the year before the completion of the transcontinental line, and Omaha was certain to become a thriving gateway to the West because of the railroad. Note the steamboats on the Missouri River in the foreground.

Map 484 (*left, center*).
Wyandotte, now the riverfront part of Kansas City, Kansas, was laid out in 1857. This bird's-eye dates from 1869. The Missouri is in the foreground; the Kansas flows in from the left.

Map 485 (*left, bottom*).
This 1892 map, published a year after Oklahoma Territory was created, shows *Oklahoma* City at the intersection of the *Choctaw Coal & Ry* and the *Atch[ison] Top[epka]* & Santa Fe Railroad lines. The Choctaw Coal and Railway Company, later the Choctaw, Oklahoma and Gulf Railroad, built a line out onto the Plains, reaching Amarillo in the Texas Panhandle in 1902. The company was merged with the Chicago, Rock Island and Pacific Railroad in 1904.

Omaha, which actually bills itself as the Gateway to the West today, had been founded in 1854 but in 1866 found itself the start point of the Union Pacific line building west. Beginning in 1885 Omaha developed stockyards that rivaled and ultimately overtook those in Chicago.

Kansas City, today a two-state conurbation, is an amalgam of previous small cities laid out at various times. Westport was a trading post built here by John McCoy in 1833 as the last supply post before the West, and it, or Westport Landing, its wharf on the Missouri, is shown as the endpoint of the Santa Fe Trail on a number of maps rather than the military end at Fort Leavenworth, just to the north.

Kansas City's stockyards, which also rivaled those of Chicago at one point, were built in 1871 and expanded to cover 55 acres in 1878. Before their construction, farmers to the west had to accept whatever price the railroads offered, and the stockyards gave the farmers much more control. The location was ideal because of excellent connections to the rail net-

MAP 486 (*above*).
This superb and detailed bird's-eye map shows the stockyards of Kansas City in 1895 and clearly depicts the massive enterprise they were. Here was the collection point for cattle from a vast swathe of the Plains. The view is to the west, with the Missouri in the foreground and the Kansas River beyond. The Kansas–Missouri state line does not follow the river here but bisects the stockyards about where the long road bridge crosses the railroad tracks at center top. The area covered on this map is almost exactly that adjacent to the left of MAP 484, though, of course, the two views are separated by nearly thirty years. This map has been partially digitally restored.

work; at their peak the stockyards were served by no fewer than sixteen railroads. The Kansas City stockyards were destroyed by a flood in 1951 and never fully recovered. Stockyards have now tended to move nearer to producers, since refrigerated cars allow meat to be shipped more easily than cattle, and stockyards have become smaller and more dispersed; the day of the huge yard is over.

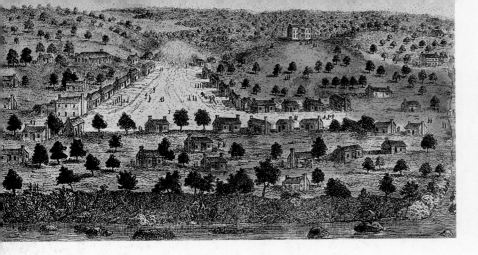

MAP 487 (*left*).
Austin, the new capital of the Republic of Texas, is depicted in this 1840 bird's-eye, which must be one of the earliest such maps of the West.

MAP 488 (*below*).
This 1873 bird's-eye map of San Antonio shows no railroad, usually a feature of this type of map because it indicates economic progress and was often included even when only planned for the future; bird's-eyes were promotional items, after all, and bending the truth was common. The railroad actually arrived in San Antonio four years later.

THE CITIES OF TEXAS

Texas is home to what are now the fourth- and sixth-largest urban regions of the United States: Dallas–Fort Worth and Houston.

The site of the 1836 Battle of the Alamo (see page 80), San Antonio retains some of its Spanish frontier feel and has only relatively recently grown into a modern urban city. Unlike most large cities, San Antonio is not surrounded by smaller ones and has grown in area by annexing unincorporated areas around it. Nearly 75 percent of its area has been acquired in this way since 1960. It is because of this that the city now ranks seventh largest in the country, while the metropolitan area is only ranked twenty-ninth among such areas.

Austin, another historic city, but one created after the declaration of the Texas Republic, was intended as the capital from the beginning. A town that had been laid out around 1835, Waterloo, was chosen as the site and renamed after Texan hero Stephen F. Austin (see page 80; a map of Austin in 1839 is MAP 157, *page 83*). The choice of site was supported by Mirabeau Lamar when he was president of the republic, but when Sam Houston, Lamar's political enemy, regained the presidency in 1841 the capital was moved to Washington-on-the-Brazos, and it was not until Anson Jones became president in 1844 and began to lobby for admission to the Union that a new state constitution named Austin as the state capital. A new Texas State Capitol building was completed in 1888.

Sam Houston, of course, had a city named after him, too. In August 1836, real estate developers and brothers John and Augustus Allen purchased nearly seven thousand acres on Buffalo Bayou, which flowed into the head of Galveston Bay. They promoted their town of Houston as the "great commercial emporium of Texas," and they would, one day, be right. No doubt the brothers thought that naming their town after the popular hero would help sell lots.

Houston was incorporated in 1837. The town later became a railroad hub and a center for exporting cotton. The Houston Ship Channel was completed in 1876 to facilitate development of the port. The devastating Galveston hurricane of 1900 encouraged the expansion of the port of Houston, and a deepwater port was completed by 1914. The city is now the largest in Texas and the fourth largest in the United States.

The largest metropolitan area in Texas, slightly bigger than Houston, is that of Dallas–Fort Worth, including Arlington, all of which grew up as, and have remained, separate cities.

John Neely Bryan in 1841 intended to establish a trading post on the Trinity River at

MAP 489 (*below*).
This fine isometric view map of the downtown area of Houston was published in 1912. Smokestacks crowd the horizon, suggesting a city humming with industry. The views include, at top left, one of the *Houston Ship Channel*. The location of the city as a railroad hub is promoted, at right: *Where 17 Railroads Meet the Sea*. Also promoted is the city's cotton trade—*Largest Inland Cotton Market in the World*—and the city as a center for rice, oil, lumber, and finance.

the site of a natural ford and an intersection of Caddo trails, but a treaty signed that year removed all Indians from northern Texas, so instead Bryan founded a settlement. It turned out that he was on land already part of the Peters Colony, granted by the republic to William Peters's Texas Emigration and Land Company of St. Louis (see page 84). While this created a few problems for Bryan, he legalized his claim and benefited from the promotional work of Peters. Dallas was incorporated in 1856, and when, in 1873, the Texas & Pacific Railway and the Houston & Texas Central Railroad both arrived in the city, an intersection of east–west and north–south lines, the city's success as a commercial center was assured.

Nearby Fort Worth was one of a string of U.S. Army forts recommended by Major General William Jenkins Worth in 1849. Worth died of cholera that year, but a fort built on the banks of the Trinity River was named in his honor.

The settlement that grew up around the fort became a cattle center on the Chisholm Trail and established stockyards, and the latter boomed following the arrival of the Texas & Pacific Railway in 1876, when Fort Worth became for a time the western railhead. As a cattle town it became famous for its rough saloons and bawdy houses frequented by cowboys and outlaws alike. By 1903 meat-packing houses were established in the city.

Even as it grew to become a part of the vast Dallas metropolitan area, Fort Worth retained some of its western flavor, and it still promotes itself as the place "where the West begins."

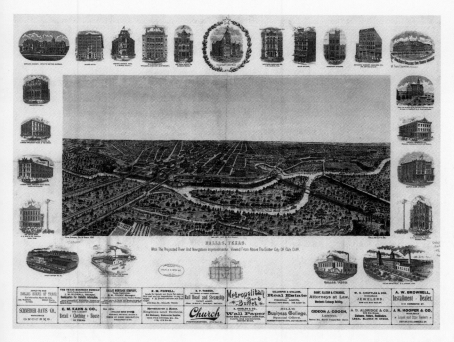

Map 490 (*left*).
An elegant bird's-eye map of *Dallas* published in 1892.

Map 491 (*above, top*).
An 1872 bird's-eye map of Dallas. The two railroads shown actually reached the city the following year.

Map 492 (*above*).
Fort Worth in 1876, the year the railroad arrived. A train is shown, unusually, in the background; the railroad would normally be portrayed front and center.

Map 493 (*below*).
Anchorage Townsite platted at Ship Creek, on *Knik Arm* of Cook Inlet, by federal General Land Office surveyors in 1915.

ANCHORAGE

The origins of Anchorage, Alaska, are more modern than those of most western cities. The site, where Ship Creek enters Cook Inlet, was selected as a construction port for the Alaska Railroad, built by the federal government—Alaska just having become a territory two years earlier. The railroad, from Seward to Fairbanks, was intended to facilitate development of the interior; it was completed in 1925. The townsite, soon called Ship Creek Anchorage, and then just Anchorage, was surveyed in 1915 (Map 493, *right*), and the first lots were sold that year. Anchorage was incorporated in 1920 and is now the largest city in Alaska.

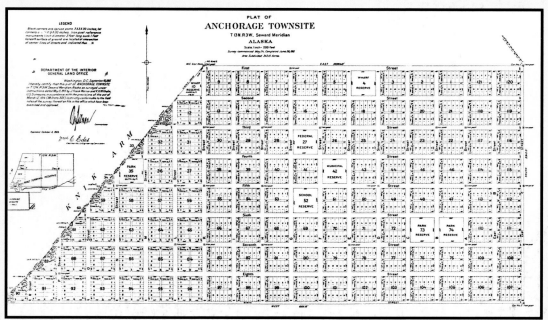

SELLING THE WEST

The romance of the West was a very saleable product to the citizens of eastern cities. The railroads evolved two businesses—bringing the people of the East to the West, as tourists, and bringing the produce of the western Eden to a hungry East; the West could be sampled without leaving home.

ENTICING THE EAST WEST—TOURISM

General William Palmer of the Denver & Rio Grande—and founder of Colorado Springs as a health resort—was not the only entrepreneur to realize that there was money to be made by selling the virtues of the West. Virtually all western railroads promoted tourism to build their traffic and add to their profitability. And the time was right. Thousands of Easterners wanted to see the West—the romantic, healthful, warm West they had read about for years but never been able to see for themselves. Indians, once a feared enemy, were turned into a spectacle not to be missed. At first the tourists were the more affluent—those who had the money and, just as importantly, the time—but the railroads proved to be a great equalizer, and soon almost anyone could travel west if they so desired—they may just have had to travel third class.

The West was promoted by photographers, whose new medium proved ideal advertising for the region's grandeur and scale. The development of the national parks system provided many bona fide destinations with which the railroads could seduce the public west. The Union Pacific promoted Yosemite and the parks of Utah, the Northern Pacific invested heavily in promoting Yellowstone, the Santa Fe outdid itself with the Indian cultures of the Southwest, and the Great Northern advertised Glacier National Park. The Southern Pacific went one step further, publishing a travel magazine, *Sunset,* which, using lavish artwork and top writers, every month transported the reader to somewhere on the railroad's route. By 1911 the magazine printed a hundred thousand copies a month and was read by half a million people. Agricultural and industrial investment was promoted as well.

Above.
This Denver & Rio Grande Western Railroad travel brochure from the 1930s has most of the elements by which the West was sold: the romance—the *Romantic Rocky Mountain Wonderlands*—the spectacular scenery, brought close by the railroad; and the cowboys of the "Old West." Even something distinctly nonscenic, the Moffat Tunnel, opened in 1928, was advertised as an engineering wonder, a "must see."

MAP 494 *(below).*
The scenic wonders of the West are displayed in the margins of this 1883 Union Pacific map highlighting the region. Although the wonders are mainly natural, the *Mormon Temple and Tabernacle* in Salt Lake City are also shown—conveniently reached via Union Pacific, of course.

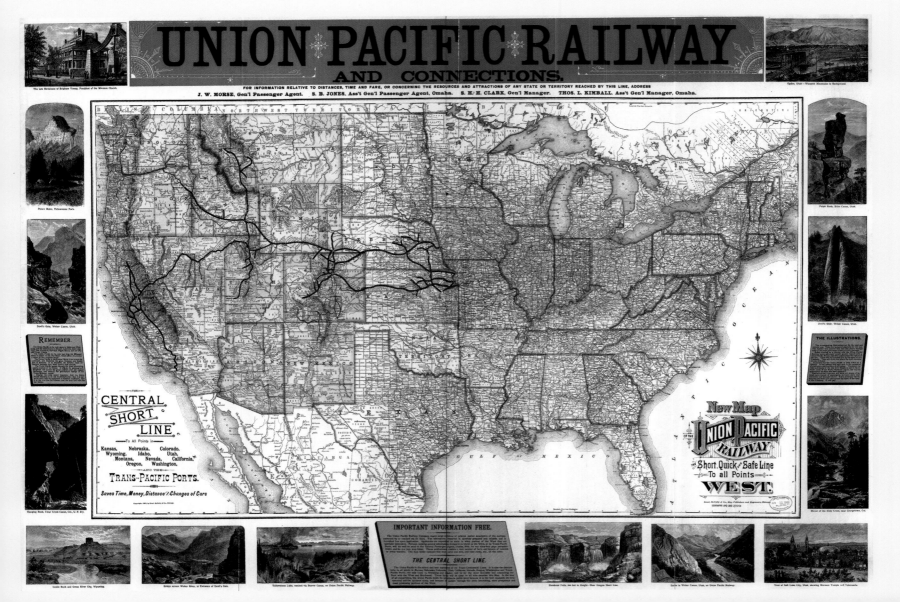

The Yellowstone National Park and Dining Car Route to the Pacific Coast.

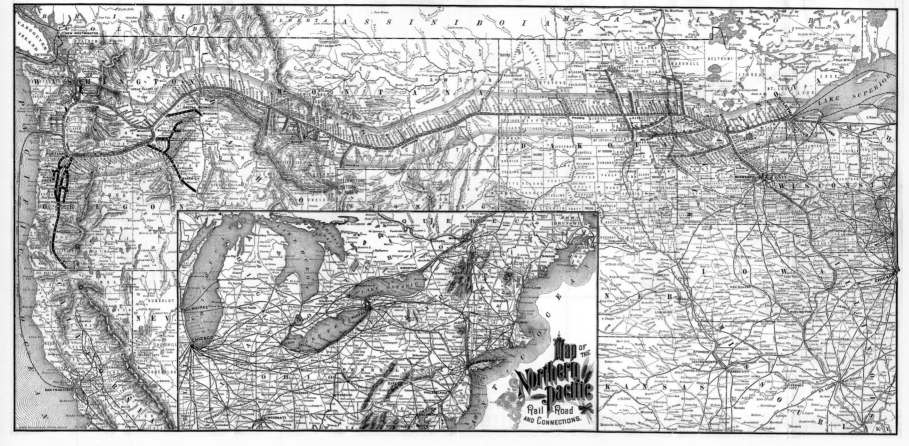

Map 495 (*above*).
Published in 1887, only four years after the transcontinental line was completed, this Northern Pacific map headlines its access to Yellowstone National Park. Yellowstone was created in 1872 following the efforts of Ferdinand Hayden in documenting its scenic wonders; it was the first federally controlled national park.

Map 496 (*below, left*).
What is it? indeed. The Santa Fe's innovative advertisement touted its route to California as the *Banana Line,* presumably to convey an impression of tropical lushness.

Map 497 (*below, right*).
The Front Range of Colorado was especially promoted as a healthful area, and thousands of affluent tuberculosis patients were recommended to recuperate there. Palmer's Colorado Springs was not only a fashionable resort for the well-off tourist but also a center for health resorts. One competitor to Colorado Springs was this summer resort near Denver, advertised with a superb bird's-eye map and the view from *Lookout Mountain,* famous as the grave site of Buffalo Bill, who was buried there in 1917.

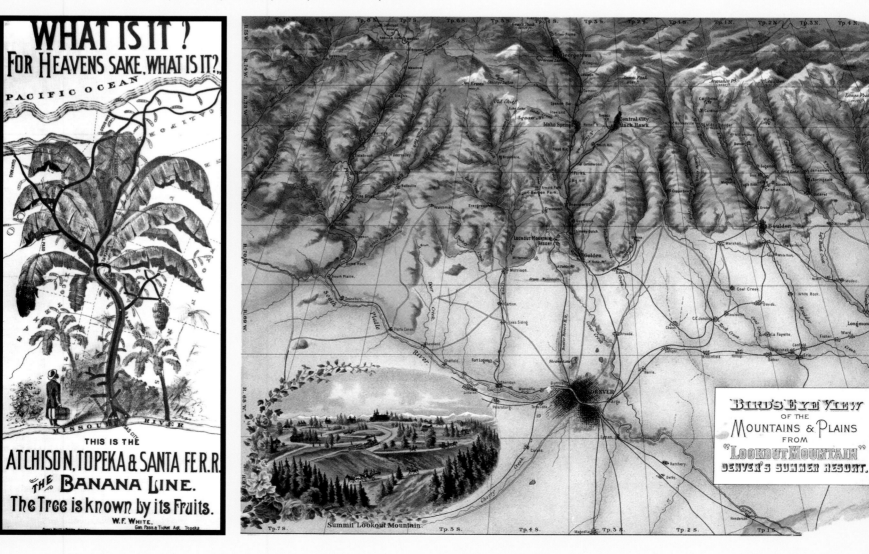

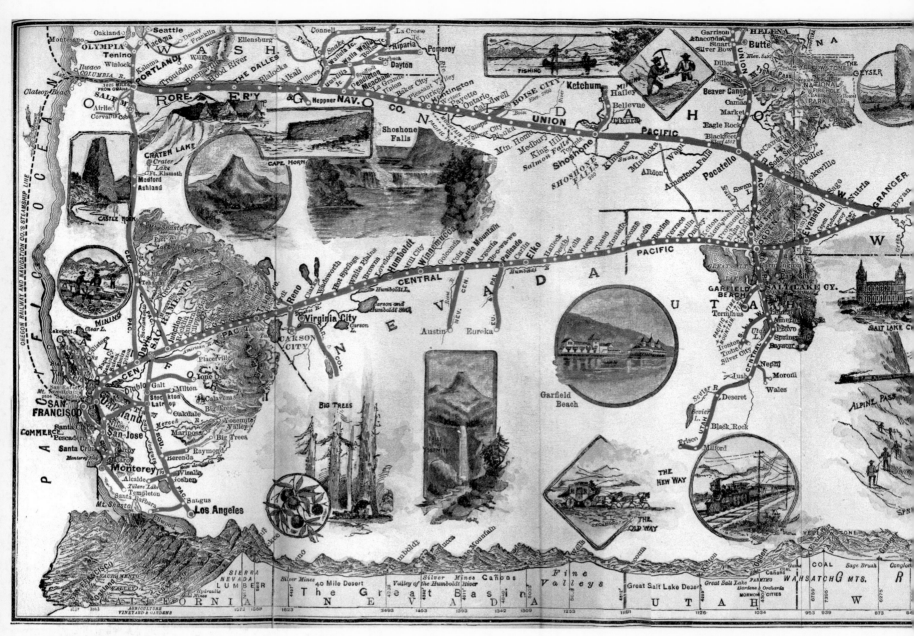

MAP 498 (*above*).
Views of the West abound on this attractive tourist map published by the Union Pacific Railroad in 1888.

MAP 499 (*below*).
Southern Pacific portrayed in bird's-eye form the *Apache Trail* from *Phoenix*, on the line, at left, to the old mining town of *Globe*, at right, via Theodore *Roosevelt Dam*, built as the first part of the Salt River federal reclamation project (see page 163). The 1908 International Harvester touring car (*right*) was used to transport tourists along the Apache Trail; it is shown here displayed in the Arizona Historical Society's museum in Tempe, Arizona. The one-way trip from Mesa to the dam took eight hours but was still an improvement over the two days it had taken by horse-drawn coach.

MAP 500 (*right, bottom*).
It must have taken a bit of imagination to see the Northern Pacific line as part of a pointer dog, but the artist did so in this combination of map and art published by the railroad in 1901. The Northern Pacific sponsored author Olin Wheeler to write travel books about places on its route, a promotional method used by many railroads.

APACHE TRAIL OF ARIZONA ON SOUTHERN PACIFIC LINES

MAP OF CRIPPLE CREEK DISTRICT

ST. PETER'S DOME – THE CRIPPLE CREEK TRIP

A whole new industry, tourism in its many forms, was born in the West. The railroad brought the people, then others—often railroad company subsidiaries—took them into a park, on a tour of the sights, or for a stay in a purpose-built hotel or resort or perhaps a dude ranch, a new western phenomenon where the guest could play at being a cowboy, soaking up the "real" West.

Some of the declining or shuttered mines of the Rocky Mountains took on a new lease on life as tourist attractions, and the railroads built to service them over the most treacherous terrain now served as scenic magic carpets to whisk tourists through the mountains to places not reachable by any other means (MAP 501, *above,* and MAP 502, *right, top*).

Much of the tourists' excitement about the West centered on the national parks. Yellowstone was the first, created in 1872, though not developed for some years afterward. Not until 1890 did the federal government assume full responsibility for the park, lobbied by the Northern Pacific to do so.

As early as 1864 Abraham Lincoln had signed a bill protecting the Yosemite Valley and the Mariposa Grove of big sequoias, conveying it to California as a state park (MAP 505, *overleaf*). It was President Theodore Roosevelt who, after camping in the valley with naturalist and activist John Muir (who in 1892 had founded the Sierra Club), made Yosemite a federally controlled national park in 1906.

MAP 501 (*above*).
The Colorado Springs and Cripple Creek District Railway, which marketed itself as the Cripple Creek Short Line, was said by some to be the most remarkable railroad construction in the world. It was opened in 1901 to serve the gold mines of the Cripple Creek district west from Colorado Springs. By 1915 it had become one of the principal tourist attractions of the region and one of the promotable features of the city. "The wonderful scenery along the Cripple Creek Short Line has been a large factor in spreading the fame of Colorado Springs as a tourist center," says the accompanying text. "I have never seen such a railroad, either for steepness or for sinuosity," said a 1914 article in *Collier's* magazine. The railroad took fifty miles to cover what in a straight line would have been eighteen. Despite appearances, the line was in trouble and was declared bankrupt in 1919. The railbed was converted into a road (see page 231). *Above.* A train on the Cripple Creek Short Line.

CONTOUR MAP—HALF-WAY TO CRIPPLE CREEK ON "CRIPPLE CREEK SHORT LINE"

MAP 502 (*above*).
The literature promoting the Cripple Creek Short Line—only half of the total line is depicted in this map, also from 1915—reached grand heights of hyperbole. "At the city's [Colorado Springs] very border terra firma itself climbs into the sky, and the Cripple Creek train goes with it," spouted one brochure; "all the wonder and thrill of aeronautics without being separated from terra firma," effused another.

MAP 503 (*below*).
National parks, buffalo reserves, ski resorts, and dude ranches come together in the central Rockies, where, this map claims, there is sunshine every day of the year. This pictorial tourist map was published about 1930 by the Denver & Rio Grande Western Railroad, *Scenic Line of the World*. Difficult terrain and difficult economics have been turned into an asset.

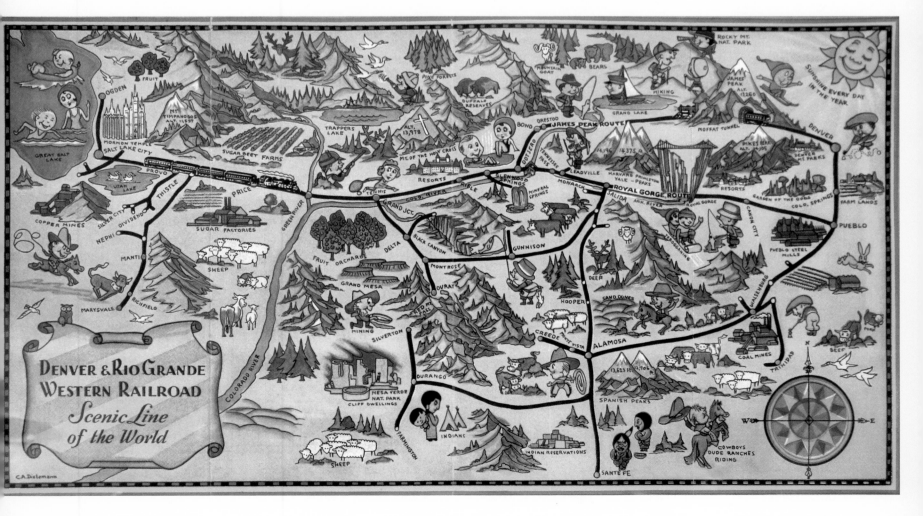

MAP 504 (*above*).
An original combination of map and artwork depicts the *North Coast Limited*, a crack deluxe train of the Northern Pacific, complete with Pullman coaches. At center is Yellowstone; one would never guess from looking at this map that it was actually at the end of a branch from the main line. Note the *Gardiner Gateway*.

Left. The artistic cover of *The Yosemite*, the book John Muir wrote about the park he loved so much.

MAP 505 (*below*).
George Wheeler (see pages 177–78) surveyed the Yosemite area, and this finely engraved map, which gives a good feel for the topography through the use of shading, was published in 1883. The red line is the boundary of the Yosemite Valley land that the federal government granted to California for park purposes in 1864. A much larger national park would be created in 1890.

One of the closest relationships a railroad had with a national park was that of the Northern Pacific with Yellowstone. The railroad was deliberately routed near the park, and in 1883, the same year the transcontinental link was completed, a branch was constructed from Livingston, Montana, to Cinnabar, about three miles north of the park boundary; in 1902 it was extended to Gardiner, on the boundary. The railroad then advertised Gardiner as the first and best of the Yellowstone gateways. As the railroad's advertising makes clear, the Northern Pacific was *the* way to get to Yellowstone.

Below.
Cover of a 1930s brochure published by the Estes Park Chamber of Commerce, whose members' livelihood was greatly affected by tourists visiting nearby Rocky Mountain National Park.

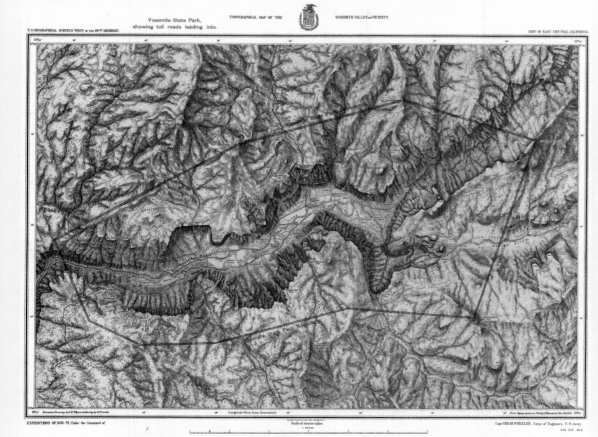

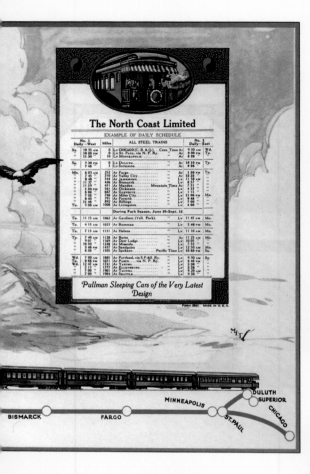

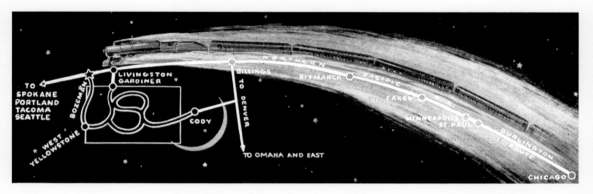

Map 506 (*above, right*).
The topography of Yellowstone National Park on a beautiful Northern Pacific brochure dated 1904.

Map 507 (*right, center*).
A Northern Pacific train is depicted as a comet and the map of Yellowstone as a star map in this illustration from a 1928 information booklet published by the railroad. The *Yellowstone Park Comet* was a Northern Pacific train from Chicago to Yellowstone in the 1920s.

Map 508 (*right, bottom*).
An advertisement for the city of *Visalia* from the 1930s dubs it the *Outing Hub, Enroute to God's Country*, emphasizing its proximity to several of the California national parks.

Map 509 (*below*).
The Alaska Steamship Company published this map in a brochure in 1936 promoting tourist travel to Alaska.

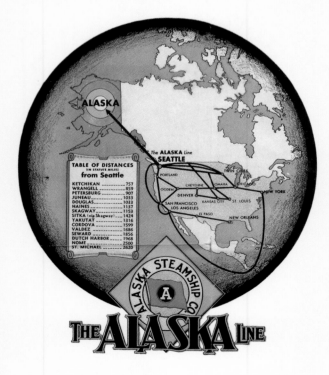

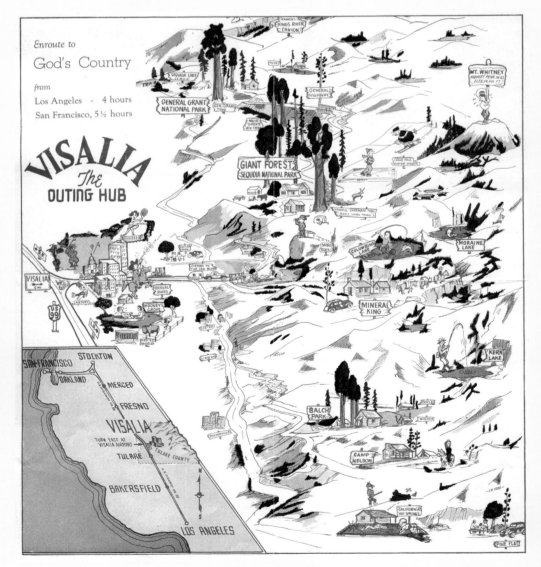

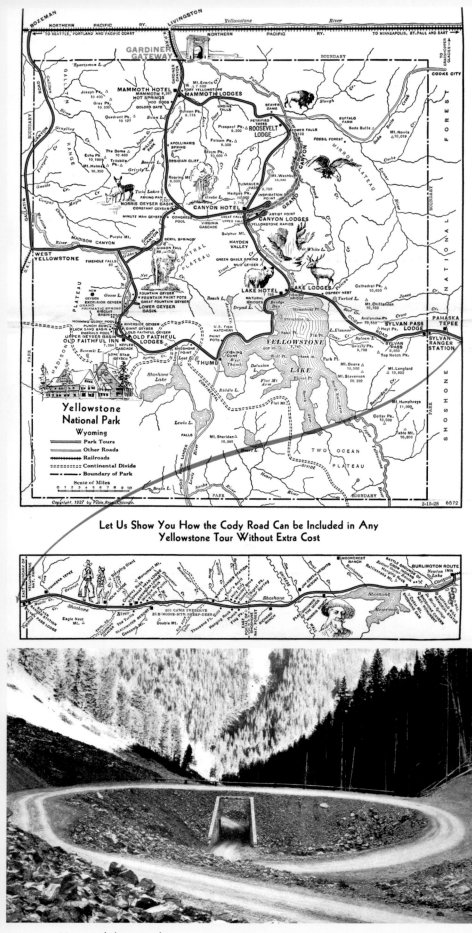

Let Us Show You How the Cody Road Can be Included in Any Yellowstone Tour Without Extra Cost

MAP 510 (*above, top*).
The Northern Pacific's map of Yellowstone in 1928. Now the railroad is cooperating with another, promoting an exit from the park via the Cody Gateway, opened in 1916, and the Cody Road, shown *above*, to Cody, Wyoming, where a connection would be made with the Chicago, Burlington and Quincy Railroad, which had built a loop through Wyoming and Billings, Montana, and added a short branch to Cody.

In the Southwest, the Atchison, Topeka & Santa Fe promoted Indians and Indian dwellings, especially the pueblos, as tourist attractions, using the Indians of the Southwest as what one writer described as "living ruins." The campaign might have been degrading to the Indians, but it sold tickets, and that was what the railroad wanted. It promoted the Southwest in a symbiotic relationship with the Fred Harvey Company, which, beginning with a single Topeka lunchroom in 1876, constructed a string of hotels and dining rooms across the West on Santa Fe lines (MAP 514, *overleaf*). The company also acted as a broker for Indian art, manufactured souvenirs, postcards, and the like, and even created a museum collection for display. However contrived it may have been, the romantic appeal of the Southwest was expertly marketed to Easterners, who became the railroad's—and Fred Harvey's—customers because of it.

MAP 511 (*below*).
In the 1920s the Union Pacific was promoting tours of Zion and Bryce Canyon national parks in Utah and the granddaddy of them all, the Grand Canyon National Park, from its line between Salt Lake City and Las Vegas. Here Union Pacific buses met the trains.

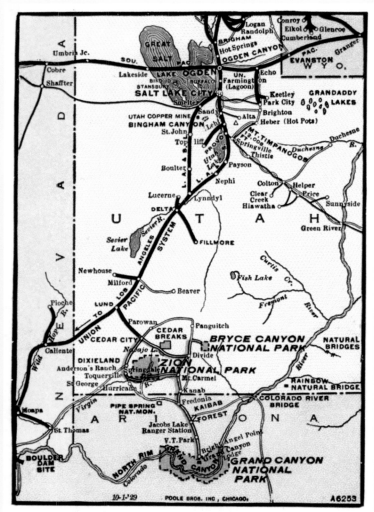

MAP OF UTAH AND NORTHERN ARIZONA
Showing locations of Zion and Bryce Canyon National Parks, Cedar Breaks, the Kaibab Forest and Grand Canyon National Park. These regions, with their gorgeous color schemes, vast canyons and amphitheatres, are reached by regular Union Pacific motor-bus tours from Cedar City, Utah, during the season, approximately June 1 to September 25.

Left.
Tour buses wait to depart in Yellowstone National Park in 1928. The railroads had promoted the use of road vehicles for sightseeing in the scenic areas beyond the reach of their systems, but before long tourists came to realize they could arrive by automobile as well.

MAP 512 (*right*).
By 1926 things were changing. This interesting and detailed pictorial bird's-eye map of the Phoenix region, complete with cameo views, does not show any railroads in *The Heart of Arizona*—just roads.

MAP 513
(*below, with cover*).
In 1929 the Santa Fe produced this imaginative brochure for the *Indian-detour*, which left the railroad for three days to visit the Indian pueblos of northeastern New Mexico, including *Santa Fe* and *Taos*. One of the railroad buses used is shown at bottom right; another is on the brochure cover.

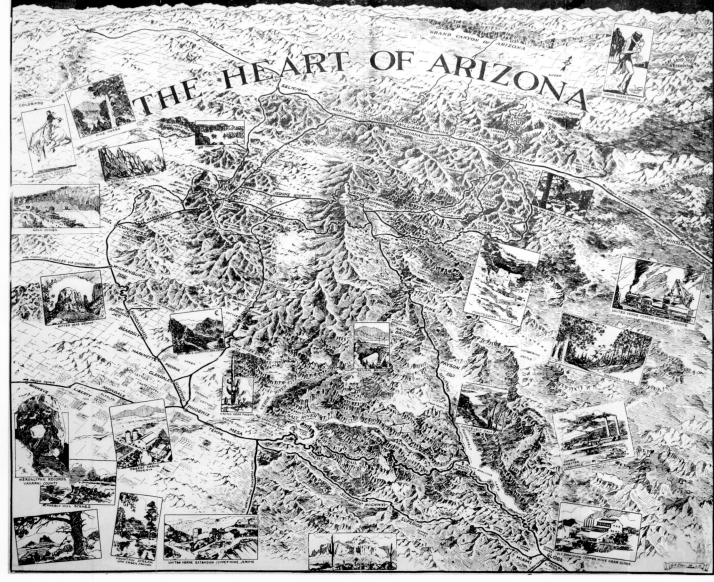

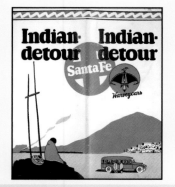

Three days and three hundred miles of sunshine and mountain air in a land of history and mystery—the Enchanted Empire

La Bajada Hill on way to Albuquerque
31

Fishing in The Upper Pecos River
32

Scene near Old Santa Fé
33

A stop is made at Santo Domingo Indian pueblo
34

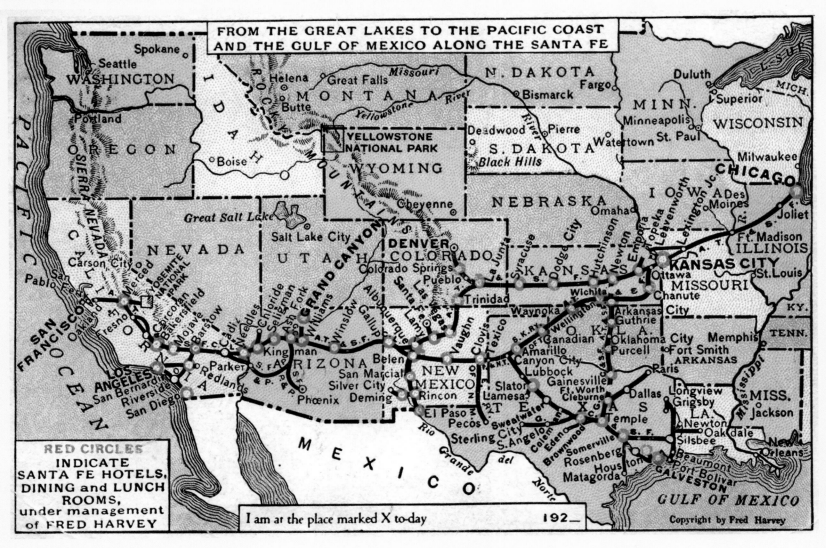

MAP 514 (*above*).
Red circles mark the locations of Fred Harvey hotels and restaurants on this map of the Santa Fe system published in 1926. Fifty locations are shown in the West, plus one in Chicago. The map was on a free postcard so that vacationers could fill in the date and mark with an "X" their location and send the card to family back East—thus spreading the advertising message.

MAP 515 (*below*).
A more modern version of MAP 494 (*page 214*) is this 1939 Union Pacific advertising map surrounded by destinations that had multiplied and been supplemented by man-made wonders such as the Boulder (Hoover) Dam and San Francisco's Golden Gate Bridge.

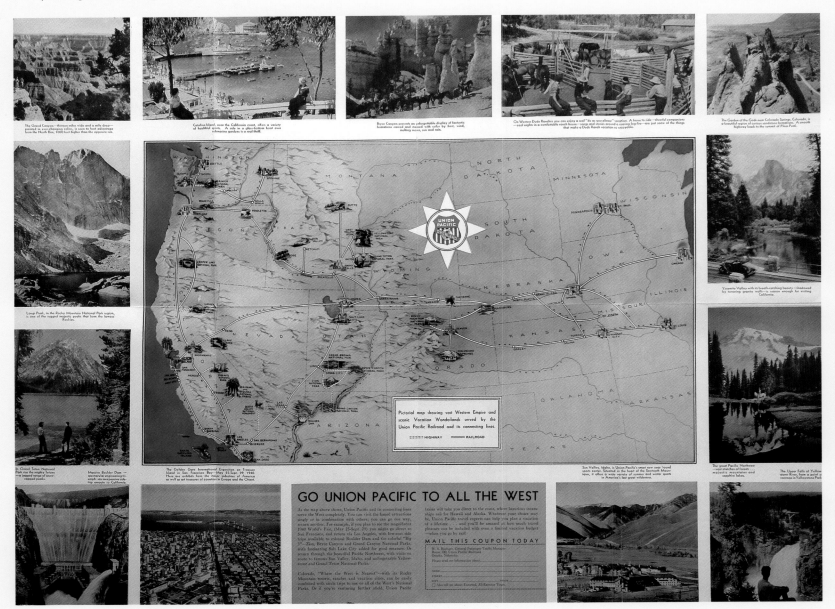

Sending the West East—Produce

If Easterners could not be persuaded to visit the West, then the harvests of the West could be brought to them. The West, with its many irrigation projects, could grow excellent produce; the East provided a market and the railroads the means of transport, and it all came together with marketing.

One of the classic examples was in Idaho, where reclamation projects, coupled with savvy marketing and the availability of a suitable variety, began a whole new agricultural industry—the Idaho potato. About 1907 farmers found that Russet Burbank potatoes grown in the Snake River valley exhibited appealing color, excellent firmness, good texture, and large size, qualities not found in this combination elsewhere. This knowledge was used to good advantage to market Idaho potatoes as superior to all others. In 1924, in a blaze of publicity, gift-wrapped Idaho potatoes were sent to President Coolidge for his Christmas dinner; two years later the state began issuing car license plates with the words "Famous Potatoes" on them. Very soon, marketing had created a new and desired western brand for eastern consumers.

A similar combination was used in California, where selling the concept of an agricultural Eden right on the eastern consumers' table developed into a high art.

The first oranges had been shipped East from California in 1877—though they only went as far as St. Louis—but by 1909 14.5 million boxes of oranges were being shipped east by rail. In 1893 about a hundred citrus growers, in an effort to increase prices, formed the Southern California Fruit Exchange (after 1905 the California Fruit Growers Exchange). In 1908 the organization began to use the term "Sunkist" as a name for its oranges in advertising, the first time a perishable food product had been advertised. The campaign was phenomenally successful, selling as it did the dream of tropical paradise. Here was a way, it seemed, everyone could share California's sunshine. The organization became adept at selling the orange as healthful, fresh, and nutritious; so successful was the advertising that in 1952 the organization adopted its brand, becoming Sunkist Growers.

The story has been repeated, though to a lesser extent, by other agricultural industries from different parts of the irrigated West, such as California's wine industry and Washington's apple growers.

MAP 516 (*right, top*) and MAP 517 (*right, center*).
Two apple crate labels featuring a map of Washington State to emphasize the apples' origins, from the 1950s and 1940s, respectively.

MAP 518 (*right*).
A late-1930s California Fruit Growers Exchange shipping poster with a pictorial map of California—and the Phoenix area of Arizona (the Salt River Project). The 14,500 grower-members referred to on the poster have since been reduced to about 6,000 owing to consolidation. The Sunkist name is prominent.

MAP 519 (*below*).
The Sunkist moniker extended to lemons as well as oranges. This crate label, featuring a map of California, is from the 1940s.

OPENING THE WEST — YET MORE

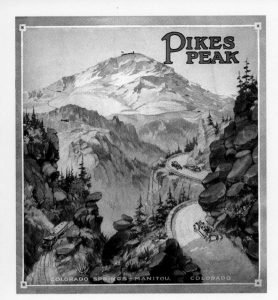

After 1900 the automobile began its rapid ascension to transportation dominance in the United States, and it spelled the beginning of the end for the railroads, at least as carriers of people. Then, after about 1950, the jet aircraft began to take over the skies, leading to a mass transportation system ideal for the vast distances of the West. Between them, they made the West accessible to all.

THE SWITCHBACKS—PIKES PEAK AUTO HIGHWAY.

Above.
A tourist bus of the day climbs the final switchbacks of the Pikes Peak road about 1912.

Above.
A brochure for Pikes Peak published in about 1915 depicts both the Pikes Peak Cog Railway, at left, and the 19-mile-long new road, completed that year. The railway, the highest in the United States, was built as a tourist attraction in 1889.

MAP 520 (*below*).
A route map for the Pacific Coast Highway, published in 1915. As can be seen from the advertisements, traveling the route took quite a few days.

GOOD ROADS EVERYWHERE

The automobile and the truck running on "good roads everywhere" would finally make the West truly accessible. Henry Ford began mass-producing automobiles in 1908; the nation boasted two million automobiles by 1915 and twenty-three million by 1929. The Lincoln Highway Association, just one of many "good roads" organizations, was formed in 1913 to lobby for a paved transcontinental highway. By 1925 there were over 250 named highways in the country, requiring detailed maps to navigate them; most were marked with signs such as those shown at right. In 1927 a numbered road system was introduced, creating 96,000 miles of "US" routes.

Ironically, perhaps, a railroad subsidiary was the first long-distance bus service. The Santa Fe's Pickwick Corporation in 1925

MAP 521 (*below*).
A map of the road from Los Angeles to Phoenix in 1914, another major expedition.

MAP 522 (*right*).
The transcontinental highways of the West in 1918. All the roads are named, and a selection of the road markers with their names is displayed in the margin. Every junction had to be marked—but they often were not. And just because a road was marked on the map did not mean it was a "good" road—that is, a paved or at least improved highway. Local merchants were not always above repositioning signs to divert traffic past their storefronts. With a rising tide of automobiles, a federally regulated system was soon essential, and it came in 1927.

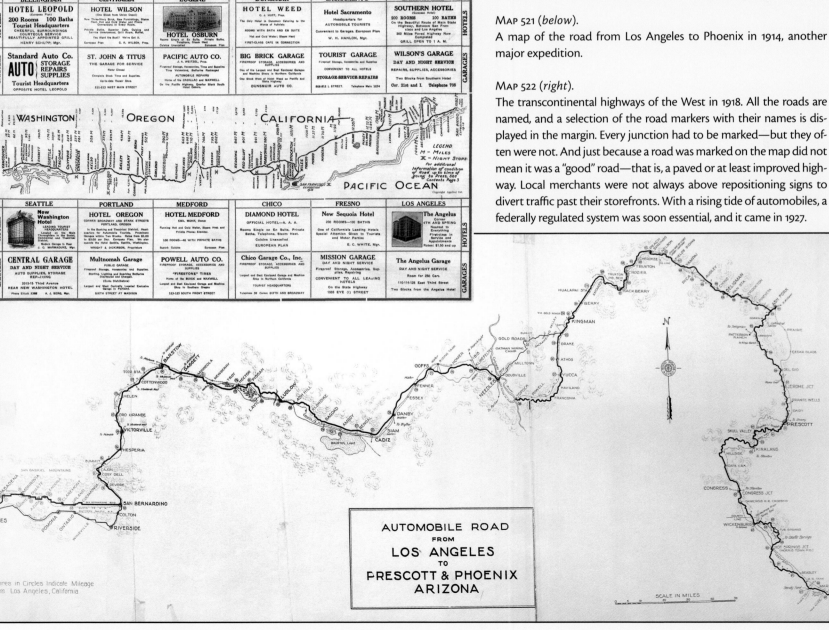

AUTOMOBILE ROAD
FROM
LOS ANGELES
TO
PRESCOTT & PHOENIX
ARIZONA

Figures in Circles Indicate Mileage
From Los Angeles, California

SCALE IN MILES

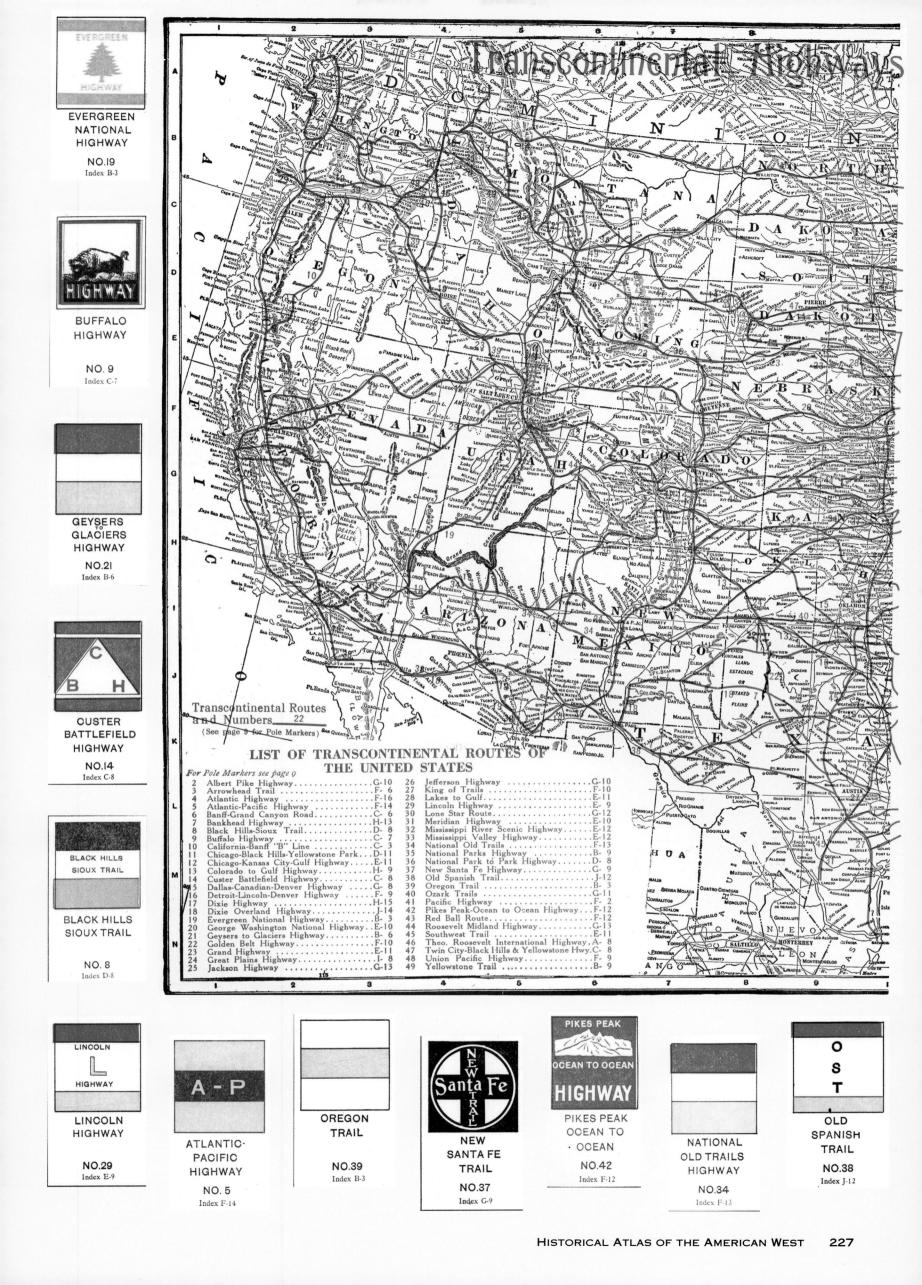

Transcontinental Highways

EVERGREEN
NATIONAL
HIGHWAY

NO. 19

Index B-3

BUFFALO
HIGHWAY

NO. 9

Index C-7

GEYSERS
TO
GLACIERS
HIGHWAY

NO. 21

Index B-6

CUSTER
BATTLEFIELD
HIGHWAY

NO. 14

Index C-8

BLACK HILLS
SIOUX TRAIL

BLACK HILLS
SIOUX TRAIL

NO. 8

Index D-8

Transcontinental Routes
and Numbers ____ 22
(See page 9 for Pole Markers)

LIST OF TRANSCONTINENTAL ROUTES OF THE UNITED STATES

For Pole Markers see page 9

2 Albert Pike Highway...............G-10	26 Jefferson Highway G-10
3 Arrowhead Trail....................F- 6	27 King of Trails F-10
4 Atlantic Highway...................F-16	28 Lakes to Gulf...................E-11
5 Atlantic-Pacific Highway...........F-14	29 Lincoln Highway ....E- 9
6 Banff-Grand Canyon Road...........B- 6	30 Lone Star Route................G-12
7 Bankhead Highway.................H-13	31 Meridian Highway...............E-10
8 Black Hills-Sioux Trail.............D- 8	32 Mississippi River Scenic Highway.E-12
9 Buffalo Highway....................C- 7	33 Mississippi Valley Highway......E-12
10 California-Banff "B" Line...........C- 3	34 National Old Trails..............F-13
11 Chicago-Black Hills-Yellowstone Park..D-11	35 National Parks Highway..........B- 9
12 Chicago-Kansas City-Gulf Highway..E-11	36 National Park to Park Highway....D- 8
13 Colorado to Gulf Highway..........H- 9	37 New Santa Fe Highway...........G- 9
14 Custer Battlefield Highway.........C- 8	38 Old Spanish Trail................J-12
15 Dallas-Canadian-Denver Highway...G- 8	39 Oregon Trail ....B- 3
16 Detroit-Lincoln-Denver Highway....F- 9	40 Ozark Trails G-11
17 Dixie Highway.....................H-15	41 Pacific Highway..................F- 2
18 Dixie Overland Highway............J-14	42 Pikes Peak-Ocean to Ocean Highway..F-12
19 Evergreen National Highway........B- 3	43 Red Ball Route..................F-12
20 George Washington National Highway.E-10	44 Roosevelt Midland Highway.......G-13
21 Geysers to Glaciers Highway.......B- 6	45 Southwest Trail.................E-11
22 Golden Belt Highway...............E-11	46 Theo. Roosevelt International Highway..A- 8
23 Grand Highway....................F-10	47 Twin City-Black Hills & Yellowstone Hwy..C- 8
24 Great Plains Highway...............I- 8	48 Union Pacific Highway...........F- 9
25 Jackson Highway G-13	49 Yellowstone Trail................B- 9

LINCOLN
HIGHWAY

NO. 29

Index E-9

ATLANTIC-
PACIFIC
HIGHWAY

NO. 5

Index F-14

OREGON
TRAIL

NO. 39

Index B-3

NEW
SANTA FE
TRAIL

NO. 37

Index G-9

PIKES PEAK
OCEAN TO
OCEAN

NO. 42

Index F-12

NATIONAL
OLD TRAILS
HIGHWAY

NO. 34

Index F-13

OLD
SPANISH
TRAIL

NO. 38

Index J-12

Map 523 (*above*).
The state highway system of *Idaho* in 1923. Note that the roads are all named; the numbers are merely map reference numbers, not highway numbers. The latter would come in four more years.

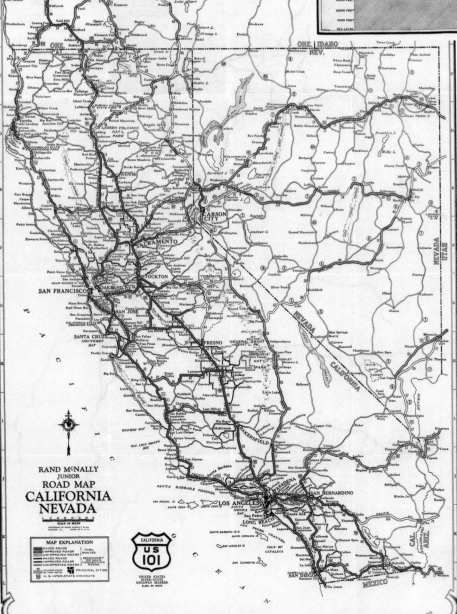

Map 524 (*left*).

In preparation for the full implementation of U.S. Highway numbers the following year, this Rand McNally road map of California from 1926 shows the "US" route numbers together with an example of what to look for. The map is of interest in that it also indicates which roads are paved, "improved," and so on; only the roads shown with a solid red line are paved, and they are certainly in the minority, even in a relatively populous state like California.

Map 525 (*right*).
Published about 1923, this map created specifically for tourists shows the road system of the Pacific Northwest, though without any reference to road condition. Most of the roads shown would not have been paved. Yellow was a strange color choice, as it is hard to read. Crater Lake National Park, shown at bottom, had allowed motor touring within the park in 1911.

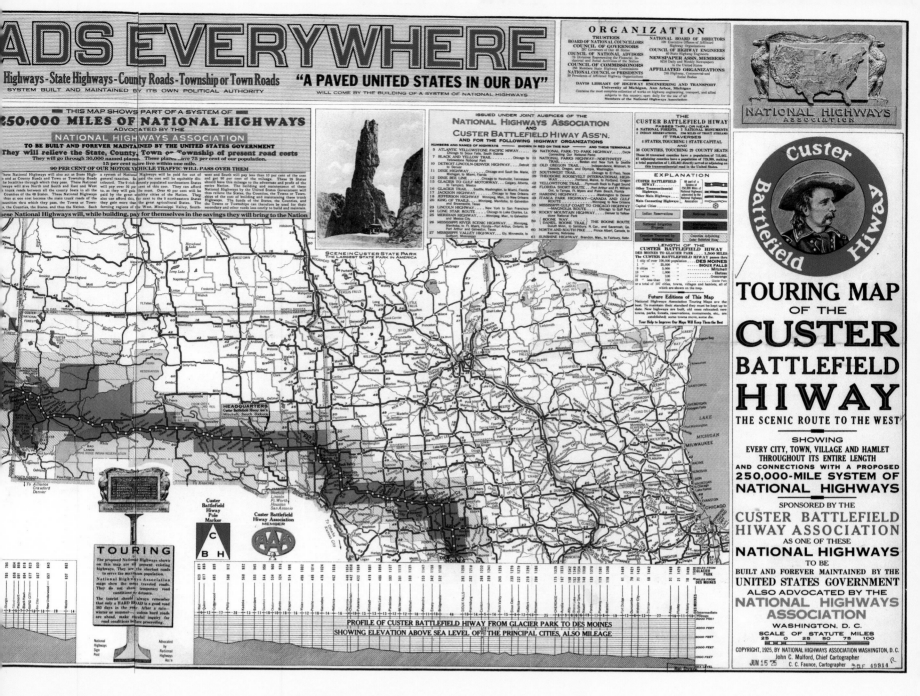

Map 526 (*above*).

A fine example of an automobile touring map published by the National Highways Association, an organization established in 1912 to lobby for *Good Roads Everywhere.* This 1925 map promotes the historical *Custer Battlefield* (see page 151) but shows roads the way the association thought they should be rather than the way they actually were at the time. In the margin the association's aims are promoted, including an interesting idea for highway airports. Early air navigation relied heavily on visual features, and roads were readily identifiable lines that planes could follow.

began a service from Portland to El Paso via California. Three years later the Yelloway Bus Line began the first transcontinental bus service from New York to Los Angeles. In 1929 these two companies merged with a third company, originally established in 1914, that from 1929 would be known as Greyhound Corporation (MAP 530, *overleaf*).

Another development due to the automobile was lodging. At first only downtown hotels were available, since they had to be in an accessible central location served by the railroad, but as automobile tourism grew, cabins began to appear aimed at the touring motorist; these then became "motor courts," then that American invention and institution—the motel.

Map 527 (*right*).

The Lincoln Highway Association prepared this map to show the U.S. secretary of agriculture—who was responsible for roads—recommended routes for federal involvement between Salt Lake City and California in 1923. The existing Lincoln Highway is shown in red.

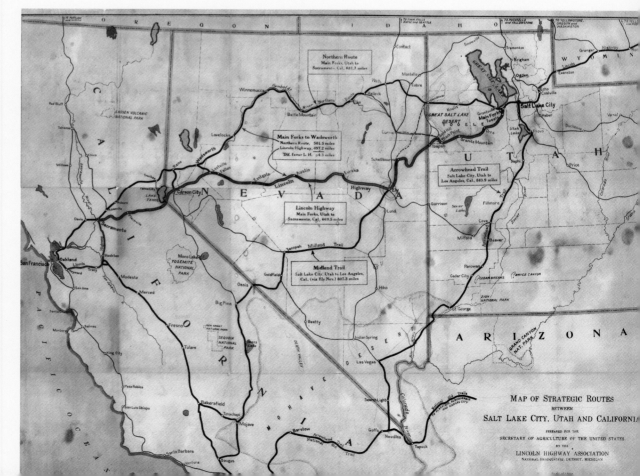

MAP OF STRATEGIC ROUTES BETWEEN SALT LAKE CITY, UTAH AND CALIFORNIA

PREPARED FOR THE SECRETARY OF AGRICULTURE OF THE UNITED STATES BY THE LINCOLN HIGHWAY ASSOCIATION

Map 529 (*left*).
The improved and partially paved *Pacific Highway* is promoted in this strip map from the 1930s. The road, from the Mexican border to Vancouver, British Columbia, was the result of intensive lobbying by the Pacific Highway Association, a group of auto clubs, formed in 1909.

Below.
A map cover for the same highway, published in 1926.

Map 530 (*right*).
A Greyhound Bus map published about 1940. The company started using this name in 1929.

Map 528 (*above*).
This stunning bird's-eye map promoted the *Columbia River Highway* in 1923 as *America's Greatest Scenic Asset.*

Map 531
(*right*, and brochure cover, *below*).
Oregon Motor Stages advertised its *Beach Route* in 1939 with this artistic design. The beaches had been served by railroads but only at selected points. The bus provided service along the coast itself.

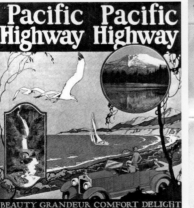

Pacific Pacific
Highway Highway

BEAUTY GRANDEUR COMFORT DELIGHT

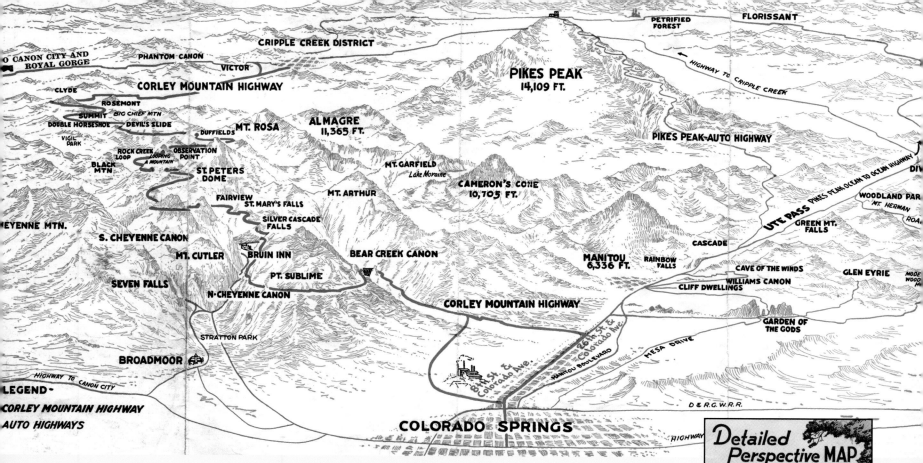

Many roads, including private toll roads, were built specifically to accommodate motor tourists. In one rather ignominious example the rails turned into a road. In 1924 the bed of the defunct Colorado Springs and Cripple Creek District Railway (Cripple Creek Short Line; see page 218) was converted into a scenic highway instead (MAP 532, *above*).

The ubiquity of the automobile led to a profusion of maps: from the twenties to the sixties oil companies tried to outdo each other with often artistically produced road maps, all given away free to their customers. An example is MAP 19, *page 16*. Auto clubs and states also issued road maps to encourage automobile tourism. Two particularly striking examples are illustrated on page 233.

Automobiles gradually became the principal way tourists arrived, and they transformed tourism into a major facet of the western economy. Roads kept improving, and in 1940 the first freeway, the Arroyo Seco Freeway in—where else—Los Angeles—was completed. It would be the first of many that would transform the West even further (see page 248).

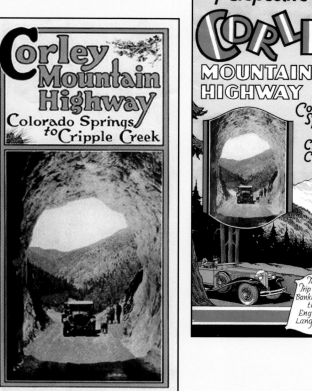

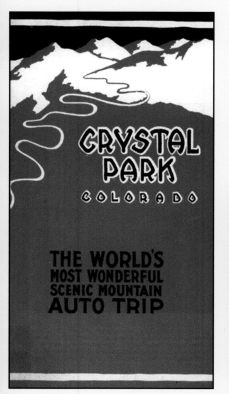

MAP 533 (*left*) and photo, *below*.
The Crystal Park Auto Highway was a toll road for tourist use. This brochure from about 1920 displays the highway as a schematic map. A 1923 guidebook sets the tone: "Every kind of car makes the trip easily in second gear," it stated. "No changing of gears on this trip." The road was promoted with the usual excess as the "Scenic Wonder Trip of the World." Crystal Park, so named because crystals of gems could be found there, is ten miles southwest of Colorado Springs.

MAP 532 (*above*) with two brochure covers.
The Corley Mountain Highway was built on the roadbed of the Colorado Springs and Cripple Creek District Railway (the Cripple Creek Short Line; see page 218) after the railway became bankrupt in 1919. W.D. Corley, a coal mine owner, purchased the railbed and turned it into a toll road, which opened in 1924. The same hyperbole that was used to promote the railroad is now being used to promote the road. Perhaps inspired by the superb bird's-eye maps used to display the railroad's route, Corley used this attractive three-dimensional map in his 1925 brochure. Other connecting roads are also shown. In the 1930s Corley sold the road to the federal government, and the U.S. Forest Service turned it into a public-use road, a free highway called the Gold Camp Road. The whole road was listed in the National Register of Historic Places in 1999.

LEGEND
U.S. Highways
91
89
40
50
33
30
6
189
191
State Highways
3
Railroads
Airlanes
Rivers

Map 534 (*left*).
This colorful pictorial map of Utah was issued by the state tourism commission in 1939. It shows railroads, roads, and what are termed *Airlanes*. The booklet that contained this map was full of photographs of the state, and two are reproduced below. At *bottom left* is British racing driver John Cobb's "Railton Special," which broke the world land speed record on the Bonneville salt flats near Wendover, Utah, on 23 August 1939. He traveled at 367.91 miles per hour. *Below, bottom,* automobiles are lined up along the beach for a day at the Great Salt Lake.

PRE-1937

HISTORIC

NEW MEXICO
U.S.
66

ROUTE

Above.
A historic marker for the pre-1937 U.S. Route 66 on a narrow street through the center of Santa Fe, New Mexico.

TRAVEL US 66
...WILL ROGERS HIGHWAY
...1296 MILES FOUR-LANE!

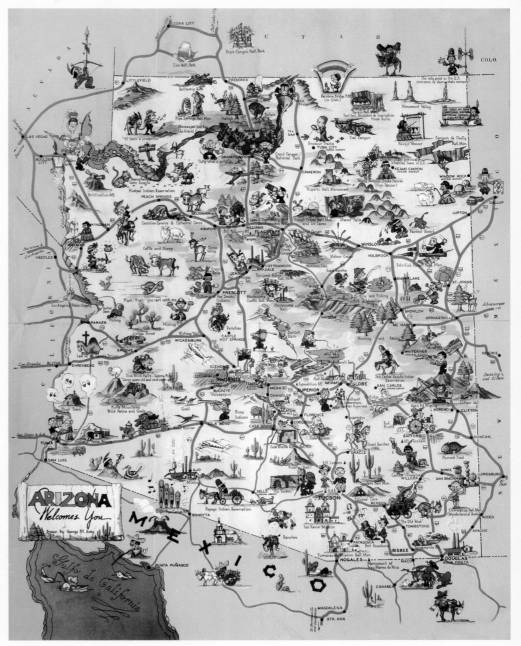

MAP 535 (*above*) and MAP 536 (*below, left*).
Perhaps the most fabled road in all of America, Route 66 was one of the original roads of the U.S. system introduced in 1926–27. The road ran from Chicago to Los Angeles, a distance of about 2,450

miles, though the exact distance varied with various realignments. The road was a major pathway for migrants to the West in the 1930s, and many businesses that grew up on the route relied on the flow of traffic along it. Route 66 was officially decommissioned in 1985, having been replaced by the Interstate Highway System. A 1952 postcard and brochure from about the same date advertise US Route 66.

MAP 538 (*below, left*) and MAP 539 (*below, right*).
Two Montana State Highway Commission road map covers just two years apart: 1940 (*left*) and 1942 (*right*). The 1940 cover evokes the classic romantic West of cowboys and Indians and buffalo, somehow transmuted into automobiles, while the 1942 cover has dispensed with the romance in favor of emphasizing patriotism and the war effort. Either way, both are superb pieces of art.

MAP 537 (*above*).
The August 1940 edition of *Arizona Highways*, a monthly magazine for the promotion of the state's tourism and economy in general, featured this detailed pictorial map of the state: *Arizona Welcomes You*. The magazine called it a "pleasure map."

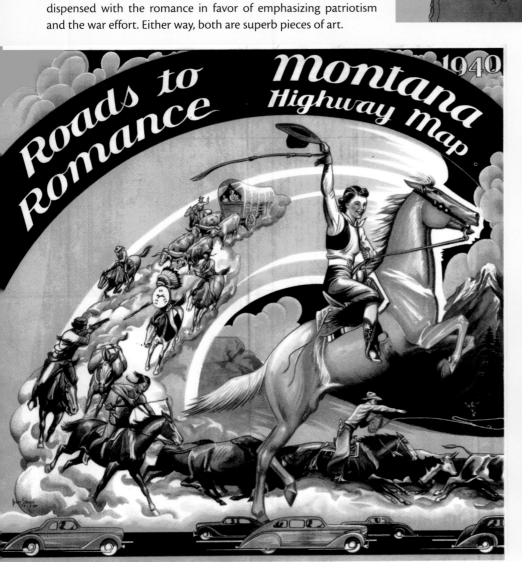

DISTANCE TAMED

Commercial flight effectively came to the West in 1925 when Congress passed the Kelly Air Mail Act, which—just as had happened in due course with stagecoaches, with the Pony Express, and with railroads—put regional mail flights up for private bid, thus encouraging regular air routes to be established. It was not long before a few adventurous passengers were also taken along.

The following year the post office also contracted out the transcontinental mail route, and William Boeing won the Chicago–to–San Francisco leg. Boeing Air Transport began flying mail to the West in July 1927. Boeing's company was split up in 1934 to create three companies, one of which was the aircraft manufacturer with its principal facilities in Seattle, Boeing Airplane Company. Another was United Air Lines, now based in Denver.

Just as World War I had demonstrated the practicality of aviation, World War II changed it again, with reliable planes such as the trusty Douglas DC-3 emerging in considerable numbers to be used by commercial airlines after the war. But still only a tiny fraction of the public flew. In the late 1950s Boeing introduced its Boeing 707 and, using this plane, American Airlines flew the first nonstop transcontinental flight in January 1959. The competitive Douglas DC-8 began service later that year, and the two planes ushered in the jet age. Now anywhere in the West—indeed, anywhere in the world (with a reasonable runway, at least)—could be reached in a matter of hours.

In 1978 airlines were deregulated and became more subject to market conditions. Some regional airlines were forced out of business—Dallas-based Braniff and Denver-based Frontier were probably the best known—but deregulation also allowed smaller airlines to fill in perceived gaps in the market—smaller cities not well served by the larger companies. And so, using smaller jets such as Boeing's 737, air service to the West was filled in, with flights to quite small cities not so long ago thought unable to provide enough customers. For tourists and for businesspeople alike, the West became integrated with the East in a way not possible before.

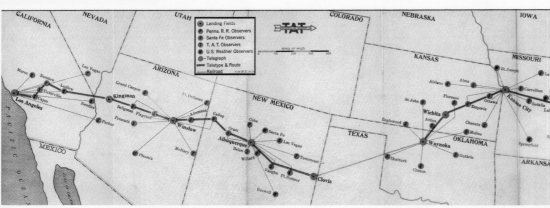

MAP 540 (*left, top*).
Vacation by air in the sunny West is the message from this American Airlines brochure in 1956.

MAP 541 (*left, center*).
Transcontinental Air Transport briefly operated a combined air and rail transcontinental service as shown on this 1929 map of the western portion of the route. The service, which lasted only sixteen months, involved a rail bridge overnight between Waynoka, Oklahoma, and Clovis, New Mexico. Planes by this time could fly at night, but nighttime flight was considered too dangerous for passengers. Tickets were expensive, and with the onset of the Depression not enough customers could be found. The airline merged with others in 1930 to create Transcontinental and Western Air—TWA—which in 1931 flew the first scheduled coast-to-coast service.

MAP 542 (*left, bottom*).
In 1929 the largest U.S. airline was Western Air Express. Its 4,700 miles of route, shown here, required thirty-nine planes. The airline was one of those merged in 1930 to create TWA.

MAP 543 (*below*).
Oakland's plans for its airport expansion, about 1946. An airport at this location was first opened in 1927 by famous aviator Charles Lindbergh and has developed into a low-cost airline and air freight center.

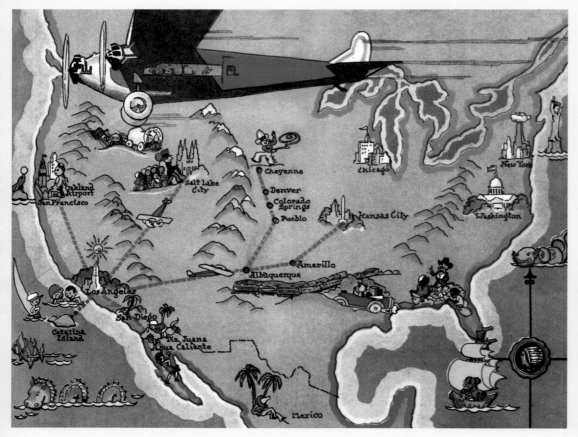

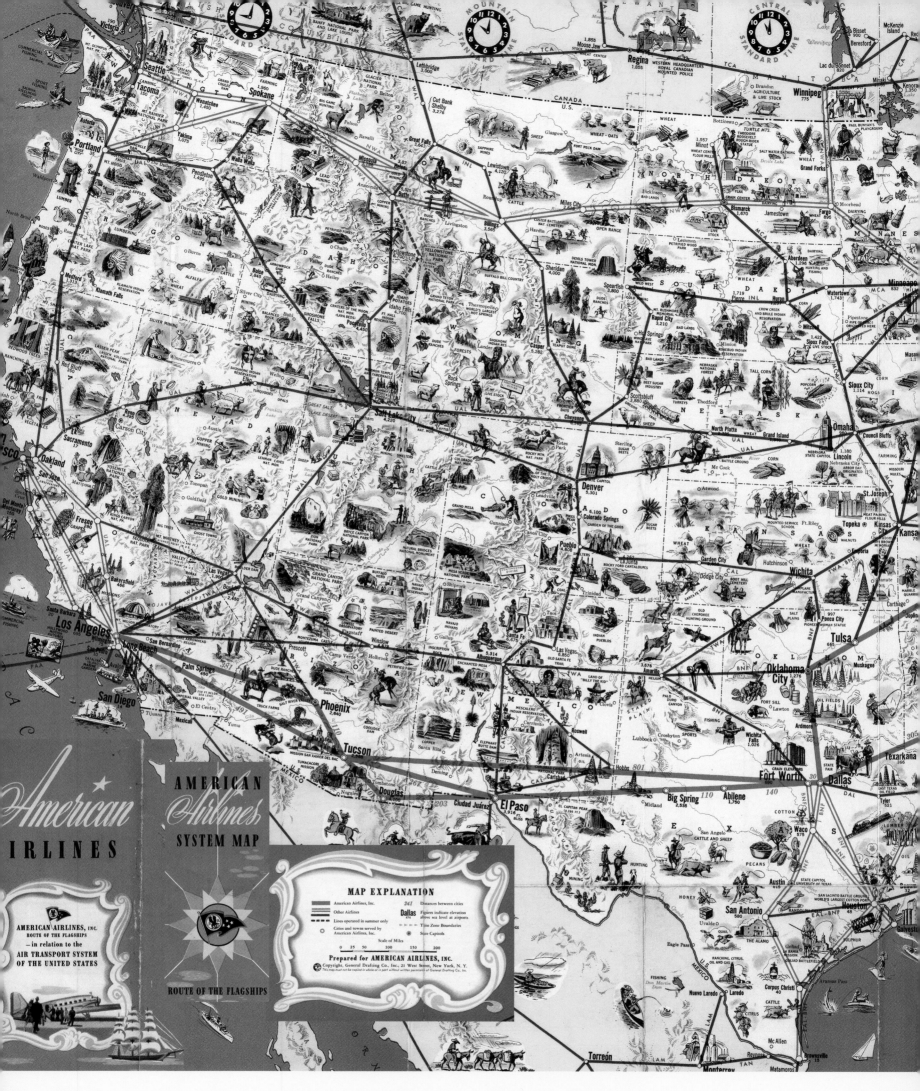

Map 544.

An amazingly detailed, intricately drawn, and colorful pictorial map of the West, published by American Airlines in 1945. Despite the fact that the map is of the entire West, as can be seen from the key, American Airlines at this time only operated flights to and from Los Angeles (in solid red), and even taking into account the routes of other airlines shown, the West is still poorly served by air. By 1954, as can partly be seen from Map 542 (left, bottom) American Airlines routes had multiplied, along with those of its competitors, and the West was serviced by a considerably greater density of routes. Note that the routes are relatively short hops, reflecting the range of the propeller-driven, piston-engined planes of the day.

WANT, WATER, AND WAR

This famous image of the Dust Bowl was taken by federal photographer Arthur Rothstein in Cimarron County, Oklahoma, in April 1936.

THE DEPRESSION YEARS

The West had, like the rest of the country, experienced mainly good economic conditions during the 1920s. Technology improved the quality of life of rural inhabitants—the automobile and the radio (MAP 547, *right*) contributing greatly in reducing the feeling of isolation. But prosperity was not uniform, and the rural population fled to the cities in greater numbers than ever. The decade saw the beginnings of the West as the most urbanized region of the United States—urbanized in terms of proportion of the population living in cities.

Then came the crash of 1929 and the onset of the Great Depression. Conditions on the central and southern Plains were made worse by the Dust Bowl—wind erosion of the soil loosened by poor agricultural practices and then subjected to years of drought—which forced many more off the land. Migrants headed west for California, where the state's own advertising had for years been telling them the living was easy. California, this time, would have preferred they stayed home. John Steinbeck's novel *The Grapes of Wrath* (1939) documented the social upheaval of the migration of the "Okies" west.

Most big cities grew shack towns on any convenient vacant piece of land; they were soon dubbed "Hoovervilles" in derision of a president who seemed to be insensitive to the plight of the homeless.

A new president, Franklin D. Roosevelt, ousted Herbert Hoover in 1933 and, determined to be seen to be "doing something" about all the misery, initiated an alphabet soup of organizations to use federal money for projects to create employment and bolster the economy. His "New Deal" had a lasting impact on the West, where funds were channeled not only to irrigation projects such as those in the Columbia Basin (see overleaf) but also to a myriad of smaller projects such as schools, hospitals, parks, roads, and municipal water supplies, some of which are illustrated on the pictorial Public Works Administration (PWA) map (MAP 548, *right, bottom*).

MAP 545 (*left, center*).
The California Pacific International Exposition was held in San Diego in 1935 using funds supplied by the federal Works Progress Administration (WPA)—money that was intended for the arts and all types of artists on relief.

MAP 546 (*left, bottom*).
A California tourist brochure published in 1936 shows an unusual bird's-eye view of California from the coast, looking east.

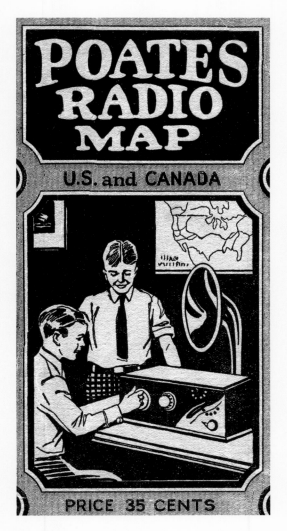

POATES
RADIO
MAP

U.S. and CANADA

PRICE 35 CENTS

MAP 547 (*right, top*).
Radio stations helped relieve the isolation of many, but they were initially few and far between and had limited range, so they had no effect in vast areas of the West. This radio station map, the cover of which is shown *above*, was published in 1924.

MAP 548 (*right, bottom*).
Published in 1935 by the Public Works Administration (PWA) under the title *PWA Rebuilds the Nation*, this map publicized projects funded by that organization to fight the Depression.

An Agricultural Adjustment Administration (AAA) made payments to farmers who reduced their acreages to eliminate surpluses, increase prices, and minimize erosion on marginal land. The flow of these direct subsidies proved vital to the agricultural West. The Rural Electrification Administration (REA) provided low-cost loans for electrification, and the Soil Conservation Service (SCS) tried to restore eroded land by planting native grasses, providing employment in the process.

In 1934 the government passed the Taylor Grazing Act, which granted cattle farmers grazing leases on 140 million acres of federal rangelands under strict conditions derived from more scientific management of the land. In the spring of 1935 Roosevelt withdrew 165 million acres of remaining public domain land, setting them aside for grazing and some other federally regulated uses. This seminal change in public policy is considered by many historians to have marked the final closing of the western frontier.

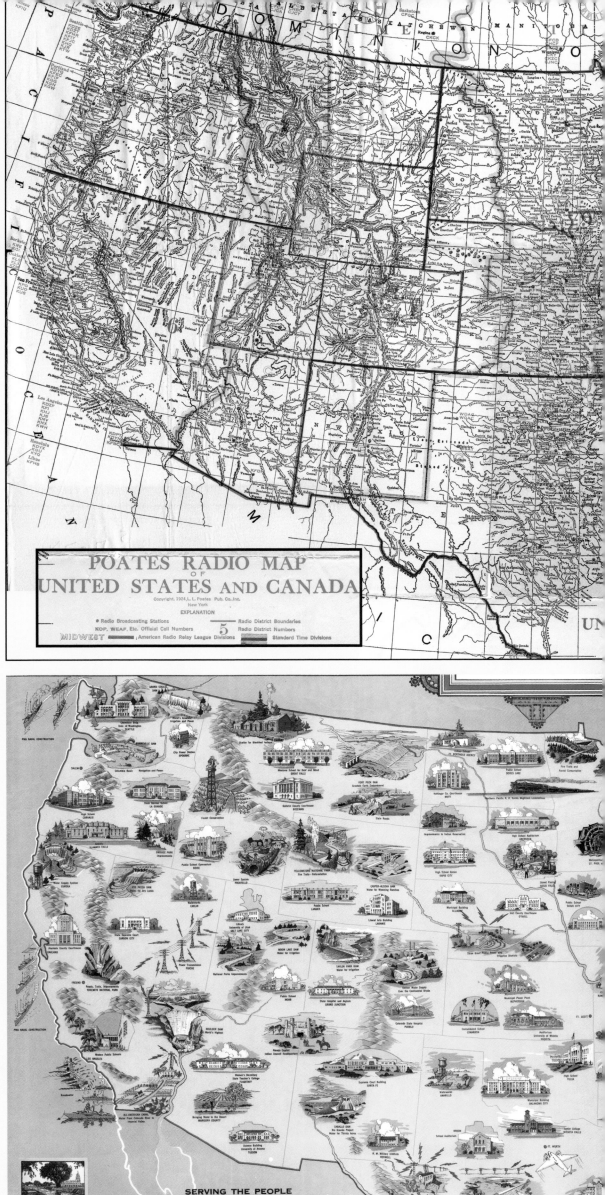

POATES RADIO MAP
OF
UNITED STATES AND CANADA

Copyright, 1924, L. L. Poates Pub. Co. Inc.
New York
EXPLANATION

● Radio Broadcasting Stations   ━━━ Radio District Boundaries
KOP, WEAF, Etc. Official Call Numbers   5 Radio District Numbers

MIDWEST ━━━━━ American Radio Relay League Divisions   ▬▬▬ Standard Time Divisions

SERVING THE PEOPLE

In picture and legend, this map indicates how the Federal Public Works Administration has aided local communities to rebuild the United States. Thousands of PWA improvements and structures, of which only a selected number of typical examples appear here, have modernized our cities—conserved and developed our resources—refurbished our school system—improved public health—advanced our recreational facilities—and helped to create a stronger, better-equipped nation for all the people. These useful PWA projects, in nearly every county in the United States, have stimulated industry and employment. As permanent national assets they are dedicated to the service of the American public.

The Big Water Projects

Of equally long-lasting significance to the West was the series of large multipurpose dams initiated in the 1930s. The Bureau of Reclamation, the PWA, and the Army Corps of Engineers began a program of dam building that would permanently alter the face of the arid West. The dams would provide not only irrigation for agriculture but also cheap electricity, flood control—and, of course, employment.

The Hoover Dam is today the single most important dam in the West, and its reservoir, Lake Mead (see also page 259) supplies water to much of the Southwest. It was planned in the 1920s, before the Depression, and work started in 1931; it became a convenient works project, outstripping most of the PWA projects in the employment it provided. The dam, which contains 4.36 million cubic yards of concrete, was completed in 1936. Its reservoir, Lake Mead, contains 28.5 million acre-feet of water, at least when full (which it rarely is these days), and stretches 110 miles back from the dam. The project required the Bureau of Reclamation to contract with six construction companies, since none was large enough by itself to raise the necessary capital.

The 1930s saw construction begin on a number of other large dams and other water projects, all of which were destined to contribute to what would add up to massive change in the West, as regional economies

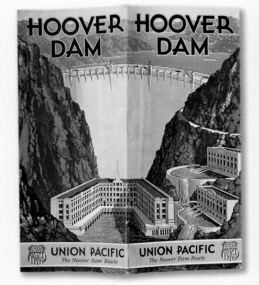

MAP 549 (*below, top*).
This 1879 map of Black and Boulder canyons shows the topography of the area long before the Hoover Dam was built and Lake Mead was created.

MAP 550 (*below, bottom*).
A modern signboard at the Hoover Dam explains how it was made and illustrates the amount of aggregate required for its concrete with a map showing the trainload spanning the distance from Las Vegas to Austin.

MAP 551 (*right, bottom*).
This magnificent 1934 Union Pacific bird's-eye map shows the Hoover Dam—then the Boulder Dam—and the lake behind it while the dam was still two years away from completion. The booming construction town of *Boulder City* competes with a smaller *Las Vegas* nearby. Today the urban area of Las Vegas and its southeastern arm of Henderson has expanded to all but encompass Boulder City. The cover of this map is shown at *top right*.

Above and far right.
The project changed its name several times. Originally planned for Boulder Canyon, it retained the name Boulder Dam when it was moved to Black Canyon. In February 1931 the name was officially changed to Hoover Dam, to reflect the name of the president who initiated it—and who would be standing for reelection the following year. When that election was lost to Roosevelt, a new secretary of the interior, Harold Ickes,

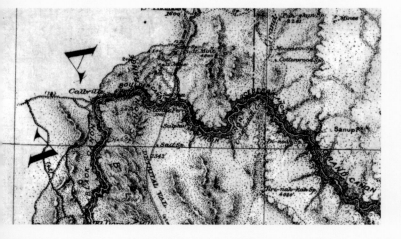

A Dam of Sand and Stone

Aggregate, the sand and stone that goes into concrete, makes up 75% of Hoover Dam's mass. Aggregate was also needed for the powerplant, spillways, and tunnels.

Aggregate came from river rocks and a gravel deposit 6 miles from the dam site. Rail cars brought aggregate to the screening and washing plant, where it was washed and separated by size. The aggregate was then hauled by trains to two concrete mixing plants.

Trains ran around the clock, bringing aggregate to the screening and washing plant, then to the concrete plants. April, 1932.

The screening and washing plant only stockpiled materials for 14 hours of operation, so trains ran constantly between the plant and the gravel deposit. February, 1932.

By the time the aggregate plant stopped operating, it had processed 4.5 million cubic yards of aggregate. November, 1934.

The Boulder Canyon Project required more concrete than was used in all Reclamation projects prior to 1931 combined. To assure success, two concrete plants and the world's largest and most sophisticated concrete production system, were built here.

High Mix concrete plant. September, 1933.

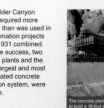

The concrete plants produced enough concrete to build a 16-foot wide highway from Seattle, Washington to Miami, Florida. Low Mix concrete plant. January, 1932.

The plants produced enough aggregate to fill a train stretching from Las Vegas to Austin, Texas—1,300 miles!

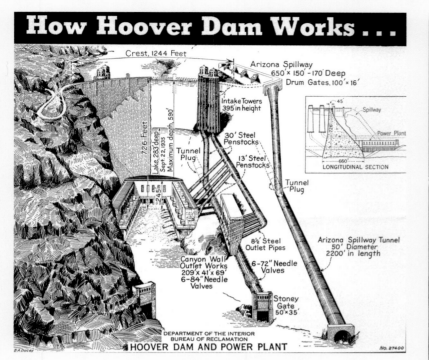

How Hoover Dam Works...

Crest, 1244 Feet

Arizona Spillway
650' x 150' -170' Deep
Drum Gates, 100' x 16'

Intake Towers
395 in height

30' Steel
Penstocks

Tunnel
Plug

13' Steel
Penstocks

Tunnel
Plug

726 Feet

Lake, 283' deep
Sept 22, 1935
Maximum depth, 590'

245 ft

Arizona Spillway Tunnel
50' Diameter
2200' in length

8½ Steel
Outlet Pipes

6-72" Needle
Valves

Canyon Wall
Outlet Works
209' x 41' x 69'
6-84" Needle
Valves

Stoney Gate
50' x 35'

Spillway

Power Plant

45

660'
LONGITUDINAL SECTION

DEPARTMENT OF THE INTERIOR
BUREAU OF RECLAMATION

HOOVER DAM AND POWER PLANT

No. 27400

MAP 552 (*above*).
A 1949 Bureau of Reclamation brochure explained, with the help of this part map, part cut-away diagram, how the dam—now Hoover Dam again—worked.

issued a memo in May 1933, instructing that the dam be known as the Boulder Dam. And so it remained until 1947 when the Truman administration officially named it the Hoover Dam once again. Herbert Hoover, who died in 1964, lived to see his dam's name restored. The covers on the 1932 and 1934 versions of MAP 551, *below*, reflect the name changes.

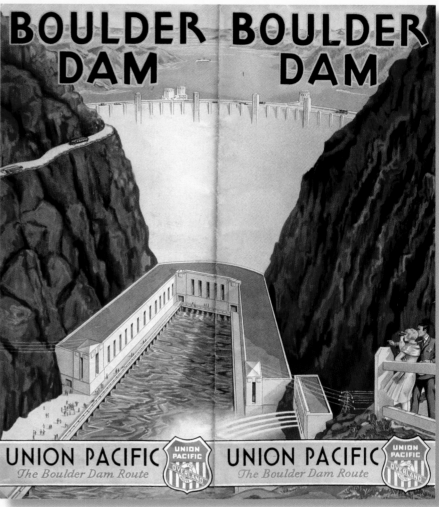

Panoramic Perspective of the Area Adjacent to
BOULDER DAM
As It Will Appear When Dam is Completed
SERVED EXCLUSIVELY BY THE
UNION PACIFIC SYSTEM
"The Boulder Dam Route"

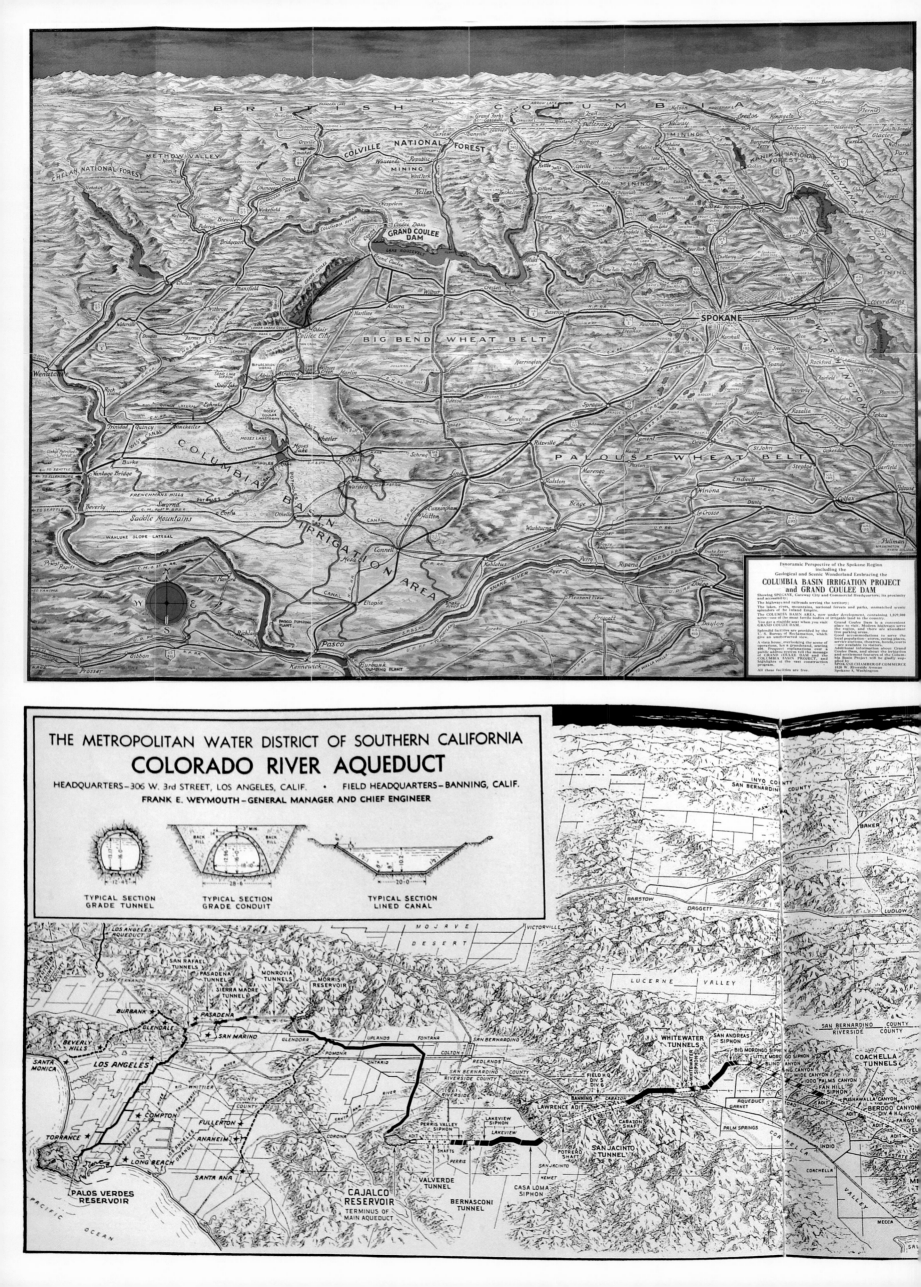

were revived and expanded, building up the local economy and making the arid West more habitable. Some, such as the Colorado–Big Thompson Project (see page 251) or California's Central Valley Project (see page 252) were so extensive that they were not completed until after World War II.

On the Columbia the U.S. Army Corps of Engineers in 1933 began work on the Bonneville Dam, a project intended to generate power and to allow larger ships to navigate the river. The first powerhouse was completed in 1937; a second one would be completed later, in 1981. Farther up the river, the vast Columbia Basin Irrigation Project also began in 1933 with the construction of the Grand Coulee Dam, completed just as the war began. This complex project involved further dam construction, notably the sealing off of part of the Grand Coulee, a deep canyon, with earthen dams at either end to create a massive holding reservoir, Banks Lake, twenty-seven miles long. The Dry Falls Dam was completed in 1949 and the North Dam in 1951. Irrigation, which had been put on hold during the war in favor of power generation for aluminum smelting, came to the Columbia Basin in the 1950s.

The other critically important western water project of the 1930s was not funded by the federal Depression agencies: the Colorado River Aqueduct, which brings water to the Los Angeles Basin and San Diego from the Colorado at the Parker Dam, was completed in 1941. Conceived in 1923 by William Mulholland, the engineer responsible for the earlier Los Angeles Aqueduct (see page 194), the ambitious project (MAP 554, *below*) overcame mountain ranges with tunnels and pumping stations. It became clear during the planning stages that even Los Angeles could not afford the project by itself, and so the Metropolitan Water District of Southern California was created, representing most of the cities of southern California. The consequent availability of water permitted the explosive growth of the region and its new wartime manufacturing industries during World War II.

MAP 553 (*left, top*) and MAP 555 (*above*).
During the Depression the Pacific Northwest was the recipient of two major projects on the Columbia River—the Bonneville Dam and the Grand Coulee Dam. This interesting bird's-eye-style map, published by the Spokane Chamber of Commerce in 1949, shows the *Columbia Basin Irrigation Project*, the *Grand Coulee Dam*, and *Lake [Franklin D.] Roosevelt* in relation to the city of *Spokane*. The *Equalizing Reservoir* in the *Grand Coulee* is Banks Lake, then unfilled, formed by earthen dams at either end. MAP 555 is the cover of the folded map, with an image of the Grand Coulee Dam.

MAP 554 (*left, bottom*).
The *Colorado River Aqueduct* is shown in this superb bird's-eye map from the report of the Metropolitan Water District of Southern California for 1939. The *Parker Dam*, where the aqueduct takes water from the river, is at right; the unnamed reservoir behind it is Lake Havasu (see page 257).

MAP 556 (*below*).
San Diego ran short of water because of wartime growth, and so in 1944 an emergency extension of the Colorado Aqueduct was authorized. The extension was not, however, completed until 1947, after the end of the war.

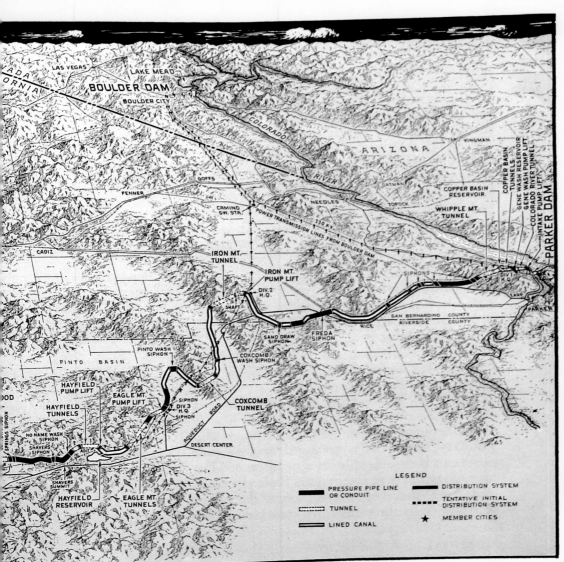

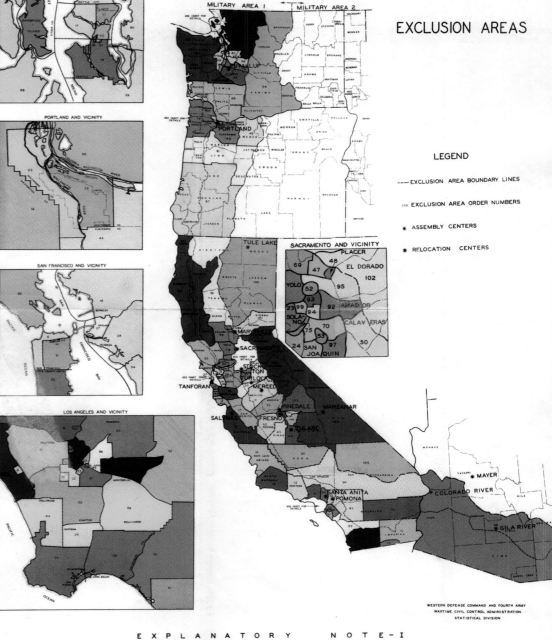

Map 557 (*above, left*).
A newspaper report the day after the "Battle of Los Angeles" showing *Where Anti-Aircraft Guns Opened Up*, despite the lack of any actual enemy planes.

Map 558 (*above*).
A map of Japanese *Exclusion Areas* in 1942, from a federal government report, *Japanese Evacuation from the West Coast, 1942*, published the following year. The map also shows the location of temporary assembly centers and the *Relocations Centers* to which persons of Japanese ancestry were then sent.

Map 559 (*left*).
This one-time top secret map shows the disposition of the American Pacific Fleet at the time of the Japanese attack on Pearl Harbor. On the West Coast, ships are at San Diego, Los Angeles, San Francisco, and Puget Sound.

Left, top.
The headline of the *Los Angeles Times* on the morning of 25 February 1942, following the "Battle of Los Angeles" the night before. Note also the subheading: *Fifth-Column Acts Reported During Raids.*

Left, center.
A manual on warplane identification published for civil defense personnel.

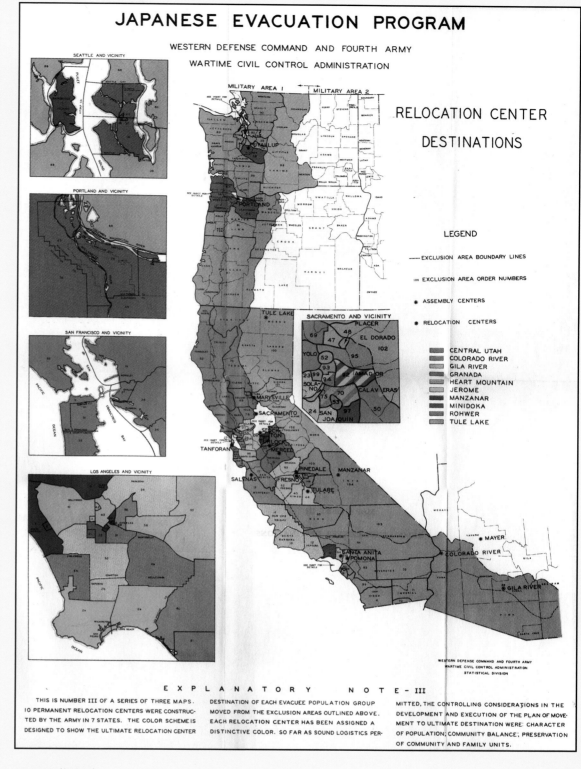

JAPANESE EVACUATION PROGRAM

WESTERN DEFENSE COMMAND AND FOURTH ARMY
WARTIME CIVIL CONTROL ADMINISTRATION

RELOCATION CENTER
DESTINATIONS

LEGEND

—— EXCLUSION AREA BOUNDARY LINES

100 EXCLUSION AREA ORDER NUMBERS

★ ASSEMBLY CENTERS

● RELOCATION CENTERS

CENTRAL UTAH
COLORADO RIVER
GILA RIVER
GRANADA
HEART MOUNTAIN
JEROME
MANZANAR
MINIDOKA
ROHWER
TULE LAKE

WESTERN DEFENSE COMMAND AND FOURTH ARMY
WARTIME CIVIL CONTROL ADMINISTRATION
STATISTICAL DIVISION

EXPLANATORY NOTE - III

THIS IS NUMBER III OF A SERIES OF THREE MAPS. 10 PERMANENT RELOCATION CENTERS WERE CONSTRUCTED BY THE ARMY IN 7 STATES. THE COLOR SCHEME IS DESIGNED TO SHOW THE ULTIMATE RELOCATION CENTER DESTINATION OF EACH EVACUEE POPULATION GROUP MOVED FROM THE EXCLUSION AREAS OUTLINED ABOVE. EACH RELOCATION CENTER HAS BEEN ASSIGNED A DISTINCTIVE COLOR. SO FAR AS SOUND LOGISTICS PERMITTED, THE CONTROLLING CONSIDERATIONS IN THE DEVELOPMENT AND EXECUTION OF THE PLAN OF MOVEMENT TO ULTIMATE DESTINATION WERE: CHARACTER OF POPULATION; COMMUNITY BALANCE; PRESERVATION OF COMMUNITY AND FAMILY UNITS.

Map 560 (*right*).
Color codes indicate the *Relocation Center Destinations* to which Japanese Americans from the coastal areas and southern Arizona were to be deported. This map comes from the same 1943 federal government report as Map 558. Temporary assembly centers are indicated, from where the deportees would be moved to an internment camp. Four of the latter—*Tule Lake, Manzanar, Colorado River* (Poston), and *Gila River* (Sacaton)—are shown.

The West at War

War with the expanding empires of Nazi Germany and imperial Japan had been threatening for years when the American fleet at Pearl Harbor was devastatingly attacked by Japan without declaration of war on the morning of 7 December 1941. The United States, and especially the West Coast, was thrown into tumult as rumors built daily of a Japanese attack similar to Pearl Harbor or even a full-scale invasion.

On the night of 10 December unidentified planes were reported approaching the south coast, and a blackout was ordered, which covered the entire area from San Diego to Bakersfield and lasted several hours. The release of casualty figures from Pearl Harbor added to the sense of impending doom—2,251 killed and 1,119 wounded. Then on 23 February 1942 a Japanese submarine fired on the oil installations at Ellwood, west of Santa Barbara, an attack that was front-page news the following morning. At seven the next evening the Navy received a warning from Washington of an imminent air attack on Los Angeles: radar screens did pick up some unidentified object 120 miles west of the city, and something thought to be a balloon was sighted over Santa Monica at three that morning. Antiaircraft batteries opened up all over the region. What actually caused all the shooting in what was dubbed the "Battle of Los Angeles" has never been properly established. It is clear, however, that there was an understandably high state of paranoia in the West in the months following Pearl Harbor.

Under these conditions of an anticipated Japanese invasion President Roosevelt had, a week before, signed Executive Order 9066, which allowed "military areas" to be designated from which "any or all persons" could be excluded at the discretion of the military commander, General John Lesesne DeWitt. As the maps show, these areas were quite arbitrary in many cases.

DeWitt initially sought to persuade Americans of Japanese ancestry to voluntarily relocate away from the coast, but when this

Map 561 (*below*).
A sample map of a 1942 *Prohibited Area*, this one in Oakland, California, from the 1943 Army report, together with the accompanying *Instructions to All Persons of Japanese Ancestry*.

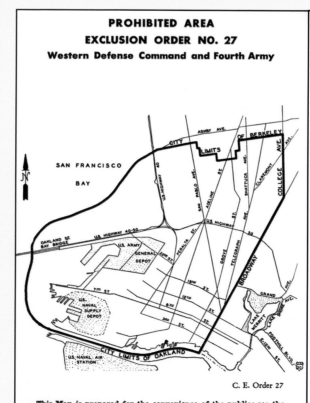

PROHIBITED AREA
EXCLUSION ORDER NO. 27
Western Defense Command and Fourth Army

C. E. Order 27

This Map is prepared for the convenience of the public; see the Civilian Exclusion Order for the full and correct description.

WESTERN DEFENSE COMMAND AND FOURTH ARMY
WARTIME CIVIL CONTROL ADMINISTRATION
Presidio of San Francisco, California

INSTRUCTIONS
TO ALL PERSONS OF
JAPANESE
ANCESTRY
LIVING IN THE FOLLOWING AREA:

All of that portion of the County of Alameda, State of California, within that boundary beginning at the point at which the southerly limits of the City of Berkeley meet San Francisco Bay; thence easterly and following the southerly limits of said city to College Avenue; thence southerly on College Avenue to Broadway; thence southerly on Broadway to the southerly limits of the City of Oakland; thence following the limits of said city westerly and northerly, and following the shoreline of San Francisco Bay to the point of beginning.

Pursuant to the provisions of Civilian Exclusion Order No. 27, this Headquarters, dated April 30, 1942, all persons of Japanese ancestry, both alien and non-alien, will be evacuated from the above area by 12 o'clock noon, P.W.T., Thursday May 7, 1942.

No Japanese person living in the above area will be permitted to change residence after 12 o'clock noon, P.W.T., Thursday, April 30, 1942, without obtaining special permission from the representative of the Commanding General, Northern California Sector, at the Civil Control Station located at:

530 Eighteenth Street,
Oakland, California.

Such permits will only be granted for the purpose of uniting members of a family, or in cases of grave emergency.

The Civil Control Station is equipped to assist the Japanese population affected by this evacuation in the following ways:

1. Give advice and instructions on the evacuation.

2. Provide services with respect to the management, leasing, sale, storage or other disposition of most kinds of property, such as real estate, business and professional equipment, household goods, boats, automobiles and livestock.

3. Provide temporary residence elsewhere for all Japanese in family groups.

4. Transport persons and a limited amount of clothing and equipment to their new residence.

Left.
A Japanese American deportee's suitcase with name and number, preserved in the Arizona Historical Society's museum in Tempe. Takeo Sakata was interned at the Gila River camp.

Below.
This striking and famous photograph of the Manzanar Relocation Center in the Owens Valley of California was taken in July 1942 by a War Relocation Authority photographer.

MAP 562 (*below*).
The vast size of the Manzanar camp is apparent from this plan of the entire installation. Over ten thousand Japanese Americans were housed here for the duration of the war.

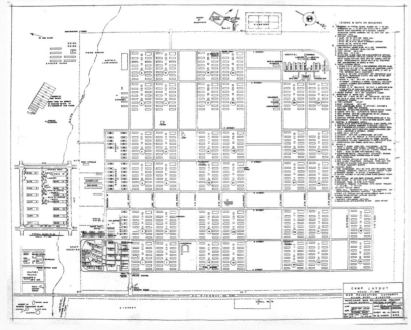

MAP 563 (*right*).
The defenses of San Diego Harbor, shown on a 1941 Army map. This is Point Loma, at the harbor entrance, now the site of the Cabrillo Monument. Several battery installations are indicated (*BTRY* or *BTRIES*). They housed massive guns, capable of firing at ships far out to sea. The gun, *inset,* is a sixteen-inch gun, with the figure standing beside it giving some notion of its immense size and power. It is one of the two big guns in *Btry Ashburn,* at right on the map. The guns are actually facing out to sea, as the map is oriented with north at the right.

strategy did not produce a response he began forcible relocation. All Japanese Americans were required to report to assembly centers, shown on MAP 560, *previous page,* from where they were transported to one of ten internment camps—officially called relocation centers—distributed throughout the West.

Federal funds poured into the West. Every western state had at least one military installation, the West Coast dozens. California, it has been said, felt like one big armed camp. Of particular military importance for the Pacific War were the naval yards at San Diego, Los Angeles–Long Beach, San Francisco, and Bremerton, on Puget Sound. Colorado Springs became a major military center, with Camp Carson housing 37,000 Army trainees. Others were at Fort Leavenworth and Fort Riley, both in Kansas. In Texas, Carswell Field in Fort Worth became a major training base for the Army Air Corps.

On the West Coast, shipbuilding and aircraft manufacture boomed. One of the primary shipbuilders was Henry J. Kaiser. His shipyards together could at their peak produce a new ship every ten hours; over the entire war Kaiser was responsible for a third of all American ships. His shipyard at Richmond, on San Francisco Bay, constructed 486 Liberty ships, freighters all built to the same design. Nearby Mare Island was the U.S. Navy's critical shipbuilding yard. California Shipbuilding Corporation built 467 ships, 336 of them Liberty ships, at its facility on Terminal Island in Los Angeles Harbor. Kaiser built the first western steel mill at Fontana, east of Los Angeles, smelting western ore to supply steel to the yards. And the West's mines, oil wells, and food farmers all fed the war effort.

Los Angeles became a critical aircraft manufacturing center, with companies such as Douglas, Lockheed, Hughes, Northrop, and North American; Consolidated Vultee and Ryan were in San Diego. The latter city grew by 75 percent between 1942 and 1945. Boeing made aircraft in Seattle and Wichita.

The West was irrevocably changed by the war. Cities all over the West bulged at the seams. Some eight million people moved to the West in the 1940–50 decade—3.5 million of those to California. Most immigrants stayed after war's end—Japan surrendered on 14 August 1945—despite the inevitable contraction in defense jobs, and the population now had expectations of a higher standard of living.

Civilian schemes replaced military—new port projects, new civilian aircraft, new power and water projects, new housing, and, with urban sprawl, new freeways. The West's prosperity and growth would hardly pause.

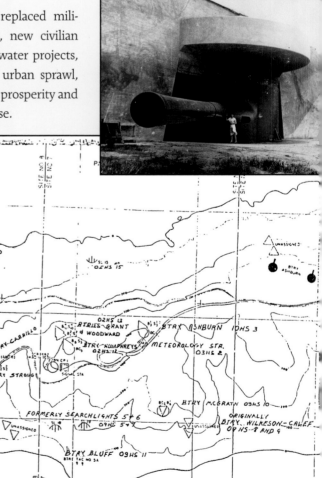

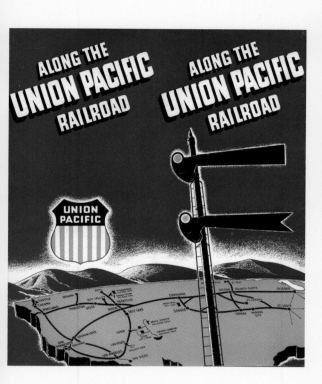

AMERICA'S ZONE OF PLENTY
Served by the Great Northern Railway

No wonder America is able to supply the vast wartime needs of United Nations the world over

MAP 564 (*above*) and MAP 565 (*right*).
The railroads were critical to the war effort, and their advertising was aimed at patriotism during the war period. MAP 564 is from a Union Pacific brochure cover published in 1944, with an interesting perspective view of the West, complete with clifflike coastline. MAP 565 is a Great Northern Railway advertisement from 1942, which emphasizes its transportation of food from the Northern Plains and the Pacific Northwest, together characterized as *America's Zone of Plenty.*

MAP 566 (*below*).
An aeronautical chart issued 12 August 1943. Much of Southern California plus an area extending out into the Pacific Ocean is a *Vital Defense Area* in which the only civilian aircraft permitted were scheduled flights.

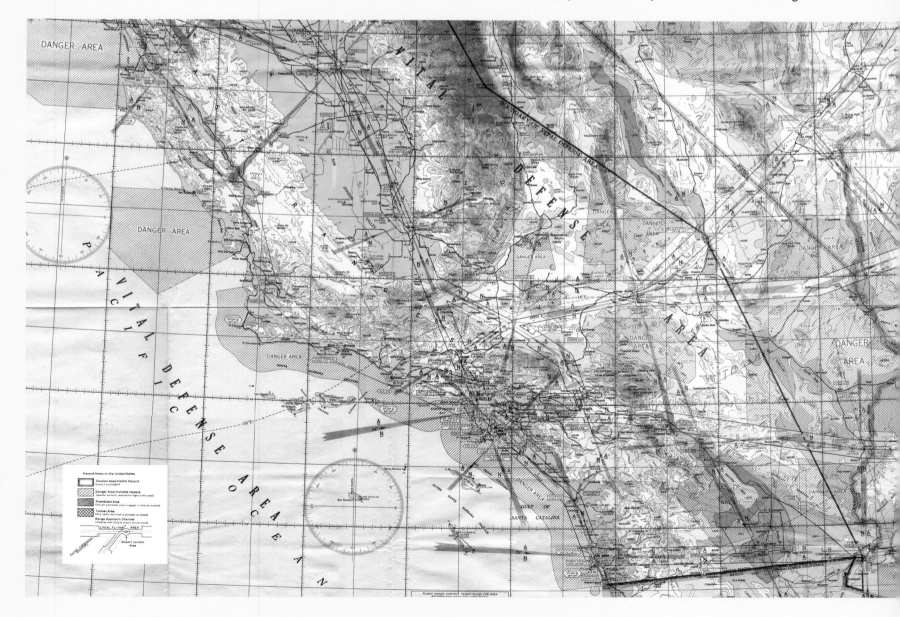

THE POSTWAR WEST

World War II jump-started the growth of the West, the growth we today almost take for granted. More than half a million people flooded into the Los Angeles Basin during the war, even more to the Bay Area. San Diego grew two and a half times, Tucson and Portland doubled, Las Vegas tripled, Seattle grew by 50 percent, Denver by 20 percent. All this growth—and although it slowed, it did not stop thereafter—placed many demands on resources such as water and power. Population growth continued, fueled by migration to the so-called sunbelt, the increasing popularity of retirement in the sun, the availability of air conditioning, and new water projects. And the transportation network also changed forever, with passenger rail declining and automobile ownership climbing, resulting in the construction of a new form of road—the freeway—and especially the federally funded interstate highway network.

RAILROADS

Improvements in standards of living, in particular widespread automobile ownership and, from about 1960 on, the rise of airline travel, were the writing on the wall for the railroad's passenger services, once truly openers of the West and responsible for much of its development up to the middle of the twentieth century.

The West lost about 22,000 miles of rail in the forty years after the war, a lower figure than for the rest of the country because much of western track remains for freight haulage, especially for bulk commodities, such as coal and wheat, that were not so reliant on the door-to-door service a truck could offer. It was essentially impossible for the railroads to compete with their adversaries the car, which could go virtually anywhere, or the plane, which could travel to any western destination within hours. For a while the railroads emphasized service and luxury even more than they had before, but it was a losing battle, one not even the introduction of shiny new diesels could win. In 1971 Amtrak began service, relieving all the railroads of their passenger obligations.

The railroads could now concentrate on their freight operations, and they improved their efficiency with several rounds of mergers; the Great Northern, for example, in 1970 merged with the Northern Pacific; the Chicago, Burlington and Quincy; and the Spokane, Portland and Seattle to create the Burlington Northern. In 1996 it merged once more, this time with the Santa Fe, and is now the Burlington Northern Santa Fe (BNSF).

MAP 567 (*below*) and cover (*right*). Railroad maps and brochures for a while continued to promote tourism in the West as it had before the war. This is a Santa Fe map published in 1946. At Santa Fe *Indian Detours* are advertised (see page 223).

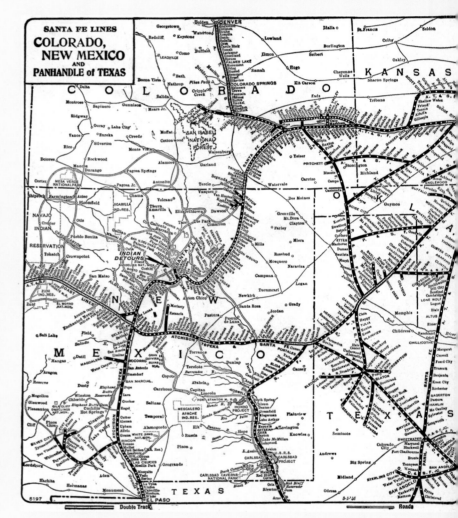

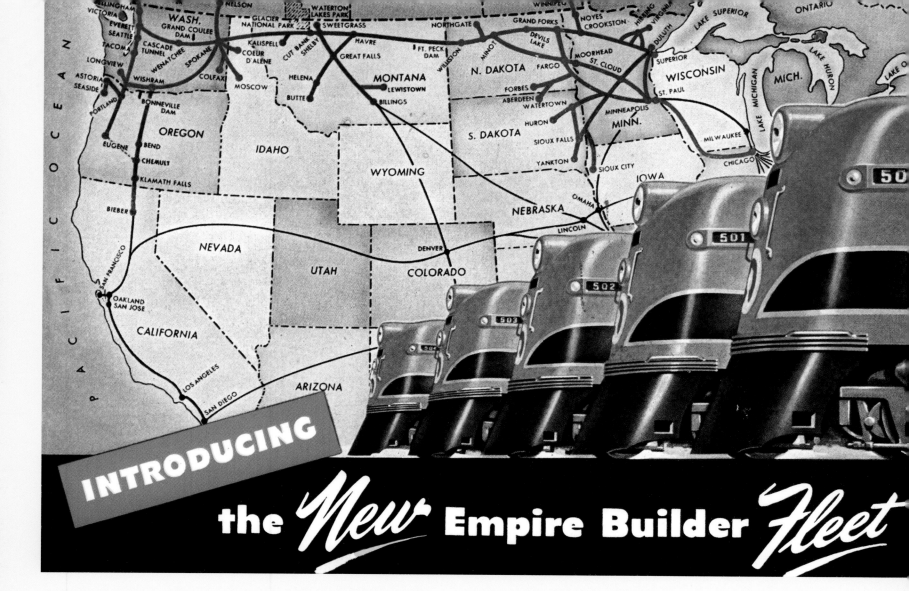

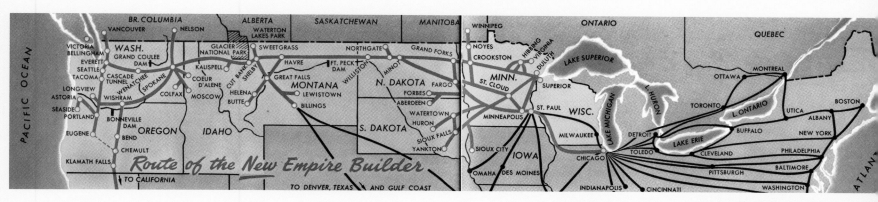

Route of the New Empire Builder

Map 568 (*above, top*), Map 569 (*above*), and illustrations (*below*).

"More luxury, more comfort, more fun" gushed a Great Northern brochure published in 1947 to promote the railroad's new *Empire Builder* transcontinental service. The railroad had to purchase five complete trains to maintain a daily service between Chicago and Seattle or Portland (the train split in Spokane), each of which, the brochure states, cost $1.5 million. That acquisition probably accounts for the fact that five are shown on the brochure cover, gracing an otherwise mundane map of the West. The Burlington, the railroad over which the trains ran from St. Paul to Chicago, owned one of the trains.

The Great Northern's original Empire Builder service was inaugurated in 1929 and was named in honor of James J. Hill, the railroad's founder responsible for a great deal of development in North Dakota and the Pacific Northwest. The Empire Builder advertised here, using new colorfully liveried, streamlined diesels, began service in February 1947. When Amtrak took over railroad passenger service in 1971, it named the train run on this route the Empire Builder. James Hill continues to be honored.

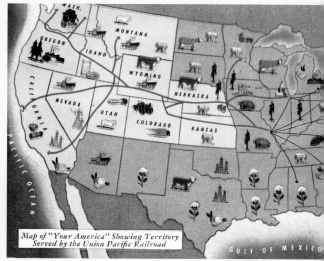

Map of "Your America" Showing Territory Served by the Union Pacific Railroad

Map 570 (*above*).
Rival railroad Union Pacific displayed its lines on this postcard in 1948; the West—or at least the Union Pacific–served West—is "*Your America.*"

FREEWAYS

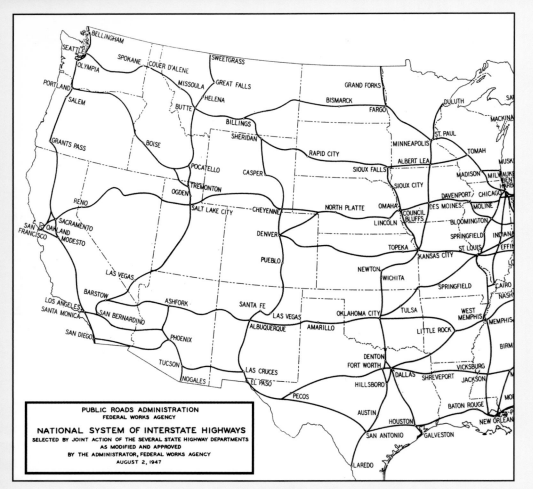

The roads that sounded the death knell of the passenger railroad—the freeways—first appeared in Los Angeles in 1940; in 1947 California passed the Collier–Burns Act, which authorized the use of fuel taxes to build a new highway system and mandated that the state would also be responsible for highways going through urban areas. The Los Angeles Master Plan of that year already envisioned a considerable network of freeways to dissect the city (MAP 572, *below*).

In 1956 Congress, urged on by President Dwight Eisenhower, passed the Federal-Aid Highway Act, which projected a 41,000-mile network of freeways across the nation. The federal government was to pay up to 90 percent of construction costs, though in many western states this climbed to 95 percent. Eisenhower had been impressed by the German autobahn system during the war and had realized its immense value.

Many people reviled the interstate highway system as a destroyer of neighborhoods, and in some instances elevated freeways were torn down. A notable example was the Embarcadero Freeway along the waterfront of San Francisco—never

MAP 571 (*above*).
The system of federally funded interstate highways in the West originally proposed in 1947 and reprinted in the 1955 "Yellow Book." Quite a few—for example, Interstate 5 down the West Coast—were built almost exactly as shown in the 1947 proposal.

MAP 572 (*left*).
The Los Angeles Regional Planning Commission adopted this freeway master plan in 1947. All of the thicker, darker lines are proposed freeways—euphemistically termed parkways, a name that made them sound so much friendlier. Many of these routes were used for freeways during the next twenty years or so. Today Angelenos can only recall with nostalgia the promise the Automobile Club of Southern California made in 1941: "Imagine," it said, "driving your car on an exclusive express highway through the congested Los Angeles metropolitan area without a stop or hindrance."

completely finished owing to local opposition—which was torn down rather than repaired following its damage from the 1989 Loma Prieta earthquake.

Nonetheless, the interstates have transformed the West, fusing it together as never before. The system was officially renamed the Dwight D. Eisenhower National System of Interstate and Defense Highways in 1993 in recognition of the president's key role in their creation.

ESCAPE

MAP 573 (*above*).
The 1955 "Yellow Book" (it had a yellow cover), correctly the *General Location of National System of Interstate Highways*, also contained larger-scale city maps such as this one for Los Angeles, which depicted the proposed interstates around and through the cities.

It will be noted that the word "defense" is part of the freeway system's name. This is because they were considered a primary way of evacuating cities if they were targeted for nuclear attack—if the "Cold War" of the 1950s to 1980s ever became "hot." This rationale provided much of the initial justification for the interstate freeways. Virtually every American city produced plans in the mid-1950s for rapid evacuation. Many roads were designated as escape routes and made one-way—away from the city to rural collection areas deemed less prone to be targeted by the enemy—the U.S.S.R., with its Intercontinental Ballistic Missiles (ICBMs). Plans for two western cities are shown at *right*.

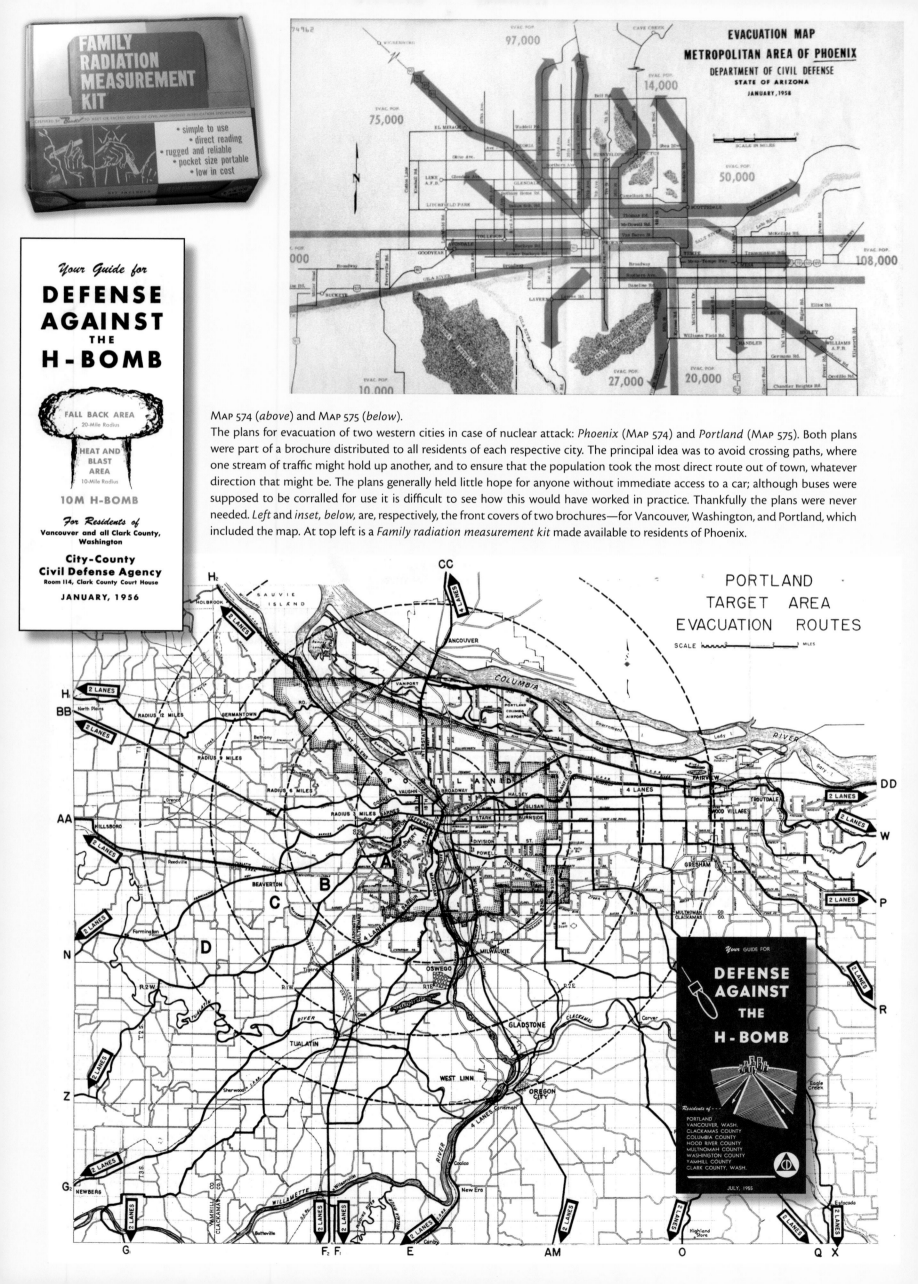

FAMILY RADIATION MEASUREMENT KIT

• simple to use
• direct reading
• rugged and reliable
• pocket size portable
• low in cost

Your Guide for

DEFENSE
AGAINST
THE
H - BOMB

FALL BACK AREA
20-Mile Radius

HEAT AND
BLAST
AREA
10-Mile Radius

10M H-BOMB

For Residents of
Vancouver and all Clark County, Washington

**City-County
Civil Defense Agency**
Room 114, Clark County Court House

JANUARY, 1956

EVACUATION MAP
METROPOLITAN AREA OF PHOENIX
DEPARTMENT OF CIVIL DEFENSE
STATE OF ARIZONA
JANUARY, 1958

SCALE IN MILES

EVAC. POP. 97,000

EVAC. POP. 14,000

EVAC. POP. 75,000

EVAC. POP. 50,000

EVAC. POP. 108,000

EVAC. POP. 10,000

EVAC. POP. 27,000

EVAC. POP. 20,000

MAP 574 (*above*) and MAP 575 (*below*).

The plans for evacuation of two western cities in case of nuclear attack: *Phoenix* (MAP 574) and *Portland* (MAP 575). Both plans were part of a brochure distributed to all residents of each respective city. The principal idea was to avoid crossing paths, where one stream of traffic might hold up another, and to ensure that the population took the most direct route out of town, whatever direction that might be. The plans generally held little hope for anyone without immediate access to a car; although buses were supposed to be corralled for use it is difficult to see how this would have worked in practice. Thankfully the plans were never needed. *Left* and *inset, below,* are, respectively, the front covers of two brochures—for Vancouver, Washington, and Portland, which included the map. At top left is a *Family radiation measurement kit* made available to residents of Phoenix.

PORTLAND
TARGET AREA
EVACUATION ROUTES

SCALE

Your GUIDE FOR

DEFENSE
AGAINST
THE
H - BOMB

Residents of ---
PORTLAND
VANCOUVER, WASH.
CLACKAMAS COUNTY
COLUMBIA COUNTY
HOOD RIVER COUNTY
MULTNOMAH COUNTY
WASHINGTON COUNTY
YAMHILL COUNTY
CLARK COUNTY, WASH.

JULY, 1955

ALASKA   the 49th State?

NEXT Tuesday the Alaskans will go to the polls to determine whether the majority favors admission to the Union as a full-fledged state. If the vote is in the affirmative, it will be up to Congress to decide whether the honor of being the 49th state will go to Alaska or Hawaii. The Hawaiians voted for statehood in 1940, but Congress has not passed on the proposal, although President Truman, in January of this year, recommended immediate action. At the same time he urged statehood for Alaska. That territory became American soil in 1867, when we bought it from Russia for $7,200,000. Its area is 586,400 square miles, more than twice the size of our largest state, Texas. The population is about 85,000, less than that of any of the 48 states. More than half are whites; the rest, Eskimos, Aleuts, and Indians. Americans became Alaska-conscious with the discovery of gold about 1890. The events of World War II have demonstrated its importance to our national defense. Existing Army and Navy installations concerning which information is available are indicated on this map. Much of the wealth of Alaska is undeveloped. In recent years, salmon and gold have been its principal exports. For the future, petroleum and platinum are among the known possibilities and a vast amount of unknown wealth may lie in the unexplored areas.

(NEWS map by Staff Artist Sundberg)

MAP 576 (*above*).
This map appeared in an Alaska newspaper in October 1946, just before a referendum was held on the question of statehood. The referendum passed by a margin of three to two, but although a statehood bill was introduced into Congress by 1948, it quickly became bogged down in political wrangling and died.

MAP 577 (*left*).
A humorous postcard published around the time Alaska became a state in 1959. Up till that time, of course, Texas had been the largest state—and proud of it.

ALASKA

After Pearl Harbor, the military mobilization of Alaska transformed the territory. The Army built the 1,390-mile-long Alaska Highway in just over eight months in 1942 to facilitate moving munitions and men required to defend Alaska. Even while the highway was under construction, the Japanese had attacked and occupied Attu and Kiska, in the Aleutian Islands. After the war, however, although many more people were now living in and aware of the territory, Alaska did not achieve statehood until 1959. After several abortive attempts a bill for statehood was passed in 1958, and the bill was signed by President Eisenhower on 7 July 1958, admitting Alaska into the Union as of 3 January 1959.

The state is now the resource powerhouse of America but has endured two traumatic events since statehood. The first was the fearsome Good Friday earthquake of 1964, the most severe earthquake ever recorded in North America. The second involved the state's new resource. Oil was discovered at Prudhoe Bay in 1968, and the Trans-Alaska Pipeline completed in 1977. Transporting oil from this pipeline, the mega-tanker *Exxon Valdez* struck a reef in Prince William Sound on 24 March 1989 and spilled an estimated 10.8 million gallons of crude oil onto 1,100 miles of coastline, killing countless wildlife.

WATER—AGAIN

The West's most precious resource continues to be water. Several major water projects were brought to fruition after World War II, though some were conceived before it.

In Colorado, the Colorado–Big Thompson Project was planned in the late 1930s, and construction began in 1938, but the project was so massive and complex that it was not completed until almost twenty years

The COLORADO-BIG THOMPSON PROJECT
BUREAU OF RECLAMATION

Map 578 (*above*), Map 579 (*right, center*), and Map 580 (*below*). The Colorado–Big Thompson Project, shown in three different types of map. Map 578 is a fine bird's-eye map executed in 1930s style but was actually published in 1959. From the same 1959 Bureau of Reclamation brochure is Map 579, a mainly cross-sectional map, vastly exaggerated vertically, but which illustrates very well the route along which water is diverted to take it over the Continental Divide through the 13.2-mile-long Alva B. Adams Tunnel. Map 580 is a regular map with relief shown by shading and color. Together these maps make understanding the complex structure of the project easy.

About 80 percent of Colorado's population lives east of the Continental Divide, while the same proportion of the state's rainfall falls on the western side. The Colorado–Big Thompson Project redresses that imbalance but could only practically do so by using the tunnel. The project was originally built for irrigation purposes, with the generation of power as a side benefit. Today, however, much of the water has been diverted to the cities of the Front Range. There are no fewer than ten reservoirs, eighteen dams, and six power plants in addition to the tunnel. The lynchpin of the project, the Alva B. Adams Tunnel, bored under the Rocky Mountain National Park and named after the Colorado senator responsible for advancing the project, was completed in June 1947, but the entire project was not completed until 1957.

later. Water is impounded in the Willow Creek Reservoir and Lake Granby on the North Fork of the Colorado before being pumped to the Alva B. Adams Tunnel across the Continental Divide. Thus the Colorado, probably the most heavily exploited river in America, sends water east right from its headwaters. One of the first project facilities built, however, was the Green Mountain Dam and Reservoir (also shown on the maps on this page), which also controls water flow west and is now one of a series of dams on the various tributaries of the upper Colorado that do the same (Map 581, *overleaf*).

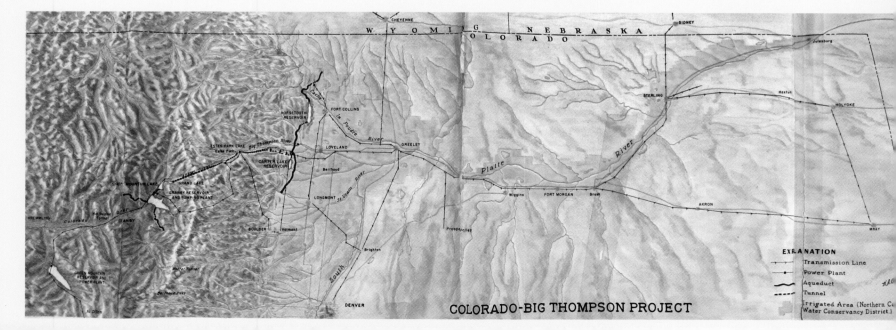

COLORADO-BIG THOMPSON PROJECT

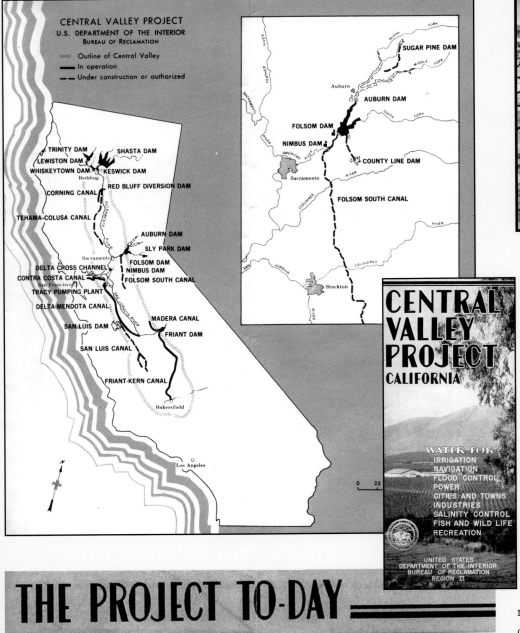

CENTRAL VALLEY PROJECT
U.S. DEPARTMENT OF THE INTERIOR
BUREAU OF RECLAMATION

~~~~ Outline of Central Valley
▬▬ In operation
▬▬ Under construction or authorized

(Map labels, left map:) TRINITY DAM, LEWISTON DAM, WHISKEYTOWN DAM, KESWICK DAM, SHASTA DAM, Redding, RED BLUFF DIVERSION DAM, CORNING CANAL, TEHAMA-COLUSA CANAL, AUBURN DAM, SLY PARK DAM, Sacramento, DELTA CROSS CHANNEL, FOLSOM DAM, NIMBUS DAM, FOLSOM SOUTH CANAL, CONTRA COSTA CANAL, San Francisco, TRACY PUMPING PLANT, DELTA-MENDOTA CANAL, MADERA CANAL, FRIANT DAM, SAN LUIS DAM, SAN LUIS CANAL, FRIANT-KERN CANAL, Bakersfield, Los Angeles

(Inset map labels:) SUGAR PINE DAM, Auburn, AUBURN DAM, FOLSOM DAM, NIMBUS DAM, COUNTY LINE DAM, Sacramento, FOLSOM SOUTH CANAL, Stockton

0   25

CENTRAL VALLEY PROJECT CALIFORNIA

WATER FOR
IRRIGATION
NAVIGATION
FLOOD CONTROL
POWER
CITIES AND TOWNS
INDUSTRIES
SALINITY CONTROL
FISH AND WILD LIFE
RECREATION

UNITED STATES
DEPARTMENT OF THE INTERIOR
BUREAU OF RECLAMATION
REGION II

THE PROJECT TO-DAY

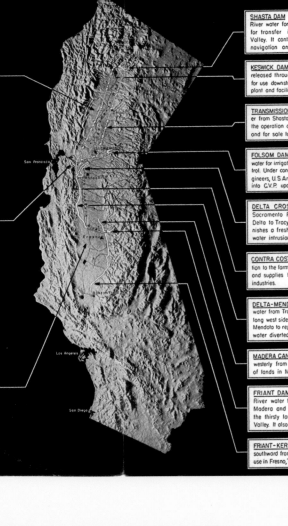

THE PROBLEM

SACRAMENTO VALLEY While two-thirds of the Central Valley's water supply originates in this section, the Sacramento Valley contains but one-third of the agricultural lands. Stream flows reach their crests in late winter and spring, allowing the greater percentage of valuable water resources to waste unused into the Pacific Ocean and occasionally causing destructive floods. In summer low river stages often are inadequate to meet irrigation needs, and prevent river navigation for any considerable distance upstream from Sacramento.

DELTA REGION This fertile farming area is threatened by the inflow of salt water from San Francisco Bay during the late summer months when fresh water in the Sacramento and San Joaquin Rivers reaches low stage and is insufficient to repel the incursion of salt tides. As a result, thousands of rich, irrigated acres face permanent damage and the cities and industries of the Delta and northern Bay areas suffer for lack of adequate fresh water supply.

SAN JOAQUIN VALLEY This section of the Central Valley contains two-thirds of the agricultural lands, but is provided by nature with only one-third of the water supply. During the summer when irrigation reaches its peak there is not enough water to meet crop needs. A large portion of these lands are irrigated by pumping and the overdraft on subsurface supplies resulting from expansion of agriculture has caused a serious water deficiency. Thousands of acres already have been abandoned because of the lack of water, and many additional thousands of acres are similarly threatened. Located in this section are many thousands of acres of dry land which can be made productive by an assured irrigation supply.

THE SOLUTION

SHASTA DAM — stores Sacramento River water for use downstream and for transfer into the San Joaquin Valley. It controls floods, aids river navigation and generates power.

KESWICK DAM — reregulates the water released through Shasta Power Plant for use downstream. It also has a power plant and facilities for fish conservation.

TRANSMISSION LINES — convey power from Shasta and Keswick Plants for the operation of project pumping works and for sale to other agencies.

FOLSOM DAM — stores American River water for irrigation, power and flood control. Under construction by Corps of Engineers, U.S. Army, it is to be integrated into C.V.P. upon completion.

DELTA CROSS CHANNEL — carries Sacramento River water across the Delta to Tracy Pumping Plant and furnishes a fresh water supply to repel salt water intrusion.

CONTRA COSTA CANAL — brings irrigation to the farms of Contra Costa County and supplies fresh water to towns and industries.

DELTA-MENDOTA CANAL — carries water from Tracy pumps southward along west side of San Joaquin Valley to Mendota to replace San Joaquin River water diverted at Friant Dam.

MADERA CANAL — diverts water northwesterly from Friant Dam for irrigation of lands in Madera County.

FRIANT DAM — stores San Joaquin River water for diversion through the Madera and Friant-Kern Canals onto the thirsty lands of the San Joaquin Valley. It also provides flood control.

FRIANT-KERN CANAL — diverts water southward from Friant Dam for irrigation use in Fresno, Tulare and Kern Counties.

MAP 581 (*above*).
An unusual perspective map showing the proposed Blue Mesa Dam, on the Gunnison River, a Colorado headwater tributary, and the extent of the Blue Mesa Reservoir once filled. The dam was constructed between 1962 and 1966.

In California, the Central Valley Project was similarly planned a long time before it was completed. Conceived in the 1920s, it was begun in the 1930s but not completed until after the war. The project was an attempt at a coordinated plan for the whole Central Valley—to move abundant water from the north to the dry south and also to control floods. The work was authorized in 1933 but failed because of lack of financing in the Depression years until it was taken over by the federal Bureau of Reclamation in 1935. Construction began on the Shasta Dam, on the northern Sacramento River, in 1938, and was completed in 1945. The Friant Dam, on the San Joaquin, was also completed in 1945. It diverts water into the Madera Canal, also completed that year. The Friant-Kern Canal was completed four years later, and the Delta-Mendota Canal down the west side of the San Joaquin Valley was finished in 1951. The Delta-Mendota, under a complex legal swap arrangement, replaces water lost from the San Joaquin by diversion into the Madera and Friant-Kern canals with water from the delta. Other dams and reservoirs, such as Folsom Dam and Lake on the American River above Sacramento, completed in 1955, hold water from westward-flowing Sierra streams and are now integrated into the Central Valley system, illustrated in MAP 582 and MAP 583, *left*.

Finally, the California Aqueduct, completed in 1968, carries water farther south still, into the Los Angeles Basin. It is part of the State Water Project, authorized in 1960. Water originates from Lake Oroville, behind the Oroville Dam on the Feather River, another tributary of the Sacramento. Leaving the Central Valley involves a number of pumping stations and a two-thousand-foot lift over the Tehachapi Mountains. Urban and industrial uses take 70 percent of this water, with the rest going to irrigation projects. California alone now has over eight million acres of irrigated land.

The Colorado River is the source of water for the Central Arizona Project, approved in 1968. Its centerpiece is a 336-

MAP 582 (*above, left*) with map cover (*inset*).
The components of the Central Valley Project are shown in this 1966 map of the entire system.

MAP 583 (*left*).
This cartographically interesting, topographically shaded 1954 map also shows the components of the Central Valley Project, with a description of their functions listed at right.

mile-long aqueduct from Lake Havasu to a point 14 miles southwest of Tucson (MAP 584, *below*), begun in 1973. The aqueduct requires a number of tunnels and pipeline siphons to carry water over the highest and lowest points. The project, declared substantially complete in 1993, uses Arizona's entitlement to Colorado River water under agreements worked out in the 1940s. The Central Arizona Project supplies water to the burgeoning urban areas of the central part of the state. It is the largest and most expensive water distribution system in the United States, having cost $4 billion to construct.

The arid parts of the West are full of water projects, large and small, all contributing to the transformation of the agricultural economy and urban landscape. The Bureau of Reclamation even claimed in the

MAP 584 (*below*).
A section of the extensive planning maps for the Central Arizona Project from 1972, the year before construction began. This map shows the area northeast of Phoenix, with the *Granite Reef Aqueduct*, later renamed the Hayden-Rhodes Aqueduct, and the *Salt-Gila Aqueduct*, now renamed the Fannin-McFarland Aqueduct, all after individuals material to the project's success. The sites of proposed dams and power lines are also shown, including the *Orme Dam Site*, with the

proposed area to be flooded outlined behind it. The Orme Dam was never built. This planned flood-control and storage reservoir, at the confluence of the Salt and Verde rivers, would have flooded 15,000 acres of the Fort McDowell Indian Reservation; its residents opposed the project, and it was abandoned in 1977. *Above* is the Central Arizona Project Aqueduct today, looking west from Hovatter Road near Interstate 10, about one hundred miles west of Phoenix.

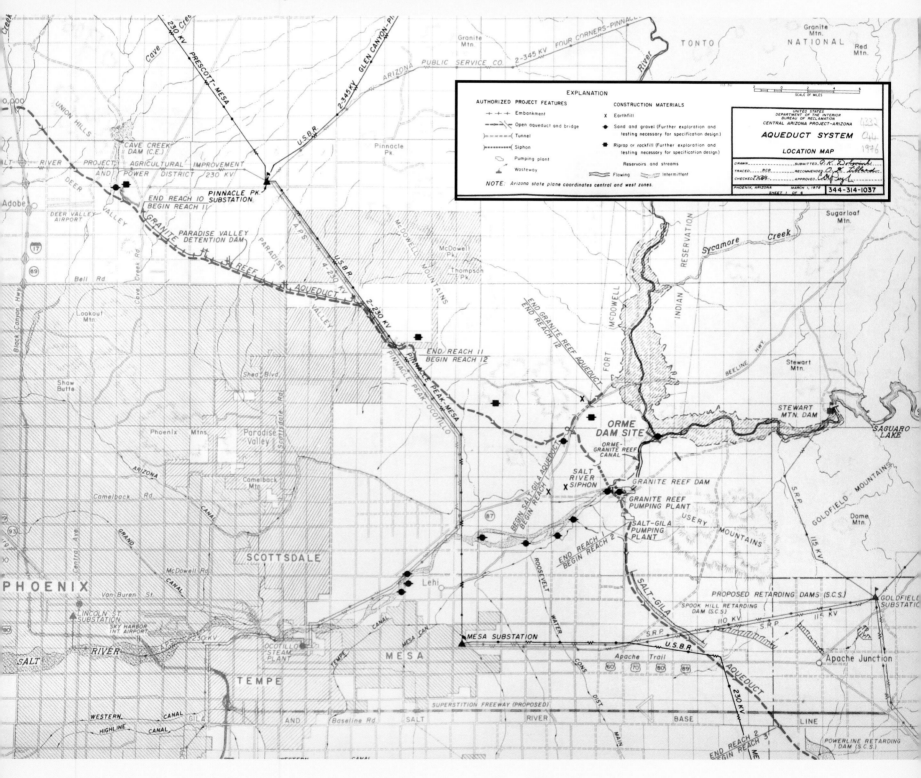

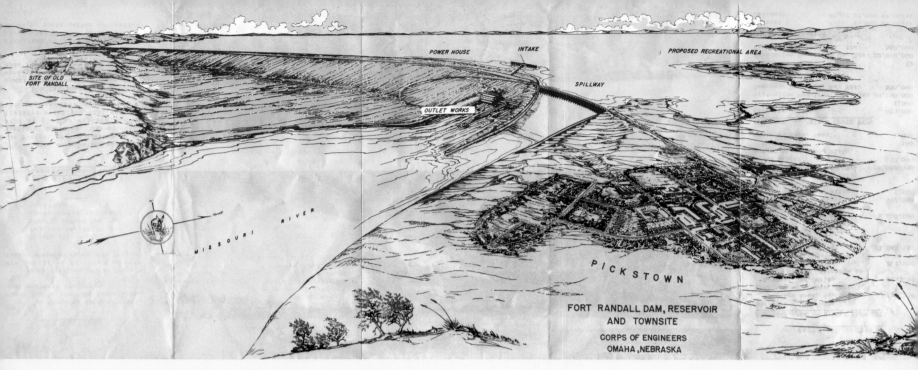

PICKSTOWN

FORT RANDALL DAM, RESERVOIR
AND TOWNSITE
CORPS OF ENGINEERS
OMAHA, NEBRASKA

late 1980s that "the arid West essentially has been reclaimed," meaning that no significant streams of water remained to be diverted for human use elsewhere. It was quite a claim but nonetheless correct; the West remains largely arid, but there is no more water to distribute.

Energy

Coal has had a remarkable revival as an energy source, owing not in small part to increases in the price of oil. Coal-fired generating plants have sprung up in many places in the Southwest, the complex at Farmington–Four Corners being perhaps the largest—and most notorious. High-voltage transmission lines allow electricity to be sent to distant markets. The coal mines of the West, unlike most of their counterparts in the East, use strip mining to access the coal, an infinitely more efficient way of extracting the resource. The North Antelope Rochelle Mine in Wyoming, for example, boasts an open eighty-foot-high wall of coal. The region that has seen considerable coal mine development is the Powder River Basin in Wyoming and Montana (Map 586, right). So-called unit trains carrying nothing but coal in uniform wagons transport coal to power plants as far away as Michigan and Texas. Wyoming is now the top coal-producing state in the country.

The Fun West

Now arriving more by air and car than by rail, tourists have continued to flood to the scenic West. Winter tourism has flourished with the development of ski resorts at favorable locations. In 1936 W. Averell Harriman, then chairman of the Union Pacific, opened the first major western ski resort at a place deliberately named

Map 585 (*above*).
The U.S. Army Corps of Engineers was responsible for many water projects throughout the West. Projects focused on flood control, power generation, and the improvement of navigation. This interesting bird's-eye map is from an information brochure published in 1951 showing the Fort Randall Dam, then under construction, and Lake Francis Case behind it, at Pickstown, on the Missouri River in South Dakota, almost at the Nebraska state line. Built under the Flood Control Act of 1944, the dam generated its first power in 1954, and the project was completed in 1956.

Map 586 (*below*).
The coal-mining areas of the Powder River Basin in east-central Wyoming, shown on a detailed 1984 U.S. Geological Survey map. Coal mines, active and inactive, are the areas shown (appropriately) in black; for details refer to the key at left. Casper, Wyoming, is at bottom, Buffalo at top.

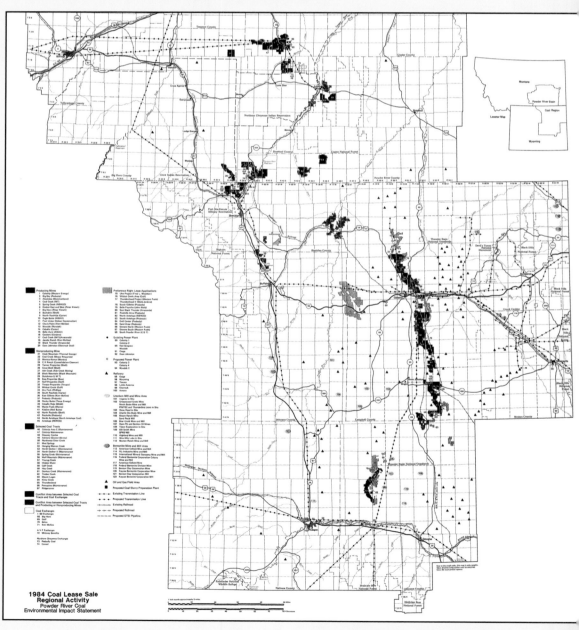

1984 Coal Lease Sale
Regional Activity
Powder River Coal
Environmental Impact Statement

ARIZONA...
land of adventure

Map 587 (*above*).
The romance of the Old West is featured against a map of *Arizona* on this 1957 tourist information booklet cover.

Sun Valley, in central Idaho, carefully selected for its ski potential with the help of a ski expert, an Austrian count. Sun Valley installed the world's first chairlifts.

Although interrupted by the war, other ski resort developments followed, notably Aspen in 1946; Vail in 1962; and Snowbird, at Ketchum, Utah, in 1971, the latter just twenty-five miles southeast of Salt Lake City. While most ski resorts boosted the prospects of existing small towns, the one at Vail actually created the town, incorporated in 1966.

No mention of fun in the West would be complete without noting the creation of Disneyland, in Anaheim, in 1955, the first of a number of destination theme parks.

Map 589 (*below*).
The major ski areas of the West are compressed together in this innovative pictorial map from a magazine advertisement by United Airlines. "Ski the West at Piker's Prices"— and fly there on Denver-based United, of course.

Map 588 (*above*).
A 1940s map advertising the *Sandia Mountain* ski area, twenty miles northeast of Albuquerque.

Map 590 (*below*).
A 1940s map of ski areas in Colorado prepared by the U.S. Forest Service and published by the state of Colorado's tourist office.

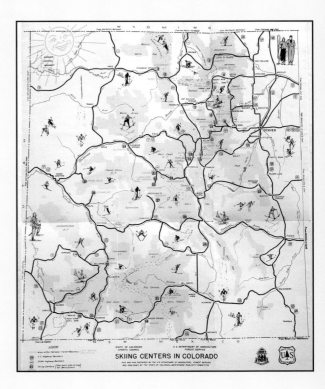

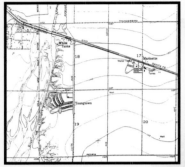

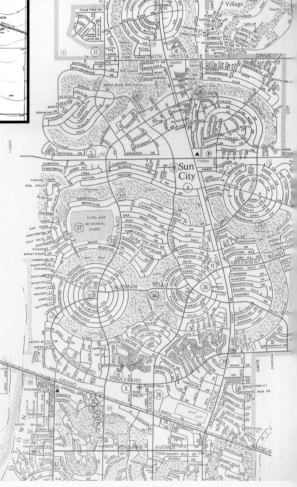

RETIREMENT AND RESORTS

But, of course, the main reasons the West continues to be a major tourist destination are its scenery and the sun. And the climate also attracts new retiree residents.

In 1954 two developers purchased 320 acres northwest of Phoenix and began work on Youngtown—deliberately so named—the first master-planned community exclusively for retirees. Youngtown was incorporated in 1960, the same year developer Del E. Webb opened his Sun City nearby, a massive subdivision and self-contained new town now housing nearly forty thousand residents. A similar development, Sun City West, was opened in 1978 to accommodate overflowing demand.

MAP 592 (*above*).
Now part of the urban area that includes Sun City South, Youngtown was the first master-planned adult community for retirees. This map is dated 1956. The Santa Fe railroad track into Phoenix and adjacent Grand Avenue run diagonally across the map.

MAP 591 (*above*).
A very detailed pictorial "recreational" map of New Mexico filled with tourist attractions. The map was the work of artist Wilfred Stedman and was published in 1946. Here the map form has been used to advertise all the tourist-worthy features of the state at once.

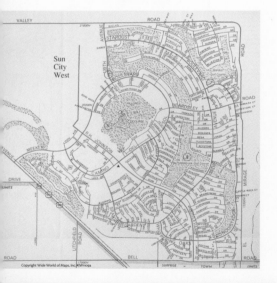

MAP 593 (*left*) and MAP 594 (*right*).
Sun City West (MAP 593) opened in 1978 and was essentially the second phase of the original Del Webb development, *Sun City* (MAP 594). To qualify to live at Sun City at least one member of the household had to be fifty or older. Sun City clearly supplied a demand. During the first three days of sales in January 1960, 272 houses were sold, and 1,301 were sold in the first year. Entirely residential except for retail and community services including churches, hospitals, and medical clinics, the subdivisions were based on circles rather than the more traditional rectangular street pattern. On both of these maps *Grand Avenue* runs diagonally. These maps show development as it was in 1984. *Below* is the main entrance to Sun City West, and *right, inset,* is part of the original Sun City subdivision along Grand Avenue showing how it was separated from that arterial street by a wall.

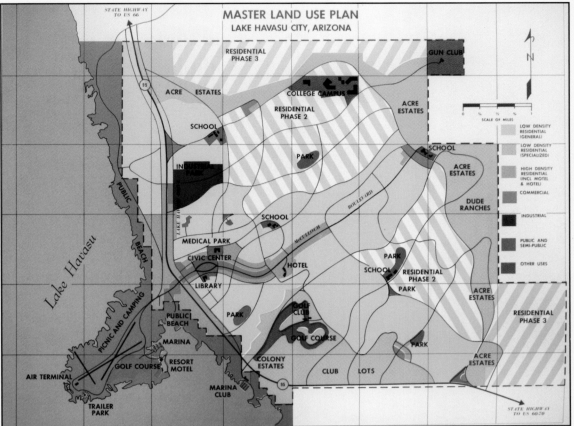

MASTER LAND USE PLAN
LAKE HAVASU CITY, ARIZONA

MAP 595 (*right*).

The original *Master Land Use Plan* for *Lake Havasu City*, drawn up in 1965 soon after chainsaw company industrialist Robert McCulloch purchased the site. The city is probably the best-known example of a planned resort in the West. The entire waterfront was to be devoted to public and semipublic uses (shown in blue). The peninsula, Pittsburg Point (not named on this map) was made into an island to accommodate London Bridge when it was installed between 1968 and 1971 after being shipped from London as individually numbered stones. The residential areas are phased to allow for orderly growth, and there are two golf courses. The city's 16,700 acres are divided into 33,514 lots, most of which sold within a few years, although many lots were not immediately built upon. The city has many retirees but has also attracted many younger people.

MAP 596 (*below*).

Lake Havasu City is the center of the Southwest and near the junction of four states in this map from a 1965 promotional booklet.

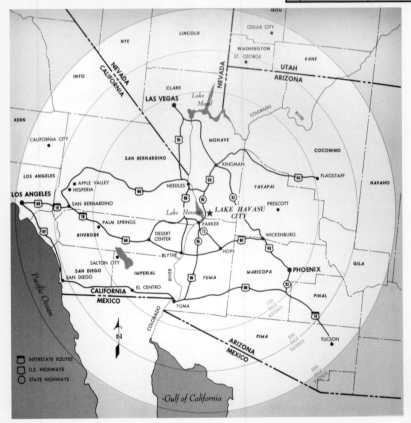

MAP 597 (*below*).

The 1965 promotional booklet contained this persuasive map showing the percentage of days with sunshine in the United States, with the city's location in the highest zone, with over 85 percent of days with sunshine.

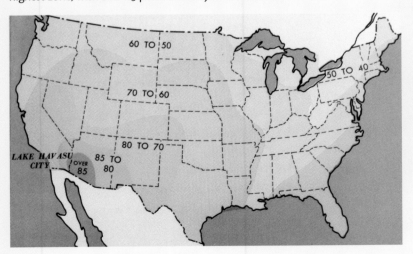

Life in the sun for the non-retired, either with a primary residence or a vacation home, has been a lure for a number of large western planned real estate projects started from scratch on arid lands. One of the largest such projects was Rio Rancho, eleven miles northwest of Albuquerque, on 54,000 acres (later increased to 91,000 acres), begun in 1961. For years the fastest-growing community in New Mexico, Rio Rancho, incorporated in 1981, now has about eighty thousand inhabitants.

Perhaps the most famous resort community, created from scratch in the desert, is Lake Havasu City, in Arizona, on Lake Havasu, filled by the Parker Dam beginning in 1938. It is famous as the home of London Bridge, shipped in stone by stone from London, England, and reconstructed, opening in 1971. It was likely worth the $2.5 million it cost in its advertising value alone and provides a classic example of adding value to an investment. Lake Havasu City was the brainchild of Robert McCulloch, of chainsaw fame, who established the community in 1964. The city, incorporated in 1978, now has about 45,000 residents.

Above.

Lake Havasu City's famous landmark, London Bridge, spanning a channel cut through Pittsburg Point to make it an island—thus necessitating a bridge.

Map 598.
Arizona seems to have produced more than its fair share of pictorial maps over the years. This superb example of the art was created by artist Bob Martin in 1972. Naturally enough, *London Bridge,* completed the previous year in its new location at Lake Havasu City, is prominently shown, at left.

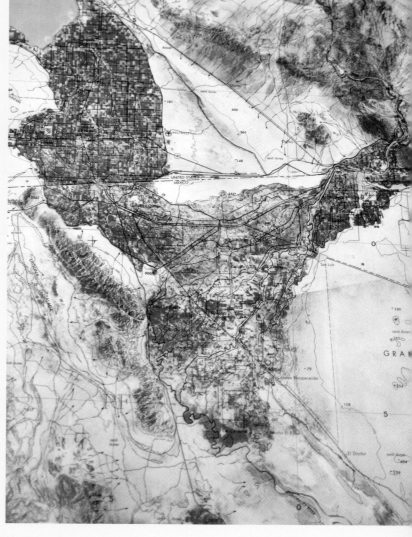

Map 599 (*left*).
A roadside marker in the form of a map of Arizona commemorating the old mining town of Chloride, established in 1864. Once home to two thousand, it is still a small village, but most of it is a ghost town (see page 142). Hundreds, if not thousands of failed or played-out settlements are found all over the West.

THE WEST TODAY

If global warming is a reality, the West will continue to face challenges to its growth and continued prosperity. As one drives through the West today, one is struck by the burgeoning of suburbia around the big cities and the never-ending network of new roads and freeways, yet traffic flows ever more slowly on many routes—witness the Santa Monica Freeway on a weekday afternoon or the I-25 through Denver on the morning commute.

At the same time reservoir levels are sinking, exposing the remnants of forests and settlements unseen since they first disappeared under the waters of new lakes. Growth can only continue if compromises can be reached, making every new resident's footprint on the land smaller, by harnessing alternative forms of energy and using those we have now more intelligently. Conservation is the new watchword; waste is no longer an option.

The extensive western public lands will remain; in 1976 Congress passed the important Federal Land Policy and Management Act to preserve their public ownership. Map 603 (*overleaf*) shows the modern extent of federal land in the West.

Security has become a concern in the wake of the 9/11 (2001) attacks, as so many water projects, dams, and aqueducts are so utterly critical to the West's current and future well-being. A project to reroute US 93 away from the strategic Hoover Dam was dramatically speeded up; in the meantime no truck traffic is allowed across the dam, and all other vehicles are individually checked.

Creating a western Eden was a monumental achievement; maintenance and now protection are required to allow many more future residents and visitors alike to continue to enjoy its bounty.

Map 600 (*right, top*).
A "photomap" of the Imperial Valley and its extension into Mexico, published in 1969. The map is composed of "rectified" photography (that is, adjusted to allow for the curvature of the earth) from Gemini 3 and Gemini 5 in 1965; Apollo 6 in 1968; and Apollo 9 in 1969, combined with an aeronautical chart. The composite gives an excellent overview of the region.

Map 601 (*below*).
A relief map of Lake Mead, behind the Hoover Dam, a model in the Lake Mead National Recreation Center office. The extensive size of the lake is evident, though the water level has dropped by about 120 feet in the last ten years (photo, *inset*) and is now at less than half the lake's capacity.

Map 602 (*below*).
A map illustrating the Colorado River Bridge and new route for US 93, under construction in 2007 to avoid routing the existing road across the Hoover Dam in the wake of 9/11.

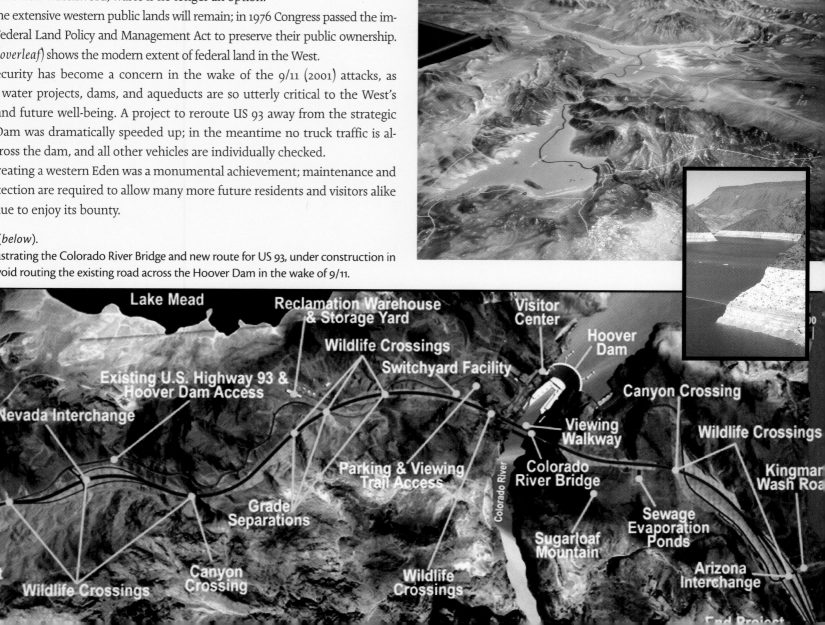

Lake Mead
Reclamation Warehouse & Storage Yard
Visitor Center
Wildlife Crossings
Existing U.S. Highway 93 & Hoover Dam Access
Switchyard Facility
Hoover Dam
Nevada Interchange
Canyon Crossing
Viewing Walkway
Colorado River Bridge
Wildlife Crossings
Parking & Viewing Trail Access
Colorado River
Colorado River Bridge
Kingman Wash Road
Grade Separations
Sewage Evaporation Ponds
Begin Project
Sugarloaf Mountain
Wildlife Crossings
Canyon Crossing
Wildlife Crossings
Arizona Interchange

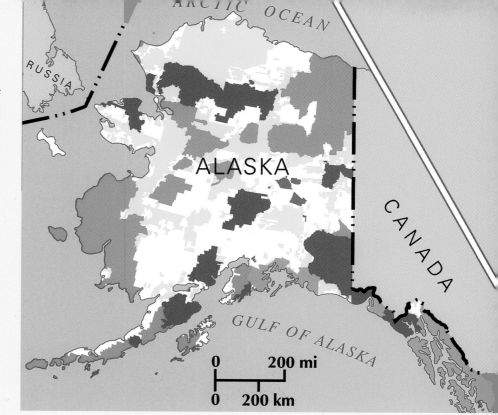

Map 602 (*left, western part; right, Alaska; and below, right, whole map*). One of the major realities of the American West is that a huge proportion of it is owned by the federal government. Here we have a map of federal land ownership in the West from the *National Atlas of the United States*, 2009. Note that Alaska is shown at a smaller scale than the rest of the West. The map is computerized and web based, allowing the user to zoom in for more detail. The colors denote management by different federal agencies; the key is shown, enlarged, below.

As can be seen from the map of the entire United States, *below, right*, the proportion of land owned by the federal government in the region from the Rocky Mountains west is very high. Federal ownership in the West originated from the expansion of the United States, through purchase or conquest, from the Louisiana Purchase forward, including the Oregon Treaty with Britain, which added the Oregon Country in 1846; the Treaty of Guadalupe Hidalgo, which in 1848 added most of the West after the war with Mexico; the Gadsden Purchase of 1853–54, which extended today's Arizona and New Mexico southward; and the purchase of Alaska from the Russians in 1867. The federal government did recognize most privately held land—such as land previously granted by the Mexican government to individuals—but this was nevertheless a small percentage of the total.

The majority of federal land is administered by the Bureau of Land Management (and is shown in yellow on the map). The agency administers about 248 million acres of land in the eleven westernmost states (including Alaska), or about 22 percent of all land in the region. This represents about one-eighth of the total land mass of the United States. The bureau was established by Congress as the General Land Office in 1812. The Bureau of Land Management, a division of the Department of the Interior, was created in 1946 by the merger of the General Land Office with the U.S. Grazing Service; the latter had been established in 1934 by the Taylor Land Grazing Act to manage public rangelands. Most of the federal land is away from rivers and is particularly absent from the coastal areas, because the latter areas either held most of the prime land that was claimed by individuals under the various land grant schemes over the years or was the best land of the original grantees, such as the railroads, and hence sold more readily. All of the land grant programs were aimed at drawing settlement westward, and they succeeded in no small measure.

The National Forest Service manages the second-largest amount of federal land in the West, some 155 million acres. Other large federal holdings include the national parks system, which include national preserves, national recreational areas, and national historic parks. Alaska, not surprisingly, holds the largest: Noatak National Preserve and Gates of the Arctic National Park and Preserve (on the map the large band of green in northern Alaska) total 14.2 million acres; the Wrangell–St. Elias National Park and Preserve (where Alaska meets its panhandle) is 11.7 million acres; Denali is 6 million acres. For comparison, it may be noted that the total area of the state of Maryland is 6.7 million acres. The largest national parks in the lower forty-eight are Death Valley National Park, with 3.3 million acres, and the Mojave National Preserve, with 1.5 million acres. Yellowstone National Park, in Wyoming, Montana, and Idaho, has 2.2 million acres. Huge areas for the preservation of wildness—early conservationist and park advocate (and founder of the Sierra Club) John Muir would be proud.

He would likely not be so proud of the large tracts of western lands controlled by the Department of Defense (shown in blue). These are military bases and weapons-testing ranges, where the unpopulated, wide-open spaces are an essential element.

Indian reserves are also shown on this map (in red), though with a few exceptions they are still relatively small. A comparison with the earlier reservation maps (Map 319 and Map 320, *page 155*) is worthwhile. The largest Indian reserve today is that at the "Four Corners" (of Arizona, New Mexico, Colorado, and Utah), home of the self-governing Navajo Nation. American Indians have rebounded from the dark days of the 1890s and have been quite successful at reclaiming their rights and gaining more control over their lands. An economic stimulus based on land control has been found in casinos, which have sprouted on Indian land all over the West; today 184 Indian nations belong to the National Indian Gaming Association. There are now some 4.5 million American Indians and Alaskan Natives, and a cultural resurgence is evident in the fact that 27 percent of those over five years old speak a language other than English at home.

Areas still managed by the Bureau of Reclamation (shown in dark maroon) are relatively small, being limited to a few river valleys, but here the map does not tell the whole story, for some 10 million acres of private farmland are supplied with that critical western resource—water—by the bureau. The bureau also supplies water to more than 31 million people in the West and is the second-largest (after the Army Corps of Engineers) producer of hydroelectric power in the West. Founded in 1902, the Bureau of Reclamation, perhaps more than any other federal agency, has been responsible for the West's transformation.

- Bureau of Indian Affairs
- Bureau of Land Management
- Bureau of Reclamation
- Department of Defense
- Fish and Wildlife Service
- Forest Service
- National Park Service
- Tennessee Valley Authority
- Other agencies

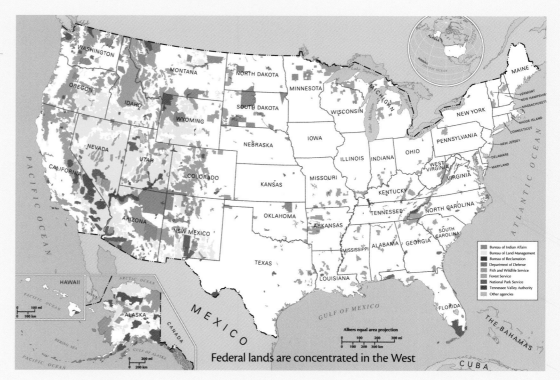

Federal lands are concentrated in the West

Map Catalog

Note: Where a source is not given, the map is from the author's or a private collection.

Map 1 (half-title page).
[Composite image with part of an 1879 map of the United States]

Map 2 (page 4).
Arizona
Arbuckle Coffee Co., 1889

Map 3 (page 4).
Wyoming
Arbuckle Coffee Co., 1889

Map 4 (page 6).
The Geographic Face of the Nation:
Land Cover of the Conterminous
United States
U.S. Geological Survey, 1992
Library of Congress G3701.D2 2001 .U5

Map 5 (page 7).
Map of Glacier–Waterton International
Peace Park
Great Northern Railway, 1939

Map 6 (page 8).
Map of Linguistic Stocks of American
Indians
Bureau of Ethnology, Annual Report,
1890
Library of Congress G3301.E3 1890 .M3 TIL

Map 7 (page 9).
Originalkarte der Urwohnsitze der
Azteken und Verwandten Pueblos in
New Mexico
O. Loew, Petermanns Geographische
Mitteilungen, 1876

Map 8 (page 10).
Map of Prehistoric Irrigation Canals
Omar A. Turney, 1929

Map 9 (page 10).
U. States Indian Frontier in 1840
From: George Catlin, Illustrations of the
Manners, Customs, & Condition of the
North American Indians, 1876

Map 10 (page 11).
[Map of the Missouri and its tributaries]
Drawn by the Feathers or ac ko mok ki
a Blackfoot chief 7 Feby. 1801
Ac ko mok ki, copied by Peter Fidler,
1801
Hudson's Bay Company Archives
E3/2 folios 106 verso - 107

Map 11 (page 12).
[Part of a map of the world]
Giovanni Contarini (Engraved by
Francesco Rosselli), 1506
British Library Maps.C.2.cc.4

Map 12 and Map 13 (page 12).
Universalis Cosmographia Secundum
Ptholomaei Traditionem et Americi
Vespucci Aliou[m]que Lustrationes
Part of main map and inset map
Martin Waldseemüller and Matthias
Ringmann, 1507
Library of Congress G3200 1507 .W3
Vault

Map 14 (page 13).
[Part of a world map]
Faicte A Arques par Pierre Desceliers
PBRE: L AN 1550
Pierre Desceliers, 1550
British Library Add. MS 24065

Map 15 (page 14).
[Southern North America]
Battista Agnese, portolan atlas, 1544
Library of Congress G1001.A4 1544

Map 16 (page 15).
[Mapa del Golfo y costa de la Nueva
España desde el Rio de Panuco hasta el
cabo de Santa Elena]
Alonso de Santa Cruz, c. 1544
Library of Congress
G3860 1572 .S3 Vault

Map 17 (page 15).
[Map of California, Japan, and the
Pacific Ocean]
Joan Martines, 1578
British Library
Harley MS 3450, Map 10 in atlas

Map 18 (page 16).
[Map engraved on copper plate on
display at the Coronado Monument,
New Mexico]

Map 19 (page 16).
Kansas Parco Motor Trails Map
[cover]
Producers and Refiners Corporation,
1931

Map 20 (page 17).
[Baja California and adjacent coasts]
Hernán Cortés, 1535–37
Facsimile of map in Archivo General
des Indias, Seville, Spain

Map 21 (page 17).
Nueva España
From: Hernán Cortés, Historia de
Nueva España, 1770

Map 22 (page 17).
[Globe gores]
Alonso de Santa Cruz, 1542
National Library of Sweden

Map 23 (page 17).
[Part of world map]
Sebastian Cabot, 1544
Bibiothèque nationale de France
RES Ge AA 582 Rc C 2486

Map 24 (page 18).
[Baja California and adjacent coasts]
Domingo del Castillo, 1541
From: Hernán Cortés, Historia de
Nueva España, 1770

Map 25 (page 19).
Universale Descittione di tutta la terra
conosciuta fin qui
Paolo Forlani, c. 1565
Library of Congress G3200 1565 .F6
Vault

Map 26 (page 19).
Universalis exactissima atque non
recens modo
Giacomo Gastaldi, 1555

Map 27 (page 20).
[Globe gores called the Ambassadors'
Globe]
c. 1533, reproduced in
A.E. Nordenskiöld, Facsimile-Atlas
to the Early History of Cartography,
Stockholm, 1889

Map 28 (page 20).
Typus Orbis Terrarum
Abraham Ortelius, 1570
From: Theatrum Orbis Terrarum
Library of Congress
G1006 .T5 1570b Vault

Map 29 (page 21).
Carta de los reconocimientos hechos
en 1602 por el Capitan Sebastian
Vizcayno
From: Relación del Viage . . . Atlas, 1802

Map 30 (page 21).
[San Diego Bay and vicinity]
Antonio de la Ascension, diary
(facsimile), 1602

Map 31 (page 21).
Tartariae Sive Magni Chami Regni
Abraham Ortelius, 1570
From: Theatrum Orbis Terrarum
Library of Congress
G7270 1570.O7 Vault

Map 32 (page 22).
[Map of the Americas]
From: Descripcion de las Indias
Occidentales
Antonio de Herrera y Tordesillas, 1622

Map 33 (page 22).
The North part of America
Henry Briggs, 1625
Library and Archives Canada NMC 6582

Map 34 (page 22).
[Island of California]
Joan Vinckeboons, c. 1650
Library of Congress G3291.S12coll .H3
Harrisse No. 10

Map 35 (page 23).
Audience de Guadalajara Nouveau
Mexique, Californie, &c.
Nicolas Sanson, c. 1657, c. 1683 edition
Bill Warren Collection

Map 36 (page 23).
Passage par terre À La Californie
Découvert par le R.P. Eusibe François
Kino, Jesuite
[Eusebio Kino, 1701], 1705
Bill Warren Collection

Map 37 (page 24).
Vera Totius Expeditionis Nauticae
descriptio D. Franc. Draci
Joducus Hondius, 1595
Library of Congress
G3201.S12 1595 .H6 Vault

Map 38 (page 24).
Portus Novæ Albionis, inset in
Vera Totius Expeditionis Nauticae
descriptio D. Franc. Draci
Joducus Hondius, 1595
Library of Congress
G3201.S12 1595 .H6 Vault

Map 39 (page 24).
La herdike enterprinse faict par le
Signeur Draeck D'Avoir cirquit toute
la Terre
Nicola van Sype, 1581
Library of Congress G3201.S12 1581 .S9

Map 40 (page 24).
[Silver medal struck to commemorate
Sir Francis Drake's circumnavigation]
Michael Mercator, 1589

Map 41 (page 25).
Illustri Viro, Dimino Philippo Sidnaes
Michael Lok Civis Londinensis Hanc
Chartum
Michael Lok, 1582
From: Richard Hakluyt, Divers Voyages
touching the Discoverie of America,
1852

Map 42 (page 25).
Chart of North and South America
From: Thomas Jefferys, A General
Topography of North America and the
West Indies, 1768
Library of Congress G1105 .J4 1768

Map 43 (page 26).
Nova et Rece Terraum et Regnorum
Californiæ
Gabriel Tatton, c. 1600

Map 44 (page 27).
[Sketch map of New Mexico and the
Plains]
Enrico Martínez/Juan de Oñate, c. 1602
Archivo General des Indias, Seville

Map 45 (page 27).
Plano Dela Villa de Santa Fee, Capital del Reino del nuebo Mexico, situada segun mi observacion en 36° y 10 minutos de latitud boreal
José de Urrutia, 1766–67
British Library Add. MS. 17,662.m

Map 46 (page 28).
North America divided into its III principall parts
Philip Lea, 1685
Library of Congress
G3300 1685 .L4 TIL Vault

Map 47 (page 28).
Le Nouveau Mexique appele aussi Nouvelle Granade et Marata. Avec Partie de Californie
Vincenzo Coronelli, 1742 (1688)
Library of Congress G4420 1742 .C6 TIL

Map 48 (page 28).
Nuevo Reyno de la Nueva Navara con sus confinantes otros Reynos 1710
Eusebio Kino, 1710

Map 49 (page 29).
Mapa Geografico que presento con su Ynforme al virrey dela Nª España, Don Juan de Olivan Rebodello (Geographical Map presented along with his report to the viceroy of New Spain by Juan de Olivan Rebodello), 1717
Center for American History, University of Texas, Austin, di_03257

Map 50 (pages 30–31).
Plano Corographico e Hydrographico de las Provincias de el Nuevo Mexico
Francisco Álvarez Barreiro, 1729
Hispanic Society of America

Map 51 (page 32).
Nuevo Mexico Tejas Nueva Vizcayna
Anon., 1746
W.B. Stephens Collection, University of Texas, Austin

Map 52 (page 33).
Segunda Parte/Quarta Parte Del Mapa, que comprende la Frontera, de los Dominios del Rey, en la America Septentrional
José de Urrutia and Nicolás de Lafora, 1769
Library of Congress
G4410 1769 .U7 TIL Vault

Map 53 (page 33).
Primera Parte Del Mapa, que comprende la Frontera, de los Dominios del Rey, en la America Septentrional
José de Urrutia and Nicolás de Lafora, 1769
Library of Congress
G4410 1769 .U7 TIL Vault

Map 54 (page 34).
Primera Parte Del Mapa, que comprende la Frontera, de los Dominios del Rey, en la America Septentrional
José de Urrutia and Nicolás de Lafora, 1769
Library of Congress
G4410 1769 .U7 TIL Vault

Map 55 (page 34).
Plano del Presidio de Nuestra Señora del Pilar del paso del Rio del Norte, dependiente dela governacion del nuebo Mexico
José de Urrutia, 1766–77
British Library Add. MS. 17,662.n

Map 56 (page 35).
Primera Parte Del Mapa, que comprende la Frontera, de los Dominios del Rey, en la America Septentrional
José de Urrutia and Nicolás de Lafora, 1769
Library of Congress
G4410 1769 .U7 TIL Vault

Map 57 (page 36).
Mapa de toda la Frontera de los dominios del Rey en la America septentrional
Nicolás de Lafora, 1816
Library of Congress G4410 1771 .F6 Vault Oversize

Map 58 (page 37).
Plano Corografico del Rey Nuevo Mexico
Anon., c. 1770
British Library Add. MS. 17,651/ Arizona State University Map Library

Map 59 (page 38).
Plano de Puerto de S. Diego
Anon., c. 1799 (map dated 1779)
Library of Congress
G3351.P5 1799.C Vault

Map 60 (page 38).
Mapa de lo substancial del Famosa Puerto y Rio de San Francisco
Juan Crespi, 1772
Copy of original in Archivo Generale des Indias
Bancroft Library
G4362.S22 1772 .C7 Case XB

Map 61 (page 38).
Carta Reducida del Oceano Asiatico, o Mar del Sur
Miguel Costansó, 1770
Bancroft Library G4230 1770.C6 Case XD (copy from papers of Neal Harlow, Special Collections, University of British Columbia)

Map 62 (page 39).
Carta Reducida del Oceano Asiatico ô Mar del Sur que contiene la Costa dela California
José de Cañizares, 1774
U.S. National Archives RG 77, "Spanish maps of unknown origin," No. 67

Map 63 (page 39).
Carta Reducida de las Costas, y Mares Septentrionales de California
Juan Francisco de la Bodega y Quadra and Francisco Antonio Maurelle, 1775
Archivo General de Indias MP, Mexico 581

Map 64 (page 39).
Plano del Rada de Bucareli
Bruno de Hezeta, 1775
Archivo General de Indias Mexico 532

Map 65 (page 40).
Carta Geographica de la Costa y Parte de la Peninsula de la California
Manuel Villavicencio, 1781

Map 66 (page 41).
Plano que contiᵉ las Provincias de Sonora, Pimerias, Papagueria, Apacheria, Rios Gila y Colorado, y tierras descubiert . . .
From the diary of Francisco Garcés, 1775–76

Map 67 (page 41).
Mapa Correspondiente Al Diario Que Formo el P.F. Pedro Font del Viage que Hizo a Monterey
From the diary of Pedro Font, 1775–76

Map 68 (page 42).
Plan o mapa del viage hecho desde Monterey al gran Puerto de S. Francisco
Pedro Font, 1777
British Library Add MS 17651, folio 9

Map 69 (page 42).
Plano del Puerto de Sn Francisco
José de Cañizares, 1776
Bancroft Library
G4362 S22 1776 C4 Case C

Map 70 (page 43).
Plano geografico de la tierra descubierta, y demarcada, por Dn Bernardo de Miera y Pacheco al rumbo del Noroeste, y oeste del nuevo Mexico
Bernardo Miera y Pacheco, 1777
British Library Add. MS 17,661 C

Map 71 (page 43).
Derrotero hecho por Antonia Vélez y Escalante, misionero para mejor conocimiento de las misiones, pueblos de indios
(Silvestre Vélez de Escalante), 1777
Library of Congress G4300 1777 .V4 Vault

Map 72 (page 44).
[Pueblo de San José]
Land case map, 1840s
Bancroft Library Land case 228 ND

Map 73 (page 44).
[Pueblo lands of Los Angeles]
Land case map, 1840s[1781] (1)
Bancroft Library Land case 386 SD

Map 74 (page 44).
[Map of San Antonio, Texas]
[?] Morfi, 1780

Map 75 (page 44).
Mapa geografico de una parte de la America Septentrional
Manuel Agustin Mascaró, 1782
British Library Add. MS 17,652a

Map 76 (page 45).
Carta Reducida de las Costas y Mares Septentrionales de California
Anon., c. 1779
Archivo General des Indias
MP Mexico 359

Map 77 (page 45).
Carta de los descubrimientos hechos en la Costa N.O. America Septentrional
Juan Francisco de la Bodega y Quadra, 1792
Library of Congress
G3350 1792 .B6 TIL Vault

Map 78 (page 46).
La America Septentrional desde su extremo Norte hasta 10° de Latitud segun las ultimas observaciones y descubrimientos para el Curso de Geografia de D. Isidoro de Antillon
From: Isìdoro de Antillon, *Carta de la America Septentrional*, 1802

Map 79 (pages 46–47).
Carte du Mexique et de Pays Limitropher Situres ou Nort et E'est
Alexander von Humboldt, Paris: F. Schoell, 1811
University of Texas at Arlington
00217@140/1

Map 80 (page 48).
[Map of Western North America]
Juan Pedro Walker, c. 1817
Huntington Library

Map 81 (page 48).
Carta Esferica de los Territorios de la Alta y Baja Californias y Estado de Sonora
José M. Narváez, 1823
Library of Congress
G4300 1823 .N3 TIL Vault

Map 82 (page 49).
Map of North America from 20 to 80 Degrees North Latitude Exhibiting the Latest Discoveries, Geographical and Nautical
James Wyld, 1823
David Rumsey Collection

Map 83 (page 50).
Carte des environs du Mississipi
Guillaume De L'Isle, 1701
Service Historique de la Marine, Vincennes, Recueil 69, No. 4

Map 84 (page 51).
[Canada ou Nouvelle France]
Jean-Baptiste-Louis Fraquelin, 1699
Service Historique de la Marine, Vincennes, Recueil 66, Nos. 12–15

Map 85 (page 51).
Carte de la Louisiane et du Cours du Mississipi
Guillaume De L'Isle, 1718
Library of Congress G3700 1718 .L5 Vault

Map 86 (page 52).
Carte Nouvelle de la Partie de l'ouest de la Province de la Louisiane sur les observations & decouvertes de Sieur Benard de La Harpe
Sieur de Beauvilliers (?) from Benard de La Harpe, 1720
Service historique de la Marine, Vincennes, Recueil 69, No. 7

MAP 87 (*page 52*).
Carte Nouvelle de la Partie de L'Ouest de la Louisianne
Jean de Beaurain (after Bénard de La Harpe), 1723–25
Library of Congress Manuscripts, Louisiana Miscellany Coll.

MAP 88 (*page 53*).
Rivière des Panis jusqu'a l'île aux Cèdres [Missouri]
Guillaume De L'Isle, c. 1716
Service historique de la Marine, Vincennes, Recueil 69, No. 20

MAP 89 (*page 53*).
Plan du Fort D'Orleans
J. P. L. S. Dumont de Montigny
Centre des archives d'outre-mer, Aix-en-Provence, DFC Louisiane, portefeuille VI B, No. 63

MAP 90 (*page 53*).
[Map showing the connection of Lake Michigan to the Mississippi]
Jacques Marquette, 1673
Archives de la Compagnie de Jésus, Saint-Jérôme, Québec

MAP 91 (*page 54*).
Carte d'une partie du lac Supérieur avec la découverte de la Rivière depuis le grand portage A jusqu'à la Barrière B
Christophe Dufrost de La Jemerais, 1733
Service historique de la Marine, Vincennes, Recueil 67, No. 88

MAP 92 (*page 54*).
Carte contenant les nouvelles découvertes de L'ouest en Canada, mers, rivieres, lacs et nations qui y habittent en l'année 1737
Pierre Gaultier de Varennes et de la Vérendrye, 1737
Service historique de la Marine, Vincennes, Recueil 67, No. 42

MAP 93 (*page 54*).
Carte que les Gnacsitares/Carte de la Riviere Longue
Louis-Armand de Lom d'Arce, Baron de La Hontan, 1703
From: *Nouveaux Voyages de Mr. le Baron de Lahontan dans L'Amérique Septentrionale*, 1703

MAP 94 (*page 54*).
Carte Marine entre Californie et une Partie de l'Asie la plus Orientale (left part of map shown) and
Carte Marine de Amerique Septentrionale Partie de la Be d'Hudson (right part of map shown)
Isaac Brouckner, 1749
Library and Archives Canada NMC 14044/14043

MAP 95 (*page 55*).
A Map of the British and French Dominions in North America
John Mitchell, 1755
Library of Congress G3300 1755 .M51 Vault

MAP 96 (*page 55*).
A New Map of North America From the Latest Discoveries
From: Jonathan Carver, *Travels through the Interior Parts of North America in 1766, 1767 and 1768*, 1778

MAP 97 (*page 56*).
[Map of the North Pacific]
Anon., c. 1702
Library and Archives Canada NMC 133187

MAP 98 (*page 56*).
[Map of the discoveries of Maerten Vries, 1643]
Isaak de Graaf, c. 1644
Nationaal Archief, Netherlands

MAP 99 (*page 56*).
[Map of Mikhail Gvozdev's voyage]
Martin Spanberg, c. 1734
A.V. Efimov, 1964, Map 69

MAP 100 (*page 56*).
Carte Representant la Situation et la Distance de la Tartarie Orientale jusqaux Terres les plus voisines de L'Amerique
Joseph-Nicolas De L'Isle, 1731
A.V. Efimov, 1964, Map 78

MAP 101 (*page 57*).
[Map of Aleksei Chirikov's voyage]
Ivan Elagin, c. 1742
A.V. Efimov, 1964, Map 98

MAP 102 (*page 57*).
[Map of Bering's 1741 voyage]
Probably by Sven Waxell, 1742 or 1743
A.V. Efimov, 1964, Map 101

MAP 103 (*page 58*).
A Map of the Discoveries made by the Russians on the North West Coast of America
From: Thomas Jefferys, *A General Topography of North America and the West Indies*, 1768
Library of Congress G1105 .J4 1768

MAP 104 (*page 58*).
[Geographical map showing the discoveries of the Russian sea-going vessels on the northern part of America]
Anon., c. 1773

MAP 105 (*page 58*).
A Map of the New Northern Archipelago discover'd by the Russians in the Seas of Kamtschatka & Anadir
Jacob von Stählin, 1774
From: *Account of a New Northern Archipelago Lately Discovered by the Russians*, 1774

MAP 106 (*page 59*).
L'Amérique septentrionale divisée en ses principaux états
Jean Janvier, 1762
Library of Congress G3300 1762 .J31 Vault

MAP 107 (*page 59*).
Mappe Monde ou Globe Terrestre en deux Plans Hemispheres
Jean Covens and Corneille Mortier, c. 1780

MAP 108 (*page 59*).
Amerique Septentrionale
Jean B. Nolin, Plate 33, Atlas Général a L'Usage des Colleges et Museums d'Education, 1783
Library of Congress G1015.N68 1783

MAP 109 (*page 60*).
Chart of Part of the NW Coast of America Explored by Capt. J. Cook in 1778
Map enclosed in letter to Philip Stephens, Secretary to the Admiralty, sent 20 October 1778 from Unalaska
National Archives (U.K.) MPI 83

MAP 110 (*page 60*).
Esquisse d'une Carte and *Extrait de la Carte*
Samuel Engel, 1781
Beinecke Rare Book Library, Yale University

MAP 111 (*page 60*).
Chart of the NW Coast of America and part of the NE of Asia with the track of his Majestys Sloops Resolution & Discovery from May to October 1778 by George Vancouver
American Geographical Society Collection, University of Wisconsin

MAP 112 (*page 61*).
Carte de la Côte Ouest de l'Amérique du Nord, de Mt. St. Elias à Monterey, avec la trajectoire l'expédition de La Pérouse et la table des données de longitude compilées par Bernizet et Dagelet
Joseph Dagelet and Gérault-Sébastien Bernizet, 1787
Archives nationales, Paris 6 JJ1: 34B

MAP 113 (*page 61*).
A Chart Shewing part of the Western Coast of America
Joseph Baker and George Vancouver, 1792
U.K. Hydrographic Office 226 on Ac1

MAP 114 (*page 61*).
[Preliminary chart of the N.W. Coast of America]
George Vancouver, 1792
National Archives (U.K.) MPG 557 (4), removed from CO 5/187

MAP 115 (*page 62*).
Copy of a Map presented to the Congress by Peter Pond, a native of Milford in the State of Connecticut
Anon. (Peter Pond, 1784), 1785
Service Historique de la Marine Recueil 67 No. 30

MAP 116 (*pages 62–63*).
A Topogra[phical] Sketch of the Missouri and Upper Missisippi Exhibiting the various Nations and tribes of Indians who inhabit the Country
Antoine Soulard, 1795 (English copy)
Beinecke Rare Book Library, Yale University

MAP 117 (*page 63*).
[North America from the Mississippi River to the Pacific]
Anon., c. 1798
Library of Congress G3300 179-.N6 TIL Vault

MAP 118 (*page 63*).
Columbia's River
Robert Gray, 1792
National Archives (U.K.) MPG 557 (1), removed from CO 5/187

MAP 119 (*page 63*).
A Chart shewing part of the N.W. Coast of North America with the Tracks of His Majesty's Sloop Discovery *and Armed Tender* Chatham . . .
Joseph Baker and George Vancouver, 1798
From: George Vancouver, *A Voyage of Discovery to the North Pacific Ocean and Around the World*, Plate 5 of atlas, 1798

MAP 120 (*page 64*).
[Sketch map of the Missouri west of the Mandan villages, derived from Indian sources]
John Evans, 1796–97
Beinecke Rare Book Library, Yale University

MAP 121 (*page 64*).
A Map Exhibiting All the New Discoveries in the Interior Parts of North America
Aaron Arrowsmith, 1802
Library of Congress G3300 1802 A7 Vault Casetop

MAP 122 (*page 65*).
[Map of the Missouri River from Saint Charles to the Mandan villages of North Dakota]
James Mackay or Nicolas de Finiels, 1797 or 1798
Library of Congress G4127 .M5 1798 .F5 Vault Oversize

MAP 123 (*page 65*).
[Bend of the Missouri River]
David Thompson, 1798
Library of Congress G4127.M5 1798 B4 TIL Vault

MAP 124 (*page 65*).
A Map of North America
John Luffman, 1803
Library of Congress G3300 1803 .L8 TIL

MAP 125 (*page 66*).
Carte du Mississipi et de ses embranchemens
James Pitot, 1802
Service Historique de la Marine, Vincennes, Recueil 69, 9

MAP 126 (*page 67*).
Draught of the Falls and Portage [of the Missouri]
William Clark, 1805
American Philosophical Society
Clark Journal, Codex E: 132–133

MAP 169 (*page 88*).
Croquis del terro, camino, bosques, cerro y beredas de Cerro-gordo con las posiciones de las topas Mejicanas y Americanas
Rafeal Zamora, 1847
Library of Congress
G4412.C4 1847 .Z3 Vault

MAP 170 (*page 89*).
[American attack on Mexico City, 13–14 September 1847]
Joseph Goldsborough Bruff, 1847
Library of Congress
G4414 .M6S44 1847 .B7 Vault

MAP 171 (*page 90*).
Mapa de los Estados Unidos de Méjico
J. Disturnell, 1847 (revised edition)
(Map used to negotiate the Treaty of Guadalupe Hidalgo)
U.S. National Archives

MAP 172 (*page 90*).
Plan of Santa Fé New Mexico
J.F. Gilmer, 1846
New Mexico Museum of History, Santa Fe

MAP 173 (*page 91*).
Map of the United States of America
J.H. Colton, 1848
David Rumsey Collection

MAP 174 (*pages 92–94*).
Topographical Map of the Road from Missouri to Oregon, commencing at the Mouth of the Kansas in the Missouri River and ending at the Mouth of the Walla-Wallah in the Columbia
Charles Preuss, 1846
Library of Congress
G4127.O7 1846 .F7 TIL Vault (7 sheets)

MAP 175 (*page 92*).
Map of Oregon
From: Hall Kelley, *A Geographical Sketch of That Part of North America Called Oregon*, 1830

MAP 176 (*page 92*).
[Proposed city at the confluence of the Columbia and the Multnomah (Willamette)]
From: Hall J. Kelley, *General Circular*, 1830

MAP 177 (*page 93*).
Map of an Exploring Expedition to the Rocky Mountains in the Year 1842 and to Oregon & North California in the Years 1843–44
John Charles Frémont, 1845
Library of Congress
G4051.S12 1844 .F72 Vault

MAP 178 (*page 93*).
Map of Oregon Territory
Samuel Parker, 1838
Beinecke Rare Book Library, Yale University

MAP 179 (*page 94*).
Map of Oregon and Upper California
John C. Frémont and Charles Preuss, 1848
David Rumsey Collection

MAP 180 (*page 95*).
Line of Original Emigration to the Pacific Northwest Commonly Known as the Old Oregon Trail
Double postcard, Ezra Meeker, 1907

MAP 181 (*page 95*).
Pays des Porteurs
Pierre Jean De Smet, c. 1846
Manuscripts, Archives, and Special Collections, Washington State University WSU 2

MAP 182 (*page 96*).
[Bird's-eye maps comparing Deseret to Canaan as the Promised Land]
From: *Pointer to Prosperity*, Denver & Rio Grande Western brochure, 1896

MAP 183 (*page 96*).
Map of the Great Salt Lake and Adjacent Country in the Territory of Utah
Howard Stansbury, 1852
David Rumsey Collection

MAP 184 (*page 96*).
Map of the Emigrant Road Independence Mo. to S^t. Francisco
T.H. Jefferson, 1849
Library of Congress G4051.P25 1849 .J4

MAP 185 (*page 97*).
Map to Illustrate Horn's Overland Guide to California and Oregon
J.H. Colton, 1852
From: *Horn's Overland Guide, From the U.S. Indian Sub-Agency, Council Bluffs, on the Missouri River, to the City of Sacramento, in California.*
Hosea B. Horn, 1852
Beinecke Rare Book Library, Yale University

MAP 186 (*page 97*).
Route of the Mormon Pioneers from Nauvoo to Great Salt Lake, Feb'y 1846–July 1847
Millroy & Hayes, 1899
Library of Congress G4051.S1 1899 .M5

MAP 187 (*page 98*).
Map of the Emigrant Road Independence Mo. to S^t. Francisco
T.H. Jefferson, 1849
Library of Congress G4051.P25 1849 .J4

MAP 188 (*page 98*).
Map of the Emigrant Road Independence Mo. to S^t. Francisco
T.H. Jefferson, 1849
Library of Congress G4051.P25 1849 .J4

MAP 189 (*page 99*).
Map of the Valley of the Sacramento including the Gold Region
John Bidwell, 1848
Warren Heckrotte Collection

MAP 190 (*page 100*).
Map of the United States The British Provinces Mexico &c.
J.H. Colton, 1849
David Rumsey Collection

MAP 191 (*page 100*).
Map of the Gold Regions of California, Showing the Routes via Chagres and Panama, Cape Horn, &c.
Ensigns and Thayer, 1849
David Rumsey Collection

MAP 192 (*page 101*).
Bai San Francisco und Vereinigung de Sacramento mit dem San Joaquin
Henry Lange, 1854
David Rumsey Collection

MAP 193 (*page 101*).
San Francisco
M. and N. Hanhart, after Francis Samuel Marryat, 1851
Library of Congress

MAP 194 (*page 101*).
Virginia City, Nevada Territory, 1861
Charles Conrad Kuchel, 1861
Library of Congress
PGA-Kuchel--VirginiaCity

MAP 195 (*page 102*).
Map of Virginia Gold Hill and Devil's Gate Mining Districts, Nevada Territory
James Butler, 1864
Storey Co. Recorder's Office, Nevada

MAP 196 (*page 102*).
Map of Virginia, Gold Hill, Devil's Gate, American Flat Gold & Silver Mining Districts
Higginson & Goldworthy, 1865
Mary B. Ansari Map Library, University of Nevada, Reno

MAP 197 (*page 103*).
Washoe Silver Region
H.H. Bancroft and Company, 1862
Mary B. Ansari Map Library, University of Nevada, Reno

MAP 198 (*page 103*).
Nevada
U.S. General Land Office, 1866
David Rumsey Collection

MAP 199 (*page 104*).
Birds Eye View of Virginia City, Storey County, Nevada. 1875
Augustus Koch, 1875
Library of Congress
G4354.V4A3 1875 .K6

MAP 200 (*page 104*).
Map of the Comstock Lode and the Washoe Mining Claims in Storey & Lyon Counties, Nevada
T.D. Parkinson, 1875
Special Collections, University of Nevada, Reno

MAP 201 (*page 105*).
Map of the Indian Territory, Northern Texas and New Mexico, Showing the Great Western Prairies by Josiah Gregg
From: Josiah Gregg, *The Commerce of the Prairies*, 1844

MAP 202 (*page 105*).
[Map of the Western Territory showing the *Route of the Dragoons under the command of Col. Dodge in 1835*]
Senate Document, 1861, reprinted from 1836 Senate document, Gaines Pierce Kingsbury, *Journal of a March of a Detachment of Dragoons under the Command of Colonel Dodge during the Summer of 1835*

MAP 203 (*page 106*).
New Map of the Pikes Peak Gold Region Showing all the Routes from the Mississippi and Missouri Rivers and the Out fitting points
Parker & Huyett, 1859
Beinecke Rare Book Library, Yale University

MAP 204 (*page 106*).
Map of the Recently Discovered Gold Regions in Western Kansas & Nebraska. From Actual Surveys and Notes & Observations by Hartley French Dickson & Co.
Hartley French Dickson & Co., 1859
Library of Congress G4201.H2 1859 .H3

MAP 205 (*page 107*).
The Direct Route to Pikes Peak and the Gold Regions via the Toledo Wabash & Great Western Rail Road Line and the Hannibal & St. Joseph R.R.
1859
Beinecke Rare Book Library, Yale University

MAP 206 (*page 107*).
Routes to the Pikes Peak Gold Regions
Anon., for J.S. Fillmore, c. 1860
Library of Congress G4051.P1 186-.R6

MAP 207 (*page 107*).
General Map of the United States & their Territory between the Mississippi and the Pacific Ocean
John T. Fiala, 1859
Library of Congress G4050 1859 .F5 RR 175

MAP 208 (*page 107*).
Routes from the Missouri River to the Kansas Gold Mines
O.B. Gunn, 1859, inset in *Gunn & Mitchell's New Map of Kansas and the Gold Mines Embracing all the Public Surveys up to 1862*, O.B. Gunn and David T. Mitchell, 1862
David Rumsey Collection

MAP 209 (*page 108*).
Colorado Territory
U.S. General Land Office, 1866
David Rumsey Collection

MAP 210 (*page 108*).
New Mexico & Arizona Territories
U.S. General Land Office, 1866
David Rumsey Collection

MAP 211 (*page 108*).
Official Map of the Territory of Arizona
Richard Gird, 1865
David Rumsey Collection

MAP 212 (*page 109*).
United States, Territories
U.S. General Land Office, 1866
David Rumsey Collection

MAP 301 (page 145).
*Spindletop Oil Field, Beaumont
District, Texas*
From: *Oil Fields of the Texas–Louisiana
Gulf Coastal Plain,* U.S. Geological Survey
Bulletin No. 282, Plate 2, 1906

MAP 302 (page 145).
Geological Map of North-East Texas
(Oil fields in south-eastern Texas)
Standard Blue Print Map and Engineering
Company, Fort Worth, c. 1930

MAP 303 (page 146).
*George Catlin's Map of the Indian
Country*
George Catlin, 1833
From: *Eleventh Census of the United
States* (1890), vol. 8. *Report on Indians
Taxed and Indians Not Taxed,* 1894

MAP 304 (page 147).
*Map Showing the Lands Assigned to
Emigrant Indians West of Arkansas &
Missouri*
From: Senate document, Gaines Pierce
Kingsbury, *Journal of a March of a
Detachment of Dragoons under the
Command of Colonel Dodge during the
Summer of 1835*
United States Topographical Bureau, 1836
Library of Congress G4051.E1 1836 .U5 TIL

MAP 305 (page 147).
*Map of Nebraska and Kansas
Territories, Showing the Location of
the Indian Reserves According to the
Treaties of 1854*
Indian Office, Washington, 1854
U.S. National Archives, Center for
Legislative Archives RG 46, SEN 35B-C1

MAP 306 (page 148).
*Colton's New Map of the State of
Texas, the Indian Territory and
Adjoining Portions of New Mexico,
Louisiana, and Arkansas*
G.W. & C.B. Colton, 1872
Library of Congress G4030 1872 .C6 Vault

MAP 307 (page 148).
[Map showing areas reserved for each
tribe according to the Treaty of Fort
Laramie, 1851]
Pierre-Jean De Smet, 1851
Library of Congress G4052.S14 1851 .S6

MAP 308 (page 149).
*Map of a Reconnaissance of the Black
Hills, July and August 1874, With
troops under command of Lt. Col. G.A.
Custer, 7th Cavalry*
William Ludlow, 1874

MAP 309 (page 150).
[Map of the Battle of Little Bighorn,
25 June 1876]
Robert Patterson Hughes, 1876
Contained with letter 30 June 1876
Library of Congress Manuscript
Division, 46C.1b

MAP 310 (page 151).
[Map of the Battle of Little Bighorn,
25 June 1876]
White Bird, c. 1895
West Point Museum Art Collection,
United States Military Academy, West
Point, New York

MAP 311 (page 151).
*Department of Columbia Map of the
Nez Perce Indian Campaign Brig. Gen.
O.O. Howard Commanding*
Inset: *Scene of the Outbreak*
Robert H. Fletcher, United States War
Department, 1877

MAP 312 (page 152).
*Department of Columbia Map of the
Nez Perce Indian Campaign Brig. Gen.
O.O. Howard Commanding*
Robert H. Fletcher, United States War
Department, 1877

MAP 313 (page 152).
*Map Showing the Nez Perce Indian
Reser^{vn} and the Wallowa Valley*
Clay Wood, 1877

MAP 314 (page 153).
*Map Illustrating the Extermination
of the American Bison*
W.T. Hornaday, 1889
Library of Congress G3301.D4 1889

MAP 315 (page 153).
*Texas and Part of Mexico & the
United States, Showing the Route of
the First Santa Fe Expedition*
Wiley and Putnam, 1844
Beinecke Rare Book Library, Yale University

MAP 316 (page 154).
*Diagram of the Situation at the Battle
of Wounded Knee at the Time the
Indians Opened Fire*
The Bee, 1891
Denver Public Library

MAP 317 (page 154).
[Cherokee Outlet Lands]
Atlas map, c. 1893
Western History Collection
University of Oklahoma

MAP 318 (page 154).
Dakota Territory
U.S. General Land Office, 1866
David Rumsey Collection

MAP 319 (page 155).
*Map . . . showing . . . Constitutional
Population . . . To Which is Added a
Sketch of the Principal Indian
Reservations and Ranges*
Francis A. Walker, 1871
From: U.S. Census Office, *Statistical
Atlas of the United States,* 1874

MAP 320 (page 155).
*Indian Reservations West of the
Mississippi River*
United States Office of Indian Affairs, 1923
Library of Congress G4051.E1 1923 .U5 TIL

MAP 321 (page 156).
Plat of the Seven Ranges of Townships
Thomas Hutchins, 1785
From: Mathew Carey, *Carey's General
Atlas,* 1814
David Rumsey Collection

MAP 322 (page 156).
New Mexico
U.S. General Land Office, 1879
David Rumsey Collection

MAP 323 (page 157).
United States, Territories
U.S. General Land Office, 1866
David Rumsey Collection

MAP 324 (page 157).
Wyoming Territory
U.S. General Land Office, 1879
David Rumsey Collection

MAP 325 (page 158).
*Bird's eye View of Greeley, Colo.,
County Seat of Weld Co.*
Beck & Pauli, 1882
Library of Congress G4314.G8A3 1882 .S7

MAP 326 (page 158).
Greeley and Additions
Charles E. Littell, 1910
Greeley History Museum

MAP 327 (page 159).
*Map of the Colony Lands as Laid Out
by Union Colony of Colorado 1871*
Anon., 1871
Greeley History Museum

MAP 328 (page 159).
Map of the State of Colorado
U.S. General Land Office, 1897
Colorado State University, Boulder,
Map Library

MAP 329 (page 159).
*Map of the Irrigated Farms of Northern
Colorado*
R.W. Gelder, 1915
Greeley History Museum

MAP 330 (page 159).
*Chicago Colorado Colony
Plan of Town Site*
Unknown, c. 1871
Colorado State University, Boulder

MAP 331 (page 160).
*Western Part of the United States Showing
Location of Areas Irrigated in 1889*
F.H. Newell, 1889
From: *Eleventh Census of the United
States,* vol 8, part 2, *Agriculture by
Irrigation in the Western Part of the
United States,* 1894

MAP 332 (page 160).
*Plat of Irrigated Portion of Water
District No. 22 in Rio Grande Division
(No. 3) State of Colorado*
State Engineer's Office, 1894
Colorado State University, Boulder

MAP 333 (page 160).
*Map of Wyoming Showing Areas Irrigated
in 1889*
From: *Eleventh Census of the United
States,* vol 8, part 2, *Agriculture by
Irrigation in the Western Part of the
United States,* 1894

MAP 334 (page 161).
*Plan of the Truckee River System of
Irrigation and Water Storage*
Francis G. Newlands, 1890
Mary B. Ansari Map Library,
University of Nevada, Reno

MAP 335 (page 161).
*Map of Colorado Showing Areas Irrigated
in 1889*
From: *Eleventh Census of the United
States,* vol 8, part 2, *Agriculture by
Irrigation in the Western Part of the
United States,* 1894

MAP 336 (page 161).
*Plat of Irrigated Portion of Water
District No. 8 in South Platte Division
(No. 1) State of Colorado*
State Engineer's Office, 1894
Colorado State University, Boulder

MAP 337 (page 162).
*Plat of Irrigated Portion of Water
District No. 9 in South Platte Division
(No. 1) State of Colorado*
State Engineer's Office, 1894
Colorado State University, Boulder

MAP 338 (page 162).
*Commemorating the Dedication of the
American Falls Dam*
Newspaper advertisement, 1927

MAP 339 (page 162).
Irrigated Areas of Arizona
From: *Report of the Governor,* 1901

MAP 340 (page 162).
*The Roosevelt Dam and the Salt River
Valley*
Real estate promotional map, 1908

MAP 341 (page 163).
Salt River Project and Central Arizona
Unknown origin, c. 1947
Arizona State University Map Library

MAP 342 (page 163).
[Untitled map of the Salt River Project]
T.A. Hayden, 1934
Arizona State University Map Library

MAP 343 (page 164).
[Bird's-eye map of the Umatilla Project,
Hermiston, Oregon]
Umatilla Project Development League,
1910

MAP 344 (page 165).
*Umatilla Project – East Branch –
Oregon General Map*
U.S. Reclamation Service, 1910

MAP 345 (page 166).
*Map of the San Joaquin, Sacramento
and Tulare Valleys State of California*
California Irrigation Commission, 1873
David Rumsey Collection

MAP 395 (*page 183*).
Map of Arizona or the Gadsden Purchase with the Position of its Silver Mines as Now Worked, 1859
Sopori Land and Mining Company, charter and by-laws, John R. Bartlett, 1859
Beinecke Rare Book Library, Yale University

MAP 396 (*page 184*).
Johnson's Nebraska and Kansas
Johnson & Browning, 1860
David Rumsey Collection

MAP 397 (*page 184*).
Territory of Kansas and Indian Territory
Henry D. Rogers and Alexander K. Johnston, 1857
From: *Atlas of the United States of North America*, 1857
David Rumsey Collection

MAP 398 (*page 184*).
Territory of Nebraska
Henry D. Rogers and Alexander K. Johnston, 1857
From: *Atlas of the United States of North America*, 1857
David Rumsey Collection

MAP 399 (*page 184*).
Territory of Minnesota
Henry D. Rogers and Alexander K. Johnston, 1857
From: *Atlas of the United States of North America*, 1857
David Rumsey Collection

MAP 400 (*pages 184–85*).
Map of Part of the Boundary between Colorado and New Mexico on the 37th Parallel
Ehud N. Darling, 1868
New Mexico Museum of History

MAP 401 (*page 185*).
Map of Public Surveys in Colorado Territory
U.S. General Land Office, 1866
David Rumsey Collection

MAP 402 (*page 185*).
South–Western States
Unknown, 1864

MAP 403 (*page 186*).
Colton's Map of the United States of America
J.H. Colton, Johnson & Browning, 1861

MAP 404 (*page 186*).
Bacon's Military Map of the United States Shewing the Forts & Fortifications
Bacon and Company, 1862

MAP 405 (*page 186*).
Map of the Territory of the United States from the Mississippi River to the Pacific Ocean
Gouverneur Kemble Warren, 1858, with addition of state and territorial boundaries to 1863
Library of Congress
G4050 1863 .W35 Fil 250

MAP 406 (*page 186*).
The American Continent. Topographical and Railroad Map of the United States, West Indies, Mexico and Central America
Ch. Lubrecht & Co., 1864
David Rumsey Collection

MAP 407 (*page 186*).
Territory of Utah
Henry Johnston Rogers and Alexander Keith Johnston; Edward Stanford, 1857
David Rumsey Collection

MAP 408 (*page 186*).
Map of the United States, Showing the Territory in Possession of the Federal Union
Bacon and Company, 1864

MAP 409 (*page 187*).
Territory of New Mexico
Henry Darwin Rogers and Alexander Keith Johnston; Edward Stanford, 1857
David Rumsey Collection

MAP 410 (*page 187*).
Johnson's California, Territories of New Mexico and Utah
From: *Johnson's New Illustrated Family Atlas of the World*, A.J. Johnson, 1862

MAP 411 (*page 187*).
Official Map of the Territory of Arizona
Richard Gird, 1865
David Rumsey Collection

MAP 412 (*page 187*).
United States
Unknown, 1861

MAP 413 (*page 188*).
Washington and Oregon
J.H. Colton, 1856
David Rumsey Collection

MAP 414 (*page 188*).
Map of Oregon, Washington, and Part of British Columbia
Samuel Augustus Mitchell, 1860

MAP 415 (*page 188*).
Colton's Map of Oregon, Washington, Idaho and British Columbia
J.H. Colton, 1863

MAP 416 (*page 188*).
Map of the Country from Lake Superior to the Pacific Ocean
G.W. & C.B. Colton & Co., 1867 (1868 reprint)

MAP 417 (*page 188*).
Map of the Indian and Oklahoma Territories
Rand McNally, 1892
Library of Congress
G4021.E1 1892 .M2 TIL Vault

MAP 418 (*page 188*).
Diagram Showing Cut-Offs Made by Red River
U.S. Geological Survey, 1895

MAP 419 (*page 189*).
[Map of Alaska]
U.S. Exploring Expedition, 1841
U.S. National Archives

MAP 420 (*page 189*).
[Map of the northern part of North America]
Vasili Berkh, 1821
A.V. Efimov, 1964

MAP 421 (*page 189*).
North Western America Showing the Territory Ceded by Russia to the United States
United States Coast and Geodetic Survey, 1867
Library of Congress G4370 1867 .U5 TIL

MAP 422 (*page 189*).
Map of the Canadian Pacific Railway and Connections Showing Routes to the Yukon Gold Fields, Alaska, Klondike and the Northwestern Mining Territories of Canada
Poole Brothers, 1898
Library of Congress

MAP 423 (*page 190*).
[Bird's-eye view of San Francisco]
G.H. Goddard, 1868
Library of Congress G 4364.S5A3 1868 .G6

MAP 424 (*page 190*).
Oakland, California, 1900
Fred Soderberg, c. 1900
Library of Congress G4364.O2A3 1900 .S6

MAP 425 (*page 191*).
City of San Jose, Cal., 1875
Charles B. Gifford, 1875
Library of Congress G4364.S6A3 1875 .G5

MAP 426 (*page 191*).
[San Francisco Burned District]
From: Frank Thompson Searight, *The Doomed City*, 1906
David Burkhart Collection

MAP 427 (*page 191*).
The Exposition City San Francisco
North American Press Association, 1912

MAP 428 (*page 191*).
[Distribution system of] *Spring Valley Water Co. San Francisco – California*
Spring Valley Water Company, 1922

MAP 429 (*page 191*).
[Bird's-eye map of the Hetch Hetchy Aqueduct]
From: *San Francisco and Its Great Water Project*, 1930
San Francisco Public Library

MAP 430 (*page 192*).
Map of the City of Los Angeles
E.O.C. Ord, Henry Hancock, George Hansen, Bancroft & Thayer, 1857
David Rumsey Collection

MAP 431 (*page 192*).
Los Angeles, Cal., Looking South-west to Pacific Ocean
W.W. Elliott Lithographer, 1887
Huntington Library BV/L-2

MAP 432 (*page 193*).
Los Angeles, California, 1894
B.W. Pierce, 1894
Library of Congress G 4364.L8A3 1894 .P5

MAP 433 (*page 193*).
Map of Hollywood
H.H. Wilcox & Co., 1887
Huntington Library 442300

MAP 434 (*page 194*).
Topographic Map of the Los Angeles Aqueduct and Adjacent Territory
City of Los Angeles Board of Water and Power Commissioners, 1908
Library of Congress G4361.N44 1908 .C5

MAP 435 (*page 194*).
Map Showing Territory Annexed to the City of Los Angeles, California
Homer Hamelin (Los Angeles City Engineer), 1916
Library of Congress G 4364.L8F7 1916 .H3

MAP 436 (*page 195*).
Map of Palmdale
Palm Valley Land Company, 1888
Huntington Library 471218

MAP 437 (*page 196*).
New San Diego [and inset]
Sketch of the Port of San Diego
A.B. Gray and T.D. Johns, 1850
Huntington Library 431875

MAP 438 (*page 196*).
Map of Horton's Addition San Diego
L.L. Lockling, 1867

MAP 439 (*page 196*).
Bird's Eye View of Coronado Beach, San Diego Bay and City of San Diego, Cal, in distance
E.S. Moore, c. 1886
Library of Congress
G4364.C77A3 188- .M6 MLC

MAP 440 (*page 196*).
San Diego, The Southwestern Gateway. The Future Great Seaport of the Southwest
Promotional postcard, 1915

MAP 441 (*page 196*).
Bird's-eye View of the City of Sacramento, State Capital of California, 1870
Britton & Rey, 1870

MAP 442 (*page 197*).
Map of Sacramento City & West Sacramento
William Warner, 1850
Sutter's Fort State Historical Park

MAP 443 (*page 197*).
Sacramento
W.W. Elliott & Company, 1890s
Library of Congress G4364.S2A3 189- .E5

MAP 444 (*page 197*).
Fresno, California
L.W. Klein, Britton & Rey, 1901
Library of Congress G4364.F8A3 1901 .K5

MAP 552 (*page 239*).
How Hoover Dam Works
U.S. Bureau of Reclamation, 1949

MAP 553 (*page 240*).
Panoramic Perspective of the Spokane Region Including the Geological and Scenic Wonderland Embracing the Columbia Basin Irrigation Project and Grand Coulee Dam
Spokane Chamber of Commerce, 1949

MAP 554 (*pages 240–41*).
The Metropolitan Water District of Southern California, Colorado River Aqueduct
From: *Annual Report of the Metropolitan Water District of Southern California*, 1939

MAP 555 (*page 241*).
Columbia Basin Irrigation Project
Brochure and map cover,
Spokane Chamber of Commerce, 1949

MAP 556 (*page 241*).
[Southern part of the San Diego Aqueduct]
From: *Annual Report of the Metropolitan Water District of Southern California*, 1953

MAP 557 (*page 242*).
["Battle of Los Angeles"]
Galveston Daily News,
26 February 1942

MAP 558 (*page 242*).
Japanese Evacuation Program Exclusion Areas
Western Defense Command and Fourth Army Wartime Civil Control Administration, 1942
From: *Final Report: Japanese Evacuation from the West Coast*, 1943

MAP 559 (*page 242*).
Disposition of U.S. Pacific Fleet 7 Dec. 1941
Classified United States Government map (now declassified), c. 1941

MAP 560 (*page 243*).
Japanese Evacuation Program Relocation Center Destinations
Western Defense Command and Fourth Army Wartime Civil Control Administration, 1942
From: *Final Report: Japanese Evacuation from the West Coast*, 1943

MAP 561 (*page 243*).
Prohibited Area Exclusion Order No. 27
U.S. Army, 1942
Western Defense Command and Fourth Army Wartime Civil Control Administration, 1942
From: *Final Report: Japanese Evacuation from the West Coast*, 1943

MAP 562 (*page 244*).
Camp Layout, Manzanar War Relocation Project
War Relocation Authority, 1945
Japanese American National Museum
NRC.1999.43.7

MAP 563 (*page 244*).
[Harbor defenses on Point Loma, San Diego]
U.S. Engineer's Office, 1941
U.S. National Archives RG 407, Box 118, Supplement to harbor defense project

MAP 564 (*page 245*).
Along the Union Pacific Railroad
Brochure cover, Union Pacific Railroad, 1944

MAP 565 (*page 245*).
America's Zone of Plenty
Magazine advertisement,
Great Northern Railway, 1942

MAP 566 (*page 245*).
Regional Aeronautical Chart
[of Southern California]
U.S. Coast and Geodetic Survey, 1943

MAP 567 (*page 246*).
Santa Fe Lines, Colorado, New Mexico, and Panhandle of Texas
Atchison, Topeka & Santa Fe Railroad, 1946

MAP 568 (*page 247*).
Introducing the New Empire Builder Fleet
Brochure, Great Northern Railway, 1947

MAP 569 (*page 247*).
Route of the New Empire Builder
Brochure, Great Northern Railway, 1947

MAP 570 (*page 247*).
Map of "Your America" Showing Territory Served by the Union Pacific Railroad
Postcard, 1948

MAP 571 (*page 248*).
National System of Interstate Highways
[as approved, 1947]
From: *General Location of National System of Interstate Highways*, Bureau of Roads, U.S. Department of Commerce, Washington, D.C., 1955

MAP 572 (*page 248*).
Master Plan of Metropolitan Los Angeles Freeways
Regional Planning Commission, 1947

MAP 573 (*page 248*).
[Los Angeles Area]
From: *General Location of National System of Interstate Highways*, Bureau of Roads, U.S. Department of Commerce, Washington, D.C., 1955

MAP 574 (*page 249*).
Evacuation Map Metropolitan Area of Phoenix
Department of Civil Defense, State of Arizona, 1958
Arizona Historical Society

MAP 575 (*page 249*).
Portland Target Area Evacuation Routes
Civil Defense brochure and map, *Defense against the H-Bomb*, 1955

MAP 576 (*page 250*).
Alaska the 49th State?
Anchorage *Sunday News*, 6 October 1946

MAP 577 (*page 250*).
Alaska 49th State
Postcard, 1959

MAP 578 (*page 251*).
The Colorado–Big Thompson Project
U.S. Bureau of Reclamation, 1959
University of Colorado, Boulder, Map Library

MAP 579 (*page 251*).
[Colorado–Big Thompson Project]
U.S. Bureau of Reclamation, 1959
University of Colorado, Boulder, Map Library

MAP 580 (*page 251*).
Colorado–Big Thompson Project
H.A. Grout, 1948
University of Colorado, Boulder, Map Library

MAP 581 (*page 252*).
[Blue Mesa Reservoir projected boundary]
Curecanti Unit, Colorado River Storage Project, 1960
University of Colorado, Boulder, Map Library

MAP 582 (*page 252*).
Central Valley Project
U.S. Bureau of Reclamation, 1966

MAP 583 (*page 252*).
The Project To-day
[Central Valley Project]
U.S. Bureau of Reclamation, 1954

MAP 584 (*page 253*).
Central Arizona Project – Arizona Aqueduct System
U.S. Bureau of Reclamation, 1972
Arizona State University Map Library

MAP 585 (*page 254*).
[Proposed] *Fort Randall Dam, Reservoir and Townsite*
U.S. Army Corps of Engineers, 1951

MAP 586 (*page 254*).
1984 Coal Lease Sale Regional Activity Powder River Coal Environmental Impact Statement
United States Geological Survey, Central Energy Resources Team, Denver, 1984

MAP 587 (*page 255*).
Arizona . . . Land of Adventure
Tourist booklet, 1957

MAP 588 (*page 255*).
Sandia Mountain Winter Sports Area
Albuquerque Ski Club and the Albuquerque Chamber of Commerce, 1940

MAP 589 (*page 255*).
[Pictorial map of western ski resorts]
United Airlines advertisement, 1972

MAP 590 (*page 255*).
Skiing Centers in Colorado
U.S. Forest Service, c. 1946

MAP 591 (*page 256*).
Recreational Map of New Mexico
Wilfred Stedman, New Mexico State Tourist Bureau, 1946

MAP 592 (*page 256*).
[Map showing Youngtown, Arizona]
Unknown, c. 1956
Arizona State University Map Library

MAP 593 (*page 256*).
[Sun City West]
Wide World of Maps, Phoenix, 1984
www.maps4u.com

MAP 594 (*page 256*).
[Sun City]
Wide World of Maps, Phoenix, 1984
www.maps4u.com

MAP 595 (*page 257*).
Master Land Use Plan, Lake Havasu City, Arizona
McCullough Corporation, 1965
Arizona State University

MAP 596 (*page 257*).
[Map showing distances from Lake Havasu City]
McCullough Corporation, 1965
Arizona State University

MAP 597 (*page 257*).
[Percentage of days with sunshine]
McCullough Corporation, 1965
Arizona State University

MAP 598 (*page 258*).
[Pictorial map of] *Arizona*
Bob Martin, 1972
Arizona State University Map Library

MAP 599 (*page 259*).
[Historical highway marker for Chloride in shape of map of Arizona]
Author photograph, 2007

MAP 600 (*page 259*).
[Photomap of Imperial Valley area]
U.S. Geological Survey and NASA, 1969
Arizona State University Map Library

MAP 601 (*page 259*).
[Relief map/model of Lake Mead]
Lake Mead National Recreation Center office, author photograph, 2007

MAP 602 (*page 259*).
[Hoover Dam bypass road project]
Sign at Hoover Dam, U.S. Bureau of Reclamation, 2007

MAP 603 (*pages 260–61*).
Federal Lands and Indian Reservations
From: *The National Atlas of the United States* (www.nationalatlas.gov)
U.S. Department of the Interior/U.S. Geological Survey, 2009

MAPS 604, 605, 606, 607
(*page 276, below*).
Arbuckle Coffee Co. cards, 1890
David Rumsey Collection

MAP 608 (*page 277, right*).
West/Scenic Route Across America
Northern Pacific Railway brochure,
1936

SOURCES OF OTHER ILLUSTRATIONS

By page number.
All modern photographs are by the author.
Brochure and map covers are from the same source as corresponding maps.
Uncredited items are from the author's or other private collections.

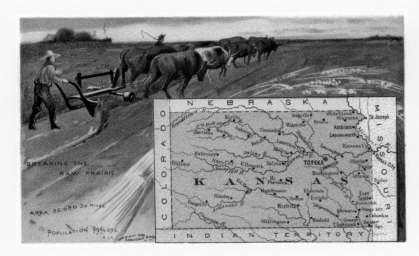

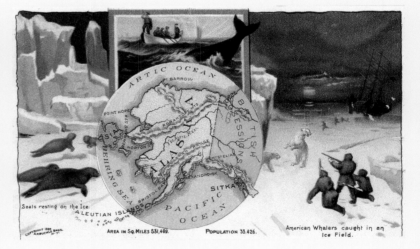

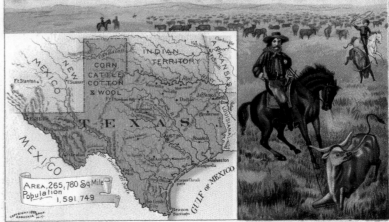

MAP 604 – MAP 607.
Geographically educational cards issued with packages of coffee in 1890 by the Arbuckle Coffee Company.
From top left, clockwise: Kansas, Alaska, Texas, and New Mexico. See also Arizona and Wyoming cards illustrated on page 4.

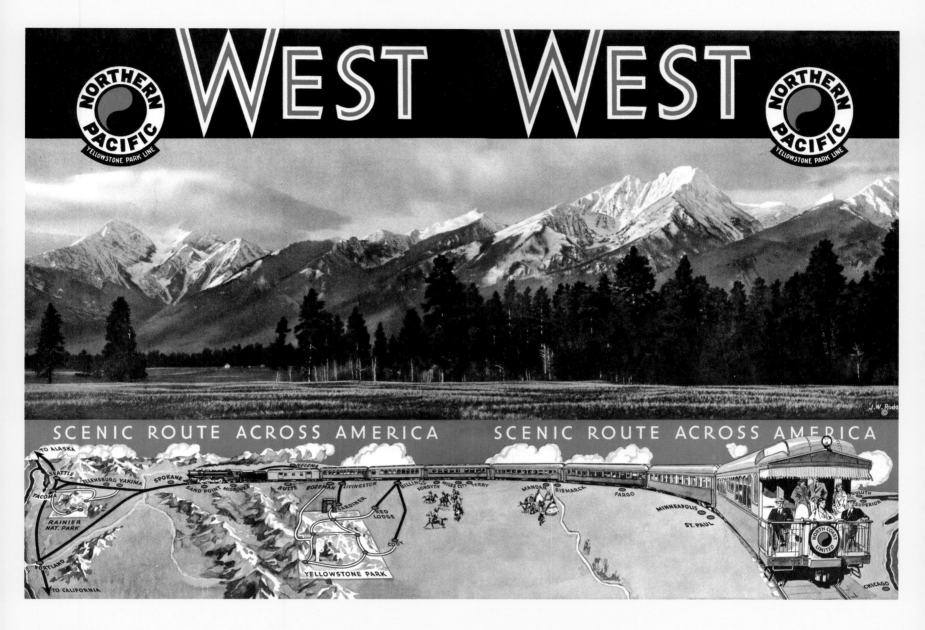

MAP 608.
This beautifully designed cover is from a brochure advertising the Northern Pacific's *North Coast Limited* and the *scenic route* across the West. It was published in 1936. The train stretches from Chicago to Spokane, and the national parks, *Rainier* and *Yellowstone,* are also larger than life.

BIBLIOGRAPHY

Abbott, Carl, Stephen J. Leonard, and David McComb. *Colorado: A History of the Centennial State.* Niwot: University Press of Colorado, 1994.

Ambrose, Stephen E. *Nothing Like It in the World: The Men Who Built the Transcontinental Railroad, 1863–1869.* New York: Simon & Schuster, 2000.

Anderson, Alex. D. *The Silver Country or The Great Southwest.* New York: G.P. Putnam's Sons, 1877.

Beck, Warren A., and Ynez D. Haase. *Historical Atlas of New Mexico.* Norman: University of Oklahoma Press, 1969.

———. *Historical Atlas of California.* Norman: University of Oklahoma Press, 1974.

———. *Historical Atlas of the American West.* Norman: University of Oklahoma Press, 1989.

Becker, Robert H. *Diseños of California Ranchos: Maps of Thirty-Seven Land Grants, 1822–1846, from the Records of the United States District Court, San Francisco.* San Francisco: Book Club of California, 1964.

———. *Designs on the Land: Diseños of California Ranchos and Their Makers.* San Francisco: Book Club of California, 1969.

Bowles, Samuel. *Our New West: Records of Travel between the Mississippi River and the Pacific Ocean.* Hartford, CT: Hartford Publishing Co., 1869.

Brechin, Gray A. *Imperial San Francisco: Urban Power, Earthly Ruin.* Berkeley: University of California Press, 1999.

Brown, Dee. *Bury My Heart at Wounded Knee.* New York: Bantam Books, 1978.

Burkhart, David. *Earthquake Days: The 1906 San Francisco Earthquake & Fire in 3-D.* San Bruno: Faultline Books, 2005.

Carberry, Michael E. *Patterns of the Past: An Inventory of Anchorage's Heritage Resources.* Anchorage: Municipality of Anchorage Historic Landmarks Commission, 1979.

Carle, David. *Introduction to Water in California.* Berkeley: University of California Press, 2004.

Caughey, John, with Norris Hundley Jr. *California: History of a Remarkable State.* Englewood Cliffs, NJ: Prentice Hall, 1982.

Chávez, Thomas E. *An Illustrated History of New Mexico.* Niwot: University Press of Colorado, 1992.

Clee, Paul. *Photography and the Making of the American West.* North Haven, CT: Linnet Books, 2003.

Cohen, Paul E. *Mapping the West: America's Westward Movement, 1524–1890.* New York: Rizzoli, 2002.

Collins, Robert. *Kansas Pacific: An Illustrated History.* David City, NE: South Platte Press, 1998.

Commission on Wartime Relocation and Internment of Citizens. *Personal Justice Denied: Report of the Commission on Wartime Relocation and Internment of Citizens.* Seattle: University of Washington Press/Washington: Civil Liberties Public Education Fund, 1997 (original report 1982 and 1983).

Conkling, Roscoe P., and Margaret B. Conkling. *The Butterfield Overland Mail, 1857–1869,* Vol. III, Atlas. Glendale, CA: Arthur H. Clark Co., 1947.

Cross, Coy F., II. *Go West Young Man!: Horace Greeley's Vision for America.* Albuquerque: University of New Mexico Press, 1995.

Dawdy, Doris Ostrander. *George Montague Wheeler: The Man and the Myth.* Athens, OH: Swallow Press/Ohio University Press, 1993.

DeVoto, Bernard. *The Course of Empire.* New York: Mariner/Houghton Mifflin, 1998 (original edition 1952).

Dicken, Samuel N., and Emily F. Dicken. *The Making of Oregon: A Study in Historical Geography.* Portland: Oregon Historical Society, 1979.

Engerman, Stanley L., and Robert E. Gallman (eds.) *The Cambridge Economic History of the United States.* Cambridge, U.K.: Cambridge University Press, 1996.

Etulain, Richard W. *Beyond the Missouri: The Story of the American West.* Albuquerque: University of New Mexico Press, 2006.

Fey, Marshall, R. Joe King, and Jack Lepisto. *Emigrant Shadows: A History and Guide to the California Trail.* Virginia City, NV: Western Trails Research Association, 2002.

Ficken, Robert E. *Washington Territory.* Pullman: Washington State University Press, 2002.

Ficken, Robert E., and Charles P. LeWarne. *Washington: A Centennial History.* Seattle: University of Washington Press, 1988.

Fiege, Mark. *Irrigated Eden: The Making of an Agriculture Landscape in the American West.* Seattle: University of Washington Press, 1999.

Fradkin, Philip L. *Stagecoach: Wells Fargo and the American West.* New York: Simon and Shuster, 2002.

———. *The Great Earthquake and Firestorms of 1906: How San Francisco Nearly Destroyed Itself.* Berkeley: University of California Press, 2006.

Francaviglia, Richard V. *Mapping and Imagination in the Great Basin: A Cartographic History.* Reno: University of Nevada Press, 2005.

Garber, Paul Neff. *The Gadsden Treaty.* Gloucester, MA: Peter Smith, 1959.

Goetzmann, William H. *Exploration and Empire: The Explorer and the Scientist in the Winning of the American West.* Austin, TX: Texas State Historical Association, 2000 (original edition 1966).

Gutiérrez, Ramón A., and Richard J. Orsi (eds.). *Contested Eden: California before the Gold Rush.* Berkeley: University of California Press, 1998.

Harlow, Neal. *California Conquered: War and Peace on the Pacific, 1846–1850.* Berkeley: University of California Press, 1982.

Hayden, Dolores. *Seven American Utopias: The Architecture of Communitarian Socialism, 1790–1975.* Cambridge: Massachusetts Institute of Technology Press, 1976.

Hayes, Derek. *Historical Atlas of the Pacific Northwest.* Seattle: Sasquatch Books, 1999.

———. *America Discovered: A Historical Atlas of North American Exploration.* Vancouver: Douglas & McIntyre, 2004.

———. *Historical Atlas of the United States.* Berkeley: University of California Press, 2006.

———. *Historical Atlas of California.* Berkeley: University of California Press, 2007.

Hidy, Ralph W., et al. *The Great Northern Railway: A History.* Boston: Harvard Business School Press, 1988.

Hill, William E. *The Mormon Trail: Yesterday and Today.* Logan: Utah State University Press, 1996.

Hornbeck, David. *California Patterns: A Geographical and Historical Atlas.* Palo Alto: Mayfield Publishing, 1983.

Hudson, Alice, and Barbara Cohen-Stratyner. *Heading West, Touring West: Mapmakers, Performing Artists, and the American Frontier.* New York: New York Public Library, 2001.

Hundley, Norris, Jr. *The Great Thirst: Californians and Water: A History.* Berkeley: University of California Press, 2001.

Hunt, Michael E., et al. *Retirement Communities: An American Original.* New York: The Haworth Press, 1983.

Jones, Holway R. *John Muir and the Sierra Club: The Battle for Yosemite.* San Francisco: Sierra Club, 1965.

Kahrl, William L. (ed.). *The California Water Atlas.* Sacramento: Governor's Office of Planning and Research, 1979.

———. *Water and Power.* Berkeley: University of California Press, 1982.

Kalani, Lyn, Lynn Rudy, and John Sperry (eds.). *Fort Ross.* Fort Ross, CA: Fort Ross Interpretive Association, n.d. [c. 2006].

Kessel, John L. *Spain in the Southwest: A Narrative History of Colonial New Mexico, Arizona, Texas, and California.* Norman: University of Oklahoma Press, 2002.

Kreyche, Gerald F. *Visions of the American West.* Lexington: The University Press of Kentucky, 1989.

Land, Barbara, and Myrick Land. *A Short History of Las Vegas*. Reno: University of Nevada Press, 1999.

Larson, T.A. *History of Wyoming*. Lincoln: University of Nebraska Press, 1965.

Lavender, David. *Fort Laramie and the Changing Frontier*. National Park Service Handbook 118. Washington, DC: U.S. Department of the Interior, 1983.

Leonard, Stephen J., and Thomas J. Noel. *Denver: Mining Camp to Metropolis*. Niwot: University Press of Colorado, 1990.

Lubetkin, M. John. *Jay Cooke's Gamble: The Northern Pacific Railroad, the Sioux, and the Panic of 1873*. Norman: University of Oklahoma Press, 2006.

Luckingham, Bradford. *Phoenix: The History of a Southwest Metropolis*. Tucson: University of Arizona Press, 1989.

MacPhail, Elizabeth C. *The Story of New San Diego and of Its Founder, Alonzo E. Horton*. San Diego: San Diego Historical Society, 1979.

Malone, Michael P., and Richard W. Etulain. *The American West: A Twentieth-Century History*. Lincoln: University of Nebraska Press, 1989.

Malone, Michael P., and Richard B. Roeder. *Montana: A History of Two Centuries*. Seattle: University of Washington Press, 1976.

Meinig, D.W. *The Shaping of America: A Geographical Perspective on 500 Years of History*. Vol. 2, *Continental America, 1800–1867*; Vol. 3, *Transcontinental America, 1850–1915*. New Haven, CT: Yale University Press, 1986, 1993, and 1998.

Metropolitan Water District of Southern California. *Fifteenth Annual Report, 1953/Report for the Fiscal Year July 1, 1952, to June 30, 1953*. Los Angeles: Metropolitan Water District of Southern California, 1953.

Montoya, María E. *Translating Property: The Maxwell Land Grant and the Conflict over Land in the American West, 1840–1900*. Berkeley: University of California Press, 2002.

Mulholland, Catherine. *William Mulholland and the Rise of Los Angeles*. Berkeley: University of California Press, 2000.

Noel, Thomas J., Paul F. Mahoney, and Richard E. Stevens. *Historical Atlas of Colorado*. Norman: University of Oklahoma Press, 1993.

Nofi, Albert A. *The Alamo and the Texas War for Independence*. [New York?]: Da Capo Press, 2001.

Ng, Wendy. *Japanese American Internment During World War II: A History and Reference Guide*. Westport, CT: Greenwood Press, 2002.

Olien, Diana Davids, and Roger M. Olien. *Oil in Texas: The Gusher Age*. Austin: University of Texas Press, 2002.

Ormsby, Waterman L. *The Butterfield Overland Mail*. San Marino, CA: Huntington Library, 1942.

Orsi, Richard J. *Sunset Limited: The Southern Pacific Railroad and the Development of the American West, 1850–1930*. Berkeley: University of California Press, 2005.

Powell, John Wesley. *Report on the Lands of the Arid Region of the United States*. Cambridge, MA: Belknap Press of the Harvard University Press, 1962.

Price, Edward T. *Dividing the Land: Early American Beginnings of Our Private Property Mosaic*. Chicago: University of Chicago Press, 1995.

Rawls, James J., and Walton Bean. *California: An Interpretive History*. New York: McGraw-Hill, 1993.

Reinhartz, Dennis, and Charles C. Colley (eds.). *The Mapping of the American Southwest*. College Station: Texas A & M University Press, 1987.

Reinhartz, Dennis, and Gerald D. Saxon (eds.). *The Mapping of the Entradas into the Greater Southwest*. Norman: University of Oklahoma Press, 1998.

———. *Mapping and Empire: Soldier-Engineers on the Southwestern Frontier*. Austin: University of Texas Press, 2005.

Rolle, Andrew F. *California: A History*. Wheeling, IL: Harlan Davidson, 1998.

Root, Frank A., and William E. Connelley. *The Overland Stage to California*. Topeka: the authors, 1901.

Sackman, Douglas Cazaux. *Orange Empire: California and the Fruits of Eden*. Berkeley: University of California Press, 2005.

Schwantes, Carlos. *In Mountain Shadows: A History of Idaho*. Lincoln: University of Nebraska Press, 1990.

Schwantes, Carlos, et al. *Washington: Images of a State's Heritage*. Spokane: Melior Publications/1989 Washington Centennial Commission, 1988.

Schwantes, Carlos A., and James P. Ronda. *The West the Railroads Made*. Seattle: University of Washington Press, 2008.

Sheridan, Thomas E. *Arizona: A History*. Tucson: University of Arizona Press, 1995.

Simmons, Marc. *New Mexico: An Interpretive History*. Albuquerque: University of New Mexico Press, 1988.

Solomon, Brian. *Union Pacific Railroad*. Osceola, WI: MBI Publishing, Railroad Color History, 2000.

Smith, Henry Nash. *Virgin Land: The American West as Symbol and Myth*. Cambridge, MA: Harvard University Press, 1950.

Snyder, Eugene E. *Early Portland: Stump-Town Triumphant*. [Portland:] Binford and Mort, 1970.

Starr, Kevin. *Embattled Dreams: California in War and Peace, 1940–1950*. New York: Oxford University Press, 2002.

———. *California: A History*. New York: Random House, 2005.

Storm, Colton (compiler). *A Catalogue of the Everett D. Graff Collection of Western Americana*. Chicago: University of Chicago Press, 1968.

Stover, John F. *The Routledge Historical Atlas of the American Railroads*. New York: Routledge, 1999.

Stroud, Hubert B. *The Promise of Paradise: Recreational and Retirement Communities in the United States since 1950*. Baltimore: Johns Hopkins University Press, 1995.

Texas State Historical Association. *Handbook of Texas Online*. http://www.tshaonline.org/handbook/online/

Thompson, Erwin N. *The Guns of San Diego: San Diego Harbor Defenses 1796–1947*. San Diego: National Park Service, 1991. Online: http://www.cr.nps.gov/history/online_books/cabr/hrs7.htm

Viola, Herman J. *Exploring the West*. Washington, DC: Smithsonian Books, 1987.

Wagner, Henry Raup. *Spanish Voyages to the Northwest Coast of America in the Sixteenth Century*. San Francisco: California Historical Society, 1929.

———. *Cartography of the Northwest Coast of America to the Year 1800*. Mansfield Center, CT: Martino Publishing, 1965 (original publication 1937).

Walker, Henry P., and Don Bufkin. *Historical Atlas of Arizona*. Norman: University of Oklahoma Press, 1979.

Walker, Steven L. *The Southwest: A Pictorial History of the Land and Its People*. Scottsdale: Camelback Design, 1993.

Warner, Ted J. (ed.), and Angelico Chavez (trans.). *The Domínguez–Escalante Journal: Their Expedition through Colorado, Utah, Arizona, and New Mexico in 1776*. Salt Lake City: University of Utah Press, 1995.

Watkins, T.H. *California: An Illustrated History*. New York: American Legacy Press, 1983.

Weber, David J. *The Spanish Frontier in North America*. New Haven, CT: Yale University Press, 1992.

West, Elliott. *The Contested Plains: Indians, Goldseekers & the Rush to Colorado*. Lawrence: University Press of Kansas, 1998.

Wishart, David J. *The Fur Trade of the American West, 1807–1840: A Geographical Synthesis*. London: Croom Helm, 1979.

Wrobel, David M. *The End of American Exceptionalism: Frontier Anxiety from the Old West to the New Deal*. Lawrence: University Press of Kansas, 1993.

———. *Promised Lands: Promotion, Memory, and the Creation of the American West*. Lawrence: University Press of Kansas, 2002.

Wrobel, David M., and Patrick T. Long (eds.). *Seeing and Being Seen: Tourism in the American West*. Lawrence: University Press of Kansas, 2001.

Index

irrigation in 168
Land Company 81
and the Mexican War 87–91
oil industry in 144–45
& Pacific Railway 130–34, 195, 213
Panhandle 150, 153, 180, 210
Republic of 70, 80–84, 182, 212
Santa Fe Expedition 182
Spanish 26, 30, 31, 33, 34, 46, 49, 50, 51
State 7, 124, 125, 131, 132, 180–82, 185, 188, 244, 250, 271
Theodore Roosevelt Dam 162, 163, 216
Thompson, David 65
Todd, Alexander 112
Tonopah City, Nevada 142
tourism 120, 137, 169, 198, 209, 214–21, 226, 228, 229, 231, 232, 233, 234, 246, 254, 255, 256
Toussaint L'Ouverture, François-Dominique 65
Trans-Alaska Pipeline 250
Transcontinental Air Transport 234
Transcontinental and Western Air (TWA) 234
Transcontinental Arc 179
transcontinental railroad 111, 114–19, 120–41, 157, 158, 169, 171, 183, 200, 202, 209, 210, 215, 220
treaty(ies)
of Cahuenga 88
of Fontainebleau 33
of Fort Laramie 148, 150
of Guadalupe Hidalgo 78, 90, 91, 182, 183, 261
Louisiana Purchase 65, 66, 67, 146, 180, 189, 209, 261
Nootka 45
Oregon 86, 261
of Paris 55
of San Ildefonso 65
Transcontinental 48, 49, 73, 180
Trist, Nicholas 90, 91
Truckee River 161, 163
Truckee Valley 119, 161
Truteau, Jean Baptiste 64
Tubac presidio 34, 40, 41
Tucson, Arizona 26, 34, 108, 133, 186, 187, 205, 246, 253
Tyler, John 83

U
Ulloa, Francisco de 14, 17, 18
Umatilla Project Development League 164, 165
Umpqua River 75, 165
Unassigned Lands, Oklahoma 155
Union Colony of Colorado 124, 158, 159
Union Pacific Railroad 4, 112, 116–19, 120–27, 130, 137, 198, 202, 209, 210, 211, 214, 216, 222, 224, 238, 245, 247, 254
Union Pacific Railway, Eastern Division 122, 124, 149.
See also Kansas: Pacific Railway
United Air Lines/Airlines 234, 255
Upper California 37, 174, 181, 182, 189. See also Alta California
Urrutia, José de 27, 33, 34, 36
U.S. Army Corps of Engineers 238, 241, 254, 261. See also U.S. Army Corps of Topographical Engineers
U.S. Army Corps of Topographical Engineers 73. See also U.S. Army Corps of Engineers
U.S. Bureau of Ethnology 8, 178
U.S. Bureau of Reclamation 163, 164, 166, 238, 239, 252. See also U.S. Reclamation Service
U.S. Coast and Geodetic Survey (USCGS) 179
U.S. Coast Survey (USCS) 179, 189
U.S. Exploring Expedition 85, 94, 174, 189
U.S. Forest Service 231
U.S. General Land Office 108, 109, 118, 154, 156, 157, 185, 213, 261
U.S. Geological and Geographical Survey of the Territories 178
U.S. Geological Survey (USGS) 177, 178
U.S. Reclamation Service 162, 163, 164, 165, 166, 205. See also U.S. Bureau of Reclamation
US routes 226, 228, 232, 233, 259
Utah 42, 49, 91, 110–11, 113, 114, 115, 118, 119, 140, 168, 180, 181, 182, 186, 187, 202, 203, 232

Lake 42, 43, 96, 97, 168
War. See Mormon(s): War
Territory 181, 182, 186, 202
Ute Indians 78, 150

V
Vail, Colorado 255
Valdés, Cayetano 45
Valverde, Battle of 111
van Sype, Nicolas 24
Vancouver, George 11, 21, 45, 60–61, 63–64, 66
Vancouver Island 39, 45, 61, 85–86, 182
Véniard, Étienne de, Sieur de Bourgmont 51
Veracruz. Mexico 89
Viana, Francisco 70
Villahermosa (Tabasco), Mexico 89
Villalón, Pedro de Rivera y 31
Villard, Henry 129, 131
Villasur, Pedro de 31, 36, 51, 52
Vinckeboons, Joan 22
Vioget, Jean Jacques 77
Virginia City, Montana 109
Virginia City, Nevada 101, 102, 104, 106
Virginia City, New Mexico 78
Visalia, California 221
Vizcaíno, Sebastian 18–21, 22, 23, 37
von Egloffstein, Frederick 115, 177
Vries, Maerten 56
Vulture Mine 108, 109

W
Wagon Box Fight 150
wagon trains 92, 93, 94, 98, 111, 114, 147, 150
Waldseemüller, Martin 12
Walker, Joseph Reddeford 93
Walker, Juan Pedro 48
Wallula, Washington 93, 127, 130, 200
Ward, Aaron Montgomery 137
Warner, William 196, 197
Warren, Gouverneur K. 116
war(s). See also battles
"Bleeding Kansas" 110, 111, 184
Civil 102, 110, 111, 114, 116, 149, 150, 155, 184, 185, 187
Cold 248
Colfax County 78
of 1812 73, 180
for Independence 45, 55, 156
Indian, 11, 83, 148–53
Mexican 49, 84, 85, 87–89, 182, 261
Mexican, for Independence 49, 77
Modoc 153
Mormon 110–11, 114, 177
of the Quadruple Alliance 30
Red Cloud's 150
Red River 153
Revolutionary. See war(s): for Independence
Seven Years' 33
World, II 234, 241, 243, 246
Washington
admission to the union 200
apple industry 136, 225
-on-the-Brazos, Texas 212
State 95, 127, 128, 130, 142, 182
surveys of 39, 40, 45, 60, 61, 86
Territory 109, 114, 182, 186, 188
Washoe silver region, Nevada 102
water projects 160–68, 191–95, 204, 205, 206, 207, 238–41, 246, 250–54. See also irrigation
Waxell, Sven 57
Webb, Del E. 198, 256
Weber, Charles 197
Wells, Henry 114
Wells Fargo 114
Welsh Indians 64
West Coast
Japanese evacuation from the 242
mapping the 9, 12, 17–21, 24, 25, 37, 39, 45, 56, 60, 61, 179
railroads to the 126, 133, 134

Russia and the 75
and World War II 243–44
Western Air Express 234
Western Pacific Railroad 134, 137
Westport Landing (endpoint of the Santa Fe Trail) 211
Weyerhaeuser, Frederick 136
Wheeler, George Montague 177, 178, 206, 220
Wheeler, Olin 216
Whipple, Amiel Weeks 114, 116
White Bird 151
White Bird Canyon, Battle of 152
Whitman, Marcus and Narcissa 93, 94
Whitman Massacre 94
Whitney, Josiah 174
Whitney Glacier, Mount Shasta 174
Wichita, Kansas 27, 124, 244
Wickenburg, Arizona 108, 109
Wickenburg, Henry 109, 205
Wilcox, Harvey Henderson 193
Wilkes, Charles 85, 86, 94, 174, 189
Wilkinson, James 70
Willamette River 67, 75, 92, 93, 130, 198, 199
Willamette Valley 6, 93, 94, 199
Williamson, Robert S. 116, 177
Willow Creek Reservoir 251
Wilson, Stephen 81
Wilson and Exeter Land Grant 81
Wind River Range 71, 72, 73, 96
wine industry, California 225
Winter Quarters, Nebraska 96
Wood Lake, Battle of 149
Woodbury Grant 81
Wool, John E. 89
Works Progress Administration (WPA) 236
World War II 234, 241, 243, 246
Worth, William Jenkins 89, 213
Wounded Knee, Battle (Massacre) of 150, 154
Wovoka and Ghost Dance religion 154
Wrangell–St. Elias National Park and Preserve 261
Wyandotte, Kansas 122, 210. See also Kansas: City, Kansas/Missouri
Wyeth, Nathaniel 92, 93
Wyld, James 85, 86
Wyoming 4, 54, 178, 182, 22
mining in 109, 140, 178, 254
Territory 126, 157, 160, 186, 188

Y
Yankton Cession 154
Yankton Sioux 154
Yelloway Bus Line 229
Yellowstone National Park 70, 109, 148, 177, 178, 214, 215, 220, 221, 222, 261
Yellowstone River 70, 151, 152
Yerba Buena 77, 190
Yesler, Henry L. 199
Yosemite National Park 174, 192, 214, 218, 220
Young, Brigham 96, 97, 110, 111, 201, 202, 203
Young, Ewing 93, 94
Youngtown, Arizona 256
Yuma Irrigation Project 167

Z
Zaikov, Potap 45
Zion National Park 222
Zuni pueblos 15

Back endpaper.
This 1819 map shows the American Missouri Territory, the area covered by the Louisiana Purchase of 1803 less the state of Louisiana, created in 1812. The West is divided between Britain, to the north; the United States, in the center; and Spain, to the south. In 1818, following the War of 1812, the United States negotiated a boundary with Britain at the forty-ninth parallel west to the Rocky Mountains (the top boundary). The area west of the mountains—the Oregon Country—remained an area of "joint occupancy" with Britain until the boundary was finally fixed in 1846. In 1819 the United States obtained by treaty Spanish claims north of 42° (today's northern boundary of California), but the border with Spanish territory (the bottom boundary) remained ill-defined. To the south was the Spanish northern province of New Mexico, from which Spain was ousted in 1821 by the Mexican Revolution. The United States finally gained control of most of the West in 1848 following the Mexican War.

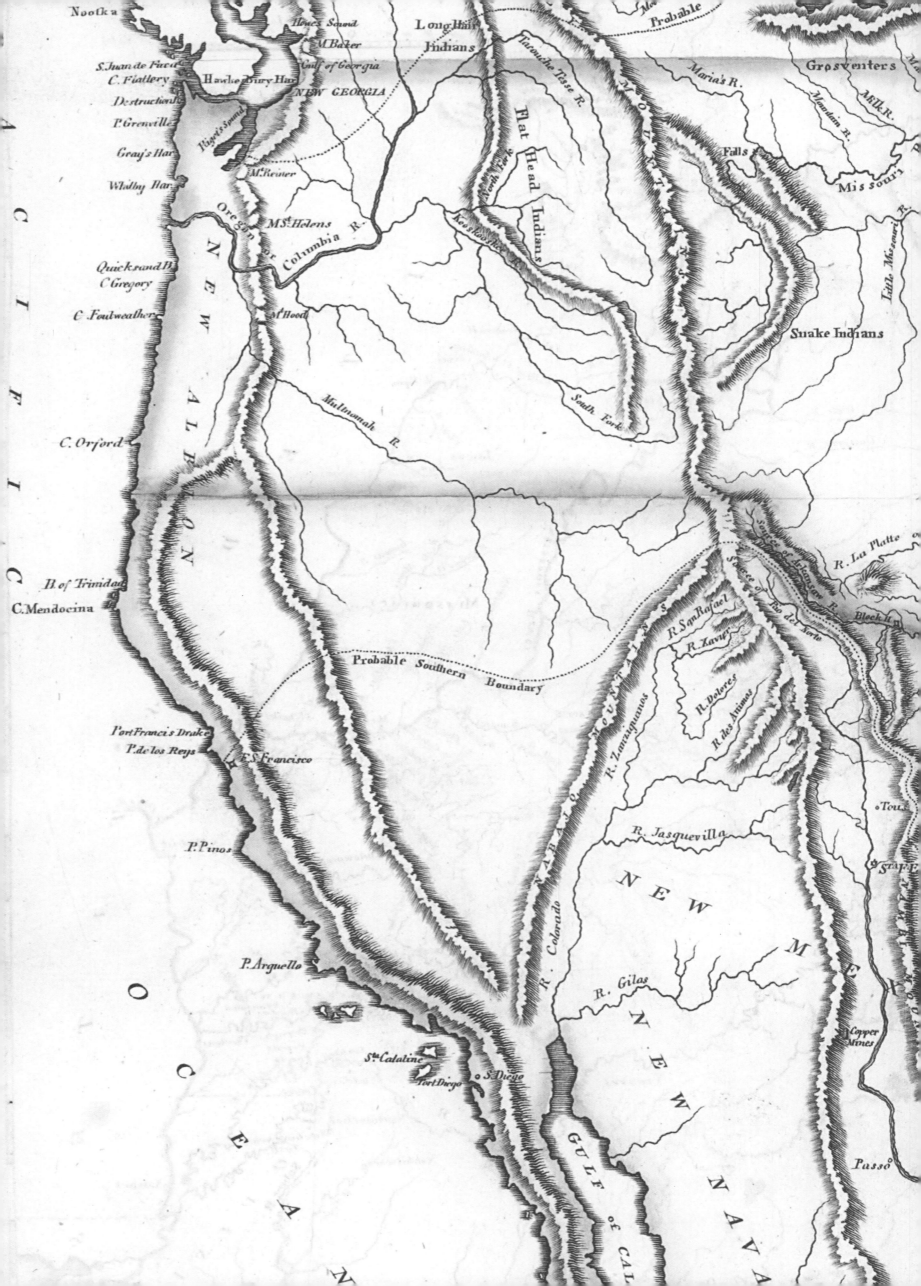